**FROM THE LIBRARY OF:**

**FREDK. P JOHNS**

THE LOVE OF LEARNING, THE SEQUESTERED NOOKS,
AND ALL THE SWEET SERENITY OF BOOKS.

–*Henry Wadsworth Longfellow*

# THE EARLY DYNASTIC TO AKKADIAN TRANSITION

THE UNIVERSITY OF CHICAGO
ORIENTAL INSTITUTE PUBLICATIONS
VOLUME 129

*Series Editors*

Leslie Schramer

*and*

Thomas G. Urban

EXCAVATIONS AT NIPPUR
MCGUIRE GIBSON • NIPPUR SERIES EDITOR

# NIPPUR V

# THE EARLY DYNASTIC TO AKKADIAN TRANSITION

# THE AREA WF SOUNDING AT NIPPUR

*by*

AUGUSTA McMAHON

*with*
*contributions*
*by*

McGUIRE GIBSON, ROBERT D. BIGGS,
DAVID REESE, PAMELA VANDIVER, *and* K. ASLIHAN YENER

THE ORIENTAL INSTITUTE OF THE UNIVERSITY OF CHICAGO
CHICAGO • ILLINOIS

Library of Congress Control Number: 2006936403
ISBN: 1-885923-38-4
ISSN: 0069-3367

*The Oriental Institute, Chicago*

© 2006 by The University of Chicago. All rights reserved.
Published 2006. Printed in the United States of America.

*Series Editors' Acknowledgments*

The assistance of Alexandra Witsell is acknowledged in the production of this volume.

*Cover Illustration*

Cylinder seal of Lugal-DÚR, a scribe (18 N 174; see p. 121 for description; pl. 157:2)

*Spine Illustration*

Upright-handled jar (19 N 44; see p. 47 for description; pls. 143–44)

*Printed by Edwards Brothers, Ann Arbor, Michigan*

The paper used in this publication meets the minimum requirements of American National Standard for Information Services — Permanence of Paper for Printed Library Materials, ANSI Z39.48-1984.

# TABLE OF CONTENTS

| | |
|---|---|
| LIST OF ABBREVIATIONS | vii |
| LIST OF FIGURES | ix |
| LIST OF PLATES | xi |
| LIST OF TABLES | xvii |
| PREFACE. *McGuire Gibson* | xix |
| BIBLIOGRAPHY | xxiii |
| INTRODUCTION: THE AREA WF SOUNDING AT NIPPUR | 1 |
| CHAPTER 1. DETAILED DESCRIPTION OF LEVELS AND STRATIGRAPHY | 13 |
| CHAPTER 2. BURIALS | 37 |
| CHAPTER 3. POTTERY | 59 |
| CHAPTER 4. OBJECTS FROM AREA WF | 119 |
| CHAPTER 5. CONCLUSION | 145 |
| APPENDIX 1. SCIENTIFIC ANALYSIS OF TWO AKKADIAN GLASS BEADS. *Pamela Vandiver and K. Aslıhan Yener* | 149 |
| APPENDIX 2. ANIMAL BONES AND SHELLS. *David Reese* | 161 |
| APPENDIX 3. THE INSCRIPTIONS. *Robert D. Biggs* | 165 |
| INDEX | 171 |
| PLATES | 175 |

# LIST OF ABBREVIATIONS

| | | | |
|---|---|---|---|
| AbS | Abu Salabikh | lgth. | length |
| abv. | above | L. | locus |
| Ach. | Achaemenid | max. | maximum |
| Akk. | Akkadian | mm | millimeter(s) |
| Br | Bronze | m | meter(s) |
| C | Celsius | n(n). | footnote(s) |
| ca. | *circa*, approximately | N | Nippur |
| cf. | *confer*, compare | NA | Neo-Assyrian |
| ch(s). | chapter(s) | N/A | not available |
| cm | centimeter(s) | NB | Neo-Babylonian |
| col. | column | no(s). | number(s) |
| cont. | continued | NT | Nippur tablet |
| Cu | copper | OB | Old Babylonian |
| diam. | diameter | obv. | obverse |
| D.O.G. | Deutsche Orient-Gesellshaft | pcb | plano-convex brick |
| ED | Early Dynastic | pers. comm. | personal communication |
| e.g. | *exempli gratia*, for example | pers. obs. | personal observation |
| et al. | *et alii*, and others | pl(s). | plate(s) |
| etc. | *et cetera*, and so forth | rev. | reverse |
| (et) passim | (and) here and there | Sel. | Seleucid |
| f(f). | and following | sk(s). | skeleton(s) |
| fig(s). | figure(s) | Std. Dev. | Standard Deviation |
| fl(s). | floor(s) | T. | Tell |
| gm | gram(s) | th. | thickness |
| Gr(s). | grave(s) | Uch | Uch Tepe |
| H | eighteenth season at Nippur | UmmJ. | Umm el-Jīr |
| ht. | height | unpubl. | unpublished |
| I | nineteenth season at Nippur | UT | untyped |
| ibid. | *ibidem*, in the same place | w. | width |
| i.e. | *id est*, that is | wt. | weight |
| incl. | including | | |

# LIST OF FIGURES

1. Map of South Mesopotamia Showing Location of Nippur ....................................................... 2
2. Topographic Map of Nippur with Areas WA 50c and WF Indicated ....................................... 6
3. Areas WF and WA 50c ............................................................................................................. 8
4. Combined Plans of Area WF, Level XIIIB and WA 50c, Level X, Floor 7 ........................... 18
5. Combined Plans of Area WF, Level XIIB and WA 50c, Level X, Floors 6–1 ....................... 20
6. Combined Plans of Area WF, Level XI and WA 50c, Level IX ............................................. 22
7. Combined Plans of Area WF, Level X and WA 50c, Level VIII ........................................... 24
8. Wireframe Reconstruction of Burial 14, Deep Shaft Phase with Chambers for Skeletons 7 and 8 ........ 40
9. Wireframe Reconstruction of Burial 14, Deep Shaft Phase with Chambers for Skeletons 6–8 .............. 41
10. Wireframe Reconstruction of Burial 14, Deep Shaft Phase with Chamber for Skeletons 2–4 ............... 45
11. Burial 14 Schematic Sections, All Phases .............................................................................. 46
12. Reconstructed Seal Impression from Nippur, Area TB, Level II ........................................... 122

# LIST OF PLATES

1. General View of Area WF, from Northeast, and General View of Area WF, from Southwest
2. Area WF, Looking Down into Trench, from Southeast, and Area WF, Looking Up from Base of Trench, Northeast Corner
3. Plan of Level XIXB, Loci 68–70 and 72
4. Level XIXB, from Above and West, and South End of Level XIXB, from North
5. Plan of Level XIXA, Locus 67
6. Plan of Level XVIII, Loci 65–66
7. Plan of Level XVIIC, Loci 64 and 71
8. Plan of Level XVIIB, Loci 62–63 and 71
9. Plan of Level XVIIA, Loci 61 and 71
10. Plan of Level XVI, Locus 59
11. Plan of Level XVB, Loci 57 and 60
12. Level XV, from Southwest, and Level XV, from Northwest
13. Plan of Level XVA, Loci 53 and 57
14. Plan of Level XIVB, Loci 44, 47, 54, and 73
15. Detailed Plan of Level XIVB, Locus 47, Objects and Features at Floor 5
16. Plan of Level XIVA, Loci 40, 44, 54, and 73
17. Detailed Plan of Level XIVA, Locus 40, Objects and Features at Floor 2
18. Level XIVA, Locus 40, Detail of Western End of Room, and Level XIVA, Locus 40, Northwest Corner with Foundation Deposit Bowls
19. Detailed Plan of Level XIVA, Locus 40, Objects and Features at Floor 1
20. Detail of Superimposed Walls AS, AQ, and AM in Southeast Corner, and Detail of East End of Locus 40
21. Plan of Level XIIIC, Loci 39, 43, and 51–52
22. Plan of Level XIIIB, Loci 39, 43, and 50
23. Plan of Level XIIIA, Loci 42–43 and 50
24. Plan of Level XIIB, Loci 34, 38, and 41
25. Level XIIB, Wall AG Leaning Outward into Courtyard, from East-Northeast, and Level XIIB, from Above and Northwest
26. Plan of Level XIIA, Loci 34–35 and 38
27. Plan of Level XIB, Loci 34–36
28. Level XIB, Toilet in Locus 36, and Level XIA, Equid Skeleton in Locus 34
29. Plan of Level XIA, Loci 31 and 34–35
30. Plan of Level X, Loci 27, 30, and 32–33
31. Level X, from Above and South, and Level X, from Northeast
32. Plan of Level IX, Loci 24–26
33. Plan of Level VIII, Loci 20, 22, 29, and 45
34. Plan of Level VII, Loci 17, 20, and 29
35. East Section at Level VI, and South Section at Levels VII and VI

# LIST OF PLATES

36. Plan of Level VI, Loci 13–14, 16, 19, and 28
37. Level VI from Above and North and Level VI, Detail of Mudbrick Bin and Walls P and L
38. Plan of Level VB, Loci 13, 18, and 23
39. Plan of Level VA, Loci 15, 18, 21, and 23
40. North Section Showing Multiple Pits, Wall R, and Erosion Layer, Locus 15
41. Plan of Level IV, Loci 10–12 and 46
42. Level IV from Above and South
43. Plan of Level IIIB, Loci 6–8
44. Level IIIB, Drain at Locus 8, Floor 4, with Baked-brick Cover, and Level IIIB, Drain at Locus 8, Floor 4, with Cover Removed
45. Level IIIB, Exterior of Building, Detail of Drain, and Level IIIB, Outlet of Drain at Locus 8, Floor 3
46. Level IIIB, Corner of Building from Above and East, with Drain at Locus 8, Floor 3, and Level IIIB, Drain at Locus 8, Floor 3, Close-up from North
47. Plan of Level IIIA, Loci 4–5 and 9
48. Level IIIA, Building from Above and Northeast, with Drain in Locus 4, and Level IIIA, Drain in Locus 4, from Northwest
49. Plan of Level II, Locus 2
50. Burial 22 and Burial 19
51. Burial 21, Skeleton 2, and Burial 21, Skeleton 1
52. Burial 18 and Burial 17
53. Burial 14, Skeleton 5, and Burial 14, Skeleton 5 Grave Goods
54. Burial 16 and Burial 11
55. Burial 15 and Burial 15, Registered Grave Goods
56. Burial 14, Skeleton 8, Burial 14, Skeleton 8, Registered Grave Goods, and Burial 14, Skeleton 7
57. Deep Shaft of Burial 14, Skeleton 6, and Burial 14, Skeleton 6
58. Plan of Burial 14, Level XIIIB Chamber, and Detailed Plan of Burial 14, Skeleton 2
59. Burial 14, Level XIIIB Chamber
60. Burial 14, Skeleton 3, Burial 14, Skeletons 3 and 4, and Burial 14, Skeleton 3, Grave Goods
61. Burial 14, Skeleton 4, and Burial 14, Skeleton 4, Grave Goods
62. Burial 14, Skeleton 2, and Plan of Burial 14
63. Burial 14, Equid Skeleton, and Burial 14, Skeleton 2 Jewelry, Cylinder Seal
64. Burial 14, Skeleton 2, Copper/Bronze Vessels, and Burial 14, Skeleton 2, Pottery
65. Ash-filled Baked-brick Box Above Burial 14, and Plan of Burial 14, Skeleton 1
66. Burial 14, Skeleton 1, Jewelry and Bronze Filter, and Burial 14, Skeleton 1, Weapons
67. Burial 14, Skeleton 1, Copper/Bronze Vessels
68. Burial 14, Skeleton 1, Registered Pottery, and Burial 14, Skeleton 1, Registered Pottery
69. Burial 9 and Burial 9 Pottery
70. Burial 12 and Burial 12 Pottery
71. Burial 8 and Associated Grave Goods
72. Burial 6, Unopened and Opened
73. Burial 4 and Burial 4 Grave Goods
74. Burial 3, Unopened and Opened
75. Burial 5, Burial 7, and Burial 1

76. Type O-1
77. Type O-2
78. Type O-3
79. Type O-4
80. Type O-5
81. Type O-6
82. Types O-7, O-8
83. Type O-9
84. Type O-10
85. Type O-10 (*cont.*)
86. Type O-11
87. Type O-12
88. Type O-13
89. Types O-14, O-15, O-16
90. Type O-17
91. Types O-18, O-20
92. Type O-19
93. Type O-21
94. Types O-22, O-23
95. Types O-24, O-25
96. Type C-1
97. Type C-2
98. Type C-3
99. Types C-4, C-5
100. Types C-6, C-7
101. Types C-8, C-11
102. Type C-9
103. Type C-10
104. Type C-12
105. Type C-13a
106. Type C-13b
107. Type C-14
108. Type C-15
109. Type C-16a
110. Type C-16b
111. Type C-16c
112. Type C-17
113. Type C-18
114. Type C-18 (*cont.*), Type C-19
115. Type C-20
116. Type C-21
117. Type C-22

118. Type C-24
119. Type C-25a
120. Types C-25b, C-28
121. Types C-26, C-27
122. Type C-29
123. Bases and Foundation Deposit Bowls
124. Foundation Deposit Bowls
125. Foundation Deposit Bowls
126. Miscellaneous Third-millennium B.C. Pottery
127. Miscellaneous Third-millennium B.C. Pottery
128. Third-millennium B.C. Grave Groups, Burials 20 and 19
129. Third-millennium B.C. Grave Group, Burial 19 (*cont.*)
130. Third-millennium B.C. Grave Group, Burial 19 (*cont.*)
131. Third-millennium B.C. Grave Group, Burial 19 (*cont.*)
132. Third-millennium B.C. Grave Groups, Burial 21, Skeletons 1 and 2, and Burial 18
133. Third-millennium B.C. Grave Group, Burial 14, Skeleton 5
134. Third-millennium B.C. Grave Groups, Burials 16 and 13
135. Third-millennium B.C. Grave Groups, Burials 15 and 11
136. Third-millennium B.C. Grave Group, Burial 14, Skeleton 6
137. Third-millennium B.C. Grave Group, Burial 14, Skeleton 6, Bowls
138. Third-millennium B.C. Grave Groups, Burial 14, Skeleton 6, and Burial 14, Skeleton 7
139. Third-millennium B.C. Grave Group, Burial 14, Skeleton 8
140. Third-millennium B.C. Grave Group, Burial 14, Skeleton 8 (*cont.*)
141. Cosmetic Shells from Burial 19; Burial 14, Skeleton 7; and Burial 14, Skeleton 3
142. Third-millennium B.C. Grave Groups, Burial 14 Southwest Shaft and Burial 14, Skeleton 3 or 4
143. Third-millennium B.C. Grave Group, Burial 14, Skeleton 3
144. Goddess-handled Jar with Burial 14, Skeleton 3
145. Third-millennium B.C. Grave Groups, Burial 14, Skeleton 3, and Burial 14, Skeleton 4
146. Third-millennium B.C. Grave Group, Burial 14, Skeleton 2, Objects
147. Third-millennium B.C. Grave Group, Burial 14, Skeleton 2, Bowls
148. Third-millennium B.C. Grave Group, Burial 14, Skeleton 2, Pottery and Copper/Bronze Vessels
149. Third-millennium B.C. Grave Group, Burial 14, Skeleton 2, Pottery and Copper/Bronze Vessel
150. Third-millennium B.C. Grave Group, Burial 14, Skeleton 2, Pottery and Copper/Bronze Vessel
151. Third-millennium B.C. Grave Group, Burial 14, Skeleton 2, Pottery and Copper/Bronze Objects
152. Third-millennium B.C. Grave Group, Burial 14, Skeleton 1
153. Third-millennium B.C. Grave Group, Burial 14, Skeleton 1 (*cont.*)
154. Third-millennium B.C. Grave Group, Burial 14, Skeleton 1 (*cont.*)
155. Third-millennium B.C. Grave Group, Burial 14, Skeleton 1 (*cont.*)
156. Third-millennium B.C. Grave Group, Burial 14, Skeleton 1 (*cont.*)
157. Cylinder Seals, Burial 14, Skeleton 1
158. Cylinder Seals from Burial 14, Skeleton 2 and from Level XVIII
159. Sealings, Levels XIIB and XIIIB

## LIST OF PLATES

160. Cylinder Seals, Stamp Seals, and Scarab, Non-burial
161. Third-millennium B.C. Stone and Copper/Bronze Vessels, Non-burial
162. Third-millennium B.C. Copper/Bronze Objects and Pins, Non-burial
163. Third-millennium B.C. Baked-clay and Stone Objects
164. Third-millennium B.C. Miniature Pottery Vessels
165. Foundation Deposit 19 N 97, Level XIIIC
166. Third-millennium B.C. Miscellaneous Objects
167. Third-millennium B.C. Glass Beads
168. Second-millennium B.C. Grave Groups, Burials 9 and 12
169. First-millennium B.C. Grave Group, Burial 6
170. First-millennium B.C. Grave Group, Burial 8
171. First-millennium B.C. Grave Groups, Burials 5, 2, and 3
172. First-millennium B.C. Grave Group, Burial 4
173. First-millennium B.C. Grave Group, Burial 7
174. First-millennium B.C. Pottery Bowls
175. First-millennium B.C. Pottery Bowls
176. First-millennium B.C. Pottery Bowls
177. First-millennium B.C. Pottery Jars and Other Forms
178. First-millennium B.C. Pottery and Metal Hoard
179. First-millennium B.C. Objects
180. First-millennium B.C. Objects
181. West Section
182. North Section and East Section
183. South Section
184. Area WF North and East Sections
185. Area WF South and West Sections
186. Spherical Translucent Dark Olive Green and Opaque White Glass Bead (18 N 95, H840, 27.2.89), Side View Showing a Miniscus at Each End, and Cylindrical Opaque Yellow and Translucent Bluish Green Bead (18 N 96, H107, 1.3.89), Side View Showing Barrel Shape
187. Section of Opaque White Glass of 18 N 95 Showing Conchoidal Fracture and Bubble or Pore, Taken with Scanning Electron Microscope (S.E.M.) in Secondary Mode at ×1,600, and Freshly Fractured Surface of Opaque Yellow Glass of 18 N 96 Showing Rough, Polycrystalline Surface Texture and Round Bubble. Taken with S.E.M. in Secondary Mode at ×500
188. Green Glass Showing Lead-tin II or Lead-stannate Phases Surrounded by Calcium-magnesium-silicate Phase Identified by X-ray Diffraction as Diopside. Flat Polished Cross Section of Yellow Glass Showing Lead-stannate and Diopside Phases Concentrated at Surface to Give Opaque Yellow Color (backscattered at ×370)
189. The Same 0.3 mm Polished Chip of Yellow Glass Shown Using Optical Microscopy in Transmitted and Reflected Light at ×400
190. Two Small Droplets of Lead Phosphate Phase (see table A.2 for composition) Shown in Backscattered S.E.M. at ×1,800 and As Concentration of Brown-colored Droplets in Transmitted Light Micrograph at ×400
191. Replication of the Yellow-green Glass Composition, Melted in a Fireclay Crucible at Three Different Temperatures for Twelve Hours in Oxidation
192. Third-millennium B.C. Tablets
193. Third-millennium B.C. Tablets

# LIST OF TABLES

1. Brick Sizes, by Level ..... 11
2. Concordance of Loci, Walls, Pits, and Burials ..... 34
3. Concordance of Loci and Levels ..... 35
4. Orientations of Third-millennium B.C. Burials ..... 53
5. Contents of Third-millennium B.C. Burials ..... 54
6. Concordance of Burials and Levels ..... 58
7. Ratios of Third-millennium B.C. Closed to Open Vessels, Sherd Counts, and Relative Percentages ..... 88
8. Third-millennium B.C. Open and Closed Vessel Sherd Counts by Level ..... 89
9. Presence/Absence of Third-millennium B.C. Open Types by Level ..... 90
10. Presence/Absence of Third-millennium B.C. Closed Types by Level ..... 91
11. Number of Third-millennium B.C. Types Present per Level, and Ratios of Open to Closed Types ..... 92
12. Pottery Type O-1 Third-millennium B.C. Bowl Height by Level ..... 93
13. Pottery Types O-1 through O-13: Third-millennium B.C. Sherd Counts and Relative Frequencies by Level ..... 94
14. Pottery Types O-14 through O-25, Third-millennium B.C. Sherd Counts and Relative Frequencies by Level ..... 95
15. Pottery Types C-1 through C-15, Third-millennium B.C. Levels Sherd Counts and Relative Frequencies by Level ..... 96
16. Pottery Types C-16a through C-29, Third-millennium B.C. Levels Counts and Relative Frequencies by Level ..... 97
17. Third-millennium B.C. Sherd Counts, Bases, Spouts and Vat Fragments by Level ..... 98
18. Third-millennium B.C. Decorated Sherd Counts by Level ..... 99
19. Pottery Type O-1 Relative Percentages by Third-millennium B.C. Levels ..... 100
20. Pottery Type O-2 Relative Percentages by Third-millennium B.C. Levels ..... 100
21. Pottery Type O-3 Relative Percentages by Third-millennium B.C. Levels ..... 100
22. Pottery Type O-4 Relative Percentages by Third-millennium B.C. Levels ..... 101
23. Pottery Type O-5 Relative Percentages by Third-millennium B.C. Levels ..... 101
24. Pottery Type O-6 Relative Percentages by Third-millennium B.C. Levels ..... 101
25. Pottery Type O-7 Relative Percentages by Third-millennium B.C. Levels ..... 102
26. Pottery Type O-8 Relative Percentages by Third-millennium B.C. Levels ..... 102
27. Pottery Type O-9 Relative Percentages by Third-millennium B.C. Levels ..... 102
28. Pottery Type O-10 Relative Percentages by Third-millennium B.C. Levels ..... 103
29. Pottery Type O-11 Relative Percentages by Third-millennium B.C. Levels ..... 103
30. Pottery Type O-12 Relative Percentages by Third-millennium B.C. Levels ..... 103
31. Pottery Type O-13 Relative Percentages by Third-millennium B.C. Levels ..... 104
32. Pottery Type O-14 Relative Percentages by Third-millennium B.C. Levels ..... 104
33. Pottery Type O-15 Relative Percentages by Third-millennium B.C. Levels ..... 104
34. Pottery Type O-16 Relative Percentages by Third-millennium B.C. Levels ..... 105
35. Pottery Type O-17 Relative Percentages by Third-millennium B.C. Levels ..... 105

| | | |
|---|---|---|
| 36. | Pottery Type O-18 Relative Percentages by Third-millennium B.C. Levels | 105 |
| 37. | Pottery Type O-19 Relative Percentages by Third-millennium B.C. Levels | 106 |
| 38. | Pottery Type O-20 Relative Percentages by Third-millennium B.C. Levels | 106 |
| 39. | Pottery Type O-21 Relative Percentages by Third-millennium B.C. Levels | 106 |
| 40. | Pottery Type O-22 Relative Percentages by Third-millennium B.C. Levels | 107 |
| 41. | Pottery Type O-23 Relative Percentages by Third-millennium B.C. Levels | 107 |
| 42. | Pottery Type O-24 Relative Percentages by Third-millennium B.C. Levels | 107 |
| 43. | Pottery Type O-25 Relative Percentages by Third-millennium B.C. Levels | 108 |
| 44. | Pottery Type C-1 Relative Percentages by Third-millennium B.C. Levels | 108 |
| 45. | Pottery Type C-2 Relative Percentages by Third-millennium B.C. Levels | 108 |
| 46. | Pottery Type C-3 Relative Percentages by Third-millennium B.C. Levels | 109 |
| 47. | Pottery Type C-4 Relative Percentages by Third-millennium B.C. Levels | 109 |
| 48. | Pottery Type C-5 Relative Percentages by Third-millennium B.C. Levels | 109 |
| 49. | Pottery Type C-6 Relative Percentages by Third-millennium B.C. Levels | 110 |
| 50. | Pottery Type C-7 Relative Percentages by Third-millennium B.C. Levels | 110 |
| 51. | Pottery Type C-8 Relative Percentages by Third-millennium B.C. Levels | 110 |
| 52. | Pottery Type C-9 Relative Percentages by Third-millennium B.C. Levels | 111 |
| 53. | Pottery Type C-10 Relative Percentages by Third-millennium B.C. Levels | 111 |
| 54. | Pottery Type C-11 Relative Percentages by Third-millennium B.C. Levels | 111 |
| 55. | Pottery Type C-12 Relative Percentages by Third-millennium B.C. Levels | 112 |
| 56. | Pottery Type C-13 Relative Percentages by Third-millennium B.C. Levels | 112 |
| 57. | Pottery Type C-14 Relative Percentages by Third-millennium B.C. Levels | 112 |
| 58. | Pottery Type C-15 Relative Percentages by Third-millennium B.C. Levels | 113 |
| 59. | Pottery Type C-16a Relative Percentages by Third-millennium B.C. Levels | 113 |
| 60. | Pottery Type C-16b Relative Percentages by Third-millennium B.C. Levels | 113 |
| 61. | Pottery Type C-16c Relative Percentages by Third-millennium B.C. Levels | 114 |
| 62. | Pottery Type C-17 Relative Percentages by Third-millennium B.C. Levels | 114 |
| 63. | Pottery Type C-18 Relative Percentages by Third-millennium B.C. Levels | 114 |
| 64. | Pottery Type C-19 Relative Percentages by Third-millennium B.C. Levels | 115 |
| 65. | Pottery Type C-20 Relative Percentages by Third-millennium B.C. Levels | 115 |
| 66. | Pottery Type C-21 Relative Percentages by Third-millennium B.C. Levels | 115 |
| 67. | Pottery Type C-22 Relative Percentages by Third-millennium B.C. Levels | 116 |
| 68. | Pottery Type C-24 Relative Percentages by Third-millennium B.C. Levels | 116 |
| 69. | Pottery Type C-25a Relative Percentages by Third-millennium B.C. Levels | 116 |
| 70. | Pottery Type C-25b Relative Percentages by Third-millennium B.C. Levels | 117 |
| 71. | Pottery Type C-26 Relative Percentages by Third-millennium B.C. Levels | 117 |
| 72. | Pottery Type C-27 Relative Percentages by Third-millennium B.C. Levels | 117 |
| 73. | Pottery Type C-28 Relative Percentages by Third-millennium B.C. Levels | 118 |
| 74. | Pottery Type C-29 Relative Percentages by Third-millennium B.C. Levels | 118 |
| 75. | Third-millennium B.C. Beads by Shape and Material | 128 |
| 76. | First-millennium B.C. Beads by Shape and Material | 130 |
| 77. | Concordance of Objects, by Level | 136 |
| 78. | Catalogue of Objects by Object Number | 139 |

# PREFACE

*McGuire Gibson*

This book, *Nippur* V, is both the fifth monograph in the series of Oriental Institute Publications devoted to Nippur and the third that reports on a renewed program of research that was initiated in 1972. The previous reports on the renewed program have included *Nippur* III, Richard L. Zettler's treatment of Kassite houses in Area WC-1, and Steven W. Cole's *Nippur* IV, dealing with an important cache of early Neo-Babylonian texts.

Although Nippur, the most important religious center in Mesopotamia (fig. 1), had been excavated by the University of Pennsylvania in the 1890s, and by Chicago since 1948, when I became Director of the Expedition, I was convinced that we needed a new, long-term, expanded research focus. Beginning in the eleventh season (1972/73), we proposed to investigate all parts of Nippur, not just the religious quarter, and especially to work on the West Mound, which had not been touched since the 1890s. We set out to establish a fresh stratigraphic scheme that would confirm, complement, or correct the ceramically based sequences derived from excavations at TA-TB (McCown and Haines 1967) and the Inanna Temple (Hansen 1965). The relatively unbroken stratigraphy of the earlier part of the Inanna Temple sequence, from the Uruk through the Early Dynastic, when combined with the TA-TB sequence, which spanned the Akkadian through the Achaemenid, had been widely accepted as a sound ceramic chronology. But in adopting the Inanna Temple sequence, the field was made conscious of some flaws in the other early standard sequence for Mesopotamia, the one established in the Diyala Region (Delougaz 1952).

The TA-TB sequence, however, also had some problems. The sharp division at the Old Babylonian-Kassite line, reflected dramatically in table 1 of *Nippur* I (McCown and Haines 1967), should have raised doubts as to the soundness of the scheme. Pottery just does not respect the change of dynasties in that way. Pottery and other artifacts do change through time, presumably sometimes at the direction of a new set of rulers, but the changes cannot be immediate, and there is considerable style lag from historical period to historical period. Even artifacts of administration and economy, such as seals and coins, which directly reflect changes in dynasty take a considerable time to abandon the older style.

In the eleventh season, we turned to the West Mound intending not only to create a new stratigraphy, but to investigate especially the Akkadian and Kassite periods, two eras which until then had been given too little attention, despite their importance politically, historically, and artistically. We knew that the Pennsylvania Expedition of the 1890s had found administrative tablets of the Kassite period in an area which we called WA (fig. 2). Here, Pennsylvania had made a huge excavation, leaving a pit more than one hundred meters on a side, but filled with dumps, foundations of gigantic buildings of the Seleucid and Parthian periods, and recently arrived sand dunes. Taking WA as a major area of operations meant that we could be down into Babylonian historical levels much more quickly than if we were to start at an undisturbed part of the mound, where we would have to excavate, record, and remove meters of later occupation.

As part of the WA operation, we sank a stratigraphic pit in a 5 × 5 meter sub-unit called WA 50c, going down about five meters. This pit was meant not only to indicate the sequence of layers we would be meeting in the larger operation, but would also indicate whether or not we had a chance of reaching the Akkadian level. The Akkadian period, the critical juncture between the Inanna Temple and TA-TB sequences had not yet been well defined at Nippur or elsewhere. Up to that time, the number of sites with excavated Akkadian remains was surprisingly small. Tell Asmar and the Ur Cemetery presented major information, but the temporal placement of much of the material was not secure. Kish, which should have yielded crucial information on the period because of Sargon's early linkage to the site, did not yield those data to the excavators. Tell al-Wiliyah was clearly a key excavation, but a reworking of the material by Subhi Anwar Rashid (1963) called for a rethinking of the situation as laid out by the excavator (Madhlum 1960). As it happens, Rashid's re-analysis, using the Diyala sequence as a guide, led to crucial errors in the dating of this most important site. My own excavation at Umm el-Jīr, in cooperation with Dr. Rashid (Gibson 1972b), was a deliberate attempt to expose more of the Akkadian assemblage, but it was a minor operation. At the time, I was not thinking as much about the transition into Akkadian as I was about the assemblage of the period itself and I was still taking the Diyala sequence as a guide.

The WA 50c pit did allow us to reach the Akkadian level, although we mistakenly thought we had also reached the Early Dynastic (Gibson 1975). At that point, we were still several meters above plain level and knew that we had a very good chance of reaching very early levels in the area, if we opened a large enough operation. We hoped to be able to show, eventually, how early the West Mound was occupied, perhaps in the Uruk or even the Ubaid.

The relative richness of Akkadian artifacts in WA 50c argued for a deeper and larger stratigraphic pit, even if we did not expand the WA operation as a whole. But it appeared that we would be expanding WA because there we exposed part of a temple of the Neo-Babylonian period, resting on a series of earlier temples, going down to at least the Ur III period. This temple, not initially identified, was potentially as important as the Inanna Temple as a source for a new sequence of artifacts and architectural information. But rising costs in the 1970s economic boom in Iraq, and logistical problems related to the dunes that continually filled the excavations, forced us to leave WA after three seasons. It was only in the late 1980s, after the dunes had migrated off the mound, that we returned to this area. During the eighteenth and nineteenth seasons (1988/89, 1990), we were able to identify the temple as being devoted to Gula (earlier, Nin-Isin-na). We then began to plan for a much expanded operation of 100 × 100 meters, which did not come to fruition because of the Gulf War.

In those last two seasons, we also sank a new stratigraphic trench, WF, right beside WA 50c. This time, the main aim was to reinvestigate the Akkadian level, but in a much more informed manner.

The new approach to the Akkadian material incorporated work that we had carried out in the meantime at Nippur, Umm al-Hafriyat (a site in the desert 30 km east of Nippur), and at Uch Tepe in the Hamrin Salvage area. Earlier in the 1970s, excavation on and under the late Ur III city wall in area WC-3 at Nippur had given us a very fine, sealed assemblage of Ur III pottery, fixed in time by dated tablets. This material allowed us to see very clearly that there were certain types that have come to be thought of as diagnostic of the Akkadian period (e.g., multiple-ridge-shouldered jars) but were, in fact, introduced very late in that period and were even more at home in the earlier part of Ur III.

Unfortunately, our emphasis on this lag from the Akkadian to Ur III has led some scholars to conclude that the pottery assemblages of the Akkadian and Ur III periods are so similar that they cannot be distinguished. We can, in fact, distinguish the full assemblages of both periods, but must allow a set of types to remain in a "transitional" category, since they can occur on both sides of the time line unless we can fix them by reference to dated tablets or seals. There are new types in Ur III, and one of them seems to occur very early in the period and to last throughout it, with only a rare occurrence still in the earliest part of the Isin-Larsa period. This is the type we have called the band-rimmed bowl. When this type is present, its context can be dated with more than usual confidence to Ur III. There are other more subtle indicators that are easily recognized, once one knows the assemblage in a particular site.

Although we could define the Ur III types at area WC-3, we could not demonstrate the complete succession of pottery types from the Akkadian into the Ur III because there were no Akkadian levels under the Ur III levels in this operation. We thought we had a chance to investigate the succession from Early Dynastic through Akkadian and into Ur III at Umm al-Hafriyat, an important industrial site that we have presented only in very preliminary form (Gibson 1978). Plentiful sherds on one of the mounds seemed to indicate that all three periods (Early Dynastic, Akkadian, Ur III) were present. But our judgment of the pottery was, at that time, still greatly colored by the Diyala sequence (Delougaz 1952). Robert McC. Adams had discovered this site (NS 1088) in his survey of the Nippur area in 1973, and brought it to my attention, saying that it was the largest Akkadian site he had ever seen, and that it was being looted extensively by nomads. Later, the Nippur staff visited the site and found it to consist of four or five mounds, none more than five meters high, lying beside exceptionally visible ancient canal traces. The looting had occurred on only one of the mounds, where Akkadian pottery was tossed up out of graves, along with bronze artifacts. The looters seemed interested only in cylinder seals and beads. The looted mound (later our Area C) had pottery that Adams identified as Early Dynastic through Ur III. A somewhat higher mound (Area A) to the northwest had Ur III, Isin-Larsa, and Old Babylonian sherds. Yet another was covered with Kassite material and another with Seleucid sherds. There was also a very small mound with remains of one public building with plastered floors, datable to the Ur III period. Lastly, the site had a low Uruk period mound with its own small canal, which Adams had not seen, probably because of the dunes.

After several years, we gained permission to excavate the site in 1977. The season was very productive. A detailed, systematic collection showed that rather than being a very large site, it was in fact a relatively small one that shifted through time. Masking its true nature was a halo of pottery kilns with wasters and sherds that were located in part on the mounds, but were mainly spread out onto the plain from each of the mounds. The reason that the site seemed to be so large in the Akkadian period was that sherds that we now identify as Ur III were being identified as Akkadian, adding to the presumed size of the site at that time. The Akkadian mound did, in fact, have a larger than normal group of pottery kilns spread to the north and east. In 1989 we returned to the site to locate with a theodolite and date more than 400 kilns of all periods of occupation. The continued concentration on ceramic production, implied by the numerous kilns, produced enormous amounts of ash that built up within the houses, even when the kilns were located at a distance from the settlement, forcing the inhabitants to shift the location of the town fairly often. In short, rather than being a large site, Umm al-Hafriyat was a relatively small industrial town that moved through time.

Excavation in pits under the earliest levels in three of the mounds at Umm al-Hafriyat yielded the surprising information that virgin soil was reached 50 cm above the present plain in each case. This observation gave us for the first time a graphic illustration of the power of wind erosion as a force in landscape formation in southern Iraq. In one of these pits in Area C, virgin soil was a black, marshy deposit, with some remnants of marsh plants. The first occupation here was Akkadian in date, with no sign of Early Dynastic wares. Adams' identification of Early Dynastic sherds here and in other parts of the site could not be confirmed. In Area A, virgin soil was sandy and its first occupation was in the Ur III period. Another pit under the clay-floored public building of Ur III times, mentioned above, had a similar sandy layer as virgin soil directly under the walls of the building.

In Area C, remains of mudbrick houses were sandwiched between virgin soil and a surface layer that had Ur III kilns but little architecture. The houses were filled with heavy deposits of ash over multiple floors. An unusually rich assortment of artifacts, including cuneiform tablets, cylinder seals, stamp seals, and bronze tools and weapons was recovered from the rooms. There were also eighteen burials, most containing cylinder seals. The seals and cuneiform tablets dated the houses firmly in the later half of the Akkadian period. Here, then, we had a very good sample of later Akkadian ceramics. Among our most important conclusions was that the typical jar of the Akkadian period was one with a single ridge, or only a hint of a ridge, at the shoulder. Multiple ridges did occur, but were rare. Several of our late Akkadian types were those that in WC-3 at Nippur we had seen continuing into the Ur III period. But the bit of Ur III stratigraphy on top of the Akkadian houses also yielded a few types that continued from the late Akkadian, and it also included the important Ur III hallmark, the band-rimmed bowl.

At this point, we had a good stratigraphic transition from the Akkadian to the Ur III. But we did not have the assemblage of the earlier part of the Akkadian period nor the transition from the Early Dynastic to the Akkadian. The next stage in our understanding of the artifacts of the entire Akkadian period was our two seasons at Uch Tepe, in the Hamrin Salvage Project (Gibson et al. 1981). Here, in one tell, Tepe al-Atiqeh, we exposed a house with easily identified "Akkadian" pottery, accompanied by a mature Akkadian seal. With some local variations, the pottery was very much like that in the houses at Umm al-Hafriyat. Under that house were other buildings with pottery similar to material labeled "Protoimperial" in the Diyala.

A second mound at Uch Tepe, Tell Razuk, had burials cutting down into an earlier round building. These burials were furnished with pottery that was akin to the "Protoimperial" level at Tepe al-Atiqeh. In searching for parallels, we looked beyond the Diyala and found them in the A Cemetery at Kish. By comparing the Kish and Diyala artifacts, we became convinced that the Diyala sequence had masked the early Akkadian pottery types under the label "Protoimperial." Further search of original Diyala field records made it clear that an unfortunate set of decisions about the dating of certain materials and levels had led to the misidentification of early Akkadian material under the term "Protoimperial." Continued analysis led to the conclusion that even some Early Dynastic IIIb levels in the Diyala were really early Akkadian in date (Gibson 1982).

The excavation of WF in the eighteenth and nineteenth seasons at Nippur (1988/89, 1990) was aimed specifically at delineating the transition between the Early Dynastic and Akkadian periods, and this goal has been realized. Augusta McMahon took on this task through two seasons, working tirelessly with increasingly unhappy workmen, whose climbs to the dump became even more arduous. The danger of collapse of the sandy baulks at the top of the pit, and the constant threat of a sherd or rock being dislodged and falling on someone meters below meant that the work had to be halted on occasion to carry out remedial measures. Usually, this meant the widening of the top of the pit to make a ledge that would catch debris or slumping sand. We were lucky in that there was no collapse and no injury.

Stratigraphic exposure of floor after floor of artifacts was slowed drastically by a complex stack of burials that took up almost half of the space in the pit. The gain in whole forms offset the diminution of stratified sherds in the living debris. McMahon succeeded in taking the pit down until we could safely say that we had reached Early Dynastic IIIa, and thus had the material to assess the passage from Early Dynastic to Akkadian in artifactual terms.

It is abundantly clear that further work at WA in these ranges of time will be extremely rewarding. All plans for expansion were canceled by the Gulf War, but we hope to return to the work eventually.

Research during the eighteenth and nineteenth seasons was made possible by the permission and encouragement of Dr. Moayyad Sa'id, Director of Antiquities, and our other friends in the Directorate. During the eighteenth season (December 27, 1988 to March 22, 1989), I served as Director. Abbas Fadhil al-Obaydi was the representative of the Department of Antiquities. James A. Armstrong was Associate Director and archaeologist in charge of the WG operation to the southwest of WF. John C. Sanders was the architect, and the plans in this volume are his. Peggy Sanders was artist, photographer, and assistant to the architect. Augusta McMahon was in charge of WF. Robert D. Biggs was epigrapher. Lorraine Brochu was a square supervisor and registrar. Krzysztof Edward Ciuk served as Sasanian/Islamic pottery specialist for the WG operation, working on the subsequent analysis under the supervision of Edward J. Keall of the Royal Ontario Museum. Margaret Brandt was environmental specialist. Pamela Vandiver, a research scientist from the Smithsonian's Conservation Analytical Laboratory, joined us for two weeks in late February to begin a project on the deterioration of glazed ceramics. During the season, we hired up to twenty-seven workmen, who were under the supervision of our foreman, Khalaf Bedawi. The fact that we were working during the Iran-Iraq War meant that we did not have the usual complement of workmen, especially of the trained pickmen, some of whom had been killed at the front. We did, however, find enough trained men to work beside new trainees. Our local expert pickman, Abda Sadeh, was especially important in helping us to train the new men. During this season, work on the Sasanian/Islamic transition was partially supported by a grant from the National Geographic Society.

During the nineteenth season (January 4 to March 25, 1990), conditions were greatly improved because the Iran-Iraq War had ended and there was a general atmosphere of optimism and promise. The Directorate of Antiquities was planning new salvage projects in key areas of Assyria, which could be as productive of new insights about those areas as the Hamrin, Haditha, and Eski Mosul projects had been. The nineteenth season was the most relaxed, productive, and hopeful one in years. I once more served as Director, while Abbas Fadhil al-Obaydi was the government representative, along with Ahmad Hamud Abdullah. James A. Armstrong was Associate Director and supervised the excavation of Area WA. Augusta McMahon continued the digging of WF. John Sanders was the architect and Peggy Sanders assisted him, while also acting as the staff artist. Miguel Civil was epigrapher. Catherine Sease was general conservator while Margaret Schroeder was cuneiform tablet conservator. David Reese was responsible for animal bones and shells. Joel Sweek and Jennifer Artz were square supervisors in WA. John Hudson did the photography. Two Friends of Nippur, Marnie Akins and Alice R. Hayes, joined us for part of the season, giving valuable help in pot-mending and cataloguing of human bones. A team of Smithsonian conservation researchers, comprised of Pamela Vandiver, Martha Goodway, Bylthe McCarthy, and Amy Vandiver, carried out a variety of studies on glaze deterioration and bronze composition.

In both seasons, we were aided financially by the generosity of Friends of Nippur, who have been supporting our efforts since the early 1970s.

We would like to acknowledge the work of Richard L. Zettler, who, as a graduate student in the early 1970s, elaborated our initial typology for the Akkadian–Ur III ranges of ceramics from WC-3 and Umm al-Hafriyat. Guillermo Algaze somewhat later took the WA 50c material and created another very helpful preliminary analysis.

During the preparation of the manuscript for this volume, a number of persons did valuable work on layout, preparation of photographic and computerized plates, computerization of lists, proofreading, and other tasks. These include Clemens Reichel, Jason Ur, and Lamya Khalidi. John and Peggy Sanders were very important in the preparation of final plans and sections.

# BIBLIOGRAPHY

Abu al-Soof, Behnam
 1967 "The Relevance of the Diyala Sequence to South Mesopotamian Sites." *Iraq* 29: 133–42.

Adams, Robert McCormick
 1965 *Land Behind Baghdad: A History of Settlement on the Diyala Plains.* Chicago: University of Chicago Press.
 1981 *Heartland of Cities: Surveys of Ancient Settlement and Land Use on the Central Floodplain of the Euphrates.* Chicago: University of Chicago Press.

Adams, Robert McCormick, and Hans Jörg Nissen
 1972 *The Uruk Countryside: The Natural Setting of Urban Societies.* Chicago: University of Chicago Press.

al-Kassar, Awad
 1979 "Tell Abu Qassem." *Sumer* 35: 473–76.
 1983 "Tell Abu Qasim Excavation." *Sumer* 40: 59–60.

Amiet, Pierre
 1961 *La glyptique mésopotamienne archaïque.* Paris: Centre national de la recherche scientifique.

Andrae, Walter
 1970 *Die archäischen Ischtar-Tempel in Assur.* Wissenschaftliche Veröffentlichungen der Deutschen Orient-Gesellschaft 39. Osnabrück: Otto Zeller. Reprint of 1922 edition.

Armstrong, James A.
 1993 "Pottery." In *Nippur, Volume 3: Kassite Buildings in Area WC-1*, by Richard Zettler, pp. 67–80. Oriental Institute Publications 111. Chicago: The Oriental Institute.

Armstrong, James A., and Margaret C. Brandt
 1994 "Ancient Dunes at Nippur." In *Cinquante-deux réflexions sur le Proche-Orient ancien offertes en hommage à Léon de Meyer*, edited by H. Gasche, M. Tanret, C. Janssen, and A. Degraeve, pp. 255–63. Leuven: Peeters.

Bahrani, Zainab
 1989 The Administrative Building at Tell Al Hiba, Lagash. Ph.D. dissertation, New York University.

Baker, Heather
 1995 "Neo-Babylonian Burials Revisited." In *The Archaeology of Death in the Ancient Near East*, edited by Stuart Campbell and Anthony Green, pp. 209–20. Oxbow Monograph 51. Oxford: Oxbow Books.

Banks, Edgar James
 1912 *Bismya, or the Lost City of Adab: A Story of Adventure, of Exploration, and of Excavation among the Ruins of the Oldest of the Buried Cities of Babylonia.* New York: G. P. Putnam.

Barag, Dan P.
 1962 "Mesopotamian Glass Vessels of the Second Millennium B.C." *Journal of Glass Studies* 4: 9–27.
 1970 "Mesopotamian Core-Formed Glass Vessels (1500–500 B.C.)." In *Glass and Glassmaking in Ancient Mesopotamia: An Edition of the Cuneiform Texts Which Contain Instructions on Glassmakers with a Catalogue of Surviving Objects*, by A. Leo Oppenheim, Robert H. Brill, Dan Barag, and Axel von Saldern, pp. 129–99. Corning Museum of Glass Monographs 3. Corning: Corning Museum of Glass.
 1975 "Rod-Formed Kohl-Tubes of the Mid-First Millennium B.C." *Journal of Glass Studies* 17: 23–36.
 1985 *Catalogue of Western Asiatic Glass in the British Museum*, Volume 1. London: British Museum Press.

Beck, Horace C.
 1931 "Beads from Nineveh." *Antiquity* 5: 427–37.
 1934 "Glass before 1500 B.C." *Ancient Egypt and the East* 19: 7–21.

Biggs, Robert D.
  1973  "On Regional Cuneiform Handwritings in Third Millennium Mesopotamia." *Orientalia*, n.s., 42: 39–46.
  1974  *Inscriptions from Tell Abū Ṣalābīkh*. Oriental Institute Publications 99. Chicago: University of Chicago Press.

Bimson, M., and I. C. Freestone
  1988  "Some Egyptian Glasses Dated by Royal Inscriptions." *Journal of Glass Studies* 30: 11–15.

Bimson, M., and A. E. Werner
  1967  "Two Problems in Ancient Glass: Opacifiers and Egyptian Core Material." *Annales du 4ᵉ Congrès des Journées Internationales du Verre*, pp. 262–63.

Böck, B.; R. M. Boehmer; J. Boessneck; M. van Ess; G. Meinert; L. Patzelt; and M. Peter-Patzelt
  1993  "Uruk 38 (1989)." *Baghdader Mitteilungen* 24: 3–126.

Boehmer, Rainer Michael
  1965  *Die Entwicklung der Glyptik während der Akkad-Zeit*. Berlin: Walter de Gruyter.
  1967  "Die Entwicklung der Hörnerkrone von ihren Anfängen bis zum Ende der Akkad-Zeit." *Berliner Jahrbuch für Vor- und Frühgeschichte* 7: 273–91.
  1991  "Lugalzagesi, der Bauherr des Stampflehmgebäudes in Uruk." *Baghdader Mitteilungen* 22: 165–74.
  1993  "Kleinfunde." In "Uruk 39 (1989)," edited by Barbara Böck, Rainer Michael Boehmer, Joachim Boessneck, Margarete van Ess, Günter Meinert, Lambert Patzelt, and Michaela Peter-Patzelt, pp. 18–48. 1993. *Baghdader Mitteilungen* 24: 3–126.

Boehmer, Rainer Michael; Freidhelm Pedde; and Beate Salje
  1995  *Uruk: Die Gräber*. Deutsches archäologisches Institut, Abteilung Baghdad, Ausgrabungen in Uruk-Warka, Endberichte 10. Mainz: Philipp von Zabern.

Braidwood, Robert J., and Linda S. Braidwood
  1960  *Excavations in the Plain of Antioch, Volume 1: The Earlier Assemblages, Phases A–J*. Oriental Institute Publications 61. Chicago: University of Chicago Press.

Braun-Holzinger, Eva
  1993  "Die Ikonographie des Mondgottes in der Glyptik des III. Jahrtausends v. Chr." *Zeitschrift für Assyriologie* 83: 119–35.

Brill, Robert H.
  1969  "The Scientific Investigation of Ancient Glass." In *Proceedings of the Eighth International Congress on Glass*, pp. 47–68.
  1970  "The Chemical Interpretation of the Texts." In *Glass and Glassmaking in Ancient Mesopotamia: An Edition of the Cuneiform Texts Which Contain Instructions on Glassmakers with a Catalogue of Surviving Objects*, by A. Leo Oppenheim, Robert H. Brill, Dan Barag, and Axel von Saldern, pp. 105–28. Corning Museum of Glass Monographs 3. Corning: Corning Museum of Glass.

Brill, Robert H., and Nicholas D. Cahill
  1988  "A Red Opaque Glass from Sardis and Some Thoughts on Red Opaques in General." *Journal of Glass Studies* 30: 16–27.

Buchanan, Briggs
  1981  *Early Near Eastern Seals in the Yale Babylonian Collection*. New Haven: Yale University Press.
  1966  *Catalogue of Ancient Near Eastern Seals in the Ashmolean Museum*, Volume 1: *Cylinder Seals*. Oxford: Clarendon Press.

Carter, Elizabeth
  1980  "Excavations in Ville Royale 1 at Susa: The Third Millennium B.C. Occupation." *Cahiers de la Délégation archéologique française en Iran* 11: 11–134.

Cholidis, Nadja
  1992  *Möbel in Ton: Untersuchungen zur archäologischen und religionsgschichtlichen Bedeutung der Terrakottamodelle von Tischen, Stühlen und Betten aus dem Alten Orient*. Altertumskunde der Vorderen Orients 1. Münster: Ugarit-Verlag.

Civil, Miguel
  1975  "Appendix A: Cuneiform Texts." In *Excavations at Nippur: Eleventh Season*, by McGuire Gibson, pp. 125–42. Oriental Institute Communications 22. Chicago: University of Chicago Press.

Colbow, Gudrun
- 1997 "More Insights into Representations of the Moon God in the Third and Second Millennium B.C." In *Sumerian Gods and Their Representations*, edited by I. L. Finkel and M. J. Geller, pp. 19–31. Groningen: Styx Publications.

Collon, Dominique
- 1982 *Catalogue of the Western Asiatic Seals in the British Museum, Cylinder Seals*, Volume 2: *Akkadian, Post-Akkadian, Ur III Periods*. London: British Museum Press.
- 1987 *First Impressions: Cylinder Seals in the Ancient Near East*. Chicago: University of Chicago Press.
- 1995 "Mondgott." *Reallexikon der Assyriologie und vorderasiatischen Archäologie* 8/5–6: 371–76.
- 1997 "Moon, Boats and Battle." In *Sumerian Gods and Their Representations*, edited by I. L. Finkel and M. J. Geller, pp. 11–17. Groningen: Styx Publications.

Damerji, Muayad Said Basim
- 1999 *Gräber assyrischer Königinnen aus Nimrud*. Jahrbuch des römisch-germanischen Zentralmuseums 45. Mainz: Römisch-germanisches Zentralmuseum.

Delougaz, Pinhas
- 1940 *The Temple Oval at Khafājah*. Oriental Institute Publications 53. Chicago: University of Chicago Press.
- 1952 *Pottery from the Diyala Region*. Oriental Institute Publications 63. Chicago: University of Chicago Press.

Delougaz, Pinhas; Harold D. Hill; and Seton Lloyd
- 1967 *Private Houses and Graves in the Diyala Region*. Oriental Institute Publications 88. Chicago: University of Chicago Press.

Delougaz, Pinhas, and Seton Lloyd
- 1942 *Pre-Sargonid Temples in the Diyala Region*. Oriental Institute Publications 58. Chicago: University of Chicago Press.

Druc, Isabelle
- 1989 "La poterie." In *Ḥabl aṣ-Ṣaḫr 1986, nouvelles fouilles: L'ouvrage défensif de Nabochodonosor II au nord de Sippar*, edited by Hermann Gasche, pp. 39–53. Northern Akkad Project Reports 2. Ghent: University of Ghent.

Edzard, D. O.
- 1980 "Keilschrift." *Reallexikon der Assyriologie und vorderasiatischen Archäologie* 5: 544–68.

de Feyter, Theo
- 1988 "The Metal Finds." In *Hammam et-Turkman*, Volume 1: *Report on the University of Amsterdam's 1981–84 Excavations in Syria 2*, edited by Maurits N. van Loon, pp. 609–25. Nederlands Historisch-Archeologisch Instituut te Istanbul. Leiden: Nederlands Instituut voor het Nabije Oosten.

Fielden, Kate
- 1977 "Tell Brak 1976: The Pottery." *Iraq* 39: 245–55.

Finkbeiner, Uwe
- 1991 *Uruk, Kampagne 35–37, 1982–1984: Die archäologische Oberflächenuntersuchung (Survey)*. Deutsches archäologisches Institut, Abteilung Baghdad, Ausgrabungen in Uruk-Warka, Endberichte 4. Mainz: Philipp von Zabern.

Fischer, Claudia
- 2002 "Twilight of the Sun-God." *Iraq* 64: 125–34.

Forest, Jean-Daniel
- 1980 "Kheit Qasim 1: Un cimetière du début du troisième millénaire dans la vallée de Hamrin, Iraq." *Paléorient* 6: 213–20.

Foster, Benjamin R.
- 1977 "Commercial Activity in Sargonic Mesopotamia." *Iraq* 39: 31–43.
- 1982 *Umma in the Sargonic Period*. Memoirs of the Connecticut Academy of Arts and Sciences 20. Hamden: Archon Books.

Frankfort, Henri
- 1934 *Iraq Excavations of the Oriental Institute 1932/33*. Oriental Institute Communications 17. Chicago: University of Chicago Press.
- 1955 *Stratified Cylinder Seals from the Diyala Region*. Oriental Institute Publications 72. Chicago: University of Chicago Press.

Garner, Harry
- 1956 "An Early Piece of Glass from Eridu." *Iraq* 18: 147–49.

Gasche, Hermann
    1989    *La Babylonie au 17ᵉ siècle avant notre ère: Approche archéologique, problèmes et perspectives.* University of Ghent Mesopotamian History and Environment Series 2, Memoirs 1. Ghent: University of Ghent.

Gasche, Hermann; James A. Armstrong; Steven W. Cole; and V. G. Gurzadyan
    1998    *Dating the Fall of Babylon: A Reappraisal of Second-Millennium Chronology.* Mesopotamian History and Environment Series 2, Memoirs 4. Ghent: University of Ghent; Chicago: The Oriental Institute.

Gelb, I. J.
    1959    "Hurrians at Nippur in the Sargonic Period." In *Festschrift Johannes Friedrich zum 65. Geburtstag am 27. August 1958 gewidmet,* edited by Richard von Kienle, pp. 183–95. Heidelberg: C. Winter.

Gelb, I. J.; Piotr Steinkeller; and Robert Whiting
    1991    *Earliest Land Tenure Systems in the Near East: Ancient Kudurrus.* Oriental Institute Publications 104. Chicago: The Oriental Institute.

Gibson, McGuire
    1972a    *The City and Area of Kish.* Edited by Henry Field and Edith M. Laird. Miami: Field Research Projects.
    1972b    "Umm el-Jīr, A Town in Akkad." *Journal of Near Eastern Studies* 31: 237–94.
    1975    *Excavations at Nippur: Eleventh Season.* Oriental Institute Communications 22. Chicago: University of Chicago Press.
    1981    *Uch Tepe 1: Tell Razuk, Tell Ahmed al-Mughir, Tell Ajamat.* Edited by McGuire Gibson. Hamrin Report 10. Chicago: The Oriental Institute.
    1982    "A Re-evaluation of the Akkad Period in the Diyala Region on the Basis of Recent Excavations at Nippur and in the Hamrin." *American Journal of Archaeology* 86: 531–38.
    1992    "Patterns of Occupation at Nippur." In *Nippur at the Centennial,* edited by Maria deJong Ellis, pp. 33–54. Papers Read at the 35ᵉ Rencontre Assyriologique Internaionale, Philadelphia, 1988. Occasional Publications of the Samuel Noah Kramer Fund 14. Philadelphia: The University Museum.
    1993    "Introduction." In *Nippur,* Volume 3: *Kassite Buildings in Area WC-1,* by Richard L. Zettler, pp. 1–9. Oriental Institute Publications 111. Chicago: The Oriental Institute.

Gibson, McGuire; Judith A. Franke; Miguel Civil; Michael L. Bates; Joachim Boessneck; Karl W. Butzer; Ted A. Rathbun; and Elizabeth Frick Mallin
    1978    *Excavations at Nippur: Twelfth Season.* Oriental Institute Communications 23. Chicago: The Oriental Institute.

Gibson, McGuire; James A. Armstrong; and Augusta McMahon
    1998    "The City Walls of Nippur and an Islamic Site Beyond: Oriental Institute Excavations, 17th Season, 1987." *Iraq* 60: 11–44.

Gibson, McGuire, and Augusta McMahon
    1995    "Investigation of the Early Dynastic-Akkadian Transition: Report of the 18th and 19th Seasons of Excavation in Area WF, Nippur." *Iraq* 57: 1–39.

Gibson, McGuire, and Augusta McMahon
    1997    "The Early Dynastic-Akkadian Transition, Part 2: The Authors' Response." *Iraq* 59: 9–14.

Goetze, A.
    1968    "Akkad Dynasty Inscriptions from Nippur." *Journal of the American Oriental Society* 88: 54–59.

Green, Anthony
    1993    *The 6G Ash-Tip and Its Contents: Cultic and Administrative Discard from the Temple?* Edited by Anthony Green. Abu Salabikh Excavations 4. London: British School of Archaeology in Iraq.

Green, Margaret W., and Hans J. Nissen
    1987    *Zeichenliste der archäischen Texte aus Uruk.* Ausgrabungen der Deutschen Forschungsgemeinschaft in Uruk-Warka 11, Archäische Texte aus Uruk 2. Berlin: Mann.

Hackman, George Gottlieb
    1958    *Sumerian and Akkadian Administrative Texts from Predynastic Times to the End of the Akkad Dynasty.* Babylonian Inscriptions in the Collection of James

B. Nies, Yale University 8. New Haven: Yale University Press.

Haerinck, Ernie
1980 "Les tombes et les objets du sondage sur l'enceinte de Abū Ḥabbah." In *Tell ed-Dēr* 3: *Sounding at Abū Ḥabbah (Sippar)*, edited by Léon de Meyer, pp. 53–79. Leuven: Peeters.

Hall, Harry R.
1930 *A Season's Work at Ur*. London: Methuen.

Hall, Harry R., and C. Leonard Woolley
1927 *Ur Excavations*, Volume 1: *Al-'Ubaid*. Oxford: Oxford University Press.

Haller, Arndt
1954 *Die Gräber und Grüfte von Assur*. Wissenschaftliche Veröffentlichung der Deutschen Orient-Gesellschaft 65. Berlin: Mann.

Hallo, W., and W. Simpson
1971 *The Ancient Near East: A History*. New York: Harcourt, Brace, and Javanovich.

Hansen, Donald P.
1965 "The Relative Chronology of Mesopotamia, Part 2: The Pottery Sequence at Nippur from the Middle Uruk to the End of the Old Babylonian Period (3400–1600 B.C.)." In *Chronologies in Old World Archaeology*, edited by Robert W. Ehrich, pp. 201–13. Chicago: University of Chicago Press.
1973 "Al-Hiba, 1970–1971: A Preliminary Report." *Artibus Asiae* 35: 62–78.
1992 "Royal Building Activity at Sumerian Lagash in the Early Dynastic Period." *Biblical Archaeologist* 55: 206–11.

Harley, Rosamond D.
1970 *Artists' Pigments c. 1600–1835: A Study in English Documentary Sources*. New York: American Elsevier Publishing; London: Butterworth Scientific.
1982 *Artists' Pigments c. 1600–1835: A Study in English Documentary Sources*. Second Edition. London: Butterworth Scientific.

Hauptmann, Ralf
1991 "Ein akkadzeitliches Relieffragment aus Ḫafāǧī." *Mitteilungen des Deutschen Orient-Gesellschaft zu Berlin* 123: 149–56.

Hedges, R. E. M.
1976 "Pre-Islamic Glazes in Mesopotamia—Nippur." *Archaeometry* 18: 209–13.

Hedges, R. E. M., and P. R. S. Moorey
1975 "Pre-Islamic Glazes at Kish and Nineveh in Iraq." *Archaeometry* 17: 25–43.

Hrouda, Barthel
1977 *Isin-Išān Baḥrīyāt* 1: *Die Ergebnisse der Ausgrabungen 1973–1974*. Edited by Barthel Hrouda. Philosophisch-historische Klasse Abhandlungen, neue Folge, 79. Munich: Bayerische Akademie der Wissenschaften.
1981 *Isin-Išān Baḥrīyāt* 2: *Die Ergebnisse der Ausgrabungen 1975–1978*. Edited by Barthel Hrouda. Philosophisch-historische Klasse Abhandlungen, neue Folge, 87. Munich: Bayerische Akademie der Wissenschaften.
1987 *Isin-Išān Baḥrīyāt* 3: *Die Ergebnisse der Ausgrabungen 1983–1984*. Edited by Barthel Hrouda. Philosophisch-historische Klasse Abhandlungen, neue Folge, 94. Munich: Bayerische Akademie der Wissenschaften.

Hrouda, Barthel, and K. Karstens
1967 "Zur inneren Chronologie des Friedhofs 'A' in Ingharra/Chursagkalama bei Kiš." *Zeitschrift für Assyriologie* 58: 256–98.

Jacobsen, Thorkild
1957 "Early Political Development in Mesopotamia." *Zeitschrift für Assyriologie* 52: 91–140.

Killick, Robert, and Michael Roaf
1979 "Excavations at Tell Madhhur." *Sumer* 35: 534–42.

Krecher, J.
1987 "IGI+LAK-527 SIG$_5$, gleichbedeutend GIŠ.ÉREN; LAK-647." *Mari, Annales des recherches interdisciplinaires* 5: 623–25.

Kühne, Hartmut
1976 *Die Keramik von Tell Chuēra und ihre Beziehungen zu Funden aus Syrien-Palästina, der Türkei und dem Iraq*. Berlin: Gebr. Mann.

Laird, Marsa
1984  Linear-Style Cylinder Seals of the Akkadian to Post-Akkadian Periods. Ph.D. dissertation, New York University.

Langdon, Stephen
1924  *Excavations at Kish,* Volume 1: *1923–1924.* Paris: Paul Geuthner.

Lebeau, Marc
1985  "Rapport préliminaire sur la séquence céramique du chantier B de Mari (III$^{ème}$ millénaire)." *Mari, Annales des recherches interdisciplinaires* 4: 93–126.

Legrain, Leon
1926  *Royal Inscriptions and Fragments from Nippur and Babylon.* Publications of the Babylonian Section, University Museum 15. Philadelphia: University Museum.
1930  *Terra-Cottas from Nippur.* University of Pennsylvania, The University Museum, Publications of the Babylonian Section 16. Philadelphia: University of Pennsylvania Press.
1951  *Seal Cylinders.* Ur Excavations 10. London: British Museum Press; Philadelphia: The University Museum.

Lewy, Julius
1935  *Texte und Materialen der Frau Professor Hilprecht Collection of Babylonian Antiquities im Eigentum der Universität Jena.* Vorsargonische und Sargonische Wirtschaftstexte 5. Leipzig: J. C. Hinrichs.

Limper, Klaudia
1988  *Uruk, Perlen, Ketten, Anhänger, Grabungen 1912–1985.* Deutsches archäologisches Institut, Abteilung Baghdad, Ausgrabungen in Uruk-Warka, Endberichte 2. Mainz: Philipp von Zabern.

Lindemeyer, Elke, and Lutz Martin
1993  *Uruk, Kleinfunde* 3. Deutsches archäologisches Institut, Abteilung Baghdad, Ausgrabungen in Uruk-Warka, Endberichte 9. Mainz: Philipp von Zabern.

Lloyd, Seton, and Fuad Safar
1943  "Tell Uqair, Excavations by the Iraq Government Directorate of Antiquities in 1940 and 1941." *Journal of Near Eastern Studies* 2: 131–58.

Longacre, William
1991  "Ceramic Ethnoarchaeology: An Introduction." In *Ceramic Ethnoarchaeology,* edited by William Longacre, pp. 1–10. Tucson: University of Arizona Press.

Mackay, Ernest
1925  *Report on the Excavations of the "A" Cemetery at Kish, Mesopotamia,* Part 1. Chicago: Field Museum of Natural History.
1929  *A Sumerian Palace and the "A" Cemetery at Kish, Mesopotamia,* Part 2. Chicago: Field Museum of Natural History.

Madhlum, Tariq A.
1960  "The Excavations at Tell al-Wilayah." *Sumer* 16: 62–92 (Arabic section).

Mallowan, M. E. L.
1947  "Excavations at Brak and Chagar Bazar." *Iraq* 9: 1–259.

Martin, Harriet P.
1982  "The Early Dynastic Cemetery at al-'Ubaid: A Re-evaluation." *Iraq* 44: 145–85.
1983  "Settlement Patterns at Shuruppak." *Iraq* 45: 24–31.
1988  *Fara: A Reconstruction of the Ancient Mesopotamian City of Shuruppak.* Birmingham: Chris Martin.

Martin, Lutz
1993  "Teil 1: Steingefässe." In *Uruk, Kleinfunde* 3: *Kleinfunde im Vorderasiatischen Museum zu Berlin: Steingefässe und Asphalt, Farbreste, Fritte, Glas, Holz, Knochen/Elfenbein, Muschel/Perlmutt/ Schnecke,* by Elke Lindemeyer and Lutz Martin, pp. 3–235. Deutsches archäologisches Institut, Abteilung Baghdad, Ausgrabungen in Uruk-Warka, Endberichte 9. Mainz: Philipp von Zabern.

Martin, Harriet P.; Jane Moon; and J. Nicholas Postgate
1985  *Graves 1 to 99.* Abu Salabikh Excavations 2. London: British School of Archaeology in Iraq.

Matson, Frederick R.
1986  "Glazed Brick from Babylon: Historical Setting and Microprobe Analysis." In *Ceramics and Civilization,* Volume 2:

*Technology and Style,* edited by W. D. Kingery, pp. 133–56. Columbus: American Ceramic Society.

Matthews, Donald
1997 "The Early Dynastic-Akkadian Transition, Part 1: When Did the Akkadian Period Begin?" *Iraq* 59: 1–7.

Matthews, Roger J.; J. Nicholas Postgate; and E. J. Luby
1987 "Excavations at Abu Salabikh, 1985–86." *Iraq* 49: 91–119.

McCown, Donald E., and Richard C. Haines
1967 *Nippur: Excavations of the Joint Expedition to Nippur of the University Museum of Philadelphia and the Oriental Institute of the University of Chicago,* Volume 1: *Temple of Enlil, Scribal Quarter, and Soundings.* Oriental Institute Publications 78. Chicago: University of Chicago Press.

McCown, Donald E.; Richard C. Haines; and Robert D. Biggs
1978 *Nippur: Excavations of the Joint Expedition to Nippur of the University Museum of Philadelphia and the Oriental Institute of the University of Chicago,* Volume 2: *The North Temple and Sounding E.* Oriental Institute Publications 97. Chicago: University of Chicago Press.

McMahon, Augusta
1998 "The Kuyunjik Gully Sounding, Nineveh, 1989 and 1990 Seasons." *Al-Rāfidān* 19: 1–32.

Moon, Jane A.
1981 "Some New Early Dynastic Pottery from Abu Salabikh." *Iraq* 43: 47–75.
1982 "The Distribution of Upright-handled Jars and Stemmed Dishes in the Early Dynastic Period." *Iraq* 44: 39–69.
1987 *Catalogue of Early Dynastic Pottery.* Abu Salabikh Excavations 3. London: British School of Archaeology in Iraq.

Moorey, P. R. S.
1970 "Cemetery A at Kish: Grave Groups and Chronology." *Iraq* 32: 86–128.
1982 "The Archaeological Evidence for Metallurgy and Related Technologies in Mesopotamia, c. 5500–2100 B.C." *Iraq* 44: 13–38.
1985 *Materials and Manufacture in Ancient Mesopotamia: The Evidence of Archaeology and Art.* British Archaeological Reports, International Series 237. Oxford: British Archaeological Reports.
1994 *Ancient Mesopotamian Materials and Industries: The Archaeological Evidence.* Oxford: Clarendon Press.

Moortgat, Anton
1966 *Vorderasiatische Rollsiegel.* Berlin: Gebr. Mann.

Moortgat-Correns, Ursula
1988 *Tell Chuēra in Nordost-Syrien: Vorläufiger Bericht über die zehnte Grabungskampagne, 1983.* Berlin: Gebr. Mann.

Müller-Karpe, Michael
1993 *Metallgefäße im Iraq 1 (von den Anfängen bis zur Akkad-Zeit).* Prähistorische Bronzefunde, Abteilung 2, Band 14. Stuttgart: Franz Steiner.

Nissen, Hans Jörg
1966 *Zur Datierung des Königsfriedhofes von Ur unter besonderer Berücksichtigung der Stratigraphie der Privatgräber.* Bonn: Rudolf Habelt.

Oates, David; Joan Oates; and Helen McDonald
2001 *Excavations at Tell Brak,* Volume 2: *Nagar in the Third Millennium B.C.* Cambridge: McDonald Institute for Archaeological Research; London: British School of Archaeology in Iraq.

Oppenheim, A. Leo; Robert H. Brill; Dan Barag; and Axel von Saldern
1970 *Glass and Glassmaking in Ancient Mesopotamia: An Edition of the Cuneiform Texts Which Contain Instructions on Glassmakers with a Catalogue of Surviving Objects.* Corning Museum of Glass Monographs 3. Corning: Corning Museum of Glass.

Parrot, André
1948 *Tello, vingt campagnes de fouilles (1877–1933).* Paris: Albin Michel.
1956 *Le temple d'Ishtar.* Mission archéologique de Mari 1; Bibliothèque archéologique et historique 65. Paris: Paul Geuthner.
1959 *Le palais.* Mission archéologique de Mari 2; Bibliothèque archéologique et historique 68. Paris: Paul Geuthner.

1967 *Les temples d'Ishtarat et de Ninni-zaza.* Mission archéologique de Mari 3; Bibliothèque archéologique et historique 86. Paris: Paul Geuthner.

Partington, J. R.
1935 *Origins and Development of Applied Chemistry.* London: Longmans, Green and Co.

Philip, Graham
1997 "The Metal Objects." In *Excavations at Tell Brak,* Volume 1: *The Mitanni and Old Babylonian Periods,* edited by David Oates, Joan Oates, and Helen McDonald, pp. 113–24. London: British School of Archaeology in Iraq and McDonald Institute for Archaeological Research.

Pollard, A. M., and P. R. S. Moorey
1982 "Some Analyses of Middle Assyrian Faience and Related Materials from Tell al-Rimah in Iraq." *Archaeometry* 24: 45–50.

Pollock, Susan
1985 "Chronology of the Royal Cemetery of Ur." *Iraq* 47: 129–58.
1991 "Of Priestesses, Princes and Poor Relations: The Dead in the Royal Cemetery of Ur." *Cambridge Archaeological Journal* 1: 171–89.

Pomponio, Francesco
1984 "Notes on Fara Texts." *Orientalia,* n.s., 53: 1–18.

Pongratz-Leisten, Beate
1988 "Keramik der frühdynastischen Zeit aus den Grabungen in Uruk-Warka." *Baghdader Mitteilungen* 19: 177–319.

Porada, Edith; Donald P. Hansen; Sally Dunham; and Sidney H. Babcock
1992 "The Chronology of Mesopotamia, ca. 7000–1600 B.C." In *Chronologies in Old World Archaeology,* edited by Robert W. Ehrich, pp. 77–121. Third edition. Chicago: University of Chicago Press.

Postgate, Nicholas J.
1977 "Excavations at Abu Salabikh, 1976." *Iraq* 39: 269–99.
1980 "Excavations at Abu Salabikh, 1978–79." *Iraq* 42: 87–104.
1984 "Excavations at Abu Salabikh, 1983." *Iraq* 46: 95–113.
1990 "Excavations at Abu Salabikh, 1988–89." *Iraq* 52: 95–106.
1997 "Mesopotamian Petrology: Stages in the Classification of the Material World." *Cambridge Archaeological Journal* 7: 205–24.

Postgate, Nicholas J., and Jane A. Moon
1982 "Excavations at Abu Salabikh, 1981." *Iraq* 44: 103–36.
1984 "Late Third Millennium Pottery from Abu Essalabikh." *Sumer* 43: 69–79.

Postgate, Nicholas J., and P. R. S. Moorey
1976 "Excavations at Abu Salabikh, 1975." *Iraq* 38: 133–69.

Potts, Timothy
1993 "Stone Vessels." In *The 6G Ash-Tip and Its Contents: Cultic and Administrative Discard from the Temple?,* edited by Anthony Green, pp. 159–61. Abu Salabikh Excavations 4. London: British School of Archaeology in Iraq.
1994 *Mesopotamia and the East: An Archaeological and Historical Study of Foreign Relations ca. 3400–2000 B.C.* Oxford University Committee for Archaeology Monograph 37. Oxford: Oxbow Books.

Rashid, Fawzi
1983 "Akkadian Texts from Tell Sleima." *Sumer* 40: 55–56.

Rashid, Subhi Anwar
1963 "Die Ausgrabung von Tell el-Wilayah und die Bedeutung ihrer Rollsiegel." *Sumer* 19: 82–106.

Rashid, Subhi Anwar, and Hayat Abd 'Ali Huri
1983 *The Akkadian Seals of the Iraq Museum.* Baghdad: State Organization of Antiquities and Heritage.

Rathje, William L.
1977 "New Tricks for Old Seals: A Progress Report." In *Seals and Sealing in the Ancient Near East,* edited by McGuire Gibson and Robert D. Biggs, pp. 25–32. Bibliotheca Mesopotamica 6. Malibu: Undena.

Reade, Julian E.
1968 "Tell Taya (1967): Summary Report." *Iraq* 30: 234–64.

Rmaidh, Salah Salman
    1983    "Tell Sleima Excavations (Second Season)." *Sumer* 40: 57–58.

Roaf, Michael
    2001    "Doubts about the Two-lobed Burial and the Survival of Early Dynastic to Akkadian Transitional Building Levels in Area WF at Nippur." *Iraq* 63: 55–66.

Roaf, Michael; Deborah Downs; Jane A. Moon; Philip Watson; Robert Miller; and Janie Rees Miller
    1984    "Tell Madhhur: A Summary Report on the Excavations." *Sumer* 43: 108–67.

Rutten, K.
    1996    "Late Achaemenid and Hellenistic Pottery from the Tombs of Maḥmūdīyah, Abū Qubūr and Tell ed-Dēr." *Northern Akkad Project Reports* 10: 7–38.

Salje, Beate
    1992    "Keramik der neubabylonischen Zeit aus den Grabungen in Uruk-Warka." *Baghdader Mitteilungen* 23: 371–464.
    1996    "Becher für die Toten? Bronzene Trinksets und ihre Bedeutung im Grabkult." *Baghdader Mitteilungen* 27: 429–46.

Sax, Margaret; Dominique Collon; and M. N. Leese
    1993    "The Availability of Raw Materials for Near Eastern Cylinder Seals during the Akkadian, Post-Akkadian and Ur III Periods." *Iraq* 55: 77–90.

Saxe, Arthur A.
    1970    Social Dimensions of Mortuary Practices. Ph.D. dissertation, University of Michigan.

Sayre, Edward V.
    1963    "The Intentional Use of Antimony and Manganese in Ancient Glasses." In *Advances in Glass Technology* 2, edited by F. R. Matson and G. E. Rindone, pp. 263–82. New York: Plenum Press.

Sayre, Edward V., and R. W. Smith
    1967    "Some Materials of Glass Manufacturing in Antiquity." In *Archaeological Chemistry: A Symposium*, edited by M. Levy, pp. 279–311. Philadelphia: University of Pennsylvania Press.
    1974    "Analytical Studies of Ancient Egyptian Glass." In *Recent Advances in Science and Technology of Materials* 3, edited by A. Bishay, pp. 47–70. New York: Plenum Press.

Sayre, Edward V.; K. Aslıhan Yener; Emile C. Joel; J. M. Blackman; and H. Özbal
    2001    "Stable Lead Isotope Studies of Black Sea Anatolian Ore Sources and Related Bronze Age and Phrygian Artefacts from Nearby Archaeological Sites. Appendix: New Central Taurus Ore Data." *Archaeometry* 43: 77–115.

Selz, Gebhard J.
    1993    *Altsumerische Verwaltungstexte aus Lagash*, Part 2: *Altsumerische Wirtschaftsurkunden aus amerikanischen Sammlungen* 1. Freiburger altorientalische Studien 15:2. Stuttgart: Franz Steiner.
    1994    "Verwaltungsurkunden in der Eremitage in St. Petersburg." *Acta Sumerologica* 16: 207–29.
    1995    "Den Fährmann bezahlen! Eine lexikalisch-kulturhistorische Skizze zu den Bedeutungen von addir." *Altorientalische Forschungen* 22: 197–209.

Speiser, Ephraim
    1935    *Excavations at Tepe Gawra*, Volume 1: *Levels I–VIII*. American Schools of Oriental Research. Philadelphia: University of Pennsylvania Press.

Starr, Richard F. S.
    1937    *Nuzi: Report on the Excavations at Yorgan Tepa near Kirkuk, Iraq, 1927–1931*, Volume 2. Cambridge: Harvard University Press.
    1939    *Nuzi: Report on the Excavations at Yorgan Tepa near Kirkuk, Iraq, 1927–1931*, Volume 1. Cambridge: Harvard University Press.

Steinkeller, Piotr, and J. N. Postgate
    1992    *Third-Millennium Legal and Administrative Texts in the Iraq Museum, Baghdad*. Winona Lake: Eisenbrauns.

Steve, Marie-Joseph, and Hermann Gasche
    1971    *L'acropole de Suse*. Mémoires de la Délégation archéologique en Iran 46. Paris: Paul Geuthner; Leiden: Brill.

Stone, Elizabeth C.
    1987    *Nippur Neighborhoods*. Studies in Ancient Oriental Civilization 44. Chicago: The Oriental Institute.

Strommenger, Eva
- 1964 "Grabformen in Babylon." *Baghdader Mitteilungen* 3: 157–73.

Stronach, David
- 1978 *Pasargadae: A Report on the Excavations Conducted by the British Institute of Persian Studies from 1961 to 1963*. Oxford: Clarendon Press.

Tallon, Françoise
- 1987 *Métallurgie susienne 1: De la fondation de Suse, au XVIII$^e$ siècle avant J.-C*. Paris: Musées nationaux.

Tinney, Steve
- 1998 "Death and Burial in Early Mesopotamia: The View from the Texts." In *Treasures from the Royal Tombs of Ur*, edited by Richard L. Zettler and Lee Horne, pp. 26–28. Philadelphia: University of Pennsylvania Museum.

Tosi, Maurizio
- 1974 "The Problem of Turquoise in Protohistoric Trade on the Iranian Plateau." *Studi di paletnologia, paleoantropologia, paleontologie e geologia del quaternario*, nova series, 2: 147–62.

Trumpelmann, Leo
- 1982 "Tell Abqaʿ, Vorläufiger Bericht über die Ausgrabungen der Hamrin Expedition der Ludwig-Maximilians Universität, München, 1. Kampagne." *Sumer* 38: 40–49.

Tunca, Önhan
- 1987 *Tell Sabra*. Edited by Önhan Tunca. Akkadica Supplementum 5. Leuven: Peeters.

Turner, W. E. S., and H. P. Rooksby
- 1959 "A Study of the Opalising Agents in Ancient Opal Glasses throughout Three Thousand Four Hundred Years, Part 1." *Glastechnische Berichte* 8: 17–28.
- 1963 "A Study of the Opalising Agents in Ancient Opal Glasses throughout 3400 Years, Part 2." In *Advances in Glass Technology*. New York: Plenum Press.

Vandiver, Pamela B.
- 1982 "Mid-Second Millennium B.C. Soda-Lime-Silicate Technology at Nuzi (Iraq)." In *Early Pyrotechnology: The Evolution of the First Fire-Using Industries*, edited by Theodore A. Wertime and Steven F. Wertime, pp. 73–92. Washington, D.C.: Smithsonian Institution Press.
- 1983 "Glass Technology at the Mid-Second-Millennium B.C. Hurrian Site of Nuzi." *Journal of Glass Studies* 25: 239–47.

Vandiver, Pamela B.; McGuire Gibson; and Augusta McMahon
- 1995 "Glass Manufacture in the Late Third Millennium B.C. at Nippur in Iraq." In *The Ceramics of Cultural Heritage*, edited by P. Vincenzini, pp. 331–41. Techna Monographs in Materials and Society, Vol. 2. Faenza: Techna.

van Ess, Margarete
- 1988 "Keramik von der Akkad bis zum Ende der altbabylonischen Zeit aus den Planquadraten N XV und XVI und aus dem Sînkāšid-Palast in Uruk-Warka." *Baghdader Mitteilungen* 19: 321–442.
- 1993 "Inventarisierte Keramik." In "Uruk 39 (1989)," edited by B. Böck, R. M. Boehmer, J. Boessneck, M. van Ess, G. Meinert, L. Patzelt, and M. Peter-Patzelt, pp. 52–83. *Baghdader Mitteilungen* 24: 5–126.

van Ess, Margarete, and Friedhelm Pedde
- 1992 *Uruk, Kleinfunde 2*. Deutsches archäologisches Institut, Abteilung Baghdad, Ausgrabungen in Uruk-Warka, Endberichte 7. Mainz: Philipp von Zabern.

Waetzoldt, Hartmut
- 1972 *Untersuchungen zur neusumerischen Textilindustrie*. Studi Economici e Tecnologici 1. Rome: Centro per le Antichità e la Storia dell'Arte del Vicino Oriente.

Wainwright, Ian N. M.; John M. Taylor; and Rosamond D. Harley
- 1986 "Lead Antimonate Yellow." In *Artists' Pigments: A Handbook of Their History and Characteristics*, Volume 1, edited by R. L. Feller, pp. 219–54. Cambridge: Cambridge University Press.

Wall-Romana, Christophe
- 1990 "An Areal Location of Agade." *Journal of Near Eastern Studies* 49: 205–45.

Wallenfels, Ronald
- 1994 *Uruk: Hellenistic Seal Impressions in the Yale Babylonian Collection 1: Cuneiform Tablets*. Deutsches archäologisches Ins-

titut, Abteilung Baghdad, Ausgrabungen in Uruk-Warka, Endberichte 19. Mainz: Philipp von Zabern.

Warburton, R. C.
- 1989 "Keramik und Kleinfunde (1987)." In *Abū Qubūr 1987–1988, Chantier F: La résidence achéménide*, edited by Hermann Gasche, pp. 25–34. Northern Akkad Project Reports 4. Ghent: University of Ghent.

Watkins, Trevor
- 1983 "Cultural Parallels in the Metalwork of Sumer and North Mesopotamia in the Third Millennium B.C." *Iraq* 45: 18–23.

Westenholz, Aage
- 1987 *Old Sumerian and Old Akkadian Texts in Philadelphia,* Part 2: *The "Akkadian" Texts, the Enlilemaba Texts, and the Onion Archive.* Carsten Niebuhr Institute Publications 3. Copenhagen: Museum Tusculanum Press.

Woolley, C. Leonard
- 1934 *The Royal Cemetery.* Ur Excavations 2. London: The British Museum; Philadelphia: The University Museum.
- 1962 *The Neo-Babylonian and Persian Periods.* Ur Excavations 9. London: The British Museum; Philadelphia: The University Museum.

Zettler, Richard L.
- 1977 "The Sargonic Royal Seal: A Consideration of Sealing in Mesopotamia." In *Seals and Sealing in the Ancient Near East,* edited by McGuire Gibson and Robert D. Biggs, pp. 33–39. Bibliotheca Mesopotamica 6. Malibu: Undena.
- 1978 Review of *Die Keramik von Tell Chuēra und ihre Beziehungen zu Finden aus Syrien-Palästina, der Türkei und dem Iraq,* by Hartmut Kühne. *Journal of Near Eastern Studies* 37: 345–50.
- 1984 The Ur III Inanna Temple at Nippur. Ph.D. dissertation, University of Chicago.
- 1993 *Nippur,* Volume 3: *Kassite Buildings in Area WC-1.* Oriental Institute Publications 111. Chicago: The Oriental Institute.

# INTRODUCTION
## THE AREA WF SOUNDING AT NIPPUR

The results presented here formed part of the University of Chicago excavation program at Nippur during 1989 and 1990. One of the expressed goals of the excavations since 1972 has been the investigation of chronological questions, which Nippur, strategically located near the center of southern Mesopotamia (fig. 1) and carrying great religious significance, may be uniquely equipped to answer. The specific question which the excavation of the Area WF sounding addressed was that of the archaeological characterization of the third-millennium B.C. transition from the Early Dynastic to the Akkadian period. In Area WF, an unbroken sequence of domestic occupation levels was exposed for the Early Dynastic IIIa through the late Ur III or Isin-Larsa periods, with additional levels of Kassite and first-millennium B.C. date. This volume represents the final report on the entire excavation, with the main focus on the third-millennium B.C. levels.

### The Early Dynastic III–Akkadian Transition and the Akkadian Period

The transition from the city-states of the Early Dynastic period to the unified national entity of the Akkadian period was one of the most important transitions in southern Mesopotamian political history. The new nation, while not long-lived, became an administrative and ideological template for later rulers to recreate and expand upon. Since the Early Dynastic and Akkadian periods are marked by quite distinct political structures, there has perhaps been a general assumption that there should be equally distinct differences between the archaeological records of each period. "Late Early Dynastic" and "Akkadian" are used to describe styles of artworks and material culture as well as history and politics. But while stylistic change may be relatively rapid in some media (e.g., cylinder seals, public art), injection or development of a new style in these media does not necessarily drive out a previous style completely. Change is potentially far slower in other forms of cultural expression (pottery, architecture), with previous types and traditions frequently extending well across historical boundaries. It may be a very long time after a historical event occurs for its effects to become visible in the structure of a site or in a regional settlement pattern. The archaeological use of the "Early Dynastic" and "Akkadian" labels and the assemblages ascribed to these periods are due for reassessment.

The inevitable difficulty in the archaeological definition of historical transitions is, in this case, compounded by variability in breadth of the archaeological record for the crucial periods. The late Early Dynastic period is reasonably well represented historically and very well represented archaeologically. But while many specific historical events of the Akkadian period are well known from contemporary and later texts, the archaeological evidence is variable, with numerous artworks and grave groups attested but domestic and public contexts underrepresented. Not only has the transition between the two periods, in archaeological terms, remained unclear, but so has the definition of the archaeological assemblage(s) within the Akkadian period.

The Diyala sites, especially Tell Asmar and Khafajah, have the best-known and best-published material from the late Early Dynastic and Akkadian periods (Delougaz 1940, 1952; Delougaz, Hill, and Lloyd 1967; Frankfort 1955; Delougaz and Lloyd 1942). But more recent work by the University of Chicago at Nippur in Area WC-3 and at the site of Umm al-Hafriyat, northeast of Nippur, in textually dated levels of the late Akkadian and Ur III periods, indicates that the dating of some of the Diyala material should be revised (Gibson 1982). From those excavations, it became clear that some pottery types called "Akkadian" in the Diyala publications (and elsewhere since those excavations are widely used for comparanda throughout Mesopotamia) actually belonged only to the later half of the Akkadian period and continued into the following Ur III period.

In addition to the reassessment and redating of "Akkadian" pottery types, Gibson's critical look at the Diyala records in conjunction with excavation of late Early Dynastic and early Akkadian material from the Hamrin resulted in a redating of earlier levels of the Diyala sites (Gibson 1981, 1982). Much of the "Early Dynastic IIIb" and all the "Protoimperial" material were relabeled as early Akkadian. However, this redating has not been applied consistently to material from southern Mesopotamia excavated since that time, nor has it been possible up till now

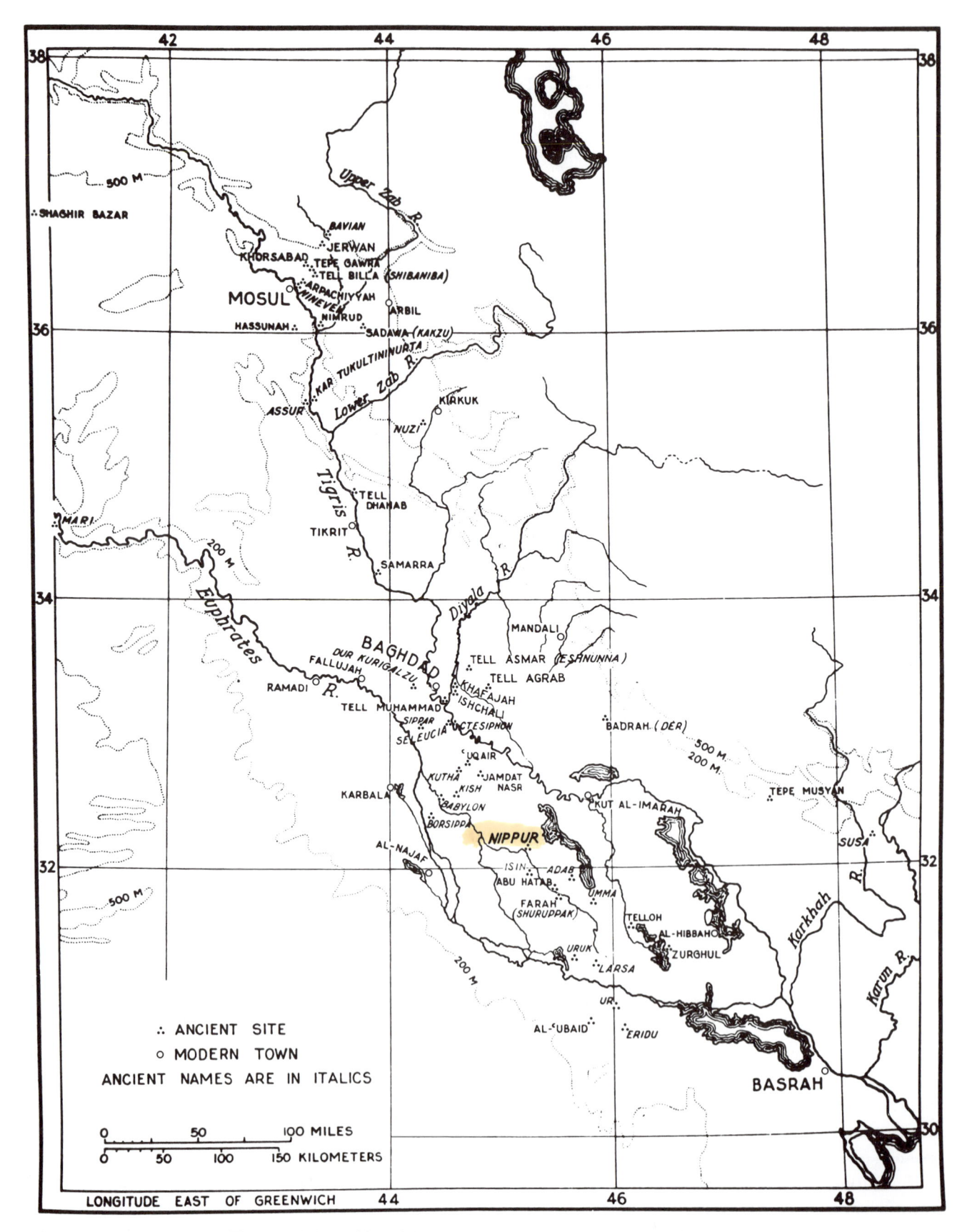

Figure 1. Map of South Mesopotamia Showing Location of Nippur

to present a comprehensive pottery assemblage for the early part of the Akkadian period. The result has been that the archaeological transition from Early Dynastic to Akkadian has remained unclear.[1] The use of the "Early Dynastic IIIb" label at some sites but not at others has added to the confusion surrounding the archaeological identification of the historical transition.[2]

The archaeological evidence for the Akkadian period is only slightly less problematic than that for the transition between the late Early Dynastic and early Akkadian. There are cemeteries in southern Mesopotamia from which Akkadian material is known, and a few levels within sequences of large public buildings can be assigned to the Akkadian period. In addition, deposits belonging to the end of the Akkadian period and the following Ur III period have been investigated at a few sites.[3] But excavated domestic occupational material of the early Akkadian period is rare, as are stratigraphic columns giving the entire internal sequence of the Akkadian period. While a great deal has been published about the artistic development in the Akkadian period, most of the cylinder seals on which this research has been based come from graves or the art market, while the reliefs and statues have commonly been found out of their original contexts. No clear sequence of pottery, architecture, or objects has been published for the Akkadian period as a whole, either from a single site or as a combination of all the available data.

The phenomenon of archaeological type continuity from one historical period into the next is unsurprising, but it has not been consistently acknowledged and incorporated into many previous studies. As with the continuity of types from late Akkadian into Ur III, proven by the excavations at Nippur Area WC-3 and at Umm al-Hafriyat, there should also be a continuity or lag of pottery types from the late Early Dynastic into the Akkadian period. The redefinition of the former "Akkadian" assemblage as "late Akkadian/Ur III" should have an impact upon how we look at the early part of the Akkadian period and the late Early Dynastic period. One question remaining is the depth of type continuity from one period to the next. Does continuity occur to the same depth in all types or might it be possible to discern a few pottery types which could be used for a tighter definition of either the late Early Dynastic III or the early Akkadian period? Perhaps what is needed is a wider recognition and use of the term "late Early Dynastic/early Akkadian" to describe material which, in fact, is transitional and cannot be assigned with certainty to one period or the other. But while archaeological data favor overlapping or combined labels (e.g., Early Dynastic III–early Akkadian, late Akkadian–Ur III), the presence of texts and our knowledge of historical events and agents make such compromises awkward. If these issues could be resolved, more transitional material may be identified, "Akkadian" levels at various sites might be pinned down to early or late in the period, cemetery sequences could be reshuffled, and the copious historical information we have about the Akkadian period would be better contextualized.

---

1. Other sites with excavated material of the late Early Dynastic period which may continue into the early Akkadian period include Kish (Mackay 1925, 1929), Tell Uqair (Lloyd and Safar 1943), Tell Deylam (unpubl.), Umm el-Jīr (Gibson 1972b), Abu Salabikh (Martin, Moon, and Postgate 1985; Matthews, Postgate, and Luby 1987; Moon 1981, 1987; Postgate 1977, 1980, 1984, 1990; Postgate and Moon 1982, 1984; Postgate and Moorey 1976), previous excavations at Nippur (McCown and Haines 1967; McCown, Haines, and Biggs 1978), Tell al-Wilayah (Madhlum 1960; Rashid 1963), Fara (Martin 1988), Adab (Banks 1912), Tell al-Hiba (Bahrani 1989; Hansen 1973), Ur (Woolley 1934), Uruk (Boehmer 1991), Tell Razuk (Gibson 1981), Tepe al-Atiqeh (unpubl.), Tell Abu Qasem (al-Kasar 1979, 1983), and Tell Madhhur (Killick and Roaf 1979; Roaf et al. 1984). At many of these sites, the relevant material comes from graves and is not fully representative of the cultural assemblage of the period. In most cases, the material is published as late Early Dynastic, with the possibility of extension into the Akkadian period briefly mentioned. The dating of cemeteries by their stratigraphy and associated art objects is fraught with difficulty; some attempts have been made to redate the material from some of these sites (Hrouda and Karstens 1967; Martin 1982; Moorey 1970; Nissen 1966; Pollock 1985), but with mixed results.
2. See, most importantly, Porada et al. 1992: 112–13; Hansen 1992.
3. Umm al-Hafriyat (unpubl.) and Tell Asmar (Delougaz 1952; Delougaz and Lloyd 1942; Delougaz, Hill, and Lloyd 1967) have well-excavated samples of stratified material of Akkadian date; at Abu Salabikh (Postgate and Moon 1984) and Fara (Martin 1988), there is late Akkadian–Ur III pottery in drains and pits, though the associated settlements have eroded away. There are graves at Ur and Kish from throughout the Akkadian period, and excavations at Adab, Isin (Hrouda 1977, 1981), Uruk (van Ess 1988), Tepe al-Atiqeh (unpubl.), Tell Sleima (Rmaidh 1983, Rashid 1983), and the Inanna Temple and Area TB at Nippur have produced material of Akkadian date, but their placement within that period has suffered from the lack of a full independent southern sequence for comparison. Excavation at Umm el-Jīr (Gibson 1972b) did uncover a relevant sequence for apparently all of the period, but in a very small exposure. In northern Mesopotamia, sequences including strata of the Akkadian period have been excavated at Nineveh, Tell Brak, Tell Leilan, Tell Taya, Tell Mozan, Tell Chuera, and Tell Hamoukar, among others, with more levels of Akkadian date being revealed every year as excavation in northern Mesopotamia intensifies. But the northern pottery and architectural traditions have little in common with the southern. Similarly, there are contemporary levels excavated at Susa, but parallels with southern Mesopotamian material culture are few.

Regional surveys for settlement pattern reconstruction would also be aided by reassessment of terms and by identification of a tighter group of pottery types for determination of site dates. Surveys are always plagued by the difficulties inherent in defining and then finding distinct sets of pottery types (upon which they must necessarily rely) to match historically defined periods. It is unfortunate but inevitable that a settlement pattern attributed to the latter half of one (politically defined) period and the beginning of another (e.g., Early Dynastic III–Akkadian) may cover variant forms of government, different locations of capital cities, shifts in foreign contact corridors, and vastly different "mental maps." Surveys in south Mesopotamia have used various strategic groupings to deal with the pottery of the later third millennium B.C.: Early Dynastic I–III, Akkadian/Guti, and Ur III groups for the Diyala (Adams 1965); Early Dynastic II–III and Akkadian–Ur III for the area around Uruk (Adams and Nissen 1972); Early Dynastic II–III, Akkadian, and Ur III for the central plains (Adams 1981); Early Dynastic I–III, Akkadian, and Ur III–Isin-Larsa for the area around Kish (Gibson 1972a); Early Dynastic II–III and Akkadian for the site survey of Fara (Martin 1983, 1988); and Early Dynastic II–III, Akkadian–Ur III, and Ur III–Isin-Larsa for the Uruk site survey (Finkbeiner 1991b).

In each survey, the Early Dynastic III and Akkadian assemblages have been assumed to be distinct enough that they can be firmly and completely separated from each other, although they have been variously combined with earlier or later material, respectively. The "Akkadian" types generally used can now be shown to be late Akkadian types, and it can be shown that the "Early Dynastic III" types may continue into the early Akkadian. Given the assumptions of a consistent division between Early Dynastic and Akkadian (notably acknowledged as problematic only by Gibson 1972a), the "Akkadian" pattern discerned in these studies (whether the extent of occupation of a site or pattern of sites in an area) probably applies only to the late Akkadian period and the earlier part of the Ur III period, while the "Early Dynastic" pattern must also include a picture of the situation in the early Akkadian period.

## Chronological Problems

The problem with the definition of the end of the Early Dynastic and beginning of the Akkadian period in the archaeological record is magnified by the difficulty in defining a single historical moment for this change. The moment might be attached to a specific agent, such as the first attestation of Sargon. But if the focus is on events, rather than the presence of an agent, we might pin the historical term "Akkadian" to the military evidence, to the date at which the "empire" was established according to the texts, rather late in Sargon's reign. The historical moment might also be political or economic, for instance when the Akkadian administration took hold, unfortunately a more difficult point to pinpoint. Or, if emphasis is placed on ideological aspects, we would need to look for the moment of visible impact in the artistic and archaeological record (which could be during the reign of Manishtushu or more probably represented by the monuments and building programs of Naram-Sin). Finally, we might have to look for the point at which use of the Akkadian language became widespread. All these first occurred at slightly different times and then spread unevenly across the Mesopotamian landscape.

While this is not the place to go in depth into the historical and social setting for the Akkadian "empire," it should be noted that it is possible that Lugalzagesi, the last "Early Dynastic" king of Uruk, probably overlapped with Sargon during much of the latter's reign.[4] This overlap has an effect on those kings supposed to have immediately preceded Lugalzagesi at Uruk and Lagash in particular, bringing some of them potentially into an overlap with Sargon as well. Since it seems that some of those individuals may themselves have overlapped with Lugalzagesi, the stacking-up of kings makes the historical situation exceedingly complicated. Most relevant for understanding the archaeological sequence is the fact that, depending on the depth of overlap of Lugalzagesi and Sargon, some of the kings of Lagash for whom the "Early Dynastic IIIb" label was adopted (possibly Enanatum II, Enentarzi, Lugalanda, and Urukagina) probably overlapped with Sargon. Thus any level, artifact, or group of pottery types defined as Early Dynastic IIIb (or "Protoimperial" in the Diyala) might equally be early Akkadian.

---

4. A situation with Sargon in control of the northern alluvial plain and Lugalzagesi in control of the south, based at Uruk, is plausible. Such a situation would partially explain why Lugalzagesi never claimed to be "king of Kish," although he was apparently militarily powerful. A substantial temporal overlap of Sargon and Lugalzagesi may be indicated by the continued presence of Lugalzagesi as *ensi* of Umma during the reign of Sargon's son and successor Rimush (Hallo 1971: 57; Foster 1982: 155). An Urukagina is listed on the Manishtushu Obelisk (Gelb, Steinkeller, and Whiting 1991: side A3, column xv, lines 7–10), which may indicate the overlap of this "ED IIIb" *ensi* of Lagash with Sargon and Lugalzagesi (Jacobsen 1957). A Meskigal, *ensi* of Adab, appears to have been a contemporary of both Lugalzagesi (Hackman 1958: no. 26) and Rimush (Legrain 1926: no. 41, an Old Babylonian copy).

# The Excavation of Area WF

During the eighteenth and nineteenth seasons of the University of Chicago excavations at Nippur (1989 and 1990), a deep sounding, Area WF, was made on the West Mound. The intent was to clarify the archaeological sequence of the late Early Dynastic through early Akkadian periods for southern Mesopotamia. The background to the Area WF sounding goes back to 1972 (the eleventh season of excavations at Nippur), when a stratigraphic trench (Area WA 50c) was sunk in the same area (fig. 2); the intention at that time was to supplement the Inanna Temple sequence for the Early Dynastic and Akkadian periods. The sounding was located at the bottom of a runoff *wadi*, about ten meters lower than the highest point of the West Mound (pl. 1). This low area was chosen in order to avoid the overburden of late occupations and to reach levels of the third millennium B.C. as quickly as possible. The Area WA 50c sounding reached a depth of 8 m, with levels dating from the Akkadian through the Parthian period.[5]

Area WF is located just north of Area WA 50c (figs. 2 and 3).[6] Since 1972, the third-millennium B.C. material from WA 50c has been augmented by further excavations at Nippur in Area WC-3 in 1975, 1976, and 1987 and at Umm al-Hafriyat, ca. 30 kilometers east of Nippur, in 1977. The Area WC-3 excavations recovered sufficient material to characterize the entire Ur III period in terms of pottery and other artifacts and Umm al-Hafriyat provided an excellent sample of late Akkadian through Ur III material. But the assemblages of the late Early Dynastic and early Akkadian periods remained underexplored.

Over two seasons of excavation, Area WF reached a depth of 12 m, with nineteen definable stratigraphic levels ranging in date from Early Dynastic IIIa through Parthian (pl. 2).[7] The dating of the levels rests primarily on a number of independently datable seals, sealings, tablets, and other objects located throughout the stratigraphic column. The lowest six meters of the sounding uncovered an essentially unbroken sequence for the third millennium B.C., from Early Dynastic IIIa through late Ur III or Isin-Larsa (Levels XIX–VI). There was then an abandonment during the Old Babylonian period, followed by a Kassite level (Level V) and then a second abandonment. Finally, there were three first-millennium B.C. levels (Level IV–II), and a modern sand layer (Level I).[8]

Area WF was laid out as a 10 × 10 m square. Since the upper 2–3 m consisted of sand, a one meter wide inward step was made for safety at a depth of 2 m, reducing the excavated area to approximately 8 × 8 m. With each successive level removed, the excavated area was further curtailed by the necessity of leaving access stairs intact (pl. 182); at Level XIX, the lowest level reached, the excavation was about 5.0 × 4.5 m in extent (pl. 2a and b). Despite these limitations, a representative range of domestic contexts was identified, both indoor and outdoor spaces, rooms, courtyards, and open areas.[9] If a larger horizontal exposure had been attempted, the excavation would not have been able to reach the depth it did. It should be noted that excavation of the trench was stopped at just under 84 m above datum, about 1 m above the modern plain level around the site. From the evidence in trenches excavated by Carl Haines in the West Mound, it can be assumed that there are an additional 5 or 6 m of occupation now below plain level, and that there is a very good chance that an expanded and deepened stratigraphic pit could have reached layers of Uruk or even Ubaid date in this location (Gibson, pers. comm.).

---

5. See Gibson 1975, especially pp. 71–103. In the original publication, the lowest level in WA 50c was tentatively attributed to the late Early Dynastic period. The excavation in WF indicates that it should be dated within the Akkadian period.

6. Between the 1972 and 1989 seasons, a single site grid was created for Nippur, replacing the individual architecture-related grids used for each area. The change to the new site-wide grid involved a shift from Area WA's prior orientation to a directly north–south orientation, a movement of about 21 degrees toward the north. Thus, as can be seen in figure 3, Areas WA 50c and WF are at an angle to each other.

7. For a preliminary report on Area WF, see Gibson and McMahon 1995.

8. The two abandonments within the WF sequence are further evidence for the two site-wide abandonments reconstructed for the occupational history of Nippur. For the Old Babylonian period abandonment, see Gibson 1992; Stone 1987; for the post-Kassite abandonment, see Gibson 1992; Armstrong and Brandt 1994.

9. The Nippur system of excavation recording revolves around identification of three-dimensional loci, usually defined by ancient walls or pits or the excavation sections. Loci are assigned numbers in a sequence that is unique for a specific area. All walls are given letter designations that are also unique within that area (a wall in Area WA may have the same letter designation as one in Area WF, but no two walls in Area WF have the same letter, and the same applies to locus numbers). In general, a single locus number is retained until the bottom of any wall (or walls) defining that locus is reached. Then a new locus number is assigned and used until the bottom of the next wall is reached. Thus a single wall may be associated with a series of locus numbers, which are variously shaped in plan according to their other defining walls. Loci usually run continuously from wall to wall, from wall to section, or from wall to a cut or other later disturbance; but there are a few loci which may be associated with one architectural feature but which thin out and stop before reaching a section or second wall.

Individual loci are horizontally subdivided into floors, usually harder surfaces within accumulated layers of occupational debris. Floors are numbered as they are excavated, smaller numbers being higher and larger numbers lower in the stratigraphic column. With each new locus number, the sequence of inter-

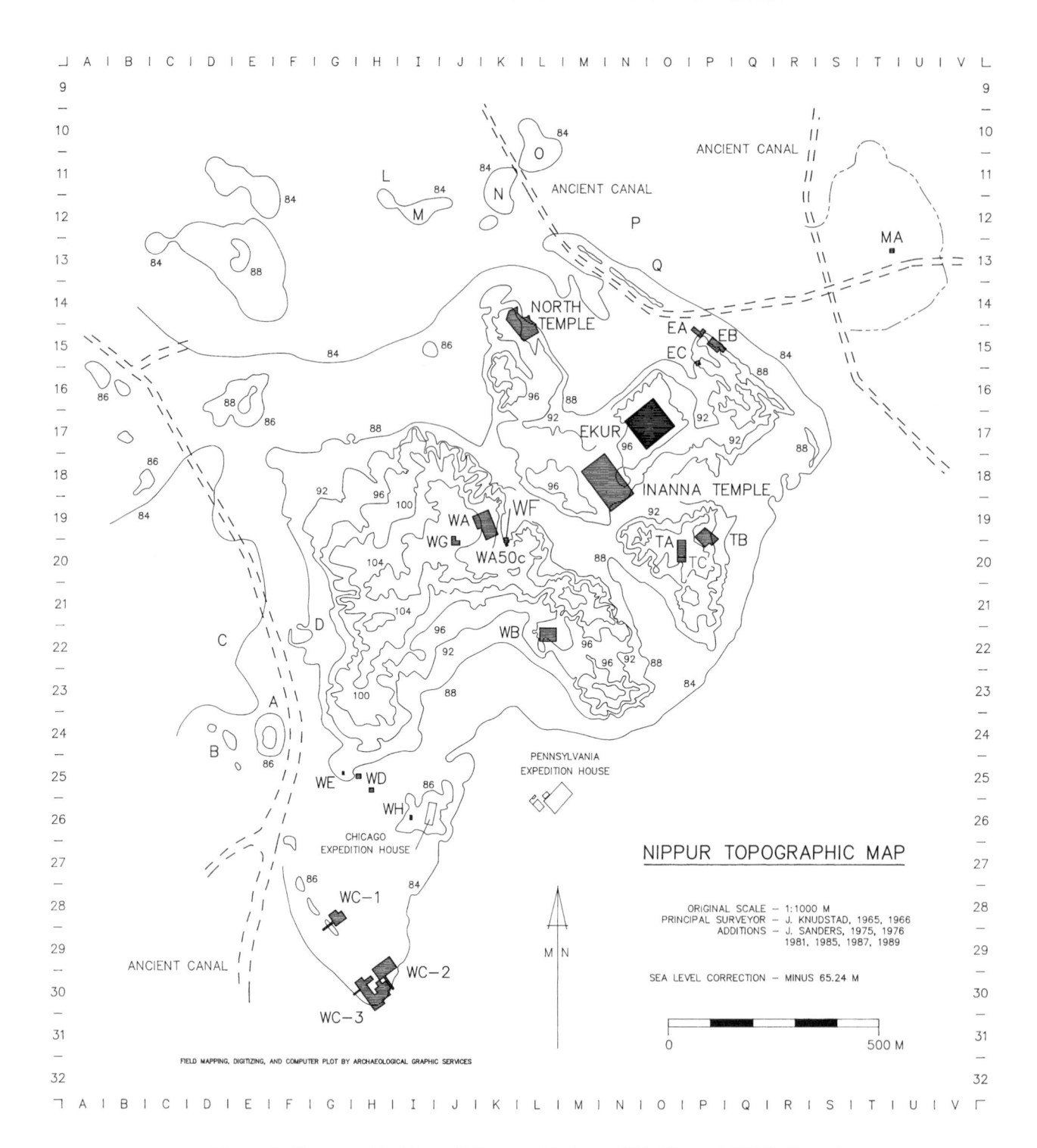

Figure 2. Topographic Map of Nippur with Areas WA 50c and WF Indicated

nal floor numbers begins again. In Area WF, the floors identified and numbered were selected from among a large potential number of surfaces within the occupational buildup. Generally, they were distinguished from others by reason of color change, slightly harder feel, or density of pottery, any of which made it possible to trace that surface successfully. The material from the excavated layers between identified floors is here noted as "above floor x"; this does not mean that the object in question was floating or was deposited in an unusual way. Most of these objects were originally deposited or dropped on a floor or surface, but a minor floor to which we did not assign a number and which was excavated together with a number of other minor surfaces. In a few cases, a layer above a floor will be the result of one event — trash dumping or other deliberate fill, identified as "deliberate fill above floor x" — but in Area WF the layers between labeled floors generally represent gradual accumulation over time.

Burials are numbered in sequence, with the sequence being unique to an area. Finally, ancient cuts or pits are also assigned numbers within yet another area-specific sequence. In the plans of the individual levels included here, burial numbers are indicated on the plan of the level from which the burial was made;

The area of the WF excavation was domestic in function almost throughout the entire sequence of occupation, as indicated by the type of construction, nature of the accumulated deposits, presence of burials below the structures in many levels, and the buildings' contents. This continuity affords a look at the consistency of privately organized construction techniques over time. The only possible exceptions to the domestic function are in the Kassite and final first-millennium B.C. levels.

## Architectural Plans

Due to the small size of the sounding, aimed at investigation of a diachronic, rather than a synchronic question, entire building plans were not recovered in any level. However, even in the absence of complete information, some aspects of the buildings, particularly those of the third millennium B.C., are worth further discussion. The architecture of the very lowest levels of the sounding (Levels XIX–XV) was quite variable. However, from Level XIVB (pl. 14) and above, the area had a distinctive and consistent arrangement. In the area exposed, a courtyard took up the northeastern part of the excavation, with a small room to the southeast. At the west was another space reached by a door from the courtyard; and at the northwest corner of the excavation was a final room or wall corner, perhaps belonging to a separate building. This building plan was retained, with the exception of one level and some minor alterations, through the next eight levels (through Level VI). The persistence of this arrangement through levels that can be dated to the Akkadian period and into the Ur III period indicates the stability of property lines and the likelihood that the property ownership was held by a single family throughout.

It is not clear in what portion of the building the Area WF excavation was located, despite the presence of a courtyard in the majority of levels. The ideal Mesopotamian house may have had a central courtyard surrounded by rooms, but the larger exposure of contemporary houses in Area TB at Nippur (McCown and Haines 1967: pl. 52, Levels XI–X) indicates that in a tightly packed urban situation, this ideal plan was not often realized. The courtyard might be at the side or front of the house as often as at the center. It is also not certain in which direction the entrance and the main core of the structure are to be found. Area WA 50c, immediately south of Area WF, contained levels contemporary with Area WF Level XIII and above with a comparable domestic structure. The two areas might together reveal part of the same building, in which case most of the house probably lies south of Area WF. However, no walls could be connected between the two excavations with absolute certainty, and it cannot be proved that the two areas did not expose parts of two separate structures, perhaps with party walls.

Only a single architectural fragment of the Kassite period (Level V) was excavated. The exposed portion of the better-preserved structure in the seventh century B.C. level (Level IV) has only two rooms. Only the corner of a structure was exposed in Level III. To judge by the presence of graves below building floors, the area was still domestic in character during Level IV, but more formal construction in Levels V and III may indicate that the area had a different nature during those phases of occupation.

## Construction Details

The buildings in all levels of Area WF were of mudbrick, with occasional drains, door sockets, and other features in baked brick. Throughout the entire sequence, the thickness of the walls was such that it is not likely that any structure was more than one story, with the roof presumably used for domestic activities and even household-based manufacture but not itself bearing any substantial superstructure. The width of walls in the Early Dynastic through Ur III levels varied from a flimsy 30 cm to almost a meter, with most around 60–70 cm wide.

---

where the burial pit intrudes into levels below that, it is shown on those plans but labeled simply as "cut." Other installations, such as drains, firepits, ovens, or other small features, are labeled as such but were not assigned any other designations.

The minimum collection unit used in Nippur excavations is a "lot." Any object, bag of pottery, bag of bones, etc. collected is assigned a lot number. Each lot is given a unique designation: the excavation season is signified by a letter (here "H" for the eighteenth season and "I" for the nineteenth), and there is a sequence of numbers, beginning with 1, used during that season among all the areas under excavation. So, for instance, lots H1–99 may have been used in WF, lots H100–99 in WA, and so on; there is no overlap of lot numbers among areas. In general, separate lot numbers were given to pottery collected from on and from above a defined floor. In some instances the excavation of a layer above a floor was carried out over two or more days, in which case new lot numbers were assigned to collections from different days.

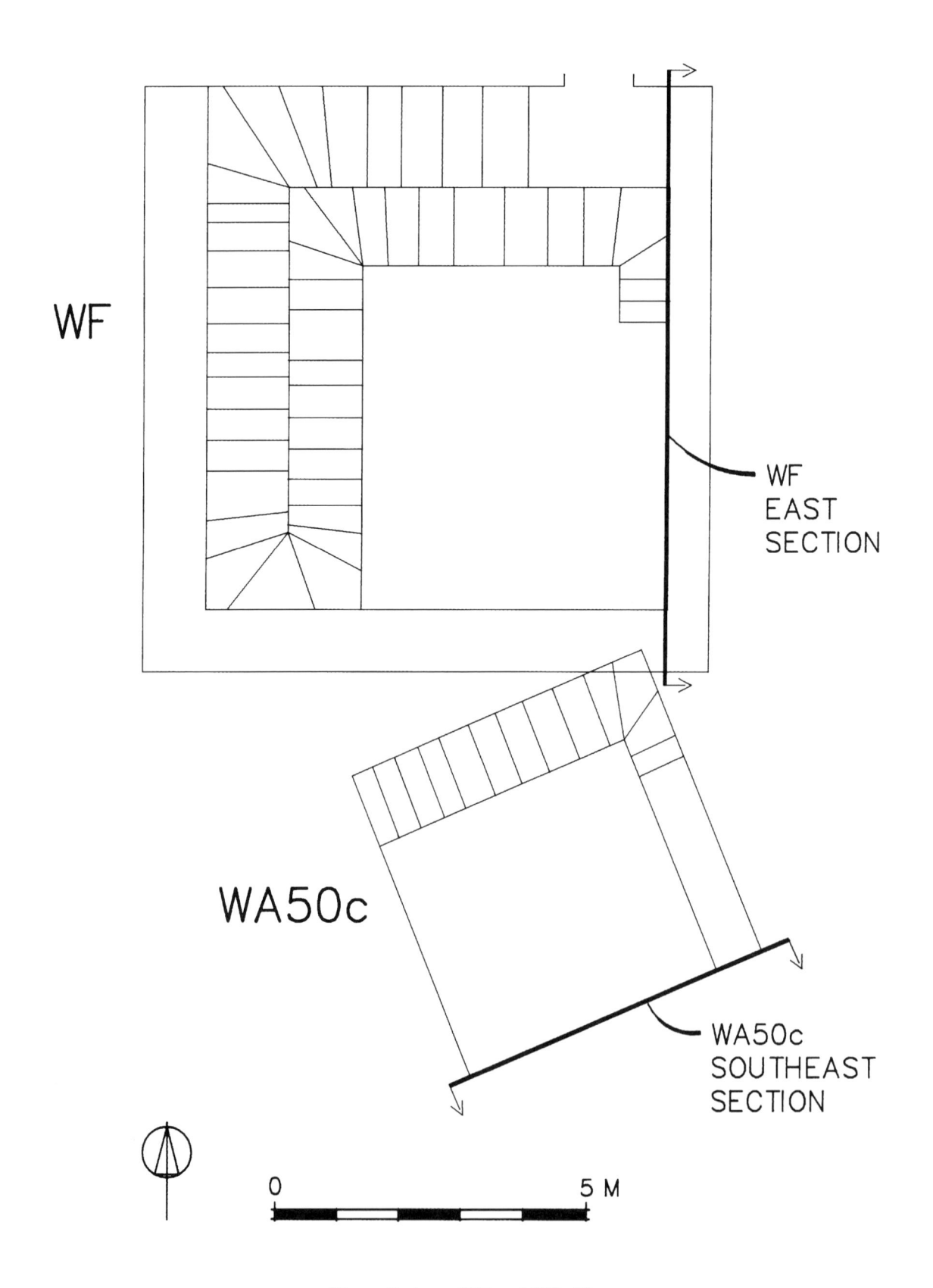

Figure 3. Areas WF and WA 50c

The most striking aspect of the construction was the persistence of plano-convex bricks from the Early Dynastic levels through all the Akkadian levels and right into the Ur III levels. In most cases, these bricks were small and relatively regular, laid in horizontal courses as stretchers and covered with mud plaster. Customary dimensions are 18–22 cm long × 14–15 cm wide × 7–8 cm thick at the maximum, although slightly smaller bricks are also attested. (See table 1 for measurements of bricks in all walls.) There was almost none of the distinctive herringbone effect created by laying alternately slanting courses. The single exception in Area WF, Wall X in Level X, had a course of horizontal bricks topped by a course of slanted bricks; unfortunately, two courses were all that were preserved of this wall. Wall AD of Level XIA also exhibits some variation and care in construction, with its alternation of headers and stretchers. The plano-convex bricks often are almost oval in section, instead of having the distinctive flat base and curved top customarily associated with these bricks from their form in the Diyala sites. The simple shape of the bricks, together with the lack of complexity in construction technique, may be related to the domestic function of the buildings and the absence of formal planning or specialist builders.

For construction of most levels, earlier walls were leveled and new walls were built directly on top of their remains or in the same location but on top of a thin layer of fill. In at least two cases, a reed mat had been placed over a razed wall before the new wall was built, for example, between Walls AI and AE in Levels XIIA and XIB and between Walls Z and W of Levels X and IX. In the former case, the top of Wall AI had been cut to a slope, and the mat may have been intended to keep Wall AE from slipping. The presence of reed mats between building phases in which later walls were built on the stubs of earlier walls is recorded elsewhere at Nippur in Area TB (McCown and Haines 1967: 335), at al-Hiba in Area C between Levels IB and IA (Bahrani 1989), and at Tell Asmar in the Private Houses (Delougaz, Hill, and Lloyd 1967: 151, 156), as well as being noted in Area WC-3 and other more recent excavations at Nippur. The mats are thought to have been placed to spread the load of the later walls evenly, to prevent differential settling of the upper walls. There were no instances of foundation trenches in any of the third-millennium levels. When built on the same surface at the same time, the corners of walls were bonded; however, there were frequent cases in which a wall was reused and a later wall was built abutting it.

A number of walls survived through several different building levels. Most often, reused walls would persist through at most two or three levels and survive to a height of about a meter, but Wall S, for example, was built in Level XIIB and survived until Level VIII, preserved to a height of 2.4 m. Wall AG was also reused and repaired across several levels, and during the course of its reuse it gradually sagged outwards, toward the courtyard to its north. The reuse of walls across architectural levels and the deliberate razing and immediate rebuilding of other walls, supports the reconstruction of the third-millennium B.C. levels as an essentially unbroken sequence.

Bricks were mostly yellowish brown, occasionally reddish brown or gray brown, with light straw temper. In a few walls, the bricks had probably been made with soil from earlier occupational deposits and were dark brown or dark gray with inclusions of charcoal, bits of bone, and other domestic trash. The construction and bricks were unusual and distinctive in three walls (Wall BI in Level XVIIC, Wall BE in Level XVB, and Wall AR in Level XIVB). In each of these walls the bricks were made from a distinctive gray green sticky clay without visible temper, and on average the brick-like lumps are at least twice the size of normal bricks. These walls were otherwise not notably different from others of more regular construction, either in width or function. The color and consistency of the clay may point to a source for the bricks' raw material in a canal or riverbed.[10]

Most walls had one coat of mud plaster, some as many as three or four, each correlated with specific floors within rooms or with the construction of special features. Layers of plaster were yellow, reddish, or gray, usually with a light straw temper component. In some places the faces of walls that defined outdoor spaces had become eroded at the base or had partially collapsed due to action of rainwater, salinity, or wind erosion; in such cases they had generally been repaired with thick plaster (as in Walls BR and BP in Level XIXB). In some repairs, handfuls of sherds were used as strengthening material, being pressed against the collapsing wall before the repair plaster was applied.

In Level VI there was a mixture of plano-convex bricks (in walls reused from earlier levels) and rectangular bricks (in new walls). These rectangular bricks measure 26–28 cm long × 16–17 cm wide × 8–9 cm thick — a standard set of dimensions found in Ur III levels elsewhere at Nippur (in houses in Area WC-3 and the city wall in Area EB).

---

10. In a geomorphological trench outside the city walls northeast of the ziggurat, dug by Stephen Lintner in 1976, a layer of very similar dense gray green clay more than 1 m thick was uncovered (M. Gibson, pers. comm.). This layer has been identified as representing an ancient water-related deposit.

The rectangular bricks of the single Kassite wall were also extremely regular in size (20 × 27 × 9 cm) and the construction was rigorously even and well controlled. The deep foundation trench for this wall is unusual in the Area WF sequence. However the severe erosion of this level and its subsequent disturbance by first-millennium B.C. burial pits have meant that the building cannot be reconstructed and nothing can be assumed about its function.

The seventh-century B.C. structure was also unusual in that there was a foundation cut made for the northern wall. This was apparently only a half trench with an open northern side, cut in order to regularize an existent slope in the site so that a stable surface was created for construction of the wall. The square bricks used in the building's construction measured a consistent 29–32 × 29–32 × 10–13 cm.

## Floors

As briefly detailed in the explanation of excavation procedures (n. 9), floors identified and labeled during the excavation were only a few of the possible floors or surfaces that existed in columns of stratified material. None of the floors was paved or consciously laid but consisted of trampled earth surfaces of variable density and hardness. The floors identified and singled out for exposure tended to be the harder or more continuous surfaces within a great many superimposed floors, which were often interleaved and discontinuous. There were a few instances of the plaster of a wall continuing out horizontally onto the associated surface, but the plastering in such cases usually did not extend more than 20 or 30 cm from the wall face.

Table 1. Brick Sizes, by Level

| Level | Wall: Measurement (cm) | Level | Wall: Measurement (cm) |
|---|---|---|---|
| IIIA | A: 30–34 × 30–34 × 9–10 (rectangular)<br>B: 30–34 × 30–34 × 9–10 (rectangular)<br>C: 30–34 × 30–34 × 9–10 (rectangular) | XIIB | AI: 12–22 × 10–15 × 5–8 max. (pcb)<br>AU: 15–18 × 10–12 × 7–8 max. (pcb)<br>S: 18–22 × 16–17 × 7–8 max. (pcb)<br>AF: 15–22 × 12–15 × 5–8 max. (pcb)<br>AG: 15–20 × 12–15 × 7–8 max. (pcb)<br>AH: 12–22 × 12–15 × 7–8 max. (pcb)<br>AI: 12–22 × 10–15 × 5–8 max. (pcb)<br>AU: 15–18 × 10–12 × 7–8 max. (pcb) |
| IIIB | D: 30–34 × 30–34 × 9–10 (rectangular)<br>E: 30–34 × 30–34 × 9–10 (rectangular)<br>F: 30–34 × 30–34 × 9–10 (rectangular) |   |   |
| IV | G: 29–32 × 29–32 × 10–13 (rectangular)<br>H: 29–32 × 29–32 × 10–13 (rectangular)<br>I: 29–32 × 29–32 × 10–13 (rectangular)<br>J: 29–32 × 29–32 × 10–13 (rectangular) | XIIIA | AJ: 15–25 × 13 × 6 max. (pcb)<br>AM: 12–25 × 7–12 × 5–8 max. (pcb)<br>AO: 14–21 × 10–15 × 6–8 max. (pcb)<br>BA: 15–25 × 13 × 6 max. (pcb) |
| V | R: 26–27 × 20 × 9 (rectangular) | XIIIB | AJ: 15–25 × 13 × 6 max. (pcb)<br>AM: 12–25 × 7–12 × 5–8 max. (pcb)<br>AO: 14–21 × 10–15 × 6–8 max. (pcb)<br>BA: 15–25 × 13 × 6 max. (pcb) |
| VI | L: 25–27 × 16–17 × 8–9 (rectangular)<br>M: 25–27 × 16–17 × 8–9 (rectangular)<br>N: 25–27 × 16–17 × 8–9 (rectangular)<br>O: 25–27 × 16–17 × 8–9 (rectangular)<br>P: 24–25 × 17–18 × 7–8 max. (pcb) | XIIIC | AM: 12–25 × 7–12 × 5–8 max. (pcb)<br>AO: 14–21 × 10–15 × 6–8 max. (pcb)<br>BB: 15–25 × 13 × 6 max. (pcb)<br>BC: 15–25 × 13 × 6 max. (pcb) |
| VII | P: 24–25 × 17–18 × 7–8 max. (pcb)<br>T: 25–26 × 17–18 × 7–8 max. (pcb)<br>W: 20–28 × 14–19 × 7–8 max. (pcb) | XIVA | AR: 10–15 × 8–10 × 5–8 max. (pcb)<br>AQ: 10–20 × 8–12 × 5–9 max. (pcb)<br>BD: 15–25 × 10–12 × 5–8 max. (pcb)<br>BF: 12–26 × 8–10 × 5–8 max. (pcb)<br>BG: 10–15 × 8–10 × 5–8 max. (pcb) |
| VIII | P: 24–25 × 17–18 × 7–8 max. (pcb)<br>Q: 24–25 × 17–18 × 7–8 max. (pcb)<br>S: 18–22 × 16–17 × 7–8 max. (pcb)<br>T: 25–26 × 17–18 × 7–8 max. (pcb)<br>U: 15–20 × 8–10 × 5–8 max. (pcb)<br>W: 20–28 × 14–19 × 7–8 max. (pcb) | XIVB | AR: 10–15 × 8–10 × 5–8 max. (pcb)<br>AS: 10–20 × 8–12 × 5–8 max. (pcb)<br>BD: 15–25 × 10–12 × 5–8 max. (pcb)<br>BF: 12–26 × 8–10 × 5–8 max. (pcb)<br>BG: 10–15 × 8–10 × 5–8 max. (pcb) |
| IX | S: 18–22 × 16–17 × 7–8 max. (pcb)<br>U: 15–20 × 8–10 × 5–8 max. (pcb)<br>W: 20–28 × 14–19 × 7–8 max. (pcb) | XVA | AS: 10–20 × 8–12 × 5–8 max. (pcb)<br>BE: 15–27 × 15–20 × 9–15 (pcb and irregular lumps) |
| X | S: 18–22 × 16–17 × 7–8 max. (pcb)<br>U: 15–20 × 8–10 × 5–8 max. (pcb)<br>X: 15–23 × 14–15 × 6–8 max. (pcb)<br>Y: 15–20 × 8–10 × 5–8 max. (pcb)<br>Z: 25–26 × 16–17 × 6–9 max. (pcb)<br>AC: not measurable | XVB | BE: 15–27 × 15–20 × 9–15 (pcb and irregular lumps)<br>BH: 12–18 × 8–11 × 8 max. (pcb) |
| XIA | S: 18–22 × 16–17 × 7–8 max. (pcb)<br>AA: 18–22 × 16–17 × 7–8 max. (pcb)<br>AB: 18–22 × 16–17 × 7–8 max. (pcb)<br>AD: 20–25 × 10–15 × 8–10 (pcb)<br>AF: 15–22 × 12–15 × 5–8 max. (pcb) | XVI | BH: 12–18 × 8–11 × 8 max. (pcb) |
|   |   | XVII | BI: 20–30 × 15–20 × 9–20 (pcb and irregular lumps)<br>BJ: 12–18 × 8–11 × 8 max. (pcb)<br>BK: 12–18 × 8–11 × 8 max. (pcb) |
| XIB | S: 18–22 × 16–17 × 7–8 max. (pcb)<br>AA: 18–22 × 16–17 × 7–8 max. (pcb)<br>AB: 18–22 × 16–17 × 7–8 max. (pcb)<br>AD: 20–25 × 10–15 × 8–10 (pcb)<br>AE: 14–22 × 12–15 × 5–8 max. (pcb)<br>AF: 15–22 × 12–15 × 5–8 max. (pcb) | XVIII | BM: 12–18 × 8–11 × 8 max. (pcb)<br>BO: 12–18 × 8–11 × 8 max. (pcb) |
|   |   | XIXA | BN: 12–18 × 8–11 × 8 max. (pcb)<br>BP: 12–18 × 8–11 × 8 max. (pcb) |
| XIIA | S: 18–22 × 16–17 × 7–8 max. (pcb)<br>AF: 15–22 × 12–15 × 5–8 max. (pcb)<br>AG: 18–22 × 16–17 × 7–8 max. (pcb)<br>AH: 12–22 × 12–15 × 7–8 max. (pcb) | XIXB | BP: 12–18 × 8–11 × 8 max. (pcb)<br>BQ: 12–18 × 8–11 × 8 max. (pcb)<br>BR: 12–18 × 8–11 × 8 max. (pcb) |

# CHAPTER 1
# DETAILED DESCRIPTION OF LEVELS AND STRATIGRAPHY

## Level XIX, Phases B–A

The lowest level, Level XIX, was divided into two phases: B (earlier) and A (later). In Phase B (pls. 3–4), the excavation exposed part of a building or buildings consisting of two walls (Walls BP and BR/BQ) separating three rooms or spaces (Locus 68 at the east, 69 at the southwest, and 70/72 at the northwest). All the walls were built of small plano-convex mudbricks ranging from carefully made tan sandy bricks in Wall BP to softer trash-filled ones in Wall BR.

During occupation of Level XIXB, in Locus 68, the eastern space, the base of Wall BP was badly eroded, indicating that Locus 68 was probably unroofed and subject to exposure to water. At the face of Wall BP in this locus was a series of bowls at each of the three floors identified within the accumulated layers, bowls which may have been intended as apotropaic foundation deposits.[11] Burial 22 was interred from Floor 1 near Wall BP (see *Chapter 2* for description of this and all other burials). In Locus 69, the southwest space, the accumulated layers of debris were ashy and the lowest floor in particular (of three identified) had scattered large sherds and basalt fragments. The base of Wall BR had eroded in this area, like Wall BP in Locus 68, and had been repaired with a thick coating of mud plaster. North of Wall BQ, Locus 70 was filled with striated trash lenses, greenish debris, and a high density of sherds and animal bones. A later burial intervened between Locus 70 and 72, at the west section, north of Wall BR (pls. 181 and 184). Although we did not excavate the connection between Locus 70 and Locus 72, it is clear that Wall BP did not continue north to separate these two loci, so they must have made up a single space.

In this level we may have uncovered the party walls of three separate structures. The erosion at the bases of Walls BP and BR and the quantities of large sherds and debris that we interpret as kitchen trash in all three loci mean that each of the spaces could have been an outdoor area. The presence of large sherds is more typical of outside areas than of interior rooms, from which large pieces would probably be removed or be broken down by traffic. The fact that no doorways were found in any of the walls to connect the loci indicates that the three spaces probably belonged to separate structures. However, the spaces might have been courtyards of houses or open public areas.

Level XIXA (pl. 5) consisted of a brief occupation followed by a period of localized use as a rubbish dump. At the west side of Area WF, a poorly preserved wall, Wall BN, approximately parallel to but just south of the location of BR in the previous phase, was the only new construction of this level. The southern end of Wall BP, from the earlier phase, was still visible. Wall BN may originally have reached to near the center of the excavation and formed a corner with BP but this junction had eroded, and only the top of the southern end of Wall BP was still visible. Its northern end and the other walls of Level XIXB were apparently cut down or allowed to collapse and the entire area was covered with mottled debris (Locus 67). The southwest space, possibly bounded by Walls BN and BP, had filled with a continuation of the debris of Locus 67, cut by three later burials. It appears that the structure represented by Wall BN was short-lived and the area was then used as a rubbish dump since the mottled debris is typical of intermittent dumping of kitchen ash and trash, in contrast to the horizontally striated layers created by habitation. The average depth of the trash deposit was ca. 20 cm, and the absence of internal layering indicates that this episode was of short duration.

---

11. The bowls are indicated by small circles on plate 3; a single bowl was placed upright at Floor 3 (1774; pl. 123:8), one was inverted at Floor 2 (1689; pl. 123:9), and there were two, horizontally separated by about a meter, at Floor 1 (1675; pl. 123:10). The placement of these bowls is frequent in Area WF, occurring in most of the third-millennium B.C. levels. In most cases the bowls are empty; the upright bowls may have originally held liquids but it is the act of bowl placement and the incantation spoken at the moment which are apparently more important than any offering. See Gibson, Armstrong, and McMahon 1998 for foundation deposits of bowls in other Early Dynastic IIIa (Area EA) and Ur III (Area WC-3) domestic contexts at Nippur. Bowls inverted at the corners of rooms and in doorways are already known from Old Babylonian, Kassite, and seventh century B.C. contexts at Nippur (Gibson et al. 1978). The placement of inscribed incantation bowls below floors of buildings in Sasanian/Early Islamic times is well attested, particularly at Nippur, and it is proposed that these later bowls are a survival of an ancient practice.

## Level XVIII

As in Level XIXA, the architecture of Level XVIII was poorly preserved (pl. 6). In the southeast portion of the excavated area were the remains of two walls, Walls BM and BO, both constructed of small plano-convex mudbricks. From the orientation of the remaining wall faces, these walls originally formed a corner, defining a space at the southeast and stretching beyond the south and east sections. The material both outside (Locus 65) and within the walls (Locus 66) was similar to the mottled trash dumping debris of Level XIXA. In Locus 66 this material was grayish, while that outside (Locus 65) was mottled and burned orange brown to black, with broken baked bricks, mudbricks, and large sherds. The nature of this material suggests that the area was an open dumping ground for kitchen debris, presumably from houses just outside the excavated area. One burial (Burial 20) and a shallow pit (Cut 17) were cut from this level.

The pottery assemblages of Levels XIX and XVIII date to Early Dynastic IIIa (see *Chapter 3*). A single object was found in Level XVIII in Locus 65 near the north section: a translucent green stone cylinder seal with an Early Dynastic II-style scene (19 N 108, pl. 158:2, see *Chapter 4* for detailed description of all objects).

## Level XVII, Phases C–A

Level XVII was divided into three phases. In the initial phase, Level XVII, Phase C (pl. 7), Wall BI was built at the north end of Area WF, using large, irregular, greenish gray clay bricks (20–30 × 15–20 × 9–20 cm). The western end of Wall BI and part of the space to its north (Locus 71) were removed by a later burial cut. South of the wall, the debris covering the excavated area (Locus 64) was similar to Locus 65 of Level XVIII, an orange brown mottled layer, so there seems to have been little change in use of the area, although the placement of Wall BI may indicate an encroachment of the surrounding buildings into the open space. One object was found in this layer, a miniature hole-mouthed, pointed-based jar (19 N 62; pl. 164:1). Burial 19, at the south section, was sealed by Locus 64, Floor 1.

In the northeastern half of Area WF, a thin (0.3–1.5 cm) layer of sand was laid down between Level XVII, Phases C and B. It is possible that this sand was deposited by a single brief event such as a sandstorm. The brevity is indicated by the fact that Wall BI remained in use in Level XVIIB; two more walls were built during Phase B but were unfortunately poorly preserved (pl. 8). These new walls were located approximately above Walls BM and BO of Level XVIII and, like them, probably defined a space that extended beyond the excavation to the south and east (Locus 63). The remains of Wall BJ are actually a corner formed by two adjoining walls, one running to the northeast and the other to the southeast; Wall BK was a mere fragment disappearing into the south section but may have been oriented northeast–southwest. Both were built of small plano-convex mudbricks. North and west of the walls, the area had an accumulation of ashy surfaces and sherds (Locus 62) and adjacent to Wall BI was a conical bread oven (*tannur*) surrounded by a thick patch of mixed red and white ash. Also belonging to Phase B of Level XVII were Burial 21 and Cut 16.

Near the northwest end of Wall BJ, loose in the dirt, was a single "Fara" tablet (19 N 80; pl. 192:1), a type usually dated to Early Dynastic IIIa. This tablet serves as an important *terminus post quem* for later levels, but the pottery of this level includes types that may postdate Early Dynastic IIIa (see *Chapter 3* for a full discussion), and this tablet may be a holdover in this level. The context is occupational, but the likelihood of this being an unroofed space is a strong indication that this tablet was not in its original context.

In Phase A (pl. 9), Walls BJ and BK were covered by horizontally laid layers of built-up debris (Locus 61), traceable across the entire area and running up against Wall BI. The *tannur* near Wall BI continued to be used, implying that Walls BJ and BK had not been standing for long or were only low structures. The walls and the oven had been built on the same surface, and it is unlikely that the oven was used for more than a few years. A second dense, thick (1–3 cm) patch of mixed bright red and white ash surrounded the *tannur*. The walls of the three phases of this level are so eroded or damaged by later activity that reconstruction of an overall plan is impossible, but the presence of the oven and nature of the deposits still point to a mostly unroofed space, though closely attached to neighboring structures.

## Level XVI

For the duration of Level XVI (pl. 10), Area WF was an open space (Locus 59), with only one wall or mudbrick feature at its southeast corner (Wall BH). There were two firepits, a *tannur*, and several burials in the exposure, from which evidence we assume that the inhabitants of the surrounding buildings utilized the area intensively and it may have been a large courtyard attached to a house. The area had filled up with striated ashy layers that sloped down slightly from north to south, covering Wall BI of Level XVII.

The initial two skeletons in a sequence of eight burials, recorded as Burial 14, were interred from a deep rectangular shaft during occupation of this level, but precise correlation of the burials with specific floors in Locus 59 was not possible. Near the firepit at the center of Area WF, associated with Floor 3, was a cluster of bowls: two pairs of upright and inverted bowls (19 N 58 and 19 N 59, I419:1–2; pls. 125:1–2, 123:13–14).[12] In the debris nearby was a copper/bronze pin with a bent tang (19 N 63; pl. 162:7).[13] East of the firepit was an infant grave (Burial 18), cut from Floor 3.

Wall BH was built on Floor 2 of Locus 59 and constructed of small, gray plano-convex mudbricks. At the time of its construction, the firepit mentioned above was still in use, as evidenced by a second group of bowls, two upright and nested together (19 N 56 and I408:1; pl. 125:3–4) plus one inverted (I410; pl. 124:1) placed next to it. Farther away but still in association with the oven was a fourth bowl (19 N 57; pl. 125:5). To the southeast a second firepit was dug, and a conical *tannur* was built on this floor at the north section. At the final floor level, Floor 1, Burial 17 was interred in the southern half of Area WF. Level XVI is the last stratum in the sequence without substantial architecture. The graves and fire installations, however, are indications that the space was owned and utilized by a specific family and was not a public area.

## Level XV, Phases B–A

Level XV had two phases. In the initial phase, Level XV, Phase B (pls. 11, 12a–b), Wall BE, running northeast to southwest across Area WF, subdivided the large open space of Level XVI into two spaces, either two courtyards or possibly a courtyard and an open area (Loci 57 and 60). The recurrent ovens and similar buildup of ashy layers indicate continuity of use from Level XVI. Both spaces were fairly large and are unlikely to have been roofed, as there were bread ovens (*tannurs*) on both sides of the wall. Bread ovens observed in archaeological and modern contexts are usually outdoor installations; where they do appear inside rooms they are usually placed near the doorway for ventilation of smoke (e.g., unpublished examples at Tepe al-Atiqeh, M. Gibson, pers. comm.), which is not the case here. A single conical bowl was found inside the *tannur* in Locus 60 (I385; pl. 123:11). At the eastern end of Wall BE, as exposed, a doorway connected Loci 60 and 57. The wall was built of large, irregular, greenish gray clay bricks, similar to those used in Wall BI in Level XVII. Locus 60, the southern space, contained two objects above Floor 1: a flint scraper (19 N 68; pl. 166:10)[14] and an Ubaid or early Uruk period stamp seal (19 N 74; pl. 160:2).

In the later phase of Level XV, Phase A (pl. 13), Wall BE was still in use and both north and south spaces (Loci 57 and 53) retained their appearance as unroofed areas. At the southeast corner, Wall AS, built of small regularly laid plano-convex mudbricks, was constructed on the remains of Wall BH. The oven built in Phase B in the southern area was still in use.

A burial, numbered incorrectly during excavation as Burial 14, Skeleton 5, was probably interred from Floor 1 of Locus 57 (see *Chapter 2* for discussion of this burial and the reasoning behind its attribution to this level).

---

12. These are the same conical bowl type as was used for foundation/apotropaic deposits elsewhere, although these examples may instead have been equipment related to use of the firepit. However, in Area WB at Nippur, in Old Babylonian levels, there are similar bowls placed at firepits or hearths and there may have been a necessity for apotropaic practice related to these features. An additional bowl was found in this same general area on Floor 4, prior to creation of the firepit (I425: pl. 123:12).

13. Until analysis of the metal objects can be done, it is not clear whether any of the "bronze" objects from Area WF are in fact tin-bronze, copper, or arsenical copper.

14. Flint tools, especially scrapers and small blades, are relatively common in late Early Dynastic through Akkadian levels at Nippur Area WF and in Akkadian levels at Umm al-Hafriyat (M. Gibson, pers. comm.), despite the assumed increased availability of copper/bronze for tools at that time.

## Level XIV, Phases B–A

With Level XIVB (pls. 13, 15), Area WF underwent a change from being a mostly unroofed/outdoor area to encompassing both indoor and outdoor spaces in a tighter building arrangement. A courtyard (Locus 44) in the northern part of the excavated area continues the open space in this area of Level XV. A door in Wall BD provided access to a small room at the southeast (Locus 47). At the southwest was another space (Locus 54) with a door from the courtyard. At the northwest corner of the excavation was a small portion of a final room (Locus 73).

Among the walls bounding the southeast room (Locus 47), Wall AR was built of the same large, irregular, greenish gray clay bricks seen in previous levels, while Wall BD was built of smaller plano-convex bricks. Wall AS was still in use from the preceding level, Level XV, and Wall AR had been built abutting its western end.

The first event of this level was a burial (Burial 16 at the northeast corner of the trench), which was then partly sealed by construction of Wall BF immediately above it. This is an unusual arrangement for a burial and might be interpreted as involving a substantial passage of time between accumulation of Levels XVA and XIVB, with Burial 16 interred during that intervening period. This is unlikely, however, given the continued use in Level XIV of Wall AS from the previous level. Burial 15 (a child's burial) was cut from the lowest of the five floors in the southeast room (Locus 47, Floor 5) and then covered by multiple layers of ashy debris (pl. 15). At Floor 4, an installation at the east end of the room was created, consisting of a small open box made of baked-brick fragments and a reused baked-brick door socket.

During accumulation of the floors in the southeast room, the space may have been used for storage of tools and other objects since these layers contained five copper/bronze pins (18 N 143, 144, 146–47 and 151; pl. 162:10, 9, 12, 11, 8, respectively), a copper/bronze dagger (18 N 122; pl. 162:2), a copper/bronze spearhead (18 N 121; pl. 162:3), a copper/bronze chisel or adze (18 N 172; pl. 162:1), along with a flint blade and scraper (18 N 156 and 160; pl. 166:11–12), a conch shell bead (18 N 152; pl. 166:2), and a number of related nonregistered objects: a basalt grindstone, two whetstones, and three unbaked clay jar stoppers (see pl. 15 for location of objects). At the final two floors there were also bowl deposits: a single inverted bowl at the face of Wall AS at Floor 1 (too fragmentary to register or draw) and a pair, one inverted above the other, in the southwest corner of Walls AS and AR at Floor 2 (H1101:1–2, pl. 124:2–3). Also at Floor 2, a pile of broken vessels and sherds had been placed against the south face of Wall BD as a repair, including two nearly complete small jars (I327, 325; pl. 126:1–2) and two bowls, one containing a miniature pot (19 N 55, I113, 115; pls. 125:6, 127:4–5).

In the courtyard (Locus 44), the accumulation of dark ashy debris was mostly cut away by Burial 14 from Level XIIIB. At the northeast corner of Area WF, the northeast boundary wall of the courtyard, Wall BF, barely protruded into the excavation area; it too was built of small plano-convex bricks. The northwest courtyard wall, Wall BG, was mostly removed by Burial 14, but Wall AR, the southwest boundary, was intact. A doorway through Wall AR led from the courtyard to Locus 54 on the west.

The only change in plan from Level XIV, Phases B to A (pl. 16), was that Wall AS, the southeast wall of the southeast room, was leveled at about 30 cm from its base and partially covered with a thin layer of gray ashy fill and Wall AQ was built above it (pl. 20a). The courtyard side of the corner of Walls BD and AR was repaired in this phase, but the other walls remained unchanged. The horizontal layers of debris in the southeast room (Locus 40) consisted of very similar material to Locus 47 of Level XIVB. At Floor 2 of Locus 40, a mudbrick bin was built in the western end of the room and a ribbed-sided vat was partially sunk into the floor within it (see pl. 17 for detailed plan of this room at this floor, pl. 18a for photograph of the vat feature). On the floor outside the vat was an ovoid jar with a wide ring base (18 N 134; pl. 126:3) and a copper/bronze bracelet (18 N 120; pl. 162:6). About 10 cm of debris accumulated in the vat, at which point, with the vat sides still visible, a miniature four-footed pot was placed upright at its center and covered with an inverted bowl (18 N 137, 18 N 136; pl. 127:2–3).

The purpose of this last installation is unclear. In its initial arrangement, just the vat and brick feature, it may have been an installation for making burial offerings, placed as it is directly above Burial 15. The young child in that grave seems an unusual figure to have merited such treatment since presumably it would not have had enough time to become an important figure in the household structure. Potentially, the child may have had some special status (such as being the firstborn) or its ghost had been perceived as being particularly demanding. The vat's final function, with the small pot and inverted bowl at its center, may be related to the deposits of single bowls or pairs of bowls at other floors in this room or may be another aspect of post-burial ritual. There was another single inverted fragmentary bowl in the northeast corner of the room in this phase (not registered or drawn).

Just outside the mudbrick feature, near Wall AQ (pl. 17), was a shallow copper/bronze ladle (18 N 170; pls. 19, 161:5) and near the room's center was a shell cylinder seal with a scene of Shamash in a "god-boat" preceded by a lion, with a plow and two jars in the field (18 N 111; pls. 17, 160:1).[15] The style of carving is comparable to Boehmer's "Akkadisch I b/c" to "II," implying a date at least as late as the reign of Rimush or Manishtushu (Boehmer 1965: 81, 135–36). This seal is unequivocal proof that by this level, at least, the occupation must belong to the Akkadian period.

At the subsequent floor (Floor 1, see pls. 18b and 19 for details of features and locations of objects), the almost-buried vat was covered with a reed mat, visible as a white powdery layer with a woven pattern, extending beyond the vat and curving up against the brick feature on the north and west and against the wall of the room on the south. Below the mat on Floor 1 in the northwest corner was a group of baked-clay objects: two animal figurines (18 N 130 and 166; pl. 163:8, 10) and two model chariots (18 N 162, 18 N 133; pl. 163:2–3) along with two bowls, inverted next to each other (18 N 123–124; pls. 18b, 125:7–8). On the same floor in the southwest corner was another pair of bowls, one inverted over the other (18 N 190, 18 N 189; pl. 125:9–10), along with a pair of taller conical cups (18 N 138, H1009; pl. 125:12–13). A final bowl was inverted on Floor 1 near the center of the room (H536; pl. 124:4). Burial 13, a child burial sealed by Floor 1, was made in a shallow cut just east of the vat feature.

The occupational material above Floor 1 contained two copper/bronze pins (18 N 153, 18 N 150; pl. 162:14–15), and more baked-clay objects: a third chariot above the two in the northwest corner (18 N 165; pl. 163:1), a model boat fragment and a broken animal figurine (both too fragmentary to register), as well as a stone axhead (18 N 139; pl. 166:17). The number and variety of objects found in this room during both phases of this level may indicate a special use of the space. The frequent recurrence of the apotropaic bowl deposits surely indicates an unusual importance attached to the room, probably linked to the two burials.

In the courtyard of Level XIVA, as in Level XIVB, most of the material was removed by the second phase of Burial 14, belonging to Level XIIIB. But the deep cut, the first phase of that burial (fig. 9), was possibly still in use and Skeleton 6 may have been interred during this level. Two more objects were found in the ashy debris of the courtyard, south of the Burial 14 cut: a copper/bronze pin with a rolled head (19 N 13; pl. 162:13) and an obsidian blade (19 N 61; pl. 166:13). Four inverted foundation deposit bowls were found along the east face of wall AR at or below Floor 1 (I1:1–4; pl. 124:5–8).

Similar baked-clay objects, especially the plain-fronted chariots, are primarily from Akkadian levels at other sites. Parallels for the many metal objects from this room (pins, tools, and ladle) are most often found in burials at other sites, where they are usually dated to the late Early Dynastic and Akkadian periods. The presence of the early Akkadian seal (18 N 111), however, rules out a pre-Akkadian date for this level.

## Level XIII, Phases C–A

Level XIII represents a brief diversion from the building plan established in Level XIV. Much of that plan was retained, but the southeast room no longer existed, the courtyard having been expanded in that direction. In Level XIIIC (pl. 21), the first phase of three into which this level was divided, Wall AM was built directly above Wall AQ in the southeast corner (pl. 20a), while the other walls of the southeast room were leveled. Wall AM was built of small plano-convex bricks. At the southwest, the junction of two walls, Walls BB and BC, the northern corner of Locus 52, projected into Area WF. Both were built of irregular, plano-convex mudbricks. Below the east wall, Wall BC, there was a foundation deposit consisting of a broken jar base atop a baked brick, the jar base holding a cluster of weights and beads (19 N 97; pl. 165). This is one of the few such foundation deposits in which the vessel clearly had contents.

---

15. The jar, bronze bracelet, bronze ladle, and cylinder seal from this immediate area are more typical of the contents of graves than of gradually accumulating occupational material, yet no traces of associated bones were found here, nor was there any evidence of cut-lines of a burial pit at this level. These items definitely were not part of either of the two nearby burials (Burial 15 and Burial 13), and the collection of other complete and unusual objects at the next floor in this room reinforces the assumption they were stored objects rather than burial contents.

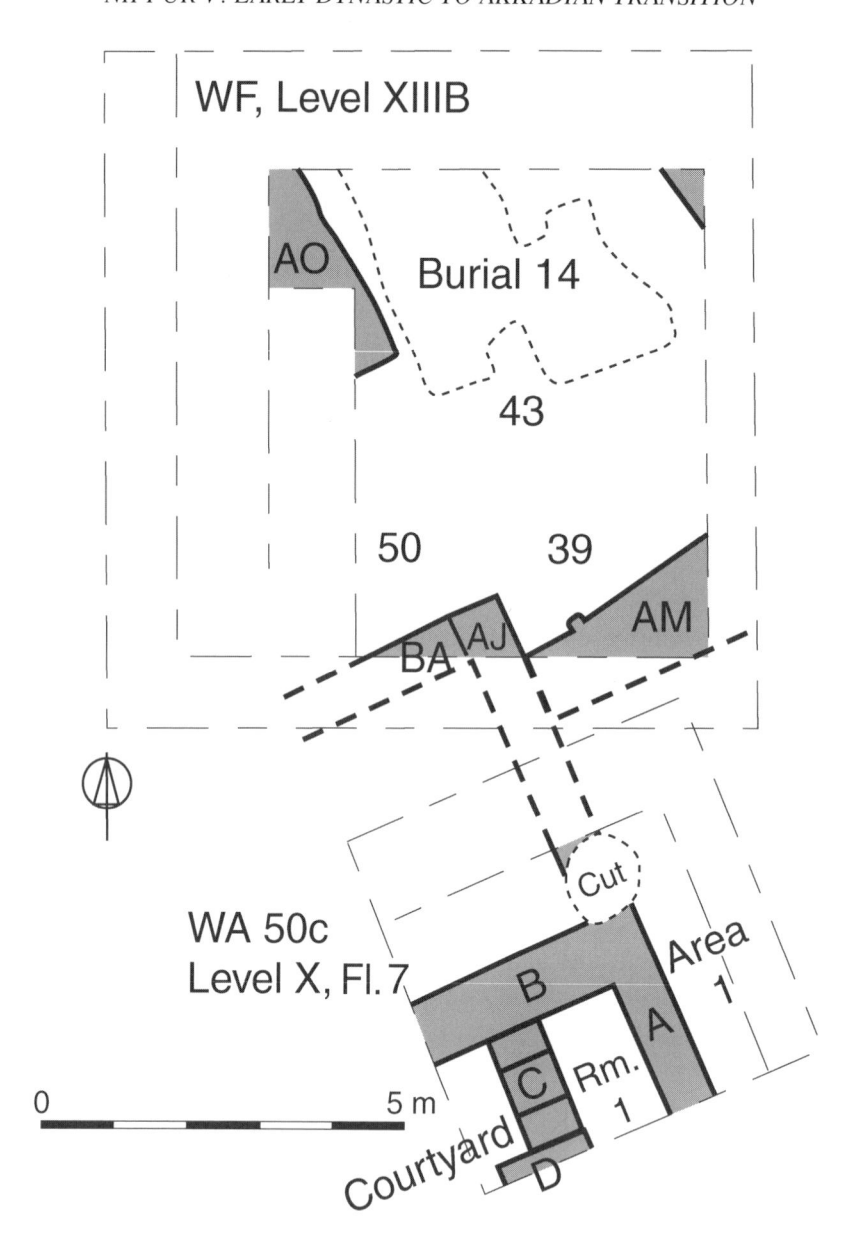

Figure 4. Combined Plans of Areas WF, Level XIIIB, and WA 50c, Level X, Floor 7

At the northwest corner of Area WF, Wall AO (the lowest in the series of thick wall corners which were maintained through the next five levels) was built above Walls AR and BG.[16] The corner was constructed of small plano-convex bricks. Finally, in the northeast corner of Area WF, there was a mudbrick feature, possibly a wall defining the open area, but difficult to judge with so little present in the excavation area. The debris in the courtyard[17] contained a number of baked-clay objects: a "game-piece" (18 N 116; pl. 163:14), a fragment of a model chair or bed (18 N 167; pl. 163:7), a dog figurine fragment (18 N 169; pl. 163:9), and a model boat (18 N 128; pl. 163:6).

---

16. The walls of the corner in this and later levels were so thick that they had the appearance of a solid platform. Although this corner was used as a boundary wall for the courtyard and the southwest space exposed in WF, the much greater thickness of the corner, when compared to the other walls, may mean that it belonged to a separate structure. A comparison with the Akkadian houses in Level XI of Area TB at Nippur is useful (McCown and Haines 1967: pl. 52, C). Several houses with party walls were excavated in that area and a wall corner of comparable thickness surrounded Room 297 and projected into Locus 292 of an adjacent building.

17. Because of the occasional necessity of leaving walls in place for mapping, while at the same time continuing to excavate into earlier levels, the courtyard of Level XIIIC was recorded under three locus and floor numbers: 39 Floor 1, 43 Floor 3, and 51 Floor 2, respectively its southern, northern, and western portions. Once the later walls were removed, connections between these excavated areas could be made, and it was clear that they form a single soil layer.

In Level XIIIB (fig. 4, pl. 22), all the walls of Level XIIIC were still in use except Walls BB and BC, which were replaced by Walls AJ and BA, a wall corner that maintained the same orientation but was shifted slightly to the south and east. The walls were built in the same manner as Walls BB and BC, of small plano-convex bricks.[18] In the northern portion of the courtyard, the debris included an unbaked-clay sealing with a late Akkadian style scene of combat (18 N 110; pl. 159:2); the sealing is in Boehmer's "Akkadisch III" style, dated to Naram-Sin or later (Boehmer 1965: 136). Also in the courtyard debris were a flint blade (18 N 157; pl. 166:14), a stone weight (18 N 158; pl. 163: 16), two pieces of basalt grindstone, and the end of a copper/bronze blade (19 N 14; pl. 162:4). The southern portion of the courtyard in particular was very ashy, with many large sherds.[19] Near the east face of Wall AO was a deposit of a pair of bowls, one inverted over the other (H1078 and 1077; pl. 84:6–7). A repair of clay and brick had been made at the base of Wall AO on the south side of the corner.

It was at the end of the occupation of Level XIIIB that a large burial chamber (the second phase of Burial 14) was dug in the courtyard, then sealed by Level XIIIA. During the short span of time covered by Level XIIIA (pl. 23), the walls of Level XIIIB remained unchanged. The evidence of Level XIIIA consisted of a heavy ash layer (Locus 42) in the northwest corner of Area WF, covering part of Locus 43. This layer was particularly thick and dense at the face of Wall AO but lensed out to the south and east. It may have been deliberate fill, brought in to cover the Burial 14 chamber.[20]

The late Akkadian sealing in the courtyard material confirms the late Akkadian date of this level, which is further supported by pottery and objects in the burials (see *Chapter 2*).

## Level XII, Phases B–A

The next level was divided into two phases; and in the first, Level XII, Phase B (pl. 24), the plan again resembles the one seen in Level XIV, with a southeast room connected by a doorway to the courtyard at the northeast. Another thick wall corner (Wall AF) was built at the northwest and there was a corridor or narrow room to the southwest (Locus 34). In the southeast room, Wall AI was built directly on top of the leveled Wall AM. The other walls of this room, despite approximately 50 cm of intervening debris, were built in the same locations as their counterparts in Level XIV. The only change was the shift of the eastern wall (Wall AH), which in previous levels may be assumed to lie beyond the east section, toward the west. The three new walls (Walls AG, AH, S) were built of regularly formed plano-convex mudbricks.

In the southeast room, Locus 38, Floor 3 was associated with a mudbrick sill across the doorway in Wall AG, making a step up to the contemporary surface in the courtyard, Locus 41, Floor 2. At the corner of Walls AG and S, built on this surface, was an L-shaped feature of mudbricks. Both of these walls, but especially AG, developed a severe lean outward into the courtyard (pl. 25a–b) and the feature may have been intended to keep them from collapsing. In the debris of the courtyard were a clay sealing with an Early Dynastic III combat scene (18 N 109; pl. 159:1), a broken spacer bead (18 N 155; pl. 166:3), and a broken baked-clay dog figurine (not registered). Near the corner where Wall AG meets Wall AH was a copper/bronze axhead (18 N 171; pl. 162:5) next to a conical bowl. The ax is of a type recognized as Akkadian/Ur III in date at Ur (see *Chapter 4*).

The new wall corner at the northwest, Wall AF, built directly on Wall AO, was constructed of small plano-convex mudbricks. Extensions of Wall AF and Wall S created a doorway that gave access to a narrow room on the west (Locus 34). The lowest floor of the courtyard, Floor 2, ran through the doorway to merge with the lowest floor

---

18. For WF, Level XIII, a tentative connection between Area WF and Area WA 50c can be made. This connection is mostly based on the tablet-based link between the following levels in both areas (see n. 24), but there are supporting pottery parallels between WA 50c Level X, Floor 7, and both Levels XIV and XIII in WF. Of the two, the plan of Level XIII is a better match with the plan of WA 50c, Level X, Floor 7 (Gibson 1975: fig. 55). Wall A of WA 50c may become Wall AJ of Level XIIIB in Area WF. The scale and orientation of these walls is well matched, and they are of similar construction: very small, irregular plano-convex mudbricks with large patches of unshaped mud and plaster. Wall AM in Area WF thus becomes the northwest boundary of Area WA 50c's Area 1, a courtyard or open space (see fig. 4).

19. As in Level XIIIC, the same adaptation to the Nippur locus system was made in Level XIIIB in order to make connections across open spaces below still-standing walls: Locus 43, Floors 2 and 1, Locus 39, Floor 0, and Locus 50, Floor 1 were excavated as separate units but merged once later walls had been mapped and removed.

20. As a simple soil layer not associated with any change in architecture and not extending over the entire square, Locus 42 should perhaps not have been singled out as a distinct phase, Level XIII, Phase A, but retained as the final episode of Level XIIIB. However, it does represent a genuine change in accumulation pattern from the occupational accumulation of Level XIIIB, and thus has been assigned a separate phase designation.

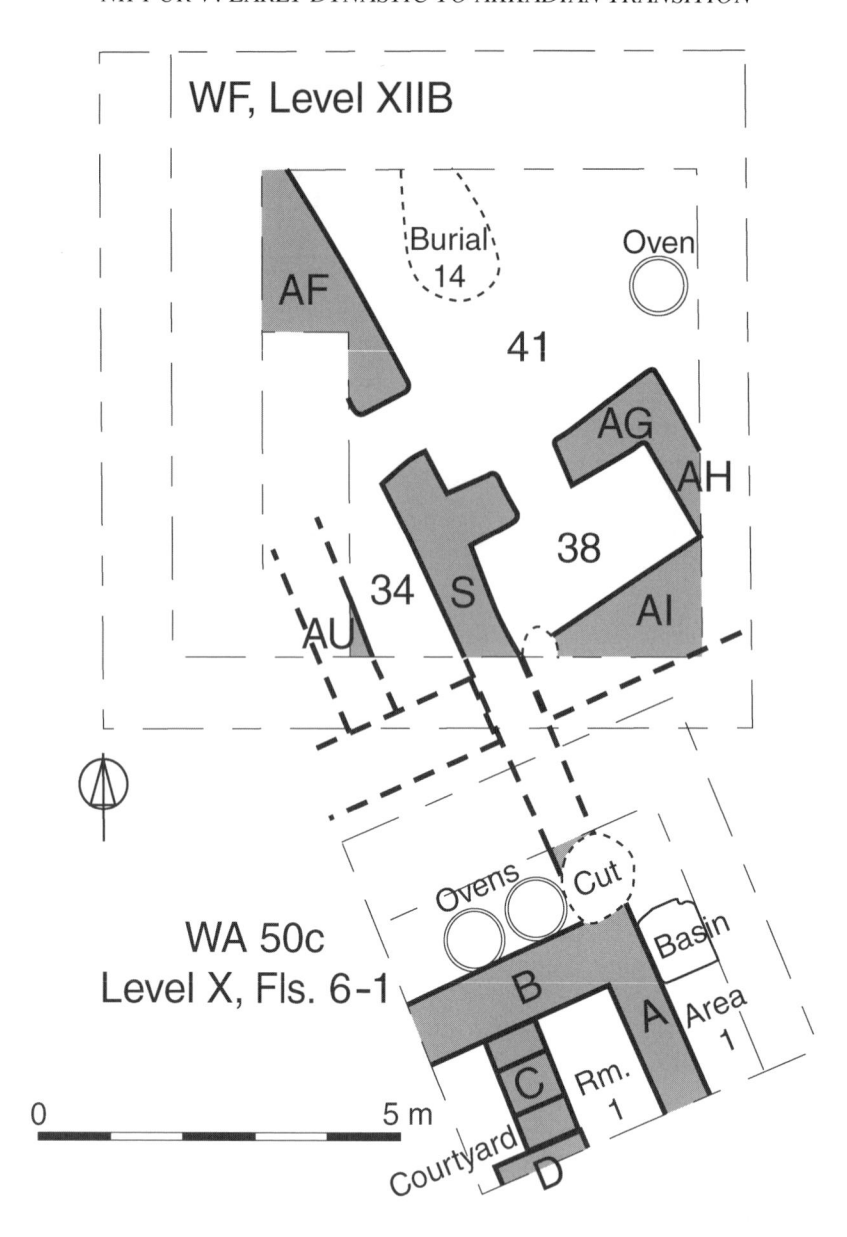

Figure 5. Combined Plans of Areas WF, Level XIIB, and WA 50c, Level X, Floors 6–1

in that narrow room (Locus 34, Floor 3). Set into this floor at the northern side of the door was a baked-brick door socket. Only a small stretch of Wall AU, its southwest boundary, was visible in the excavation. The material in the narrow space (Locus 34) was dark brown with a higher than average quantity of sherds and animal bones.

Additional floors belonging to this phase were traced in the southeast room and courtyard. The upper floor in the southeast room (Locus 38, Floor 2; pl. 27) was a slightly harder surface between layers of debris dense in sherds. The material above the floor contained a number of objects, the most important being an Old Akkadian tablet near Wall AI (18 N 106; pl. 193:1 a–b),[21] as well as a stone weight (18 N 89; pl. 163:17) and a copper/bronze pin with a rolled head (18 N 112; pl. 162:16). A yellow plaster layer across the doorway connected it to the contemporary floor in the courtyard (Locus 41, Floor 1).

No architectural changes were made in the courtyard at Floor 1, but immediately before the surface was formed (i.e., sealed by this floor), two pits were cut at the northern end of Area WF. They form the final phase of the Burial 14 sequence. The first pit contained an ash-filled box made of rectangular baked bricks, the second adjacent to it held

---

21. The text is a list of grain, textiles, and other objects. The orthography of the tablet indicates that it was at least later than the reign of Sargon, but no date is given in the text itself. See n. 24 for similar tablets from Level XIIA. See *Appendix 3* for a description of all inscriptional material.

the final skeleton (Skeleton 1) of Burial 14. Locus 41, Floor 1 sealed the burial pit and a layer of debris, including some eroded mudbrick, accumulated on this floor. Within this final layer were two objects: a straight copper/bronze pin (18 N 142; pl. 162:17) and a miniature conical lid (18 N 164; pl. 164:3).[22]

In Level XIIA (pl. 26), all the walls of Level XIIB remained in use, while two more floors accumulated in the courtyard (Locus 35, Floors 5–4) and one floor in the southeast room (Locus 38, Floor 1).[23] In the doorway through Wall AG at this floor an oblong basalt grindstone was reused as a sill. Near the center and in the east corner of the southeast room (Locus 38), on Floor 1 and on the minor floor surfaces above it, were four more Old Akkadian tablets (18 N 104–05, 107–08; pls. 192:2–3, 193:2–3).[24] Elsewhere in the room were a baked-clay model wheel (18 N 163; pl. 163:4) and a stone weight (18 N 141; pl. 163:18). Another important object from this level was a cylindrical yellow and pale blue green glass bead (18 N 96; pl. 167:2; see *Appendix 1*) found in the stratified occupational debris at the east end of the room.

This floor within the room corresponded to a hard grayish floor at the south end of the courtyard (Locus 35, Floor 5). Above this floor were several dense patches of fish bones and separate patches of ash. Among these layers were an unfinished shell cylinder seal (18 N 113; pl. 160:3), a baked-clay "game-piece" (18 N 115; pl. 163:15), a perforated stone disk (18 N 159; pl. 163:19), and a straight copper/bronze pin (18 N 148; pl. 162:18). Near the face of Wall AG was a miniature spouted pot (18 N 85; pl. 164:10). Near the center of the courtyard, a runoff drain consisting of a cylindrical pit just large enough to hold a jar with its base broken away was cut down from Floor 5. Another pair of bowls was found in Locus 34, above Floor 3, near the west face of Wall S (I3:1–2; pl. 124:10–11).

## Level XI, Phases B–A

During the two phases of Level XI, the plan of Level XII was continued with modifications. In Level XIB (pl. 27) Wall AF was repaired and replastered. In the southeast room Wall S continued in use, while the other walls were cut down. A thin layer of ashy fill was laid over the area of the room to level it before rebuilding new walls in the same locations as previously. The doorway in Wall AB was established directly above the doorway in Wall AG, Wall AA was built over Wall AH on the northeast, and Wall AE was built over Wall AI, with a reed mat laid between. All the walls were built of horizontally laid plano-convex mudbricks. Only Wall AE had not been very carefully built; its base subsequently eroded and was repaired with clay lumps, sherds, and pieces of bitumen in a matrix of mud plaster. Wall AE was built on the same surface as the other walls but its different construction may indicate that it was not bonded to them and had been added after the plan was established.

---

22. Sherds of four additional miniature vessels came from Floors 2 and 1 in Locus 41 and a further miniature from Locus 35 in Level XIIA, the courtyard in that phase. This is an above average number of miniatures but is not linked with any significant changes in use of space or nature of deposits. See *Chapter 4*.

23. Although all the walls of Level XIIB were still in use, a rebuilding in Wall AG at Floor 5 of Locus 35 and other minor architectural changes were the reasons for assigning a new phase here.

24. The tablets include lists of textiles and other goods and a list of personal names. Among the names in this last text, 18 N 108, is possibly Lugal-iti-da (obverse line 9), which appeared on a tablet excavated in Area WA 50c (Level X, Floor 4; 11 NT 19, a list of date growers; obverse line 2, see Civil 1975). An individual of the same name also appears in texts from the Nippur "Onion Archive" (Westenholz 1987) as a receiver of onion seeds and a harvester of onions. Since the Onion Archive possibly originated in the immediate area of Area WF (see Westenholz 1987: 88, fig. 2, where the findspot of the Onion Archive is reconstructed as along the northwest edge of the erosion gully in which Area WF lies), it is possible that this is the same individual who appears in our text, although the name was not an uncommon one. If so, this provides an invaluable dating aid for this level of WF since the Onion Archive is dated to the reign of Sharkalisharri. In particular, two of the tablets from that archive which include the name Lugal-iti-da are dated to the third and fourth years of this king. Tablet 18 N 106, from the same location in Level XIIB, is so similar in palaeography and content to the Level XIIA tablets as to be ascribed to the same date, and the separation of Level XII into phases is not intended to imply the passage of a substantial length of time (see above).

Although the connection with the Onion Archive is a tenuous one, the connection between Areas WF and WA 50c is much firmer. As well as sharing at least one personal name, the tablets are of similar content (mostly lists of small amounts of goods), so we can make a provisional connection between Areas WF, Level XII, and WA 50c, Level X, Floor 4. The architectural remains of Areas WF, Level XII, and WA 50c, Level X, Floors 6–1, are compatible (see fig. 5). Wall A of Area WA 50c, Level X, Floors 6–1, was restored and rebuilt during the accumulation of those floors, which would match the shift from Wall AJ to Wall S in Area WF. The depth of occupation in Area WA 50c, Level X, Floors 6–1, indicates that more than one level in Area WF may be associated, and the continued use of Wall S in Area WF from Levels XII through XI may mean that Level XI relates to the upper floors of Level X in Area WA 50c.

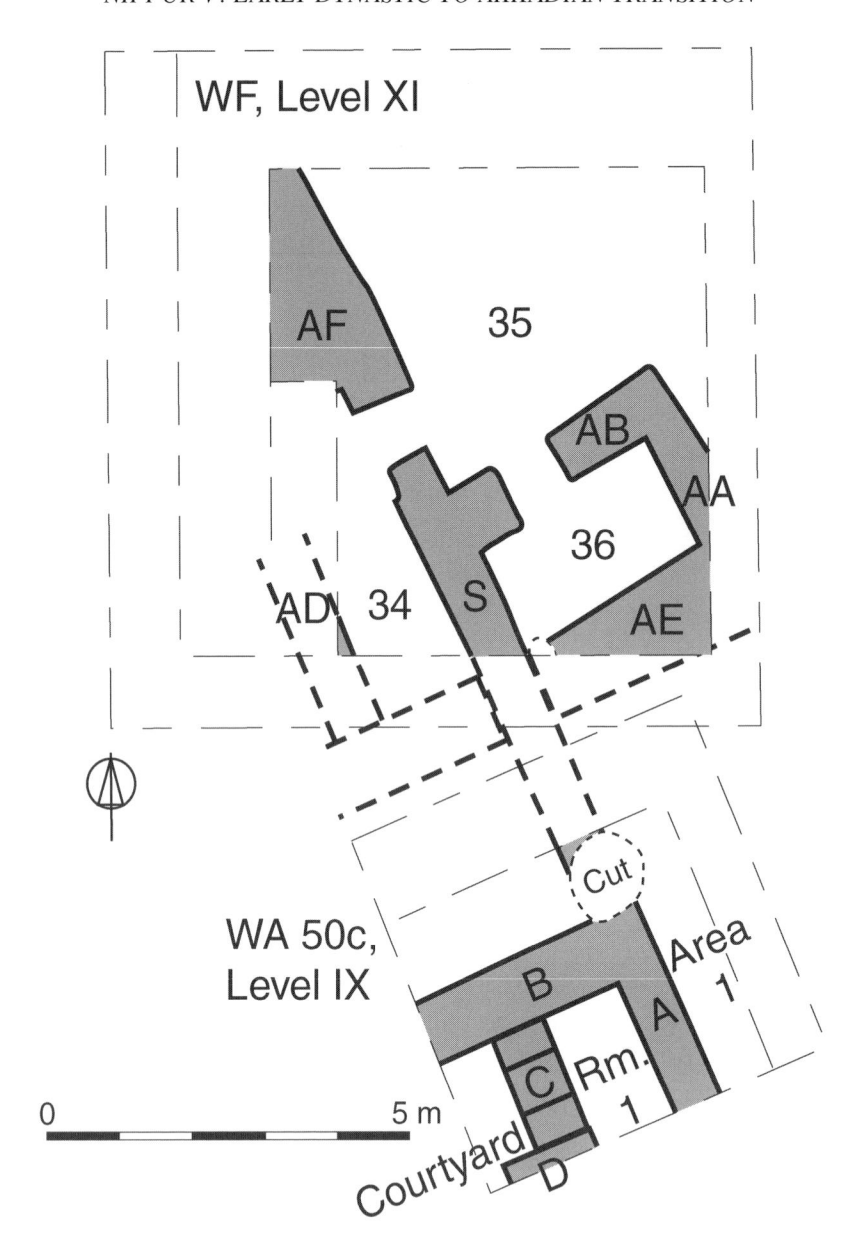

Figure 6. Combined Plans of Areas WF, Level XI, and WA 50c, Level IX

A toilet was found at the lowest floor of the southeast room (Locus 36, Floor 4). A cylindrical pit had been dug in the northeast corner of the room and two vats, one inverted over the other, both with their bases broken through, had been placed inside. On the floor was a baked brick that covered the hole in the base of the upper vat (pl. 28). The greenish soil filling the pit dug for these vats indicates this was certainly a toilet, a radical shift in function from the use for storing "special" items in Level XIV and tablets in Level XII. Chance inclusions within the pit were a small round-bodied jar (18 N 131; pl. 121:1) and a date-shaped agate bead (18 N 154; pl. 166:4). At the west jamb of the doorway through Wall AB, just below the floor, was an upright bowl, a repetition of the foundation deposits of earlier levels (not registered). A mudbrick doorsill ran across the outer edge of the doorway.

The lowest floor in the room (Locus 36, Floor 4) was covered with a layer of trash including lenses and patches of light brown porous soil with a dense component of plant casts, probably animal manure. Cut into this layer from Floor 2 or 3 was Burial 11, against Walls S and AB. The use of this room for a burial is consistent with the earlier interments, in Level XIV, Phases B and A, but in those earlier levels, the special function of the room was marked by the presence of high-quality artifacts. The use of the room in this level as a toilet for humans and then probably for housing animals, and almost immediately thereafter for a human adult burial, is surprising.

At Floor 3, a stone door socket was set into the floor at the west side of the doorway. In the doorway itself, at the west jamb, was a second bowl deposit (H138:1; pl. 124:9). The accumulation above the floor was similar to that below, with traces of animal manure. Floor 2 was a hard blackish surface and the debris above it was almost entirely animal manure with very few sherds, but included was a sherd with an incised B-shaped potter's mark (18 N 79; pl. 166:20). The subsequent accumulation in the room lacked the manure of earlier floors, so the function seems to have reverted to human occupational use. The final floor (Floor 0) was a softer, less well-defined surface than the earlier floors, consisting of brownish soil with an accumulation layer derived mainly from trash dumping: greenish patches, a large amount of pottery, especially large jar sherds, and animal bones. A few additional objects were recovered from the upper layers: a flint blade (18 N 66; pl. 166:15) and a copper/bronze rivet (18 N 145; pl. 162:19).

Two floors were traced in the courtyard. The lowest (Floor 3) ran at the base of Wall AB and at the bottom of the doorsill of that wall (thus contemporary with Locus 36, Floor 4, within the southeast room). Above this floor was a change in the plastering on Wall AF. Level XII originally had a single yellow plaster coating, while from Level XIB up, it had a thicker triple coat of plaster, a gray coat between two coats of red. The mudbricks of AF were uniformly small and reddish brown and no break could be seen in the courses, so the same wall was still in use, rather than being rebuilt.

Locus 35, Floor 3, sealed a 1.5 meter deep pit, Cut 15, which may be a burial comparable to the large chamber of Burial 14. Unfortunately it is located almost completely north of the excavated area and is only just visible at the north section. The fill of the cut was not the loose greenish soil usually observed in drains and its depth suggests a burial. Its location, only slightly north and west of the final phase of Burial 14, suggests that it may be a continuation of the practice of burying in the courtyard.

Floor 3 of the courtyard was a hard surface covered with eroded green and pink mudbrick or plaster. Within the accumulated debris near the center of the excavated space was a second glass bead (18 N 95; pl. 167:1).[25] Other objects from this layer include a miniature bowl (18 N 83; pl. 164:11), a copper/bronze pin (18 N 84; pl. 162:20), and a baked-clay bird figurine (18 N 168; pl. 163:11). The next floor in the courtyard (Floor 2) could be traced through the doorway into Locus 36, where it was designated Floor 3.

The doorway between Loci 34 and 35 continued in use in this level. Wall AD replaced Wall AU as the southwest boundary of the western space. Floor 2 of Locus 34, the only floor traced in this room for this phase, ran at the base of Wall AD and was marked by a reed mat across the doorway, leading to and lying on Floor 3 of Locus 35. A baked-brick door socket was set below this floor within Locus 34, at the north jamb.

In the second phase of this level, Level XIA (pl. 29), the courtyard (Locus 35) and western corridor (Locus 34) remained essentially unchanged, but the southeast room (Locus 31) was modified by the removal of Wall AE, thereby extending this space to the southeast. After Wall AE had been leveled, a pit, Cut 11, was dug into its remains and filled with mottled debris. A layer of striated material then accumulated over the pit and the remains of Wall AE, and filled in the rest of the room (Locus 31).

A single floor in the courtyard (Locus 35, Floor 1) belonged to this phase. At the outer corner of Walls AA and AB, a semicircular pit about 50 cm deep was cut, and its interior was lined with five courses of baked plano-convex bricks, laid on edge slanted in alternate directions; the pit was then covered with a cap of baked plano-convex bricks. It was too shallow to have been a drain, and the utilization of the wall of the house for one side of the feature and the care with which the bricks were laid suggest a storage installation.

The upper floor in the southwest corridor (Locus 34, Floor 1) was the equivalent of the single floor in the courtyard. On this floor at the south section was the still-articulated skeleton of a small equid (pl. 28b). It had perhaps been buried in a shallow pit in accumulated debris, meaning that this area was probably an outdoor space with little traffic at this time. In the trash in this area was a baked-clay rattle in the shape of an animal (18 N 129; pl. 163:12). Above this floor, Wall AD had slumped eastward and partially eroded. It was probably part of a building to the west, beyond our excavation (either part of the same building as Wall AF or a third building), and its collapse may indicate that this particular building was abandoned at the time, although the house on the east continued in use. The upper portion of Wall AD was built of very large, red clay, plano-convex bricks.[26]

---

25. Glass during this period is clearly unusual, and objects as small as beads may easily be shifted from their original contexts by postdepositional processes. However, the excavation of two glass beads in two slightly different levels and in different loci supports the integrity of the findspot for both beads (see also 18 N 96, Level XIIA, and *Appendix 1*).

26. The construction of this wall could be easily defined and was more regular than that of many other walls in Area WF, perhaps due to the larger size of the bricks (23 × 16 × 9 cm.). The courses consist of either central stretchers flanked by headers on each side, or alternatively central headers flanked by stretchers. This bonding pattern is seen in other Akkadian structures, i.e., Umm el-Jīr, Phase IV, Area D (Gibson 1972b: fig. 15).

## Level X

The plan of Level X is comparable to Level XIB (fig. 7, pls. 30, 31a–b). A new wall corner, Wall Z, was built on top of Wall AF, and the walls of the southeast room were rebuilt. Wall S was reused; Wall U was built over Wall AB, with a doorway in the same location; and Wall Y was built over Wall AA. Despite an intervening layer of debris in Level XIA, Wall X was built above Wall AE of Level XIB. At the southeast corner, a fragment of the rest of this structure was visible: Wall AC ran perpendicular to Wall X, forming another room or space, Locus 32, farther south and offset to the east. No access from Locus 30 into Locus 32 was visible within Area WF, and the probable location of a corner of Walls X and Y makes it unlikely that any door did exist in Wall X. At the southwest of the excavation, the former corridor was replaced by a wider space (Locus 33), therefore the building in that direction present in previous levels, already possibly abandoned in Level XIA, had been pulled down or eroded completely.[27]

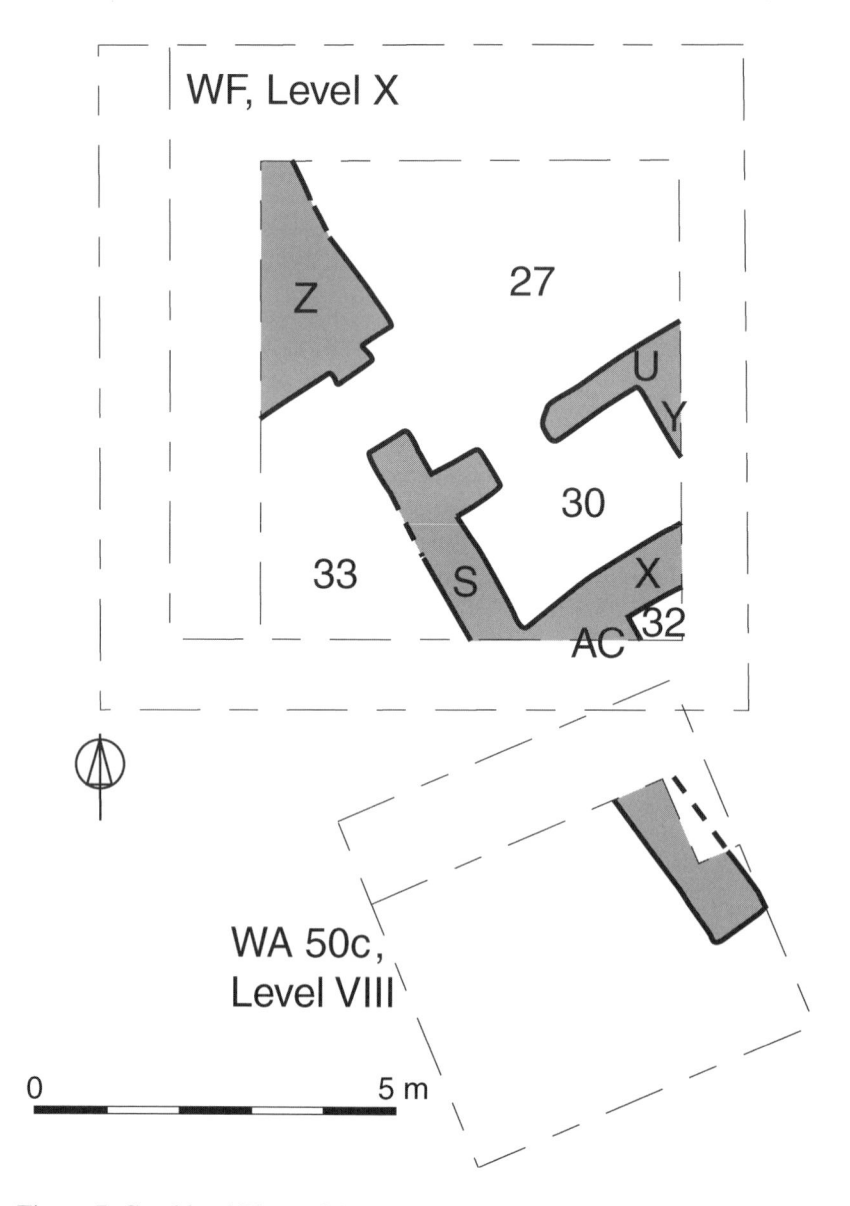

Figure 7. Combined Plans of Areas WF, Level X, and WA 50c, Level VIII

---

27. A connection between Areas WF, Level X, and WA 50c, Level IX, is based primarily on the firm connection made between the areas at the previous level (see n. 24) but is supported by similar ceramic assemblages and objects of comparable date. The rebuilding of Area WA 50c, Level IX, on the same plan as Level X would match the reorganization of the area in Area WF from Level XIA to Level X, but with the continued use of Wall S. The connection should probably be extended to include Area WF, Level IX, as well (see fig. 7).

The western jamb of Wall U may be the reused Wall AB since there was no change in construction at this level. But the eastern half of Wall U and all of Wall Y were newly built and less substantial, constructed of soft brown plano-convex mudbricks, while Wall X was built of harder gray plano-convex mudbricks.[28] A single floor was traced in the southeast room (Locus 30, Floor 1), a hard ashy surface with traces of a reed mat over it, covered by a layer of trash debris with a large amount of pottery.

A two course high mudbrick sill was laid across the outer side of the doorway in Wall U at the level of the first floor in the room. A gap in the sill at the west end may have allowed drainage from the room. This floor corresponded to the lowest floor in the courtyard (Locus 27, Floor 4), the surface on which Walls Z and U were built. At this floor, there was a *kisū*-like footing added to Wall Z on the courtyard side (pl. 31b). This construction was three courses high and two bricks wide and abutted the jamb of the doorway. Wall Z was built of gray and yellow plano-convex mudbricks; its east face was covered with gray and reddish yellow mud plasterings, while its south face had a single coat of gray mud plaster.

The courtyard debris in this level consisted of many thin, discontinuous ash surfaces and lenses. In general, the surfaces sloped down on all sides away from the walls toward the center, but they were cut by many small shallow pits and were made difficult to follow by lenses sloping in slightly different directions. On the lowest courtyard floor (Floor 4), near the east edge of Area WF, was half of a U-shaped mudbrick bin, partially demolished by the foundation trench of a later wall. The following floor (Floor 3) was a brownish surface with several patches of fish bones, such as were found in this area in Level XI. At the next highest floor (Floor 2), a second doorsill had been built across the doorway in Wall U. The debris above this floor and above the final floor (Floor 1) was mostly ash and trash. In this debris above Floor 1 was a fragment of a marble mace-head with traces of an incised inscription (18 N 78; pl. 166:21) and a baked-clay model wheel (18 N 161; pl. 163:5).

The lowest floor of the courtyard (Floor 4) ran through the doorway between Walls S and Z to merge with the lowest floor in the western space (Locus 33, Floor 1). This floor sloped up to the west, over the remains of Wall AD of Level XI. In the doorway at this floor was a copper/bronze pin with a rolled head (18 N 90; pl. 162:21). The debris above the floor in Locus 33 was similar to that in the main courtyard: greenish and ashy. At the level of the final floor in the courtyard (Floor 1), there was a doorsill one brick wide across the doorway between the two spaces. This level was slightly damaged along the north section by three separate deep pits that cut down from Levels V and III through all the intervening levels to Level X.

## Level IX

During occupation of Level IX (pl. 32), the eastern house may at last have been abandoned since the room in the southeast corner of the trench was unused, the walls were allowed to erode, and a layer of debris built up over them. The debris was then cut by a wide shallow pit, Cut 6. The pit was filled with large sherds, animal bones, baked-brick fragments, and carbonized pieces of reed matting. Wall S remained standing from Level X as a boundary for Locus 26 on the southwest. Wall U from Level X was still visible, but its faces were badly eroded, and Walls Y and X had been destroyed and completely covered by debris. However, a new wall, Wall W, was built above and directly upon the wall corner Wall Z of Level X. This new construction, built at the same time that the other walls in WF were derelict, reinforces the interpretation that all the walls in this location had belonged to a separate building, throughout Levels XIV–X.

Wall W was built of dark gray and yellow plano-convex mudbricks and was faced with red mud plaster. The bricks were larger and more regularly sized than the bricks of the earlier (Early Dynastic and Akkadian) levels, but they were still plano-convex, although Level IX can be dated to the Ur III period by pottery and objects. Wall W was set directly on top of the remains of Wall Z, but its east and south faces projected slightly beyond those of Wall Z, and a reed mat was laid between the two constructions. Just before construction of Wall W, a small pit was cut into the top of Wall Z and a small round-based jar (18 N 135; pl. 127:1) was set upright inside and the pit sealed by Wall W. Although the jar was empty, the care taken in its placement may indicate that it was intended as a foundation deposit. In the lowest course of W, between two bricks, was a baked-clay male figurine typical of Ur III date (18 N 81; pl. 163:13).

---

28. The disjuncture between Walls U and Y seen in the plan was the result of later erosion (see Level IX plan, pl. 32); the two walls were presumably originally bonded. Like Wall AD of Level XI, the bricks of Wall X were easily articulated; the wall consisted of two courses of bricks (18–22 × 14–15 × 7–8 cm), the lower lying flat and the upper slanted, the beginning of what would have been an alternating "herringbone" arrangement.

In the former courtyard space, a single floor was traced (Locus 25, Floor 1). The layer above this surface, in Locus 25 and south of the remains of Wall U in Locus 24, was a rubble of fallen mudbrick, ash, and trash. A few objects were recovered: a whetstone (18 N 69; pl. 166:16), a fragment of basalt grindstone, and a broken baked-clay animal figurine.

As in earlier levels, a doorway between Walls W and S led to an open area at the southwest corner of the trench (Locus 26). The space was filled with an accumulation of striated ashy floors that sloped up to the west, echoing the slope of floors in Level X below, over the rise made by Wall AD of Level XI. On Floor 1, a splash course of yellow plano-convex mudbricks was laid vertically against the base of Wall W. Because this area was filled with accumulated occupational debris, rather than trash and rubble, it may be that it was associated with the structure represented by Wall W, although it utilized Wall S of the now abandoned southeast room as one of its boundaries.

## Level VIII

The subsequent level, Level VIII (pl. 33), datable to the Ur III period, was the final level in which plano-convex mudbricks were found. It is already widely recognized that plano-convex bricks were still used in the Akkadian period, but the evidence from Area WF indicates that their use continued even after that.[29] The employment of this type of brick well into the Ur III period is surprising but may be explained by the fact that the buildings in which they were found were domestic structures, built with traditional, conservative techniques.

The plan of Area WF, Level VIII, is in some ways similar to earlier plans. The top of Wall W was still visible but had been leveled so that it resembled a mudbrick pavement or platform, with debris accumulated around it. Wall P was built on top of it, along its south edge. Wall S was still in use and a doorway between it and the corner of W and P allowed access into a rectangular space (Locus 22) at the southwest corner of Area WF. This space was bounded by a new wall, Wall Q, on the west. The rest of Area WF was taken up by a courtyard on the northeast (Locus 20).[30]

Walls P and Q were built of gray plano-convex mudbricks, mostly laid horizontally, but with some irregular slanted fragments. Both walls had received three mud plasterings, a gray coat between two red. A baked-brick door socket was set inside the passage between Walls P and S, just below the first floor of the room (Locus 22, Floor 1). This floor ran through the doorway in Wall S and merged with Floor 2 in Locus 20; a mudbrick sill ran across the doorway at this floor. Farther west was a doorway through Wall Q into Locus 45.

Wall T, the southern wall of the courtyard, was built just above the debris covering Wall X. It also formed the north wall of a room, Locus 29, which lay south and east of the excavation. Wall T was built of hard, sandy, yellow plano-convex mudbricks, laid in horizontal courses in red mortar. At the junction of Walls T and S, the south end of Wall S (reused from earlier levels) had been cut down and Wall T was built partially across the cut, but in such a way as to leave a niche on the Locus 22 side, a peculiarly unstable arrangement that could not be fully investigated due to its proximity to the south section.

Two floors were traced in the courtyard. The lower floor (Locus 20, Floor 2), in places bearing traces of a reed mat, was the construction floor for Wall T. The top of the eastern portion of Wall U was still visible at this floor but only as an eroded line of mudbrick. The second floor (Floor 1) was also partially covered by a reed mat and ran over Wall U and up to the face of Wall T. These reed mats may mark specific work areas within the courtyard. In the layer above the floor, about a meter east of the doorway between Walls S and P, were a number of unbaked clay sealings. None bore seal impressions, but their reverses had impressions of smooth flat surfaces, possibly from a wooden door or box. A door between Walls P and S, leading into Locus 22, is the most likely candidate for sealing because of its proximity; in this case, Loci 22 and 45 may have formed a discrete unit of rooms without access to the rest of the house.

---

29. The presence of plano-convex bricks in the Ur III period at Nippur has additionally been attested in the WA 50c sounding (Gibson 1975) and in Area WC-3, in houses under the city wall, dated by inscriptions to the reign of Amar-Sin (M. Gibson, pers. comm.).

30. A connection between Level VIII in Area WF and Level VIII in Area WA 50c is more tentative than the connections made between the two areas in lower levels. The architectural remains of Level VIII in Area WA 50c consist of a single plano-convex brick wall at the northeast corner of the square (Gibson 1975: fig. 58). The alignment of this wall does not fit well with the orientation of the architecture in Area WF, nor can it be proven to continue across the intervening unexcavated space to emerge in Area WF. The connection at these levels is made primarily on the basis of pottery parallels, the use of plano-convex bricks for the final time, and the reorganization in WF that took place from Level IX to VIII and would allow for a new building farther to the south, represented by Level VIII in Area WA 50c.

## Level VII

In Level VII (pl. 34), Area WF underwent a localized lapse in occupation; parts of Walls T, W, and P were visible but certainly the structure and probably even the entire area were temporarily abandoned, while a sloping layer of ashy debris accumulated over the southwestern portion of Level VIII. Most of the courtyard (Locus 20) and the top of Wall W remained clear and visible during this accumulation, therefore the time span covered by this level was probably not long. The debris layer (Locus 17) ran over Wall Q, up to the south face of Wall P, completely covered Wall S, and covered about half a meter of the western end of Wall T. Farther east, however, the layer thinned out and eventually disappeared over Locus 20, and the eastern portion of Locus 20 and part of Wall T remained visible (a wall of the next level was built directly on top of Wall T; see pl. 35a). Since the accumulation of this level was mainly inside the walls of an earlier building, it appears that the structure stood as a ruin and trash from a neighboring house or houses to the southwest was thrown into it.[31]

## Level VI

Level VI (pls. 36–37a) was the first in Area WF in which rectangular mudbricks were used. Even so, the plan of the level echoes earlier ones and the reuse of Wall P implies temporal and functional continuity with earlier levels. There were two rooms at the southeast corner of the trench (Loci 13–14), with a courtyard to the north (Locus 16) and an open space or separate courtyard to the southwest (Locus 19). The main change in plan was that there was no longer a doorway from the courtyard into the southwest space, a change which could indicate that the western locus may have changed hands or was used for a different function. Instead, Wall L was carried across to Wall P (reused from Level VII). Wall L was built directly above Wall S, despite the intervening debris. Wall M was built on top of T (pl. 35a–b); Wall O was built over Wall Y, which had not been visible since Level X; and Wall N was built above Wall U (last visible in Level IX), with a doorway in the same location as the doorway in Wall U.

All these new walls were built of small rectangular bricks. Those of Walls L, N, and O were soft and gray, while those of Wall M were hard and yellow, set in red mortar. Wall M was the first built and Wall L was then constructed around its western end. The foundation of Wall L sloped down toward the north, and Walls N and O were also at a lower elevation than Wall M (see Area WF east section, pls. 35a, 184), meaning that the base of the level as a whole sloped downward to the north. This slope is mostly due to the fact that the underlying Wall T had been leveled off at a higher point than that of the eroded remains of Wall U.

Two floors were traced in Locus 14. The lowest (Floor 2) was a hard surface on which the walls were built; the upper floor (Floor 1) was another hard surface covered with flat-lying pottery.

The excavation did not reveal the means of access to the room south of Wall M (Locus 13), just barely visible in Area WF. Only one end of it was exposed and the upper layers there were cut away by a later pit, but it is clear that there was no door from Locus 14. One floor was traced in the corner of Locus 13, and resting on this was a three course high feature of rectangular mudbricks. The bricks covered a pit (Cut 9), which reached down as far as Level XI. The pit may have been a grave with bricks as a tomb marker, but the excavation exposed only its edge and no bones or grave contents. The excavation also just reached the northwest corner of a room east of Locus 14 (Locus 28), bounded on the north by Wall N and on the west by Wall O. There was no access to Locus 28 through Wall O.

Two floors were traced in the open space north of the building, Locus 16. The debris there was mostly trash and brick rubble with a large quantity of sherds. The top of Wall W may have still been visible as a platform or paving at the lower floor, but by the second, debris had covered it to a depth of 10 cm and run against the north face of Wall P. If another wall was built on top of Wall W it was completely removed by the later Pit 5. On the upper surface in the courtyard (Locus 16, Floor 1) was a U-shaped mudbrick bin just east of the corner of Walls L and P, connected to that corner by a low block of mudbricks (pl. 37).

---

31. Once again, a tenuous connection may be made between Level VII in Area WA 50c and Levels VII–V in Area WF. Area WA 50c, Level VII, includes a plano-convex brick wall, just at the south corner of the square, with an associated hearth and oven, while most of the rest of the level is a trash layer of Ur III or Isin-Larsa date, cut by a Kassite period grave (Gibson 1975: fig. 59). The wall and trash layer should be approximately contemporary with Area WF, Levels VII, VI, and VB; while the grave should be contemporary with Area WF, Level VA, which includes two Kassite graves (see below).

The upper layers of Locus 19, at the southwest of Area WF, were cut away by a large pit from the next level up, leaving only a layer of striated floors a few centimeters thick (pl. 35b). The bottom of this layer (Floor 1) sloped up to the west, following the slope of earlier surfaces in this area. Many other later pits intruded into this level, including the large pits at the north section which removed parts of every level down to Level X, plus five different burials associated with Levels V and IV.

## Level V, Phases B–A

The occupation sequence of Levels XIX through VI in Area WF was finally broken at the beginning of the second millennium, in the Isin-Larsa period. Level V comprises a mixed group of layers, of which the earliest (Level VB; pl. 38) contained pottery which is Isin-Larsa at the latest. The next remains in the area (Level VA; pl. 39), comprising several burials, a single wall at the northeast, and the space adjacent to it, are Kassite. There is virtually no pottery identifiable as Old Babylonian from Area WF, and what few sherds there are come from later mixed contexts.

We know from excavated areas elsewhere on the site that Nippur was abandoned during much of the Old Babylonian period.[32] Although early Old Babylonian occupation in Areas WB, TA, TB, and others is attested, from the evidence of Area WF, some scattered abandonment within the site might have occurred at the beginning of the Old Babylonian period when the city began to contract (Gibson 1992: fig. 5). Although the processes of site abandonment cannot be reduced to a formula, it is logical that sites undergoing a gradual abandonment did not merely shrink in overall area but also became more sparsely inhabited within their diminishing boundaries. It is possible that there had been an early Old Babylonian occupation in Area WF that was later completely eroded or consciously leveled and removed, but no evidence points to this. The reconstruction of a hiatus in occupation during the entire Old Babylonian period is a better fit with the evidence. It is tempting to link the occupational hiatus in Area WF to the known reduced occupation at the site-wide scale, which in turn was part of a wider regional trend, but at this scale of excavation, it cannot be ruled out that the lack of Old Babylonian occupation in Area WF was linked only to a smaller scale situation in the neighborhood.

The location of the earliest identifiable event of Level VB is to the west of Wall L, where a wide shallow pit (Locus 18) was dug down into Locus 19 of Level VI and gradually filled in with striated ash layers, clumps of mudbrick, and sand (pl. 38). None of the pottery from the pit dates later than the Isin-Larsa period and it seems probable that the pit was dug and filled shortly after the abandonment of the Level VI building.

A second pit in the northern part of Area WF probably also belongs to Level VB. Pit 10 was a wide shallow cut, reaching down as far as Locus 27 of Level X. Its horizontal extent is unknown, as it was later cut on the west by Pit 5 (Level III) and on the east by the foundation trench for Wall R of Level VA (pl. 40). The surface from which it was cut is also unclear, as it was partially covered by an erosion layer (Locus 15, Level VA), which may indicate that the original surface in this area had been higher. A final pit, Pit 8, was a shallow cut at the southeast that removed much of Locus 13, including the top of the mudbrick feature covering Pit 9. A complete outline of the pit could not be traced, as it ran into the south and east sections (pls. 183, 184, 185).

A layer of debris covered the remains of the Level VI room in the southeast corner (Locus 23) but thinned out or had eroded before it reached the north section. Walls L and M of Level VI still protruded slightly above this layer, but it ran over the tops of Walls N and O, which had been deliberately cut down to two or three courses high. Later burials had cut into Locus 23 near the trench center, and the foundation trench of Wall R of the next phase removed it at the northeast. It should be noted here that the presence of the cut for Burial 5 of Level III makes the east section in this area difficult to interpret (pl. 184).

Level VA is dated to the Kassite period by pottery. It comprises three burials and a single wall, Wall R, running northwest–southeast at the northeast corner of Area WF (pl. 39). It was difficult to ascertain whether the wall

---

32. The last datable Old Babylonian text from Nippur belongs to the twenty-ninth regnal year of Samsuiluna (Gasche 1989; Gasche et al. 1998; Stone 1987: 26–28). Both Stone (1987) and Gibson (1992: 42–44) attribute the near abandonment of the site in the late Old Babylonian period to a westward shift of the Euphrates which had provided the area with water. Gasche (1989) has gathered the evidence of datable Old Babylonian texts from southern Mesopotamia, revealing a pattern of gradual abandonment of regional centers over the course of the Old Babylonian period, beginning in the far south in the early years of Samsuiluna and reaching Nippur late in his reign.

and two of the burials (Burials 9 and 12) were strictly contemporary, as no surface between them was traced. Any occupation surfaces in the area had been destroyed and replaced by a subsequent erosion level (Locus 15) in the north and west portions of the square; in the southeast portion of the square, any Kassite material had been completely removed for construction of the next level, Level IV. In addition, both Level VA graves were disturbed by later burial cuts (from Levels IV and III). The third burial, Burial 10, was in the northeast corner of Area WF, just inside Wall R.[33]

Wall R was built of large, hard brown clay rectangular bricks (26–27 × 20 × 9 cm) set in sandy mortar. It was two bricks wide, alternating from course to course with headers or stretchers on each side. Seven courses of the wall foundations were preserved, set into a trench that cut down as far as Level VIII. On the west, the foundation trench was at least 10–20 cm wider than the wall and was packed with large sherds and sandy fill. The wall, as opposed to the foundations, was only preserved within Area WF right at the north section. There were no floors preserved on either side of it; much of the upper portion had been deliberately cut down and the walls of Level IV were built directly above. The deep foundation trench and the care with which the foundations were built may indicate that this wall belonged to a structure more substantial than a simple house. Yet the proximity of roughly contemporary burials should point to a continued domestic use of the general area. Without extension of the excavation area to the east and north, it is impossible to say anything about the function or status of this building.

The foundation space east of Wall R (Locus 21) was filled with homogenous brown soil, within which was a mudbrick feature with bricks of similar size and composition to the bricks of Wall R. The restricted exposure in this area did not allow a complete plan of this feature, but it seemed to be a rectangular paving one course high, covering a pit only partly filled with broken bricks and debris. Although no bones or burial offerings were visible, this feature and pit were called Burial 10. The cut for this pit must have originated from some unpreserved floor associated with Wall R.

The other two burials (9 and 12) may have been cut from floor levels within a contemporary structure or from outdoor surfaces, but the structure or surfaces were not preserved. Instead, the burials were left almost entirely without context, although they could be dated to the Kassite period on the basis of internal ceramic evidence. Above these two burials, signs of abandonment and erosion were visible as a layer of fine gravel, washed and tumbled sherds, and laminated lenses of sand of varying thickness (Locus 15). This layer sloped down radically from south to north, gradually becoming thicker in that direction. At the northeast end of the trench this layer ran against the upper courses of Wall R, where they were visible in the north section (pl. 40). This final erosion layer may be associated with the second of the major site contractions or abandonments known to have occurred at Nippur, in the late to post-Kassite period, ca. 1225 to 750 B.C.[34]

## Level IV

Level IV (pls. 41, 42) is dated to the seventh to early sixth century B.C. by the objects in associated burials and by pottery. Two rooms of a substantial building were exposed, with burials below the floors. The exposed architecture consisted of one long wall (Wall G) running northeast–southwest, south of which were two rooms (Loci 10–11), separated by Wall H. Locus 10, the eastern room, was additionally defined by Wall I to the east and Wall J to the south; the other walls of Locus 11 remain unexcavated. All the walls were built of square mudbricks, 29–32 × 29–32 × 12–13 cm, either crumbly and trash-filled or hard and gray with green and tan inclusions. Although all were constructed on the same floor, none of the corners was bonded. What appears to be a cut in Wall H is presumably a damaged doorway. As Wall G was not preserved very high and was cut in several places by later burials, there is the possibility that there was also a door with a high threshold, leading outside to the north.[35]

---

33. In Area WA 50c, there is also minimal Kassite occupational material (and again no Old Babylonian material of any kind). The final event of Level VII in that square was a Kassite grave (Gibson 1975: fig. 59, burial 3), which is cut into a layer of debris which dates to the Ur III or Isin-Larsa period; the grave is approximately contemporary with the graves of Area WF, Level VA.

34. See Gibson 1992 and Gibson 1993. Again, the shrinking or abandonment of the site may have been related to a westward shift in the course of the Euphrates.

35. There is nothing contemporary with Area WF, Level IV, preserved in Area WA 50c. The builders of a substantial building in Level VI in that square had removed all occupation material in the area down to Level VII, which is contemporary with Area WF, Levels VII through V.

The foundation course of Wall G is a brick's width narrower on either side than the width of the wall above. At its south face this lowest course appeared to be set into a foundation trench that cut down as far as Loci 14 and 16 of Level VI. But at its north face the entire area had been leveled to that depth and filled with a soft, yellow, sandy layer of oatmeal-like consistency (Locus 12). That layer ran up to the foundation course of Wall G as well as against the upper part of the wall as it stepped out over the foundation course. The foundation cut for Wall G did not remove a traditionally trench-shaped area of earlier material but apparently involved a larger-scale leveling of earlier material, and later deliberate filling. The pottery in Locus 12 was of first-millennium B.C. date at the latest.[36] The north edge of this fill material was cut away by Pit 5, so its horizontal extent is unclear. In addition, the top of the fill was removed by both Pit 5 and the later Pit 1, so its original depth is unknown; there were no occupational surfaces preserved north of Wall G.

Three floors were cleared in the eastern room, Locus 10. The first, Floor 3, was the floor on which the walls were constructed and was an even gray surface. It was covered by a layer of eroded gray clay mudbricks and other debris, a layer which appears to have been deliberately added as leveling and paving before the room was used. Above this layer was Floor 2, the first "use" surface. At the northwestern end of the room, parallel to wall G, Burial 8, an adult in a baked-clay coffin (H756; pl. 170:5), was cut down from Floor 2. The final floor in Locus 10 (Floor 1) was a medium-hard surface within greenish ashy occupational buildup. On this floor, above the northeast end of Burial 8, was a nearly complete pot of a type known to be Ur III to Isin-Larsa in date, with comb-incision on the sides and a rectangular multiple-ridged rim. It was upright, contained a small quantity of animal bones, and appeared to be properly in situ despite the fact that the sherds from the room included first-millennium B.C. types at the latest. The best explanation is that this jar had been dug up from Level VI during the excavation of the burial pit or the earlier leveling operation and was then reused above the grave for supplying offerings to the dead. Other objects from above Floor 1 include the upper and lower halves of two different baked-clay human figurines (18 N 26; pl. 180:1 and one unregistered).

Two floors were traced in the western room, Locus 11. The lowest (Floor 2), was formed prior to construction of the walls since this surface ran at the bottom of the narrow foundation of Wall G. This surface was uneven, as was the bottom of Wall G in this area; near the center of the room the base of the wall dipped by the depth of one brick course, filling in a low place left by uneven erosion of the earlier architecture. Presumably, this unevenness was the reason the area north of the structure was more extensively leveled.

The "use" floor in this room (Floor 1) ran at the base of Wall G proper, where it stepped out over the foundation. On this floor near the south section was a feature of mudbricks one course high, laid in a zigzag, with both seventh century B.C. and Isin-Larsa sherds in the mortar. Immediately east of it was Burial 6, parallel to Wall H, which was covered by a similar one-course high feature of mudbricks. There was no burial under the first feature, but it possibly had something to do with post-burial offerings for Burial 6. From the fill above Locus 11, Floor 1, was a fragment of a baked-clay camel figurine (unregistered), confirming the first-millennium date of the level.

## Level III, Phases B–A

Level III is divided into two phases, B and A. The architecture of this level was located in the southwest corner of the trench, where the northeastern corner of a building was uncovered. Originally there may have been other structures within the area of Area WF, but the northeast portion of the excavation was badly damaged at this point by Pit 1 of Level II. The pottery of both Phases B and A points to a date in the sixth to fifth centuries B.C. At Level IIIB (pl. 43), Wall D, running northwest–southeast, and Wall E, running northeast–southwest, form the exterior walls of the corner of the building. On the northern side, at the corner, was a doorway through Wall E. Wall F ran parallel to Wall D from the doorjamb on Wall E, creating a narrow corridor (Locus 8) leading in from the doorway; the corner of a room to the west was also exposed (Locus 6).

---

36. One result of this leveling and disturbance of earlier levels was the presence of a large number of Ur III and Isin-Larsa sherds in the occupational debris within the Level IV building. There were almost as many diagnostic sherds of the late third millennium B.C. as there were of the seventh–sixth century B.C.

All the walls of this building were built of square mudbricks (30–34 × 30–34 × 9–10 cm). While the construction of Walls E and F was fairly straightforward, Wall D was built as two thick faces of mudbrick with the space between filled with gray occupational debris and a few broken pieces of mudbrick. Below Wall D was a layer of sand about 4 cm thick, presumably to even out the foundation. In this sand was found a baked-clay rattle (18 N 59; pl. 180:2). Walls E and F were built directly on top of Locus 11 and Wall G of Level IV. Directly below Wall F was a broken baked-clay female figurine, with hands crossed over the chest (unregistered).

Five floors were cleared in Locus 8 and four in the tiny area exposed of Locus 6. The first floor in Locus 8, Floor 5, ran at the bottoms of Walls D and F and corresponds to Floor 4 of Locus 6, similarly at the bottom of Walls F and E. In the corridor, the bases of both Walls D and F suffered badly from erosion and this seems to have been the reason for a repair program: about 20 cm of fill was added to the room, at the top of which was Floor 4. At that level, a repair was made to the face of Wall F: a thick layer of mud plaster was spread over the wall face and a veneer of half bricks laid as stretchers was set against the mud plaster. A thicker plastering was also applied to Wall D from the level of Floor 4 and upward, contemporary with the repair on Wall F. Floor 4 itself was an ashy surface littered with globs of plaster probably derived from that repair work.

In the corner doorway at Floor 4 was a horizontal drain of baked brick, the cover of which served as a doorsill. The base of the channel was made of single bricks and a single course of half bricks on either side formed the channel edges; the channel was lined with bitumen (pl. 44a–b). Within the doorway, the drain was covered by a sill two and a half bricks wide and three and a half bricks across. Once clear of the building's walls, the drain turned about 30 degrees to the east and sloped downward. On the north face of the building's corner, just to the east of the drain, was a repair or splash course of mudbricks, slanted against the wall face, probably to protect it from overflow from the drain (pl. 45a). At the outflow of the drain was a sandy greenish soakaway area. Clearly a substantial amount of water was being moved out of the building and this water was responsible for the damage to the walls seen at Floor 5. The repair program at Floor 4 was well conceived but was not large scale. The lack of a drain actually within the corridor is curious, but there may originally have been a drain in this location, the baked bricks of which were removed and reused.

Floor 3 in Locus 6 is at about the same absolute elevation as Floor 4 in Locus 8, but at Floor 2 of Locus 6 there were repairs to Walls F and E that could have been made at the same time as those associated with Floor 4 of Locus 8. Either the accumulation was faster in Locus 6 than in Locus 8 so that the contemporary floor was higher in the room than in the corridor or these repairs were made at different times. At Floor 2, the faces of both Walls E and F were covered by a 4 cm thick layer of red mud plaster. Wall F in particular had eroded away near the base.

At the next floor in Locus 8, Floor 3, a second drain was constructed, this one reaching all the way across the room.[37] The drain consisted of a V-shaped baked-brick channel that filled almost entirely the width of the corridor (pls. 45b, 46a–b). It seems likely that it had originally been covered, otherwise all traffic through the door would have stepped into the drain; but the upper bricks had been removed for some other purpose. The covering bricks were still in place in the doorway, forming the doorsill. The sloped channel barely projected beyond the walls, but again there may have been a continuation of the drain outside, the valuable baked bricks having been reused in another context. In Locus 6 it was again unclear what floor was contemporary with Floor 3 of Locus 8. Floor 1 in Locus 6 was at a lower elevation than the drain, but it too had a baked-brick installation at that point. This installation, as far as it could be uncovered, consisted of two broken baked bricks flat on the floor in the Wall E/F corner and another placed vertically against the face of Wall F.

The final two floors in Locus 8 were ashy surfaces separated by thin layers of striated occupation material which filled in and covered the drain. In Locus 6, no higher floors were traced within the occupational layers, but at about 15 cm above the baked bricks on Floor 1 of this locus was another heavy red mud plastering on Wall E.

The area outside the building was designated Locus 7. As was mentioned above, it was cut away on the north and east by Pit 1. Only one floor was traced in this area, Floor 1, the surface running at the bottom of walls D and E. The material above it consisted of striated grayish material with occasional areas of mudbrick debris, but no floors

---

37. The corner of the building in Level IIIB–A is almost certainly part of the structure partially revealed in WA 50c Level VI (Gibson 1975: figs. 60–62). Wall F is continued by the wall in WA 50c at this level, and the baked-brick drain at Locus 8, Floor 3, almost certainly connects to the curving drain of Area WA 50c, Level VId. This connection between the two areas must include the reconstruction of a second doorway in Wall F within the unexcavated material between the two squares, plus a probable corner in Wall D, which does not emerge into Area WA 50c.

were distinctive enough to clear across the whole locus. The area was open and had been used for a number of pits and burials. Pit 5, the top of which was removed by Pit 1, was dug in the northern area of Area WF from a floor probably within Locus 7. In some places Pit 5 cut the lowest floor of Locus 7, but the pottery from Pit 5 is the same as that from Level III, so it originated either in Locus 7 or possibly in Locus 5, which covered Locus 7 in Phase A of Level III. Pit 5 also removed the top and north edge of the yellow fill (Locus 12) associated with Wall G of Level IV and cut as far down as Level X. Burials 2–5 and 7 all originated from surfaces within Locus 7. Another small cut, Pit 7, may belong to a now eroded surface in Locus 7 or to Locus 5 of Level IIIA. This pit cuts into and therefore postdates Pit 5 but was itself cut by Pit 1.

From just outside the building, below the projecting bricks of the drain at Locus 8, Floor 3, was a baked-clay plaque with a molded relief of a lion and a short cuneiform inscription identifying its owner (18 N 51; pl. 180:3, *Appendix 3*). Other objects from Locus 7 include a stone axhead (18 N 38; pl. 166:18), several pieces of a copper/bronze bracelet and a flat copper/bronze triangular fragment (unregistered), a piece of diorite with opposing indentations (part of an ancient door socket, unregistered), a fragmentary baked-clay horse-and-rider figurine, and an unbaked-clay ball (both unregistered).

Level IIIA was a rebuilding of Level IIIB along slightly different lines (pl. 47). Again, the only structure preserved in Area WF was the northeast corner of a building, and much of the rest of the level was cut away by Pit 1. This building corner had the same arrangement as in Level IIIB: a corridor with a door leading outside plus an adjacent room. Wall A was built directly on Wall D but was set about 15 cm farther east; Wall C was built above and slightly farther south than Wall E; Wall B was built above and offset about 5 cm to the east of Wall F. The bricks were the same size as those in Walls D, E, and F and construction was solid all the way across. The bricks varied from orange brown and fairly hard to soft brown trash-filled ones. The east face of Wall A was damaged by Pit 1, and further pits cut into Walls B and C.

Locus 4, between Walls A and B, corresponds to Locus 8, the corridor of Level IIIB; the corresponding area above the inner room of Level IIIB, Locus 6, was cut away by Pit 3, but a room may be reconstructed there on analogy with the plan of the building in Level IIIB. Locus 5 was the outside space to the north of the building corner, above Locus 7. This could not be traced all the way around to the east of the building due to the intrusion of Pit 1, therefore, despite the fact that it was probably the same material, it is called Locus 9. Very little of this outdoor material was preserved.

Three floors were traced in Locus 4. The lowest one, Floor 3, was a harder surface within a number of striated layers, while the upper floors, Floors 2 and 1, were marked by the construction of baked-brick drains. The drains were only preserved in the doorway between Walls A and C, but they may originally have run across the room (pl. 48a–b). Burial 1 of Level II (or possibly from an eroded floor of Level III) removed most of the fill of the room at the center of the exposed area and would have removed the bricks of any drains within the room. The earliest drain at Floor 2 was a simple channel at the western edge of the doorway, with a paving and sides made of broken baked-brick fragments. No cover was preserved and although this may have been removed when the second drain was built, the drain's placement to one side of the doorway suggests that it may have been an open channel. The subsequent drain at Floor 1 was centered in the doorway and reused the eastern side of the first drain for its western side. The base was made of baked half bricks and the eastern side was built of broken baked bricks, set upright. The channel was covered by whole and half baked bricks. The east side of the channel was preserved extending outside into Locus 5 for about 80 cm; the entire drain construction may have originally reached that far or farther, but had been dismantled for reuse. The sequence of rebuilt drains and the layer of mud plaster on the face of Wall A within the corridor both point to the Level IIIA building having the same function or the same water removal problem as the Level IIIB building. Within Locus 4, set slightly below Floor 1 at the corner of Walls B and C, was a door socket made of a broken baked brick with a central hollow. The doorsills at various floors and this door socket indicate that although the corner is an unusual location for a door, one was certainly present here.

# Level II

Level II consisted of a number of small- to medium-sized pits that cut down into earlier levels, a single burial (Burial 1), and the enormous Pit 1, which removed the tops of most of the smaller pits and a large area of the north and east of Area WF (pl. 49). Most of the small pits did not contain any pottery or enough pottery to give a secure dating, but the latest material from Pit 1 was Seleucid. Burial 1 preceded Pit 1 and was probably not far removed in date from Level IIIA, into which it cut, since it was placed within the corridor of the Level IIIA building parallel to its walls. The walls still may have been visible, even if the structure was no longer in use. Pits 3 and 4 were small shallow cuts made into the tops of Walls B and C. Pit 3 removed the west face of Wall B and the south face of Wall C, as well as the corner of the room which presumably lay between them. Pit 4 cut into Wall C at the west section of Area WF. Pit 6 was a similar, approximately contemporary, cut made just north of Wall C into Locus 5.

Pit 2 was a small oval pit that cut down into Locus 7. Since its top was only seen from within Pit 1, its attribution to this level is tentative. It is possible that it originated from an upper floor in Locus 7 during Level IIIB or from within Locus 9 of Level IIIA. Alternatively, it may belong among the similar small pits of Level II and was made just before Pit 1. Pit 2 was a traditional "cooking pit" with lightly burned sides and a fill of charcoal, ash, and bones. There was a small hole at the east end of the pit, however, that contained a hoard — or a single necklace — of 285 beads of various semiprecious stones, faience, shell, copper/bronze, and iron (18 N 7; pl. 179:4). Also included were a faience scarab (18 N 8; pl. 160:4) and a stone stamp seal (18 N 9; pl. 160:5).

Another hoard was found about 1 m west of Pit 2. This one appeared to be simply placed in the fill of Pit 1, although the possibility exists that it was in a small cut within that pit, the edges of which were difficult to identify in the mixed pit fill. This hoard consisted of a small ovoid jar packed with scrap silver and copper (18 N 126, 127; pl. 178:5). It seems likely that these two hoards were assembled and buried at approximately the same time, perhaps by a jeweller. They may even have been contemporary with the occupation of Level IIIA, but all stratigraphic connections were removed by Pit 1.

Pit 1 covered the entire area of Area WF. It had at least two visible phases, where a cut was made into a previously partially filled cut, but it was all of Seleucid date. At its deepest it cut as far down as Level IV and was more than 3 m deep. The fill consisted of soil that graded from pink to gray with varying amounts of charcoal and ash. Within it were several discrete lenses of red material, possibly debris from cleaning an oven or floor. There was a massive amount of broken pottery, including types ranging from Kassite to Seleucid in date. The pit was probably dug for raw material for brickmaking (the usual purpose of pits of this size) and was subsequently used as a trash pit.[38]

A great many objects of varying date came from the fill of Pit 1, including a baked-clay disk with a molded scorpion-man (18 N 15; pl. 180:5) and a copper/bronze tool handle (18 N 60; pl. 179:2). However, most of the objects were too broken and out of context to register. These include several fragments of baked-clay objects: four horse-and-rider figurines, two horses, three unidentifiable figurines, two boat model pieces, a corner of a model bed, and three spindle whorls, plus a cubic rubbing stone, the corner of an uninscribed stone tablet, a pottery lamp, two Uruk period clay cones, and a broken copper/bronze finger ring.

At the eastern side of Area WF, Pit 1 was sealed by Locus 2, an erosion/wash layer. It may have been relatively modern in formation, but the latest material in it — sherds of blue glazed slipper coffins — is Parthian. The layer consisted of coarse gray debris with a large quantity of weathered pottery, a few baked-brick and mudbrick fragments, and lenses of ash. The top sloped down from southwest to northeast, as did the top of Pit 1, even at the west where it was not sealed by Locus 2. Objects from this layer include a baked-clay figurine of a tambourine player (18 N 11; pl. 180:4), a Seleucid bronze coin (18 N 28; pl. 179:3), three baked-clay horse-and-rider figurines, a spindle whorl, and more Uruk clay cones (all unregistered).[39]

# Level I

The final level in Area WF was a modern layer of sand that had washed and blown into the erosion gully bottom from the trapped dune that lies to the south and west of the excavation. The top of the layer was fairly level, but the bottom sloped down steeply from southwest to northeast over the top of Level II. The layer averaged about 2.0 m in depth but varied from only 1.4 m at the center of the south section to over 3.0 m at the north section (pls. 184, 185).

---

38. A similar large, trash-filled pit of approximately the same date was the dominant feature at the top of Area WA 50c (Gibson 1975: Level V). The subsequent layers of occupational material and a final building level (Level II) in Area WA 50c were not represented in Area WF.

39. These Uruk clay cones surely originally decorated a public building of this date somewhere on the site. It is likely that they had been dug up and incorporated into the large debris-filled bricks typical of the Parthian period and that they came from another part of the site entirely, most probably north of the ziggurat.

Table 2. Concordance of Loci, Walls, Pits, and Burials

| Loci | Walls | Pits | Burials |
|---|---|---|---|
| 1 | — | — | — |
| 2–3 | — | 1–4, 6 | Burial 1 |
| 4–5, 9 | A, B, C | — | — |
| 6w–8 | D, E, F | 5, 7 | Burials 2–5, 7 |
| 10–12 | G, H, I, J | — | Burials 6, 8 |
| 15, 21 | R | — | Burials 9, 10, 12 |
| 18, 23 | L, M | 8, 10 | — |
| 13–14, 16, 19, 28 | L–P | 9 | — |
| 17, 20, 29 | P, T, W | — | — |
| 20, 22, 29, 45 | P–Q, S–U, W | — | — |
| 24–26 | S, U, W | 6 | — |
| 27, 30, 32–33 | S, U, X–Z, AC | — | — |
| 31, 34–35 | S, AA–AB, AD, AF | 11 | — |
| 34–36 | S, AA–AB, AD–AF | 15 | Burial 11 |
| 34–35, 38 | S, AF–AI, AU | — | — |
| 34, 38, 41 | S, AF–AI, AU | — | Burial 14, Skeleton 1 |
| 42, 43, 50 | AJ, AM, AO, BA | — | — |
| 39, 43, 50 | AJ, AM, AO, BA | — | Burial 14, Skeletons 2–4 |
| 39, 43, 51–52 | AM, AO, BB–BC | — | — |
| 40, 44, 54, 73 | AR, AQ, BD, BF–BG | — | Burial 13, Burial 14, Skeleton 6 |
| 44, 47, 54, 73 | AR–AS, BD, BF–BG | — | Burials 15–16 |
| 53, 55–57 | AS, BE | — | Burial 14, Skeleton 5 |
| 57, 60 | BE, BH | — | — |
| 58–59 | BH | — | Burial 14, Skeletons 7–8, Burials 17–18 |
| 61–64, 71 | BI–BK | 16 | Burials 19, 21 |
| 65–66 | BM, BO | 17 | Burial 20 |
| 67 | BN, BP | — | — |
| 68–70, 72 | BP–BR | — | Burial 22 |

Table 3. Concordance of Loci and Levels

| Locus Number | Level |
|---|---|
| 1 | I |
| 2 | II |
| 3 | II (part of Pit 1) |
| 4 | IIIA |
| 5 | IIIA |
| 6 | IIIB |
| 7 | IIIB |
| 8 | IIIB |
| 9 | IIIA |
| 10 | IV |
| 11 | IV |
| 12 | IV |
| 13 | VI |
| 14 | VI |
| 15 | V |
| 16 | VI |
| 17 | VII |
| 18 | V |
| 19 | VI |
| 20 | VIII and VII |
| 21 | V |
| 22 | VIII |
| 23 | V |
| 24 | IX |
| 25 | IX |
| 26 | IX |
| 27 | X |
| 28 | VI |
| 29 | VIII and VII |
| 30 | X |
| 31 | XIA |
| 32 | X |
| 33 | X |
| 34 | XIIB and A and XIB and A |
| 35 | XIIA and XIB and A |
| 36 | XIB |
| 37 | Not used |

| Locus Number | Level |
|---|---|
| 38 | XIIB and A |
| 39 | XIIIC and B |
| 40 | XIVA |
| 41 | XIIB |
| 42 | XIIIA |
| 43 | XIIIC, B, and A |
| 44 | XIVB and A |
| 45 | VIII |
| 46 | Not used |
| 47 | XIVB |
| 48 | Not used |
| 49 | Not used |
| 50 | XIIIB and A |
| 51 | XIIIC |
| 52 | XIIIC |
| 53 | XVA |
| 54 | XIVB and A |
| 55 | XVA (merged with 53) |
| 56 | XVA (merged with 53) |
| 57 | XVB and A |
| 58 | XVI (merged with 59) |
| 59 | XVI |
| 60 | XVB |
| 61 | XVII |
| 62 | XVII |
| 63 | XVII |
| 64 | XVII |
| 65 | XVIII |
| 66 | XVIII |
| 67 | XIXA |
| 68 | XIXB |
| 69 | XIXB |
| 70 | XIXB |
| 71 | XVII |
| 72 | XIXB |
| 73 | XIVB and A |

# CHAPTER 2
# BURIALS

Twenty-two burials were excavated in the Area WF sounding, placed throughout the levels from Levels XIXB through II (table 6). Scientific analysis of the skeletal material was planned for the 1991 excavation season but was overtaken by political events, therefore no precise ages are attributable to any of the skeletons, nor was any attempt made to determine sex.[40] In general, the condition of the bones was very poor. The earliest skeletons suffered from their relative proximity to the water table and from the weight of many meters of overburden, while the more recent skeletons, even those protected by jars or coffins, suffered from salt damage. Detailed discussion of the associated pottery is included in *Chapter 3* and of the objects in *Chapter 4*.

## Third-millennium B.C. Burials

There were twelve burials in Levels XIV–X that can be dated to the Early Dynastic IIIa through the late Akkadian period. Most of these burials were located in a courtyard or an open area in close proximity to a house or houses. Three burials were made within the room at the southeast corner of Area WF, which maintained a similar plan throughout Levels XIV–X. Recurring apotropaic deposits under the floors and a generally high quantity and quality of objects are characteristic of this room (see *Chapters 1* and *4*).

Most of the burials were single interments, but two burials were double interments, while one, recorded as "Burial 14," was a three-phased sequence of seven interments, containing at least two and possibly three generations of adults from what can be assumed was a single family group.

The burial pits were generally oval or slightly squared cuts made into the underlying occupational material, not lined, and without any interior construction.[41] Burial 14 was more complex, beginning with a deep shaft in the earliest phase, off the sides of which were cut several chambers, followed by a very large chamber containing several burials in the second phase, and a final single interment in the third phase (figs. 8–11).

Among the third-millennium B.C. skeletons, infants, children, and adults were represented, as well as a wide range in the quantity and quality of burial offerings. Most burials contained at least a few pottery vessels, the better-endowed were buried with jewelry, metal and/or stone vessels, and occasionally other objects. The twenty skeletons that belong to the third-millennium B.C. levels probably do not represent the total population of the excavated structures in Area WF during the years of occupation; there are probably other burials below unexcavated rooms of the buildings.

While two of the third-millennium B.C. skeletons are remarkable for their wealth of associated objects (Burial 14, Skeletons 1 and 2), the main importance of these graves comes from the support they lend to the pottery sequence in the occupational layers for the crucial Early Dynastic through Akkadian sequence (see *Chapter 3*). The co-occurrence of independently datable objects and of specific pottery types in graves, where there is no possibility of redeposition from other levels, greatly reinforces the redating of some of these types proposed on the basis of the level-by-level sherd collection.[42]

---

40. The skeletons, stored in the Nippur excavation house, were destroyed when the house was partially burned in the aftermath of the 1991 Gulf War. The pottery type collection, brought together from all the recent excavations at Nippur, was destroyed at the same time.

41. Burial 11 in Level XIB is the only exception. The pit was a normal subrectangular shape but was lined with a layer of hard gray clay. A similar clay layer was encountered during the 1987 season in an early Ur III grave in Area WC-3 (Gibson, Armstrong, and McMahon 1998: 26).

42. Given the specialized context, the pottery group contained in any one grave is not representative of a contemporary household assemblage. Nevertheless, the preservation in burials of complete examples of vessels seen elsewhere only as sherds is of great value for characterizing the assemblages. In most cases the quality of vessels from graves is neither better nor worse than the pottery found on living floors. There are a few types that seem to be, if not restricted to use in burials, at least strongly linked with burial contexts; these types are less well represented in occupational contexts.

Burial 14, beyond providing chronological information, links with other aspects of the architecture and artifact assemblages to indicate a shift in the nature of the occupation in Area WF during the late third millennium B.C. During this time, Area WF retained its domestic character but entered a phase of more intensive use. The building plan remained stable and old structures were rebuilt or repaired immediately, without even minor episodes of disuse. In addition, the maintenance of a single location for burial over two or more generations — including more than one skeleton from each generation — represents a shift from the more scattered occurrence of single burials seen earlier. The creation of a multiple-burial tomb below the house may have been the response to increased demand for urban land, which would have both decreased space available for burial and made proof of land ownership more important than it previously had been.[43]

Most of the third-millennium skeletons were buried with a few pottery vessels only, and it seems from this that they were neither exceptionally wealthy nor particularly poor. But two richer burials in Levels XIIIB and XIIB indicate that by the late Akkadian period, the family that owned the property was not without economic power. This wealth, and the probable accompanying high status, may have been present earlier but were not recognizable.

## Level XIXB

Burial 22, at the face of Wall BP, was cut from the uppermost floor (Floor 1) in Locus 68, a courtyard or open area (pl. 3). The oval pit was just over half a meter deep and just large enough to contain the skeleton of an older child, possibly around ten years old (pl. 50a). It lay on its left side with the head to the west, legs flexed, left arm extended below the body, and right arm bent forward. A basalt grindstone was placed over the legs, but no other grave goods were included. The pit was filled in and not marked at the surface. The presence of a grindstone or stone slab in a grave is unusual at Nippur but has parallels from Early Dynastic graves at Abu Salabikh, where sandstone slabs and occasional grinding stones appear.[44]

## Level XVIII

Burial 20 was in a pit cut in the open area (Locus 65, Floor 1) at the outside corner of an eroded mudbrick wall (pl. 6). The cut was deep and irregular and the bottom was not reached, even after it had been cleared to a depth of about a meter. The main skeleton, which presumably lies still lower, could not be recovered due to lack of time at the end of the nineteenth season. Higher up in the pit was a partial skeleton, consisting of a disarticulated set of bones accompanied by two conical bowls (19 N 106 and I685; pl. 128:2–3) and a small plain-rimmed jar (I684; pl. 128:1). This group of bones and pottery was in the upper 30 cm of fill at the eastern edge of the cut. It may represent part of an earlier and unrelated burial encountered during the course of excavating a new burial pit or an earlier skeleton in the same pit encountered when the pit was reopened for a related interment. The set of pottery, consisting of one jar and two bowls, may be a minimum requirement for use by the dead in the afterlife and appears frequently in other graves at Nippur and elsewhere in southern Mesopotamia. The grave had no covering or marker of its location.

---

43. "Hypothesis 8," formulated by Saxe (1970) in his work on death and burial, is relevant here. The dead — more specifically, formal burial of the dead — can become useful markers of a group's ownership of scarce resources or property rights. Saxe was thinking of larger territories, of land used for subsistence and of the contrast between sedentary versus nomadic control, or lack thereof, of such territories. But the hypothesis is valid at the Mesopotamian domestic scale, such as the linkage of a formal, visible burial place with ownership of a house by the descendants of those buried there. Even single burials below houses may be associated with the house's inhabitants being owners, rather than renters, of the building; multiple burials then perhaps indicate an intensification of this aspect and a need to indicate ownership. The clustering of the dead in a common burial would have created (either consciously or unconsciously) a new group to which reference could be made, not simply dead ancestors scattered singly throughout the structure but specifically an assembly of dead ancestors. There remains the question of the scale involved in this tightening of property ownership, whether it was site-wide, neighborhood-specific, or unique to the family. There is a tempting link to be made to the fact that Nippur reached its largest size in the Ur III period (Gibson 1992), an expansion which surely had begun in the later Akkadian period and may be visible in Area WF as greater density of occupation. Other possibilities for explanation of the introduction of the multiple burial include a change in the structure of the family. The presence of an extended family in a single house possibly led to a larger number of burials being made in a restricted space.

44. Martin, Moon, and Postgate 1985: Graves 1, 4, 26, 28, 37, 61, 73, 83–84, 88, 94, 96.

## Level XVIIC

Burial 19 was in a deep ovoid cut (ca. 75 cm deep) that ran into the south section (pl. 185) and could therefore not be completely excavated (pls. 7, 50b). Like Burial 20 of the previous level (upon which it intruded slightly), Burial 19 was in the open area outside a wall corner (Locus 64, Floor 1), and the pit was simply filled in after the interment. The skeleton was that of an adult, flexed on its right side with the head to the west. At its feet was a pile of at least twenty-eight conical bowls, mostly stacked upright (19 N 126–28, I664:1–25; pls. 129–31),[45] covering a spouted jar (I666; pl. 128:4). North of and slightly separated from the pottery bowls was a deep alabaster bowl with concave sides (19 N 83; pl. 128:5) and a pair of cockle shells containing traces of light green cosmetic paste (19 N 81, 82; pl. 141:1). The combination of pottery types already seen in Burial 19, comprising a serving or storage container and drinking/eating vessels, reappears here, but the large number of bowls in this case perhaps points to use by a group in a ritual meal at the interment event, rather than being intended for use by the dead alone. This expanded pottery set appears frequently in graves, at Nippur and elsewhere, and the contrast with the jar and one- or two-bowl sets may signal different death rituals and expectations.[46]

## Level XVIIB

Burial 21 was a double burial in a deep (1.25 m) rectangular pit at the southeast corner of Area WF, in an open space, Locus 63, cut from within the layer of occupational surfaces above Floor 1 (pl. 8). The initial interment was an adult (Skeleton 2) lying on its back with arms bent and the head to the west, consistent with the orientations of the skeletons in both Burial 22 and 19 (see table 4). Only the upper part of the body was exposed during the excavation (pl. 51a). A pair of small jars and a conical bowl (I773:1–2, 19 N 155; pl. 132:3–5) were placed south of the head, while a polished bone tool made from a equid tibia (19 N 144; pl. 132:6) was placed north of the body. A second but virtually contemporary interment was made after the pit had been partially filled; an infant was placed in the grave, on its back with the head to the north and arms and legs bent toward the east (Skeleton 1, pl. 51b). A small jar and a small shallow conical bowl (I686–87; pl. 132:1–2) were placed near its head. The location of the burial was not marked at the surface. The sets of pottery with each skeleton, consisting of a few vessels only, match that of Burial 20, presenting both storage and eating/drinking functions, and presumably they were intended for use by the dead only. This speculation is reinforced by the small size of the vessels interred with the infant skeleton.

## Level XVI

Two single burials were made from surfaces in the open area exposed in this level (pl. 10). Burial 18 was located just east of a firepit, near the center of Area WF. It was a small, shallow ovoid pit only about 30 cm deep, cut from Floor 3 of Locus 59. The pit contained the skeleton of an infant placed on its back, its arms crossed over the chest, and the head toward the southwest (pl. 52a). A single conical bowl (19 N 60; pl. 132:7) was placed near the head and the pit was filled and left unmarked.

Burial 17 was cut from the final surface of Locus 59, Floor 1, in the southern half of Area WF (pl. 10). The cut was ovoid, only approximately 40 cm deep, with the body placed in the wider southern portion (pl. 52b). The head was missing and the body had been partially dismembered; the upper body was still articulated but lay, chest down, folded over on top of the upper legs, while the lower legs had been removed and placed, also still articulated, to the west of the body. No burial offerings accompanied the skeleton. The best explanation for its gruesome condition may be that this individual had died elsewhere and was partially dismembered for transport home for burial; but the absence of the head is strange and disarticulated burials are not common in Mesopotamia during the historic periods. The condition of the bones was much better than most of the other skeletons in Area WF, also difficult to explain. Again, the pit was unmarked.

---

45. Three bowls from this burial were registered; the other twenty-five were not registered but were drawn and recorded. The pile of bowls extended into the south section and not all were recovered, so this is only a partial count. However, since most of the skeleton was exposed, it is probable that the majority of the bowls were found.

46. See also the essay by Tinney (1998) suggesting that grave goods may be intended as gifts to the deities of the underworld as well as or instead of implements for daily use by the dead. This is a convincing explanation for some "luxury" objects found in many graves, but the stack of (apparently empty) bowls in this grave would presumably not make a particularly appealing gift.

I assume, from stratigraphic analysis and from parallels between the sherds from occupation surfaces and the vessels found with the earliest skeletons of the Burial 14 sequence (Skeletons 7–8), that the first phase of that burial took place during formation of Level XVI. This first phase involved the excavation of a deep rectangular shaft with at least two chambers cut from its base (figs. 4, 8). There is a slight possibility that the shaft was dug during the occupation of Level XV. The top of the shaft was removed during the second phase of the burial (Level XIIIB, see below), so it is not possible to be exactly certain from which of these levels it was cut. The shaft cuts a wall of Level XVII, so it must postdate that level, and since its top was removed by a cut from Level XIII, it precedes that level. In addition to Skeletons 8 and 7, which were buried in chambers cut from the base of the shaft, the shaft continued to be used for at least three more burials, which I assume are later than the two cut from the base. Two of these additional burials were not able to be excavated but were visible as chamber openings cut from the shaft sides and running beyond the section to the west and north. Skeleton 6, in a chamber clearly cut from the south end of the shaft at a higher level than Skeletons 8 and 7, was the third of these burials (fig. 9; see *Level XIV*).

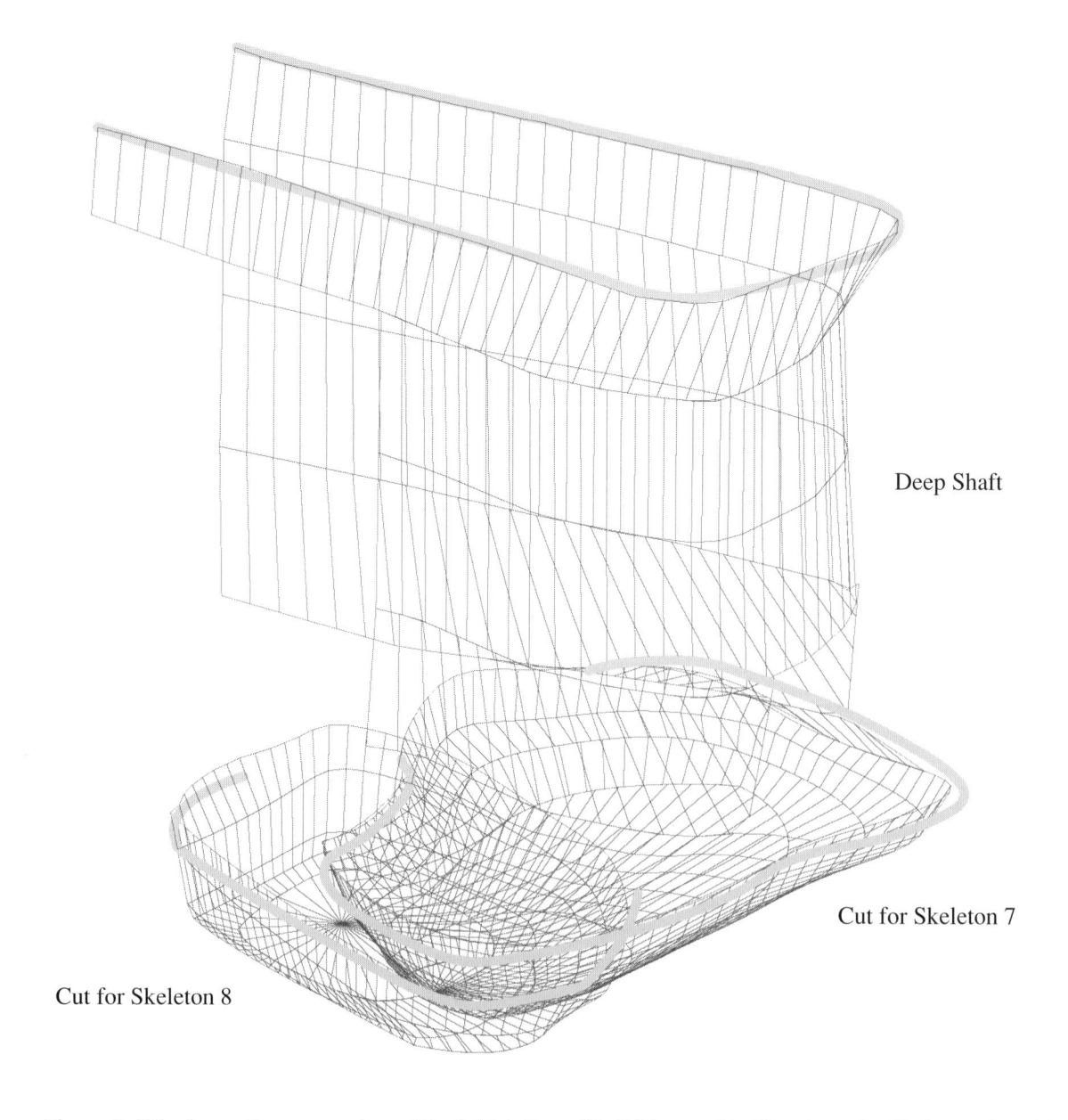

Figure 8. Wireframe Reconstruction of Burial 14, Deep Shaft Phase with Chambers for Skeletons 7 and 8

The pottery interred with Skeleton 7 is paralleled by pottery from floors in Levels XVII through XVI of Area WF, while pottery with Skeleton 6 is best paralleled in floor material of Level XIV. The pottery thus fits with the evidence from the stratigraphy, as far as the range of levels to which the shaft must belong. The interment of at least three adults, and possibly as many as five individuals in total, supports the assumption that some time passed during use of the shaft, which I assume would have been used by inhabitants of the associated building only. Thus it is certainly the case that the shaft was utilized for more than a single architectural level. I therefore propose that the shaft was dug from Level XVI or XV and was in use into Level XIV.[47] This continuity of use through at least two levels means that the location of the shaft in the courtyard was marked at the surface and the shaft was partially re-excavated each time a new interment was made.

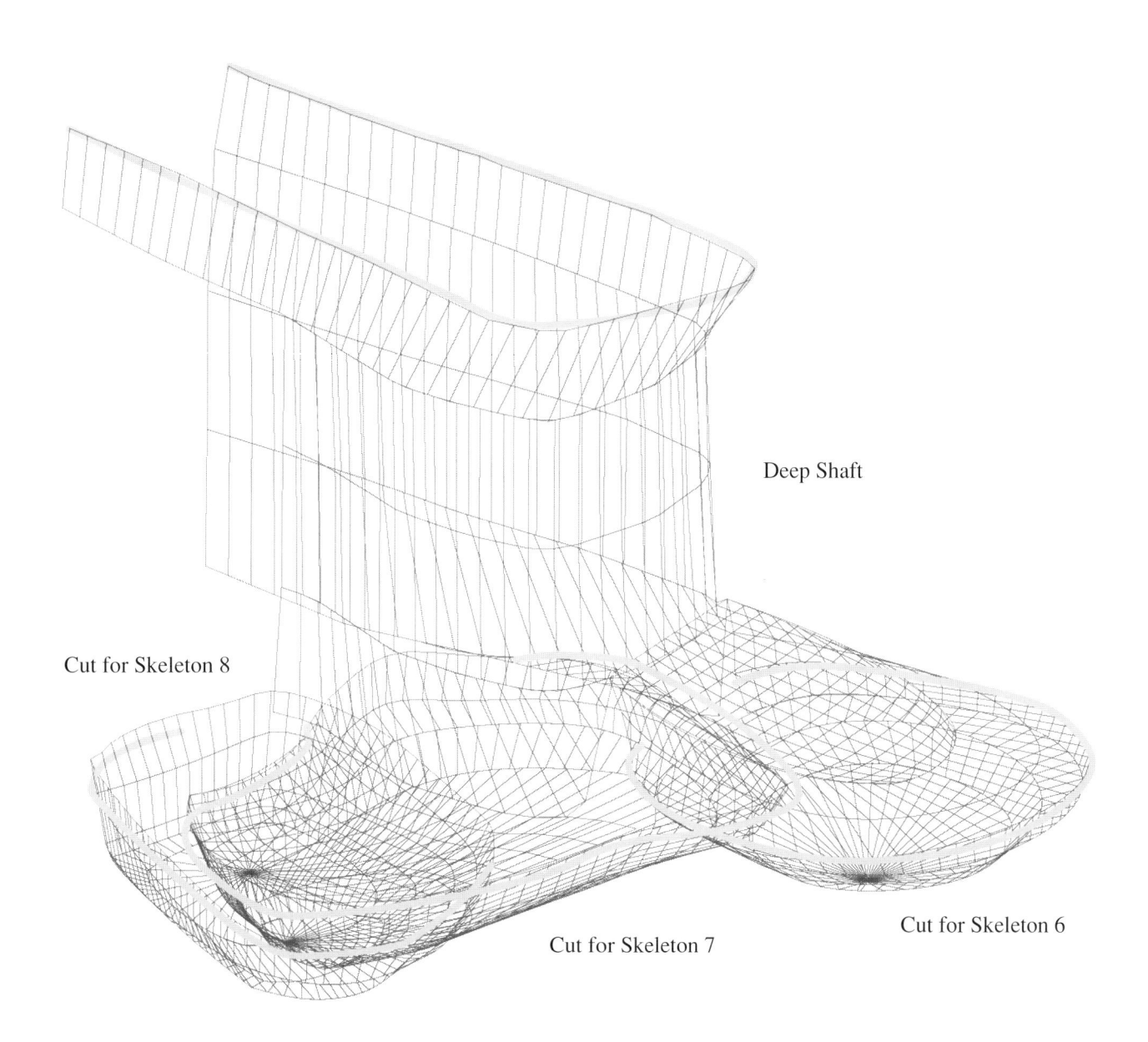

Figure 9. Wireframe Reconstruction of Burial 14, Deep Shaft Phase with Chambers for Skeletons 6–8

---

47. The possibility of the shaft being dug from Level XVI *or* XV is an amendment to the preliminary report (Gibson and McMahon 1995), which proposed that the shaft was dug in Level XVI.

The deep rectangular shaft as preserved measured ca. 0.8 m wide × 2.0 m long × 1.7 m deep.[48] The fill was a distinctive mottled orange, gray, and dark brown (probably mainly derived from the debris layer of Locus 65, Level XVIII, through which it cut), easily distinguished from the grayish striated floor layers into which the pit was made. This mottled fill was also found in the chambers cut from the shaft sides, so they were identifiable even where they ran beyond the excavation area.

The earliest interment off the deep shaft was Skeleton 8, in a shallow chamber running west from the shaft base into the section (fig. 8). Only the skull was exposed in the excavation, while the rest of the body remained beyond the west section (pls. 10, 56a). At the north edge of the burial chamber was a pile of eighteen conical bowls and two narrower cups (19 N 156, I780:1–19; pls. 56b, 139–40).[49] Within this pottery pile was a small flint blade (19 N 150; pl. 166:6), but it is unclear whether it was a deliberate or chance inclusion. This large group of bowls may be related (as those of Burial 19) to an event at interment, rather than being intended for use by the dead. A small, rounded-base jar with an everted rim and horizontal combing on the lower neck and shoulder (19 N 145; pls. 56b, 139:1) lay north of the skull, between it and the pile of bowls. This vessel is either an import from northern Syria or is strongly influenced by the Syrian/northwestern Mesopotamian tradition and I argue its date to run from late Early Dynastic III into early Akkadian — that is, it is potentially a transitional Early Dynastic/Akkadian type (see *Chapter 3*; Type C-11). Sherds of this jar type appeared in the occupation material of Area WF only in Levels XVIIB and XVI.

Skeleton 7 was placed in a shallow cut just above Skeleton 8 (fig. 8). The orientation of the body was exactly the opposite of the latter; the head was to the west and the entire body was within the excavated area (pls. 10, 56c; table 4). It was placed on its back with the arms and legs bent toward the north. There were only a few burial offerings: next to the skull was a small plain-rimmed jar covered by a conical bowl (I682:2, 1; pl. 138:3–4) and next to the left arm was a pair of cockle shells with traces of green cosmetic paste (19 N 105a–b; pl. 141:2). The arrangement of jar and bowl was certainly intended to keep dirt out of the jar and its contents; the dual function of the bowl, as a lid that could also be used for eating and drinking, is a useful check against ceramic typologies that insist upon tight reconstruction of function. Given their proximity to each other and placement at the very bottom of the shaft, the burial of Skeleton 7 must have followed closely on that of Skeleton 8, and both probably belong to the first use of the shaft, in either Level XVI or XV (fig. 11).[50]

## Level XVA

A burial, recorded during excavation as Burial 14, Skeleton 5, was probably interred from Floor 1 of Locus 57 of this level (pl. 13). When it was initially discovered, it was thought that this burial was cut from the base of a large multiple-burial chamber (the second phase of the Burial 14 sequence). The bottom of that chamber cut into Floor 1 of Locus 57 in places and had removed the top of the pit for Skeleton 5, making it appear that this skeleton had been placed in a cut made from the bottom of that chamber. The mottled fill surrounding Skeleton 5 was similar to the fill in the large chamber. In post-excavation analysis, however, the pottery associated with Skeleton 5 was found to be demonstrably earlier than that with the skeletons in the large chamber and comparable to pottery from Level XV. Since Floor 2 of Locus 57 was not cut by the large chamber, the cut for Skeleton 5 must have been made from the upper floor — Floor 1 — of this locus (fig. 11, pl. 13).

---

48. If the shaft was first dug from Level XVI, its initial depth would have been approximately 1.0 m; if dug from Level XV, approximately 1.5 m. Its final total depth, after accumulation of occupational floors and subsequent recutting of the shaft through Level XIVA, would have been approximately 2.2 m. Similar graves with rectangular shafts and side chambers at Abu Salabikh are in the range of 2 to over 3 m deep (Martin, Moon, and Postgate 1985: graves 29–30, 63).

49. A trend in decreasing height of conical bowls during the Early Dynastic through Akkadian period has been identified in Area WF and at other sites (see *Chapter 3* and table 12). The average height of the conical bowls with Skeleton 8 (7.3 cm) is closest to the average for Level XVII (7.6 cm) and less than the averages for Level XVI (6.7 cm) and Level XV (6.2 cm). This supports the attribution of the shaft and Skeleton 8 most probably to Level XVI (given that XVII is a stratigraphic impossibility).

50. The single conical bowl with Skeleton 7 was 7.3 cm high, the same as the average for the bowls with Skeleton 8. This is only a single example and thus cannot be conclusive proof, but it should be noted that bowls more than 7 cm high were consistently found only in architectural levels up through Level XVI, with just two rare exceptions thereafter (see table 12).

This reconstruction makes the pit somewhat shallow, only ca. 45 cm deep, but the skeleton was of a child about five years old and the other infant and child burials in Area WF (Burials 13, 15, and 18, for instance) are similarly shallow.[51] The body had been placed on its left side with the legs slightly flexed and head to the south (pl. 53a). The pit was at the face of Wall BE, which separated two courtyards or a courtyard from an open area. At the skeleton's head was a tall band-rim jar (19 N 39; pls. 53b, 133:1), at the knees a small spouted jar (19 N 41; pls. 53b, 133:2), and at the feet were another small jar (19 N 45; pls. 53b, 133:3) and a conical bowl (19 N 46; pls. 53b, 133:6). At the head was a ring-shaped bone bead (19 N 22; pl. 133:7). The body was covered with a horizontal line of mudbricks within the burial cut and a further pair of conical bowls was placed at the north end of these bricks (I359:1, 19 N 34; pls. 53b, 133:4–5). In the pit fill around the bricks were a flint scraper and blade, possibly chance inclusions (19 N 78, 19 N 30; pl. 166:8–9). Three jars is the largest number of storing or serving containers in a burial seen thus far and some of the contents may have been intended as gifts for deities in the underworld, not just for consumption by the dead. The presence of such a range of vessels in a child's grave is unusual.

## Level XIVB

Burial 16, lying directly below and partly sealed by Wall BF in the northeast corner of the excavation (pl. 14) was the first event of Level XIVB. The cut was oval, almost a meter deep and slightly bell-shaped in profile, and ran into the north and east sections (pls. 54a, 184). The skeleton was that of an adult lying on its right side, legs flexed, and head to the north-northwest. At the head was a pair of conical bowls (I403:1–2; pl. 134:2, 7). Three more bowls, upright and containing fish bones, were placed next to the pelvis (I426:1–3; pl. 134:5–6, 3) and a single bowl was between the legs (I422; pl. 134:4). A piriform jar with a small ledge rim, in burnished redware, was at the feet (I428; pl. 134:1).[52] Six bowls are more than one individual would use, so this may be remnants of a ritual meal. Fish bones also appear in several bowls with Burial 14, Skeleton 6 (see below), but it is extremely unusual to see remains of vessel contents in the Area WF burials. Although only a portion of one face of Wall BF was exposed in the excavation, the construction was such that it can be assumed to be a load-bearing wall, or at least a significant boundary for the courtyard, rather than a marker of the burial.

Burial 15 was sealed by the lowest floor in the western portion of the southeast room, Locus 47, Floor 5 (pls. 14–15). The cut was almost circular, the skeleton that of an infant lying flexed on its left side with the head to the west (pl. 55a). In front of the body, to its north, was a group of five conical bowls (H1103:1–2, H1104, H1106, 18 N 192; pls. 55b, 135:3–7) and between the hands a small "fruit stand" (18 N 191; pls. 55b, 135:2). Near the head was a medium-sized jar with a distinctive wide shoulder and wide ring base (18 N 193; pls. 55b, 135:1). The cut was shallow (approximately 40 cm deep) and was left unmarked, with occupation floors in the room covering it immediately. This burial is the second child within the Area WF sequence to be buried with a fairly wide range of personal effects (the first was Burial 14, Skeleton 5), and this contrasts with the less well-equipped burials of Levels XIXB, XVIIB, and XVI. While this is not a large sample, a similar increase in range and number of grave goods was present among contemporary adult burials (see discussion of Burial 14).

## Level XIVA

Burial 13, sealed by Floor 1 of Locus 40, was an extremely shallow (ca. 30 cm deep) rounded cut in the western portion of the southeast room (slightly farther north and east of Burial 15 of the previous level; pls. 16, 19). The skeleton was that of a child flexed on its right side, head to the north. A stack of four shallow conical bowls was placed in front of the face (H535:1–4; pl. 134:10, 8–9, 11), a copper/bronze bracelet was worn on each wrist (18 N

---

51. It might be argued that Burial 14, Skeleton 5, was interred from a higher level, within Level XIV for instance. But in that case, the burial pit would have been almost exactly at the center of the courtyard in that level. While this placement is not an impossibility, it would be unusual for a single grave to be so located; most of the comparable graves in Area WF are adjacent to walls, at the edges of the courtyard or room in which they lie (burials in larger open areas and the large multi-skeleton chamber of Burial 14 are separate cases).

52. The pottery from this burial was so broken that none was registered, though at least partial profile drawings could be made. The jar was partly hidden beyond the east section and the sherds that were recovered from it were too shattered to reconstruct. The burnished redware of this jar has been found elsewhere in a number of Akkadian contexts, such as Umm el-Jīr, where its propensity to shatter into many tiny fragments has also been noted (M. Gibson, pers. comm.).

118a–b; pl. 134:12), and a string of lapis, gold, and silver beads was around the neck (18 N 119; pl. 134:13). The absence of a jar or other container vessel is unusual for a grave in the Area WF sequence. The grave was awkwardly placed almost on axis with the only doorway to the room and therefore was directly below all traffic into and out of that space, a situation at odds with the possible wealth and regard expressed in the necklace and bracelets. The shallowness of the pit is also troubling, but the grave was sealed by Floor 1 of the locus, which was traced across the room, and it cut slightly into the mudbrick surround of the vat in the west end of the room, built at Floor 2.

Skeleton 6 of the Burial 14 sequence has been attributed to this level, mainly on the basis of pottery parallels. The skeleton lay in a circular chamber with a low arching roof dug into earlier occupational layers off the south end of the deep shaft, originally cut for Skeletons 8 and 7 (fig. 9). Once the body and burial offerings had been laid out the rest of the chamber was filled and the entrance from the shaft was sealed with a blocking of plano-convex mudbricks that plugged the hole in the shaft side (pl. 57a).

The skeleton was at the east edge of the cut, tightly flexed on its left side, head oriented to the south-southwest. Skeleton 6 had a richer set of items than did either Skeleton 7 or 8: a number of pottery vessels, two copper/bronze pins, and an alabaster bowl. The pottery and other objects had been pushed into the chamber after the body (pls. 16, 57b). On the southwest, farthest from the access between shaft and pit, was a group of nine conical bowls, many containing fish bones (19 N 93–95, I482:1–6; pl. 137:6, 3–5, 2, 9–10, 8). Between this group of bowls and the skull and separated from the body were two long copper/bronze pins: one straight with a short tang (19 N 64; pl. 136:1), the other with a flattened and pierced section near one end and a long bent tang (19 N 65; pl. 136:2). At the head was a small ovoid jar (19 N 84; pl. 136:7), in the mouth of which was set an upright alabaster bowl (19 N 96; pl. 136:4). Next to the jar was a fruit stand (19 N 85; pl. 136:5) and at the knees was a pair of jars (19 N 88, 19 N 89; pl. 138:2, pl. 136:3), two more conical bowls (19 N 92, 19 N 9; pl. 137:7, 12), and a third jar (19 N 87; pl. 136:6). At the feet was a fourth jar (19 N 90; pl. 138:1) with a conical bowl (I480; pl. 137:1) set upright in its mouth.

A sloping, slightly harder surface within the fill of the shaft, about 20 cm from its base, may mark the surface created when the cut for Skeleton 6 was made. The ancient excavators would have stood or squatted on this surface while scooping the earth out of the side chamber. Inverted on this surface was a thick-walled, horizontally ridged bowl (19 N 52; pl. 142:1). There was no intact stratigraphic indication for the occupational level with which Skeleton 6 should be associated, but its connection to the deep shaft was clear from within the shaft itself, with the bricks plugging a hole in the shaft side. The arched top to the chamber, cutting into occupational material and undermining remnants of earlier walls, made it clear that the pit had not been cut straight down from a surface above (fig. 9).

Two of the jars found with Skeleton 6 are very distinctive (19 N 88 and 19 N 89; pls. 138:2, 136:3); Nissen (1966) assigned an early Akkadian date to identical types from the Ur Cemetery (Woolley 1934).[53] The conical bowls from this grave are shallow, comparable to the average heights for bowls from Level XIIIB. However, since it is clear from the stratigraphy (including the north section; see pl. 182) that the large chamber was cut during occupation of that level, and since burial in that chamber replaced burial from the shaft, Skeleton 6 must predate Level XIIIB. At the lower end of the potential time range, the cutting of the Skeleton 6 chamber from the side of the shaft, at a higher elevation than Skeletons 7 and 8, indicates that it was interred after Level XVI or XV, to which they probably belong. The specific jar types from the burial only became common in floor material in Level XIV and comb-incised decoration, such as that on the fruit stand, first appeared in floor material at Level XIIIC. Thus, Skeleton 6 was probably interred during occupation of Level XIV or XIIIC and has been assigned to Level XIVA.

The fill of the shaft contained many sherds and a number of objects, all of which were apparently chance inclusions: a stone ring-shaped bead (19 N 23; pl. 166:1), a stone rectangular spacer bead, and a flint blade (19 N 29; pl. 166:7). One object from the shaft is potentially more important: from the upper fill came a copper/bronze pin with a flattened, rolled head, probably an early Akkadian type.[54]

---

53. The other vessels in the grave are more ambiguously dated. At Abu Salabikh, graves with vessels comparable to 19 N 84 include graves 32, 73, 168, 182, and 184 (Moon 1987: nos. 378, 377, 376, 381, and 388, respectively). All are dated to late Early Dynastic there, but graves 73 and 182 both include jar types which might continue into the early Akkadian period. See *Chapter 3* for discussion of all pottery.

54. This pin was too corroded and broken to register or illustrate, but compare 18 N 146 from Level XIVB (pl. 162:12).

## Level XIIIB

During occupation of Level XIIIB, a large chamber (containing Burial 14, Skeletons 2–4) was cut in the courtyard of the building, removing the occupational debris at the top of and surrounding the deep shaft (fig. 11). Either the shaft could no longer be used or other circumstances (e.g., the unusual death of three related individuals during a short span of time) forced a change in the form of burial. The large chamber was the second phase of the Burial 14 sequence. The third phase occurred in Level XIIB, when a single skeleton (Skeleton 1) was interred in a cut that intruded into this larger chamber (see fig. 11 for cross sections of Burial 14).

Since the top of the Phase 1 deep shaft was cut away by the Phase 2 chamber, it was initially thought during excavation that the shaft was dug down at the same time and as an adjunct of the large chamber. The mottled fill in the shaft was similar to that in the larger chamber and there was no distinct base to the chamber where it intersected the top of the shaft. The grave goods associated with the shaft skeletons were not as rich as those with the skeletons in the upper chamber, but placement in shaft versus chamber might have been argued to have signified a differential in wealth or prestige. Only on closer analysis of the pottery with each skeleton was it determined that the cutting of the chamber and of the deep shaft must have been temporally separate events and that the shaft itself had been in use over a substantial amount of time before being succeeded by the chamber. Thus the differences among pottery types and other grave goods found with the skeletons in the two different parts of Burial Complex 14 are due to temporal differences, rather than status distinctions. This revelation relieves the need for reconstructing the death of at least six (and quite probably more) related individuals during a short period.

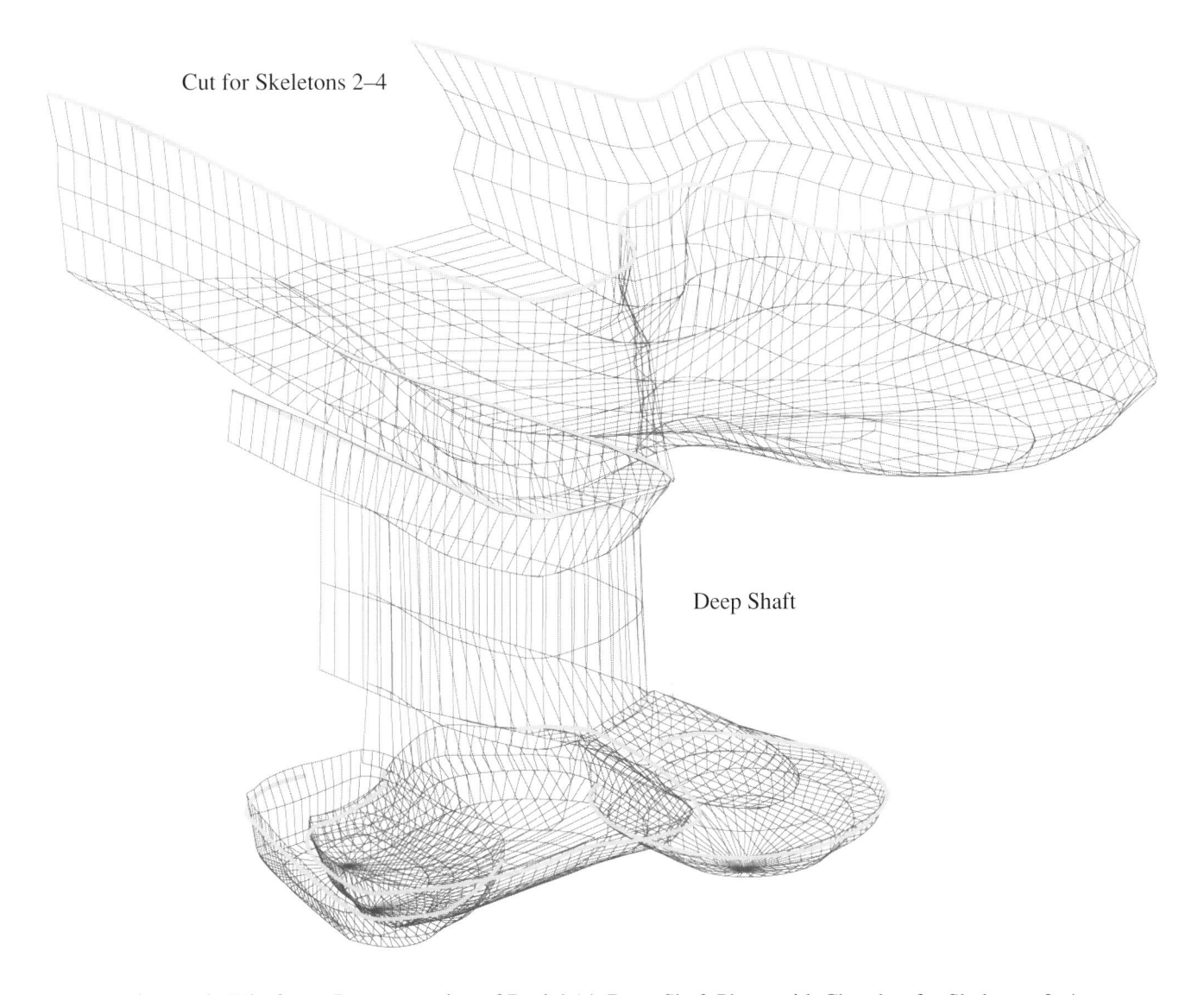

Figure 10. Wireframe Reconstruction of Burial 14, Deep Shaft Phase with Chamber for Skeletons 2–4

It is safe to assume that the individuals in the collective grave belonged to a single extended family that owned the associated building. Although it is difficult to determine the number of years that would have elapsed during accumulation of Levels XVI through XIIB, it seems likely that at least two, and probably three, generations were involved. The deep shaft alone, with up to five possible burials, may belong to two generations; and the main chamber of Level XIIIB was simply an expansion for the next generation of a habitual burial spot. Skeletons 2, 3, and 4 appear to have been interred at nearly the same time. Internal placement of skeletons and objects, and some disturbance of two of the skeletons, suggest that not much time passed between interment of two of the skeletons and that of the third, but all three were buried during the course of accumulation of a single architectural/occupational level. In the next level, Level XIIB, the final interment (Skeleton 1) was then made in a separate pit that was cut partially into the Level XIIIB chamber, perhaps with the knowledge that it was already filled to capacity. It is likely that Skeleton 1 was of the same generation as those in the chamber since these two levels were not separated by much accumulation and the objects and pottery indicate much the same date.

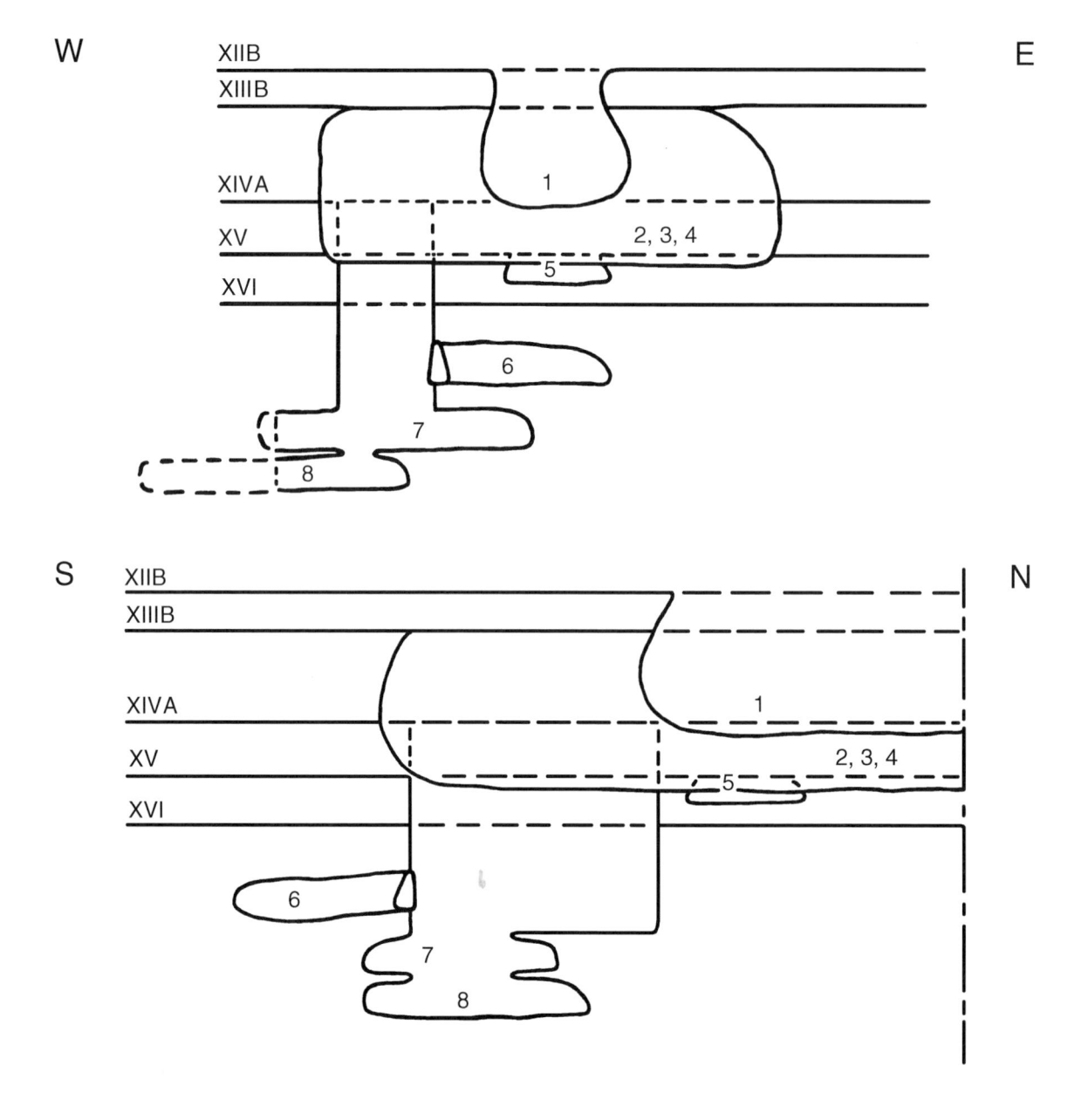

Figure 11. Burial 14 Schematic Sections Showing Levels and Skeletons of All Phases, Looking North (top) and West (bottom)

## Burial 14, Skeletons 2–4

The burial chamber for Skeletons 2–4 had an irregular outline (pls. 22, 58a–b, 59, 62). While its southwest corner preserved the rectangular shape of the earlier deep shaft, this was extended to the north, creating a long narrow trench that ran beyond the excavation limits, forming the western half of the burial chamber. The floor of the western half was flat and its west side was vertical and easily distinguished along its entire length from the horizontally striated material into which it cut. A large irregular lobe was cut from the east side of the trench to form an arched chamber approximately 1 m high. The curve of the ceiling was visible in the earlier layers of occupational material into which it was cut, especially at the east edge. Two stubs of intact earlier occupational material separated the eastern chamber and western trench and helped to give structural support.[55]

The entire tomb was at least 3.5 m northwest to southeast and 3.5 m at its greatest extent from northeast to southwest, with a depth of more than 1 m. It seems likely that there was an entrance ramp providing access into the open trench on the west, although none was visible within the excavated area. Since the chamber sides were well preserved and easily traced everywhere within the excavation, the entrance probably lay beyond the north section.[56] The tomb held skeletons of three humans, one equid, and three sheep (one a lamb). All three humans (and Skeleton 1 of Level XIIB), two of the sheep, and the equid were placed with their heads to the north (see table 4).

Skeleton 3 of Burial 14 was situated partially above the infilled deep shaft belonging to Phase 1. The body was flexed on its right side with the head toward the north. The skull, however, had been removed and, along with the legs of Skeleton 4, had been shifted to the west edge of the burial cut, north of its original position (pls. 58–59, 60a–b). The best explanation for this disturbance may be that the interment of Skeleton 2 was slightly later than the interments of Skeletons 3 and 4 (see below). Skeletons 3 and 4 were presumably the original occupants of the tomb and when Skeleton 2 came to be buried, the chamber was reopened and portions of the two previous burials were encountered and moved to the edge of the burial cut. At the right shoulder of Skeleton 3 was a copper/bronze pin (19 N 28; pls. 60c, 145:1) and a pair of shells with traces of white and black paste (19 N 27a–b; pls. 60c, 141:3). Behind the pelvis was a large upright-handled jar with elaborate incised decoration: four pendant triangles filled with herringbone design on the shoulder and a wide "handle" with carefully applied and incised anthropomorphic features (19 N 44; pls. 143–44). The details and careful work make this one of the finest recorded examples of the "goddess-handled" jar.

The base of a large fruit stand (H1097; pl. 142:5) and three conical bowls (19 N 11, I117:2, 1; pls. 61b, 142:2–4) were found between Skeletons 3 and 4, to the northwest of Skeleton 3.[57] When the pit was dug for Skeleton 2, it disturbed Skeletons 3 and 4 and this fruit stand was encountered; the stem and dish of the vessel were separated from the base and redeposited in the burial pit fill about half a meter higher. Due to the disturbance of the area and the close proximity of Skeletons 3 and 4 to each other, it is unclear to which skeleton this fruit stand originally belonged. In contemporary graves at other sites — that is, in the Diyala, at Kish, and at Ur, fruit stands may appear at either the head or feet of the skeleton.[58]

The objects associated with Skeleton 3 — the straight pin, cosmetic shells, conical bowls, fruit stand, and goddess-handled jar — might easily be called Early Dynastic if viewed out of context. But the presence of this group in the same burial pit as another skeleton with a late Akkadian seal (Skeleton 2) is important evidence that the range of dates for this assemblage must be extended, evidence supported by sherds from the occupational material (see *Chapter 3*). The assertion by Roaf (2001) that this is an Early Dynastic grave separate from Skeletons 2 and 4 is untenable, given the clarity of the pit edge in this location, clear sequence of events and absolute stratigraphic placement.

---

55. Similar supporting blocks of unexcavated material appear between portions of two chambers in the early Akkadian Burials 11–12 and 16 at Tell Razuk (Gibson 1981).

56. Supporting evidence that the entrance was in that direction is that the final skeleton (Skeleton 1) was placed in a cut near the north end of the chamber. As the final interment in the sequence, one could expect that it would have been placed near the entrance of the earlier chamber to avoid disturbing previous burials. In the Ur Cemetery (Woolley 1934), among tombs with access shafts or ramps preserved, the majority were on the northeast, although it must be admitted that all directions are attested.

57. The fruit stand was unfortunately too broken to register; one of the bowls was registered, the two others were drawn and discarded. The fill in this area also included a much smaller, lightly fired bowl or lid (19 N 16; pl. 142:6).

58. The fruit stand would have been at the head of Skeleton 3 or at the feet of Skeleton 4; fruit stands and goddess-handled jars do often appear in graves elsewhere paired as a "set," and it is slightly more probable, therefore, that the fruit stand belongs with Skeleton 3.

Skeleton 4 was laid on its back along the northeast edge of the burial chamber (pls. 58a–59, 60b, 61a). The head was to the north and remained unexcavated beyond the north section. The left arm crossed over the chest and the right was extended along the side. As mentioned above, when Skeleton 1 was interred the legs of Skeleton 4 were removed at the pelvis and stacked, disarticulated, at the edge of the cut south of the body, along with the skull of Skeleton 3. Next to the right arm were a stone bowl (19 N 4; pls. 61b, 145:2) and a copper/bronze bowl (19 N 72; pls. 61b, 145:3) with traces of woven reed preserved on its interior and exterior. At the right side of the torso was a copper/bronze spearpoint (19 N 7; pls. 61b, 145:4), pointed end toward the head. Loose in the fill nearby was a single ring-shaped carnelian bead (19 N 24; pls. 61a, 145:5).

Burial 14, Phase 2 Animal Skeletons

Between Skeletons 2 and 3 was a pile of animal skeletons (pls. 58a–59, 60a, 63a). The lowest, an equid (pl. 63a), preceded Skeleton 2, since it was partially overlapped by the latter, with an intervening thin layer of fill. From this arrangement it appears that the equid was interred with Skeleton 4 and/or 3 as the first burials in the chamber, with Skeleton 2 added subsequently. There can have been only a minimal difference in time, however, since the burial chamber as a whole is associated with a single architectural level and the placement of Skeleton 2 avoided an overlap with the other human burials (although its interment did disturb their arrangement).

The remaining three animal skeletons in Burial 14 were sheep: two adults and one lamb. They were piled between Skeletons 2 and 3, partially above the equid, and may have been associated with either Skeleton 2 or 3. The lowest sheep was placed on its right side with its forequarters to the north; the head had been intentionally removed. The lamb was laid in the same pose on top of the latter sheep's legs. A thin layer of fill separated this pair from the final adult sheep, also with its head to the north but on its left side. Associated with this last sheep was an unworked conoid *Strombus* shell (19 N 33; pl. 166:19). Comparable piles of goat skeletons were found in at least two graves in the Ur Cemetery[59] and animal skeletons have also been found in several graves at Abu Salabikh.[60] The remains in all these cases are distinct from the animal bone fragments found in many burials, bones which may have been food offerings or chance inclusions. The best reconstruction of the sequence of sheep interments here is that the first adult and lamb were placed in the grave together with the equid at the time of burial of Skeletons 3 and 4; the final sheep was then interred with Skeleton 2.

Burial 12 at Tell Razuk[61] is particularly relevant for comparison with this phase of the Nippur Area WF, Burial 14. The Razuk burial, like the Area WF example, was in a double chamber, its two parts separated by a short discontinuous wall (a stump of earlier occupational material left intact, as in Area WF) and a pair of equids had been placed in one lobe of the chamber and a human skeleton in the other.[62] The same arrangement may have occurred initially in Area WF, Burial 14, with Skeleton 4 or 3 (or both) as the first human interment in the western portion of the chamber, and the equid in the arched eastern portion.[63] The placement of Skeletons 3 and 4 with regard to each other is an argument for their having been contemporary interments. Skeleton 3, with cosmetic shells and a pin, was situated closer to the equid; but Skeleton 4, with a spear and copper and stone bowls, is the more likely candidate for close association with, or ownership of, the equid. It may be that weapons on the one hand (spears, daggers, etc.) and cosmetic shells and fine straight pins on the other are respectively male and female gender-sensitive artifacts for later third-millennium B.C. Mesopotamia. They may be actively linked to gender-specific activities or could be simply gender-reflective symbols. There is little crossover or overlap of these two classes of items in contemporary graves at Kish, Ur, and elsewhere. The "male" nature of the weapons with Skeleton 4 is a better cognitive fit with the equid; in representations in contemporary artworks, only males are shown in association with equids, which may make up part of a package of "masculine technology" or "masculine presentation."

---

59. Woolley 1934: PG/1850 and PG/1422.
60. Grave 1 at Abu Salabikh contained a sheep skeleton, like the Area WF example in that it lacked its skull, and graves 48 and 89 contained nearly whole animal skeletons (Martin, Moon, and Postgate 1985: 26, 103, 168).
61. Gibson et al. 1981: 73ff.
62. Similar Early Dynastic and Akkadian burials with an equid or an equid pair have been recorded at Tell Madhhur (Roaf et al. 1984: graves 7D, 6G, 5G), where it has been suggested that they were the burials of local "chieftains." The earlier cart burials in the Y Sounding at Kish and some of the Ur Royal Cemetery graves with equids are possibly tangentially related to these later examples.
63. The logistics of putting the equid in the eastern chamber are unpleasant to contemplate but would have been made easier if the animal had been brought down into the western trench portion of the cut while still alive. It could have been killed there, then pushed (rear-first, as is suggested by the arrangement of leg bones; see pl. 63a) into the eastern chamber, a difficult but not impossible operation. The human dead would necessarily have been brought in after that messy and disruptive operation and laid in the western trench.

Skeleton 2, at the eastern edge of the east chamber, appears to have been the most important burial in the chamber (pls. 58b–59, 62–64). The body was bedecked with jewelry and partially covered with a number of copper vessels and there were three separate groups of pottery, copper vessels, and other objects placed around it (pls. 62–63). The skeleton lay on its back with the hands on the chest and the legs bent up and to the east (its left). The face was turned to the east, but the head had fallen forward onto the chest.[64] A rectangular gold foil fillet (19 N 38; pls. 63b, 146:1) was bent around the forehead and spiral gold earrings (19 N 37a–b; pls. 63b, 146:2) were beside the skull. There was a silver bracelet (19 N 21a–b; pls. 63b, 146:3) on each wrist and a complicated double-strand necklace of more than 300 beads plus two agate and gold pendants (19 N 20; pls. 63b, 146:4), around the neck. A straight copper/bronze pin, with a hole through the shaft near the top (19 N 5; pls. 64a, 151:2), rested on the upper right arm and a lapis lazuli cylinder seal carved with a combat scene in late Akkadian style (19 N 26; pls. 63b, 158:1) lay on the pin.[65] This seal dates the grave, and Level XIIIB, to the late Akkadian period.

At each shoulder of Skeleton 2 was a small copper/bronze bowl (19 N 9, 19 N 71; pls. 64a, 148:8–9) and near the left side was a small shallow copper/bronze pan (19 N 73; pls. 64a, 149:5). Inverted next to this, adjacent to the pelvis, was a larger copper/bronze frying pan-like vessel (19 N 103; pl. 64a, 151:3). These four metal vessels are paralleled in the Ur Cemetery, where they have been primarily dated to Early Dynastic with provisional extension to early Akkadian; their association here with a late Akkadian seal indicates that this range should be extended.

Three discrete groups of items were placed around the body: one at the head and two at the feet. Immediately north of the head was a friable redware jar with a small triangular rim and horizontally ridged shoulder and base (I159/315; pls. 64b, 148:6). Next to it were the extremely fragile and decayed remains of a small wooden box with a lid inlaid with bone mosaic decoration (19 N 136; pl. 146:7). Next to the inlaid box was a round copper/bronze box with a separate lid (19 N 19; pls. 64a, 148:7). Near the boxes and separate from the body were a second elaborate necklace (19 N 18; pls. 63b, 146:5) and a loose cylindrical copper bead (19 N 25; pl. 146:6).[66]

At the feet of Skeleton 2 was a group of three jars, two with distinctive double-ridged rims, long necks, and ovoid bodies (19 N 42, 19 N 47; pls. 64b, 150:1–2). One of these jars, 19 N 42, had fallen over and spilled the yogurt it had contained, now a solid white substance,[67] over the legs and left side of the body. The other jar of the group was a large ovoid vessel with a hole near the slightly convex base (19 N 43; pls. 64b, 151:1). This last type appears in graves at Tell Razuk (Gibson 1981), Tell Madhhur (Roaf et al. 1984), and at Kish (Mackay 1929) and may have been used for processing or storing beer.

While the items so far, all in close association with the body, can be interpreted as intended for use or consumption by the deceased, the final group of objects could be a set used at the interment. The set consists of four pottery jars, a copper/bronze bucket, and a cluster of fifteen bowls, all placed in an undercut at the south end of the burial chamber. Two of the jars are identical, globular round-based pots of an unusual yellow buff fabric (19 N 40, 19 N 53;

---

64. See table 4 for the direction faced by each skeleton in Area WF, as well as the direction to which the head was oriented. Only Burial 14, Skeletons 1 and 2, the two richest burials in the area, face to the east; the rest face west or north. Although this is admittedly a small sample, the consistency may mean that there is an unstudied correlation between direction faced by the dead and status and/or wealth. Orientation of burials in private houses is usually not formulaic (see, e.g., the many different orientations for graves below the houses at Khafajah; Delougaz, Hill, and Lloyd 1967), although cemeteries may show more consistency (such as the Early Dynastic I cemetery at Kheit Qasim; Forest 1980).

65. Presumably the seal had been tied through the hole in the pin by a string run through its central perforation, but no trace of the attachment was preserved. The pin then should have been attached to the clothing of the dead, but no traces of this were preserved either.

66. The placement of the second necklace apart from the body raises the question of whether or not it was a possession of the deceased. Alternatively, it could have been a final offering from a burial attendant at the interment or a gift to one of the deities of the underworld. The practice of "extra" jewelry offerings may be attested in several tombs in the Ur Cemetery (i.e., PG/800 of Shub-ad/Pu-abi and PG/755 of Meskalamdug; Woolley 1934), where there were spare headdresses near the body. While those individuals were wealthy enough to have owned large quantities of jewelry (more than could be placed on the body at one time), similar occurrences of extra jewelry were noted in several less-rich private burials (e.g., PG/1133, PG/1312). In another grave (PG/337) there was an actual pile of jewelry — necklaces, hair ribbons, earrings, headdresses, etc. — in the access shaft, as if dropped there by mourners as the grave shaft was filled. A much later instance of this practice may be seen in the Neo-Assyrian queens' tombs at Nimrud, uncovered by the Iraqi Department of Antiquities in 1988 and 1989. In one of these graves in particular were hundreds of gold earrings strewn over the bodies, far too many to have belonged to the occupants of the tomb (Damerji 1999 and pers. obs.). In addition, many of the earrings were identical, which argues against their having belonged to a single person. These may have been final gifts from other members of the court.

67. A sample of this material was brought back to the U.S. and analyzed in the Conservation Analysis Laboratory of the Smithsonian Institution, which has confirmed that it was a dairy product (M. Gibson, pers. comm.).

pls. 64b, 149:3–4). They were stacked at the side of a copper/bronze bucket (19 N 36; pls. 64a, 150:3). The bucket held a small version of the round-based jars (19 N 35; pls. 64b, 149:2). The cluster of conical bowls (19 N 31, 19 N 32, 19 N 48–50, I184, I332:1, 2, I338:1–7; pls. 64b, 148:5, 147:5, 148:1, 147:9, 147:4, 147:7, 147:10, 147:1, 147:2, 147:6, 147:3, 147:8, 148: 2–4) was partially below those jars but extended farther west. Another conical bowl (19 N 17; pl. 147:11) was separated from the group and placed slightly to the north, nearer the skeleton. West of the bowls was the final jar of the group, an ovoid-bodied vessel with a narrow neck (19 N 51; pls. 64b, 149:1).

In the fill near the arched ceiling of the chamber, directly above Skeleton 2, was a cluster of five gray and brown river-worn stones. Their similarity to the foundation deposit below Wall BC of Level XIIIC (see *Chapters 2* and *4*) is notable, but their meaning and significance are obscure. A similar handful of pebbles and shells was found in a corner of Grave 1 at Abu Salabikh (Postgate and Moorey 1976: pls. 6 and 21d; Postgate 1997), so such items may have had a symbolic meaning or function.

In the initial assessment, the absence of weapons with Skeleton 2 would seem to indicate that it was female.[68] The presence of a cylinder seal, in theory unusual in a female burial, might be explained by its lack of an inscription and the slight crack in the seal. It may have been a "cast-off" of the woman's husband or another male relative and worn as an ornament or amulet.[69] Alternatively, a woman may have been powerful enough to have been doing business and sealing documents on her own or her family's behalf,[70] although in such a case, one would expect the seal to be inscribed with her name and to have a presentation scene, marking it as a personal seal, rather than the scene of figures in combat, which seems to be an official motif linked to the Akkadian administration.[71] It is extraordinarily difficult to identify seals owned and/or used by women in the Early Dynastic and Akkadian periods. Representations of women on seals are rare, and inscriptions identifying seal owners as women are rarer still.

The relative social status of the three skeletons in the Phase 2 chamber is difficult to assess. On the basis of quantity, quality, and variety of burial goods alone, it would seem that Skeleton 2, with its seal, jewelry, and large number of pottery and metal vessels, was the most important. However, if one takes into account the time and energy expended on the process of burial, which may be as relevant for status determination as the cost of grave goods, then the effort of carving out the large double chamber and burying the equid (a valuable item in its own right) would indicate that Skeletons 4 and/or 3 might have held the higher status. In addition, there may have been intangible or perishable indicators of status involved.

---

68. The bones of this and other skeletons at this depth in the excavation were in such poor condition and so badly warped due to the weight of material above and their proximity to the water table that they were not well preserved nor could accurate measurements be made in situ for identification of gender or age. The teeth and some fragmentary remains were collected in this case and these were stored in the Nippur Expedition house but have since been destroyed by fire.

69. Examples of seals worn as jewelry, rather than for their original function, are found in the Ur Cemetery (Woolley 1934): PG/263 contained the lower half of a broken seal which had been smoothed down and used as a bead; PG/867 had two seals worn on bracelets, at least one of which was an Early Dynastic "heirloom" in a late Akkadian grave; and both PG/35 and 543 had seals included in strings of beads. The location of the WF seal, however, in association with a pin and prominently displayed on the upper body, argues that it was still serving its original function as a marker of identity and authority.

70. One approximately contemporary example of a woman involved in business is recorded in the "Ur-Shara" archive from Umma (Foster 1977, 1982). Numerous texts in this group mention Ama-e, the wife of a businessman, doing business in her own right, controlling large amounts of land and dealing with quantities of grain, wool, metals, wood, etc. She continued doing business after her husband disappeared from the records (presumably deceased). This example is only one of several known seal-using women, and therefore she may have been unusual but was not unique.

71. Following J. H. Humphries, W. Rathje proposed long ago (1977) that seal scenes are important for more than chronological determinations and art historical studies and can shed light on occupation or social identity. It has been proposed that the "heroes and animals" combat scene was taken up by the Akkadian government as an "official" motif (see Gibson and McMahon 1995). Although the scene appeared on Early Dynastic seals, there was greater standardization in the number of figures and increased formality in their poses during the Akkadian period. The majority of Akkadian seals identified as belonging to scribes, as well as almost all of the so-called "royal" seals, those identifying their owner as a servant of the king, have this motif (Zettler 1977). In addition, in many cases in which burials contain a pair of seals, one is a scene of presentation showing an image of the deceased, while the other is a combat seal (see *Chapter 4*). From this, Gibson (pers. comm.) proposes that the combat seals were used for official business and presentation seals for private business. See also the discussion of Burial 14, Skeleton 1, below, and *Chapter 4*.

The very different types of goods with the skeletons (an equid, spear, and a few vessels versus a cylinder seal, gold, semiprecious stones, and a large number of vessels) may have been almost equivalent in absolute value but served as markers of different "social identities." The status of Skeleton 2 is indicated by what is to modern eyes a more understandable presentation of wealth, so that our tendency is to ascribe higher status to that individual, where an indigenous valuation might have been different. However, in Mesopotamia, gold and lapis lazuli items were powerful markers of status and wealth, as is proven by texts and by the association of such media with kings. Cylinder seals in particular were symbols of recognized authority and property ownership. Thus their combination may still outweigh the possibly greater effort expended on the interment of Skeletons 3 and 4.[72] The difference in identity among the skeletons remains elusive, since their burial in the same grave implies a family connection; age (generational) differential is one possibility.

## Level XIIB

The third and final phase of the Burial 14 sequence (Skeleton 1) belongs to Level XIIB (pl. 24). First, a rectangular box of baked bricks was built in a small pit cut down into the Level XIIIB chamber (pl. 65a). This box contained a single bowl (19 N 12; pl. 125:11) and was full of loose ash; it was probably used to burn offerings to the dead of Level XIIIB.[73] After the box was built, the final skeleton (Skeleton 1) was buried adjacent to it. The pit was oval, slightly bell shaped in section, and a little over a meter deep. Skeleton 1 was an adult placed in the same pose as Skeleton 2: on its back, head to the north, face turned to the east, arms crossed over the chest, and knees bent up and slightly to the east (pl. 65b). Like Skeleton 2, this body was equipped with a large amount of pottery and other objects, including two cylinder seals.

A gold foil fillet (18 N 175; pls. 66a, 152:10) was found at the neck, where it had probably slipped from the forehead. Near the upper left arm was a green stone cylinder seal with a skillfully carved presentation scene in late Akkadian style (18 N 174; pl. 157:2). The procession of gods includes Sin, the moon-god and a storm-god on a lion-griffin leading a human figure toward an unidentified seated god. The inscription identifies the seal owner as Lugal-DÚR, a scribe.[74] A second seal, of rock crystal with a combat scene of workmanship equal to that of the presentation scene (18 N 173; pl. 157:1), was found at the lower left arm, along with a long copper/bronze pin (18 N 188; pls. 66a, 152:3).

The different motifs on these seals reinforce the theory mentioned above (with description of Skeleton 2) that in cases of ownership of two seals, one would have been used for personal transactions (the presentation scene, with its depiction of the owner) and the other for official business (the standardized combat scene). The presence of original inscriptions (no traces of recutting) on both seals indicates that neither was an heirloom nor had a previous owner. The fine carving and elaborate, well-organized scenes mark both seals as superior products, possibly from a royal workshop.

---

72. Unfortunately, we cannot rule out that Skeletons 3 and 4 may have originally been buried with some of the objects found with Skeleton 2. In communal burials in which there is some time (even if only a day) between interments, there must always be a question as to whether goods were shifted among bodies, either illicitly or openly. Since the inhabitants of communal tombs are almost always related, the items can be said to belong to the lineage as a whole, thus sanctioning their reuse. Each individual may have been lowered into the tomb accompanied by the same objects, which were later removed for use with the next burial. The last individual to be buried in the tomb then ends up with all the burial items and may appear to have been the wealthiest or of the highest status. In this case, due to the arrangement of the bodies and the animal skeletons, it is clear that Skeleton 2 was the last of the three to be interred in the chamber and that Skeletons 3 and 4 were partially uncovered when Skeleton 2 was interred. While this practice of removing and reusing grave goods is not mentioned in Mesopotamian texts, it is possibly not the type of practice that is likely to have been recorded.

73. A related installation may be found at Abu Salabikh, above grave 1, where there was a series of clay lenses with burned areas and traces of "post holes" (Postgate and Moorey 1976). The excavators propose that the holes were made by standards set up over the graves, while the burned patches probably indicate offerings made to the dead. Alternatively, the holes might have been for the pouring-in of liquid offerings.

74. The reading of the second element of the name, -DÚR, is uncertain. See *Chapter 4* for full discussion of this and other seals.

A number of copper/bronze weapons was found on the body: an axhead at the left side of the pelvis (18 N 177; pls. 66b, 152:2), a spear point between the legs (18 N 176; pls. 66b, 152:1), and a group of small blades and a pin at the feet (19 N 6a–c; pls. 66b, 152:5–6, 4). At the top of the head were a short copper/bronze pin (18 N 179; pls. 66a, 152:8), a single ball-shaped lapis bead (18 N 194; pls. 66a, 152:11), and an oval bone spacer bead with an inset on one side filled with red powdery pigment, all possibly parts of a hair ornament.[75] Near the right hand was a broken gold object, a twisted wire ring with a foil band along one side, possibly the setting for a now-missing stone (19 N 8; pls. 66a, 152:12).

West of the body was a large group of vessels, both pottery and copper/bronze, most similar to vessels found with Skeleton 2. One large copper/bronze pan partially overlapped the chest (18 N 180; pls. 67b, 155:4). It held two hemispherical copper/bronze bowls (18 N 181, 18 N 182; pls. 67a, 156:3–4) and a quantity of organic material, the remains of a loosely woven reed mat or possibly a sheaf of loose reeds. At the pelvis and right knee were two tall, narrow pottery jars (18 N 187, H1111; pls. 68b, 154:2–3). West of the shoulder was a cluster of copper/bronze vessels, including a large cauldron-like pan (18 N 183; pls. 67b, 156:1) containing a bucket (18 N 184; pls. 67b, 156:2) nearly identical to the one buried with Skeleton 2. Next to that was a smaller deep, footed bowl with a long trough spout (18 N 185; pls. 67a, 155:5). Lying among these vessels was a second short pin (18 N 178; pls. 66a, 152:7) that may have come loose from the hair when the body was being moved into the grave.

To the north and south of these copper/bronze vessels were two more groups of pottery vessels. At the south were three nearly identical large storage jars with holes near the convex bases (H1109, I105, I104; pl. 155:1–3).[76] These were accompanied by a badly smashed medium-sized long-necked jar (I40/103; pl. 154:1) and five conical bowls (19 N 10, I107, I102, I106, I109; pls. 68a, 153:2, 7, 9–11). North of the group of copper/bronze vessels was a cluster of six more conical bowls (H1118–23; pl. 153:1, 6, 5, 4, 12, 8) and a shattered jar of brittle redware (H1124; pl. 154:4) containing a perforated hollow copper/bronze conical filter with traces of a reed inside (18 N 186; pls. 66a, 152:9).

The quantity and quality of the goods associated with this skeleton mark him as having been a wealthy and important individual. The name Lugal-DÚR, however, is not known from any late Akkadian period documents from Nippur.[77] It is tempting to equate the degrees of wealth associated with this skeleton and with Skeleton 2 and to identify them as a married pair. The name Lugal-DÚR is clear evidence that Skeleton 1 was male; this conclusion is further supported by the array of weapons with which he was buried. The gender of Skeleton 2 is less clearly marked, indicated as female more by an absence of "male" items. Near the top of the Mesopotamian social hierarchy, as represented by these two individuals and many more in the Ur Cemetery, there are items that may be found in either male or female burials, including gold, lapis lazuli, and even cylinder seals. However, weapons remain an important non-crossover item apparently associated virtually exclusively with males.[78] At the bottom of the social hierarchy it is similarly difficult to ascribe gender on the basis of burial items because burial items are generally few and are often limited to pottery. Nearer the middle of the social scale items without much crossover, such as hairpins and weapons, may prove to be valuable markers of gender.

---

75. Unfortunately, the bone bead disintegrated completely shortly after excavation.

76. None was in good enough condition to be registered; note that a single example of this same type of jar was buried with Skeleton 2.

77. A Lugal-DÚR[ki] is mentioned in an account of sesame from Nippur (Lewy 1935: no. 136 (HS 886) verso I, 2). But the writing of the šu sign in that text, with the wedge of the vertical stroke pointing down, dates the tablet to around the reign of Sargon. From the late Akkadian style of the seals with Skeleton 1 and the presence in Level XII of tablets probably dated to the reign of Sharkalisharri (see *Chapters 1* and *5*), the Lugal-DÚR of Burial 14 lived much later and cannot be the same individual in that text.

78. Pollock (1991) identifies some specific types of jewelry in the Ur Royal Cemetery as useful identifiers of males versus females, but these types are unfortunately rare outside Ur.

## Level XIB

Cut into the use layers in the southeast room (Locus 36) and sealed by Floor 3 was Burial 11, an adult skeleton in a shallow (ca. 45 cm deep) rectangular pit at the corner of Walls AB and S (pl. 27). The body was flexed on its left side with the head to the south and hands in front of the face (pl. 54b). The sides of the cut were lined with a layer of gray clay and there was a layer of very hard gray clay below the skeleton. This treatment with clay is unique in Area WF, although there was an Ur III burial in Area WC-3 (Gibson, Armstrong, and McMahon 1998) that had a similar bed of hard clay. The only goods in this grave were two conical bowls (18 N 114, H885:1; pl. 135:8–9) placed beneath the legs.

The third-millennium B.C. burials in Area WF exhibit a range of dates, richness, and complexity (see table 5 for a compilation of objects found in each grave). The domestic context, however, remained constant throughout. Most burials were in the courtyard or a room of a house and even if a burial was in a more open area, the nature of the accumulated debris implies that domestic structures were nearby. At the most basic, the third-millennium burials provide important information on some of the ways the dead were treated in ancient Mesopotamia. These burials are perhaps more significant in the context of this excavation because they add whole forms to support the pottery sequence outlined in the stratigraphy.

Table 4. Orientations of Third-millennium B.C. Burials

| Burial Number | Level | Head Orientation | Face Orientation | Location | Approximate Age |
|---|---|---|---|---|---|
| 22 | XIXB | West | North | Courtyard, at wall face | Child |
| 20 | XVIII | Disarticulated | — | Open area | ? |
| 19 | XVIIC | West | South | Open area | Adult |
| 21/Skeleton 2 | XVIIB | West | Up | Open area | Adult |
| 21/Skeleton 1 | XVIIB | North | Up | Open area | Infant |
| 18 | XVI | Southwest | Up | Open area | Infant |
| 17 | XVI | North | — | Open area | Adult |
| 14/Skeleton 8 | XVI or XV | East | North? | Shaft in courtyard | Adult? |
| 14/Skeleton 7 | XVI or XV | West | Up | Shaft in courtyard | Adult |
| 14/Skeleton 5 | XVA | South | West | Courtyard, at wall face | Child |
| 16 | XIVB | North-northwest | West | Courtyard | Adult |
| 15 | XIVB | West | North | Southeast room | Infant |
| 13 | XIVA | North | West | Southeast room | Child |
| 14/Skeleton 6 | XIVA? | South-southwest | Northwest | Shaft in courtyard | Adult |
| 14/Skeleton 4 | XIIIB | North-northwest | Unexcavated | Courtyard | Adult |
| 14/Skeleton 3 | XIIIB | North | West-Southwest | Courtyard | Adult |

## Table 5. Contents of Third-millennium B.C. Burials

| Burial Number/ Skeleton | Pottery* | Stone Vessel | Cu/Br Vessel | Flint or Bone Tool | Weapon | Shell | Pin | Bead/ Necklace | Earring | Bracelet | Gold Object | Cylinder Seal, etc. |
|---|---|---|---|---|---|---|---|---|---|---|---|---|
| 22 | — | — | — | — | — | — | — | — | — | — | — | — |
| 20 | O-1 × 2<br>C-4 | — | — | — | — | — | — | — | — | — | — | — |
| 19 | O-1 × 28<br>C-1 | 1 | — | — | — | 1 | — | — | — | — | — | — |
| 21/2 | O-1<br>C-1<br>C-4 | — | — | 1 | — | — | — | — | — | — | — | — |
| 21/1 | O-1<br>C-4 | — | — | — | — | — | — | — | — | — | — | — |
| 18 | O-1 | — | — | — | — | — | — | — | — | — | — | — |
| 17 | — | — | — | — | — | — | — | — | — | — | — | — |
| 14/5 | O-1 × 3<br>C-1<br>C-4<br>C-17 | — | — | 2(?) | — | — | — | 1 | — | — | — | — |
| 16 | O-1 × 6<br>C-UT | — | — | — | — | — | — | — | — | — | — | — |
| 15 | O-1 × 5<br>O-9<br>C-9 | — | — | — | — | — | — | — | — | — | — | — |
| 13 | O-1 × 4 | — | — | — | — | — | — | 1 | — | 2 | — | — |
| 11 | O-1 × 2 | — | — | — | — | — | — | — | — | — | — | — |
| 14/8 | O-1 × 20<br>C-11 | — | — | 1(?) | — | — | — | — | — | — | — | — |
| 14/7 | O-1<br>C-4 | — | — | — | — | 2 | — | — | — | — | — | — |
| 14/6 | O-1 × 12<br>O-9<br>C-1<br>C-14<br>C-17 × 2<br>C-UT | 1 | — | — | — | — | 2 | — | — | — | — | — |
| 14/4 | — | 1 | 1 | — | 1 | — | — | 1 | — | — | — | — |
| 14/3 | C-6 | — | — | — | — | 2 | 1 | — | — | — | — | — |
| 14/3 or 4 | O-1<br>O-12 × 2<br>O-9 | — | — | — | — | — | — | — | — | — | — | — |
| 14/2 | O-1 × 7<br>O-10 × 2<br>O-11<br>C-13 × 2<br>C-16b<br>C-20<br>C-22<br>C-23 × 3 | — | 6 | — | — | — | 1 | 2 | 2 | 2 | 1 | 1 plus wood box |
| 14/1 | O-1 × 5<br>O-10 × 3<br>O-11<br>O-12 × 2<br>C-16a<br>C-17<br>C-22 × 3<br>C-UT × 2 | — | 6 | — | 4 | — | 4 | 1 | — | — | 2 | 2 |

* For a description of pottery vessels listed here by Type Number, see *Chapter 3*.

# Second-millennium B.C. Burials

There are only two burials of the second millennium B.C., both datable to the Kassite period from the pottery vessels included as burial offerings. A contemporary feature (recorded as Burial 10; see *Chapter 1*) may be a third grave, but only the edge of the pit was encountered and no skeleton or grave goods were uncovered.

## Level VA

Burial 9 was a double-jar burial of an adult in a simple oval pit (pls. 39, 69a). The pit was cut down probably from Locus 15 into Level VI. It was subsequently disturbed by Burial 6 (Level IV), which removed the uppermost halves of the burial jars and the top of the pit, erasing the stratigraphic connection. The skeleton was extended on its back with the head to the south-southeast and feet to the north-northwest. The arms were crossed over the chest and there were two Kassite goblets (18 N 55, 18 N 56; pls. 69b, 168:1–2), one on either side of the head. Although the body was relatively undisturbed, the damage done to the burial jars by the cut for Burial 6 indicates that there may have been additional objects on the body which were looted when the grave was exposed. Morphological details of the Kassite jars indicate that this grave was approximately contemporary with Level III/II of Area WC-1 at Nippur, or late Kassite (Armstrong 1993; and see *Chapter 3*). These findings agree with the late Kassite (and early post-Kassite) date reconstructed for this type of double-jar burial (Baker 1995: type 1A).

Burial 12 was a simple inhumation of an adult in an irregularly shaped pit that cut down into the junction of Walls S and AB of Level X (pls. 39, 70a). The top of the pit was later disturbed by the cut for Burial 4 (Level III), therefore the locus from which it was cut is not known for certain, though it was probably also Locus 15. The body was flexed on its left side with the head to the east, facing south, and the feet to the west. The arms were bent such that the hands were in front of the face. A Kassite goblet (18 N 102; pls. 70b, 168:3) and a Kassite ovoid jar (18 N 103; pls. 70b, 168:4) were placed behind (north of) the head.[79] Details of the pottery indicate that this burial may be slightly earlier than Burial 9 (see *Chapter 3*).

The area to the northeast of Wall R, running into the sections on north and east, was labeled Burial 10 (pl. 39), although no bones or grave items were found. In the tiny area exposed were several bricks laid over a cavity loosely filled with broken bricks and debris. The feature might have been a burial, but other possibilities are a pit or drain or even foundation fill.

# First-millennium B.C. Burials

Eight burials were interred during occupation of Levels IV, III, and II. The tops of many of these burials had been disturbed by later activity and pits. For the two graves of Level IV, some preserved stratigraphy and their placement with respect to the walls of the building indicate that they were interred under the floors while the building was in use. The placement of the five graves of Level III, mostly cutting directly into the walls of the Level IV building, implies that the building was not even visible as a ruin at that time. These five graves may form a miniature cemetery in an open area outside the building at the southwest corner of the excavation, although there is a possibility that they were placed below the floors of a building that was later completely obliterated by Pit 1. Jar and coffin burials were customary in Levels IV and III, rather than simple inhumation.

## Level IV

Burial 8 was an adult in a "bathtub" coffin (pl. 71a). The rectangular pit for the coffin was cut from Locus 10, Floor 1, down as deep as Level VI (pl. 41). The coffin had a ridged vertical strap handle on each end and a horizontal ridge around the body, halfway down (H756; pl. 170:5); it was placed in the pit with the rounded end to the southwest. Despite the protection of the coffin, the skeleton was in very bad condition, flattened and reduced to powder. The body had been placed in the coffin flexed, with the head to the northeast and feet to the southwest. The legs were bent to the right, while the body was twisted to the left, with the arms bent to the left and the face looking

---

79. In the fill of the cut for Burial 4 (Level III) was a nearly complete small Kassite goblet (H378:1; pl. 168:5) that may have derived from this earlier burial. As with Burial 9, we cannot rule out the possibility that this Kassite burial contained more precious objects that were removed when encountered by the ancient excavators of the later grave.

south. In front of the face, in the corner of the coffin, were two small glazed jars (18 N 42, 18 N 43; pls. 71b–c, 170:1–2). Next to the pelvis and partially overlapping it was a medium-sized bowl with a beveled rim (18 N 45; pls. 71e, 170:4) and, above that, an ovoid jar (18 N 44; pls. 71d, 170:3). Loose in the fill of the coffin were a broken bronze pin and a stone bead, but these may have been chance inclusions not originally part of the grave offerings. Above the coffin the pit was filled with mixed gray clay and sand and a salvaged Ur III/Isin-Larsa jar had been placed above the grave at Floor 1. The fragments of animal bones in this jar were probably offerings to the dead.

The morphological development of the bathtub coffin from ca. 800 to 350 B.C., and its geographical spread from Assyria into Babylonia, have been analyzed by Strommenger (1964) and revisited by Baker (1995). The almost-parallel sides and relatively large height-to-length ratio (0.55 m deep × 1.15 m long) place the Burial 8 coffin fairly early within the Babylonian development of the type, though not among the earliest examples, which tend to be even higher. The coffin appears to belong to approximately the eighth to seventh centuries B.C.; the glazed pottery refines this date to the seventh century B.C. (see *Chapter 3*).

Burial 6 was a double-pot burial of an adult (pl. 72a–b). The pots were placed end to end in an oval cut parallel to and immediately adjacent to Wall H, near the south section, in Locus 11 (pl. 41). The bottom of the pit had disturbed the Kassite Burial 9. The southeastern vessel was cylindrical with a ring base, while the northwestern one was "bowl"-like, with a slightly wider mouth, tapering sides, and a thick pointed base. This combination is a later variant of the late Kassite double-jar burial, which had two of the same jar type. This form of double-pot burial ranges in date from approximately the early post-Kassite to the sixth century B.C. (Strommenger 1964; Baker 1995: type 1B).[80]

The body was on its back, partially flexed with the head and upper body in the southeast jar and the legs, bent up and to the right, in the northwest pot. The arms were crossed over the chest and the head had probably originally been facing up but had slid down, ending up on its side on top of the upper ribcage. At the right side of the pelvis was a bronze chain with a short pin attached to either end (18 N 37; pl. 169:5). A few carnelian, lapis, and agate beads were found near the pelvis and more around the neck (18 N 36; pl. 169:6). Four jars were associated with the burial, outside and above the northwest burial jar. East of the burial jar was a small ovoid glazed jar (18 N 16; pl. 169:1) and on the west was a larger plain jar with lug handles (18 N 24; pl. 169:4). Inside the latter were two more small glazed jars (18 N 22, 18 N 23; pl. 169:2–3).

## Level IIIB

Burials 2 and 4 were two parts of a single grave, an infant (Burial 2) and an adult (Burial 4). The deep cylindrical pit was dug down from Floor 1 of Locus 7, just east of Wall D, and it had disturbed the top of Burial 12 (pl. 43). About half a meter southwest of the grave, inverted on Floor 1 of Locus 7, was a medium-sized bowl (18 N 62; pl. 178:1) that may have been associated with post-interment offerings to these burials. At the bottom of the cut was a single large jar with a ring base, slightly tipped on its side (pl. 73a). The adult skeleton was tightly flexed inside this jar, lying on its left side with the head to the southwest and feet to the northeast. The hands were under the head and around one wrist was a bronze bracelet (18 N 35; pls. 73b, 172:4). Around the neck and spilling out of the coffin was a string of stone, faience, and shell beads (18 N 30; pls. 73b, 172:5). Just southwest of the skull was a pair of small plain jars, one short and nearly spherical with a small flat base (18 N 32; pls. 73b, 172:1) and one with a high neck, ovoid body, and nipple base (18 N 54; pls. 73b, 172:2). Below the jars was a square stone palette with an attached bronze chain (18 N 33; pls. 73b, 172:7). In the fill around and above the body were a curved bronze pin (18 N 149; pls. 73b, 172:3), a shell (18 N 34; pls. 73b, 172:6), and a round stone weight (not registered). Other objects which were probably intrusive in the grave fill were a small Kassite goblet (probably from Burial 12) and a piece of a basalt grindstone (unregistered). Single jar burials such as this had a fairly long time range, from the late eighth century B.C. through the Achaemenid period (Baker 1995), but the pottery points to a date near the middle of this range (see *Chapter 3*).

Burial 2 was located about 30 cm above the burial jar of Burial 4. It is likely that the two were interred at the same time since a separate cut for the second burial was not visible. Burial 2 contained the body of an infant in an ovoid pot with a ridged rim (H352; pl. 178:6). The body was in poor condition, but appeared to be flexed on the left side with the head to the south. Around the neck was a string of faience or glass beads (18 N 10; pl. 171:3).

---

80. Approximately contemporary examples of this double-pot burial from Babylon have a much shorter or shallower "bowl" than do the Nippur examples. This should probably be attributed to regional variation.

Burial 3 was a double-pot burial of an adult, similar to Burial 6 of Level IV in that one pot was cylindrical with a ring base, while the second had sloped sides and a heavy pointed base (pl. 74a–b). The cut for the burial was oval and oriented northwest–southeast, cutting down from Locus 7 and actually undercutting Wall J of Level IV (pl. 43). The body was tightly flexed and placed mostly in the northwestern cylindrical jar. The skeleton lay on its right side with the head to the northwest and feet to the southeast. Within the cut but outside the burial jars, to the south of the northwestern jar, was a small ovoid jar (18 N 25; pl. 171:4) that held a faience "eye-bead" (18 N 40a; pl. 171:6a) and a ball-shaped agate bead (18 N 40b; pl. 171:6b). In the fill of the burial jars, above the body, was another small carnelian bead (18 N 39; pl. 171:5).

Burial 5 was a single-jar burial of an adult, only partially within the excavated area and running into the eastern section (pl. 43). It was the same type as Burial 4, with a single upright ring-based burial jar in a cylindrical pit (pl. 75a). The grave cut down as far as the top of Wall R of Level V, but the top of the burial cut had been removed by Pit 1. The exact position of the body could not be determined due to the incomplete excavation, but it seemed to be tightly flexed or perhaps even disarticulated, with the head to the west and the rest of the body to the east. The skull lay on its left side, facing north. In front of the face were two jars, a small ovoid glazed jar (18 N 46; pl. 171:1), and a larger plain jar (18 N 53; pl. 171:2). The carbonized remains of a reed mat covered the jars and body. In the upper fill of the burial jar, acting as a lid, was a single baked plano-convex brick, reused from a much earlier context.

The final grave of Level III was Burial 7, a child buried in a small "bathtub" coffin. The cut for the grave was located immediately north of Burial 4 in Locus 7; it was an oval pit just large enough for the coffin (pls. 43, 75b, 173:3). The rounded end of the coffin pointed to the southwest. The body was slightly flexed on the left side, with the head to the northeast and feet to the southwest. The right arm was crossed over the chest and the left hand was below the face. Two square baked bricks were placed over the coffin as a lid and a small green glazed jar (18 N 17; pl. 173:1) lay at the south corner of the southwestern brick. The grave was covered by a further layer of mudbricks. In the fill of the coffin was a single half clam shell (18 N 41; pl. 173:2), possibly a chance inclusion. The coffin shape, in plan view, with its slightly incurved sides, is later in the developmental sequence of the bathtub coffin than that of Burial 8, with its parallel sides.

Pit 7 (pl. 43) was not assigned a burial number during excavation because it was unclear whether the few bones it contained belonged to a human or an animal and there were no associated grave goods. This small cylindrical pit cut into Pit 5 and Locus 12 near the face of Wall G. Its top was removed by Pit 1, so it is only tentatively ascribed to this level. It was only partially excavated since it ran into the north section. The skeleton was that of an infant or young animal with small, extremely friable bones. The poor condition of the bones, as well as the partial excavation, made it impossible to determine the orientation of the body.

## Level II

Burial 1 was a simple adult inhumation in a shallow oval cut, with no accompanying grave goods (pl. 49). The cut was made into Locus 4, centered between and parallel to Walls A and B, so it is likely that they were still visible, although no longer in use, at the time. The body seems to have been disturbed after burial, as it was partially disarticulated. It had been laid in the grave flexed on the right side with the head to the northwest (pl. 75c).

Table 6. Concordance of Burials and Levels

| Burial Number | Level | Burial Number | Level |
|---|---|---|---|
| Burial 1 | II | Burial 14, Skeleton 3 | XIIIB |
| Burial 2 | IIIB | Burial 14, Skeleton 4 | XIIIB |
| Burial 3 | IIIB | Burial 14, Skeleton 5 | XVA |
| Burial 4 | IIIB | Burial 14, Skeleton 6 | XIVA(?) |
| Burial 5 | IIIB | Burial 14, Skeleton 7 | XVI or XV |
| Burial 6 | IV | Burial 14, Skeleton 8 | XVI or XV |
| Burial 7 | IIIB | Burial 15 | XIVB |
| Burial 8 | IV | Burial 16 | XIVB |
| Burial 9 | V | Burial 17 | XVI |
| Burial 10 | V | Burial 18 | XVI |
| Burial 11 | XIB | Burial 19 | XVII |
| Burial 12 | V | Burial 20 | XVIII |
| Burial 13 | XIVA | Burial 21, Skeleton 1 | XVII |
| Burial 14, Skeleton 1 | XIIB | Burial 21, Skeleton 2 | XVII |
| Burial 14, Skeleton 2 | XIIIB | Burial 22 | XIXB |

# CHAPTER 3
# POTTERY

## Third Millennium B.C.

The comparative material used for pottery of the late Early Dynastic through Akkadian periods by most excavations and surveys in southern Mesopotamia comes primarily from the Diyala excavations (Delougaz 1952). After additional excavation at other sites and reassessment of the Diyala records, Gibson (1982) revised the dating of some levels in the Diyala sites. Most importantly, several graves and Houses 1 and Oval III at Khafajah were redated from Early Dynastic III to early Akkadian; at Tell Asmar, Houses Vb was moved from Early Dynastic IIIb to early Akkadian, Houses Va from "Protoimperial" to early Akkadian, and Houses IVb from early to late Akkadian. In addition, the date of the Northern Palace at Tell Asmar was revised from "Protoimperial" to Akkadian and that of the Earlier Northern Palace from Early Dynastic IIIb to early Akkadian. Excavators of other sites refer to these new dates but generally do not yet fully incorporate them into their publications, although Gibson's conclusions have an impact on the analysis of material of Early Dynastic III, Early Dynastic IIIb, "Protoimperial," and Akkadian dates, shortening Early Dynastic IIIb, eliminating the Protoimperial, and moving other material across the Early Dynastic-Akkadian boundary.[81]

Some excavators do refer to potentially transitional levels or material at their sites as "Early Dynastic IIIb/Akkadian" (e.g., Tell Madhhur: Roaf et al. 1984), which is valid in the absence of any precisely datable object pointing to one or the other historic period. The retention of the term "Early Dynastic IIIb" (e.g., for Tell al-Hiba: Hansen 1973) to describe levels that may be contemporary with the early years of Sargon's reign remains a potential point of discussion.

Intertwining with the problem of the redating of some levels, the usefulness of the Diyala material for comparison with that from southern Mesopotamian sites is potentially limited.[82] Certainly the Diyala was an important location within the Akkadian state, situated as it was near an overland trade route to and from the east. The Diyala's location close to "Akkad" proper (whether Agade is located in the northern alluvial plain or on the Tigris, as reconstructed by Wall-Romana 1990) implies that the area is likely to have had a substantially "Akkadian" population, rather than the majority of Sumerian inhabitants found farther south. Thus, pottery and other artifacts produced in the Diyala could in some cases be argued to communicate an "Akkadian" ethnicity. But the potential for identification of "Akkadian" elements in the Diyala further emphasizes the need for identification of an independent pottery sequence for the Early Dynastic and Akkadian periods in southern Mesopotamia.

In southern Mesopotamia, most of the relevant excavated material comes from either the beginning or the end of the time range in question, therefore a complete ceramic sequence of the whole Akkadian period remains undescribed. The late Early Dynastic period in southern Mesopotamia is best represented by the Inanna Temple excavation at Nippur and by specific graves at Ur, Kish, and Abu Salabikh. There is not much argument over the characterization of Early Dynastic IIIa, but the usefulness of the "Early Dynastic IIIb" label and the range of material to which it should be applied are a matter of dispute. A more widespread adoption of an "Early Dynastic III/early Akkadian" label for transitional materials, rather than an insistence on one or the other period, might partially resolve this issue. The pottery of the late Akkadian period (the reigns of Naram-Sin and later) is also fairly well delineated,

---

81. Since 1982, further supportive evidence for the redating of Khafajah Oval III has been offered by Hauptmann (1991), who points out the probable early Akkadian date for a stone relief fragment found near the entrance of the temple complex in that phase.

82. Many pottery types found in the Diyala also appear in the Hamrin excavations and in northern Babylonia, but the assemblages found at sites farther south in the alluvial plain, while they have many specific points of comparison with the Diyala, lack some types while containing others not found there. While this problem has been addressed for the Uruk/"Protoliterate" period (Abu al-Soof 1967), this aspect of the Early Dynastic/Akkadian material has received virtually no discussion.

especially by material from Tell Asmar, Areas TB and WA 50c at Nippur (associated with datable tablets, sealings, and brick stamps), excavations at Uruk and Isin, graves at Ur, and unpublished material from Umm al-Hafriyat.[83]

Some pottery types have been identified in the past as typical of the Akkadian period as a whole (i.e., in the surveys of Adams 1965, 1981; Adams and Nissen 1972; Gibson 1972a; Martin 1983, 1988), but there has been no study of the internal sequence for the period nor a move to distinguish possible "early" versus "late" Akkadian pottery types in the material available. This division might be thought to be a futile exercise, given the short length of the Akkadian period in absolute dates. But the historic and political developments within the Akkadian period are known to have been expressed in the changing style of cylinder seals and these developments may also have had an effect on the ceramic portion of the archaeological record, given such innovations as standardized weights and measures. A distinction between pottery types of the early and late Akkadian period should be both possible and useful.

The early Ur III period is possibly best captured in the Area WC-3 excavation at Nippur, in which a sealing from Ur-Namma's reign, tablets from the time of Amar-Sin, and a city wall datable to Ibbi-Sin give an excellent framework of dates for the pottery assemblage.[84] This excavation and that at Umm al-Hafriyat indicate that many types identified as "Akkadian" are in fact typical largely of the later Akkadian period but continued well into the Ur III period.

## Excavation Procedures, Pottery Collection, Typological Decisions

The pottery from Area WF was collected in groups called "lots" (see *Introduction*, n. 9), each lot being linked to an occupation layer above a floor or surface or to some otherwise definable feature, such as a pit. The boundaries of each collection unit (locus and layer) from which the lots came were defined by visual differences: horizontally by walls, cuts, sections, etc.; and vertically by significant changes in texture or color (floors or surfaces). The separate floor-by-floor collection kept contamination among contexts to a minimum and allowed for relatively fine-grained temporal distinctions — the definition of an assemblage's change over time within a room, for instance.

For the data given here, the numbers of sherds of each identified pottery type have been combined by architectural level, rather than separated by locus and floor, though the original records made distinctions among the pottery assemblages in different loci and between the different floors or surfaces within loci. In most cases, the number of sherds of each type within any single locus was too small to provide significant comparisons; combination by architectural level increased the significance while still allowing temporal distinctions to be made. Both diagnostic sherds (rims, bases, decorated fragments, spouts) and nondiagnostic pottery (body sherds) were collected, but nondiagnostic sherds were counted and discarded in the field if they could not be used for vessel reconstruction. Diagnostic sherds were assigned to specific types and counted; many (far more than are illustrated here) were drawn as well, to record variations within each type.

The total number of typed diagnostic sherds from the third-millennium B.C. levels alone was approximately 12,600; about 40,000 nondiagnostics were counted and discarded.

Very few whole or reconstructible vessels were recovered from Area WF, apart from those in burials;[85] thus the typology presented here is based primarily on rim sherds from occupation floors and associated stratified layers. In most cases, the rims are distinctive enough that they can be assigned to a single whole vessel shape, but a few rims may occur on two or more vessel shapes with different sizes, bases, or body forms. In the absence of whole vessels, fragments of potentially very different vessels inevitably may have been combined as one type. Where there are

---

83. I thank McGuire Gibson for allowing me access to the records and pottery drawings from the 1977 excavation at Umm al-Hafriyat and for permission to refer to them here. Late Akkadian material has also been excavated at Umm el-Jīr and Tell al-Wilayah. Fragments of evidence for occupation during the Akkadian period at Adab, Fara, and Abu Salabikh (especially late Akkadian pottery from deep drains at the latter site, for which the associated floors have been eroded) exist but have limited usefulness. At Umm el-Jīr, Nippur, and Ur, there is the potential to identify and describe the whole sequence of Akkadian period remains, but up to this point this has not been done systematically. The northern Mesopotamian artifactual tradition during this period is quite distinct from that of the south, but quantities of closely related material have been found at Tell Brak, Assur, and other sites. At these northern sites, specific Akkadian pottery types known from southern sites may appear, but these are rare; even rarer are northern Akkadian types which were carried south of the Diyala.

84. Again, I must thank McGuire Gibson for access to the records and drawings of this excavation and permission to refer to them. The excavation in Area WC-3 was carried out during the thirteenth, fourteenth, and seventeenth seasons of excavation at Nippur (1973, 1975, and 1987). For a preliminary report, see Gibson, Armstrong, and McMahon 1998.

85. The one exception to this generalization is the ubiquitous small conical bowl (Type O-1, see below), of which there were many complete profiles and whole examples.

differences between two defined types that are only visible if a sherd is large enough to include certain important points of morphology, sherds smaller than that minimum size have been ascribed to the more common of the two types, admittedly resulting in bias.

For the third-millennium B.C. levels, the pottery is divided into six main categories, indicated by capital letters preceding individual type numbers. Open forms (bowls, or any vessel in which the rim diameter is the maximum diameter) are designated by an "O"; closed forms (jars, or any vessel with a neck or mouth narrower than its shoulder) are given a "C." These two categories together comprised the majority (ca. 72%) of the typed sherds, with open forms representing 63% and closed forms only 9% of the total. The four remaining categories consist of bases ("B"); spouts ("S"); decorated fragments that could not be assigned to a specific vessel type ("D"); and vats, or very large coarse vessels ("V"). Bases make up approximately 25% of the typed forms, decorated sherds 1%, and the other two categories less than 1% each. Spouts and vats show little change from level to level, either in form or frequency, but there are changes in bases and decoration that underscore changes visible in the more common open and closed categories.

Once the sherds were assigned a letter category, individual types were given sequential numbers, more or less according to their appearance in the stratigraphic column. (For instance, Types O-1 and C-1 both appear in Level XIX; the type numbers assigned become higher as forms were introduced in later levels.) There are a few exceptions to this: Types O-6b, C-16c, and C-25b first appear later than their numbers would seem to imply, but they are variant forms of types that appeared and were numbered earlier in the sequence. Types O-17 and C-24 are also slightly out of sequence; the reasons in each case are detailed below.

## Pottery Manufacture

The ware was remarkably homogenous from the late Early Dynastic through the Ur III period. Vessels are almost invariably wheel-made, with only the occasional handmade example. In the majority of the types, vessel walls range from 0.04 cm to 1.50 cm in thickness. Temper is predominantly fine sand with varying quantities of mica (possibly a natural inclusion in the local clay sources) and occasionally a small amount of straw or other organic material (especially in larger forms). The color of the fabric is most frequently a light brown ("buff") but ranges from a very pale tan ("cream") through pink to red, with occasional buff green or olive green resulting from overfiring. The surface is usually a shade or two lighter than the core (i.e., pink on red, or cream on buff), not the result of a slip or low firing, but due to the migration of salts and finer particles in the clay to the surface during its drying stage. The firing process then had a slightly different effect on this fine-grained layer than on the body of the vessel. A few rare types (see individual descriptions) received a slip or were made of a unique fabric. Paint is very rare; incised decoration is more common.

Ring bases, made separately and attached, are often of clay with denser organic temper than in the vessel itself. The fabric of "vats" usually has a large quantity of organic temper to keep such large vessels from breaking apart under their own weight before and during firing. There is very little that can be considered "fine-ware," comparable to the thin-walled, hard-fired vessels with little to no visible temper that were produced in northern Mesopotamia at this time.

## Analysis

Tables 13–16 give sherd counts and relative frequencies of open and closed types by level for the third millennium B.C. The "%" number is the percentage that sherds of a specific type represent within the total number of sherds within that specific category (open or closed) from the relevant level. These relative percentages were calculated only for the "open" and "closed" groups; the percentages for the remaining groups were not calculated since the numbers are generally too small to be significant (but see tables 17 and 18 for the sherd counts). For ease of reference, the relative percentages in each level for each type in the open and closed groups are also represented as bar charts (tables 19–74).

Due to the enormous numbers of plain-rimmed conical bowls (Type O-1) in all levels, the relative frequencies of other open types often appear almost negligible. (Type O-1 overall makes up 54% of the total number of typed sherds from all levels and 86% of the total open-form sherds.) Nevertheless, the ratio of closed to open types in each level was calculated and the sherd counts for each level, subdivided into open and closed forms, are presented in tables 7 and 8. By number of sherds, open forms are clearly the most common in all levels, although there is great variability. Levels XIIIC and IX through VI stand out as having a larger percentage of closed-form sherds (and, naturally, a smaller percentage of open-form sherds) than do other levels: Level XIIIC has 19% closed form sherds and Levels IX through VI have 26%, 22%, 32%, and 22%, respectively. These percentages stand in contrast to the other levels which vary between 5% and 15% closed-vessel sherds (with most levels falling in the range of 7%–10%).

The overwhelmingly large number of sherds from open forms across all levels can probably be related to the greater portability and higher frequency of use of open vessels (for eating and drinking) — factors that can be linked to higher frequency of breakage and thus to presence in the archaeological record.[86] The lower numbers of sherds from jars may either be evidence for minimal storage or evidence of infrequent access to storage since it is the use of vessels that causes breakage. Stable, long-term storage could well be present but reflected in low numbers of broken jars. In levels with a higher-than-usual percentage of sherds from closed vessels, we might be seeing a shift in function of the area or a different pattern of debris discard and accumulation. Certainly the highest percentage of sherds from closed vessels, 32% in Level VII, can be explained by the fact that in this level the area was not in domestic use but seemed to be a trash deposition area.

In this context, however, the three levels previous to the above-mentioned sequence of levels with high percentages of closed forms (Levels XIB, XIA, and X) also contained percentages of sherds from closed vessels at the top end of the usual range (12%, 15%, and 15%, respectively); these levels all contain domestic occupational strata. Therefore, all levels from Levels XIB through VI have a consistently higher-than-usual percentage of closed-vessel sherds. Pursuing this further, there is only one level (Level XIIA) within the range from Levels XIIIC through VI in which the percentage of sherds from closed vessels falls below 10%; conversely, among the levels earlier than Level XIIIC, only two have closed vessel percentages as high as 10%. If sublevels are grouped together (i.e., Levels XIIIC and XIIIB are merged, etc.), the contrast between closed-vessel percentages in pre-Level XIIIC and post-Level XIIIC levels is even more stark: 6%–9% prior to Level XIIIC versus 10%–32% after Level XIIIC.

In an investigation of possible explanations for this trend and the apparent division at Level XIII, it should be noted that Level XIIIB is confidently dated to the late Akkadian period by the cylinder seal found with Skeleton 2 in Burial 14. Notably, the plan of the building in Area WF stabilizes in the preceding level, Level XIVB; thereafter a similar plan is in use throughout almost all following levels, up through Level VI. It is also in Level XIV that a large number of closed vessel types appear for the first time. Only slightly earlier (Level XVI or XV), the practice of collective burial was introduced (see *Chapter 2*). It is tempting to link these several factors and speculate that they all point toward a greater number of individuals using the house, a shift in occupation of space that would have affected the amount of stored resources held in the house and the degree to which access to these resources was required.

The occurrence of very large sherd counts in Levels XIIA and XIB (see tables 7–8) is difficult to explain, as the architecture of these levels is not notably different from that in the levels before or after them. The depth of deposit, and thus the volume of earth, in each of those levels is also not notably larger than in other levels.

When the presence/absence of vessel types per level is plotted and the number of different vessel types for each level is calculated (see tables 9–11), another aspect of the sequence comes to light. Although there is a gradual buildup in number of types and a great deal of continuity, a distinct development occurs by Level XIV. From this level there is a generally greater range of vessel types per level (twenty-five to forty-five different types per level, with the exception of Levels VII and VI), compared with the number of types in levels earlier than Level XIV (twelve to twenty-two types). That some levels contain a larger number of types could be due to overall greater numbers of sherds (i.e., Level XI, in which forty-five different vessel types were found, also had the largest number of diagnostic sherds: 1,803). But there are also instances of similar numbers of diagnostic sherds being associated with widely different numbers of types: for instance, the fourteen types among 647 diagnostics from Level XIX versus the twenty-nine types among 621 diagnostics of Level XIII. Larger numbers of diagnostic sherds from a level are thus not the only explanation for wide vessel variety and the trend toward a greater range of types is surely significant. A larger number of house inhabitants does not provide an immediate logical link since one could expect each individual to be associated with the same approximate assemblage, leading to larger overall numbers of vessels, but not necessarily to a greater variety. However, the increased wealth/status ascribed to the house occupants, as indicated by burial and house contents from Level XIV onward, may provide the explanation. The change in social

---

86. The size of the sherds into which the vessels would have broken is also a factor in their relative presence in the archaeological record. The WF context was one of intense domestic use, the sort of context from which large sherds, such as those from jars or large vessels, might well have been consciously removed, while the smaller sherds from bowl breakage would have been more likely to be left where broken.

status could be linked to an increased range and degree of activity, which might explain the expansion of the assemblage.

The ratio of number of open types to number of closed types present in any level remains remarkably constant throughout the pottery sequence, in a tight range of 1:1 through 1:1.5 (table 11), with most levels having ratios of 1:1.4 or 1:1.5. In only three levels (Levels XIX, XVIII, and VII) are there the same number of different open types present as closed types. Therefore, although the number of open vessel sherds far outweighs the number of closed vessel sherds, the range of closed types represented within these smaller numbers of sherds is proportionally far greater. The explanation clearly lies in the overwhelming dominance of the simple conical bowl, Type O-1.

Most of the vessels in the burials are assignable to types and are in some cases instrumental in the definition of those types; but while whole vessels found in occupational levels are included in the percentages calculated for types, it would introduce bias to include the burial pottery there. Some burials contained types that are in the stratified material, and in cases where the overall numbers in any level are low, the addition of the burial pottery would give those types spurious significance, skewing the frequencies away from the assumed average household assemblage. Most of the types found in burials are represented in occupational material from associated levels, but there are a few types that may be more typical of burials than of daily use.

## Typology

Since the typology is based mainly on rim sherds, it does not pretend to identify the same categories as those used by the ancient manufacturers. Distinctions among types are made on an intuitive basis, from the form of the sherds, with reference to known types published from other sites and/or already identified from excavations in Areas WA 50c or WC-3 at Nippur and from Umm al-Hafriyat. The appearance of the sherds in profile is the most important consideration, with diameter, construction, and ware taken into account. In most cases the types are distinct enough that there is rarely a question of dividing a continuum, in which case a more quantitative analysis would have been required. Since only one person was responsible for characterizing all the material included here, internal consistency may be assumed. Virtually none of the sherds show any evidence of use-wear that might give evidence of function.

The types identified are certainly modern creations that may or may not have been culturally significant or functionally distinct at the time when the vessels were produced. The Area WF typology is a tool created for a purely contemporary purpose, as an aid in chronological determination. Temporal differences in rim form are purposely highlighted by the assignment of different type numbers (although the whole vessel to which they belonged might not have been substantially altered and retained the same function). In this sense, the types are "historical," related to the passing of time, rather than functional. Some of these separate types could probably be grouped into what in the past would have been recognized as a single functional form; other types should possibly be split into several distinct groups according to variations in size or base type. Given the current state of knowledge, however, the most useful thing to do with the Area WF data is to organize and present the types chronologically, for comparison with data from other sites and contexts and for elucidation of the sequence. Selective comparanda for each type are given in the descriptions accompanying each plate.

## Description of Area WF Pottery Types and Assemblages, by Level

### Level XIX, A and B

Open Vessels

*Type O-1:* Plain-rimmed, straight-sided conical bowl (pl. 76). The rim diameters cluster around 14 to 16 cm, but the range in Level XIX is from 12 to 18 cm. These bowls were made quickly on the wheel and without much care, with the result that many examples are slightly to very warped and offer a range of heights according to where along the circumference of the rim the measurement is taken; in such cases, the attempt was made to determine the median. These bowls invariably have flat string-cut bases (Type B-3). They are endemic at all southern Mesopotamian sites with occupations of Early Dynastic and Akkadian date and are found in domestic and burial contexts. They persist, in large numbers, through the entire Early Dynastic–Ur III sequence in Area WF (table 19). The three foundation-deposit bowls from Locus 68 in Level XIXB (pl. 123:8–10) belong to this type, which is the most common for foundation deposit bowls in all levels.

The average height of O-1 bowls in Level XIX, where measurable, is 9.1 cm (table 12). A gradual reduction in height of this bowl type from the Early Dynastic through the Akkadian period has been observed elsewhere (the Diyala sites, Fara, Abu Salabikh, Ur, and Tell al-Ubaid; see Martin 1982: 153, n. 21, and Moon 1987: 3). The reduction in height in each case is a general trend, however, and the absolute measurements from site to site are not strictly comparable.

*Type O-2:* "Fruit stand" or "stemmed dish" (Moon 1987), with a notched, impressed, or plain horizontal ridge below a thickened, rounded rim (pl. 77). Some sherds assigned to this type could belong either to the flared base or to the bowl of the stand, which are often similar in diameter, shape, and decoration; correct orientation in the absence of the whole vessel is often impossible. These fruit stands, like the small conical bowls, are found at most southern Mesopotamian sites with late Early Dynastic occupation, although there is some regional variation (Moon 1982). There is a significantly higher degree of association with burials than with domestic contexts.[87] This type is not common in the WF third-millennium B.C. sequence, and its relative percentage varies somewhat erratically (table 20).

*Type O-3:* Large, rounded- or triangular-rim bowl with almost straight to curving sides (pl. 78). The rim diameters range from 22 cm to approximately 40 cm. Sherds of this type can be difficult to distinguish from the bases of fruit stands (although since they lack decoration they are less often confused with the bowls of fruit stands). Large bowls with similar rims and ring bases appear in Early Dynastic III graves at Abu Salabikh,[88] at least one example comes from an Early Dynastic III context at Tell Asmar, and another example was excavated from an early Akkadian grave at Tell Razuk. They are not necessarily more often associated with burials than with domestic use. The frequency of this form varies through the Area WF sequence but remains significantly high across the third millennium B.C. (table 21).

*Type O-4:* Variant of the fruit stand, with a shallow bowl and a deep band rim, usually decorated with a row of notches and occasionally with a lightly grooved wavy line (pl. 79). At Nippur, this rim form appeared in the North Temple in Levels IV and III, dated to the late Early Dynastic III period,[89] in the Inanna Temple in Levels VIII and VIIB,[90] and in Area EA (Early Dynastic IIIa). This type is present at Ur (Moon 1982) and is in fact more common there than Area WF Type O-9 (a closely related form; see discussion of Level XVII and pl. 83). Its popularity at Ur could indicate it was a regional variant of far southern Mesopotamia. However, its replacement in the Area WF sequence by Type O-9, which was introduced in Level XVII at the same point that Type O-4 appeared for the last time, may instead reveal it as a temporal variant. In addition, fruit stands with this rim do appear farther north in graves at Kish and Tell Uqair and in the Diyala. It is only in the Diyala that stands of Type O-4 are said to come from Early Dynastic II contexts (Khafajah Houses 4 and 6); the rest of the findspots are dated to late Early Dynastic III at the earliest. Like Type O-2, Type O-4 is most often associated with graves and specialized contexts such as temples, an aspect that is reflected in its low frequency in Area WF (table 22).

*Type O-5:* Stem and base fragments of fruit stands (pl. 80), the upper rims of which can have any one of three shapes (Types O-2, O-4, O-9). Occasionally, sherds from bases of fruit stands are identifiable as such because of stance and placement of decoration, but some bases will have been incorporated in the Type O-3 or O-2 counts. Due to the difficulty of identification, the presence/absence of Type O-5 across the levels is not statistically or chronologically significant (table 23).

---

87. See the descriptions with the *Plates* for more extensive comparanda for all types.
88. At Abu Salabikh these large bowls are sometimes part of a four-vessel set in graves, including a small cylindrical strainer, a small cup or bowl, and a strainer funnel. No examples of such sets have been found at Nippur, but they have been identified in Early Dynastic III–early Akkadian burials at Kish, Tell ad-Deylam, Tell Madhhur, and Tell Razuk.
89. One sherd of this type is published in McCown, Haines, and Biggs 1978 (pl. 44: 11), and other sherds of this type are in the study collection in the Oriental Institute Museum. The excavators of the North Temple assigned a date of Early Dynastic III to both these levels, but in the light of the redating of the Diyala sequence (and the evidence from the WF excavation), Level III there should probably be called "ED III/early Akkadian."
90. I thank Karen Wilson for showing me drawings of the pottery from the Inanna Temple excavation and I thank her and Donald Hansen for allowing me to refer to them here. Levels VIII and VIIB are dated to Early Dynastic II and Early Dynastic IIIa; Richard Zettler (1984) refined the date of Level VIIB to "mid-ED III." The next stratum, Level VIIA, contains some pottery types probably datable to the Akkadian period.

*Type O-6a:* Handmade, flat-based tray with low vertical sides, made in a heavily organic-tempered fabric (pl. 81).[91] These trays can be circular or oval in plan view and may have been used to feed and water smaller domestic animals or for kitchen activities. They are known from Early Dynastic III and Akkadian contexts in the Diyala and Hamrin, and at Kish and Abu Salabikh. Never common in Area WF, they do appear across the third-millennium B.C. levels (table 24).

*Type O-7:* Large cylindrical strainer, open at top and base, with rows of large circular perforations (pl. 82:1–3). Cylindrical strainers in the later third millennium B.C. can be divided into two sizes, of which Type O-7 is the larger, with a diameter ranging from 20 to 35 cm. The smaller strainers, 10–15 cm in diameter, have been found in graves at Abu Salabikh (Moon 1987: 194–301), Kish (Mackay 1929: pl. 54:37–38), and Tell ed-Deylam.[92] The larger strainer makes up part of the "beer set" found in Early Dynastic III to early Akkadian graves at Abu Salabikh and Tell Razuk; it also appears in similarly dated levels of the Nippur North Temple and Area EA and at Tell Sabra in the Hamrin. The type continues through Level XVI in Area WF but also appears in some later levels (XIII, XI–IX), where it may have been redeposited from earlier contexts (table 25).

Closed Vessels

*Type C-1:* Plain rim on a vertical or slightly flared neck, usually 8–10 cm in diameter (pl. 96). This rim form has two variants: on a taller neck it is found on a variety of narrow, late Early Dynastic jars, with and without spouts, while the same rim on a shorter and more flared neck belongs to a jar with a wider shoulder. There is, however, something of a continuum between these two extremes, and small sherds that do not preserve the shoulder or height of the neck are difficult to place in one or the other subform. Jars with this plain rim appear at many southern Mesopotamian sites. They appear at the beginning of the Early Dynastic period and had their greatest popularity then, although they continued through the Akkadian period and later in significant, but gradually falling, numbers in the Area WF sequence (significant numbers through Level X; tables 15 and 44).

*Type C-2:* Band rim on a medium or long neck (pl. 97). This kind of rim can belong to both goddess-handled and spouted jars of Early Dynastic I through III and later. The most common version of the rim has a distinct band with a corresponding groove or depression at the rim interior (perhaps for seating a lid); a less common form has a shorter and more rounded band with a less pronounced internal depression or groove. Again, there is a gradual continuum between these two variants, which are distinct from each other only at the extremes. Originally, these variants were distinguished as Types C-2a and C-2b, but the separation proved difficult to maintain and was abandoned in the final analysis. In Area WF, this rim type is very common in Level XIX but decreases rapidly thereafter, though it remains present through Level VII (table 45).

*Type C-3:* Plain rim similar to C-1, with a diameter that can vary from 14 to 18 cm, on a very short, vertical or flaring neck (pl. 98). Type C-3 is found on wide-bodied vessels with rounded shoulders, both with and without spouts. Along with Type C-1, Type C-3 appears from the beginning of the Area WF sequence in the Early Dynastic period and continues through the Akkadian period and beyond, experiencing a peak in what I argue are transitional and early Akkadian levels (Levels XVII–XV; table 46).

*Type C-4:* Small jar with a plain rim, short vertical neck, rounded shoulder, and string-cut base (pl. 99:1–5). There is some possible crossover between the finer "normal-sized" versions of this vessel and "miniature" versions of comparable form. This type is common in the Abu Salabikh graves and also appears in burials at Ur, Kish, and at Fara (Early Dynastic II through Early Dynastic III/Akkadian contexts), the Diyala, and Mari. The shape and size suggests a function as a drinking vessel, but its frequent association with graves and its relative scarcity and erratic presence in the Area WF domestic context (table 47) could point to its use at specific ritual events.

---

91. Type O-6b first appears in Level XVII; see below.
92. I thank James Armstrong for permission to refer to the 1989 excavation at Area C, Tell ed-Deylam. The smaller version of the strainer was represented in Nippur Area WF by a single example only, from Level XIA, possibly out of context.

*Type C-5:* Low triangular rim of a neckless rounded-shoulder jar (pl. 99:6–12). This is an uncommon but very distinctive type, almost always in a dark plum red or scarlet redware with heavy white sand (or lime?) temper. This type was found at Nippur in Area EA (Early Dynastic IIIa) and in the North Temple excavation (Level IV, late Early Dynastic III), but so far this combination of shape and ware has not been illustrated from any other contemporary site. A shoulder sherd in the same distinctive ware from Level XVIIB (pl. 99:7) indicates that the rim may be attached to a jar with closely spaced horizontal grooves on the shoulder. The type appears in primary context in Levels XIX and XVIII only, with the few examples in subsequent levels surely being redeposited (table 48).

*Type C-6:* Elongated triangular everted rim on a medium or long, slightly flaring neck (pl. 100:1–6). These rims are most typical of goddess-handled jars or squat angular jars of Early Dynastic III and later. In the North Temple at Nippur, the Type C-6 rim appears first in Level V (Early Dynastic III). Such rims are also present in the Abu Salabikh graves, at Kish, and even in Akkadian levels at Tell Asmar. Like fruit stands, goddess-handled jars are often associated with burials and are less often found in domestic contexts. This form is similar to Type C-10 (see discussion of Level XVII and pl. 103) but differs from it in the angle of the triangular rim, here extending outward as contrasted to the downward angle of Type C-10. Type C-6 appears consistently in Area WF in the earlier levels through Level XV (table 49).

*Type C-7:* Very short, pronounced band rim, sometimes with an exaggerated groove at the interior, on a short, flared neck (pl. 100:7–12). This rim is related to Type C-2 but is shorter, heavier, and far less common. Type C-7 is found in contexts dating from as early as Early Dynastic I; they appear at least from Level IX (Early Dynastic I) at the North Temple excavation at Nippur, in Levels XI and X at the Inanna Temple at Nippur, in Early Dynastic I and II levels at Tell Razuk, and in Early Dynastic levels at the Diyala sites. Type C-7 appears in Area WF only in Levels XIX through XVII (possibly being replaced at that point by Type C-9 and/or C-10, both of which are of comparable scale and morphology; table 50; cf. tables 52–53).

Other Types

*Type D-1:* Single applied ridges with regular finger impressions (D-1a), notches (D-1b), or left plain (D-1c). These ridges could come from the shoulder-to-body carinations of medium to large jars (see pl. 143, for example) or from the bowls of fruit stands (pl. 77).

*Type D-2:* Incised decoration (usually crosshatched or parallel lines) made with a single pointed tool. This type of decoration is found most often on sherds clearly from large jar shoulders or fruit stands (pl. 80:2–5); however, there is one sherd in this level from a smaller jar shoulder bearing rows of irregular notches around the neck and shoulder, with a row of incised motifs between: a plant, an inverted V, and a square with vertical lines within it, framed by short oblique lines (I677:4; pl. 127:14).

*Type D-3:* Horizontal reserved slip, from jar shoulders. This form of decoration is rare in Area WF (see Gibson, Armstrong, and McMahon 1998: fig. 26:9, for example from Nippur Area EA).

*Type S:* Detached jar spouts are fairly common in this level. By the nature of their manufacture and use, spouts frequently broke off from their parent vessels and their stable structure and density means they were often then preserved complete. Even when shattered, their cylindrical morphology is such that they are easily identified from small fragments. All these factors contribute to the high numbers found throughout the Area WF sequence.

*Type V:* Large organic-tempered vat. Most have squared-off rims, often with heavy applied ridges with regularly spaced finger impressions just below. Fragments of these very large vessels appear throughout the sequence, and there does not seem to have been any significant morphological development over time. Like spouts, vats can be identified from very small fragments due to their thickness and heavy organic temper.

*Type B-1:* Early Dynastic I solid-footed goblet base. Early Dynastic I levels were not reached in Area WF, but like spouts, these bases tend to be well preserved and are easily identified from small sherds. There are several examples from Level XIX, obviously redeposited from earlier levels. Their scarcity in Area WF is reassuring, in that it indicates minimal upward percolation and redeposition of earlier pottery into later levels, reinforcing the integrity of the ceramic sequence (for examples of solid-footed goblets from Early Dynastic I contexts in Area EA at Nippur, see Gibson, Armstrong, and McMahon 1998: fig. 24:1–3).

*Type B-2:* Very narrow flat base with shaved sides (pl. 123:5–7). These bases probably belonged to tall plain-rimmed cups, other examples of which may be hidden among the Type O-1 rim counts. Their relationship to the similar, but less carefully made solid-footed goblets, is unclear.

*Type B-3:* String-cut bowl base. Most range from 4 to 6 cm in diameter. These belong to Type O-1, the conical bowl, and where both base and rim have been preserved on a sherd or whole vessel, the base has been subsumed in the O-1 counts. The distinctive concentric oval grooves on the base are produced when a finished vessel is cut from the top of a lump of clay while the wheel is spinning.

*Type B-5:* Separately made ring base from a jar of uncertain type. These often have heavier organic temper than would the rest of the vessel, and their separate manufacture and often careless attachment make them prone to separation (see pl. 128:4). The diameters range from 9 to 20 cm; most fall in the range of 12–16 cm.

*Type B-7:* Small pointed base, sometimes shaved down (pl. 123:1–4). These bases belong to plain-rimmed cups, complete examples of which have been found at Kish, Mari, and Tell Chuera in late Early Dynastic III contexts. They also appear at Nippur in Inanna Temple Levels VIIB and A. The rim associated with this base form is indistinguishable from Type O-1 (though perhaps smaller in diameter), so it is possible that there are examples of this distinct vessel included among the counts for Type O-1.

*Relative Frequencies and Date:* Type O-1 is the most numerous type in Level XIX, both among open forms and overall.[93] Type O-2 is the second most important open type in Level XIX, followed by Type O-3 and by a few sherds of the cylindrical strainer Type O-7. Only a single fragment of Type O-6a is represented. Type C-2 is the most common closed type in this level, followed by Type C-1 and then a substantially smaller percentage of Type C-3. Type C-5 is found in an even smaller percentage than these types, and the other types are rarer still. The most common base form is the string-cut bowl base Type B-3 (matching the popularity of Type O-1), with smaller numbers of all the remaining forms.

All the individual types and the pottery assemblage as a whole in Level XIX are securely datable to Early Dynastic IIIa. The assemblage is very similar to one excavated at Area EA at Nippur, a trench cutting the city wall northeast of the ziggurat (Gibson, Armstrong, and McMahon 1998). Comparable assemblages have been excavated at the Inanna Temple and North Temple at Nippur,[94] Fara, Umm el-Jīr, and Tell al-Hiba. Graves at Ur, Kish, and Abu Salabikh provide the best whole examples of types represented in our collection as sherds. The assemblage also has points of similarity to assemblages at relevant levels at the Diyala sites and Tell Razuk, farther to the northeast. Thus, Level XIX, the earliest point reached in the Area WF sequence, is dated to the Early Dynastic IIIa.

## Level XVIII

The pottery of this level is virtually identical to that of Level XIX, although there are two new types, one closed and one open, that did not appear earlier. In addition, Type C-2 suffered a drop in popularity from its peak in Level XIX.

*Type O-8:* Stand with a small conical bowl set at the top of a tall narrow cylinder (pl. 82:4–7). The sides of the cylinder are often vertically shaved, creating shallow facets or fluting. The small bowl was made separately and attached to the cylindrical stem, retaining its string-cut base (though hidden within the cylinder). Examples of this

---

93. When the sherds in each lot were counted, efforts were made to rejoin sherds from the same vessel to avoid double-counting. Certainly not all joins were recognized due to the large number of sherds involved; and there were probably cases of two or more sherds from one vessel being present in a lot without joins being preserved. However, the bias thus introduced should, in theory, have had the same effect on all forms. Thus the high relative percentage of Type O-1 cannot be ascribed to double-counting alone. Pottery in frequent use will break and be replaced more often than more specialized vessels, so the high percentage may reflect not only that Type O-1 was a common vessel within the assemblage but was also a commonly used vessel (not always the same thing). In addition, it has been noted that "of pots in regular use, the smaller the vessel, the shorter its use-life" (Longacre 1991: 7). As one of the smallest vessels, one can expect Type O-1 to have broken more frequently, to have been replaced more frequently, and thus to appear in the archaeological record more frequently than any other type. The high frequencies for Type O-1 may indicate more about its pattern of use than about the numbers of it present in a household at any single moment.

94. Very few sherds were illustrated in the report of the North Temple excavation (McCown, Haines, and Biggs 1978), but a selection was brought back and stored in the basement of the Oriental Institute. In addition, lists of pottery types by level were made by McCown during that excavation and these are stored with the records of that season and provide valuable information not always available from the sherd collection.

stand have been found in the Early Dynastic IIIb level of Tell al-Hiba in Area C and in Early Dynastic IIIa contexts at Fara and Abu Salabikh, as well as Level III of the North Temple and Level VII of the Inanna Temple at Nippur. In Area WF, the stand is present from Level XVIII through Level XV and was also found in Level XIII, although this last example may be a redeposited fragment from an earlier level (table 26). This type spans the late Early Dynastic and early Akkadian period and is thus potentially a "transitional" type.

*Type C-8:* Plain rim on a short neck with four applied tab handles at the rim (pl. 101:1–3). This is a well-known Early Dynastic I jar form that must have been redeposited in this level and the few others where it appears (table 51). There is a possibility that some sherds ascribed to Type C-3 from this or other levels may belong to Type C-8 since the rim and shoulder morphologies of the two types are similar and the Type C-8 determination can only be made when the handles are present.

*Type D-5:* Applied decoration; there is one example from this level: a curved ridge, decorated with punctates, applied to the flat side or shoulder of a vessel (pl. 127:15). This is distinct from the impressed or incised ridges from jar shoulder carinations and may be intended to represent a snake or other figure.

*Burial Group:* Burial 20 held two Type O-1 conical bowls (19 N 106, I685; pl. 128:2–3) and a Type C-1 jar (I684: pl. 128:1), but a shorter version than is normal for this type. This group is entirely typical of late Early Dynastic III graves in the range of pottery included, for both serving/storage and eating/drinking. The specific forms are also typically late Early Dynastic, although the bowls are rather shallow (6.6 and 6.5 cm) for so early in the sequence.

*Relative Frequencies and Date:* The relative frequencies of types in Level XVIII remain roughly the same as those of the previous level, and most of the types present in that level continue into Level XVIII (the exceptions are Types O-2, O-4, C-4, and C-6, all of which are either rare and/or do recur later in the sequence). The pottery parallels for the assemblage as a whole, and the similarity with the assemblage of Level XIX, point to a date in the Early Dynastic IIIa.

Level XVII

Level XVII is marked by the appearance of several new types that continue through Level XI and, in three cases, into Level IX or VIII (through the Akkadian and into the Ur III period). This is the first of three notable changes in the pottery assemblage to occur in the sequence (see also discussion of Levels XIV and XI), but the new types do not displace types already present, most of which continued in use. All but one of the new types of this level first appear in the second phase, Level XVII, Phase B. The new types include five jar rims and two open forms.

*Type O-9:* Fruit stand in which the upper bowl is shallower than in Type O-2, with a wide notched rim frequently having wavy grooves on the top and always a well-defined, sharply notched ridge below (pl. 83). This new variant possibly developed from the related Type O-4, which has a band rim but is similarly decorated with a line of notches and a wavy groove, and which makes its last appearance in this level. Type O-9 is the most common form of fruit stand/"stemmed dish" found at Abu Salabikh (where it is dated to Early Dynastic IIIa and b); elsewhere, it is found at Kish, in "Early Dynastic IIIb" contexts at Tell al-Hiba, and at Khafajah and Tell Asmar in contexts that Gibson (1982) dates to Early Dynastic IIIa and early Akkadian. In Area WF, this type first appears in Level XVII, reaches its peak frequency in Level XVI, and decreased thereafter, probably appearing in context for a final time in Level XII (table 27). Notably, there is an example present in Burial 14 in Level XIIIB (H1097; pl. 142:5) in the same tomb chamber with and only slightly earlier than a burial with a late Akkadian seal. This context argues against redeposition from a lower level, so this type had a greater temporal range than has hitherto been thought.

*Type O-6b:* Subtype of the handmade flat tray or animal feeder (Type O-6a, pl. 81). The shape and size of these types are the same, but in O-6b there are three or four strap handles or "bridges" reaching from the rim to the center of the interior. Sherds of this subtype are mainly recognizable from the "bridges" alone, unless a portion of the rim is preserved showing where one had been attached. The type could be present in earlier levels but was subsumed under Type O-6a, and it could be more common in other levels where it is unrecognized and unrecorded. Like Type O-6a, this type is assumed to have been an animal feeder or kitchen utensil.

*Type C-9:* Small, slightly rounded and thickened or rounded triangular rim on a slightly flaring neck of medium height (pl. 102). This rim can belong to a number of different jar shapes and was especially common in Ur III levels in Area WC-3 at Nippur and in late Akkadian to Ur III levels at Umm al-Hafriyat and Umm el-Jīr. There is some possibility for confusion of this form with the less extreme examples of Type C-10 and the smaller versions of Type C-14. Exceptionally, this type experiences two popularity peaks through the Area WF sequence: one in Level XVI and a second in Level IX (table 52). It is possible that this rim type belonged to two distinct jars, produced mainly in two different periods. A juxtaposition of the frequency charts of Type C-9 (table 52) and its closest relative, Type C-14 (table 57), however, indicates that it is at exactly the low point between the popularity peaks of Type C-9, Level XIII, that the popularity of C-14 reaches its highest mark. It is equally possible that a single jar was involved, remaining much the same, and popular, throughout, while fashion dictated minor changes in rim form.

*Type C-10:* Large overhanging triangular rim on a medium, flaring neck (pl. 103). These rims are close to Type C-6 but are angled downward rather than extended horizontally. Similar jar rims are found in the Diyala in contexts ranging from Early Dynastic I through Early Dynastic III, at Tell Razuk in Early Dynastic I and II levels, and in the Nippur Inanna Temple in Level XI (Early Dynastic I). The frequency of this type in Area WF in levels that are Early Dynastic III or later, however, indicates that this must be a different type of jar. The peak popularity of C-10 is reached in the next two levels, with a few examples persisting through Level IX (table 53). Rims with this morphology are also found in Akkadian levels at Susa and Early Dynastic–Akkadian levels at Tell Sabra.

*Type C-11:* Small, round-bodied fine-ware jar with a medium-high neck and flared rim; the shoulder and neck are lightly scored or horizontally grooved and there may be thin bands of fugitive scarlet or red paint on the shoulder and neck (pl. 101:4–7; and see also an example from a burial, pl. 139:1). The ware is fine and often friable, sometimes with an applied cream slip. The slip and paint are unusual for this period and the ware itself looks foreign to Nippur, in both its fineness and its orange or red color.

Sherds of this form are rare and only appear in Area WF in Levels XVIIB and XVI (table 54). The best parallels come from Syria, at Tell Chuera and Mari; the exact dating of the relevant levels there, either late Early Dynastic or early Akkadian, has been the subject of debate. Kühne (1976) limits these levels to Early Dynastic III; Zettler (1978) argues plausibly for their extension into the early Akkadian.[95] A dating to the early Akkadian period is a definite possibility, given the association of Type C-11 in Area WF with Type C-13, which has firm Akkadian parallels elsewhere. The closest parallels for C-11 in southern Mesopotamia come from Abu Salabikh graves (Early Dynastic IIIa), but those examples all have a small ring base, while the single whole example preserved in Area WF (19 N 145, with Burial 14, Skeleton 8; pl. 139:1) has a rounded base. The type is also attested once at Fara (unusually dated to Early Dynastic II; Martin 1988), and in a few graves at Ur (PG/1068, 1248, 1273; Early Dynastic III or early Akkadian). At Khafajah there are further examples, in graves 117, 167, and 168 and in Houses 1 (Early Dynastic III–early Akkadian). This is surely another form that should be called "transitional," belonging equally to the late Early Dynastic and the early Akkadian periods.

*Type C-12:* Rounded, rolled rim of a large storage vessel with sloping, rounded shoulder (pl. 104). This particular form of rim is apparently relatively uncommon, appearing in Area WF again only in Levels XIII through XI (table 55).

*Type C-13:* "Double-ridged" rim: a thickened rim with a ridge on the neck just below it (pls. 105–06). This rim is very distinctive and the most important of the forms introduced in this level, as it is mainly an Akkadian type. It has two internal variants, one a wide-mouth rim (ca. 16–20 cm) on a low neck (C-13a, pl. 105), which is found in this level and Level XV; the second having a smaller diameter (8–10 cm) on a taller neck (C-13b, pl. 106), which does not appear in Area WF until Level XIII and thereafter (table 56).[96] Type C-13b is found on squat egg-shaped jars with ring or round bases, the larger Type C-13a on ovoid jars with wide shoulders and ring or convex bases.

The larger version, Type C-13a, may first appear in the very late Early Dynastic III but also belongs to the early Akkadian period and was far more common then. It is a useful type as a marker of the transition between Early Dynastic and Akkadian as it seems to have been restricted to the very end of the Early Dynastic and early in the Akkadian period.

---

95. In support of Zettler's dating, an example of gray metallic ware (a part of the dating argument) found in an "Early Dynastic III" context at Nippur, from North Temple Level IV (4 P 268; Zettler 1978: 348, n. 60), is from a level that could date to late Early Dynastic III/early Akkadian, not Early Dynastic III only. The same is true of a pin type used by Kühne as evidence of Early Dynastic III date; an example from the North Temple (4 N 118; Zettler 1978: 347, n. 4) is also from Level IV and could be early Akkadian or late Early Dynastic III.

96. The Level XIII example of Type C-13 does not actually appear in the tables as it is in Burial 14, with Skeleton 2.

At Khafajah it is present in Houses 2 and 1, at Umm el-Jīr in an Akkadian level, at Abu Salabikh in graves attributed to Early Dynastic IIIa and b, at al-Hiba in Early Dynastic IIIb contexts, and at Ur in Akkadian graves.[97] In Area WF, it does not appear until the third phase of this level, Level XVII, Phase A, and it was never common (table 56). This form is evidence for the trend toward what Adams called "very articulated rims" in the Akkadian and Ur III periods (Adams and Nissen 1972: 103; see Type C-13b and Type C-28 for the extreme version of this trend).

*Type B-4:* Large flat jar base (not illustrated). This type of base remains strangely rare throughout all levels. It is possible that it is more frequent but went unrecognized due to its easy confusion with nondiagnostic body sherds.

*Type B-6:* Convex jar base (for examples on whole vessels, see pls. 151:1, 155:1–3). Only one sherd appears in this level, after which it does not recur until Level XIVA.

*Burial Groups:* Burial 19 in Level XVIIC contained a cluster of twenty-eight Type O-1 conical bowls (19 N 126–128, I664:1–25; pls. 129:7, 129:4, 129:2; 130:1, 129:5, 130:2–5, 129:9, 129:8, 130:7, 130:6, 130:8–10, 131:1–7, 131:9, 131:8, 129:3, 129:1, 129:6), plus a Type C-1 plain-rimmed spouted jar (I666: pl. 128:4). The depth of the bowls averages 7.6 cm, but there are some very deep examples (four between 10 and 12 cm deep); their combination with the spouted jar points to an Early Dynastic date in traditional terms, but both types continue into the Akkadian period in the occupational material in Area WF.

In Level XVIIB, Burial 21 held an adult with a Type O-1 bowl (I773:1; pl. 132:5) and two jars, one spouted Type C-1 and a large Type C-4 (I773:2, 19 N 155; pl. 132:3–4); plus an infant interred with child-sized versions of the Type O-1 bowl and Type C-4 jar (I686, 687; pl. 132:1–2). The limited range of types might again appear to be Early Dynastic in date, but the persistence of these types in the occupational material into later levels in Area WF indicates that the date could be early Akkadian.

*Relative Frequencies and Date:* Conical plain-rimmed bowls (Type O-1) are still the most frequently attested type in Level XVII, with an average height (in all three phases of Level XVII combined) of 7.6 cm, as compared to 9.1 cm in Level XIX. Relative frequencies of the types are for the most part as expected, without much change from the previous level. None of the types from earlier levels ceased to be produced in Level XVII, indicating continuity in the pottery manufacturing tradition and emphasizing the difficulty in pinpointing the precise change from Early Dynastic to Akkadian in the archaeological record. Significant is the introduction of a large number of new types, in particular C-9 and C-13, that are mostly associated with the Akkadian and even Ur III periods. This level should probably be labeled transitional, dated to late Early Dynastic III to early Akkadian.

Level XVI

A single new type distinguishes this level.

*Type O-10:* Conical bowl similar in most respects to the Type O-1 bowls, but with an overhanging beveled rim (pls. 84–85). It has a string-cut base and the depth is comparable to the O-1 bowls, but the diameter is generally slightly larger than even the maximum Type O-1 diameter, frequently around 17–18 cm. This new bowl type continues, increasing in frequency, through Level X, where it finally decreases again as two new bowl types gradually supplant it in Ur III levels (table 28). From Level XIII, the increased popularity of Type O-10 has an inverse effect on the frequency of Type O-1 bowls. Excavations at Nippur Area TB (Hansen 1965; McCown and Haines 1967), Umm al-Hafriyat, and Umm el-Jīr (Gibson 1972b) show Type O-10 to be typical of the Akkadian period, especially the later Akkadian period. Its appearance here is one of the main reasons this level has been assigned to the Akkadian period and supports the assertion that the previous level covered the transition from Early Dynastic to Akkadian.

There are a few changes among decorated sherds in Level XVI. Reserved slip (Type D-4), fairly common in Levels XIX through XVII, decreases sharply in this and the following levels. The same is true for finger-impressed ridges from jar shoulders (Type D-1a), which also begin to decrease in this level, although notched (Type D-1b) and plain (Type D-1c) ridges remain more constant. It is notable that all incised decoration on body sherds, as well as on sherds assigned to open or closed types (which do not appear separately in the D-counts), was still done with a single point (Type D-2), rather than a multiple-pointed comb; this is the case from Level XIX into Level XIII. (The

---

97. At Isin it is present in levels dated to Ur III (Hrouda 1977), far later than the majority of attestations elsewhere.

only exception to this is the comb incision on the rare, and possibly imported, Type C-11, which can have horizontal comb-incision on the shoulder.) The presence of comb-incision on vessels of Early Dynastic III date in the Diyala contrasts with the situation at Nippur, where this decoration does not appear until the Akkadian period; this difference could be explained as regional variation.

*Burial Groups:* Burial 18 was interred with a single Type O-1 bowl, the depth of which (7.0 cm) is appropriate for this level (19 N 60; pl. 132:7). Skeleton 8 of Burial 14 contained the only complete example of the Type C-11 jar found in the Area WF sequence (19 N 145; pl. 139:1), plus a set of eighteen Type O-1 bowls ranging from 6.3 to almost 8.0 cm in depth (I780:1–9, 11–19; pl. 140:8, 139:8, 139:7, 139:6, 140:7, 139:4, 140:4, 140:3, 139:11, 139:5, 140:10, 140:9, 140:1–2, 139:9–10, 140:5–6) and two narrower and taller cups that still fall within Type O-1 (19 N 156, I780:10; pl. 139:2–3). Only a single Type O-1 bowl and a Type C-1 jar were buried with Burial 14, Skeleton 7 (I682:2, 1; pl. 138:3–4).

*Relative Frequencies and Date:* Type O-1 bowls of this level have become quite shallow, with an average height of 6.7 cm, as compared to 7.6 cm in Level XVII. Despite the introduction of the very similar form Type O-10, all the foundation deposit bowls in this level are still Type O-1 (I425, I419:1, 2, I410, 19 N 56–59, I408:1; pls. 123:12–14, pl. 124:1, pl. 125:3, 125:5, 125:2, 125:1, 125:4). Type O-9 reaches its greatest popularity, while Type O-2 does not appear. From this level onward, Types O-4, C-7, C-8, and B-7 virtually disappear from the sequence. Type C-3 reaches its highest degree of popularity and the frequencies of Types C-9 and C-10 also make big leaps. Unfortunately, there are no well-dated early Akkadian period assemblages from domestic contexts (as opposed to burial assemblages) in other southern Mesopotamian sites with which to compare the assemblage of this level. The dating in the early Akkadian period rests mainly on the presence of Type O-10, which appears in "Early Dynastic IIIb" contexts at al-Hiba but is otherwise known to be typical of the later Akkadian period in southern Mesopotamia.

Level XV

There are two new jar rim types in the assemblage of Level XV and a single example of another new jar type is present in a grave of this level, but otherwise the tradition of the previous level continues.

*Type C-14:* Oval to rounded triangular rim on a short neck with a rounded or horizontal shoulder (pl. 107). This rim form reaches its maximum popularity in Level XIII and decreases sharply thereafter, although it persists through Level VIII (table 57). There are three other jar rim types that are particularly close in morphology and could cause some confusion. Type C-9 is the closest form but is smaller than C-14; as is mentioned in the discussion of Type C-9 under Level XVII, these two rim forms could both belong to the same very popular and long-lived jar form. Type C-7 is similar to C-14 but has a more triangular rim compared to the rounded form of C-14. Type C-22 is also similar but differs in several important respects: its neck is shorter and more sharply angled creating a flatter shoulder and the rim of C-22 is longer and narrower, almost a band rim, as opposed to the rounder, shorter rim of C-14. Whole vessels with Type C-22 rims from burials indicate that this rim form is associated with a larger jar than that with the Type C-14 rim. Most of the parallels for Type C-14 from other sites are from Akkadian contexts.

*Type C-24:* Small oval, triangular, or short band rim on a tall narrow neck (pl. 118), with the distinctive feature being the height of the neck.[98] In cases of a band rim, the distinction between this type and Type C-17 is the length of the band, with the rim of C-17 being distinctively longer and less well defined at the bottom, while the band rim of C-24 is shorter, usually slightly more rounded, and has a well-defined lower edge. In Area WF, rims of C-24 form have been found on both tall, narrow ovoid jars (with Burial 14, Skeleton 1; pl. 154:1–3; and Burial 14, Skeleton 6; pl. 136:7) and on squatter, wide-shouldered jars (with Burial 15; pl. 135:1). They appear as sherds in levels through the rest of the third millennium B.C., with maximum numbers in Level XI (table 68).

Jars of Type C-24 have been found in contexts dated to Early Dynastic IIIa and b at both Tell al-Hiba and Abu Salabikh or to the range of Early Dynastic through Akkadian at Ur. In the Nippur North Temple, however, sherds of this form first appear in Level II, dated to the late Akkadian by a tablet from the reign of Naram-Sin, and at Umm el-Jīr the type is present only in Akkadian levels.

---

98. Type C-24 has a higher type number than its appearance in Level XV would normally generate. The type was originally identified as having first appeared in the following level, Level XIV, and it was numbered accordingly. Subsequently, additional sherds of this Type were identified in Level XV, but renumbering types at that stage would have been disruptive.

*Burial Group:* Burial 14, Skeleton 5, was buried with a complete example of a Type C-17 jar (19 N 39; pls. 53a–b, 133:1), but no sherds of this type came from occupational debris (so it does not yet appear in tables 16 or 62). Type C-17 is a narrow jar with a small ovoid body, short carinated shoulder, tall neck, and elongated band rim. Nissen (1966) dates this type at Ur mainly to Early Dynastic, with an overlap into early Akkadian. At Abu Salabikh this form comes from graves called Early Dynastic III, and it is also found at Kish in the A Cemetery. At Fara, complete examples come from "Early Dynastic IIIa" graves, but Martin (1988) used a similar sherd as a survey type for Akkadian–Ur III identification. A nearly identical jar of this type was found at Tepe al-Atiqeh in the Hamrin (Uch Tepe 57) in an early Akkadian context (unpublished). Area WF, Level XV, to which the grave belongs, is to be dated in the Akkadian period, based on other pottery types found in the occupation material. Since the type does not actually become common until even later (identifiable sherds of this type appear first in Level XIVB and continue through Level VIII), an extension from late Early Dynastic into the Akkadian period must be allowed and an entirely Akkadian date may be probable. Burial 14, Skeleton 5, was also buried with a spouted C-1 jar, a large C-4 jar with rounded base, and three Type O-1 bowls (19 N 41, 19 N 45, I359:1, 19 N 34, 19 N 46; pls. 53b, 133:2–6).

*Relative Frequencies and Date:* The Type O-1 average height for the combined phases of Level XV decreased further, to 5.6 cm (from 6.7 cm in Level XVI; table 12). In addition, the Type O-1 rim diameters from this and the following levels were smaller on average, more frequently 14 than 16 cm. This is the only level in the sequence in which Type O-3 is not represented. Type C-6 reaches its maximum popularity and then abruptly disappears in the next level, Level XIV. The continuity of forms and similarity of assemblage to the previous early Akkadian level support an Akkadian date for Level XV.

Level XIV

Just as the introduction of several new types in Level XVII marks a significant change in the assemblage around the transition from Early Dynastic to Akkadian, a second change in the Area WF pottery sequence is visible at Level XIV, around the point of transition from the early to late Akkadian period.

Level XIVB

One new open form and seven new jar rim types appear in this phase.

*Type O-11:* Small to medium bowl, a variation on the overhanging rim Type O-10, but with the rim thickened and pulled up slightly (pl. 86) and with a smaller rim diameter, 16 cm or less. This form persists, along with Type O-10, through the Ur III period but always remains less well represented than O-10 (table 29). It has been found in late Akkadian and Ur III contexts at Nippur in Area WC-3 and at Umm al-Hafriyat.

*Type C-15:* Long oval rim with an overhanging lower edge and a shallow channel or groove at the interior (pl. 108). This type is rarer but more distinctive than C-14 (with which it shares some similarities) and continues to appear, inconsistently, through Level X (table 58). It appears infrequently at Abu Salabikh, where it is dated to Early Dynastic III, and seems to be unattested elsewhere.

*Type C-16a:* Small triangular jar rim on a short, sharply angled neck, with a plain shoulder (pl. 109). These jars are particularly common at Umm al-Hafriyat in late Akkadian levels, where they often have a distinctive single ridge at the juncture of shoulder and lower body.[99]

*Type C-16b:* Like C-16a, a triangular rim on a short, angled neck, but in this variant the shoulder is decorated with multiple well-spaced, separately applied, horizontal ridges (pl. 110).[100]

---

99. The version with a ridge at the shoulder carination also appears in an early Akkadian grave at Tell Razuk (Burial 12; Gibson 1981: pl. 99:1–2). The same grave also has five examples of Type C-16a without the ridge (ibid., pl. 99:3–7).

100. This type also has a variant in which the rim is less distinctive, more like the plain rim of Type C-3 or C-1, although the ridges on the shoulder are the same. This may be an eastern variant since most of the examples come from the Diyala, Hamrin, or farther east: Tell Asmar and Khafajah (Delougaz 1952: D.465.360, D.465.550, D.514.362), Tell Abqa' (Trumpelmann 1982: fig. 8), Tell Sabra (Tunca 1987: pl. 54:2), and Susa (Steve and Gasche 1971: pl. 2:12). There is, however, one from Tello (Parrot 1948: fig. 55:3483) and one from Abu Salabikh (Moon 1987: 706). This variant has not been noted at Nippur. Type C-16b should not be confused with the late Early Dynastic III jar form found at some northeastern Syrian sites, which has similarly spaced horizontal comb incision on the shoulder (i.e., Mari; Lebeau 1985). The applied ridges of Type C-16b are quite high, with a distinctive triangular cross section and a ca. 1.5–2.0 cm gap between each ridge.

Type C-16, in both these variants, is the most important new form from this level because it is elsewhere recognized as distinctive of the Akkadian period and has been used as a marker of Akkadian date in surveys of the southern Mesopotamian plains. The two types are almost equal in popularity in Area WF when they first appear (tables 59–60), but from Level XIB onward the multiple-ridged version is more numerous than the plain-shouldered version. However, since the ridges allow easy identification of this variant from shoulder sherds as well as rims (not the case for the plain-shouldered version), the higher frequency of Type C-16b in Area WF could be misleading.

Both versions of this type, but especially the multiple-ridged variant, have long been identified as Akkadian in date (Adams 1965, 1981; Adams and Nissen 1972; Delougaz 1952; Gibson 1972a; Hansen 1965). However, both forms continue into the Ur III period not only in Area WF but also at Umm al-Hafriyat and Nippur Area WC-3. This continuity, combined with the fact that this type only appears in Area WF three levels after the appearance of Type C-13 and two levels after Type O-10, also recognized Akkadian types, implies that Type C-16 is actually a marker of the late Akkadian and early Ur III, rather than of the Akkadian period as a whole. This form, especially with the multiple-ridged shoulder, is one of the few types that is also present in Akkadian and post-Akkadian levels at some sites in northern Mesopotamia (i.e., Nineveh, Tell Brak, Tepe Gawra, Nuzi, Assur); it also has been found to the east as far as Susa. The more precise dating to the late Akkadian and early Ur III periods is potentially valuable in connecting and reconciling the separate sequences of northern and southern Mesopotamia.

Of the four other newly attested jar rim types in this level, Types C-17 and C-21 are certainly datable to the Akkadian period.

*Type C-17:* Long band rim on a very elongated narrow neck (pl. 112). See the discussion of Level XV for a complete example of Type C-17 from a burial; sherds of this type first appear in Level XIVB and persist erratically through Level VIII (table 62).

*Type C-21:* Small jar with a short, plain vertical or rolled rim and short shoulder (pl. 116). This rim form differs from the very similar Type C-3 mainly in scale: the walls are thinner and the rim diameters smaller, a maximum of 12 cm for Type C-21 versus the minimum diameter of 14 cm for Type C-3. The shoulder of Type C-21 is also more sloped than the flatter shoulder of C-3. However, Type C-21 presents a problem in that there are two vessel forms on which this rim appears: a squat jar with sides tapering to a flat string-cut base and a round-based jar with a wider shoulder. The flat-based (or occasionally ring-based) version with this rim is more widespread and appears at Tell Asmar, Kish, Nippur Area WA 50c, Abu Salabikh, Tell al-Hiba, Uruk, and Ur. The round-based version could be slightly more limited in geographical extent, as it only appears at Kish, Nippur Area TB, Abu Salabikh, and Ur. Since the Area WF typology relies heavily on rim sherds, the two possible forms are grouped as Type C-21, as they are virtually indistinguishable without their bases.[101] Only three certain examples of the round-based type were identified in the Area WF excavation (Burial 14, Skeleton 2; pl. 149:2–4). In Area WF, Type C-21 is at its most common in the Akkadian period levels, Levels XIV through X, with only a few scattered examples thereafter (table 66).

The last two "new" types of Level XIV are found in late Early Dynastic or early Akkadian levels at other sites but first appear in Area WF in this level, which dates to the late Akkadian. However, their relative scarcity may explain why they do not appear in the earlier levels of Area WF.

*Type C-19:* Small, round-based bottle with a small triangular rim and rounded or carinated sides (pl. 114:4–7). This form has been found in late Early Dynastic to early Akkadian contexts in the Diyala, at Abu Salabikh, Tell al-Hiba, and elsewhere. It certainly continued to be produced late in the Akkadian period, however, as indicated by its presence in Akkadian graves and occupational material at Umm al-Hafriyat and Tepe al-Atiqeh, as well as Nippur Area TB, Level XII, upper levels at the Diyala sites, and at Nuzi and Susa. In Area WF, its greatest popularity is actually at its original appearance in Level XIV, although it was present consistently through Level VIII (table 64).

*Type C-22:* Medium to long band rim or rounded rim on a very short angled neck with a flat shoulder (pl. 117). From complete examples in Burial 14 it is clear that this rim belongs to a large storage jar with a convex base frequently perforated on one side (pls. 151:1, 155:1–3). The rim is distinct from Type C-14 by virtue of the sharper angle of the neck and shoulder and by the shorter neck. This jar has been found in levels at Khafajah (Houses 1) and

---

101. During initial analysis, the round-based form was designated Type C-23, to distinguish it from the flat-based Type C-21. However, the difference proved to be impossible to maintain on the basis of rim sherds only, and Type C-23 was ultimately omitted, with the sherds and vessels assigned to that type incorporated into C-21. Therefore, Type C-23 no longer exists and does not appear in the tables.

Asmar (Houses IV and V) dated to early Akkadian (Gibson 1982), at Umm el-Jīr in Akkadian levels, and in graves at Kish, Tell Razuk, and Tell Madhhur, which are Early Dynastic III–early Akkadian. In Area WF, it reaches a peak of popularity in Level XIII and continues through Level VII into the Ur III period (table 67).

Two unusual jars were found in fragmentary condition, having been used as packing in a repair to Wall BD (I327, 325; pl. 126:1–2). These jars are included in Type C-1, but the necks are higher, shoulders narrower, and volumes are smaller than is customary for this type.

*Burial Groups:* Burial 16 held six Type O-1 bowls (I403:1–2, I422, I426 1–3; pl. 134:2, 134:7, 134:4–6, 134:3) and a C-24 jar with a triangular rim on a long neck, with a short shoulder, similar to the Type C-17 jar with Burial 14, Skeleton 5 (I428; pl. 134:1). The jar has a distinctive red vertically burnished fabric that is extremely unusual, appearing only on one other jar in Area WF (with Burial 14, Skeleton 1, H1111; pl. 154:3). Although burnishing may decrease porosity, the effect in these cases is also decorative and may equate with the jars' use in the special burial context. However, the jar was too shattered to reconstruct; this extreme friability of burnished jars (redware in particular, but also examples in grayware) was noted in contemporary examples in Area WF and at Umm el-Jīr (M. Gibson, pers. comm.). The friability also sometimes appears in the burnished grayware of the early second millennium B.C. in northern Mesopotamia (Chagar Bazar, pers. obs.). It is not clear whether it is the process of burnishing, or the presence of specific chemical elements in the clay used for burnished jars, that reacts badly in post-depositional circumstances.

Burial 13 contained four Type O-1 bowls, all distinctively shallow, as is now expected in levels of Akkadian date (H535:1–4; pls. 134:10, 134:8, 134:9, 134:11).

Burial 15 held five shallow Type O-1 bowls (H1103:1, 2, H1104, H1106, 18 N 192; pls. 55b, 135:3–7), plus two vessels that could prove to be useful date markers. The more distinctive is a small, undecorated fruit stand with a double-ridged rim (18 N 191; pls. 55b, 135:2). This vessel is a smaller variant of Type O-9, a variant represented in the occupational debris in Area WF by only two sherds (pl. 83:6–7). This scarcity possibly indicates this was a burial-specific form. The jar from the burial has a narrow band rim on a medium-high neck (Type C-24), a very wide carinated shoulder, and a wide ring base (18 N 193; pls. 55b, 135:1). A close match for this jar comes from Level XIVA, on a slightly higher floor in the same room as the burial (18 N 134; pl. 126:3).

Both the jar and the stand have exact parallels as a pair and as individual items among graves at Abu Salabikh[102] and the A Cemetery at Kish,[103] at both of which the graves are ascribed to Early Dynastic IIIa and b. At both sites, however, some of the relevant graves include vessels better understood as Early Dynastic/Akkadian or even Akkadian types; for instance, Area WF Types C-11 and C-13 occur in some of the Abu Salabikh graves[104] and Types C-13, C-14, and C-17 appear among the relevant graves at Kish.[105] The reason for the attribution of an Early Dynastic III date could lie with the comb-incision and goddess-handled jars also found in some of the graves,[106] both of which could have been assumed to belong nearly exclusively to the late Early Dynastic period (although Delougaz allowed for the continuity of the goddess-handled jar into the Akkadian period). However, comb-incision in Area WF (see Level XIII) extends well into the Akkadian period, and a goddess-handled jar was found here in a grave of Level XIII, dated by a cylinder seal to the reign of Naram-Sin or later. The time range of the small plain fruit stand and the wide-bodied Type C-24 jar should probably be extended into the early Akkadian period and those graves that contain them should probably be labeled Early Dynastic/early Akkadian. As further confirmation, a fragmentary example of this wide-bodied jar comes from Area TB, Level XI, at Nippur, which is dated to the Akkadian period (McCown and Haines 1967: pl. 82:1).

The exclusively Early Dynastic date previously ascribed to the stand and jar types had already been brought into question in Gibson's redating of the "Early Dynastic IIIb" and "Protoimperial" levels and contemporary graves at

---

102. The fruit stand has been published from Abu Salabikh graves 4, 38, 79, 88, 93, and 146; the jar from graves 51, 73, 84, 120, 124, 143, 146, 148, 162, 168, 181, and 182 (Martin, Moon, and Postgate 1985; Moon 1987). Thus the only apparent overlap of the two types within this cemetery, as so far published, is in grave 146.

103. The fruit stand is illustrated for Kish burials 4, 40, 51, 65, 75, 123, and 153, and the jar is illustrated for burials 2, 4, 6, 14, 38, 42, 52, 75, 92, 102, 104, 106, and 123 (Mackay 1925, 1929); both appeared at least in burials 4, 75, and 123. Both types could have appeared in other graves as well, but in the absence of full illustrations and complete published catalogues these cannot be easily identified.

104. Type C-11 appears in Graves 73 and 182 and Type C-13 in grave 168 at Abu Salabikh (Martin, Moon, and Postgate 1985; Moon 1987).

105. Type C-13 appears in Kish burials 4, 6, and 14; Types C-14 and C-17 appear in burial 14.

106. Kish burials 2, 4, 40, 52, 75, and 123; Abu Salabikh graves 38, 73, 84, 143, 162, 168 (Martin, Moon, and Postgate 1985; Moon 1987).

Khafajah. To summarize the information from the Diyala, the small plain fruit stand appears at Khafajah in graves 122, 141, 161–62, and 164. A seal in Akkadian style (a combat scene in which the figures' arms have the upward bend peculiar to this period) occurs in grave 162 (Delougaz, Hill, and Lloyd 1967; Frankfort 1955: pl. 36:377).[107] In addition to this Akkadian seal, an Akkadian jar type (the small triangular rim on a short neck, Type C-16a) appears both in that grave and in grave 161, reinforcing their Akkadian date and supporting the extension of the time range of the stand into the Akkadian period.[108]

The wide-bodied Type C-24 jar was not common in the Diyala, appearing only in Houses 1 and graves 148, 161, and 164 at Khafajah and in the Earlier Northern Palace at Tell Asmar (Delougaz 1952). Both Khafajah Houses 1 and the Asmar Earlier Northern Palace have been redated to the early Akkadian period by Gibson (1982); and, as just mentioned, there is a demonstrably Akkadian pottery type in Khafajah grave 161 (Type C-16a).[109] Taken together, the Diyala material serves as further proof that the wide-bodied C-24 jar was in use during the early Akkadian period.

Another type relevant for investigation of transitional Early Dynastic/early Akkadian material is an ovoid jar with a high, trumpet-shaped foot. Vessels of this type appear in Houses 2 and above and in grave 164 at Khafajah;[110] and a similar ovoid vessel with a long spout and the same trumpet-shaped base appears at Tell Asmar in Houses Va (early Akkadian) and in the main level of the Northern Palace (late Akkadian).[111] A wide-shouldered jar with a similarly high foot appears in graves 122 and 141 at Khafajah.[112] Goddess-handled jars on very tall trumpet-like bases come from Houses 1 and above at Khafajah (early Akkadian) and the Asmar Northern Palace (late Akkadian).[113] The progression toward taller, narrower vessels within the Early Dynastic period has been noted (Delougaz 1952), but the early Akkadian material has not been consciously included in this progression. However, the trumpet bases in these contexts imply that the development continued into the early Akkadian period and may have peaked then.

The trumpet base also appears in graves at Abu Salabikh and Kish, sometimes co-occurring with both the small plain fruit stand and wide-shouldered jar.[114] The accumulating weight of evidence indicates that the possible time range assigned to this entire subassemblage should be extended (the trumpet bases, the small plain stand, the wide-bodied C-24 jar, and any vessels associated with them, including goddess-handled jars) from exclusively Early Dynastic into the late Early Dynastic through early Akkadian period. There is also the possibility that these vessels, in their various co-occurrences, form a "burial set" comparable to the "beer set" found in some approximately contemporary graves, but indicating a different identity for the dead or an alternative presumed activity in the afterlife.

---

107. Also included in this Khafajah grave were a goddess-handled jar and plain-rimmed narrow jars (Type C-1), which have been generally assumed, on the basis of the published Diyala sequence, to have been discontinued at the end of the Early Dynastic period. There was also a Type C-22 storage jar. The seal in the grave indicates that these three types were still in production in the Akkadian period, and the Area WF sequence confirms this. See also Gibson 1981: 86, n. 19.

108. There are other graves at Khafajah (144–45, 152, 159–60; Delougaz, Hill, and Lloyd 1967) in which this Akkadian jar, Type C-16a, appears, variously with upright-handled jars, conical bowls, and large decorated fruit stands with double-ridged rims (Area WF Type O-9); the presence of the late Akkadian jar type reinforces the theory that the presence of these last three types, although it can imply an Early Dynastic context, does not necessarily exclude an Akkadian one.

109. Other types in Khafajah grave 161 include conical bowls, a tall goddess-handled jar, the short fruit stand already discussed, a Type C-22 storage jar, and a Type C-21 rounded-base jar. This last type is present in Area WF in Burial 14 of Level XIII, along with a late Akkadian seal (Naram-Sin or later).

110. These are labeled C.686.420 and C.686.443 (Delougaz 1952). Gibson's (1982) redating assigns Houses 2 to late Early Dynastic III, but given some other pottery types found in that context (including Type C-13), the possibility exists that occupation of that level could have continued into the early Akkadian period. Grave 164 belongs to Houses 2 or above.

111. Types C.587.862 and B.676.422 (Delougaz 1952).

112. C.515.870 (ibid.). Grave 122 also includes an upright-handled jar and a Type C-18 wide-mouth vessel with a spout, which is very typical of the late Akkadian period (see Level XIVA, below). Grave 141 also includes an upright-handled jar.

113. C.527.471 and B.526.471 (ibid.). All the dates given here are the redated version of Gibson 1982.

114. At Abu Salabikh, trumpet-based jars have been published from graves 5, 15, 49, 51, 76, 83, 99, 118, 124, 177, and 198 (Martin, Moon, and Postgate 1985; Moon 1987); among these graves, the wide-bodied jar appears in 5, 51, and 124. At Kish, the trumpet-based jar is present at least in burials 1, 7, 9, 13–15, 24, 32, 39–40, 75, and 123 (Mackay 1925, 1929); among these, the small plain fruit stand appears in burial 40 and both fruit stand and wide-bodied jar in burials 14, 40, 75, and 123. There are also a few examples of the trumpet-based jar (types 240 and 241) from Ur, in PG/422, PG/547, and PG/574 (Woolley 1934). In the latter grave was found a cylinder seal in Akkadian style (U.9261) and Nissen (1966) gives the pottery types an Akkadian date. Two trumpet-based jars were also found in the early Akkadian Burial 16 at Tell ad-Deylam, along with several examples of bell-shaped tripods, strainers, cylindrical cups, and small jars (unpubl.), which together make up a set probably used in beer production (Gibson 1981: 74). Variations of this set have also been found in graves at Abu Salabikh, Kish, and Tell Razuk, but there were no such sets in Area WF.

Level XIVA

Four new types appear in the pottery assemblage of Level XIVA: two open forms and two jars.

*Type O-12:* Small conical bowl with an externally flattened or beveled rim, slightly thickened but without the overhanging edge of Type O-10 or the pulled-up shape of Type O-11 (pl. 87). Like both these related bowls, O-12 has a string-cut base and diameters mostly in the range from 14 to 18 cm. Like Type O-11, it was never as popular as the related Type O-10, but it did consistently increase in popularity through into Ur III levels (table 30). Type O-12 is generally dated from late Akkadian to Ur III, appearing at Tell Asmar in the Northern Palace and in the houses above it and in Houses III, as well as at Nippur in Area TB Levels XI and IX and Ur III houses in Area WC-3.

*Type O-13:* Small bowl with a plain inturning rim and either a flat string-cut base or a rounded base (pl. 88). This bowl is rare in the Area WF sequence, never amounting to even as much as 1% of the open forms present in any level; its variable popularity across Levels XIV to VIII is not significant (table 31). Type O-13 belongs primarily in the Ur III period (Tell Asmar Houses III–I, Nippur Area WC-3, Ur III–Isin-Larsa contexts at Uruk, and Ur III levels at Susa), but it also appears in late Akkadian contexts at Umm al-Hafriyat and in late Akkadian to Ur III graves at Ur.

*Type C-18:* Wide-mouth vessel with a squared-off rim, short rounded shoulder and a large spout below the rim (pls. 113–14:1–3). This is a well-known type used in surveys (Adams 1965; Gibson 1972a; Martin 1988) as a marker of the Akkadian period. In fact, most of its attestations from excavated contexts are late Akkadian: Tell Asmar Houses IVa, Nippur North Temple Level I, late Akkadian to Ur III graves at Ur, and even the "Naram-Sin Palace" at Tell Brak. The Area WF sequence also indicates that it did not appear until the later Akkadian, peaked in Level XI, and continued in use in the Ur III period (table 63).

*Type C-20:* Jar with a tall, slightly flared neck, fine plain or triangular rim, and a narrow, sharply carinated shoulder (pls. 115, 126:4). This type developed over the course of the next five levels into a tall, almost cylindrical jar with a low center of gravity and a horizontal ridge at the neck replacing the narrow shoulder (especially pl. 115:9).[115] In its final version (not present in Area WF until Level VIII), it is attested at Tell Asmar, Tell al-Wilayah, Nippur Area TB, Tello, Ur, and Susa, as well as being used in surveys as an Akkadian–Ur III type (Adams 1965; Martin 1988).[116] The earlier version is less common but does occur at Abu Salabikh (in "post-Early Dynastic" context), Ur, and even Tell Brak (Akkadian and post-Akkadian). In Area WF, the popularity of this type increases fairly consistently from its initial appearance through Level VI (table 65).

A vessel tentatively assigned to this level comes from the deep shaft that formed part of the first phase of Burial 14: a cylindrical bowl with thick, horizontally ridged sides (19 N 52, pl. 142:1).[117] It was inverted on a surface within the fill of the shaft, and this surface is associated with Skeleton 6, attributed to Level XIV by a combination of stratigraphic probabilities and pottery parallels. Similar ridged cylindrical vessels appear at other sites in Early Dynastic III–Akkadian and Akkadian contexts: at the Ur Cemetery (Woolley 1934: PG/896, along with a Type C-20 jar); at Tell Asmar Houses Vc and the Northern Palace; in Khafajah Houses 1; and at Kish in graves 62, 87, and 106. Only a single additional sherd of this vessel form came from Area WF, in Level XIIIB (H1079:6; pl. 127:6).

Unique vessels, or single examples of a type, are rare in the Area WF sequence but do occasionally appear. From Level XIVA are two sherds from such vessels: a small bowl with slightly incurved sides in an unusual dark, burnished fabric (H540:3; pl. 127:7); and a small "hole-mouthed" vessel with a double-pierced irregular lug handle near the rim (I319:3; pl. 127:8). There are no obvious contemporary parallels for either vessel, though lug handles are relatively more common in northern Mesopotamia at this time.

*Burial Groups:* The group of pottery with Burial 14, Skeleton 6, contains some useful examples of jars present elsewhere only as sherds. There is a group of vessels that might be assumed to belong to the late Early Dynastic pe-

---

115. This morphological progression can best be seen in McCown and Haines 1967, pl. 85:1–6, giving examples of this type from mid-Akkadian through early Isin-Larsa levels of Nippur Area TB.

116. In Area WF, the earlier carinated-shoulder version continues to be present as sherds in occupational material through Level VI; the later ridged version first appears in Level VIII. As with Type C-13, this probably should have been split into two types, or at least subtypes; however, the presence of some sherds that were transitional between the two distinct forms made such a split difficult, and the subtypes were left combined.

117. Since only one whole vessel and one sherd of this form were found in Area WF, it was not given a type number.

riod in the absence of other evidence: a Type O-9 fruit stand, narrow Type C-1 jar, and group of Type O-1 conical bowls (respectively, 19 N 85, 87, and 91–95, I480, I482:2–6; pls. 136:5–6, 137:12, 137:7, 137:6, 137:3–4, 137:1–2, 137:9–10, 137:8). The presence in the grave of two Type C-17 jars (19 N 90 and 88; pl. 138:1–2) and one jar each of Types C-24 and C-14 (19 N 84 and 89; pl. 136:7, 3) indicate a date in the Akkadian period. This finding reinforces the interpretation that the sherds of those former types, where present in the Area WF sequence in Akkadian levels, had been produced at the time rather than being redeposited from earlier levels. The comb incision on the fruit stand reinforces the proposed extension of this decorative technique into the Akkadian period.

*Relative Frequencies and Date*: It is from this level through Level XII that the use of convex jar bases (Type B-6, usually associated with rim Type C-22) become significant, although never common; one example appears in Level XVII, but the type's re-occurrence at this point in the sequence could mark the beginning of its more consistent use. In Level XIV, conical bowls are still the most numerous form encountered, both the plain rim (Type O-1) and the less common overhanging rim (Type O-10).[118] The average height of Type O-1 conical bowls for combined Level XIV, Phases A and B, is 5.3 cm, a further decrease from the average in Level XV (table 12). The average diameter of the Type O-1 bowl decreases again in this level, from 14 to 16 cm in previous levels down to 12 to 14 cm in this level. There are still examples with both larger and smaller diameters, but the majority of bowls are in this reduced range. There is an unusually large number of foundation deposits in this level, almost all of which are single examples or pairs of Type O-1 bowls, all apparently empty (H1101:1, 2, H536, I1:1–4; pl. 124:2–8; 19 N 55, 18 N 123 and 124, 18 N 138, H1009:1; pl. 125:6–8, 12–13). Only one pair of foundation deposit bowls was Type O-10 (18 N 190 and 189; pl. 125:9–10).

Two unusual foundation deposit groups each comprise a single Type O-1 conical bowl covering a smaller jar or cup. In Level XIVA, the bowl covered a cylindrical cup with four pinched feet and vertically incised sides (18 N 137 and 136; pl. 127:2–3);[119] in Level XIVB, the bowl covered a small version of the C-4 jar (I113 and 115; pl. 127:4–5).

The objects from this level (baked-clay figurines and copper/bronze pins and weapons) have mostly Akkadian parallels, and a cylinder seal from this level gives an unambiguous dating within the Akkadian period (*Chapter 4*). The pottery types introduced in this level could be usable as markers of later Akkadian occupation, in contrast to the forms that have been identified previously as transitional or early Akkadian forms.

## Level XIII

There are few changes in the pottery from Level XIV to XIII. At this point appeared the first examples of one new open type.

*Type O-15:* Large bowl with an everted, rounded-rectangular rim and gently carinated sides (pl. 89:4–6). Type O-15 is rare; it appears in "Early Dynastic/Akkadian" levels at Tell Sabra (Hamrin) and "Early Dynastic IIIb" levels at Tell al-Hiba but has so far not been illustrated from any other contemporary site. This type is present in Area WF in Levels XIII and XII only (table 33).

*Type B-8:* Large rounded jar base. The first recorded example of this type comes from Level XIIIB, but round base fragments could be difficult to distinguish from jar shoulders or other body sherds and may have been present, but not recorded, in prior levels. This difficulty is borne out by the fact that the recorded examples remained infrequent in subsequent levels.

*Type D-4:* The first comb-incised decoration on sherds in occupational material (versus incision with a single point, D-2) occurs in Level XIII. Single-point incision continues and includes one example of a fruit stand stem with an elaborate design of a palm tree (pl. 80:5).

---

118. Note in table 14 that there is one sherd in Level XIVA from a carinated bowl (Type O-17), an Ur III period type out of place in this Akkadian level. It seems likely that this sherd is intrusive, especially as examples of this type do not appear again in the sequence until Level XI. Several drains cut down from Ur III and Isin-Larsa levels into earlier strata, composed of pottery rings set into a cut, the sides of which were packed with sherds (see *Chapter 1*). This Type O-17 sherd comes from a room into which one of these drains cut, and it is likely that the drain supplied this sherd, which was accidentally included in the collection from occupational debris.

119. See the discussion of miniature pottery in *Chapter 4* for further examples of the four-footed cup.

Comb incision has customarily been associated with Early Dynastic III pottery (Delougaz 1952, Moon 1987) and its absence in the Area WF sounding until levels of indisputably late Akkadian date[120] demands explanation. Comb incision is so common in Area WF, once it does appear, that its absence in earlier levels is unlikely to be the result of small sampling size or some other collection or deposition factor. Other excavations at Nippur could confirm the Akkadian date for the beginning of comb incision at the site. There is only one published example of comb incision from the North Temple, from Level IV (McCown, Haines, and Biggs 1978: pl. 44:11), a stratum dated by the excavators to Early Dynastic III, but which may be transitional to early Akkadian. Among the study sherds from the North Temple at the Oriental Institute are several more examples of comb incision from Level IV, along with single-point incision; it is not until Level III that the decoration is entirely comb-produced. Other sites where comb incision is very common in Akkadian levels include Tepe al-Atiqeh in the Hamrin and Umm al-Hafriyat (M. Gibson, pers. comm.).

The introduction of comb incision at other sites seems to hover around the early Akkadian period. At the Diyala sites, comb incision first appears in levels that are published as Early Dynastic III or "Protoimperial" (Asmar Houses V, Khafajah Houses 1), and which have since been redated to early Akkadian (Gibson 1982). Similarly, in the Hamrin, it was found at Tell Sabra in occupation levels and in a grave (grave 5370) published as "Early Dynastic III/Akkadian" (Tunca 1987). However, the presence in that Tell Sabra grave of a variant of the later Akkadian Area WF Type C-16a makes a dating entirely in the Akkadian period probable.

The examples of comb-incised vessels from graves in the A Cemetery at Kish could also belong in the early Akkadian, rather than Early Dynastic III, given the expanded range of dates allowed for those graves. From Tell al-Wilayah, said to be late Early Dynastic III, both single-point and comb incision are shown in the excavation report (Madhlum 1960: fig. 9:10–11). However, occupation at this site continued into the Akkadian and even Ur III periods (some of the pottery illustrated is Akkadian or Ur III, e.g., Area WF Types O-17, C-13b, C-20, and C-28).

At Abu Salabikh there are comb-incised vessels dated to Early Dynastic III, and Abu Salabikh is too close geographically to Nippur for this temporal disparity to be caused by a regional lag in its adoption. The explanation may lie in the type of vessels on which the decoration appears. Such decoration is most often found on fruit stands and upright-handled jars; these vessels are frequent in graves (the main context for this period at Abu Salabikh) and are less common in occupational material. Both vessel types are represented in late Early Dynastic and Akkadian levels in Area WF at Nippur, but the different contexts, occupational in Area WF versus primarily burial at Abu Salabikh, may indicate a functional explanation for the apparent difference in the date of appearance of comb incision. Comb incision does not appear in the Ur Cemetery material, but it must be admitted that the two most relevant pottery types are rare there. Also, given Ur's distance from Nippur and the lack of other coincidences between the pottery assemblages of Ur and more central sites, the absence of comb incision at Ur could genuinely be ascribed to regional variation. (Even single-point incision is rare at Ur.)

Comb incision is conspicuously absent at some sites in "Early Dynastic III" levels where it might be expected if an Early Dynastic III date for this decoration is correct. At Tell al-Hiba, the "Early Dynastic IIIb" building in Area C certainly could be expected to contain examples of comb incision, but the only illustrated examples of incised decoration there are made with a single point (Bahrani 1989; the exception, pl. 41:6, is an intrusive Ur III/Isin-Larsa sherd). Similarly, at Fara, a site with a good collection of Early Dynastic IIIa material, only single-point incision decoration was found by either of the two expeditions (D.O.G. and the University of Pennsylvania; Martin 1988).

Several unique or unusual vessels are represented among the sherds from this level. These include a rim fragment of a horizontally ridged cylindrical pot (H1079:6; pl. 127:6), a smaller version of the vessel found in the shaft of Burial 14. A sherd from a carinated vessel has a finely flared rim with a vertical hole, perhaps for securing a lid (I122:5; pl. 127:9). A goddess handle separated cleanly from the body of its jar (D-8) is possibly an early and redeposited fragment, given its small dimensions and lack of detail (I31: pl. 127:16). The beveled-ledge rim from a gray burnished bowl (H1057:4; pl. 127:13) could be one of the few sherds from northern Mesopotamian Akkadian forms to percolate into the southern plains. The tall narrow jar with unusually wide mouth on a long neck could be a Type C-1 jar that warped during firing (I515:1; pl. 126:5).

---

120. Level XIII is dated by a late Akkadian sealing from the courtyard and a late Akkadian cylinder seal in Burial 14, with Skeleton 2, to at least the reign of Naram-Sin (see *Chapter 4*); the following level, Level XII, is dated to the early years of the reign of Sharkalisharri by a group of four tablets.

*Burial Groups*: Skeleton 2 of Burial 14 was interred with a number of identifiably late Akkadian jars, including two of Type C-13b (19 N 42 and 47; pl. 150:1–2), one C-16b (I159/315; pl. 148:6), one C-20 (19 N 51; pl. 149:1), and three round-based C-21 vessels in two different sizes (19 N 35, 40, and 53; pl. 149:2–4). This is the first attestation of the variant Type C-13b. The geographical distribution of this smaller version of the double-ridged rim jar is especially wide, reaching at least from Ur to Assur, in contexts of the Akkadian and Ur III periods. In southern Mesopotamia it is present at Umm el-Jīr in Akkadian and Ur III levels, at Ur in Akkadian graves, at Isin in Ur III contexts, and at Nippur in Akkadian levels of Area TB and Ur III levels of Area WC-3. There are also types with Burial 14, Skeleton 2, that continue from the late Early Dynastic to the early Akkadian, including one Type C-22 with a hole near the base, as in the Early Dynastic III–early Akkadian graves at Tell Razuk and Tell Madhhur (19 N 43; pl. 151:1). The conical bowls are mostly Type O-1 (19 N 17, 32, 49–50, I184, 332:1–2, 338:1–4; pls. 147:11, 147:5, 147:9, 147:4, 147:7, 147:10, 147:1–2, 147:6, 147:3, 147:8), but the Akkadian forms Type O-10 (19 N 48, I338:5–6, 19 N 31; pl. 148:1–3, 5) and O-12 (I338:7; pl. 148:4) also appear.

Skeletons 3 and 4 of Burial 14 were associated with vessels (goddess-handled jar and fruit stand) that, if viewed in isolation and in the absence of more tightly datable objects, could be ascribed to the late Early Dynastic period. The goddess-handled jar (19 N 44; pls. 143–44) has the exaggerated dimensions (very high neck, elongated body, and large handle placed high on the shoulder and nearly touching the rim) that mark it as late in the development of the type (Delougaz 1952:87). Delougaz refers to the progression of this trend of elongation into the "Protoimperial" period (which should now be understood as the early Akkadian), but the trend has not yet been tracked into the Akkadian period. The rarity of this vessel in its complete state in the Area WF sequence means it is not possible to illustrate the continuation of the trend here, but the A Cemetery at Kish could well hold this key sequence. The fruit stand is unusually large with a bowl almost half a meter across (H1097; pl. 142:5). Virtually no possibility exists that either could be a late Early Dynastic vessel that appears in a late Akkadian context; while seals were often retained as heirlooms, it is extremely rare for this to occur with pottery.

*Relative Frequencies and Date*: Plain-rimmed conical bowls (Type O-1) become still shallower in this level, with an average depth of 4.9 cm, as compared to 5.3 cm in Level XIV (table 12). There is a real jump in the popularity of the Type O-10 version of the small bowl, with a corresponding, though less dramatic, decrease in the frequency of the Type O-1 version. Type C-14 reaches its greatest popularity in this level (table 57), while Type C-9, possibly a variant rim on the same jar or belonging to a vessel closely comparable in size and volume, is at its lowest before increasing in popularity again through Level IX (table 52). Type C-22 also reaches a peak of popularity, while C-24 declines significantly (tables 67–68). Level XIII is securely dated to the late Akkadian period (the reign of Naram-Sin or later) by a sealing from occupational material and a cylinder seal in Burial 14.

Level XII

Three forms first appear during occupation of this level, all of which are known from late Akkadian and especially Ur III contexts elsewhere.

*Type O-14:* Small beveled-rim deep cup (pl. 89:1–3). Type O-14 is very common in Akkadian contexts at Umm el-Jīr and in Akkadian and Ur III contexts at Umm al-Hafriyat. It also occurs occasionally in Akkadian levels in the Diyala and in Nippur Area TB, as well as in one grave at Abu Salabikh (grave 79). It is not particularly common in Area WF (table 32) and its beveled rim is not as exaggerated as in the Diyala and at Umm el-Jīr.

*Type O-16:* Small lid with an exaggerated ledge rim (pl. 89:7–8). This type is so common in Ur III levels at Nippur Area WC-3 and at Umm al-Hafriyat that it has been assumed to be a purely Ur III type (Gibson, pers. comm.). It is found in Ur III contexts at Isin, Tello, and Susa, however, its presence in Level XII along with tablets probably dating to Sharkalisharri indicates that it was first produced in the late Akkadian period, although it is a rare form in Area WF (table 34). It also occurs in Tell Asmar Houses IVa (late Akkadian) and in levels from the late Akkadian period in Area TB at Nippur (Hansen 1965) and is judged to have a range from the Akkadian through Old Babylonian period at Uruk (van Ess 1988).

*Type C-25a:* Square ledge rim (pl. 119) belonging to a wide-mouth jar with a cylindrical neck, with a sharp join to a globular or piriform body. At Umm al-Hafriyat and Nippur Area WC-3, this type is dated to late Akkadian and Ur III. In the Area WF sequence, it appears in small but significant numbers through the Ur III levels (table 69). As a whole vessel, this type is closely related to C-13b and C-28, which have different rim morphologies but similar body shape and size.

Two sherds from probable northern Mesopotamian imports were found in this level: the shoulder and upper body of a bottle with fine incised lines on the shoulder and a pair of double-pierced vertical lug handles (I121:3; pl. 127:11), plus a gray, burnished, thick plain rim from a shallow conical bowl (H119:4; pl. 127:12). In both cases the ware is unusually fine with very fine and sparse mineral temper, typical of northern Mesopotamia during the Akkadian period.

*Burial Groups:* Burial 14, Skeleton 1, had clusters of vessels positioned around the body, similar to the arrangement encountered with Skeleton 2. There are two groups comprising a mixture of Type O-1 (19 N 10, I36, I1118–21; pl. 153:2–3, 153:1, 153:6, 153:5, 153:4), Type O-10 (I106, I109, H1122; pl. 153:10–12), Type O-11 (H1123; pl. 153:8), and Type O-12 bowls (I107, I102; pl. 153:7, 9), as well as three Type C-22 storage jars (H1109, I105, I104; pl. 155:1–3). In addition, four jars match quite closely the four jars interred with Burial 14, Skeleton 6. In the latter grave were two long-necked jars (Type C-17), one rounded-base jar (Type C-24), and one medium-sized jar (Type C-14); the corresponding jars with Skeleton 1 include two comparable long-necked jars (in this case slightly different versions of C-24 [I40/103, 18 N 187; pls. 68b, 154:1–2]), a Type C-24 rounded-base jar with the same red burnishing as seen on the jar with Burial 16 (H1111; pl. 154:3), and a medium-sized Type C-16a jar (H1124; pl. 154:4). It is tempting to reconstruct this set of four jars as a typical "household" assemblage of expected jar types, whether customarily used for particular functions or for containing specific resources. This set would then have been carried for use in the afterlife.

*Relative Frequencies and Date:* There is not much change among open forms found in Level XII, other than an increase in the number of small bowls with overhanging rims (Type O-10) and with thickened and upturned rims (Type O-11). The heights of Type O-1 bowls of the combined Level XII, Phases B and A, average 4.4 cm — only a 0.5 cm decrease from the 4.9 cm average in Level XIII (table 12). However, this small change is significant within the larger trend of decrease from level to level. The set of foundation deposit bowls from this level contains two Type O-1 bowls (I3:1–2; pl. 124:10–11).

Important changes in the relative percentages of closed types do occur in the assemblage of this level. The most notable change is the increased percentage of jars with sharp triangular rims on short necks, with and without the horizontally ridged shoulder (Types C-16a–b; tables 59–60). This increase coincides with the first indications of a genuine decrease in the popularity of plain-rimmed jars with short and medium necks (Types C-1 and C-3; tables 44, 46); while these latter forms are thought to have ceased to be produced after the Early Dynastic period (Delougaz 1952), it seems they did not actually do so until late in the Akkadian period. Their relatively large numbers in Levels XVII through X cannot be due only to sherds moving up from earlier levels, especially given the nature of the occupation in Area WF — few very deep pits were encountered that might have been the means of introducing the earlier types; and even the presence of earlier sherds in the bricks of later levels cannot account for the high frequencies encountered. It must be that these two forms were still in production at this late date.

This level is dated to the late Akkadian period by two cylinder seals in Burial 14, refined on the basis of tablets from occupational material probably to the reign of Sharkalisharri (*Chapter 1*). The assemblage is closely similar to that of the previous level.

## Level XI

Another major change in the ceramic assemblage, the third and final change to occur in this portion of the Area WF sequence, is marked by the introduction of nine new types in Level XI (five open forms and four closed forms). This level probably covers the transition from the Akkadian into the Ur III period.

*Type O-17:* Small bowl with a carination just below the rim that varies from a gentle bend to an exaggerated groove (pl. 90). Excavations in Area WC-3 and Area TB at Nippur and at Umm al-Hafriyat and Isin indicate that this type is typical of the Ur III through Isin-Larsa periods.[121] However, a slightly wider and deeper version is present in late Akkadian contexts at a few sites: Tell Asmar, Umm el-Jīr, Umm al-Hafriyat, Uruk, Ur, and Susa. Although a single (probably) intrusive sherd of this type appears in Level XIVA, the type is present in its proper context for the first time in Level XI and increases in percentage rapidly in subsequent levels through Level VI (table 35).

---

121. R. Zettler, in an analysis of bowls of this type from Area WA at Nippur and Umm al-Hafriyat (unpubl.), traced the gradual reduction in the depth of carination from the Ur III through the Isin-Larsa periods. This reduction trend is also visible in the Area WF examples.

*Type O-18:* Large carinated-sided bowl with a squared ledge rim (pl. 91:1–2). This is probably a development from the earlier Type O-15, with which it has much in common (and which no longer appears in Area WF, at this level). Type O-18 is present at Susa in an Ur III context but does not seem to have been common in southern Mesopotamia. In Area WF it is present only in Levels XI and X (table 36).

*Type O-19:* Large bowl with an elongated rounded-triangular rim (pl. 92). This form is related to the less distinctive Type O-3 large bowls that were still in production. Like Type O-18, this was never a common form in Area WF, though it is present in small numbers through Level VII (table 37).

*Type O-20:* Large vessel with a squared rim on a slightly constricted neck[122] and horizontally grooved sides (pl. 91:3–5). This type is attested in an Akkadian level at Nippur Area TB (Level XI) but seems to be rare beyond Nippur. Even in Area WF, sherds of this type are found only in Levels XI and IX (table 38).

*Type O-21:* Carinated-sided large bowl with a rounded, thickened rim (pl. 93). This type is clearly related to Types O-15 and O-18 but has a slightly smaller diameter, 20–24 cm compared with up to 34 cm for the latter types. Examples have been found in Early Dynastic IIIb contexts at al-Hiba and in an Akkadian level at Umm el-Jīr. The type could have begun earlier but did not appear in the Area WF sequence until well after it first began to be produced, its relative rarity explaining why it is not seen earlier. Once present, it is not common, although it occurs through Level VIII (table 39).

*Type C-16c:* Variant of the jar with small triangular rim, Type C-16, also with applied horizontal ridges as in C-16b, but with a more sloped shoulder, a far larger diameter (35 cm or greater versus the 12–20 cm of C-16b), and thicker walls (pl. 111). Type C-16c has been used as a marker of the Akkadian period for regional surveys in southern Mesopotamia (Adams 1981); it has also been found in excavated contexts at Umm el-Jīr. In Area WF it was never as popular as the C-16a and 16b variants and disappears from the sequence after Level VIII, while the other two continue (table 61).

*Type C-26:* Bag-shaped, round-based jar with a flaring neck and thickened rim bearing a narrow horizontal groove (pl. 121:1–2). Type C-26 is extremely rare, represented in Area WF by only two examples, both from Level XIB (table 71). Direct parallels are not found, but roughly similar vessels at Khafajah, Nippur Area TB, and Ur are dated from early Akkadian through Ur III.

*Type C-27:* Wide-mouth jar with a triangular or oval rim on a low neck and a rounded shoulder decorated with shallow horizontal grooves (pl. 121:3–6). Type C-27 is similar to a form found at sites in northern Mesopotamia (Nineveh, Tell Brak), but the northern version has horizontal comb incision, rather than grooves, and a more angular rim. Type C-27 is rare but very distinctive and easily recognizable. In Area WF it is found in Levels XI and IX (table 72); it may prove to be a useful archaeological indicator of the Akkadian–Ur III transition.

*Type C-28:* Triple-ridged rim on a low flaring neck from a wide-bodied, round-based jar (pl. 120:5–7). Type C-28 has been used in surveys as an Akkadian or Ur III period marker (Adams 1981; Adams and Nissen 1972; Gibson 1972a) and is widely attested in Ur III levels all over southern Mesopotamia as well as at Susa and Nuzi. Related multiple-ridged or -grooved rims also come from post-Akkadian levels at northern Mesopotamian sites such as Chagar Bazar. This type, like the closely related Type C-13b, is another example of Adams and Nissen's "very articulated rims" characteristic of the Akkadian–Ur III period (1972: 103). The double rim of Type C-13 belongs mainly in the Akkadian period, while the triple ridge is more typically a feature of the Ur III period. Both Type C-13b and C-28 are closely related to Type C-25a and b as well, in terms of vessel form (table 73).

Another sherd of a northern Mesopotamian form appears in this level: a rounded pot with very fine rim, double-pierced vertical lug handles, and a row of distinctively northern Akkadian decoration below the rim: rows of notches in alternate directions framed by incised horizontal lines (H841:5; pl. 127:10). The ware is gray, smooth, very fine and hard, with no visible temper; although the fabric is not true "stoneware," the density and hardness are notable.

---

122. Although the neck on this vessel (narrowing the rim slightly from the maximum diameter) indicates that it should technically be considered a "closed" form, the width of the mouth and its similarity to Types O-24 and O-25 (see below) places it functionally among open forms.

*Burial Group:* The two Type O-1 bowls with Burial 11 are very shallow (3.8 and 4.7 cm), as is to be expected at this level in the sequence.

*Relative Frequencies and Date:* The Type O-1 bowls undergo a further reduction in average height, to 3.8 cm (table 12). Although the popularity of Type O-1 was on the decrease from Level XIII, when there occur the first significant numbers of Type O-10 bowls, the foundation deposits throughout Area WF are still made almost entirely with Type O-1 bowls; the single inverted bowl deposit from Level XI is a Type O-1 (H138:1; pl. 124:9). The triangular-rim storage jar with horizontally ridged shoulder (Type C-16b; table 60) continues to increase in relative frequency, as does the wide-mouth spouted vessel (Type C-18; table 63). The rounded rim on a short to medium neck (Type C-14) decreases again, but the related Type C-9 increases simultaneously, resulting in a relatively stable percentage from the previous level to this, for the combination of the two forms (tables 57, 52).

The mixed dating of types from this level, ranging from late Akkadian into Ur III, and the absence of independently datable objects, indicates that Level XI probably represents a transition between the two periods. The next level is tentatively dated to the Ur III period (see below), therefore these types could be used as markers of the early Ur III period, but they may also belong to the very late Akkadian.

Level X

Two new forms, a jar and a bowl both distinctive of the Ur III period, appear in this level.

*Type O-22:* Shallow bowl with a band rim (pl. 94:1–11). These bowls have string-cut bases and there is great variation seen in the band rim, from a simple flare to an exaggerated overhang. This type, like the carinated bowl Type O-17, is known from excavations at Nippur (Areas WC-3 and TB), Umm al-Hafriyat, and Isin, to be typical of the Ur III period, with a slight continuation into the early Isin-Larsa period. In Area WF, its popularity was erratic, but its presence is consistent through Level VI (table 40).

*Type C-29:* Thickened, rounded rim with a distinctive droop in its lower surface, bent nearly perpendicular to a medium-to-high flaring neck (pl. 122). The contexts in which this jar type has been found at other sites are invariably Ur III in date. It is noted as an important Ur III type at Umm al-Hafriyat and Nippur Area WC-3 and it is also present at Abu Salabikh (in late drains), Uruk, and Susa. There are no complete examples from Area WF, but it is known from whole vessels found in graves in Area WC-3 at Nippur that the jar is large, with an elongated ovoid body and a convex base. Like Type O-22, it is present, though variable in frequency, through Level VI (table 74).

*Relative Frequencies and Date:* The first significant numbers of the small carinated bowl (Type O-17) belong to this level (table 35). Most of the open types continued in use from Level XI, but the small beveled-rim cup (Type O-14; table 32) and the double ridged-rim fruit stand (Type O-9; table 27) seem to be exclusively Akkadian since they are no longer present. The jar types from Level XI continue with little significant variation in percentages into Level X.

Examples of Type O-1 bowls preserved from rim to base are too few in number to produce a significant average height for this level or for the rest of the levels in the Area WF sequence, but what examples there are fall just to either side of 4.0 cm, which seems to be the approximate minimum functional height.

The presence of the Type C-29 jar and significant numbers of Type O-17 carinated bowls points to a probable date for this level in the early Ur III period.

Level IX

*Relative Frequencies and Date:* No new pottery types appear in this level and the frequencies of open forms remain fairly constant from the previous level. The small bowl Types O-17 and O-22 are not yet as numerous as the plain-rimmed bowls (Type O-1) but increase dramatically in percentage in the following level. Level IX also marks the beginning of the decline in popularity of Type O-10, the conical bowl with overhanging rim (table 28). Many of the less common open types of previous levels are not attested in this level. This does not mean, however, that they had ceased to be produced; unfortunately, the context for much of the pottery in this level is a trash pit, which potentially skews the frequencies within the pottery sample.

The relative frequencies of most of the jar types stays nearly the same as in Level X. However, the majority of the sherds recovered from the pit are from large jars, which surely has raised the percentage of such large types as

C-16a, C-16b, C-16c, and C-20 (tables 59–61, 65). Smaller vessels present in low frequencies or not at all, such as C-4 and C-21 (tables 47, 66), are more likely to have been allowed to lie where they were broken, rather than being removed and redeposited in the trash pit. Other types, such as C-28, are so infrequently represented in the sequence that the small sample size from this level could explain their apparent decrease in percentage or disappearance (table 73). A number of more common types do not disappear in this level, but their relative percentages within the closed form total decreases, only to be followed by an increase in the next level; these include Types C-1, C-2, C-14, and C-18 (tables 44–45, 57, 63). This decrease in percentage probably reflects the circumstance of deposition, not a decrease in their production and use.

This level is securely dated within the Ur III period by a distinctive male figurine placed below a wall (18 N 81; pl. 163:13, see *Chapter 4*). The pottery evidence underscores this dating.

Level VIII

Three new distinctive, yet relatively uncommon, types first appear in this level.

*Type O-23:* Small, hemispherical bowl-shaped strainer (pl. 94:12–13). Strainers such as this have been recovered from late Akkadian through Isin-Larsa levels in the Diyala and at Umm el-Jīr, Nippur Area TB, Uruk, and Ur. This form is also present in post-Akkadian levels in northern Mesopotamia (e.g., Nineveh, Tell Taya, Tell Brak, Chagar Bazar). There are only a few sherds of this form in Area WF, in this level and Level VII (table 41).

*Type O-24:* Massive, wide-mouth vessel with a vertically elongated triangular rim and horizontal comb incision on its sides (pl. 95:1). This form could be a variant of Type O-20, with its triangular rim contrasting with the squarish rim of Type O-20 and comb incision rather than horizontal grooves. However, the diameter of Type O-24 is far larger than that of O-20, 50 cm or more as compared to 32 to 38 cm. The frequency of this form matches that of O-23: both are present only in Levels VIII and VII (table 42).

*Type C-25b:* Variant of the wide-ledge rim vessel introduced in Level XII (pl. 120:1–4). The ledge rim in this version is an elongated, almost exaggerated, rectangle compared to the square shape of the C-25a variant and it frequently has a lightly grooved outer edge. This variant has been recognized at Umm al-Hafriyat and Nippur Area WC-3 and also appears at Tello, all in Ur III contexts. In Area WF it appears only in Levels VIII and VI (table 70).

*Relative Frequencies and Date:* In the pottery assemblage from Level VIII, some types from previous levels decreased or disappeared. The increasing popularity of the carinated-sided bowl, Type O-17, finally has an impact on the overwhelming frequency of the conical bowl, Type O-1, which Type O-17 must match in function. Both small bowl Types O-1 and O-10 decrease sharply in frequency and Type O-12 decreases slightly (tables 19, 28, 30), while their replacements, the carinated- and band-rim bowls Types O-17 and O-22, significantly increase (tables 35, 40).

Two types important in the Akkadian levels and carried over into the Ur III period, the large spouted vessel (Type C-18) and the double-ridged rim jar (Type C-13), both occur for the last time in Level VIII. Several other important types, such as C-14, C-16c, and C-17, also disappear from the sequence after this level. Meanwhile, the jar with the flared rim and a droop below (Type C-29) reaches its highest attested frequency (table 74). The later version of Type C-20, a cylindrical jar with a ridge below the rim replacing the short carinated shoulder of the earlier form, first appears in this level. This later version has been dated to late Akkadian through Isin-Larsa periods and is a widespread type, occurring at Tell Asmar, Tell al-Wilayah, Nippur Area TB, Tello, Uruk, Ur, and Susa. Given the overall continuity of assemblage from the previous level, the level is dated to the Ur III period.

Level VII

*Relative Frequencies and Date:* No new pottery types appear in this level. The relative percentages of some pottery types encountered in Level VII are unexpected, but this is probably due to the nature of the debris, that is, accumulation in an abandoned building, as well as to a rather small sample size. For instance, the combined percentages of the carinated bowl (Type O-17) and band-rim bowl (Type O-22) drop dramatically from the previous level (tables 35, 40). This decrease is an aberration, however, since both types reach their highest attested percentages in the following level.

The small sample size also creates an apparent increase in the percentage of four open vessels (Types O-3, O-19, O-23, and O-24; tables 21, 37, 41–42), which are rarer in other levels with larger, and surely more representative, samples. On the other hand, all these large vessel types could be argued to have been used in food processing, and we could be seeing the result of an alteration in pattern of use in the area. The small sample has a further impact on the relative percentages of several jar types: the ridged-shouldered jar with the triangular rim (Type C-16b) makes up almost one-fourth of the closed forms found, with the plain-shouldered version (Type C-16a) and the late version of Type C-20 (with the ridge on the neck) close behind at one-fifth each. Since these are all fairly large vessels, broken ones are more likely to have been disposed of in a convenient abandoned building, while smaller broken vessels would have been allowed to stay on floors until covered over. In addition, both Types C-16b and Type C-20 are easily identifiable from body sherds as well as rims, adding another bias in their favor. It must be acknowledged that if there were preserved habitation floors for this level, the percentages might be very different. A date within the Ur III period is probable.

Level VI

One new type is found in the assemblage of this level, the last intact level of the third-millennium B.C. sequence.

*Type O-25:* Large, wide-mouth vessel with comb-incised sides, related to Types O-20 and O-24 (pl. 95:2–3). This type, here seen for the first time in a level possibly dated to the very late Ur III or early Isin-Larsa period, is identified by Adams (1981) as an Akkadian type, but there is no evidence it appeared that early, from this or any other excavation. The comb incision on this vessel is a combination of straight horizontal and wavy lines; such decoration is common in the Ur III levels at Umm al-Hafriyat and at Nippur Area WC-3 and is also attested in Ur III levels of Nippur Area TB and Susa.[123]

*Relative Frequencies and Date:* The pottery collected from Level VI is a small sample, and thus some unusual relative percentages are encountered. Type O-1 plain-rim bowls are still the most common type, but their percentage, 71% of the total open forms, is the second lowest attested for this type in the Area WF sequence. The carinated bowls and band-rim bowls (Types O-17 and O-22) are correspondingly at their highest percentages.

The most common jar type is the small triangular rim with a ridged shoulder (Type C-16b), which reaches its highest relative percentage, 32% of the closed form total (table 60). As in the previous level, however, the easy identification of this jar and of Type C-20 from body sherds as well as rims means that these two are possibly over-represented in the diagnostic sherd count. Only very small numbers and percentages of other jar types appear in Level VI. A date late in the Ur III or within the early Isin-Larsa period is probable for this level, given the likelihood of carry-over of Ur III types into the following period.

## Second-millennium B.C. Pottery

Collection and recording techniques for the Kassite period ceramic material were the same as those for levels of the third millennium B.C. However, the analysis was necessarily far less rigorous. The amount of pottery present in the single level of Kassite occupation is too small to warrant generation of relative percentages of types or other quantitative assessment. Furthermore, the level was badly disturbed by later burial pits and also contained a substantial proportion of earlier sherd material.

The sand temper of the third-millennium B.C. pottery was replaced in the second and first millennia B.C. by mostly organic temper. In addition, there are possible firing developments, or else different clay sources were being utilized following the Old Babylonian and early Kassite near-abandonment of the site, since the Kassite pottery in particular frequently has a yellow fabric rarely seen in the material of the third millennium B.C.

Well-dated Kassite pottery from other excavation areas at Nippur (Areas WC-1 and TA) provides the best parallels for the sparse second-millennium B.C. material in Level V.

---

123. The combination of straight and wavy combed decoration also appears in northern Mesopotamia in post-Akkadian contexts (Nineveh, Assur, Tell Brak, Chagar Bazar), but the diagonal punctate motif that often appears with comb incision on vessels in the north (made by pressing the same comb instrument into the clay but without dragging it around the pot) was never made in the south.

Level V

The architecture and other in situ material from this level do not form a coherent unit and the pottery falls into a range of dates. The damage done to this level by ancient erosion and later disturbances makes the internal phasing difficult to reconstruct. The pottery from Level VA, the layer that covered the walls of Level VI (Loci 18–19), is primarily late Akkadian–Ur III in date, including the conical bowl Type O-1 and band-rim bowl Type O-22, plus sherds of horizontally ridged-shoulder jars (Type C-16b) and a triple ridged-rim jar rim (Type C-28). All these types would have been at home in the preceding levels. There is only one example of a vessel that could be later than the third millennium B.C.: the base and sides of a small bowl similar to the distinctive "wavy-sided" bowl typical of the Kassite period (for examples, see Armstrong 1993: pls. 72–74). In the absence of a complete profile and given the lack of other Kassite types in this layer, however, it is difficult to deny that this sherd could simply be a warped example of the Early Dynastic–Akkadian conical bowl.

Level VB certainly dates to the Kassite period. No diagnostic pottery is directly associated with Wall R and the accumulation of the layer of eroded material, Locus 15, also proves impossible to date more securely than sometime late in the Kassite period. This layer contains washed and tumbled sherds, the majority of which are of Akkadian–Ur III date; the latest pottery represented is Kassite, including well-known Kassite goblet sherds, jar rims, and pedestal bases.

The two burials from the second phase of Level V, Burial 9 and Burial 12, fall within the late Kassite period, with Burial 12 slightly preceding Burial 9, on the basis of the morphology of Kassite goblets and ovoid jars they contain. Burial 12 contained a single Kassite goblet and an ovoid jar (18 N 102, 18 N 103; pl. 168:3–4); Burial 9 held two Kassite goblets (18 N 55, 18 N 56; pl. 168:1–2).[124] The goblet with Burial 12 is wider and shorter than the two with Burial 9, and its base is hollowed out slightly deeper than theirs, aspects most closely paralleled by goblets from Level III of the Kassite buildings in Area WC-1 at Nippur (Armstrong 1993). This puts their date in approximately the late fourteenth to early thirteenth centuries B.C. The goblets with Burial 9 are taller and narrower and are similar to those in Levels II–III of Area WC-1, dated to the mid-thirteenth century B.C. Although not much time had elapsed between accumulation of those two strata in Area WC-1, nor between the two burials in Area WF, the analysis of well-dated material of this time range from Nippur and Tell ed-Der does allow relatively fine temporal distinctions to be made.

## First-millennium B.C. Pottery

Collection of the first-millennium B.C. ceramic material followed the same procedures as the third-millennium B.C. pottery. But, like the Level V pottery assemblage, the first-millennium B.C. material was frequently mixed with earlier material. In addition, all the first-millennium B.C. levels had suffered damage from later disturbances and the quantity of sherds from each level is too low for significant statistical analysis.

Like the Kassite pottery, the first-millennium B.C. pottery most often ranges from buff to yellow, with a far less frequent incidence of the pink to red tones that characterize the third-millennium B.C. material. Organic temper dominates. The three levels of the first millennium B.C., while not providing an unbroken sequence in which ceramic developments can be traced, do provide useful collections of material that can be dated by specific glazed pottery vessels in associated graves. Although this glazed pottery is considered to be distinctive of the mid- to later first millennium B.C., it in fact hardly appears at all in sherd material from occupation surfaces in Area WF; almost all the examples are whole vessels from graves. The typology of the first millennium B.C. at Nippur is as well established as the Kassite typology and most of the sherds from the upper levels of Area WF fall into recognized form categories. The best parallels come from other excavation areas at Nippur (Areas TA and WC-1), with further points of comparison at Babylon, Sippar, and other sites in the region of Tell ed-Der and from Neo-Babylonian and Achaemenid contexts at Ur and Uruk.

---

124. The Kassite cup found in the fill of the cut for Burial 4 (pl. 168:5) probably belongs to Burial 12.

## Level IV

The pottery collected from Level IV was very mixed in date due to earlier material being brought up by the digging of graves and excavation of a foundation or leveling cut. But the latest pottery, both glazed pottery vessels from the graves and sherds from the occupational material within the house, belongs to the seventh to early sixth centuries B.C. The assemblage from the house includes a range of medium-sized bowls with inturned plain rims (pl. 174:1–2), beveled rims (pls. 174:4, 175:1), and squared-off rims with shallow horizontal grooves beneath (pl. 175:3–5). Larger bowls with ledge rims and a ridge or groove below are also present (pl. 176:3–5). Sherds from stump-based cups are common (see Armstrong 1993: pl. 86j for complete example), and there are several examples of a fine-ware carinated bowl with a vertical plain rim (pl. 175:9). The jar types include plain rims on flaring necks (pl. 177:3–4), outwardly thickened rims (pl. 177:6–7), and double-ridged rims (pl. 177:11). One vessel with a strongly flared neck could be a large jar or more probably a pot-stand base (pl. 177:1).

The two burials in Level IV each contained glazed pottery, as well as other more common vessels. Burial 6 had three small glazed jars (18 N 16, 18 N 22, 18 N 23; pl. 169:1–3), as well as a larger undecorated jar with a double-ridged rim, two lug handles, and horizontal grooves on the neck and shoulder (18 N 24; pl. 169:4). The three glazed jars are all the same type, with squat rounded bodies and short flared necks, the only form differences among them being in the shape of the bases, which range from flat to pointed. The glazed patterns are yellow and white on a yellow green base coat and consist of horizontal lines of zigzags or circular patterns around the maximum diameter and radiating lines on the base. Both they and the unglazed jar are closely paralleled by examples from burials in Area TA at Nippur.

Burial 8 contained two glazed jars, one very similar to those with Burial 6 (18 N 43; pl. 170:2), while the other has a narrower neck and a less-dense glazed pattern consisting of horizontal bands around the body and thicker radiating lines at the base (18 N 42; pl. 170:1). This grave also contained a medium-sized bowl with an inturned and beveled rim that matches sherds from the house floors (18 N 45; pl. 170:4) and an unglazed jar similar to, but smaller than, the one with Burial 6, with the double-ridged rim and horizontally grooved shoulder, but without its lug handles (18 N 44; pl. 170:3).

## Level III

The pottery assemblages of Level III, Phases A and B, are essentially identical and are datable to the sixth to early fifth centuries B.C., especially by comparison with the contemporary levels at Nippur Area TA. Many of the bowl rim types seen in Level IV continue into Level III, in particular the inturned rims (pl. 174:3), beveled rims (pl. 174:4–6, 8, 10), and squared-off rims with grooves or ridges below (pl. 176:1–2). Stump-based cups still appear; and in addition a late variant of this form, a flat-based cylindrical cup, first appears in Level III (pl. 177:15). There are several variants of a carinated fine-ware bowl (pl. 175:7–8) and a single example each of a deep cup with a small square rim (pl. 175:6) and an exaggerated ledge rim of a cylindrical vessel (pl. 176:6). Among jars, the most common form has an outwardly thickened heavy rim, with or without a ridge on the neck (pl. 177:8, 10), but plain jar rims continued (pl. 177:2), and a finer club-rim is also present (pl. 177:5). There are single examples of a "hole-mouthed" vessel with a wide ledge rim (pl. 177:12), a fine-ware wide-mouth vessel with a ridge on the neck (pl. 177:13), and a smaller fine-ware jar (pl. 177:14).

The less-common types provide the basis for dating. Grayware appears in a variety of forms: an eggshell bowl with horizontal corrugations on the exterior (pl. 176:8), a carinated-sided bowl with a flared rim (pl. 176:9), and a shallow beveled-rim bowl (pl. 176:10). There are several body sherds with stamp-impressed designs typical of Achaemenid to Seleucid date: a small tree-like motif and a multi-petalled rosette, in both cases pressed hard into the wall of the vessel so that protrusions were made into the vessel interior. The fine carinated "cream bowls" (pl. 176:11, 13) and pale buff eggshell ware bowls (pl. 176:7) are also typical of the sixth–fifth century B.C. date. The thin and uniform walls of the latter vessels and the lack of any visible temper or impurities in the fabric mean that this is true "eggshell ware" as opposed to the "pseudo-eggshell ware" found at some sites (Warburton 1989). There are a few glazed sherds, including one decorated in yellow and white glaze with a possible fish and geometric designs (pl. 178:2–3); these are possibly contemporary with the similar glazed jars in the graves of Level IV and did not originate in this level. There are still many Kassite and third-millennium sherds mixed in with these types, the result of the pit-cutting and burial activities.

There are four burials in Level III. Burial 5 contains two jars very similar to those found with the Level IV burials: one a small, narrow-necked glazed jar (18 N 46; pl. 171:1) and one a larger unglazed jar with the same double-ridged rim and horizontal grooving seen on the jars in the Level IV burials, but in this case on a substantially taller vessel (18 N 53; pl. 171:2). While the glazed pattern on the small jar is similar to that seen on vessels from Level IV (horizontal bands, dots, swags, etc.), the base color is pale brown with additions in darker brown and black. Burial 7 also included a glazed jar, similar in shape and size to the glazed jars in Burial 6 of the previous level, with a squat round body and flared neck, but here the jar is covered with a uniform pale green glaze typical of the sixth century B.C. (18 N 17; pl. 173:1).

The other graves contain unglazed pottery only. Included with Burial 3 was a single medium-sized jar with a thickened rim that would have been at home in either Level IV or III (18 N 25; pl. 171:4). In the double grave excavated as Burials 2 and 4, the upper infant burial (Burial 2) held only the burial jar itself, a wide-mouth vessel with a ledge-rim (H352; pl. 178:6). There are two small jars with the adult skeleton farther below (Burial 4), a small squat jar like the previous glazed examples, but in this instance undecorated (18 N 32; pl. 172:1); and a fine nipple-based jar (18 N 54; pl. 172:2). On the floor above this joint grave was an inverted club-rim bowl of a type popular in the sherd assemblage of Levels IV and III (18 N 62; pl. 178:1).

## Level II

It is difficult to estimate the range of time covered by the two events of this level: the cutting and filling of Pit 1, and the accumulation of Locus 2. Pit 1 has at least two visible phases, where a second cut had been made into the already partially filled pit, but the material from both cuts is approximately contemporary. An enormous quantity of sherds came from this pit, including types as early as Kassite, but the latest belong to the Seleucid period. Notable were stamp-impressed body sherds and carinated bowls glazed uniformly in white or yellow or occasionally blue green (pl. 176:12). These bowls are remarkably similar in form to the Ur III carinated bowl (Type O-17) but are larger in diameter (20 cm or more). Types known from the previous levels, such as the inwardly beveled-rim bowl (pl. 174:8) and thickened jar rim with ridge on the neck (pl. 177:9), continued. The pottery of Locus 2, the erosion/wash layer that sealed Pit 1 at the eastern side of Area WF, consists mainly of either very small weathered sherds or of large body sherds from jars; diagnostic sherds are very few. Achaemenid and Seleucid types dominate, with a few sherds of Parthian blue-glazed slipper coffins providing the final date.

Table 7. Ratios of Third-millennium B.C. Closed to Open Vessels, Sherd Counts, and Relative Percentages

| Level | Closed | % of Total | Open | % of Total | Total | Ratio Closed:Open |
|---|---|---|---|---|---|---|
| XIXB | 30 | 7 | 415 | 93 | 445 | 1:13.8 |
| XIXA | 19 | 9 | 183 | 91 | 202 | 1:9.6 |
| XIX *total* | 49 | 8 | 598 | 92 | 647 | 1:12.2 |
| XVIII | 15 | 9 | 156 | 91 | 171 | 1:10.4 |
| XVIIC | 11 | 5 | 216 | 95 | 227 | 1:19.6 |
| XVIIB | 25 | 9 | 266 | 91 | 291 | 1:10.6 |
| XVIIA | 7 | 7 | 90 | 93 | 97 | 1:12.8 |
| XVII *total* | 43 | 7 | 572 | 93 | 615 | 1:13.3 |
| XVI | 28 | 6 | 403 | 94 | 431 | 1:14.4 |
| XVB | 15 | 8 | 167 | 92 | 182 | 1:11.1 |
| XVA | 13 | 10 | 121 | 90 | 134 | 1:9.3 |
| XV *total* | 28 | 9 | 288 | 91 | 316 | 1:10.3 |
| XIVB | 29 | 10 | 273 | 90 | 302 | 1:9.4 |
| XIVA | 29 | 7 | 395 | 93 | 424 | 1:13.6 |
| XIV *total* | 58 | 8 | 668 | 92 | 726 | 1:11.5 |
| XIIIC | 46 | 19 | 201 | 81 | 247 | 1:4.4 |
| XIIIB | 42 | 11 | 332 | 89 | 374 | 1:7.9 |
| XIIIA | — | — | — | — | — | — |
| XIII *total* | 88 | 14 | 533 | 86 | 621 | 1:6.1 |
| XIIB | 66 | 12 | 496 | 88 | 562 | 1:7.5 |
| XIIA | 95 | 8 | 1,030 | 92 | 1,125 | 1:10.8 |
| XII *total* | 161 | 10 | 1,526 | 90 | 1,687 | 1:9.5 |
| XIB | 155 | 12 | 1,111 | 88 | 1,266 | 1:7.2 |
| XIA | 80 | 15 | 457 | 85 | 537 | 1:5.7 |
| XI *total* | 235 | 13 | 1,568 | 87 | 1,803 | 1:6.7 |
| X | 112 | 15 | 655 | 85 | 767 | 1:5.8 |
| IX | 91 | 26 | 255 | 74 | 346 | 1:2.8 |
| VIII | 99 | 22 | 348 | 78 | 447 | 1:3.5 |
| VII | 25 | 32 | 54 | 68 | 79 | 1:2.2 |
| VI | 37 | 22 | 128 | 78 | 165 | 1:3.5 |

Average Closed:Open Ratio is 1:8.9

Table 8. Third-millennium B.C. Open and Closed Vessel Sherd Counts by Level

Table 9. Presence/Absence of Third-millennium B.C. Open Types by Level (types not to scale)

| Level | O-1 | O-2 | O-3 | O-4 | O-5 | O-6a | O-6b | O-7 | O-8 | O-9 | O-10 | O-11 | O-12 |
|---|---|---|---|---|---|---|---|---|---|---|---|---|---|
| XIX | + | + | + | + | + | + |  | + |  |  |  |  |  |
| XVIII | + |  | + |  | + | + |  | + | + |  |  |  |  |
| XVII | + | + | + | + | + | + | + | + | + | + |  |  |  |
| XVI | + |  | + |  | + |  |  | + | + | + | + |  |  |
| XV | + |  | + |  | + | + |  |  | + | + | + |  |  |
| XIV | + | + | + |  | + |  |  |  |  | + | + | + | + |
| XIII | + | + | + |  | + | + |  | + | + | + | + | + | + |
| XII | + | + | + |  | + | + | + |  |  | + | + | + | + |
| XI | + | + | + |  | + | + | + | + |  | + | + | + | + |
| X | + | + | + |  | + | + |  | + |  |  | + | + | + |
| IX | + | + | + |  | + | + |  | + |  |  | + | + | + |
| VIII | + | + | + | + | + | + |  |  |  |  | + | + | + |
| VII | + |  | + |  |  |  |  |  |  |  | + |  | + |
| VI | + | + | + |  |  | + |  |  |  | + | + |  |  |

| Level | O-13 | O-14 | O-15 | O-16 | O-17 | O-18 | O-19 | O-20 | O-21 | O-22 | O-23 | O-24 | O-25 |
|---|---|---|---|---|---|---|---|---|---|---|---|---|---|
| XIX |  |  |  |  |  |  |  |  |  |  |  |  |  |
| XVIII |  |  |  |  |  |  |  |  |  |  |  |  |  |
| XVII |  |  |  |  |  |  |  |  |  |  |  |  |  |
| XVI |  |  |  |  |  |  |  |  |  |  |  |  |  |
| XV |  |  |  |  |  |  |  |  |  |  |  |  |  |
| XIV | + |  |  |  | + |  |  |  |  |  |  |  |  |
| XIII |  | + | + |  |  |  |  |  |  |  |  |  |  |
| XII | + |  | + | + |  |  |  |  |  |  |  |  |  |
| XI | + | + |  | + | + | + | + | + | + |  |  |  |  |
| X | + |  |  |  | + | + | + |  | + | + |  |  |  |
| IX |  |  |  |  |  |  | + | + | + | + |  |  |  |
| VIII | + |  |  |  | + |  | + |  | + | + | + | + |  |
| VII |  |  |  |  | + |  | + |  |  | + | + | + |  |
| VI |  |  |  |  | + |  |  |  |  | + |  |  | + |

CHAPTER 3: POTTERY 91

Table 10. Presence/Absence of Third-millennium B.C. Closed Types by Level (types not to scale)

| Level | C-1 | C-2 | C-3 | C-4 | C-5 | C-6 | C-7 | C-8 | C-9 | C-10 | C-11 | C-12 | C-13 | C-14 | C-15 |
|---|---|---|---|---|---|---|---|---|---|---|---|---|---|---|---|
| XIX | + | + | + | + | + | + | + | | | | | | | | |
| XVIII | + | + | + | | + | | + | + | | | | | | | |
| XVII | + | + | + | + | | + | + | + | + | + | + | + | + | | |
| XVI | + | + | + | | + | + | | | + | + | + | | | | |
| XV | + | + | + | | | + | | | + | + | | | | + | + |
| XIV | + | + | + | | | | | | + | | | | | + | + |
| XIII | + | + | + | | | | | | + | + | | + | | + | + |
| XII | + | + | + | + | + | + | | | + | + | | + | | + | + |
| XI | + | + | + | + | + | | + | + | + | + | | + | | + | + |
| X | + | + | + | + | | | | + | + | + | | | + | + | + |
| IX | + | + | + | | | | | | + | + | | | + | + | |
| VIII | + | + | + | + | | | | | + | + | | | + | + | |
| VII | | + | + | | | | | | | | | | | | |
| VI | + | | + | | | | | | | | | | | + | |

| Level | C-16a | C-16b | C-16c | C-17 | C-18 | C-19 | C-20 | C-21 | C-22 | C-24 | C-25a | C-25b | C-26 | C-27 | C-28 | C-29 |
|---|---|---|---|---|---|---|---|---|---|---|---|---|---|---|---|---|
| XIX | | | | | | | | | | | | | | | | |
| XVIII | | | | | | | | | | | | | | | | |
| XVII | | | | | | | | | | | | | | | | |
| XVI | | | | | | | | | | | | | | | | |
| XV | | | | | | | | | | | + | | | | | |
| XIV | + | + | | + | + | + | + | + | + | + | | | | | | |
| XIII | + | + | | + | + | + | + | + | + | + | | | | | | |
| XII | + | + | | + | + | + | + | + | + | + | + | | | | | |
| XI | + | + | + | + | + | + | + | + | + | + | + | | + | + | + | |
| X | + | + | + | + | + | + | + | + | + | + | | | | + | + | |
| IX | + | + | + | + | + | + | + | | + | | + | | + | | + | |
| VIII | + | + | + | + | + | + | + | + | + | + | + | | | + | + | |
| VII | + | + | | | | | + | | + | + | | | | | + | + |
| VI | + | + | | | | + | + | + | | + | + | + | | | + | + |

Table 11. Number of Third-millennium B.C. Types Present per Level, and Ratios of Open to Closed Types

|  | XIX | XVIII | XVII | XVI | XV | XIV | XIII | XII | XI | X | IX | VIII | VII | VI |
|---|---|---|---|---|---|---|---|---|---|---|---|---|---|---|
| Number of O-Types | 7 | 6 | 10 | 7 | 7 | 10 | 12 | 14 | 19 | 15 | 13 | 16 | 9 | 9 |
| Number of C-Types | 7 | 6 | 12 | 8 | 9 | 15 | 17 | 21 | 26 | 23 | 18 | 20 | 9 | 13 |
| **Total Number of Types** | **14** | **12** | **22** | **15** | **16** | **25** | **29** | **35** | **45** | **38** | **31** | **36** | **18** | **22** |
| Ratio O:C | 1:1 | 1:1 | 1:1.2 | 1:1.1 | 1:1.3 | 1:1.5 | 1:1.4 | 1:1.5 | 1:1.4 | 1:1.5 | 1:1.4 | 1:1.3 | 1:1 | 1:1.4 |

## Table 12. Type O-1 Third-millennium B.C. Bowl Height by Level

| Level | Bowl Heights in Centimeters | Average Height per Phase | Average Height per Combined Level |
|---|---|---|---|
| XIXB | 8.3, 9.1, 10.0 | 9.1 | 9.1 |
| XIXA | No complete heights preserved | N/A | |
| XVIII (including Burial 20) | 6.5, 6.6 | 6.6 | 6.6 |
| XVIIC (including Burial 19) | 5.3, 6.2, 6.4, 6.5, 6.5, 6.8, 6.8, 6.8, 6.9, 7.0, 7.0, 7.0, 7.0, 7.1, 7.1, 7.1, 7.1, 7.2, 7.2, 7.4, 7.4, 7.9, 7.9, 8.2, 9.6, 10.0, 10.6, 11.2, 11.9 (this omits the two tall narrow cups, variants of O-1) | 7.6 | 7.6 |
| XVIIB (Burial 21/2) | 7.6 | 7.6 | |
| XVIIA | No complete heights preserved | N/A | |
| XVI (including Burial 18) | 5.0, 5.4, 5.8, 6.3, 6.5, 6.6, 6.8, 6.9, 7.0, 7.1, 7.2, 7.3, 7.5, 7.5, 7.9 | 6.7 | 6.7 |
| Burial 14, Skeleton 8 | 6.3, 6.6, 6.7, 6.9, 7.1, 7.1, 7.2, 7.3, 7.3, 7.4, 7.4, 7.5, 7.6, 7.7, 7.8, 7.9, 7.9, 7.9 | 7.3 | |
| Burial 14, Skeleton 7 | 7.3 | 7.3 | |
| XVB | 6.0 | 6.0 | 6.2 |
| XVA | 6.0, 6.4, 6.5 | 6.3 | |
| Burial 14, Skeleton 5 | 6.3, 6.5, 6.9 | 6.6 | |
| XIVB (including Burials 15 and 16) | 4.0, 4.3, 4.3, 4.5, 4.6, 4.6, 5.2, 5.3, 5.5, 5.6, 5.6, 5.7, 5.7, 5.7, 5.8, 5.9, 6.0, 6.0, 6.3, 6.4, 6.4, 6.5, 6.7 | 5.5 | 5.3 |
| XIVA (including Burial 13) | 3.9, 3.9, 3.9, 4.0, 4.2, 4.3, 4.3, 4.3, 4.4, 4.5, 4.5, 4.5, 5.3, 5.4, 5.8, 6.0, 6.0, 6.0, 6.4, 6.7, 7.5 | 5.0 | |
| Burial 14, Skeleton 6 | 4.0, 4.1, 4.5, 4.7, 4.8, 4.9, 5.0, 5.1, 5.2, 5.2, 5.6, 7.7 | 5.1 | |
| XIIIC | 4.5, 4.5, 4.5, 4.6, 4.7, 4.8, 4.8, 4.9, 5.0, 5.1, 6.5 | 4.9 | 4.9 |
| XIIIB (including Burial 14, Skeletons 2–4) | 3.8, 4.0, 4.2, 4.2, 4.3, 4.3, 4.3, 4.4, 4.4, 4.5, 4.6, 4.7, 4.7, 4.9, 5.0, 5.0, 5.3, 5.5, 5.5, 5.7, 5.7, 6.0, 6.1, 6.2 | 4.9 | |
| XIIIA | No complete heights preserved | N/A | |
| XIIB (including Burial 14, Skeleton 1) | 2.7, 3.0, 4.0, 4.2, 4.3, 4.5, 4.5, 4.8, 4.8, 4.9, 5.0, 5.1, 5.1, 5.2, 5.8, 6.2, 6.2 | 4.7 | 4.4 |
| XIIA | 3.1, 3.2, 3.6, 3.7, 3.8, 3.8, 3.8, 3.9, 4.4, 4.4, 4.6, 5.0, 5.2 | 4.0 | |
| XIB (including Burial 11) | 3.4, 3.6, 3.7, 3.7, 3.8, 3.9, 4.0, 4.0, 4.2, 4.1, 4.3, 4.6, 4.7, 4.8, 5.2 | 4.1 | 3.8 |
| XIA | 2.7, 2.9, 4.7 | 3.4 | |
| X | 2.6, 3.3, 3.4, 4.2 | 3.4 | 3.4 |
| IX | 3.6, 3.7, 4.2, 4.3, 4.3, 4.4 | 4.1 | 4.1 |
| VIII | 3.5, 4.8 | 4.2 | 4.2 |
| VI | 4.0 | 4.0 | 4.0 |

### 94 NIPPUR V: EARLY DYNASTIC TO AKKADIAN TRANSITION

Table 13. Types O-1 through O-13: Third-millennium B.C. Sherd Counts and Relative Frequencies by Level

| Level | O-1 | O-2 | O-3 | O-4 | O-5 | O-6a | O-6b | O-7 | O-8 | O-9 | O-10 | O-11 | O-12 | O-13 | Total |
|---|---|---|---|---|---|---|---|---|---|---|---|---|---|---|---|
| XIXB | 394 | 7 | 4 | 2 | 3 | 1 | – | 4 | – | – | – | – | – | – | 415 |
| XIXA | 174 | – | 6 | – | 3 | – | – | – | – | – | – | – | – | – | 183 |
| **XIX Total** | **568** | **7** | **10** | **2** | **6** | **1** | **–** | **4** | **–** | **–** | **–** | **–** | **–** | **–** | **598** |
| % Freq. | 94.98 | 1.17 | 1.67 | 0.33 | 1.00 | 0.17 | – | 0.68 | – | – | – | – | – | – | |
| XVIII | 148 | – | 3 | – | 1 | 1 | – | 1 | 2 | – | – | – | – | – | 156 |
| % Freq. | 94.87 | – | 1.92 | – | 0.64 | 0.64 | – | 0.64 | 1.28 | – | – | – | – | – | |
| XVIIC | 203 | 1 | 6 | 1 | 3 | – | – | 2 | – | – | – | – | – | – | 216 |
| XVIIB | 251 | – | 4 | 1 | 3 | – | 2 | 1 | 2 | 2 | – | – | – | – | 266 |
| XVIIA | 81 | – | 6 | – | – | 1 | – | – | 1 | 1 | – | – | – | – | 90 |
| **XVII Total** | **535** | **1** | **16** | **2** | **6** | **1** | **2** | **3** | **3** | **3** | **–** | **–** | **–** | **–** | **572** |
| % Freq. | 93.53 | 0.18 | 2.80 | 0.35 | 1.05 | 0.18 | 0.35 | 0.52 | 0.52 | 0.52 | – | – | – | – | |
| XVI | 378 | – | 6 | – | 9 | – | – | 1 | 1 | 5 | 3 | – | – | – | 403 |
| % Freq. | 93.80 | – | 1.49 | – | 2.23 | – | – | 0.25 | 0.25 | 1.24 | 0.74 | – | – | – | |
| XVB | 163 | – | – | – | – | 2 | – | – | 1 | 1 | – | – | – | – | 167 |
| XVA | 109 | – | 1 | – | 5 | – | – | – | – | 1 | 5 | – | – | – | 121 |
| **XV Total** | **272** | **–** | **1** | **–** | **5** | **2** | **–** | **–** | **1** | **2** | **5** | **–** | **–** | **–** | **288** |
| % Freq. | 94.44 | – | 0.35 | – | 1.74 | 0.69 | – | – | 0.35 | 0.69 | 1.74 | – | – | – | |
| XIVB | 255 | – | 2 | – | 1 | – | – | – | – | 1 | 13 | 1 | – | – | 273 |
| XIVA | 364 | 1 | 7 | – | – | – | – | – | – | 1 | 13 | 3 | 4 | 1 | 394 |
| **XIV Total** | **619** | **1** | **9** | **–** | **1** | **–** | **–** | **–** | **–** | **2** | **26** | **4** | **4** | **1** | **667** |
| % Freq. | 92.65 | 0.15 | 1.35 | – | 0.15 | – | – | – | – | 0.30 | 3.90 | 0.60 | 0.60 | 0.15 | |
| XIIIC | 171 | – | 8 | – | 3 | 1 | – | 1 | 1 | 1 | 14 | 1 | – | – | 201 |
| XIIIB | 268 | 3 | 6 | – | 1 | 1 | – | 1 | 1 | – | 48 | – | 1 | – | 330 |
| **XIII Total** | **439** | **3** | **14** | **–** | **4** | **2** | **–** | **2** | **2** | **1** | **62** | **1** | **1** | **–** | **531** |
| % Freq. | 82.37 | 0.57 | 2.64 | – | 0.75 | 0.38 | – | 0.38 | 0.38 | 0.19 | 11.63 | 0.19 | 0.19 | – | |
| XIIB | 380 | 1 | 12 | – | 1 | – | – | – | – | 3 | 90 | 5 | – | – | 492 |
| XIIA | 868 | 1 | 13 | – | – | 2 | 1 | – | – | – | 109 | 25 | 8 | 1 | 1,028 |
| **XII Total** | **1248** | **2** | **25** | **–** | **1** | **2** | **1** | **–** | **–** | **3** | **199** | **30** | **8** | **1** | **1,520** |
| % Freq. | 82.18 | 0.13 | 1.64 | – | 0.07 | 0.13 | 0.07 | – | – | 0.20 | 13.04 | 1.97 | 0.52 | 0.07 | |
| XIB | 907 | 3 | 22 | – | 3 | 3 | 1 | 1 | – | – | 116 | 31 | 7 | 8 | 1,102 |
| XIA | 378 | 1 | 12 | – | 1 | – | 1 | 1 | – | 1 | 43 | 10 | 3 | 1 | 452 |
| **XI Total** | **1285** | **4** | **34** | **–** | **4** | **3** | **2** | **2** | **–** | **1** | **159** | **41** | **10** | **9** | **1,554** |
| % Freq. | 81.95 | 0.26 | 2.17 | – | 0.26 | 0.19 | 0.13 | 0.13 | – | 0.06 | 10.14 | 2.62 | 0.64 | 0.57 | |
| X | 540 | 2 | 7 | – | 1 | 1 | – | 1 | – | – | 70 | 7 | 5 | 1 | 635 |
| % Freq. | 82.44 | 0.31 | 1.07 | – | 0.15 | 0.15 | – | 0.15 | – | – | 10.69 | 1.07 | 0.76 | 0.15 | |
| IX | 207 | 1 | 4 | – | 1 | 2 | – | 2 | – | – | 22 | 3 | 3 | – | 245 |
| % Freq. | 81.17 | 0.39 | 1.57 | – | 0.39 | 0.78 | – | 0.78 | – | – | 8.63 | 1.18 | 1.18 | – | |
| VIII | 241 | 2 | 8 | 1 | 1 | 1 | – | – | – | – | 9 | 8 | 3 | 2 | 276 |
| % Freq. | 69.25 | 0.58 | 2.30 | 0.29 | 0.29 | 0.29 | – | – | – | – | 2.59 | 2.30 | 0.86 | 0.58 | |
| VII | 43 | – | 2 | – | – | – | – | – | – | – | 2 | – | 1 | – | 48 |
| % Freq. | 79.63 | – | 3.70 | – | – | – | – | – | – | – | 3.70 | – | 1.85 | – | |
| VI | 91 | 1 | 2 | – | – | 3 | – | – | – | 1 | 1 | – | – | – | 99 |
| % Freq. | 71.09 | 0.78 | 1.56 | – | – | 2.34 | – | – | – | 0.78 | 0.78 | – | – | – | |

CHAPTER 3: POTTERY

Table 14. Types O-14 through O-25, Third-millennium B.C. Sherd Counts and Relative Frequencies by Level, with Total for Types O-1–O-25

| Level | O-14 | O-15 | O-16 | O-17 | O-18 | O-19 | O-20 | O-21 | O-22 | O-23 | O-24 | O-25 | Sub-total Types O-1–O-13 | Grand Total |
|---|---|---|---|---|---|---|---|---|---|---|---|---|---|---|
| XIXB | – | – | – | – | – | – | – | – | – | – | – | – | 415 | 415 |
| XIXA | – | – | – | – | – | – | – | – | – | – | – | – | 183 | 183 |
| **XIX Total** | **–** | **–** | **–** | **–** | **–** | **–** | **–** | **–** | **–** | **–** | **–** | **–** | **598** | **598** |
| % Freq. | – | – | – | – | – | – | – | – | – | – | – | – | | |
| XVIII | – | – | – | – | – | – | – | – | – | – | – | – | 156 | 156 |
| % Freq. | – | – | – | – | – | – | – | – | – | – | – | – | | |
| XVIIC | – | – | – | – | – | – | – | – | – | – | – | – | 216 | 216 |
| XVIIB | – | – | – | – | – | – | – | – | – | – | – | – | 266 | 266 |
| XVIIA | – | – | – | – | – | – | – | – | – | – | – | – | 90 | 90 |
| **XVII Total** | **–** | **–** | **–** | **–** | **–** | **–** | **–** | **–** | **–** | **–** | **–** | **–** | **572** | **572** |
| % Freq. | – | – | – | – | – | – | – | – | – | – | – | – | | |
| XVI | – | – | – | – | – | – | – | – | – | – | – | – | 403 | 403 |
| % Freq. | – | – | – | – | – | – | – | – | – | – | – | – | | |
| XVB | – | – | – | – | – | – | – | – | – | – | – | – | 167 | 167 |
| XVA | – | – | – | – | – | – | – | – | – | – | – | – | 121 | 121 |
| **XV Total** | **–** | **–** | **–** | **–** | **–** | **–** | **–** | **–** | **–** | **–** | **–** | **–** | **288** | **288** |
| % Freq. | – | – | – | – | – | – | – | – | – | – | – | – | | |
| XIVB | – | – | – | – | – | – | – | – | – | – | – | – | 273 | 273 |
| XIVA | – | – | – | 1 | – | – | – | – | – | – | – | – | 394 | 395 |
| **XIV Total** | **–** | **–** | **–** | **1** | **–** | **–** | **–** | **–** | **–** | **–** | **–** | **–** | **667** | **668** |
| % Freq. | – | – | – | 0.15 | – | – | – | – | – | – | – | – | | |
| XIIIC | – | – | – | – | – | – | – | – | – | – | – | – | 201 | 201 |
| XIIIB | – | 2 | – | – | – | – | – | – | – | – | – | – | 330 | 332 |
| **XIII Total** | **–** | **2** | **–** | **–** | **–** | **–** | **–** | **–** | **–** | **–** | **–** | **–** | **531** | **533** |
| % Freq. | – | 0.38 | – | – | – | – | – | – | – | – | – | – | | |
| XIIB | 2 | 1 | 1 | – | – | – | – | – | – | – | – | – | 492 | 496 |
| XIIA | 2 | – | – | – | – | – | – | – | – | – | – | – | 1,028 | 1,030 |
| **XII Total** | **4** | **1** | **1** | **–** | **–** | **–** | **–** | **–** | **–** | **–** | **–** | **–** | **1,520** | **1,526** |
| % Freq. | 0.26 | 0.07 | 0.07 | – | – | – | – | – | – | – | – | – | | |
| XIB | 1 | – | 1 | 1 | 1 | 2 | 1 | 2 | – | – | – | – | 1,102 | 1,111 |
| XIA | – | – | – | – | – | 1 | 1 | 3 | – | – | – | – | 452 | 457 |
| **XI Total** | **1** | **–** | **1** | **1** | **1** | **3** | **2** | **5** | **–** | **–** | **–** | **–** | **1,520** | **1,568** |
| % Freq. | 0.06 | – | 0.06 | 0.06 | 0.06 | 0.19 | 0.13 | 0.32 | – | – | – | – | | |
| X | – | – | – | 11 | 1 | 1 | – | 1 | 6 | – | – | – | 635 | 655 |
| % Freq. | – | – | – | 1.68 | 0.15 | 0.15 | – | 0.15 | 0.92 | – | – | – | | |
| IX– | – | – | – | – | 1 | 1 | 2 | 6 | – | – | – | 245 | 255 | |
| % Freq. | – | – | – | – | – | 0.39 | 0.39 | 0.78 | 2.35 | – | – | – | | |
| VIII | – | – | – | 32 | – | 2 | – | 1 | 34 | 2 | 1 | – | 276 | 348 |
| % Freq. | – | – | – | 9.20 | – | 0.58 | – | 0.29 | 9.77 | 0.58 | 0.29 | – | | |
| VII | – | – | – | 2 | – | 1 | – | – | 1 | 1 | 1 | – | 48 | 54 |
| % Freq. | – | – | – | 3.70 | – | 1.85 | – | – | 1.85 | 1.85 | 1.85 | – | | |
| VI | – | – | – | 14 | – | – | – | – | 14 | – | – | 1 | 99 | 128 |
| % Freq. | – | – | – | 10.94 | – | – | – | – | 10.94 | – | – | 0.78 | | |

Table 15. Types C-1 through C-15, Third-millennium B.C. Levels Sherd Counts and Relative Frequencies by Level

| Level | C-1 | C-2 | C-3 | C-4 | C-5 | C-6 | C-7 | C-8 | C-9 | C-10 | C-11 | C-12 | C-13 | C-14 | C-15 | Total |
|---|---|---|---|---|---|---|---|---|---|---|---|---|---|---|---|---|
| XIXB | 11 | 12 | 2 | 1 | 3 | 1 | – | – | – | – | – | – | – | – | – | 30 |
| XIXA | 4 | 11 | 2 | – | – | 1 | 1 | – | – | – | – | – | – | – | – | 19 |
| **XIX Total** | **15** | **23** | **4** | **1** | **3** | **2** | **1** | – | – | – | – | – | – | – | – | **49** |
| % Freq. | 30.61 | 46.94 | 8.16 | 2.04 | 6.12 | 4.08 | 2.04 | – | – | – | – | – | – | – | – | |
| XVIII | 7 | 2 | 1 | – | 2 | – | 2 | 1 | – | – | – | – | – | – | – | 15 |
| | 46.67 | 13.33 | 6.67 | – | 13.33 | – | 13.33 | 6.67 | – | – | – | – | – | – | – | |
| XVIIC | 5 | 3 | 2 | – | – | 1 | – | – | – | – | – | – | – | – | – | 11 |
| XVIIB | 4 | 6 | 3 | 1 | – | 1 | 1 | 1 | 2 | 1 | 3 | 2 | – | – | – | 25 |
| XVIIA | 3 | – | 1 | – | – | – | – | – | – | – | – | – | 3 | – | – | 7 |
| **XVII Total** | **12** | **9** | **6** | **1** | – | **2** | **1** | **1** | **2** | **1** | **3** | **2** | **3** | – | – | **43** |
| % Freq. | 27.91 | 20.93 | 13.95 | 2.33 | – | 4.65 | 2.33 | 2.33 | 4.65 | 2.33 | 6.98 | 4.65 | 6.98 | – | – | |
| XVI | 8 | 2 | 6 | – | 1 | 1 | – | – | 4 | 5 | 1 | – | – | – | – | 28 |
| % Freq. | 28.57 | 7.14 | 21.43 | – | 3.57 | 3.57 | – | – | 14.29 | 17.86 | 3.57 | – | – | – | – | |
| XVB | 4 | 2 | 3 | – | – | 1 | – | – | 3 | – | – | – | 1 | 1 | – | 15 |
| XVA | 4 | – | 1 | – | – | – | – | – | – | 4 | – | – | 1 | – | – | 10 |
| **XV Total** | **8** | **2** | **4** | – | – | **1** | – | – | **3** | **4** | – | – | **2** | **1** | – | **25** |
| % Freq. | 28.57 | 7.14 | 14.29 | – | – | 3.57 | – | – | 10.71 | 14.29 | – | – | 7.14 | 3.57 | – | |
| XIVB | 5 | – | – | – | – | – | – | – | 5 | – | – | – | – | 1 | 2 | 13 |
| XIVA | 6 | 2 | 1 | – | – | – | – | – | – | – | – | – | – | 6 | – | 15 |
| **XIV Total** | **11** | **2** | **1** | – | – | – | – | – | **5** | – | – | – | – | **7** | **1** | **27** |
| % Freq. | 19.30 | 3.51 | 1.75 | – | – | – | – | – | 8.77 | – | – | – | – | 12.28 | 1.75 | |
| XIIIC | 11 | 3 | 4 | – | – | – | – | – | – | 1 | – | 2 | – | 4 | 1 | 26 |
| XIIIB | 9 | 1 | 2 | – | – | – | – | – | 1 | 1 | – | – | – | 10 | 1 | 25 |
| **XIII Total** | **20** | **4** | **6** | – | – | – | – | – | **1** | **2** | – | **2** | – | **14** | **2** | **51** |
| % Freq. | 22.73 | 4.55 | 6.81 | – | – | – | – | – | 1.14 | 2.27 | – | 2.27 | – | 15.91 | 2.27 | |
| XIIB | 12 | 9 | 1 | – | – | – | – | – | 3 | 6 | – | 1 | – | 1 | – | 33 |
| XIIA | 6 | 6 | – | 1 | 1 | 1 | – | – | 8 | 6 | – | 2 | 4 | 9 | – | 44 |
| **XII Total** | **18** | **15** | **1** | **1** | **1** | **1** | – | – | **11** | **12** | – | **3** | **4** | **10** | – | **77** |
| % Freq. | 11.18 | 9.32 | 0.62 | 0.62 | 0.62 | 0.62 | – | – | 6.83 | 7.45 | – | 1.86 | 2.48 | 6.21 | – | |
| XIB | 19 | 7 | 3 | 1 | – | – | 1 | – | 17 | 5 | – | 4 | – | 5 | – | 62 |
| XIA | 3 | 1 | 1 | 1 | 1 | – | – | 2 | 7 | 2 | – | – | – | 2 | 1 | 21 |
| **XI Total** | **22** | **8** | **4** | **2** | **1** | – | **1** | **2** | **24** | **7** | – | **4** | – | **7** | **1** | **83** |
| % Freq. | 9.36 | 3.40 | 1.70 | 0.85 | 0.43 | – | 0.43 | 0.85 | 10.21 | 2.98 | – | 1.70 | – | 2.98 | 0.43 | |
| X | 7 | 4 | 2 | 1 | – | – | – | 1 | 11 | 1 | – | – | 1 | 3 | 2 | 33 |
| % Freq. | 6.86 | 3.92 | 1.96 | 0.98 | – | – | – | 0.98 | 10.78 | 0.98 | – | – | 0.98 | 2.94 | 1.96 | |
| IX | 4 | 1 | 1 | – | – | – | – | – | 16 | 2 | – | – | 5 | 2 | – | 31 |
| % Freq. | 4.40 | 1.10 | 1.10 | – | – | – | – | – | 17.58 | 2.20 | – | – | 5.50 | 2.20 | – | |
| VIII | 7 | 2 | 1 | 1 | – | – | – | – | 15 | – | – | – | 3 | 3 | – | 32 |
| % Freq. | 7.07 | 2.02 | 1.01 | 1.01 | – | – | – | – | 15.15 | – | – | – | 3.03 | 3.03 | – | |
| VII | – | 1 | 3 | – | – | – | – | – | – | – | – | – | – | – | – | 4 |
| % Freq. | – | 4.00 | 12.00 | – | – | – | – | – | – | – | – | – | – | – | – | |
| VI | 1 | – | 3 | – | – | – | – | – | 3 | – | – | – | – | – | – | 7 |
| % Freq. | 2.70 | – | 8.11 | – | – | – | – | – | 8.11 | – | – | – | – | – | – | |

## CHAPTER 3: POTTERY

Table 16. Types C-16a through C-29, Third-millennium B.C. Levels Counts and Relative Frequencies by Level, with Total for Types C-1–C-15

| Level | C-16a | C-16b | C-16c | C-17 | C-18 | C-19 | C-20 | C-21 | C-22 | C-24 | C-25a | C-25b | C-26 | C-27 | C-28 | C-29 | Sub-total Types C-1–C-15 | Closed Total |
|---|---|---|---|---|---|---|---|---|---|---|---|---|---|---|---|---|---|---|
| *XIXB* | – | – | – | – | – | – | – | – | – | – | – | – | – | – | – | – | 30 | 30 |
| *XIXA* | – | – | – | – | – | – | – | – | – | – | – | – | – | – | – | – | 19 | 19 |
| **XIX Total** | – | – | – | – | – | – | – | – | – | – | – | – | – | – | – | – | **49** | **49** |
| *% Freq.* | – | – | – | – | – | – | – | – | – | – | – | – | – | – | – | – | | |
| *XVIII* | – | – | – | – | – | – | – | – | – | – | – | – | – | – | – | – | 15 | 15 |
| *XVIIC* | – | – | – | – | – | – | – | – | – | – | – | – | – | – | – | – | 11 | 11 |
| *XVIIB* | – | – | – | – | – | – | – | – | – | – | – | – | – | – | – | – | 25 | 25 |
| *XVIIA* | – | – | – | – | – | – | – | – | – | – | – | – | – | – | – | – | 7 | 7 |
| **XVII Total** | – | – | – | – | – | – | – | – | – | – | – | – | – | – | – | – | **43** | **43** |
| *% Freq.* | – | – | – | – | – | – | – | – | – | – | – | – | – | – | – | – | | |
| *XVI* | – | – | – | – | – | – | – | – | – | – | – | – | – | – | – | – | 28 | 28 |
| *XVB* | – | – | – | – | – | – | – | – | – | – | – | – | – | – | – | – | 15 | 15 |
| *XVA* | – | – | – | – | – | – | – | – | – | 3 | – | – | – | – | – | – | 10 | 13 |
| **XV Total** | – | – | – | – | – | – | – | – | – | **3** | – | – | – | – | – | – | **25** | **28** |
| *% Freq.* | – | – | – | – | – | – | – | – | – | 10.71 | – | – | – | – | – | – | | |
| *XIVB* | 1 | 1 | – | 1 | – | 1 | – | 1 | 2 | 9 | – | – | – | – | – | – | 13 | 29 |
| *XIVA* | 2 | – | – | 3 | 1 | 1 | 1 | 3 | 1 | 2 | – | – | – | – | – | – | 15 | 29 |
| **XIV Total** | **3** | **1** | – | **4** | **1** | **2** | **1** | **4** | **3** | **11** | – | – | – | – | – | – | **27** | **57** |
| *% Freq.* | 5.26 | 1.75 | – | 7.02 | 1.75 | 3.51 | 1.75 | 7.02 | 5.26 | 19.30 | – | – | – | – | – | – | | |
| *XIIIC* | 2 | 1 | – | 4 | – | 2 | 4 | 3 | 4 | – | – | – | – | – | – | – | 26 | 46 |
| *XIIIB* | 2 | 1 | – | 1 | 1 | – | 5 | 1 | 3 | 3 | – | – | – | – | – | – | 25 | 42 |
| **XIII Total** | **4** | **2** | – | **5** | **1** | **2** | **9** | **4** | **7** | **3** | – | – | – | – | – | – | **51** | **88** |
| *% Freq.* | 4.55 | 2.27 | – | 5.68 | 1.14 | 2.27 | 11.36 | 4.55 | 7.95 | 3.41 | – | – | – | – | – | – | | |
| *XIIB* | 10 | 8 | – | 2 | – | 1 | 6 | 1 | 3 | 2 | – | – | – | – | – | – | 33 | 66 |
| *XIIA* | 9 | 8 | – | 2 | 2 | 2 | 7 | 11 | 5 | 3 | 2 | – | – | – | – | – | 44 | 95 |
| **XII Total** | **19** | **16** | – | **4** | **2** | **3** | **13** | **12** | **8** | **5** | **2** | – | – | – | – | – | **77** | **161** |
| *% Freq.* | 11.80 | 9.94 | – | 2.48 | 1.24 | 1.86 | 8.07 | 7.45 | 4.97 | 3.11 | 1.24 | – | – | – | – | – | | |
| *XIB* | 17 | 26 | 3 | 3 | 6 | 1 | 10 | 9 | 6 | 7 | 2 | – | 2 | 1 | – | – | 62 | 155 |
| *XIA* | 9 | 14 | 1 | 2 | 8 | – | 5 | 8 | 2 | 4 | 1 | – | – | 4 | 1 | – | 21 | 80 |
| **XI Total** | **26** | **40** | **4** | **5** | **14** | **1** | **15** | **17** | **8** | **11** | **3** | – | **2** | **5** | **1** | – | **83** | **235** |
| *% Freq.* | 11.10 | 17.02 | 1.70 | 2.13 | 5.96 | 0.43 | 6.38 | 7.23 | 3.40 | 4.68 | 1.28 | – | 0.85 | 2.13 | 0.43 | – | | |
| *X* | 11 | 14 | 2 | 7 | 6 | 1 | 10 | 5 | 3 | 4 | 3 | – | – | – | 1 | 2 | 33 | 102 |
| *% Freq.* | 10.78 | 13.73 | 1.96 | 6.86 | 5.88 | 0.98 | 9.80 | 4.90 | 2.94 | 3.92 | 2.94 | – | – | – | 0.98 | 1.96 | | |
| *IX* | 9 | 19 | 5 | 2 | 2 | 1 | 15 | – | 1 | – | 4 | – | – | 1 | – | 1 | 31 | 91 |
| *% Freq.* | 9.89 | 20.88 | 5.49 | 2.20 | 2.20 | 1.10 | 16.48 | – | 1.10 | – | 4.40 | – | – | 1.10 | – | – | | |
| *VIII* | 3 | 17 | 1 | 1 | 4 | 1 | 3 | 1 | 4 | 6 | 2 | 8 | – | – | – | 16 | 32 | 99 |
| *% Freq.* | 3.03 | 17.17 | 1.01 | 1.01 | 4.04 | 1.01 | 3.03 | 1.01 | 4.04 | 6.06 | 2.02 | 8.08 | – | – | – | 16.16 | | |
| *VII* | 5 | 6 | – | – | – | – | 5 | – | 1 | 2 | – | – | – | – | 1 | 1 | 4 | 25 |
| *% Freq.* | 20.00 | 24.00 | – | – | – | – | 20.00 | – | 4.00 | 8.00 | – | – | – | – | 4.00 | 4.00 | | |
| *VI* | 2 | 12 | – | – | – | 1 | 8 | 1 | – | 1 | 1 | 2 | – | – | 1 | 1 | 7 | 37 |
| *% Freq.* | 5.41 | 32.43 | – | – | – | 2.70 | 21.62 | 2.70 | – | 2.70 | 2.70 | 5.41 | – | – | 2.70 | 2.70 | | |

# NIPPUR V: EARLY DYNASTIC TO AKKADIAN TRANSITION

Table 17. Third-millennium B.C. Sherd Counts, Bases, Spouts and Vat Fragments by Level

| Level | B-1 | B-2 | B-3 | B-4 | B-5 | B-6 | B-7 | B-8 | S | V |
|---|---|---|---|---|---|---|---|---|---|---|
| XIXB | 5 | 3 | 195 | – | 30 | – | 1 | – | 25 | 10 |
| XIXA | 2 | 2 | 81 | – | 14 | – | – | – | 7 | 7 |
| **XIX Total** | **7** | **5** | **276** | **–** | **44** | **–** | **1** | **–** | **32** | **17** |
| XVIII | 6 | 1 | 65 | – | 10 | – | 6 | – | 8 | 4 |
| XVIIC | 8 | – | 57 | 1 | 5 | – | 6 | – | 5 | 2 |
| XVIIB | 16 | 2 | 114 | – | 16 | 1 | 1 | – | 5 | 4 |
| XVIIA | 3 | – | 33 | – | 2 | – | – | – | 1 | – |
| **XVII Total** | **27** | **2** | **204** | **1** | **23** | **1** | **7** | **–** | **11** | **6** |
| XVI | 9 | 2 | 115 | – | 16 | – | – | – | 7 | 2 |
| XVB | 4 | – | 40 | – | 8 | – | – | – | 1 | 1 |
| XVA | 3 | – | 57 | – | 9 | – | – | – | 2 | 2 |
| **XV Total** | **7** | **–** | **97** | **–** | **17** | **–** | **–** | **–** | **3** | **3** |
| XIVB | 1 | 1 | 97 | – | 10 | – | – | – | – | – |
| XIVA | 1 | 2 | 91 | – | 17 | 1 | – | – | 3 | 4 |
| **XIV Total** | **2** | **3** | **188** | **–** | **27** | **1** | **–** | **–** | **3** | **4** |
| XIIIC | 4 | – | 102 | 1 | 6 | 1 | 1 | – | 5 | 7 |
| XIIIB | – | – | 132 | – | 24 | 1 | – | 1 | 2 | 2 |
| **XIII Total** | **4** | **–** | **234** | **1** | **30** | **2** | **1** | **1** | **7** | **9** |
| XIIB | 2 | 2 | 154 | – | 12 | 1 | – | – | 3 | 3 |
| XIIA | – | 3 | 344 | – | 18 | 1 | – | – | 1 | 13 |
| **XII Total** | **2** | **5** | **498** | **–** | **30** | **2** | **–** | **–** | **4** | **16** |
| XIB | 10 | 4 | 413 | 4 | 28 | – | – | 1 | 4 | 12 |
| XIA | 3 | – | 158 | 7 | 14 | – | – | – | 1 | 9 |
| **XI Total** | **13** | **4** | **571** | **11** | **42** | **–** | **–** | **1** | **5** | **21** |
| X | 3 | 2 | 194 | 7 | 9 | 1 | – | – | 2 | 4 |
| IX | 2 | – | 70 | 2 | 17 | 1 | – | – | 3 | 3 |
| VIII | – | – | 94 | 1 | 13 | – | – | – | – | 2 |
| VII | 1 | – | 31 | – | 1 | – | – | 1 | – | – |
| VI | – | – | 56 | – | 4 | – | – | – | – | 1 |

Table 18. Third-millennium B.C. Decorated Sherd Counts by Level

| Level | D-1a | D-1b | D-1c | D-2 | D-3 | D-4 |
|---|---|---|---|---|---|---|
| XIXB | 6 | 2 | – | 1 | 4 | – |
| XIXA | 6 | 4 | 5 | – | 2 | – |
| **XIX Total** | **12** | **6** | **5** | **1** | **6** | **–** |
| XVIII | 1 | 3 | 2 | 1 | 3 | – |
| XVIIC | 4 | 1 | 2 | 1 | 6 | – |
| XVIIB | 7 | 1 | 3 | 1 | 3 | – |
| XVIIA | – | 2 | 2 | – | 2 | – |
| **XVII Total** | **11** | **4** | **7** | **2** | **11** | **–** |
| XVI | 2 | – | 1 | – | 3 | – |
| XVB | – | – | 3 | – | 2 | – |
| XVA | 2 | 1 | 4 | 1 | 1 | – |
| **XV Total** | **2** | **1** | **7** | **1** | **3** | **–** |
| XIVB | 1 | 2 | 1 | – | 1 | – |
| XIVA | – | 2 | 1 | 1 | – | – |
| **XIV Total** | **1** | **4** | **2** | **1** | **1** | **–** |
| XIIIC | – | 1 | 2 | 1 | – | 1 |
| XIIIB | – | 1 | 1 | – | – | – |
| **XIII Total** | **–** | **2** | **3** | **1** | **–** | **1** |
| XIIB | – | – | 2 | – | – | – |
| XIIA | – | 1 | 5 | – | 1 | – |
| **XII Total** | **–** | **1** | **7** | **–** | **1** | **–** |
| XIB | 3 | 2 | 5 | – | – | – |
| XIA | – | 3 | 2 | – | – | 2 |
| **XI Total** | **3** | **5** | **7** | **–** | **–** | **2** |
| X | 1 | 2 | 4 | – | – | 5 |
| IX | 1 | – | 2 | – | – | – |
| VIII | 1 | – | 1 | – | – | 3 |
| VII | – | – | 3 | – | – | 2 |
| VI | – | – | – | – | 1 | – |

Table 19. Type O-1 Relative Percentages by Third-millennium B.C. Levels

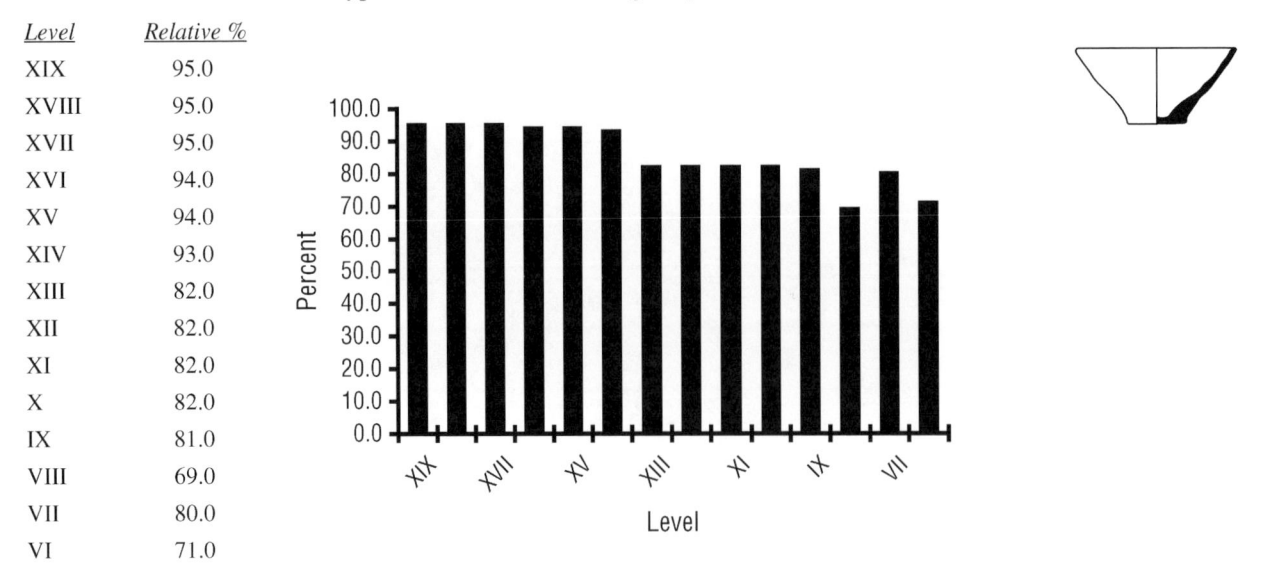

| Level | Relative % |
|---|---|
| XIX | 95.0 |
| XVIII | 95.0 |
| XVII | 95.0 |
| XVI | 94.0 |
| XV | 94.0 |
| XIV | 93.0 |
| XIII | 82.0 |
| XII | 82.0 |
| XI | 82.0 |
| X | 82.0 |
| IX | 81.0 |
| VIII | 69.0 |
| VII | 80.0 |
| VI | 71.0 |

Table 20. Type O-2 Relative Percentages by Third-millennium B.C. Levels

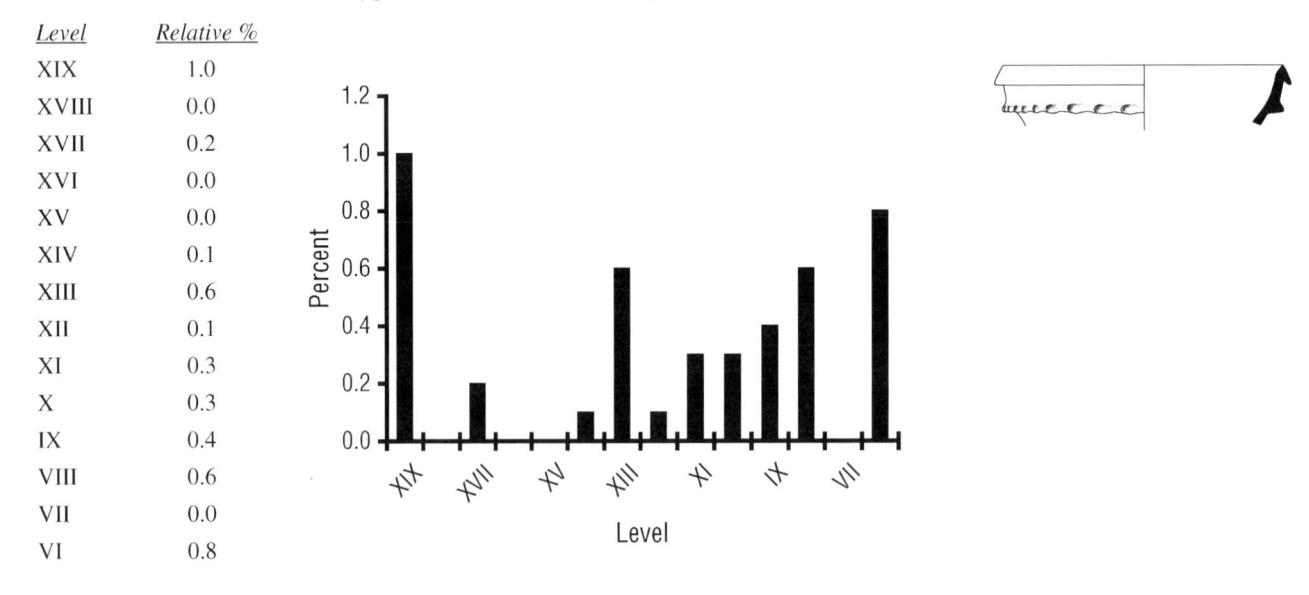

| Level | Relative % |
|---|---|
| XIX | 1.0 |
| XVIII | 0.0 |
| XVII | 0.2 |
| XVI | 0.0 |
| XV | 0.0 |
| XIV | 0.1 |
| XIII | 0.6 |
| XII | 0.1 |
| XI | 0.3 |
| X | 0.3 |
| IX | 0.4 |
| VIII | 0.6 |
| VII | 0.0 |
| VI | 0.8 |

Table 21. Type O-3 Relative Percentages by Third-millennium B.C. Levels

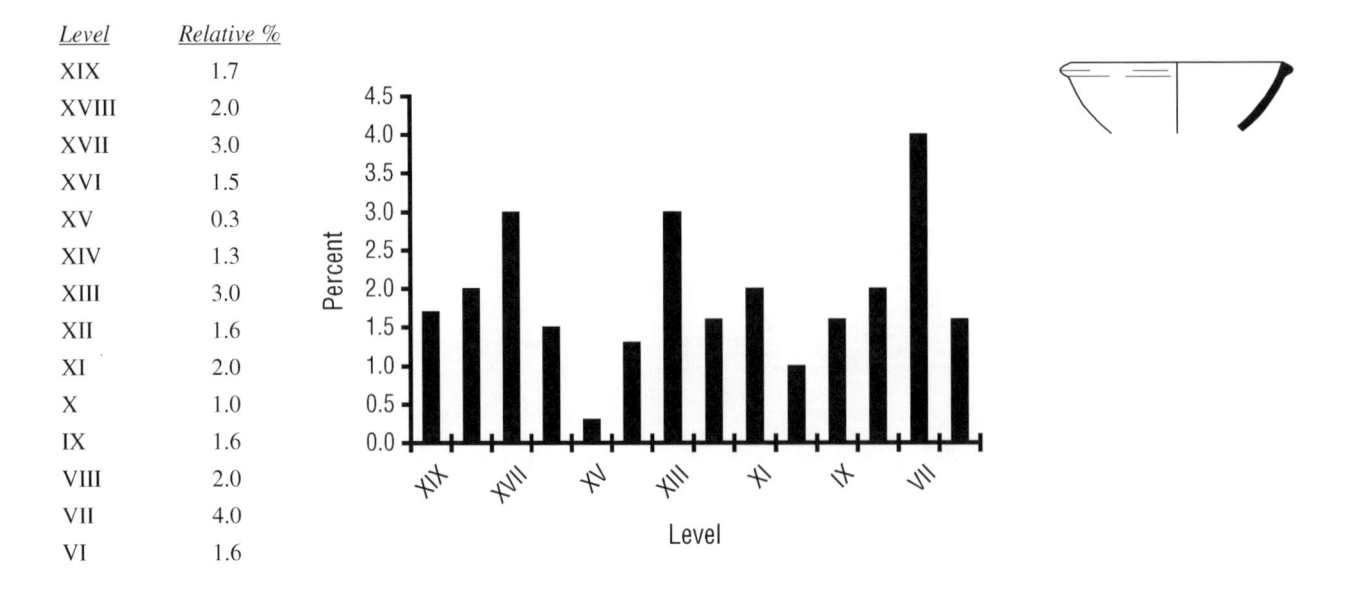

| Level | Relative % |
|---|---|
| XIX | 1.7 |
| XVIII | 2.0 |
| XVII | 3.0 |
| XVI | 1.5 |
| XV | 0.3 |
| XIV | 1.3 |
| XIII | 3.0 |
| XII | 1.6 |
| XI | 2.0 |
| X | 1.0 |
| IX | 1.6 |
| VIII | 2.0 |
| VII | 4.0 |
| VI | 1.6 |

Table 22. Type O-4 Relative Percentages by Third-millennium B.C. Levels

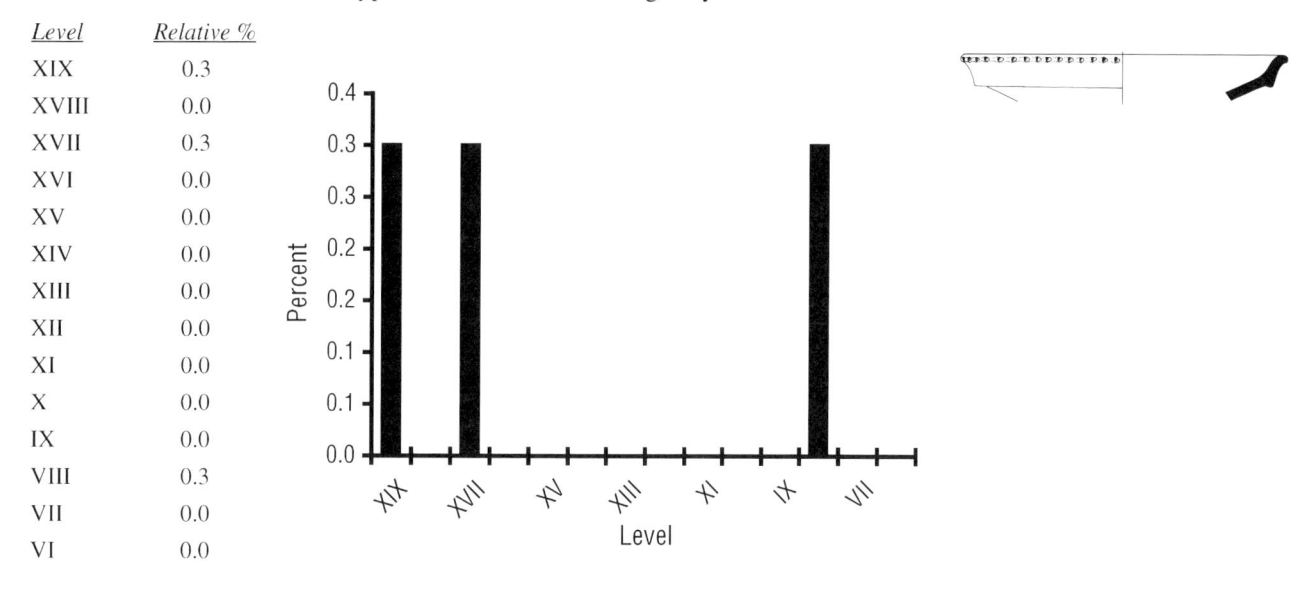

| Level | Relative % |
| --- | --- |
| XIX | 0.3 |
| XVIII | 0.0 |
| XVII | 0.3 |
| XVI | 0.0 |
| XV | 0.0 |
| XIV | 0.0 |
| XIII | 0.0 |
| XII | 0.0 |
| XI | 0.0 |
| X | 0.0 |
| IX | 0.0 |
| VIII | 0.3 |
| VII | 0.0 |
| VI | 0.0 |

Table 23. Type O-5 Relative Percentages by Third-millennium B.C. Levels

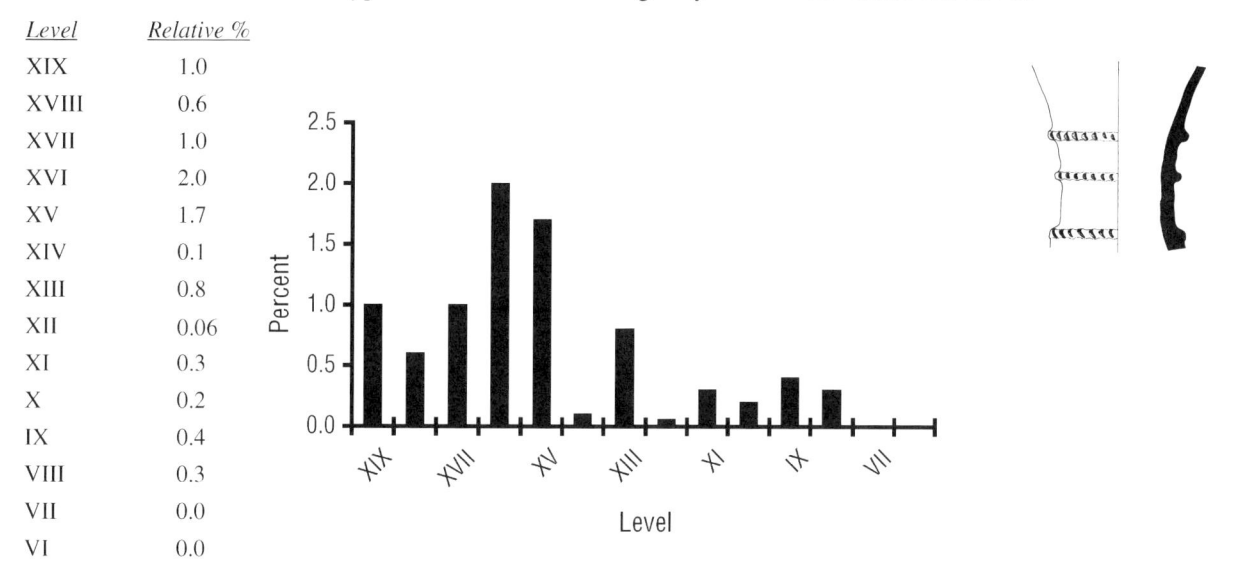

| Level | Relative % |
| --- | --- |
| XIX | 1.0 |
| XVIII | 0.6 |
| XVII | 1.0 |
| XVI | 2.0 |
| XV | 1.7 |
| XIV | 0.1 |
| XIII | 0.8 |
| XII | 0.06 |
| XI | 0.3 |
| X | 0.2 |
| IX | 0.4 |
| VIII | 0.3 |
| VII | 0.0 |
| VI | 0.0 |

Table 24. Type O-6 Relative Percentages by Third-millennium B.C. Levels

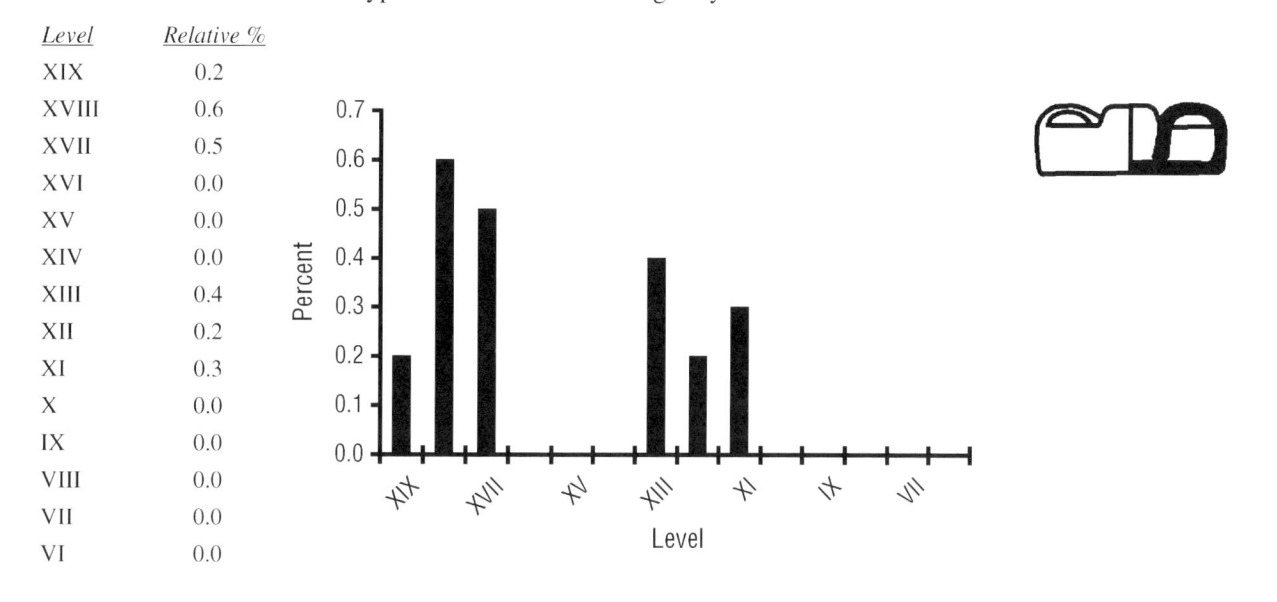

| Level | Relative % |
| --- | --- |
| XIX | 0.2 |
| XVIII | 0.6 |
| XVII | 0.5 |
| XVI | 0.0 |
| XV | 0.0 |
| XIV | 0.0 |
| XIII | 0.4 |
| XII | 0.2 |
| XI | 0.3 |
| X | 0.0 |
| IX | 0.0 |
| VIII | 0.0 |
| VII | 0.0 |
| VI | 0.0 |

Table 25. Type O-7 Relative Percentages by Third-millennium B.C. Levels

| Level | Relative % |
|---|---|
| XIX | 0.7 |
| XVIII | 0.6 |
| XVII | 0.5 |
| XVI | 0.2 |
| XV | 0.0 |
| XIV | 0.0 |
| XIII | 0.4 |
| XII | 0.0 |
| XI | 0.1 |
| X | 0.2 |
| IX | 0.8 |
| VIII | 0.0 |
| VII | 0.0 |
| VI | 0.0 |

Table 26. Type O-8 Relative Percentages by Third-millennium B.C. Levels

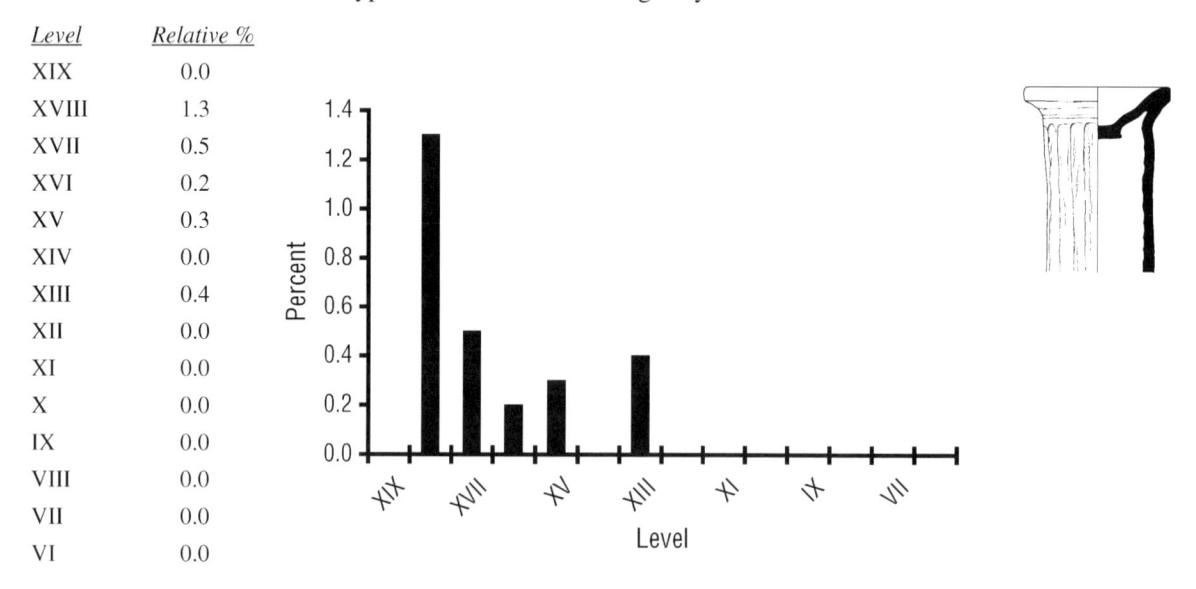

| Level | Relative % |
|---|---|
| XIX | 0.0 |
| XVIII | 1.3 |
| XVII | 0.5 |
| XVI | 0.2 |
| XV | 0.3 |
| XIV | 0.0 |
| XIII | 0.4 |
| XII | 0.0 |
| XI | 0.0 |
| X | 0.0 |
| IX | 0.0 |
| VIII | 0.0 |
| VII | 0.0 |
| VI | 0.0 |

Table 27. Type O-9 Relative Percentages by Third-millennium B.C. Levels

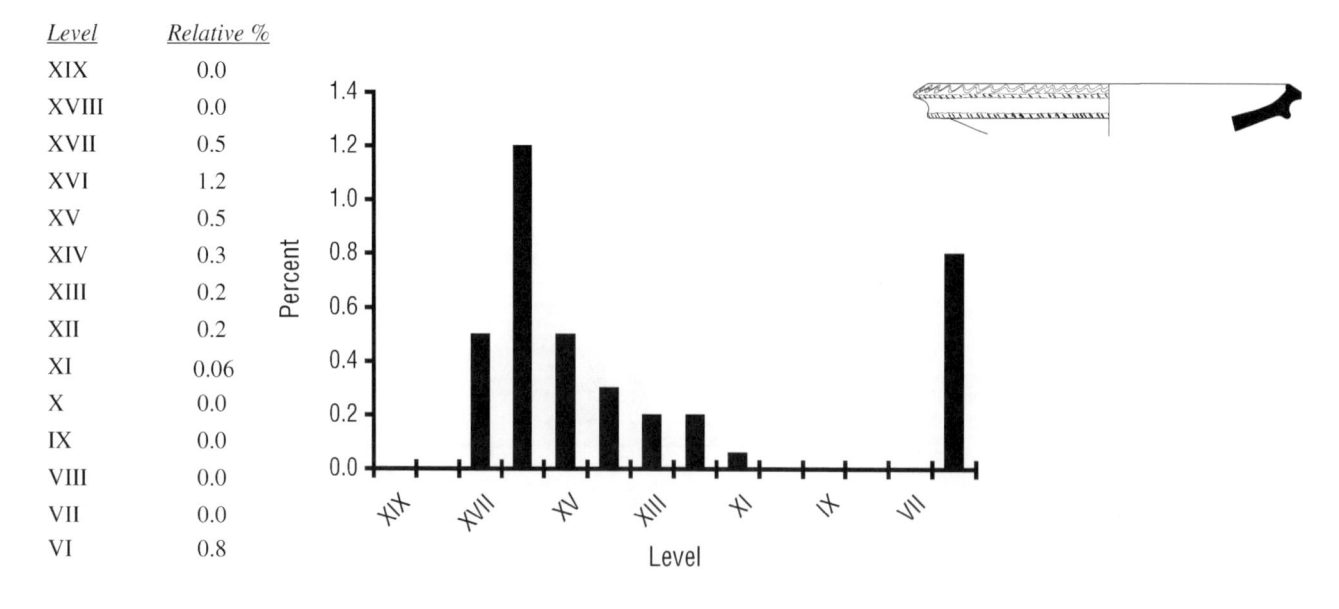

| Level | Relative % |
|---|---|
| XIX | 0.0 |
| XVIII | 0.0 |
| XVII | 0.5 |
| XVI | 1.2 |
| XV | 0.5 |
| XIV | 0.3 |
| XIII | 0.2 |
| XII | 0.2 |
| XI | 0.06 |
| X | 0.0 |
| IX | 0.0 |
| VIII | 0.0 |
| VII | 0.0 |
| VI | 0.8 |

## CHAPTER 3: POTTERY

Table 28. Type O-10 Relative Percentages by Third-millennium B.C. Levels

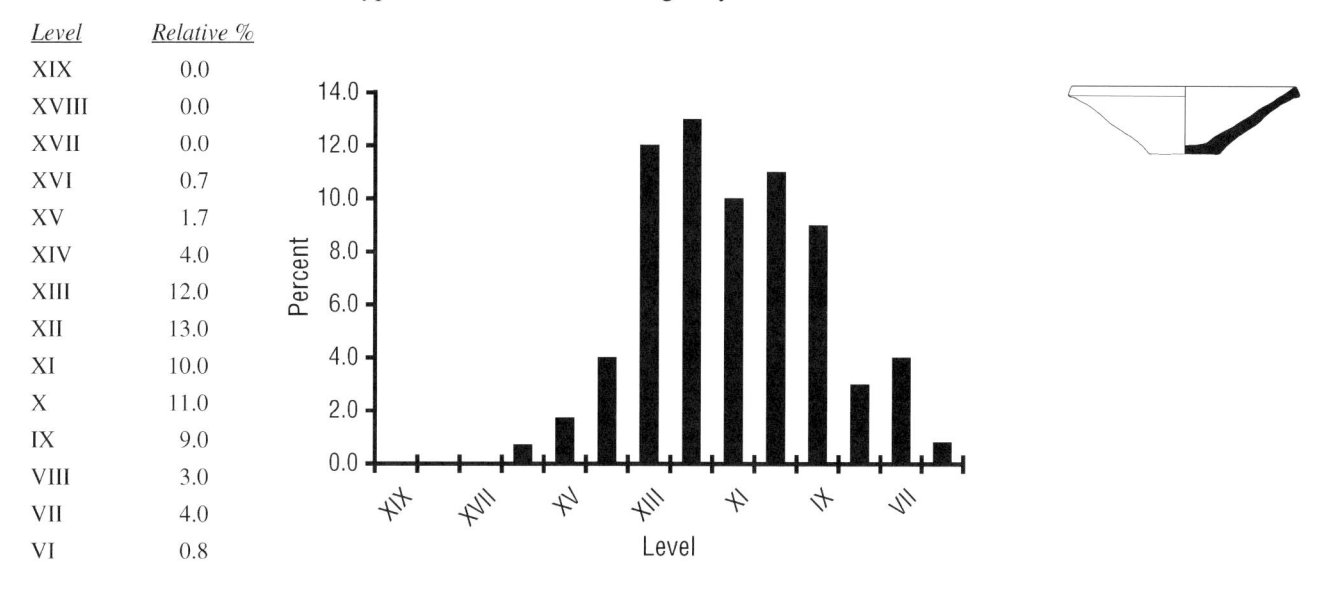

| Level | Relative % |
|---|---|
| XIX | 0.0 |
| XVIII | 0.0 |
| XVII | 0.0 |
| XVI | 0.7 |
| XV | 1.7 |
| XIV | 4.0 |
| XIII | 12.0 |
| XII | 13.0 |
| XI | 10.0 |
| X | 11.0 |
| IX | 9.0 |
| VIII | 3.0 |
| VII | 4.0 |
| VI | 0.8 |

Table 29. Type O-11 Relative Percentages by Third-millennium B.C. Levels

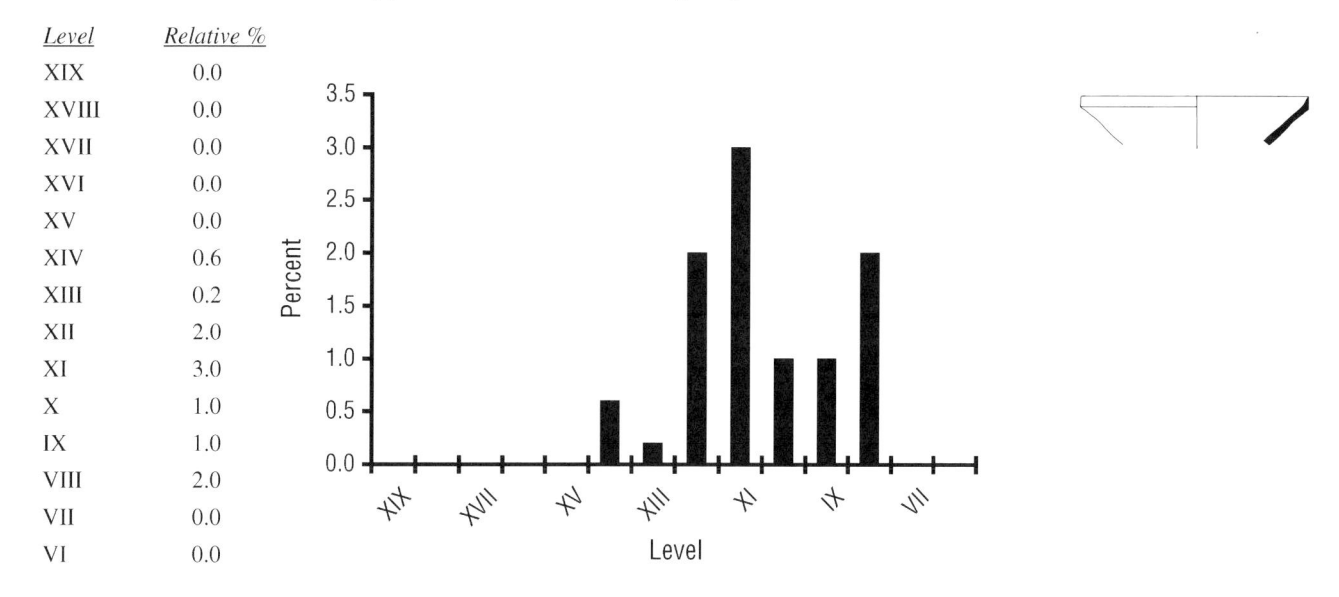

| Level | Relative % |
|---|---|
| XIX | 0.0 |
| XVIII | 0.0 |
| XVII | 0.0 |
| XVI | 0.0 |
| XV | 0.0 |
| XIV | 0.6 |
| XIII | 0.2 |
| XII | 2.0 |
| XI | 3.0 |
| X | 1.0 |
| IX | 1.0 |
| VIII | 2.0 |
| VII | 0.0 |
| VI | 0.0 |

Table 30. Type O-12 Relative Percentages by Third-millennium B.C. Levels

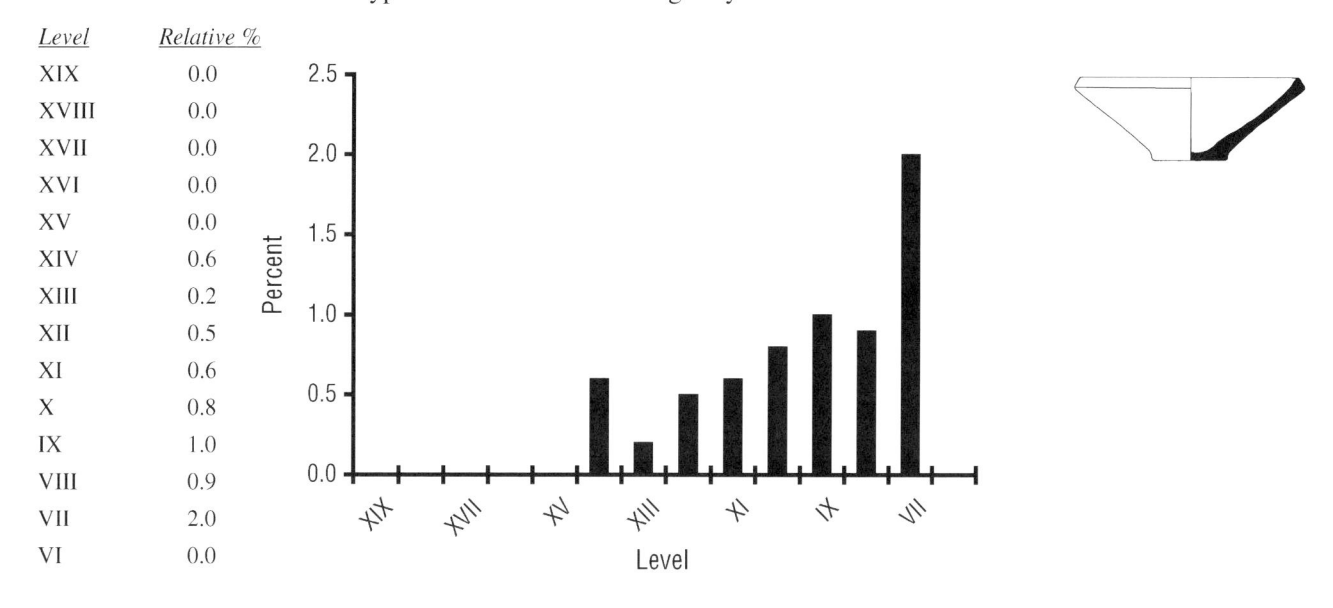

| Level | Relative % |
|---|---|
| XIX | 0.0 |
| XVIII | 0.0 |
| XVII | 0.0 |
| XVI | 0.0 |
| XV | 0.0 |
| XIV | 0.6 |
| XIII | 0.2 |
| XII | 0.5 |
| XI | 0.6 |
| X | 0.8 |
| IX | 1.0 |
| VIII | 0.9 |
| VII | 2.0 |
| VI | 0.0 |

104 NIPPUR V: EARLY DYNASTIC TO AKKADIAN TRANSITION

Table 31. Type O-13 Relative Percentages by Third-millennium B.C. Levels

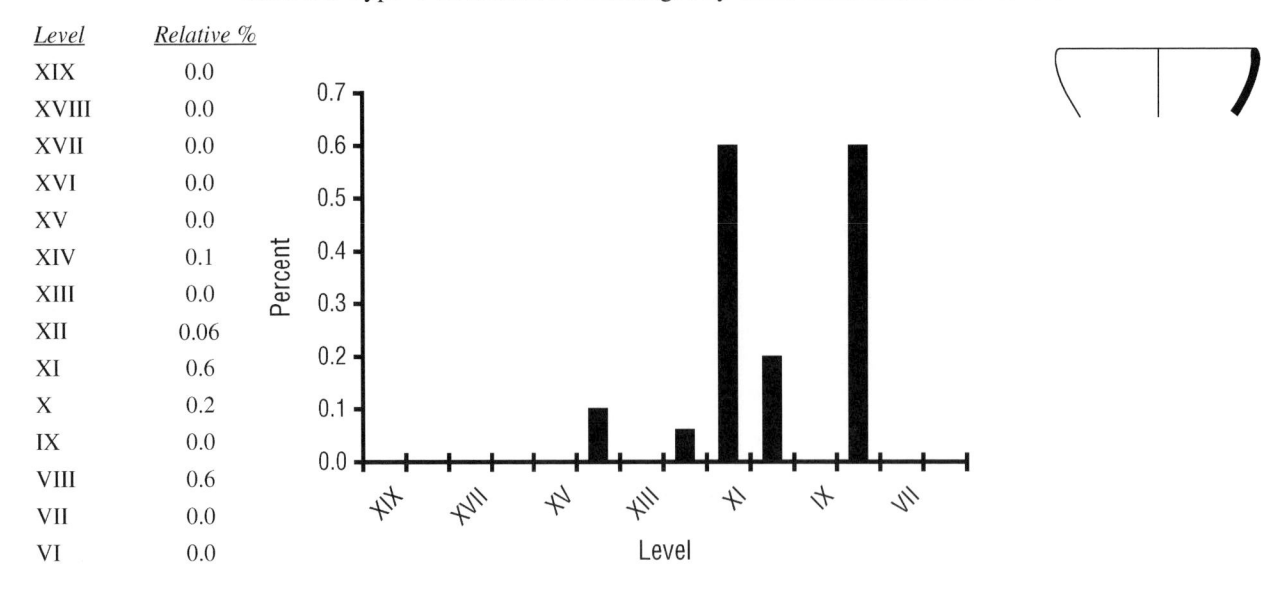

| Level | Relative % |
|---|---|
| XIX | 0.0 |
| XVIII | 0.0 |
| XVII | 0.0 |
| XVI | 0.0 |
| XV | 0.0 |
| XIV | 0.1 |
| XIII | 0.0 |
| XII | 0.06 |
| XI | 0.6 |
| X | 0.2 |
| IX | 0.0 |
| VIII | 0.6 |
| VII | 0.0 |
| VI | 0.0 |

Table 32. Type O-14 Relative Percentages by Third-millennium B.C. Levels

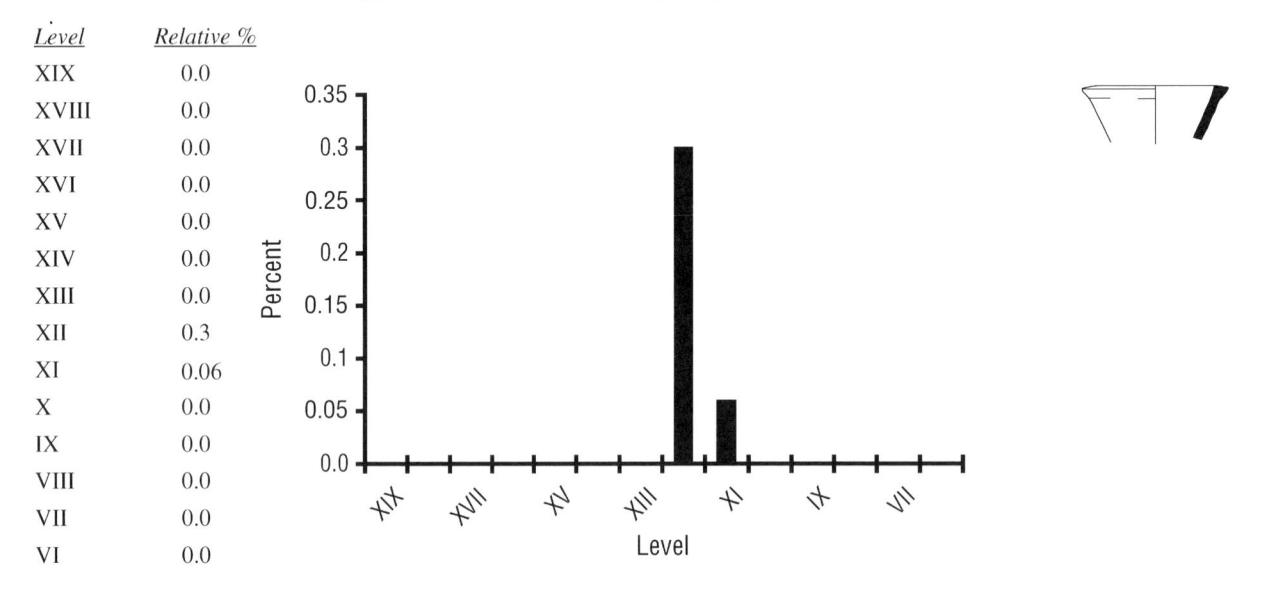

| Level | Relative % |
|---|---|
| XIX | 0.0 |
| XVIII | 0.0 |
| XVII | 0.0 |
| XVI | 0.0 |
| XV | 0.0 |
| XIV | 0.0 |
| XIII | 0.0 |
| XII | 0.3 |
| XI | 0.06 |
| X | 0.0 |
| IX | 0.0 |
| VIII | 0.0 |
| VII | 0.0 |
| VI | 0.0 |

Table 33. Type O-15 Relative Percentages by Third-millennium B.C. Levels

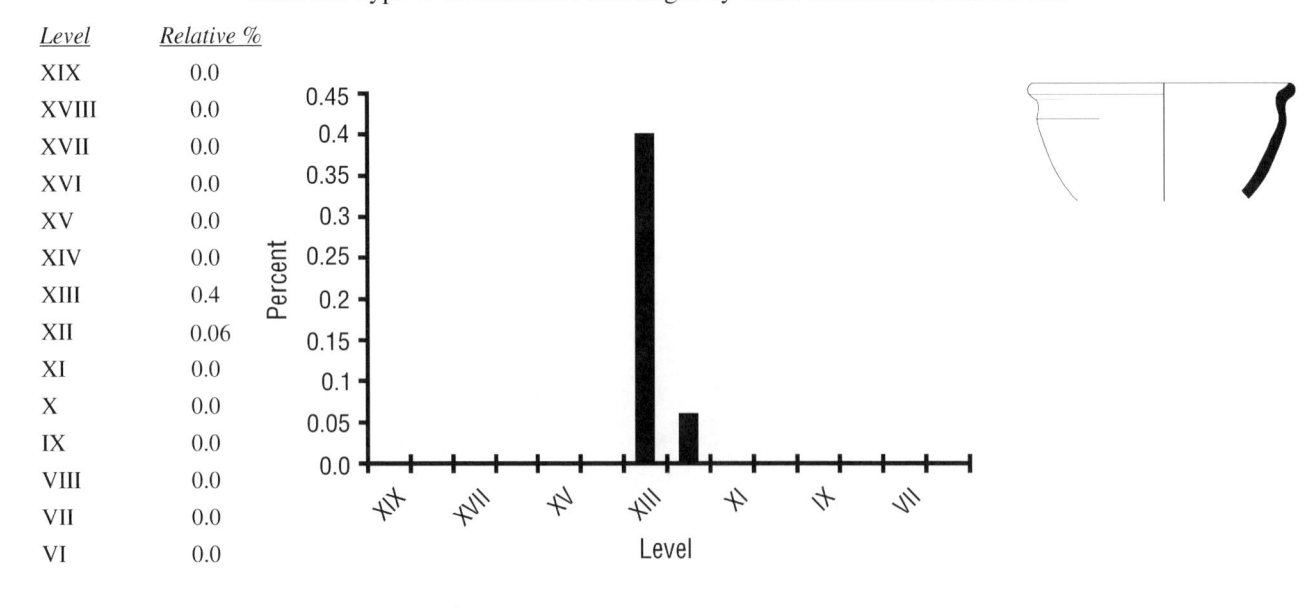

| Level | Relative % |
|---|---|
| XIX | 0.0 |
| XVIII | 0.0 |
| XVII | 0.0 |
| XVI | 0.0 |
| XV | 0.0 |
| XIV | 0.0 |
| XIII | 0.4 |
| XII | 0.06 |
| XI | 0.0 |
| X | 0.0 |
| IX | 0.0 |
| VIII | 0.0 |
| VII | 0.0 |
| VI | 0.0 |

CHAPTER 3: POTTERY

Table 34. Type O-16 Relative Percentages by Third-millennium B.C. Levels

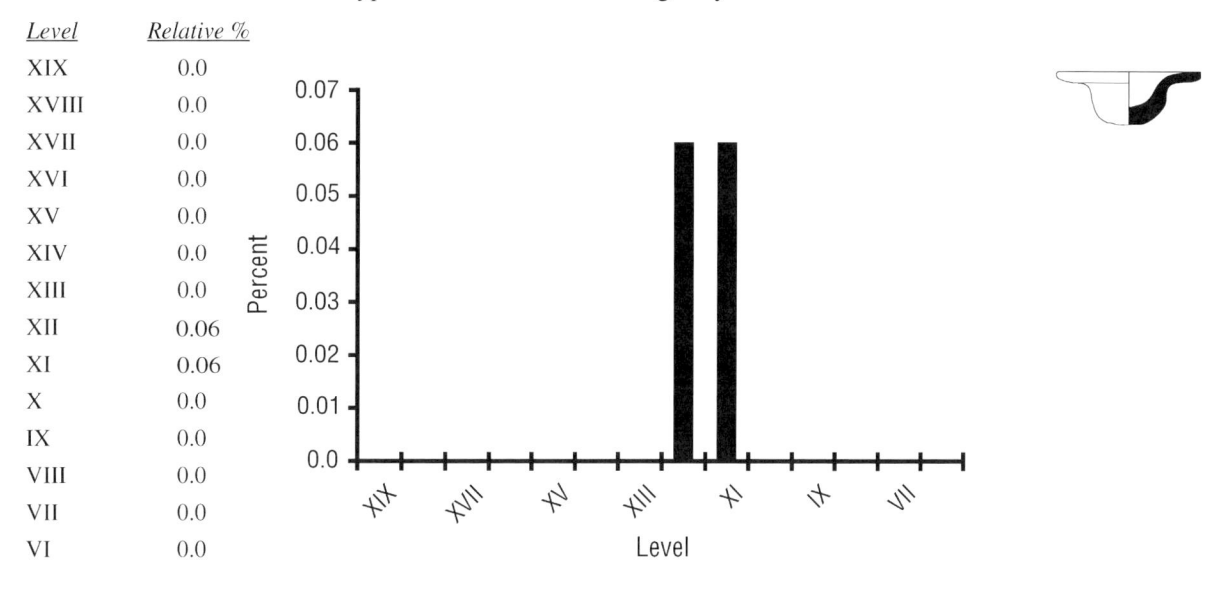

| Level | Relative % |
|---|---|
| XIX | 0.0 |
| XVIII | 0.0 |
| XVII | 0.0 |
| XVI | 0.0 |
| XV | 0.0 |
| XIV | 0.0 |
| XIII | 0.0 |
| XII | 0.06 |
| XI | 0.06 |
| X | 0.0 |
| IX | 0.0 |
| VIII | 0.0 |
| VII | 0.0 |
| VI | 0.0 |

Table 35. Type O-17 Relative Percentages by Third-millennium B.C. Levels

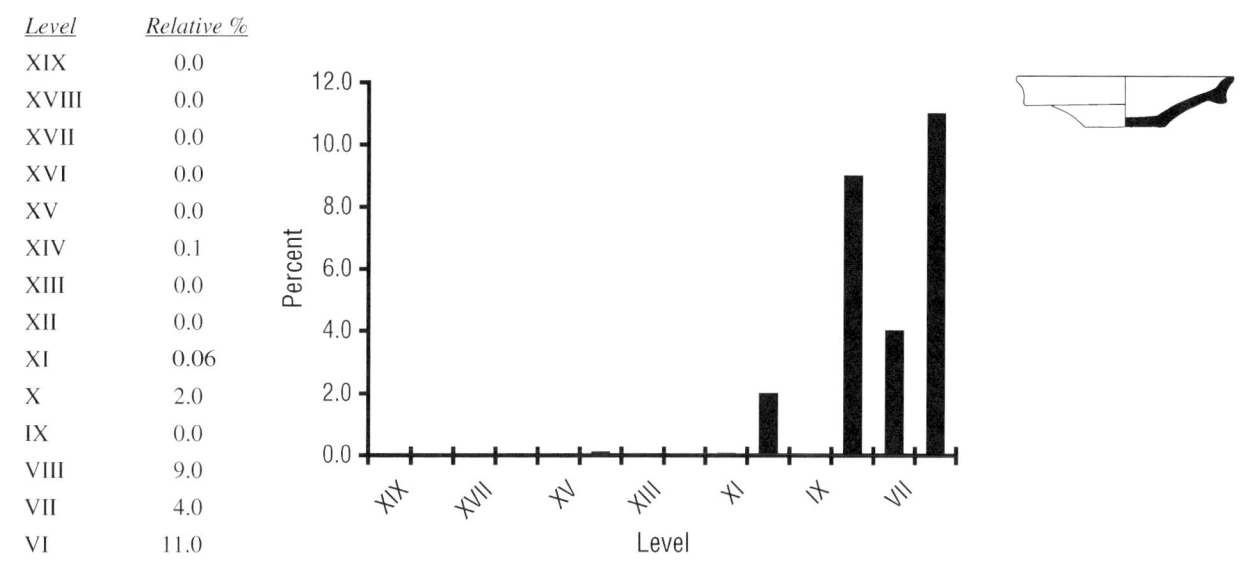

| Level | Relative % |
|---|---|
| XIX | 0.0 |
| XVIII | 0.0 |
| XVII | 0.0 |
| XVI | 0.0 |
| XV | 0.0 |
| XIV | 0.1 |
| XIII | 0.0 |
| XII | 0.0 |
| XI | 0.06 |
| X | 2.0 |
| IX | 0.0 |
| VIII | 9.0 |
| VII | 4.0 |
| VI | 11.0 |

Table 36. Type O-18 Relative Percentages by Third-millennium B.C. Levels

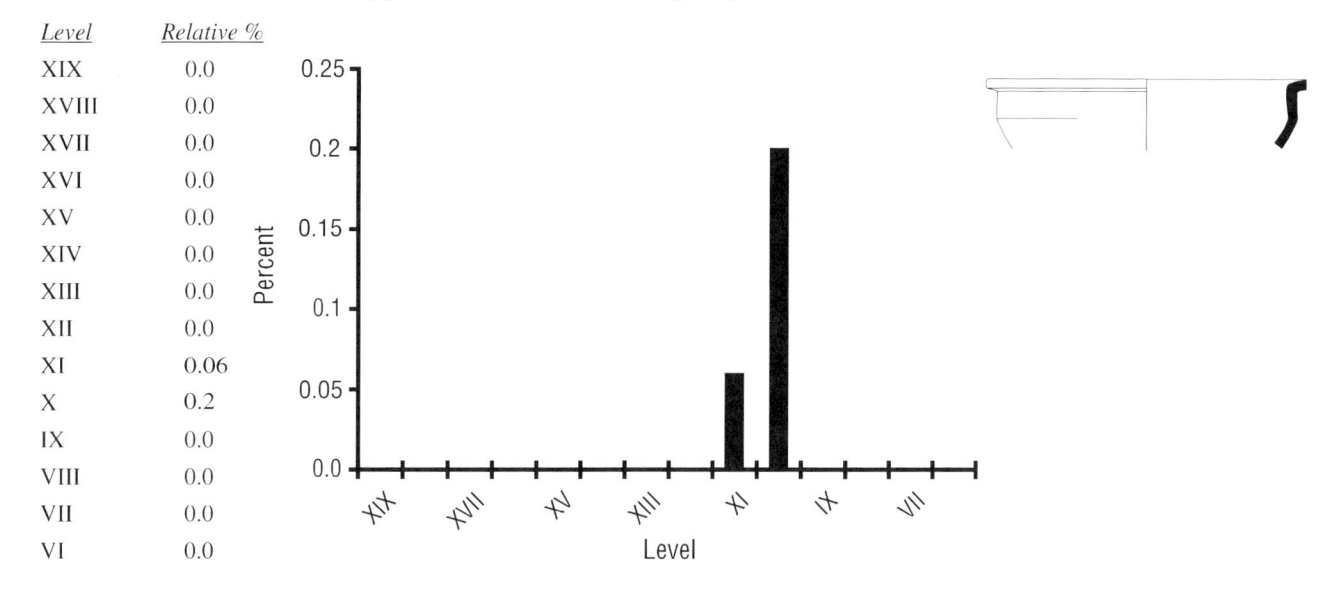

| Level | Relative % |
|---|---|
| XIX | 0.0 |
| XVIII | 0.0 |
| XVII | 0.0 |
| XVI | 0.0 |
| XV | 0.0 |
| XIV | 0.0 |
| XIII | 0.0 |
| XII | 0.0 |
| XI | 0.06 |
| X | 0.2 |
| IX | 0.0 |
| VIII | 0.0 |
| VII | 0.0 |
| VI | 0.0 |

Table 37. Type O-19 Relative Percentages by Third-millennium B.C. Levels

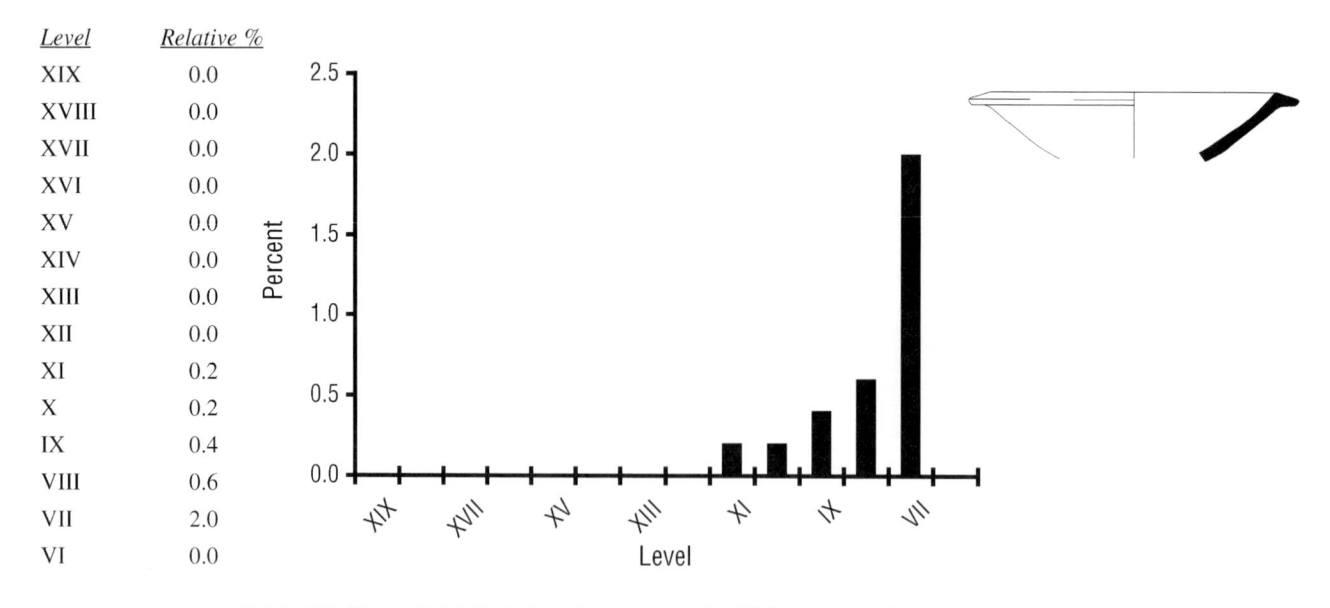

| Level | Relative % |
|---|---|
| XIX | 0.0 |
| XVIII | 0.0 |
| XVII | 0.0 |
| XVI | 0.0 |
| XV | 0.0 |
| XIV | 0.0 |
| XIII | 0.0 |
| XII | 0.0 |
| XI | 0.2 |
| X | 0.2 |
| IX | 0.4 |
| VIII | 0.6 |
| VII | 2.0 |
| VI | 0.0 |

Table 38. Type O-20 Relative Percentages by Third-millennium B.C. Levels

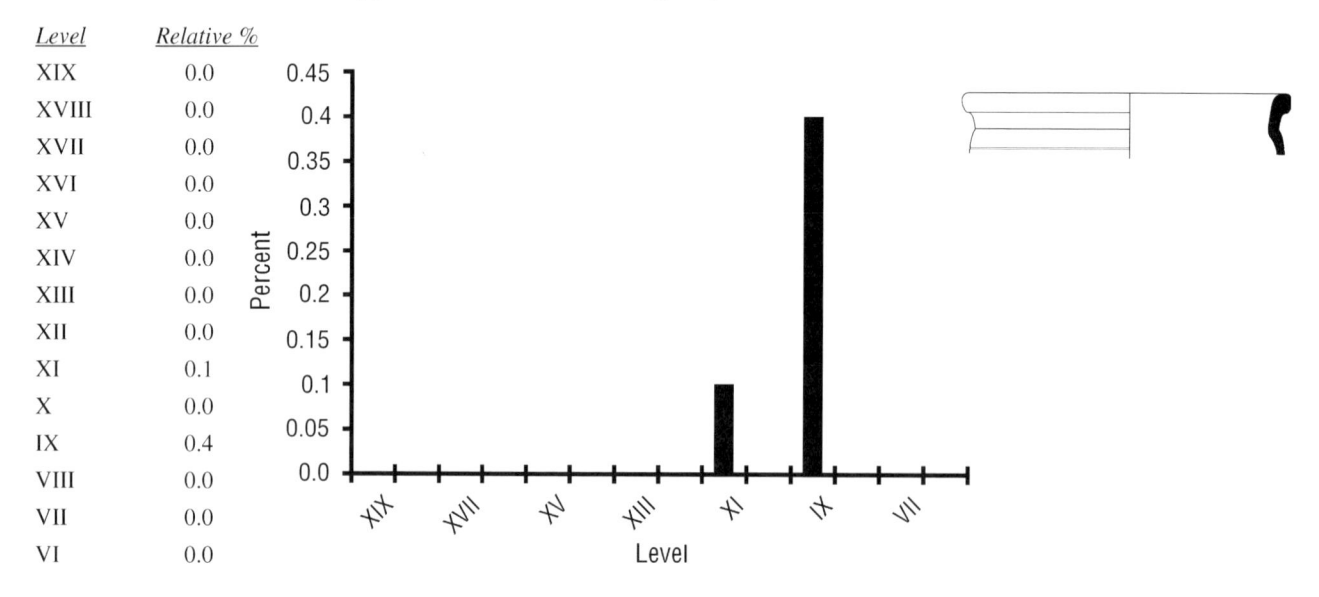

| Level | Relative % |
|---|---|
| XIX | 0.0 |
| XVIII | 0.0 |
| XVII | 0.0 |
| XVI | 0.0 |
| XV | 0.0 |
| XIV | 0.0 |
| XIII | 0.0 |
| XII | 0.0 |
| XI | 0.1 |
| X | 0.0 |
| IX | 0.4 |
| VIII | 0.0 |
| VII | 0.0 |
| VI | 0.0 |

Table 39. Type O-21 Relative Percentages by Third-millennium B.C. Levels

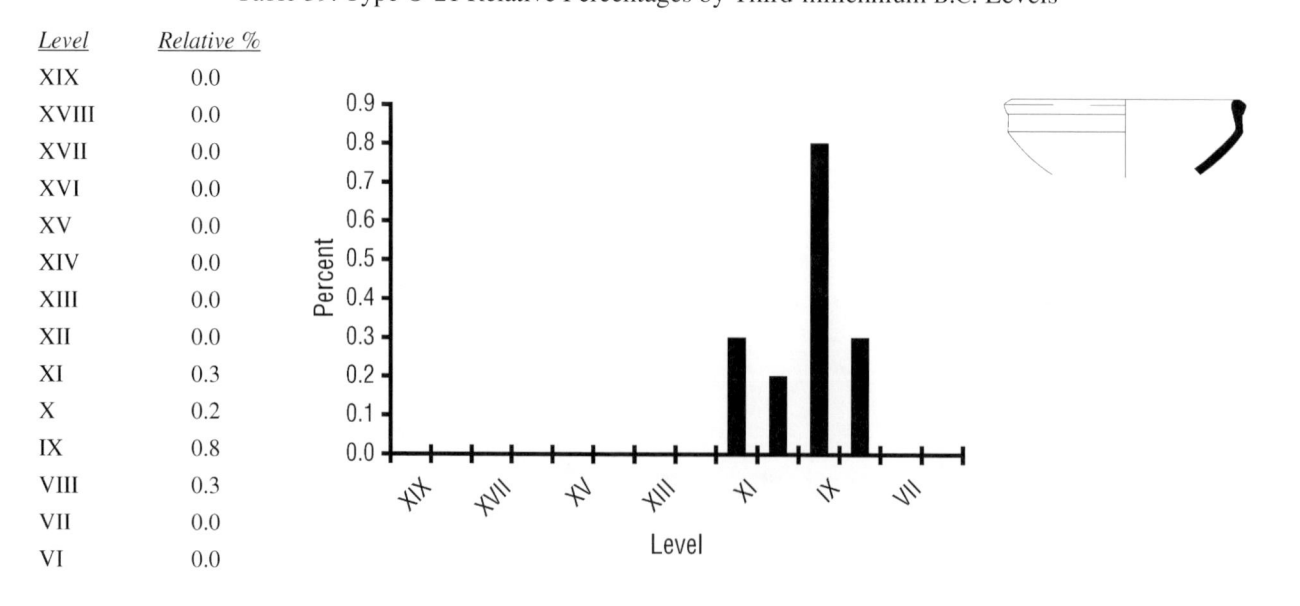

| Level | Relative % |
|---|---|
| XIX | 0.0 |
| XVIII | 0.0 |
| XVII | 0.0 |
| XVI | 0.0 |
| XV | 0.0 |
| XIV | 0.0 |
| XIII | 0.0 |
| XII | 0.0 |
| XI | 0.3 |
| X | 0.2 |
| IX | 0.8 |
| VIII | 0.3 |
| VII | 0.0 |
| VI | 0.0 |

# CHAPTER 3: POTTERY

Table 40. Type O-22 Relative Percentages by Third-millennium B.C. Levels

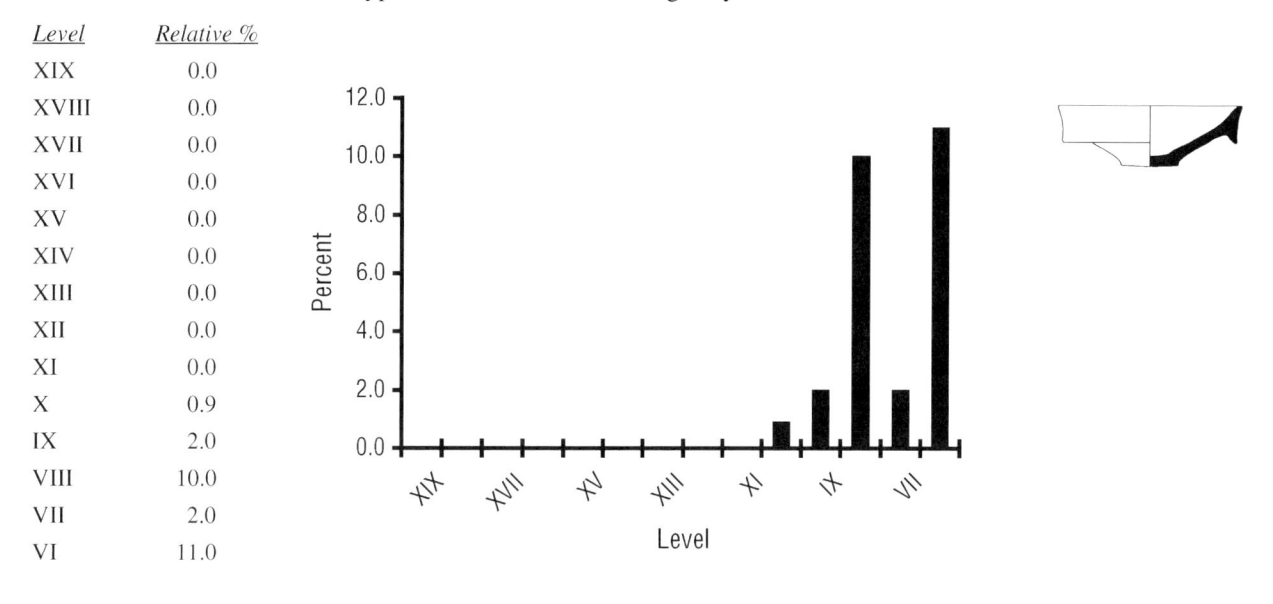

| Level | Relative % |
|---|---|
| XIX | 0.0 |
| XVIII | 0.0 |
| XVII | 0.0 |
| XVI | 0.0 |
| XV | 0.0 |
| XIV | 0.0 |
| XIII | 0.0 |
| XII | 0.0 |
| XI | 0.0 |
| X | 0.9 |
| IX | 2.0 |
| VIII | 10.0 |
| VII | 2.0 |
| VI | 11.0 |

Table 41. Type O-23 Relative Percentages by Third-millennium B.C. Levels

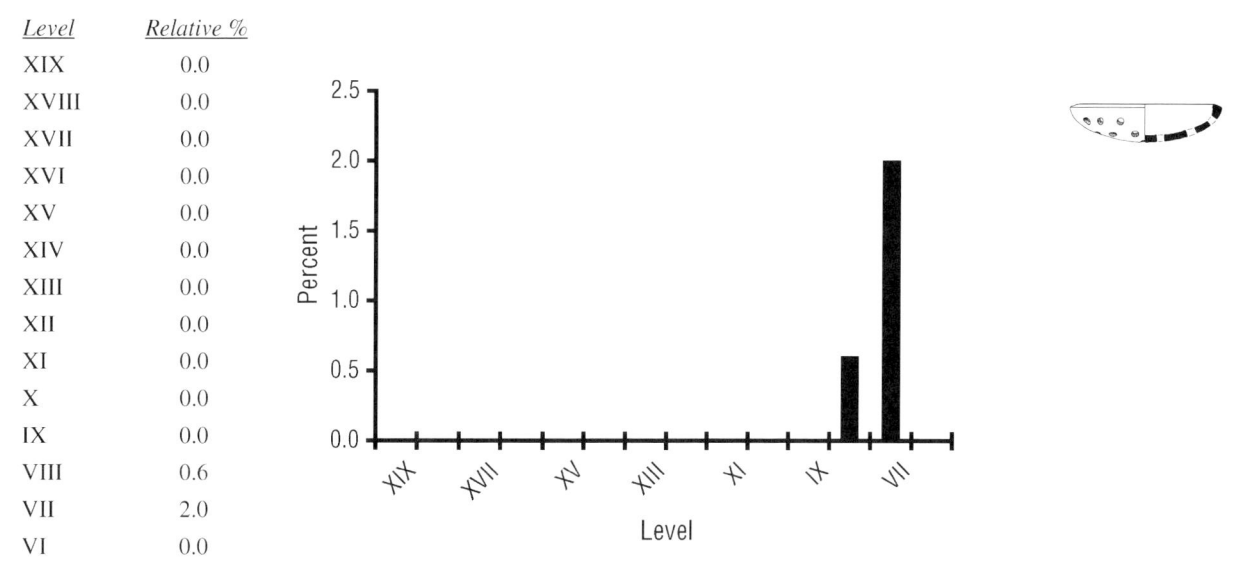

| Level | Relative % |
|---|---|
| XIX | 0.0 |
| XVIII | 0.0 |
| XVII | 0.0 |
| XVI | 0.0 |
| XV | 0.0 |
| XIV | 0.0 |
| XIII | 0.0 |
| XII | 0.0 |
| XI | 0.0 |
| X | 0.0 |
| IX | 0.0 |
| VIII | 0.6 |
| VII | 2.0 |
| VI | 0.0 |

Table 42. Type O-24 Relative Percentages by Third-millennium B.C. Levels

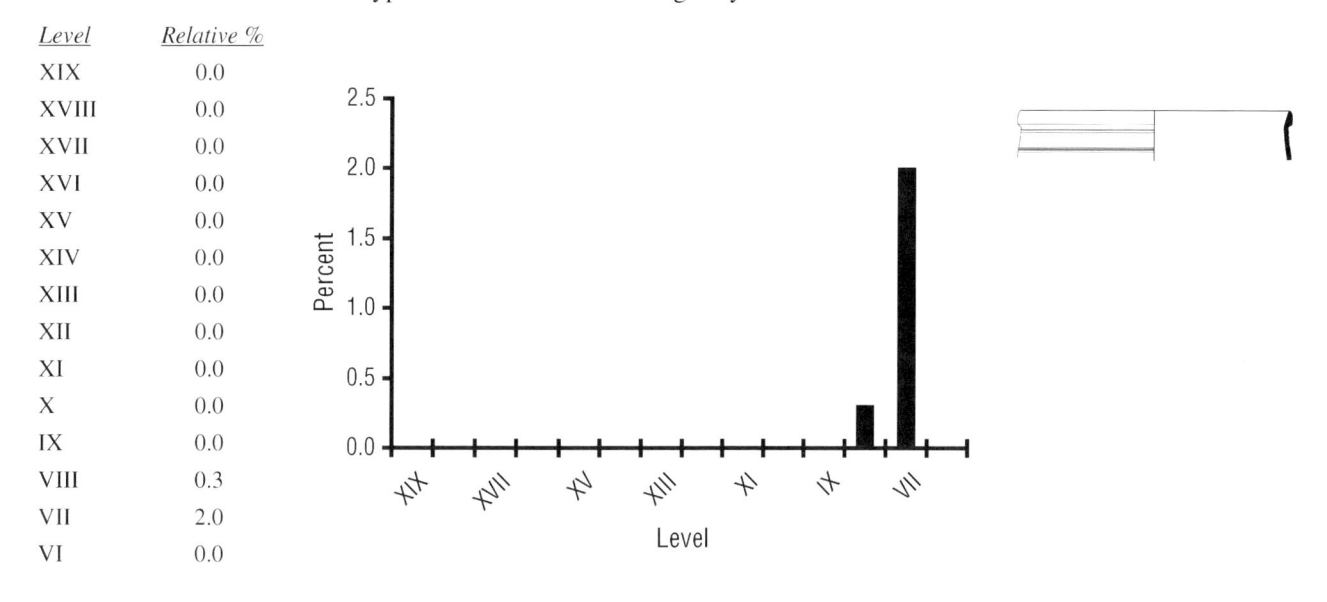

| Level | Relative % |
|---|---|
| XIX | 0.0 |
| XVIII | 0.0 |
| XVII | 0.0 |
| XVI | 0.0 |
| XV | 0.0 |
| XIV | 0.0 |
| XIII | 0.0 |
| XII | 0.0 |
| XI | 0.0 |
| X | 0.0 |
| IX | 0.0 |
| VIII | 0.3 |
| VII | 2.0 |
| VI | 0.0 |

Table 43. Type O-25 Relative Percentages by Third-millennium B.C. Levels

| Level | Relative % |
|---|---|
| XIX | 0.0 |
| XVIII | 0.0 |
| XVII | 0.0 |
| XVI | 0.0 |
| XV | 0.0 |
| XIV | 0.0 |
| XIII | 0.0 |
| XII | 0.0 |
| XI | 0.0 |
| X | 0.0 |
| IX | 0.0 |
| VIII | 0.0 |
| VII | 0.0 |
| VI | 0.8 |

Table 44. Type C-1 Relative Percentages by Third-millennium B.C. Levels

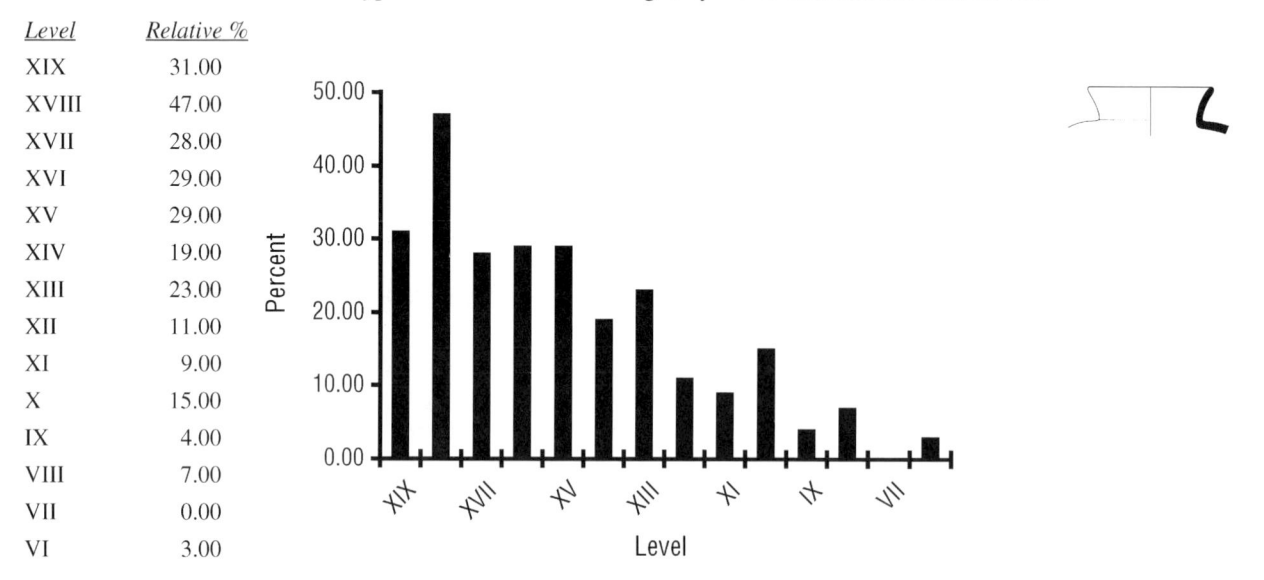

| Level | Relative % |
|---|---|
| XIX | 31.00 |
| XVIII | 47.00 |
| XVII | 28.00 |
| XVI | 29.00 |
| XV | 29.00 |
| XIV | 19.00 |
| XIII | 23.00 |
| XII | 11.00 |
| XI | 9.00 |
| X | 15.00 |
| IX | 4.00 |
| VIII | 7.00 |
| VII | 0.00 |
| VI | 3.00 |

Table 45. Type C-2 Relative Percentages by Third-millennium B.C. Levels

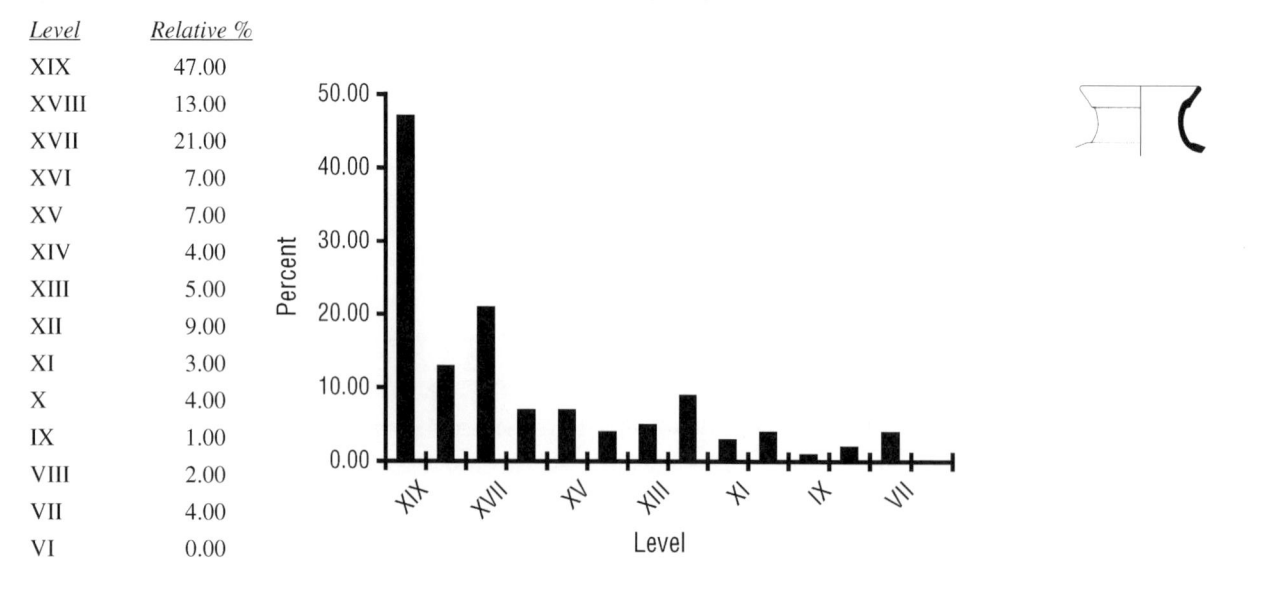

| Level | Relative % |
|---|---|
| XIX | 47.00 |
| XVIII | 13.00 |
| XVII | 21.00 |
| XVI | 7.00 |
| XV | 7.00 |
| XIV | 4.00 |
| XIII | 5.00 |
| XII | 9.00 |
| XI | 3.00 |
| X | 4.00 |
| IX | 1.00 |
| VIII | 2.00 |
| VII | 4.00 |
| VI | 0.00 |

## CHAPTER 3: POTTERY

Table 46. Type C-3 Relative Percentages by Third-millennium B.C. Levels

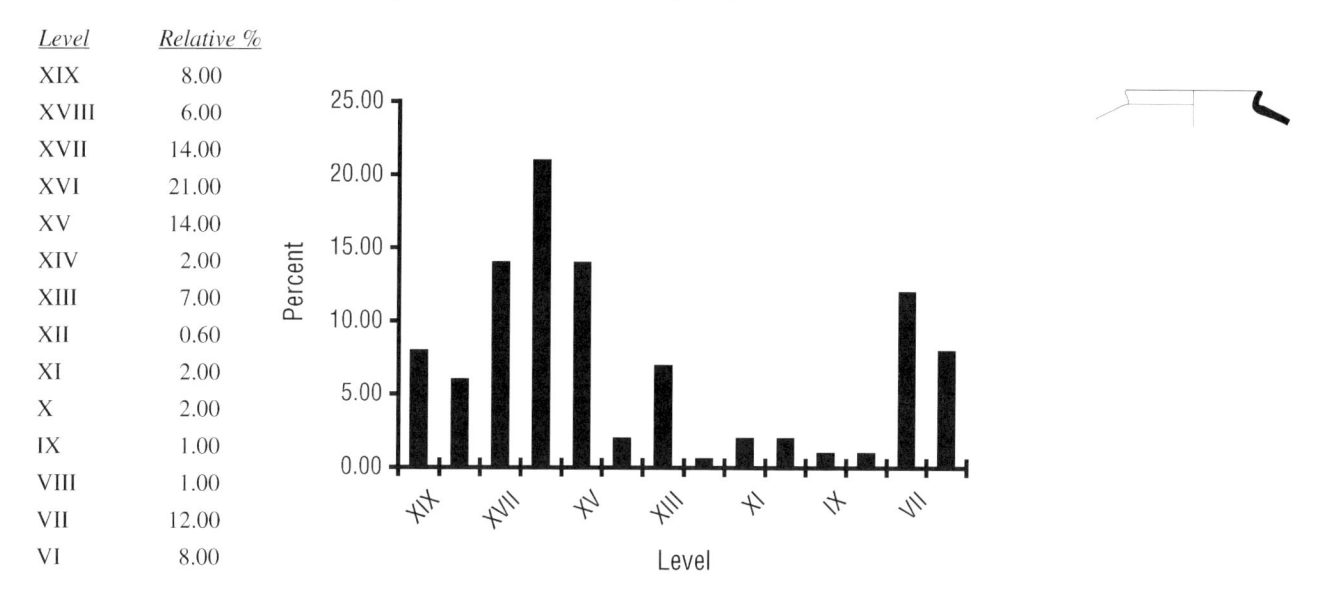

| Level | Relative % |
|---|---|
| XIX | 8.00 |
| XVIII | 6.00 |
| XVII | 14.00 |
| XVI | 21.00 |
| XV | 14.00 |
| XIV | 2.00 |
| XIII | 7.00 |
| XII | 0.60 |
| XI | 2.00 |
| X | 2.00 |
| IX | 1.00 |
| VIII | 1.00 |
| VII | 12.00 |
| VI | 8.00 |

Table 47. Type C-4 Relative Percentages by Third-millennium B.C. Levels

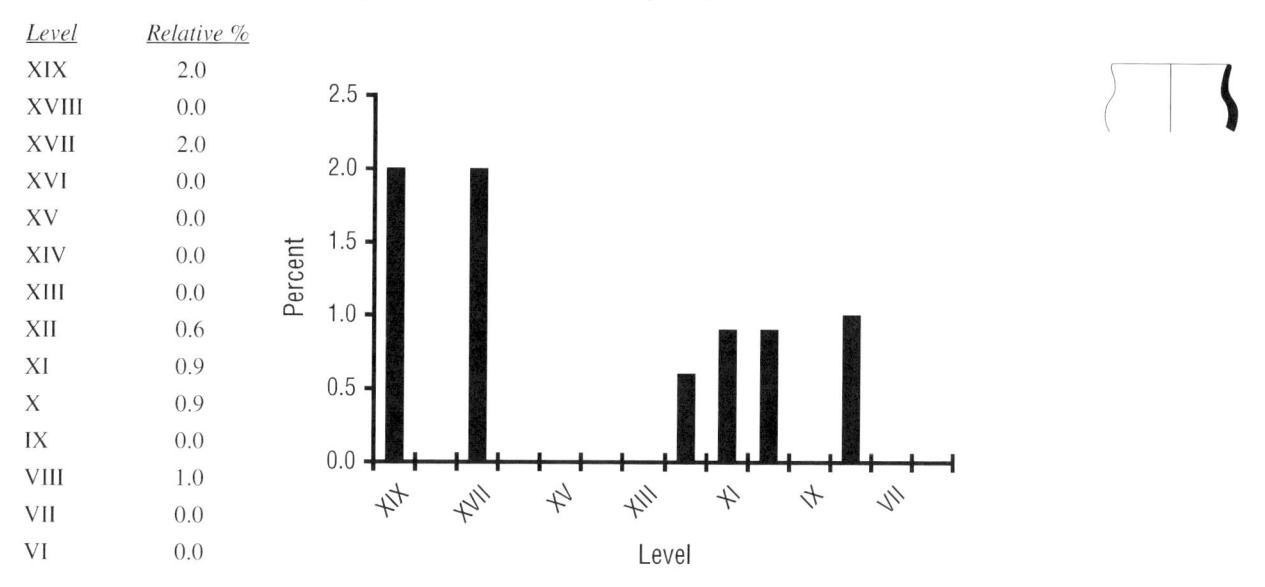

| Level | Relative % |
|---|---|
| XIX | 2.0 |
| XVIII | 0.0 |
| XVII | 2.0 |
| XVI | 0.0 |
| XV | 0.0 |
| XIV | 0.0 |
| XIII | 0.0 |
| XII | 0.6 |
| XI | 0.9 |
| X | 0.9 |
| IX | 0.0 |
| VIII | 1.0 |
| VII | 0.0 |
| VI | 0.0 |

Table 48. Type C-5 Relative Percentages by Third-millennium B.C. Levels

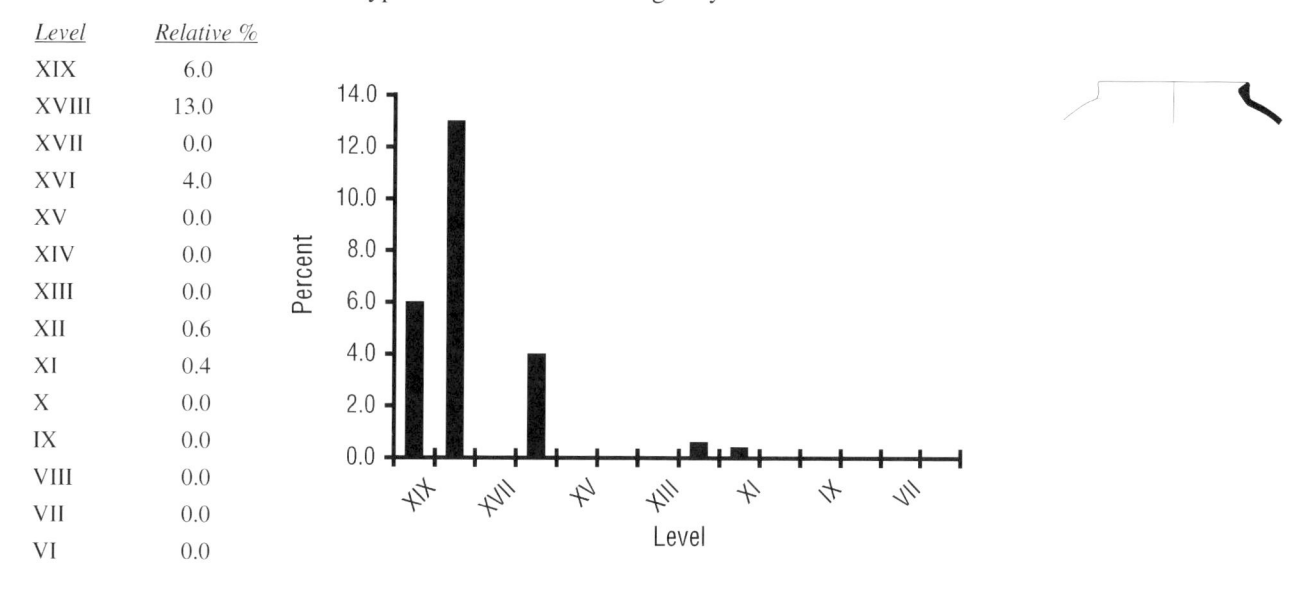

| Level | Relative % |
|---|---|
| XIX | 6.0 |
| XVIII | 13.0 |
| XVII | 0.0 |
| XVI | 4.0 |
| XV | 0.0 |
| XIV | 0.0 |
| XIII | 0.0 |
| XII | 0.6 |
| XI | 0.4 |
| X | 0.0 |
| IX | 0.0 |
| VIII | 0.0 |
| VII | 0.0 |
| VI | 0.0 |

Table 49. Type C-6 Relative Percentages by Third-millennium B.C. Levels

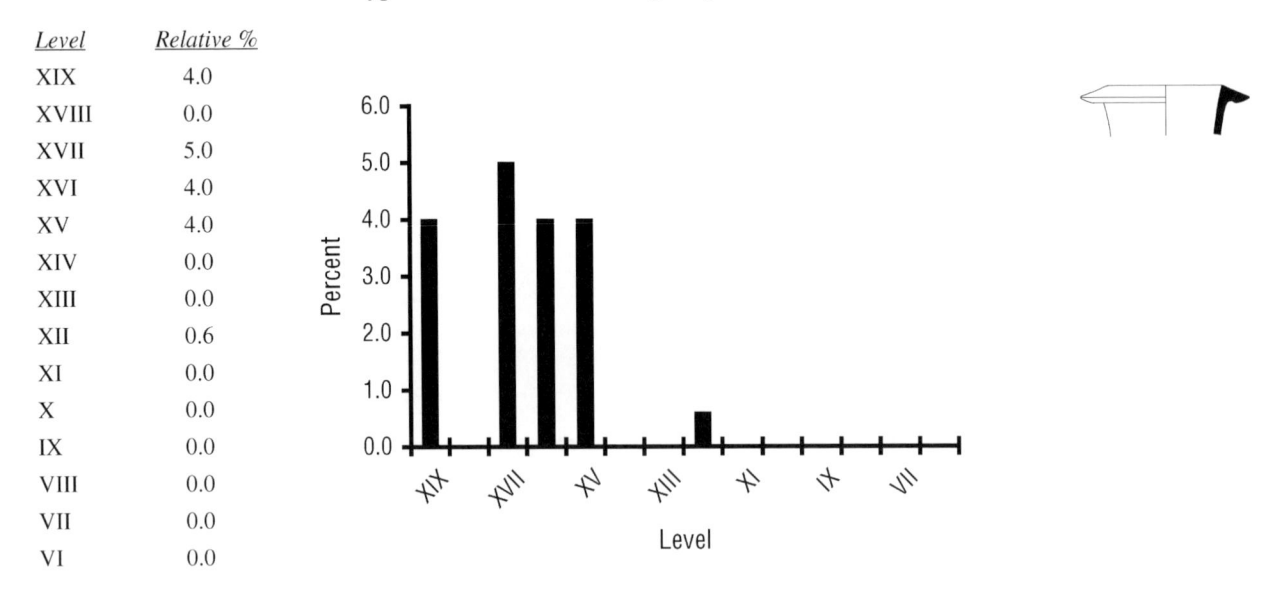

| Level | Relative % |
|---|---|
| XIX | 4.0 |
| XVIII | 0.0 |
| XVII | 5.0 |
| XVI | 4.0 |
| XV | 4.0 |
| XIV | 0.0 |
| XIII | 0.0 |
| XII | 0.6 |
| XI | 0.0 |
| X | 0.0 |
| IX | 0.0 |
| VIII | 0.0 |
| VII | 0.0 |
| VI | 0.0 |

Table 50. Type C-7 Relative Percentages by Third-millennium B.C. Levels

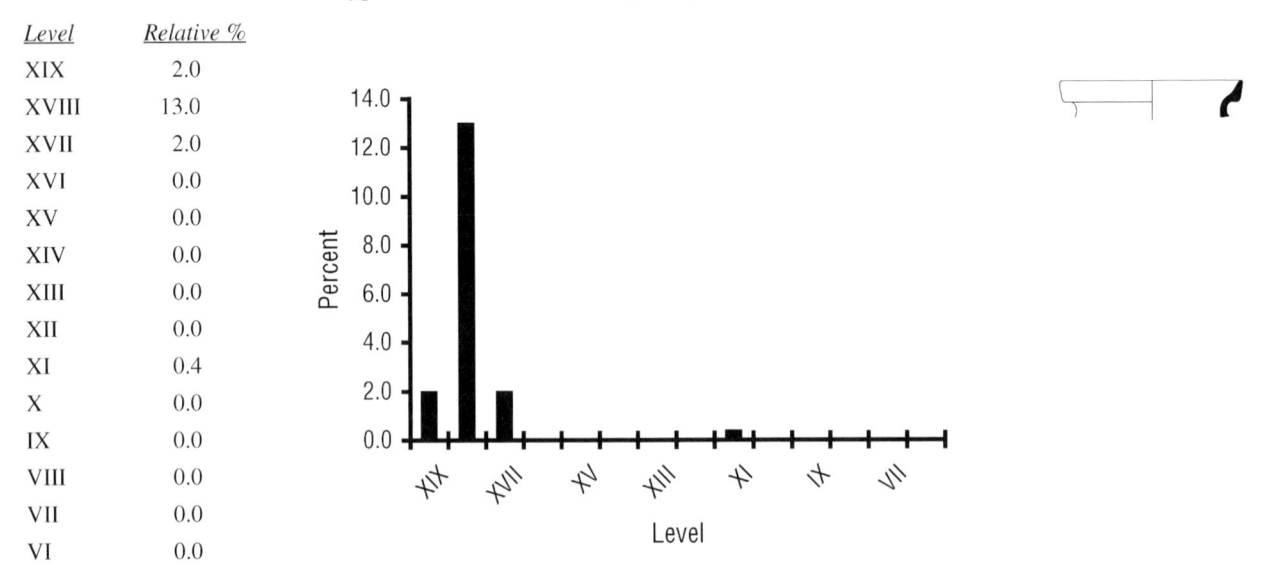

| Level | Relative % |
|---|---|
| XIX | 2.0 |
| XVIII | 13.0 |
| XVII | 2.0 |
| XVI | 0.0 |
| XV | 0.0 |
| XIV | 0.0 |
| XIII | 0.0 |
| XII | 0.0 |
| XI | 0.4 |
| X | 0.0 |
| IX | 0.0 |
| VIII | 0.0 |
| VII | 0.0 |
| VI | 0.0 |

Table 51. Type C-8 Relative Percentages by Third-millennium B.C. Levels

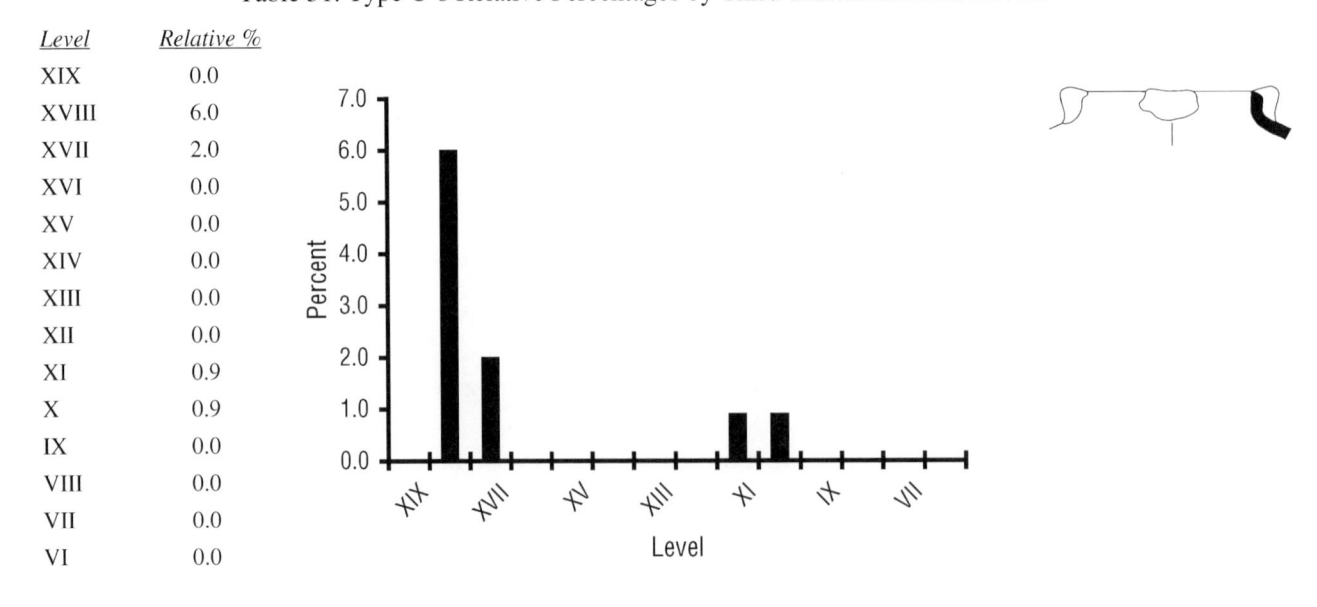

| Level | Relative % |
|---|---|
| XIX | 0.0 |
| XVIII | 6.0 |
| XVII | 2.0 |
| XVI | 0.0 |
| XV | 0.0 |
| XIV | 0.0 |
| XIII | 0.0 |
| XII | 0.0 |
| XI | 0.9 |
| X | 0.9 |
| IX | 0.0 |
| VIII | 0.0 |
| VII | 0.0 |
| VI | 0.0 |

# CHAPTER 3: POTTERY

Table 52. Type C-9 Relative Percentages by Third-millennium B.C. Levels

| Level | Relative % |
|---|---|
| XIX | 0.0 |
| XVIII | 0.0 |
| XVII | 5.0 |
| XVI | 14.0 |
| XV | 11.0 |
| XIV | 9.0 |
| XIII | 1.0 |
| XII | 7.0 |
| XI | 10.0 |
| X | 10.0 |
| IX | 18.0 |
| VIII | 15.0 |
| VII | 0.0 |
| VI | 8.0 |

Table 53. Type C-10 Relative Percentages by Third-millennium B.C. Levels

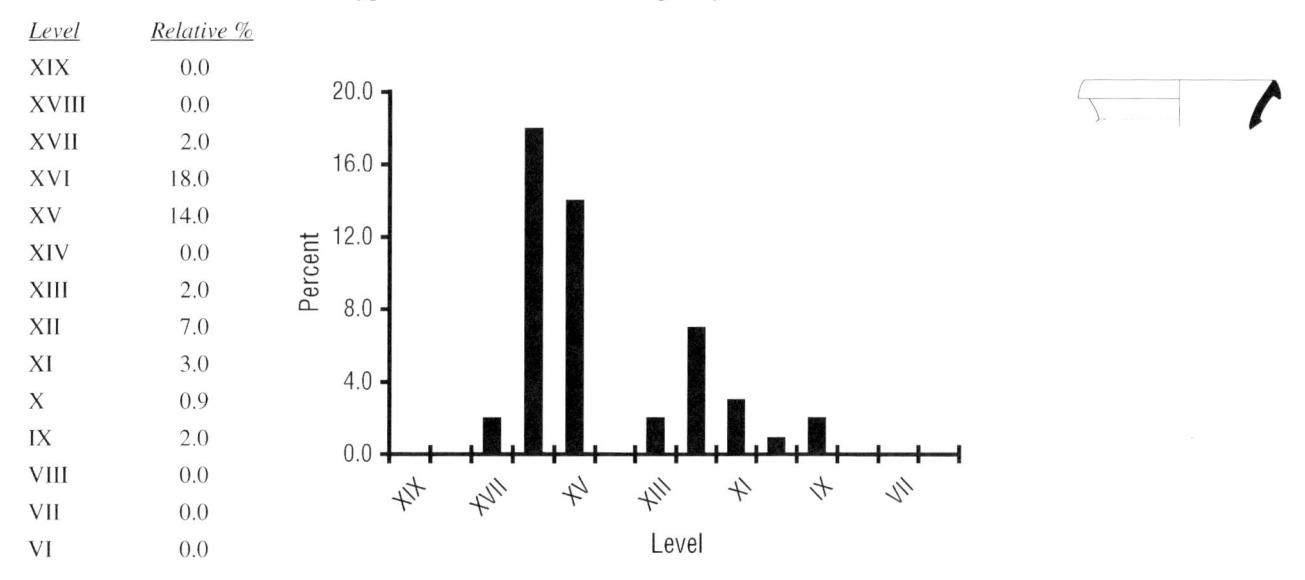

| Level | Relative % |
|---|---|
| XIX | 0.0 |
| XVIII | 0.0 |
| XVII | 2.0 |
| XVI | 18.0 |
| XV | 14.0 |
| XIV | 0.0 |
| XIII | 2.0 |
| XII | 7.0 |
| XI | 3.0 |
| X | 0.9 |
| IX | 2.0 |
| VIII | 0.0 |
| VII | 0.0 |
| VI | 0.0 |

Table 54. Type C-11 Relative Percentages by Third-millennium B.C. Levels

| Level | Relative % |
|---|---|
| XIX | 0.0 |
| XVIII | 0.0 |
| XVII | 7.0 |
| XVI | 4.0 |
| XV | 0.0 |
| XIV | 0.0 |
| XIII | 0.0 |
| XII | 0.0 |
| XI | 0.0 |
| X | 0.0 |
| IX | 0.0 |
| VIII | 0.0 |
| VII | 0.0 |
| VI | 0.0 |

Table 55. Type C-12 Relative Percentages by Third-millennium B.C. Levels

| Level | Relative % |
|---|---|
| XIX | 0.0 |
| XVIII | 0.0 |
| XVII | 5.0 |
| XVI | 0.0 |
| XV | 0.0 |
| XIV | 0.0 |
| XIII | 2.0 |
| XII | 2.0 |
| XI | 2.0 |
| X | 0.0 |
| IX | 0.0 |
| VIII | 0.0 |
| VII | 0.0 |
| VI | 0.0 |

Table 56. Type C-13 Relative Percentages by Third-millennium B.C. Levels

| Level | Relative % |
|---|---|
| XIX | 0.0 |
| XVIII | 0.0 |
| XVII | 7.0 |
| XVI | 0.0 |
| XV | 7.0 |
| XIV | 0.0 |
| XIII | 0.0 |
| XII | 2.0 |
| XI | 0.0 |
| X | 0.9 |
| IX | 5.0 |
| VIII | 3.0 |
| VII | 0.0 |
| VI | 0.0 |

Table 57. Type C-14 Relative Percentages by Third-millennium B.C. Levels

| Level | Relative % |
|---|---|
| XIX | 0.0 |
| XVIII | 0.0 |
| XVII | 0.0 |
| XVI | 0.0 |
| XV | 4.0 |
| XIV | 12.0 |
| XIII | 16.0 |
| XII | 6.0 |
| XI | 3.0 |
| X | 3.0 |
| IX | 2.0 |
| VIII | 3.0 |
| VII | 0.0 |
| VI | 0.0 |

CHAPTER 3: POTTERY

Table 58. Type C-15 Relative Percentages by Third-millennium B.C. Levels

| Level | Relative % |
|---|---|
| XIX | 0.0 |
| XVIII | 0.0 |
| XVII | 0.0 |
| XVI | 0.0 |
| XV | 0.0 |
| XIV | 2.0 |
| XIII | 2.0 |
| XII | 0.0 |
| XI | 0.4 |
| X | 2.0 |
| IX | 0.0 |
| VIII | 0.0 |
| VII | 0.0 |
| VI | 0.0 |

Table 59. Type C-16a Relative Percentages by Third-millennium B.C. Levels

| Level | Relative % |
|---|---|
| XIX | 0.0 |
| XVIII | 0.0 |
| XVII | 0.0 |
| XVI | 0.0 |
| XV | 0.0 |
| XIV | 5.0 |
| XIII | 5.0 |
| XII | 12.0 |
| XI | 11.0 |
| X | 10.0 |
| IX | 10.0 |
| VIII | 3.0 |
| VII | 20.0 |
| VI | 5.0 |

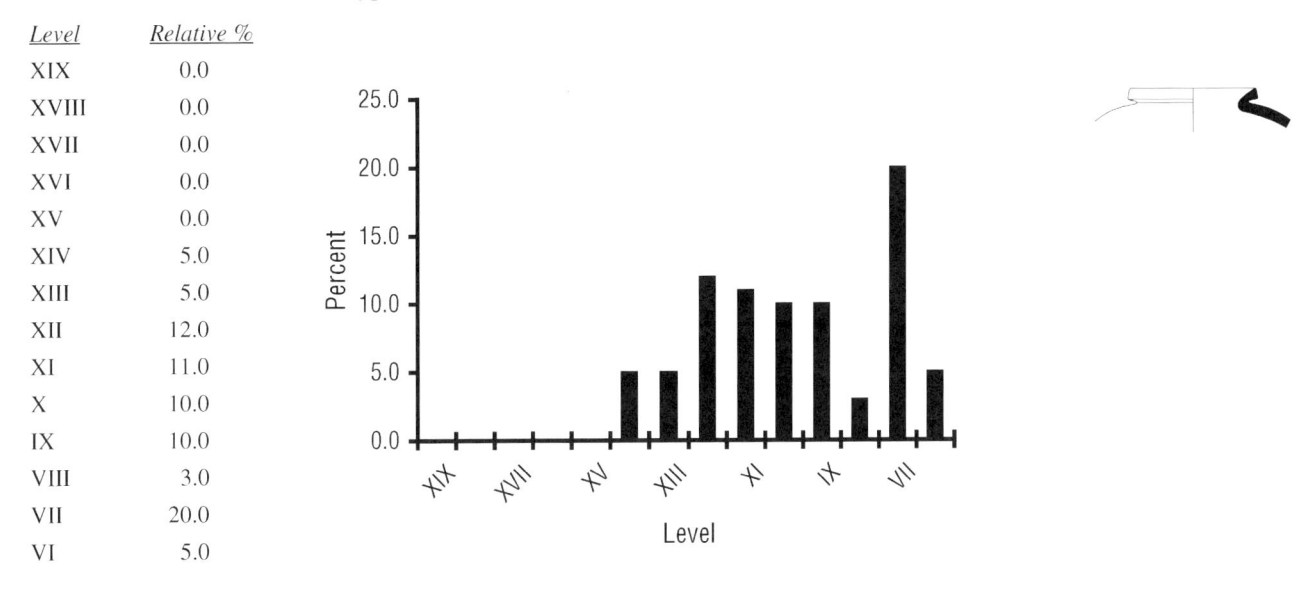

Table 60. Type C-16b Relative Percentages by Third-millennium B.C. Levels

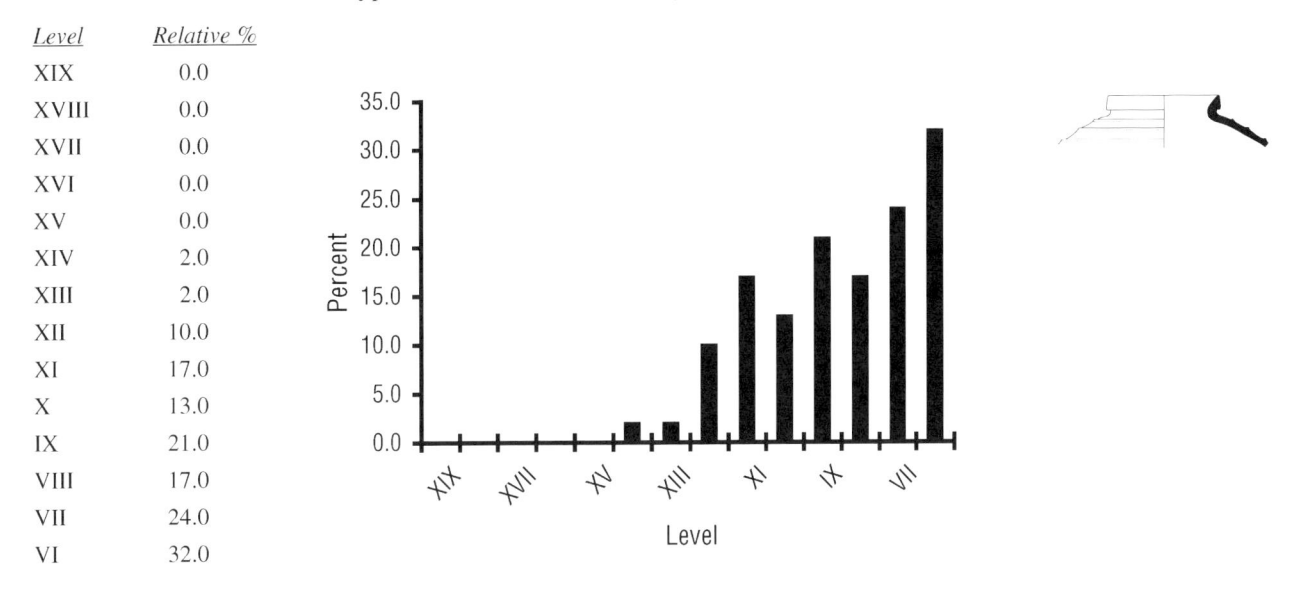

| Level | Relative % |
|---|---|
| XIX | 0.0 |
| XVIII | 0.0 |
| XVII | 0.0 |
| XVI | 0.0 |
| XV | 0.0 |
| XIV | 2.0 |
| XIII | 2.0 |
| XII | 10.0 |
| XI | 17.0 |
| X | 13.0 |
| IX | 21.0 |
| VIII | 17.0 |
| VII | 24.0 |
| VI | 32.0 |

Table 61. Type C-16c Relative Percentages by Third-millennium B.C. Levels

| Level | Relative % |
|---|---|
| XIX | 0.0 |
| XVIII | 0.0 |
| XVII | 0.0 |
| XVI | 0.0 |
| XV | 0.0 |
| XIV | 0.0 |
| XIII | 0.0 |
| XII | 0.0 |
| XI | 2.0 |
| X | 2.0 |
| IX | 5.0 |
| VIII | 1.0 |
| VII | 0.0 |
| VI | 0.0 |

Table 62. Type C-17 Relative Percentages by Third-millennium B.C. Levels

| Level | Relative % |
|---|---|
| XIX | 0.0 |
| XVIII | 0.0 |
| XVII | 0.0 |
| XVI | 0.0 |
| XV | 0.0 |
| XIV | 7.0 |
| XIII | 6.0 |
| XII | 2.0 |
| XI | 2.0 |
| X | 6.0 |
| IX | 2.0 |
| VIII | 1.0 |
| VII | 0.0 |
| VI | 0.0 |

Table 63. Type C-18 Relative Percentages by Third-millennium B.C. Levels

| Level | Relative % |
|---|---|
| XIX | 0.0 |
| XVIII | 0.0 |
| XVII | 0.0 |
| XVI | 0.0 |
| XV | 0.0 |
| XIV | 2.0 |
| XIII | 1.0 |
| XII | 1.0 |
| XI | 6.0 |
| X | 5.0 |
| IX | 2.0 |
| VIII | 4.0 |
| VII | 0.0 |
| VI | 0.0 |

## CHAPTER 3: POTTERY

Table 64. Type C-19 Relative Percentages by Third-millennium B.C. Levels

| Level | Relative % |
|---|---|
| XIX | 0.0 |
| XVIII | 0.0 |
| XVII | 0.0 |
| XVI | 0.0 |
| XV | 0.0 |
| XIV | 4.0 |
| XIII | 2.0 |
| XII | 2.0 |
| XI | 0.4 |
| X | 0.9 |
| IX | 1.0 |
| VIII | 1.0 |
| VII | 0.0 |
| VI | 3.0 |

Table 65. Type C-20 Relative Percentages by Third-millennium B.C. Levels

| Level | Relative % |
|---|---|
| XIX | 0.0 |
| XVIII | 0.0 |
| XVII | 0.0 |
| XVI | 0.0 |
| XV | 0.0 |
| XIV | 2.0 |
| XIII | 10.0 |
| XII | 8.0 |
| XI | 6.0 |
| X | 9.0 |
| IX | 16.0 |
| VIII | 3.0 |
| VII | 20.0 |
| VI | 22.0 |

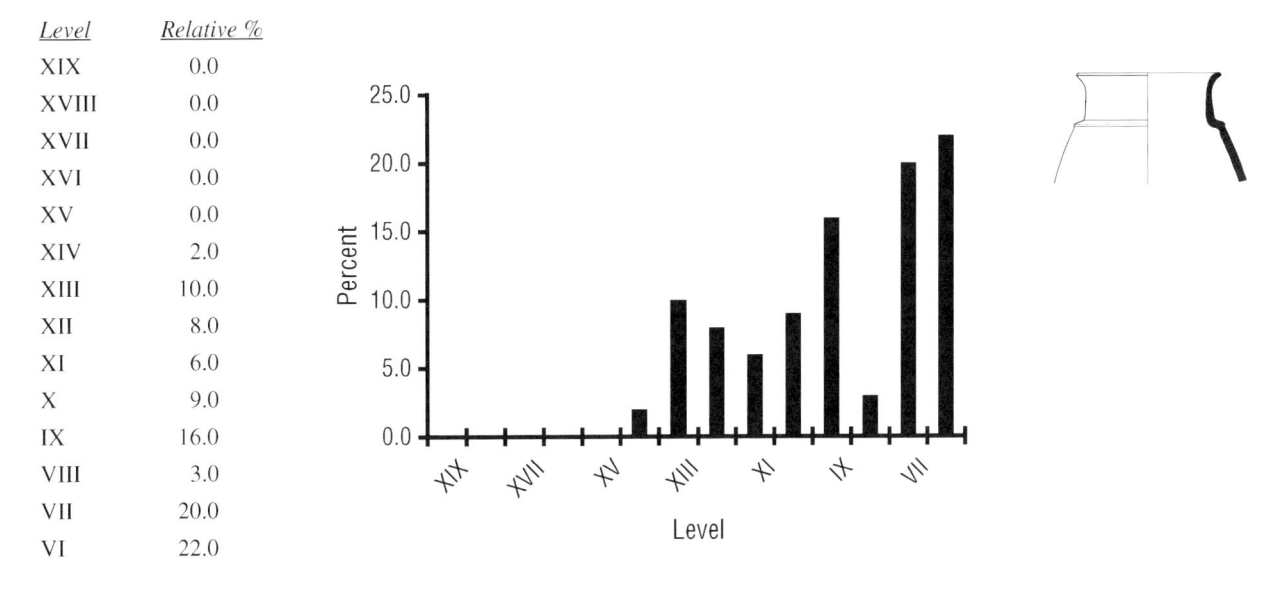

Table 66. Type C-21 Relative Percentages by Third-millennium B.C. Levels

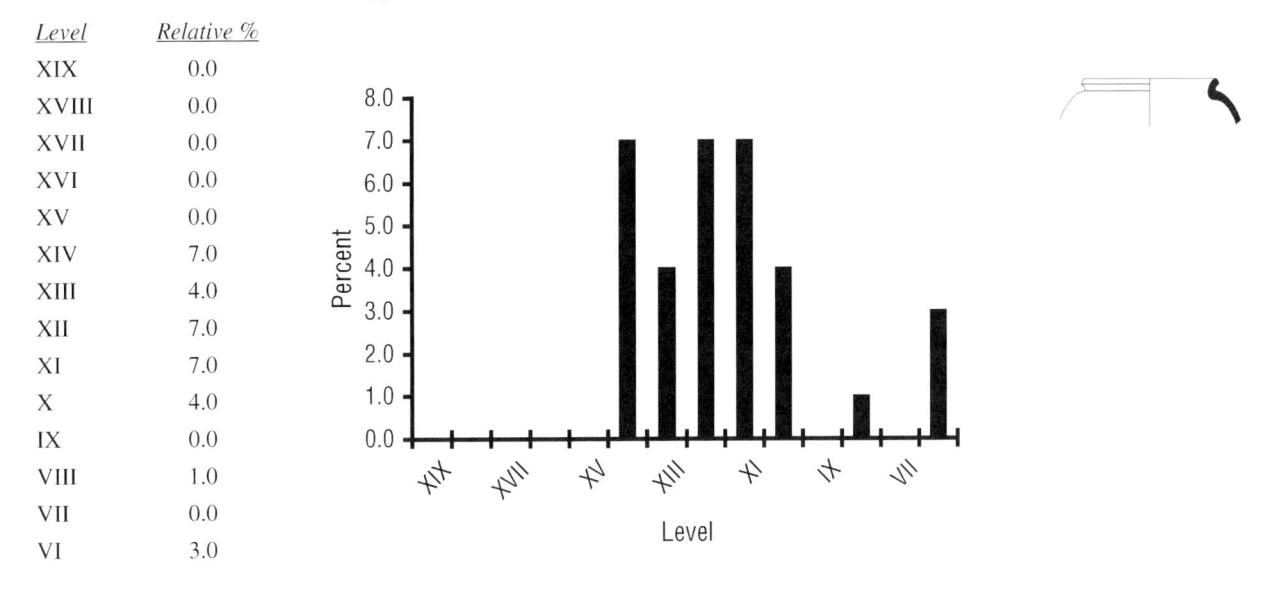

| Level | Relative % |
|---|---|
| XIX | 0.0 |
| XVIII | 0.0 |
| XVII | 0.0 |
| XVI | 0.0 |
| XV | 0.0 |
| XIV | 7.0 |
| XIII | 4.0 |
| XII | 7.0 |
| XI | 7.0 |
| X | 4.0 |
| IX | 0.0 |
| VIII | 1.0 |
| VII | 0.0 |
| VI | 3.0 |

Table 67. Type C-22 Relative Percentages by Third-millennium B.C. Levels

| Level | Relative % |
|---|---|
| XIX | 0.0 |
| XVIII | 0.0 |
| XVII | 0.0 |
| XVI | 0.0 |
| XV | 0.0 |
| XIV | 5.0 |
| XIII | 8.0 |
| XII | 5.0 |
| XI | 3.0 |
| X | 3.0 |
| IX | 1.0 |
| VIII | 4.0 |
| VII | 4.0 |
| VI | 0.0 |

Table 68. Type C-24 Relative Percentages by Third-millennium B.C. Levels

| Level | Relative % |
|---|---|
| XIX | 0.0 |
| XVIII | 0.0 |
| XVII | 0.0 |
| XVI | 0.0 |
| XV | 11.0 |
| XIV | 19.0 |
| XIII | 3.0 |
| XII | 3.0 |
| XI | 5.0 |
| X | 4.0 |
| IX | 0.0 |
| VIII | 6.0 |
| VII | 8.0 |
| VI | 3.0 |

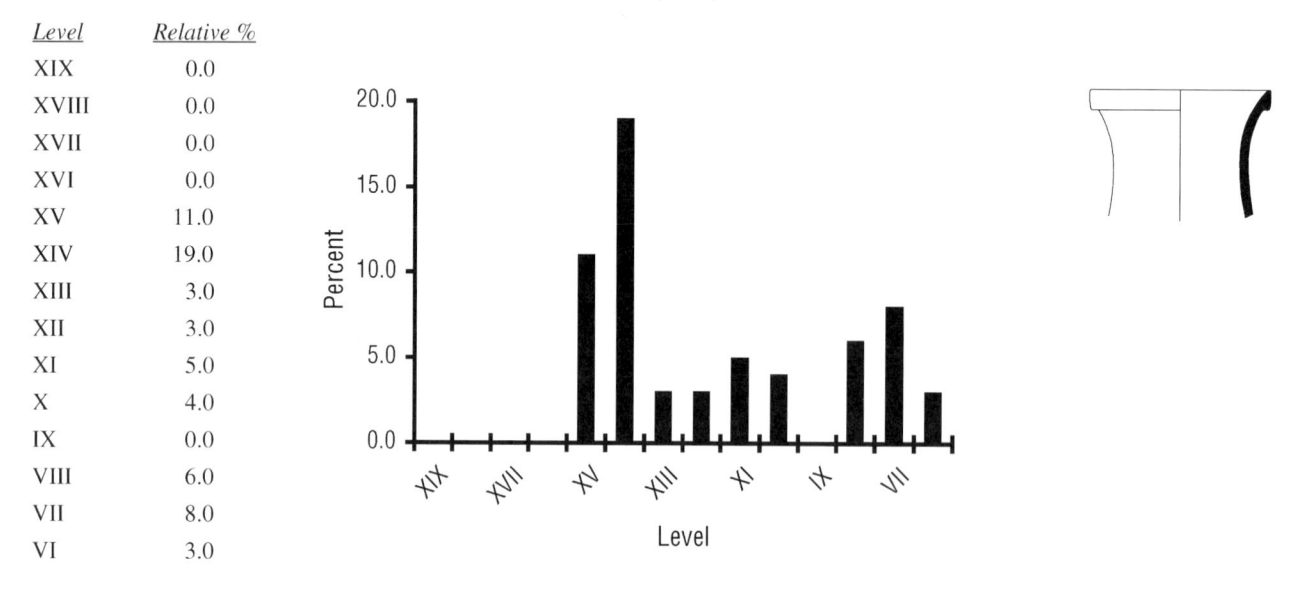

Table 69. Type C-25a Relative Percentages by Third-millennium B.C. Levels

| Level | Relative % |
|---|---|
| XIX | 0.0 |
| XVIII | 0.0 |
| XVII | 0.0 |
| XVI | 0.0 |
| XV | 0.0 |
| XIV | 0.0 |
| XIII | 0.0 |
| XII | 1.0 |
| XI | 1.0 |
| X | 3.0 |
| IX | 4.0 |
| VIII | 2.0 |
| VII | 0.0 |
| VI | 3.0 |

## CHAPTER 3: POTTERY

Table 70. Type C-25b Relative Percentages by Third-millennium B.C. Levels

| Level | Relative % |
|---|---|
| XIX | 0.0 |
| XVIII | 0.0 |
| XVII | 0.0 |
| XVI | 0.0 |
| XV | 0.0 |
| XIV | 0.0 |
| XIII | 0.0 |
| XII | 0.0 |
| XI | 0.0 |
| X | 0.0 |
| IX | 0.0 |
| VIII | 8.0 |
| VII | 0.0 |
| VI | 5.0 |

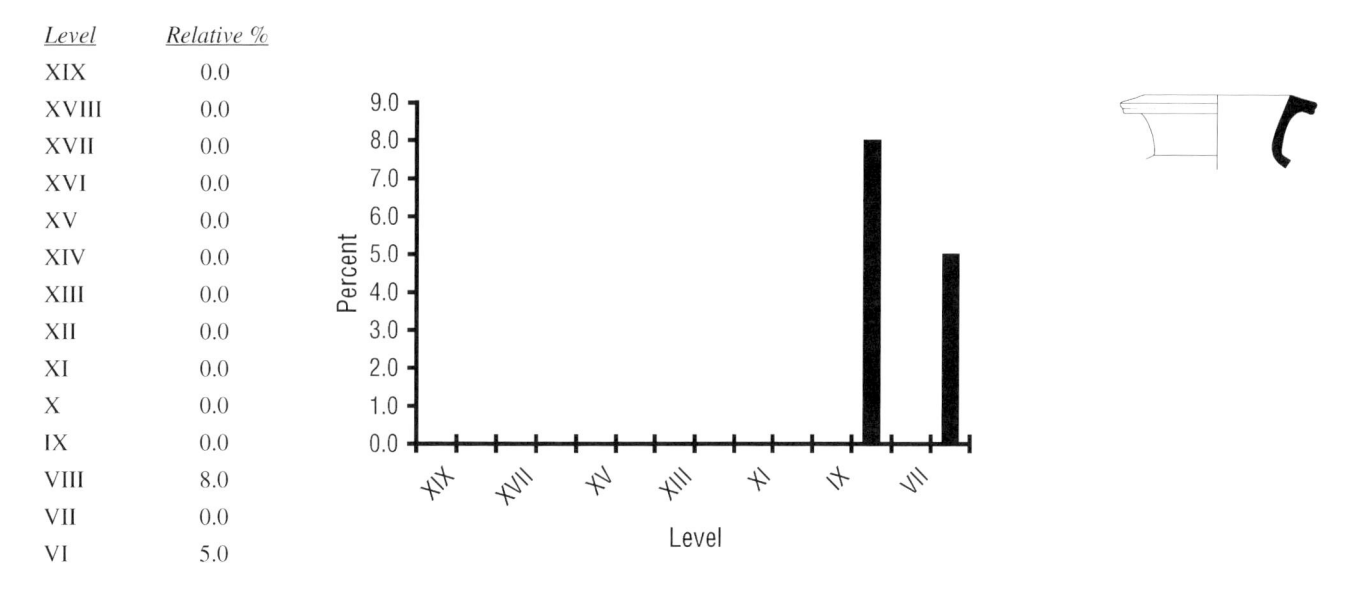

Table 71. Type C-26 Relative Percentages by Third-millennium B.C. Levels

| Level | Relative % |
|---|---|
| XIX | 0.0 |
| XVIII | 0.0 |
| XVII | 0.0 |
| XVI | 0.0 |
| XV | 0.0 |
| XIV | 0.0 |
| XIII | 0.0 |
| XII | 0.0 |
| XI | 0.9 |
| X | 0.0 |
| IX | 0.0 |
| VIII | 0.0 |
| VII | 0.0 |
| VI | 0.0 |

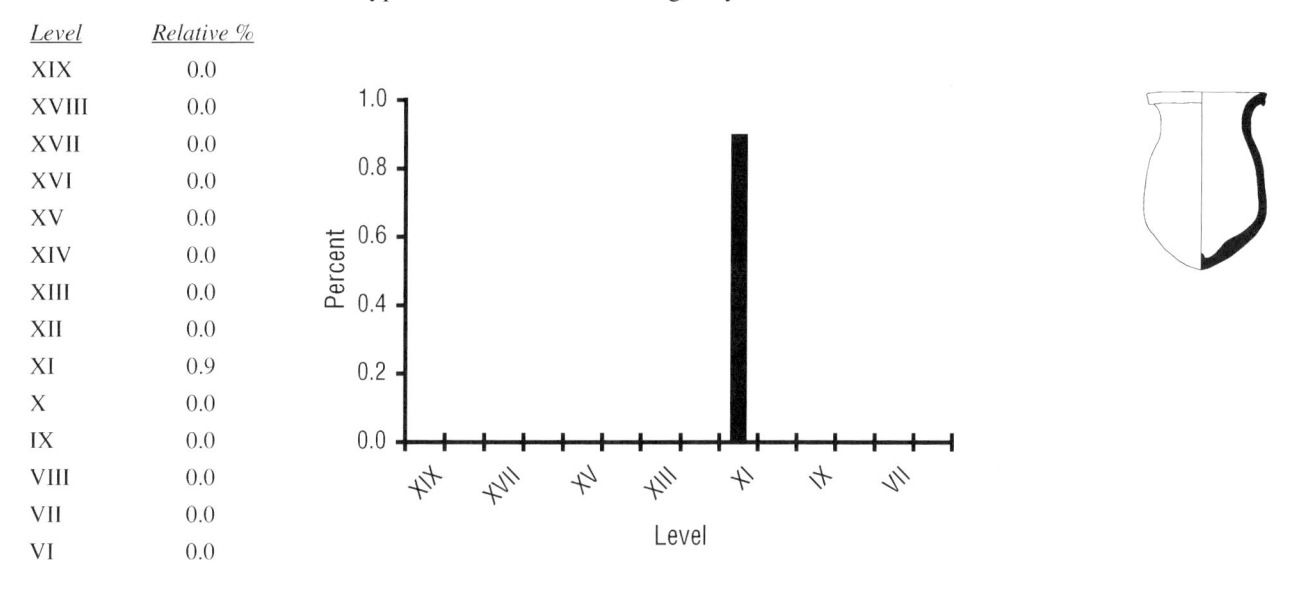

Table 72. Type C-27 Relative Percentages by Third-millennium B.C. Levels

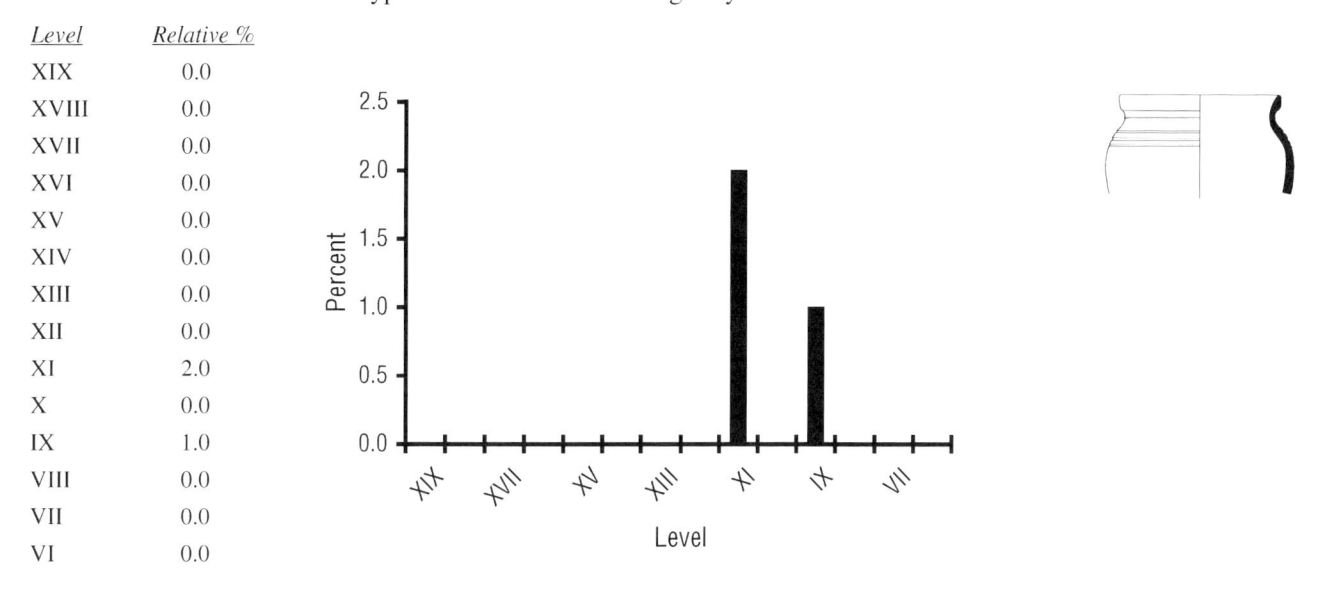

| Level | Relative % |
|---|---|
| XIX | 0.0 |
| XVIII | 0.0 |
| XVII | 0.0 |
| XVI | 0.0 |
| XV | 0.0 |
| XIV | 0.0 |
| XIII | 0.0 |
| XII | 0.0 |
| XI | 2.0 |
| X | 0.0 |
| IX | 1.0 |
| VIII | 0.0 |
| VII | 0.0 |
| VI | 0.0 |

118                         NIPPUR V: EARLY DYNASTIC TO AKKADIAN TRANSITION

Table 73. Type C-28 Relative Percentages by Third-millennium B.C. Levels

| Level | Relative % |
|---|---|
| XIX | 0.0 |
| XVIII | 0.0 |
| XVII | 0.0 |
| XVI | 0.0 |
| XV | 0.0 |
| XIV | 0.0 |
| XIII | 0.0 |
| XII | 0.0 |
| XI | 0.4 |
| X | 0.9 |
| IX | 0.0 |
| VIII | 0.0 |
| VII | 4.0 |
| VI | 3.0 |

Table 74. Type C-29 Relative Percentages by Third-millennium B.C. Levels

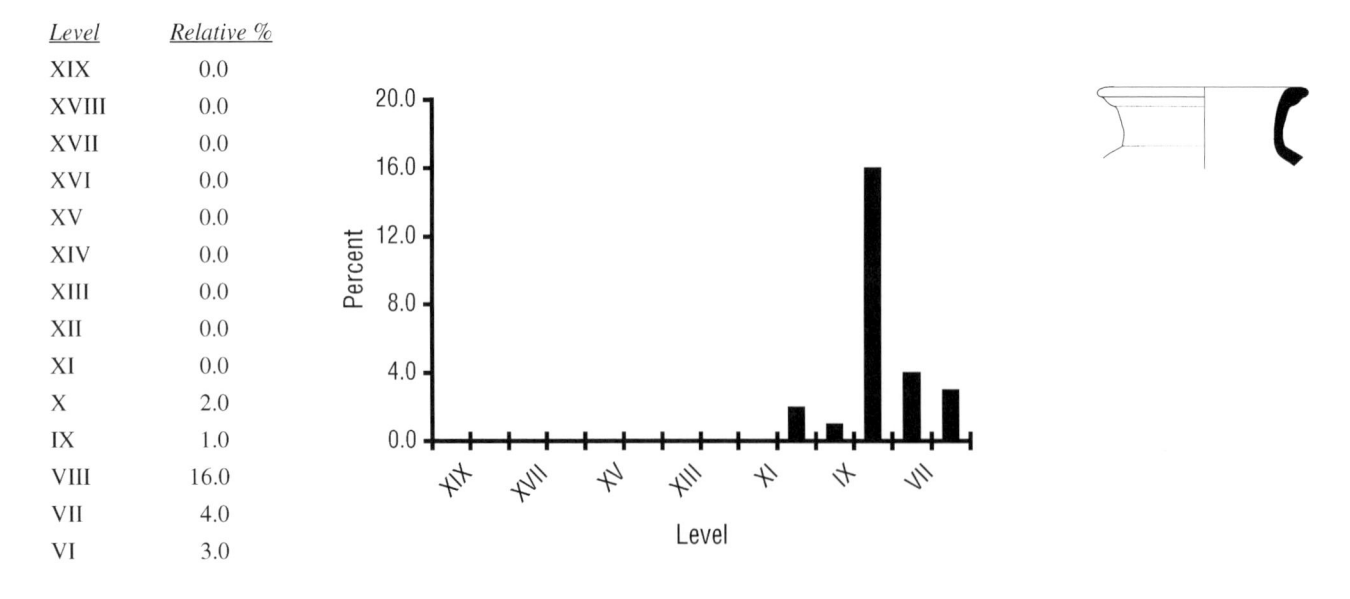

| Level | Relative % |
|---|---|
| XIX | 0.0 |
| XVIII | 0.0 |
| XVII | 0.0 |
| XVI | 0.0 |
| XV | 0.0 |
| XIV | 0.0 |
| XIII | 0.0 |
| XII | 0.0 |
| XI | 0.0 |
| X | 2.0 |
| IX | 1.0 |
| VIII | 16.0 |
| VII | 4.0 |
| VI | 3.0 |

# CHAPTER 4
# OBJECTS FROM AREA WF

The objects from Area WF are presented here by category: seals and sealings, stone vessels, metal vessels, metal objects, ornaments, baked-clay objects, miniature vessels, and miscellaneous objects. Across the accumulation of the third-millennium B.C. levels in particular, the quantity of objects increased, the range of types of objects expanded, and their quality generally improved, with very few objects appearing in levels earlier than Level XIV.[125] These trends coincide with a number of other developments in the sequence, such as the establishment of a stable building plan, shift in burial practices, and changes in the pottery assemblage. These other developments have been tentatively linked with a possible increased number of inhabitants in the building and tighter occupation of the whole area; it also seems possible that the inhabitants of the building had accrued greater wealth and status by the later Akkadian period. The entire plan of the building was not exposed, however, and the different types of objects from Level XIV and above may have to do with the specific portion of the building revealed by the excavation and the possible shifting of room function within the structure.

## Seals and Sealings

### Third Millennium B.C.

Five cylinder seals, one cylinder seal blank, one stamp seal, and two unbaked-clay sealings were recovered from the third-millennium B.C. levels. The stamp seal (19 N 74; pl. 160:2), with its drilled motif of two animals, almost certainly dates to the late Ubaid or Uruk period and is well out of its original context in Level XVB.[126] The other seals and sealings for the most part do provide useful dating anchors within the stratigraphic sequence. Three of the seals were found in burials and it is likely that they were buried close to their date of manufacture; the other two were found in occupational material and are slightly more likely to provide only a *terminus post quem*.

The earlier of the two seals from occupational material, 19 N 108 (pl. 158:2), is in Early Dynastic II style, yet it comes from a level (Level XVIII) dated to Early Dynastic IIIa on the basis of the pottery assemblage. This seal was found in a layer of outdoor accumulation, so its earlier date could be explained by the nature of the context, or by its possible continued use across more than one generation. The seal is confidently carved in a striking, pale green translucent stone. The scene consists of two horned "masters of animals," one holding an inverted goat by the horn with each hand, the other holding a rampant bull by the beard with each hand; there are numerous Early Dynastic II parallels for both the scene and the delicate style. The only flaw is that the two triads are mismatched in width; the hero with inverted goats was probably carved first, leaving a slightly smaller space for the second group, which has thus been crowded together.

The second seal from occupational debris, 18 N 111 (pl. 160:1), was found in the southeast room in Level XIVA, which also contained a quantity of other expensive items (metal tools and weapons, etc.). The context was less open and less likely to have been disturbed than that of the previous seal, and the unusual number of other objects in the room indicates that the seal could have been stored there rather than accidentally dropped. The scene is a familiar though uncommon one of the sun-god Shamash seated in the rear of a "god boat," preceded by a lion, with a schematic plow and two jars in the field above. Shamash holds the end of a steering oar, and the prow of the boat is a god who holds a punting pole; the head of this god has been destroyed by a chip in the seal. The style of carving, the presence of all the motifs that customarily make up this scene at its most standardized, and the fact that the prow of the boat has a head and arms, but not yet an extended humanoid leg, place the seal in the early Akkadian period

---

125. For a list of objects by level, see table 77; for the catalogue of objects by object number (18 N or 19 N), see table 78. The numbers are not consecutive because the full object catalogue includes items from operations other than Area WF also excavated in the eighteenth and nineteenth seasons.

126. For selected comparanda for this and all other objects, see descriptions with *Plates*.

(Boehmer's Akkadisch Ib/c or Akkadisch II; see Laird 1984). The seal was made from the central core of a conch shell and is badly worn. It is difficult to estimate how much time in use is represented by the degree of wear. Frequency of use, as well as elapsing time, is a factor in the rate of wear, as are postdepositional processes; in addition, shell wears more quickly than stone. It is possible that this seal was manufactured significantly earlier than the time of its deposition. The cylinder seal blank (18 N 113; pl. 160:3) from Level XIIA is almost identical in dimensions to this seal and was also cut from a conch shell core.

Of the two sealings, only one (18 N 110; pl. 159:2), from Level XIIIB, provides useful dating evidence. The sealing is a rounded and flattened rectangle; on the obverse is a single incomplete rolling of an Akkadian "royal style" combat seal, and on the reverse is an impression of cords and a wrinkled material (reconstruction of the sealed container was not possible). The preserved portion of the scene comprises two pairs: an inverted lion held by the feet by a bull-man, and a nude six-locked hero holding the feet of an inverted water buffalo or bull. There are no indications as to how much of the scene may be missing, but from comparison with contemporary seals, there may have been an inscription, or possibly a third pair in combat, to complete it. The fine carving style and symmetrical, well-spaced arrangement of the "heraldic" pairs of figures are characteristic of the late Akkadian period, datable to the reign of Naram-Sin or later.

The second sealing (18 N 109; pl. 159:1) is late Early Dynastic in style, but as it comes from Level XIIB, which is datable to the late Akkadian by other evidence (including other seals; see below), either the sealing had been shifted out of its original context, or (equally likely) an older seal was still in use during occupation of this level. The obverse has two partial rollings of the same seal. The crowded scene consists of a lion biting a bull held on the opposite side by a hero whose head is shown in profile; this group is followed by a combating pair of a bull-man versus a hero, and a third group of a hero versus a bull-man. There are traces of the lower border of an inscription frame, with a small scorpion in the space below it. The combination of profile and frontal heads, the lack of crossed arrangement among the figures, the scorpion filling motif, and the double line for the inscription border all point to an Early Dynastic III date. The reverse shows an impression of a cylindrical object and a knotted cord.

Finally, the three cylinder seals from burial contexts are all late Akkadian. In the large chamber of Burial 14 in Level XIIIB, with Skeleton 2, was a lapis lazuli "royal style" seal (19 N 26; pl. 158:1). The scene consists of two pairs in combat: a nude hero battling a bull or bison and a rampant lion versus a bull-man. The animal in combat with the nude hero has the heavy body hair usually associated with the bison (cf. Frankfort 1939: pl. 17h), but the lack of a beard and wider curved horns make identification as a bull more likely. There is a blank area between the hero and bull-man where an inscription has been erased; faint unreadable traces of the signs remain. The erasure could have caused the small vertical crack in the blank area and certainly removed the adjacent ear of the bull-man and the curls of the hero.[127] The style of carving and composition of the scene are comparable to those of the sealing 18 N 110 (pl. 159:2) and date to the late Akkadian period.

The two remaining seals were both buried with Skeleton 1 of Burial 14 in Level XIIB. One (18 N 174) was found near the upper left arm, and the second (18 N 173) near the lower left arm. The presence of two seals in a single grave might seem illogical, but multiple seals occur in burials fairly frequently. In the Ur Royal Cemetery, for instance, out of 322 graves in which seals were recorded as present (as published in Woolley 1934), forty-two (ca. 13%) had at least two associated seals. Of these graves, twenty-two can be dated to the Akkadian period (the rest are Early Dynastic). And of those, fourteen graves have pairs of seals that include an "official" seal with a motif of figures in combat, perhaps used by the deceased for transactions in which he represented a government office; and a second "personal" seal, with a scene of presentation, probably used for private business.[128] The Ur Royal Cemetery could include burials of relatively high status, and a higher percentage of these than would be found in a true cross section of the population could have had two seals. At least one other example of a pair of seals, one a combat scene and one a presentation scene, belonging to a single high-status individual, comes from Tell Asmar, where two different sealings of the scribe Puzurum were recovered (Frankfort 1955: nos. 517 [combat] and 649 [presentation]).

---

127. It is worth noting that this lapis seal, at 1.7 cm diameter and 3.0 cm high, is smaller than the two seals in different media with Burial 14, Skeleton 1 (see below; they are 2.1 cm in diameter × 3.4 cm high and 1.9 in cm diameter × 3.2 cm high). This adds support to the trend identified by Sax, Collon, and Leese (1993) for lapis seals of Akkadian date to be relatively small compared to seals in more common stones.

128. The Ur graves with one presentation and one combat scene are: PG/35, 59, 435, 543, 557, 559, 677, 689, 861, 867, 1003, 1381, and 1422 and possibly PG/33. The other Akkadian seal pairs include three instances of two combats (PG/635, 697, 1092), two instances of two presentations (PG/985, 1845K), and the remaining three involve one presentation together with miscellaneous scenes (PG/652, 699, 991).

The scale of the figures, details of their anatomy, and high level of artistic skill in both seals with Burial 14, Skeleton 1, mark them as the works of the same artist.[129] Seal 18 N 173 (pl. 157:1) is carved in translucent white rock crystal with a few red inclusions; the scene consists of three pairs in combat: two six-locked heroes — nude except for belts — gripping addorsed water buffaloes by the front legs, followed by a bull-man thrusting a dagger into the belly of a lion. An inscription, Lugal-DÚR DUB.SAR "Lugal-Dúr, the scribe" is arranged vertically in two compartments. There are traces of recutting between the legs of the bull-man (whose feet were originally closer together) and above the tail of the lion (the tail had curved higher and would have interfered with the hand of the bull-man as it reached around the lion's mane).

The second seal, 18 N 174 (pl. 157:2), carved in a brilliant, blue green marble-like stone with white veining, has a complex presentation scene.[130] The first figure, at the left, is a standing human male in a long fringed robe, facing right, raising his left hand before his face; this presumably represents the owner of the seal. He is preceded by a god standing on a lion-griffin that spews fire from its mouth; this god holds a whip over his shoulder and controls the lion-griffin with a leash. This storm-god first appears on seals in the late Akkadian period and persists through the Ur III and into the Old Babylonian period. The stance of the god on the shoulders and between the wings of the griffin, rather than on its back, is typical of the Akkadian period.[131] The fire spewing from the mouth of the griffin does not appear consistently; the examples with this detail tend to be late Akkadian;[132] the rein or leash running from the griffin's nose to the deity's right hand is also an unusual feature. The gracefully feathered wings and flaring tail of the griffin are a late Akkadian characteristic,[133] as earlier examples tend to have more ovoid wings and a broom-like tail.

In front of the storm-god is another god with a crescent moon resting between the horns of his crown and a crescentic ax over his right shoulder. This god stands between a pair of mountains, greeting a seated god who faces the entire procession and holds a mace in his left hand. Between the seated god and moon-god, seeming to float above one of the mountains, is a standard with two bull feet, and a staff topped with a spherical mace-head, from which hangs an object that looks like a sandal in plan view. There is a two-line inscription, the same as on 18 N 173, with a small horned animal in the field below it.

The moon-god, clearly identified here by the crescent moon on his crown, is a rare figure on cylinder seals. While a crescent moon appears often as a filler motif in the Akkadian and other periods, it is only infrequently used as a crown adornment. Boehmer (1965) cites only two examples with the crescent moon crown,[134] although Collon (1995, 1997), Colbow (1997), and Braun-Holzinger (1993) have collated more representations and expanded the possible range of attributes and appearances of this deity.[135] On other seals where Sin is identified by his crescent-moon crown he is seated, as the most powerful figure in a presentation[136] or banquet scene.[137] This is in contrast to our seal, in which he is in a subordinate pose with reference to the seated god.[138]

---

129. The same confident hand might be visible in Boehmer 1965: figs. 165, 232, 256, 548, and 725, which are all similar to the WF seals in composition, spacing, proportions, depth of carving, and details of anatomy or dress. Even the inscriptions on many of these seals and the WF seals are closely comparable in scale, spacing and depth, and weight of incision. All these seals belong to servants of the sons and daughters of Naram-Sin or Sharkalisharri; no royal connection is given on the WF seals, but the excellent carving is plausibly the product of a royal workshop.

130. Unfortunately, the stone could not be scientifically characterized; it could be green jasper or greenstone.

131. In later examples, the Ur III period and thereafter, the god has been moved toward the rear of the griffin. Compare the Ur III period griffin in Buchanan 1981: 261.

132. See Boehmer 1965: figs. 367, 371, 373.

133. See Boehmer 1965: figs. 371, 373; compare fig. 364.

134. Boehmer 1965: figs. 725 and 726.

135. These include specific figures in scenes of conflict among deities or in other groupings, a figure associated with a crescent-topped standard or with a standard with a "pennant," and a figure with one foot raised and resting on a mountain.

136. Boehmer 1965: fig. 726 (also published in Legrain 1951: 295, U.18974). The seal comes from grave 140 of the Royal Cemetery at Ur and shows the seated moon-god approached by two male deities and a human worshipper or minor deity. In an odd piece of symmetry, a second seal from the same grave (Legrain 1951: 237, U.18973) shows what could be the sun-god Shamash in an identical scene. The deity on this second seal has rays emerging from his shoulders, the traditional attribute of Shamash, although Braun-Holzinger (1993) believes these rays can also be an attribute of Sin. It is possible that two distinct aspects of the moon-god are being signified.

137. Boehmer 1965: fig. 725, a sealing from Tello showing a female and a male deity seated and raising cups toward each other, while two minor goddesses stand behind them. The inscription names the daughter of Naram-Sin, Enmenanna, and describes the seal owner as a scribe, her servant.

138. Most of the published representations of the moon-god are late Akkadian in style (Boehmer's Akkadisch III), datable to the reign of Naram-Sin or thereafter. While texts of Sargon indicate that royal attention was paid to the cult of Sin at Ur in his time, with Sargon establishing his daughter Enheduanna in an administrative capacity there, the fact that Naram-Sin included the god's name in his own name suggests an even greater importance for the cult of the moon-god later in the Akkadian dynasty. The potential for linkage between this and the expanded appearance of the moon-god as a seal motif at that time is clear.

The mountains on either side of the moon-god are slightly troubling since these are customarily associated with representations of Shamash, whose most typical appearance is rising from between mountains with rays emerging from his shoulders. The mountains here are probably intended to be associated with the seated god. The scene should be interpreted as though the moon-god is approaching the seated god (who would then be Shamash) by passing between mountains located to either side of that god's podium. In order not to obscure the feet of the two deities, the mountain on the left side of the podium has been shifted to the rear of the approaching moon-god. The absence of rays from the shoulders of the seated god could indicate that the sun has not yet risen, and the whole scene could represent the moment before dawn when the moon is setting and the sun is about to rise, a point at which the two deities might indeed meet beyond the mountains that frame their journey.

Both the seated god and the storm-god on the griffin wear high, four-horned crowns topped by hollow circles. This crown type is not peculiar to any specific deity but on other seals is worn by Ishtar and by a weather-god.[139] Boehmer (1967) labels this crown type J 27 and identifies it as late Akkadian (Akkadisch III) in style.[140] Unfortunately, it does not help in identification of the seated god.

The bull-footed standard with the dangling object bears further study. In the Area WF seal, the object looks clearly like a sandal with a foot-shaped sole and attachment straps; in other seals with the moon-god's standard, the representation is far less clear. An Akkadian-period example from the Ur Cemetery, a seal belonging to Ur-SI, a servant of Enmenanna, priestess of the moon-god, has an amorphous oval hanging from the standard. The seal shows a procession of deities, one of which must be the moon-god.[141] Another seal from the Ur Cemetery[142] shows a standard in the midst of a combat among gods; an unclear angular object hangs from the standard. The figure on the right of the standard, with one foot up on a mountain, can be identified as Sin. A seal from the Yale Babylonian Collection bears the image of a standard nearly identical to that on the Nippur seal: animal footed, mace topped, and bearing a long tapered object described by Buchanan as a pennant.[143] The same deity with one foot resting on a mountain recurs, in this case holding the staff of the standard. While the standards are roughly the same in these three cases, there is a range of shapes for the dangling object, and no convincing explanation of the standard or the object has yet been offered.

Figure 12. Scene and Dimensions Reconstructed from Several Unbaked Clay Sealings (2D328, 2D330, 2D347) Excavated in the 1949/50 Season at Nippur, Area TB, Level II. See McCown and Haines 1967: pl. 119:11–13, 17

---

139. Boehmer 1965: figs. 387 and 389 have Ishtar wearing the crown; in Boehmer 1965: fig. 373 the crown is worn by a weather-god riding in a chariot drawn by a winged griffin.
140. Boehmer 1967: 273–91.
141. See Boehmer 1965: fig. 548 or Rashid and Huri 1982: 19.
142. See Legrain 1951: 243 or Boehmer 1965: fig. 437.

143. See Buchanan 1981: 443. Buchanan hypothesizes that the standard here is related to a standard represented on an Early Dynastic III seal (Buchanan 1981: 338); this earlier standard forms the centerpiece in a banquet scene and also has animal feet. Unlike the later standards, two pendant streamers hang from the staff, but the top of the standard, significantly for comparison purposes, is a crescent moon.

An Isin-Larsa–Old Babylonian sealing from Nippur from the 1949/50 excavations in Area TB might be added as a comparison (fig. 12).[144] It shows a seated god, behind whom is a standard with animal feet. The staff has a flattened top, below which are two oval objects that, while not as clearly detailed as the object on the Area WF seal, can be best explained as a pair of sandals. Unfortunately, the leading figure in the approaching procession is not preserved.[145]

It can be argued that in all these representations, the object hanging from the standard ought to be the same, and it is only the degree of detail that varies. At its best, the object looks like a sandal or sandals; at the most schematic it is unidentifiable, but a sandal cannot be ruled out. Actual sandals from Mesopotamia are unknown, but symbolic metal sandals have been found in a few burials not very far in time from the Akkadian seals: a silver pair, along with a silver eye-patch, in grave 130 at Abu Salabikh;[146] a copper pair in a grave in Chantier I at the Ville Royale at Susa;[147] and an unpublished copper pair from a late Early Dynastic–Akkadian grave at Tell Uqair.[148] In all cases the sandals are ceremonial grave objects, impractical for use, and were found in infant or child burials. There may be an implication of a very specific kind of death in these few cases, which is being signaled by the inclusion of sandals. In tablet XII of the *Epic of Gilgamesh*, and in the Sumerian tale from which it derives, *Gilgamesh, Enkidu, and the Netherworld*, shoes are specified as an attribute of the living, and Gilgamesh is warned not to wear shoes during his visit to the Underworld, so as not to attract attention. The inclusion of shoes in a grave is thus difficult to rationalize.

The possible connection between sandals in a few child burials and the sandal(s) on standards associated with the moon-god is obscure. The rising and setting of the sun means that Shamash is sometimes considered to pass through the Underworld when the sun is not visible, and the parallel rising and setting of the moon means that such a journey could be attributed to Sin also. Shamash and Sin might have worn sandals during their passage through the Underworld in order to indicate that they do not belong there; alternatively the sandals could have been hung up and left behind during that journey, so as not to disturb the dead.

A different interpretation of the scene is also possible, however. Given that the Area WF seal comes from Nippur, it is possible that the seated god, rather than being Shamash, is Enlil, the patron deity of the city.[149] In any case, this deity has to be an important one in order to appear in a superior position to Sin. Enlil, despite being the most powerful god in the pantheon at this time, is strangely difficult to recognize in Mesopotamian representational art, as he does not have a customary attribute or identifying marker.

## First Millennium B.C.

Two seals, a stamp seal and a scarab, were included with a hoard of beads (18 N 7; pl. 179:4) placed in a jar in Pit 2 of Level II. The scarab (18 N 8; pl. 160:4) is slightly worn and of pale green faience; it has four hieroglyphic characters incised on the base and fairly fine detailing of legs and wings. The stamp seal (18 N 9; pl. 160:5) is a simple conical shape of opaque olive green stone, pierced at the top, with an oval base on which a very schematic and enigmatic figure (or figures) is incised. Depending upon the angle of view, the seal could show a standing human figure or a walking/running animal. Seen vertically, the lines could sketch out a worshipper with a staff (e.g., Wallenfels 1994: 58–61, but more schematic than those versions) or a standing archer (Wallenfels 1994: 65–71) or any one of a number of other standing deities or figures. If the orientation is horizontal, the scene could be reconstructed as a winged bull, sphinx, or other animal on a ground line with a smaller animal or filling motif below (e.g., Wallenfels 1994: 370 ff.). An inverted branch-like figure is lightly incised on the side of the seal. The minimal depth of this latter figure means it was probably not used to make an impression but may be related to the ownership or use of the seal.

---

144. The drawing shown here is a composite created from a number of sealing fragments; for photographs, see McCown and Haines 1967: pl. 119:11–13.
145. The inscription identifies the owner as a priest of Ninlil, the wife of Enlil. Given that association, as the most important figure in the scene, the seated god behind whom the standard is placed could be presumed to be Enlil.
146. Postgate 1980: 87–104.
147. Tallon 1987: fig. 38.
148. The grave is briefly mentioned in Moorey 1982: 26.
149. Fischer (2002: 127) makes the assumption that this figure is Enlil.

## Stone Vessels

Only three complete stone vessels were recovered, all from graves in Early Dynastic and Akkadian levels. Each belongs to a definable type, seen at other sites, although none of these types supplies a very precise dating. All are of the same material: a yellow and white veined alabaster or calcite. The simplest, a deep cup with plain rim, flat base, and slightly concave sides (19 N 83; pl. 128:5), comes from Burial 19 in Level XVIIC. Similar cups have been found in the Ur Cemetery in both Early Dynastic and Akkadian graves.

The other two stone bowls were buried with two of the skeletons in the Akkadian-period Burial 14 complex: with Skeleton 6 in the early Akkadian phase and Skeleton 4 in the late Akkadian chamber. The bowl with Skeleton 6 is a simple hemisphere with a beaded rim and flat disk base (19 N 96; pl. 136:4); comparable bowls come from the Ur Cemetery in late Early Dynastic graves. A rim sherd of the same type of bowl came from Level XIVA (I333; pl. 161:1), though the material is a more homogenous, white marble-like stone, rather than banded calcite. The stone vessel with Skeleton 4 (19 N 4; pl. 145:2) is a more complex form with an everted rim, carinated sides, and a rounded base; similar examples have been found in Early Dynastic and Akkadian graves at Abu Salabikh and Ur.

Additional stone vessel sherds were recovered from occupational material: two plain rims from large shallow bowls in Level XIIA (H511:1, H539:5; pl. 161:2–3) and a flat base sherd in Level XIIB (H1021:20; pl. 161:4). This base fragment is white marble and the smaller bowl rim sherd (H511:1) is carved in a white translucent marble-like stone. The larger bowl (H539:5) is of a rarer green igneous stone, possibly diorite.

A decrease in the popularity of stone vessels in post-Early Dynastic contexts has been determined for Uruk (Martin 1993), a decrease that has been linked to an increased availability of metal vessels at the time. But at Nippur, and possibly elsewhere, vessels in both media are rare and are far more likely to be found in graves or in specialized contexts than anywhere else. Their degree of popularity relative to each other may be more closely related to the amount of excavation and type of excavated contexts in the Early Dynastic versus Akkadian periods.

## Metal Vessels

Most of the metal vessels in Area WF come from graves, and the absence of even fragments of metal vessels from occupational debris could indicate that metal vessels were strictly for burial or ceremonial purposes. However, there were traces of use (i.e., ash buildup on a base, a missing handle) on some of the vessels from the burials. A more likely explanation for the absence of metal vessel fragments from occupational material is the efficient recycling process, reflecting the rarity of metals in the region.

The only metal vessel not from a burial is a shallow copper/bronze[150] ladle found among other stored objects in the southeast room in Level XIVA (18 N 170; pl. 161:5); its round bowl with subhemispherical profile and short trough spout are similar to examples from graves at Kish and Ur, but those versions have either a flat base or a low ring base, while the Area WF version has a rounded base. The projection identified here as a handle could, in fact, be a pouring spout. Closer parallels (though slightly larger) come from grave 108 at Khafajah and the Shara Temple at Tell Agrab, both of Early Dynastic II date (Müller-Karpe 1993). This date is difficult to reconcile with the mid-Akkadian date of Level XIVA given by other objects and pottery. The vessel could in this case be an heirloom, but such a time gap is very long. The scarcity of metal vessels in the archaeological record means that we must rely on scattered examples to reconstruct the full time range for production of any type attested. There may be a great deal of conservatism in metal vessel production, in contrast to the fairly rapid changes in pottery style. Rather than identifying a date of production only around the point when the earliest version is attested and assuming all later examples to be heirlooms, perhaps we should reconstruct longer time ranges for many types.

The rest of the bronze vessels were buried with the skeletons of Burial 14. Skeleton 4 in Level XIIIB had a single copper/bronze bowl (19 N 72; pl. 145:3). In the same level, six copper/bronze vessels were buried with Skeleton 2 (pl. 64a): two hemispherical bowls (19 N 9 and 19 N 71; pl. 148:8–9), a lidded cylindrical box (19 N 19; pl. 148:7), a shallow pan or ladle (19 N 73; pl. 149:5), a bucket (19 N 36; pl. 150:3), and a deeper "frying pan" vessel with a long handle (19 N 103; pl. 151:3). Skeleton 1, interred during the occupation of Level XIIB, was buried with six further copper/bronze vessels: two hemispherical bowls (18 N 181, 18 N 182; pls. 67a, 156:3–4), a deep pan (18

---

150. The metal used for this and other vessels and objects from the third-millennium B.C. levels in WF may be tin-bronze, arsenical bronze, or unalloyed copper; until chemical analysis can be done, it is described as copper/bronze.

N 180; pls. 67b, 155:4), a deep ladle or scoop (18 N 185; pls. 67a 155:5), a spouted cauldron (18 N 183; pls. 67b, 156:1), and a bucket (18 N 184; pls. 67b, 156:2).

The two assemblages of metal vessels with Skeletons 1 and 2 share strong points of comparison: both include a pair of hemispherical bowls, a bucket, and a utensil that could have served as a ladle. The unmatched items, a lidded box and "frying pan" with Skeleton 2, versus the two deep pans with Skeleton 1, might or might not be significant. The consistent grouping of the other four vessels is reminiscent of the pottery "beer sets" found in late Early Dynastic and early Akkadian graves at Kish, Abu Salabikh, Tell Deylam, Tell Razuk, and elsewhere. Other groups of metal vessels from Early Dynastic and Akkadian graves have been analyzed by Müller-Karpe (1993: 242–63). There are sets consisting of hemispherical bowls, a bucket, and a ladle in a few burials at Khafajah and in numerous graves in the Ur Cemetery. Often the ladle is replaced by a similarly shaped strainer, and the set may be accompanied by, or in part replaced by, a deep pan or pans. This more or less coherent group has been interpreted as a drinking set (Müller-Karpe 1993: 283), which is a persuasive explanation. The question that remains is the intended use of the set: if it was "ceremonial" and had been used as part of the burial ritual immediately prior to the grave's being filled in, if it was a frequently used set under normal circumstances and was included in the grave for daily use by the dead, or if it was intended as a gift that the dead could offer to one of the deities in the underworld to ensure good treatment.[151]

Hemispherical bowls are common in Early Dynastic through Akkadian period contexts. The "frying pan" vessel is also a form that is relatively frequently encountered, with several variants according to base shape — whether rounded or a flat, offset disk (as the Area WF example, 19 N 103, pl. 151:3). Examples come from the Kish A Cemetery, the Ur Cemetery, and from a floor in Level VI at Tepe Gawra. In some cases the loop at the handle end has a ring through it, which would have allowed the vessel to be hung up when not in use. The bowl with Skeleton 4 (19 N 72; pl. 145:3) has a flat base and shallower sides than the hemispherical bowls with other skeletons, which allows it to be identified as a distinct, less common, form. Examples have been found in Early Dynastic II graves at Tell Uqair and Khafajah. It is not clear, in the absence of examples that bridge the gap between these graves and Area WF Burial 14, whether the time range should be extended across Early Dynastic III and the early Akkadian into late Akkadian or whether this might be an "antique" in this context.

There are many parallels for the deep circular pan found with Skeleton 1 (18 N 180; pl. 155:4) from Early Dynastic III through Akkadian graves in the Ur Cemetery and at Tell al-Uqair. Due to warping and damage it is not clear whether the base of the bowl portion in the Area WF example was flat or convex; such vessels from other sites can have either form (see Müller-Karpe 1993: pl. 90). The details of the attachment of the base to the body of the vessel are obscured by corrosion. The "cauldron," with its wide spout and single horizontal handle (18 N 183; pl. 156:1), has no exact parallel anywhere, though it is similar in form to some Early Dynastic III vessels from the Ur Cemetery (Müller-Karpe 1993: forms 33 III and 33 IV). It has the same arrangement and type of spout and horizontal handle as other late Akkadian vessels from Ur (Müller-Karpe 1993: form 40), although those have a rounded or pedestal base.

The lidded cylindrical box (19 N 19; pl. 148:7) seems to have only two parallels, both from the Ur Cemetery in graves dating to the Akkadian period. The two buckets with Skeletons 1 and 2 belong to a single type; as drawn, their profiles vary slightly, but this is due mainly to their warped and crushed condition, which made reconstruction of the heights extremely difficult (18 N 184, 19 N 36; pls. 156:2, 150:3). Both originally had handles attached to the neck by separate riveted loops, but the handle on the Skeleton 2 bucket was missing. An "Early Dynastic IIIb" grave at Ur supplies the best parallel for the form, but the time range of this type should be extended into the Akkadian period. The "ladle," or long-handled deep cup with Skeleton 1 (18 N 185; pl. 155:5), does not have any exact published parallels, and it may be that the long trough-sectioned handle is actually a specialized pouring spout. Similar vessels with plain rounded sides or more tapering sides come from Early Dynastic III graves in the Ur Cemetery, but they lack the raised foot of the Area WF example. Finally, the flat shallow pan with solid handle with Skeleton 2 (19 N 73; pl. 149:5) does not have any parallels among published material.

---

151. The question of whether bronze "drinking sets" were used by the living at the funeral or were for use by the dead in the afterlife has been raised in the Neo-Babylonian context by Salje (1996). With either intention, there can be meanings for both religious thought and the marking of status.

## Metal Objects

### Third Millennium B.C.

The most common subcategory of metal objects, pins, is discussed under *Ornaments*, but there are several weapons or tools from graves and occupational material. A number of these come from the southeast room in Level XIV: a chisel or adze (18 N 172; pl. 162:1), a dagger (18 N 122; pl. 162:2), and a spearhead (18 N 121; pl. 162:3). The flared chisel or adze appears peculiarly fragile to have been a usable tool, but its thinness may be the result of corrosion. It had been hafted straight onto a handle, to judge by the traces of cords and wood around the short shaft end. The only close comparisons come from Susa in contexts contemporary with Early Dynastic II. The dagger and long, square-sectioned spearhead are both well-known types from Early Dynastic and Akkadian graves at Ur. The dagger has slightly bowed edges and a low central rib (which, according to Woolley, puts it "early" in the development of the shape during the mid-third millennium).[152] Daggers had wider popularity than the spear, also appearing at Kish, Abu Salabikh, Mari, Susa, and Area WA at Nippur in contexts from late Early Dynastic through Ur III. There is a second spearhead with an octagonal cross section (19 N 7; pls. 61b, 145:4) found with Skeleton 4 of Burial 14; this form is also known from the Ur Cemetery in an Early Dynastic III grave and from Susa in an Akkadian context. A bladed spearpoint with incurving sides (18 N 176; pls. 66b, 152:1) and two identical, short leaf-shaped daggers or knife blades (19 N 6a–b; pls. 66b, 152:5–6) were also found with Skeleton 1 of the same grave. All have late Early Dynastic and Akkadian parallels elsewhere. Other occupational debris yielded the curved broken end of a blade (19 N 14; pl. 162:4) that may have been part of a hammered crescentic axhead of the Akkadian period. A solid-cast socketed rectangular axhead (18 N 177; pls. 66b, 152:2) was buried with Skeleton 1 of Burial 14, and an identical axhead (18 N 171; pl. 162:5) came from occupational material in Level XIIB. This latter ax form, although present in the Ur Cemetery, is represented by only two examples there, from an Akkadian–Ur III grave. A short nail or large rivet (18 N 145; pl. 162:19) was incorporated into the bricks of a wall in Level XIB.

The final metal object is a small copper/bronze pointed filter that still retains traces of a reed drinking straw inside (18 N 186; pls. 66a, 152:9), found in a jar buried with Skeleton 1 of Burial 14. It is identical to scattered examples from northern Mesopotamia (Tell Brak, Chagar Bazar, and Hammam et-Turkman) and even farther afield, in the Levant and Anatolia (Alalakh, Megiddo, and Boğazköy among other sites; see de Feyter 1988). All the contexts in which such filters have so far been found date to the early second millennium B.C. (ca. 1900–1600 B.C.), around three centuries or more later than the Area WF example. Until now, only one example from southern Mesopotamia has been published, and this from northern Babylonia at Tell ed-Der (Gasche 1989). This type of filter is related to the long metal drinking tubes that appear infrequently in some Ur Cemetery Early Dynastic graves, but in those objects the "straw" section was also made of metal, with a bent tip — the same concept but a completely different morphology. Since the filter was found inside a jar in a sealed grave clearly dated to the late Akkadian period by seals, there is no chance it was a later object that had migrated into an earlier context.

### First Millennium B.C.

Only a single metal object came from the first-millennium levels, in Pit 1 of Level II. This is a badly corroded and damaged solid cylinder, possibly a tool handle (18 N 60; pl. 179:2). The continued absence of even fragments of metal objects in the later levels indicates that the recycling of metals, already mentioned for the third-millennium B.C. levels, presumably persisted into the later periods.

## Ornaments

### Third Millennium B.C.

#### Pins

The largest subgroup of pins is straight, with a round cross section and no distinctive detailing; included here are 18 N 84, 18 N 143, 18 N 188, 19 N 5, 19 N 28, in occupational and burial contexts from Level XIVB through Level

---

152. Watkins (1983) also puts this dagger type in the "earlier part" of the Ur Cemetery internal sequence.

XIB (pls. 60c, 162:20, 162:10, 152:3, 151:2, 145:1). Three of these straight pins are pierced laterally near the head (18 N 84, 19 N 5, 19 N 28), and it may be that others in this group were also pierced but that their ends have been obscured by corrosion. A few pins are pierced laterally below a short tang, which originally may have been decorated with a bead: 18 N 148, 18 N 153, 19 N 64, in Levels XIVA through XIIA (pls. 162:18, 14, 136:1). Among these, 18 N 153 (pl. 162:14) has traces of corrosion on its shaft that look as though a cord was wrapped spirally around it. This type of pin was used to secure clothing, as well as to attach cylinder seals to garments, and examples have been found in Early Dynastic and Akkadian graves at Kish, Abu Salabikh, Ur, and Khafajah as well as in Akkadian contexts at Nippur (Area TB, Level XI) and Susa. The example of this type from a burial in Area WF (19 N 64, with Burial 14, Skeleton 6; pl. 136:1), however, was quite long to have been worn comfortably (ca. 23 cm) and had been placed in the grave separate from the body. Three of the pins with Skeleton 1 of Burial 14 were short and straight with flattened ends: 19 N 6c, 18 N 178–179 (pls. 66a, 152:4, 7–8); two were found near the head and may have been part of a hair ornament or other headgear. The means of attachment, if any, are not clear and there are no obvious parallels published from any other site.

Two pins, 19 N 63 from occupational material in Level XVI (pl. 162:7) and 19 N 65 with Burial 14, Skeleton 6, in Level XIV (pl. 136:2), are distinctive due to their long bent tangs rising from a square or flattened cross section, with a relatively long shaft. Another pin, 18 N 151 (pl. 162:8), has a square central section and tapers abruptly at each end; it is almost certainly reworked from a longer pin, the square section perhaps indicating that it also was of the type with a long bent tang. Long-tanged pins appear in the Ur Cemetery and at Kish and Abu Salabikh in late Early Dynastic graves; Level XVI is assigned to the transitional period between Early Dynastic and Akkadian, but the burial context in Area WF (Level XIV) is Akkadian in date. With the small number of examples involved, it is difficult to determine whether the date assigned to the type should be extended or whether these could have been heirlooms saved beyond their date of manufacture. Given the recycling of metals and the relative ease with which metal objects can be reworked, however, it is likely that these were made in this style shortly before they were deposited.

A final pin type is straight and relatively short, with a round cross-sectioned shaft and a distinctive flattened and rolled head; pins 18 N 90, 18 N 112, 18 N 146, and 19 N 13 from Levels XIVB through X all fall into this category (pl. 162:21, 16, 12–13). This is a widespread type: examples come from Kish and Ur in southern Mesopotamia but also from farther away, such as Tepe Gawra and Susa. The dates ascribed to the contexts range from the Early Dynastic through Akkadian, but the type could turn out to be more distinctive of the Akkadian period. Finally, there are a number of broken fragments of straight pins with small round cross sections, which could have had the short tang or rolled head: 18 N 142, 18 N 147, 18 N 144, 18 N 150 (pl. 162:17, 11, 9, 15).

*Other Metal Ornaments*

As with the other metal objects, most of the ornaments were found in graves. Copper/bronze bracelets come from occupational material in Level XIVA (18 N 120; pl. 162:6) and Burial 13 of the same level (18 N 118a–b; pl. 134:12). In each case, the bracelet is formed of a single round-sectioned loop with overlapping ends. In the two heavier bracelets with Burial 14, Skeleton 2, the shape is the same but the material is silver (19 N 21a–b; pls. 63b, 146:3). The earrings worn by this skeleton are of a distinctive and widespread type: tapering hollow coils of gold that would have clipped onto the earlobes (19 N 37a–b; pls. 63b, 146:2). Both Skeletons 1 and 2 of Burial 14 wore thin gold foil fillets on their foreheads (18 N 175 and 19 N 38, respectively; pls. 66a, 152:10, 63b, 146:1). The first of these has a wider oval at one end, faintly embossed with crisscrossing lines; the latter is a narrow rectangular band with rounded ends and an undecorated surface. Both are pierced at the ends for a string or cord to tie the fillet around the head. A final gold object (19 N 8; pls. 66a, 152:12) was found with Burial 14, Skeleton 1: a strip of gold foil attached to a wire twisted into a double herringbone pattern. Damage to the foil makes reconstruction of the function of this object difficult, but it could have been part of a ring or pendant, or the setting for a precious stone.

*Beads*

A few single beads were found dropped or discarded on floors or in pits (19 N 23, 18 N 152, 18 N 155, 18 N 154; pl. 166:1–4), but most beads came from graves, either as disassembled but full strings, or as the occasional isolated bead. A short necklace was buried with Burial 13 in Level XIVA (18 N 119; pl. 134:13) and two longer necklaces with Burial 14, Skeleton 2, in Level XIIIB (19 N 20, 19 N 18; pls. 63, 146:4–5). A few skeletons were adorned with only a single bead, such as Burial 14, Skeleton 5 (19 N 22; pl. 133:7), and Burial 14, Skeleton 4 (19 N 24; pl. 145:5). Other examples of single beads associated with skeletons that were otherwise adorned with fuller necklaces or other ornaments are 19 N 25 from Burial 14, Skeleton 2 (pl. 146:6), and 18 N 194 from Burial 14, Skeleton 1 (pl. 152:11).

The range of both shapes and materials of third-millennium B.C. beads is wide but does not offer any startling conclusions (table 75; see plates 133–34, 145–46, 152, and 165–67 for a detailed description of the contents of individual strings). Carnelian is the most common stone (occurring in the strings 18 N 119, 19 N 18, and 19 N 20, as well as the single bead 19 N 24); lapis lazuli appears frequently (occurring in the same strings, 18 N 119, 19 N 18, and 19 N 20 and as the single bead 18 N 194). A single example of an etched carnelian bead of Indus Valley origin, with four circles filled with white paste, comes from the necklace found with Burial 14, Skeleton 2 (19 N 18, pl. 146:5k). Other semiprecious stones include agate (as beads and pendants in 19 N 20) and an unidentifiable dark green stone (in 19 N 18). Shell (the single bead 18 N 152 and one bead within 19 N 18) and baked clay (two beads in 18 N 119 and one in 19 N 18) are present but uncommon, and bone is preserved only once among the third-millennium beads (19 N 22, the single bead with Burial 14, Skeleton 5).

Gold beads are numerous, although most of them come from only two necklaces (18 N 119 and especially 19 N 20). Gold foil-covered copper (in both 19 N 18 and 19 N 20) or plain copper beads (in 19 N 20 and the single bead 19 N 25) also appear. Woolley noted (1934: 372) that gold foil-covered copper beads are common in Akkadian graves at Ur, while Early Dynastic gold beads were more likely to be solid. The two silver beads found (in 18 N 119 and 19 N 20; pls. 134:13 and 146:4) may not be completely representative of the entire number of silver beads that existed due to the high corrodibility of this metal.

Among shapes, simple ring-shaped beads are the most frequently attested (18 N 119, 19 N 18, 19 N 20, 19 N 22, 19 N 23, 19 N 24; see table 75), followed by ball shaped (18 N 119, 18 N 194, 19 N 18, 19 N 20) and date shaped (18 N 119, 19 N 18, 19 N 20), with smaller numbers of double conoid (19 N 18), cylindrical (19 N 18, 19 N 20, 19 N 25), biconvex (18 N 119), diamond shaped (19 N 18), ovoid (19 N 18), and rectangular (19 N 18). All these shapes are attested in the Ur Cemetery and appear in Woolley's bead typology (Woolley 1934: fig. 70).

Table 75. Third-millennium B.C. Beads by Shape and Material

|  | Ring | Ball | Date | Double Conoid | Cylinder | Spacer | Biconvex | Diamond | Rectangle | Ovoid | Total |
|---|---|---|---|---|---|---|---|---|---|---|---|
| Carnelian | 96 | 16 | 1 | 3 | – | – | – | – | – | – | **116** |
| Gold | 101 | 4 | – | – | – | – | – | – | – | – | **105** |
| Lapis | 35 | 11 | 1 | 17 | 9 | 5 | 3 | 1 | 1 | 1 | **84** |
| Cu with gold | 2 | 70 | – | – | – | – | – | 1 | – | – | **73** |
| Agate | – | – | 13 | – | – | – | – | – | – | – | **13** |
| Clay | – | 1 | 2 | – | – | – | – | – | – | – | **3** |
| Glass | – | 1 | – | – | 1 | – | – | – | – | – | **2** |
| Gray stone | 1 | – | – | – | – | 1 | – | – | – | – | **2** |
| Shell | 1 | – | – | – | 1 | – | – | – | – | – | **2** |
| Silver | 2 | – | – | – | – | – | – | – | – | – | **2** |
| Cu/Br | – | – | – | – | 2 | – | – | – | – | – | **2** |
| Bone | 1 | – | – | – | – | – | – | – | – | – | **1** |
| Hematite | – | – | – | – | – | – | – | – | – | 1 | **1** |
| Dark green stone | – | – | 1 | – | – | – | – | – | – | – | **1** |
| Orange and gray stone | – | – | 1 | – | – | – | – | – | – | – | **1** |
| White stone | 1 | – | – | – | – | – | – | – | – | – | **1** |
| Brown stone | 1 | – | – | – | – | – | – | – | – | – | **1** |
| **Total** | **241** | **103** | **19** | **20** | **13** | **6** | **3** | **2** | **1** | **2** | **410** |

There are a few spacer beads for double strings (19 N 20, 19 N 18; pl. 146:4–5) or multi-strand necklaces (the single fragmentary bead, 18 N 155, pl. 166:3). The second necklace with Burial 14, Skeleton 2 (19 N 18; pl. 146:5), contains five lapis lazuli spacer beads, between which are arranged three very long double-conoid carnelian beads surrounded by other beads of lapis lazuli, carnelian, shell, gold foil-covered copper, and a few rarer stones.

Although most of the strings of beads in burials had been disarranged when the string decayed, in at least one case evidence of the stringing order was partially preserved: 19 N 20 (pls. 63b, 146:4) with Burial 14, Skeleton 2, had alternating small gold, carnelian, and lapis lazuli beads, regularly interspersed with larger beads of agate and other stones. The necklace was completed by two circular pendants of agate set in gold mounts (pl. 146:4a–b); a V-shaped counterweight in agate with ends of gold foil was found at the back of the neck (pl. 146:4c). The circular pendants were carved from banded brown and white agate, with the upper surface parallel to the banding planes and the sides smoothed down so that a central brown section was left surrounded by a white ring, creating a piece that is startlingly eye-like. A very similar "eye-bead" in blue and white faience was found in a first-millennium burial (18 N 40a, from Burial 3; pl. 171:6). The eye-bead is also known at least as early as the Early Dynastic period from graves at Ur (Woolley 1934). Agate examples similar to the Area WF Akkadian eye-beads have been found in Kassite contexts and Neo-Assyrian tombs (including the queens' tombs at Nimrud; Damerji 1999), and faience versions appear in Neo-Babylonian and Parthian contexts. The function may be continued in modern glass "Evil Eye" beads.

Two beads (18 N 95 and 18 N 96, from Levels XIB and XIIA, respectively) deserve special discussion since they are manufactured of glass. One, 18 N 95, is spherical, made of dark green and white threads wrapped in spirals (pl. 167:1); it was found near the middle of the courtyard of the house in Level XIB. The other, 18 N 96, is roughly cylindrical, made of swirled pale blue green and yellow glass (pl. 167:2); it came from a floor in the small southeast room of the house in Level XIIA. Both are true glass rather than glazed faience, as they are vitreous in structure throughout. These two beads are among the earliest well-stratified, deliberately manufactured glass objects known from Mesopotamia. Together with the glass beads and other objects from Tell Judeideh, Tell Brak, Nuzi, Tell Asmar, Ur, and Eridu (Moorey 1994: 190–92), the Nippur beads form a growing collection of mid- to late-third-millennium B.C. examples of experimentation and innovation in this medium prior to the expansion of glass production in the mid-second millennium B.C. The glass in these two late Akkadian period beads seems to have been related to metal smelting in its chemical makeup and may have been the by-product of that technology. The technique of swirling the two colors of glass together and the shaping of the beads with hollow centers were deliberate actions, however, with substantial complexity of manufacture. See *Appendix 1* for a full analysis of the glass beads.

## First Millennium B.C.

### Metal Ornaments

In Burial 6 of Level IV was found an unusual item made of a pair of short bronze pins attached to each other with a length of copper/bronze chain (18 N 37; pl. 169:5). This item was located at the front of the pelvis of the skeleton and was surely part of a belt, but the total length of chain between the two pins was about 30 cm, therefore it could not have gone completely around the waist. Any organic portions of this object — presumably a leather or fabric piece that went around the back — had completely vanished. The chain and pins are similar to parts of an enigmatic object from Burial 4: a marble palette, square with a stepped top, laterally pierced for a bronze pin that protrudes slightly at both ends (18 N 33; pls. 73b, 172:7). A length of bronze chain is attached to each end of the pin so that the slab could be hung up. The form of the square with a stepped top is similar to that of calendrical clay tablets and bronze Pazuzu amulets, but there is no writing on the slab and both flat surfaces are slightly concave, as if they had been used for grinding or sharpening. However, there was no trace of pigment or any other residue visible to the eye on either side.

The small bracelet in Burial 4 of Level IIIB (18 N 35; pls. 73b, 172:4) is a single open loop of copper/bronze wire with a plano-convex cross section. The ends are badly corroded and split, but traces of surface decoration there may indicate that they had ended in heads of snakes or some other animal. A single pin (18 N 149; pls. 73b, 172:3) was found in the same burial. The tip is curved back on itself and both ends have heavy rounded finials; the corrosion is such that it is unclear whether the curve in the shaft was intentional or the result of damage.

Finally, a hoard of silver and copper was found in a jar in Pit 1 of Level II, in which a number of ornaments could be identified (18 N 126; pl. 178:4–5). Much of the hoard consisted of flat pieces or irregular fragments of copper and silver, presumably melted or hammered down from original objects and subsequently further corroded

Table 76. First-millennium Beads by Shape and Material

| | Ring | Double Conoid | Cylinder | Date | Ball | Elliptical | Lentoid | Truncated Biconical | Biconvex | Hub Shaped |
|---|---|---|---|---|---|---|---|---|---|---|
| Carnelian | 83 | 8 | 46 | 7 | 35 | 1 | 4 | 7 | 2 | 1 |
| Glass | 155 | – | – | – | – | – | 3 | – | – | – |
| Faience | 49 | – | – | 22 | 1 | – | – | 1 | – | 1 |
| Agate | – | 32 | 7 | 13 | 7 | 9 | – | – | 2 | – |
| Mottled stone | 1 | 34 | 19 | 2 | – | 1 | – | – | – | – |
| Shell | 3 | – | 23 | – | – | – | – | – | – | – |
| Lapis | 5 | 2 | 11 | 6 | – | 7 | – | – | – | – |
| Quartz | – | 14 | 2 | 4 | 1 | 2 | – | 1 | – | – |
| Orange brown stone | – | 15 | 2 | 4 | – | – | – | – | 2 | – |
| Amethyst | – | 4 | – | 4 | – | – | 6 | – | – | – |
| Turquoise | 7 | – | 1 | 5 | – | 1 | – | – | – | – |
| Hematite | 2 | 6 | – | 2 | – | 1 | – | – | – | – |
| Marble | – | 3 | – | 6 | – | 2 | – | – | – | – |
| Iron | – | – | 9 | – | – | – | – | – | – | – |
| Olive yellow stone | – | 8 | – | – | – | 1 | – | – | – | – |
| Black stone | – | 4 | 1 | – | – | – | – | – | – | – |
| Bronze | – | – | 3 | – | – | – | – | – | – | – |
| Gray stone | 1 | – | – | – | – | 1 | – | – | – | – |
| Silver | – | – | – | – | – | – | – | – | – | 3 |
| Black and white stone | – | – | – | – | 1 | – | – | – | 1 | – |
| Yellow stone | – | 1 | – | – | – | – | – | – | – | – |
| Orange and white stone | – | – | – | – | 1 | – | – | – | – | – |
| Brown stone | – | – | – | – | – | 1 | – | – | – | – |
| Tan stone | – | – | – | – | – | 1 | – | – | – | – |
| Pale orange stone | – | – | – | – | – | – | – | – | – | – |
| **Total** | **306** | **131** | **124** | **75** | **46** | **28** | **13** | **9** | **7** | **5** |

together. Most of these fragments were about 1.0–2.0 cm square and barely 0.1 cm thick, with fewer being about 2.0–8.0 cm square also about 0.1 cm thick. There are a very few pieces 4.0–6.0 cm on a side; these last are correspondingly thicker than the other pieces, about 0.3 cm. Some pieces of silver wire remained identifiable, including a clump that was folded back on itself a number of times (18 N 127e; pl. 179:1e). The other intact objects consist of a penannular earring with a spherical pendant covered with rows of granulation (18 N 127a; pl. 179:1a), three ribbed, hub-shaped beads (18 N 127b–d; pl. 179:1b–d), and a broken ring with the bezel missing but a small oval counterweight still intact (18 N 127f; pl. 179:1f).

*Beads*

Most of the first-millennium B.C. beads come from necklaces worn by the skeletons in graves of Levels IV and III: Burial 2 (18 N 10; pl. 171:3), Burial 4 (18 N 30; pls. 73b, 172:5), and Burial 6 (18 N 36; pl. 169:6). There was also a hoard of beads in a pit in Level II (18 N 7; pl. 179:4). Three single beads come from Burial 3, one loose in the grave and two found inside one of the jars that accompanied the skeleton, rather than on the body (18 N 39, 18 N 40a–b; pl. 171:5–6).

Table 76. First-millennium Beads by Shape and Material (*cont.*)

|  | Plano-convex | Rectangle | Rhomboid | Ovoid | Square Elliptical | Spacer | Hemisphere | Complex* | **Total** |
|---|---|---|---|---|---|---|---|---|---|
| Carnelian | – | – | – | 3 | – | 1 | – | 1 | **199** |
| Glass | – | – | – | – | – | – | – | – | **158** |
| Faience | 1 | 1 | 1 | – | – | – | – | 1 | **78** |
| Agate | 1 | 1 | 1 | – | 1 | – | – | 2 | **76** |
| Mottled stone | – | – | – | – | – | – | – | 1 | **58** |
| Shell | – | – | – | – | – | – | – | 27 | **53** |
| Lapis | – | 2 | – | – | – | – | – | 1 | **34** |
| Quartz | 1 | – | 1 | – | 1 | – | – | – | **27** |
| Orange brown stone | – | – | – | – | – | – | – | 4 | **27** |
| Amethyst | – | – | – | – | – | – | 1 | 1 | **16** |
| Turquoise | 1 | – | – | – | – | – | – | 1 | **16** |
| Hematite | – | – | – | – | – | – | – | – | **11** |
| Marble | – | – | – | – | – | – | – | – | **11** |
| Iron | – | – | – | – | – | – | – | – | **9** |
| Olive yellow stone | – | – | – | – | – | – | – | – | **9** |
| Black stone | – | – | – | – | – | – | – | – | **5** |
| Bronze | – | – | – | – | – | – | – | 1 | **1** |
| Gray stone | – | – | – | – | 1 | – | – | – | **3** |
| Silver | – | – | – | – | – | – | – | – | **3** |
| Black and white stone | – | – | – | – | – | – | – | – | **2** |
| Yellow stone | 1 | – | – | – | – | – | – | – | **2** |
| Orange and white stone | – | – | – | – | – | – | – | – | **1** |
| Brown stone | – | – | – | – | – | – | – | – | **1** |
| Tan stone | – | – | – | – | – | – | – | – | **1** |
| Pale orange stone | – | – | – | – | – | – | – | 1 | **1** |
| **Total** | **5** | **4** | **3** | **3** | **3** | **1** | **1** | **41** | **805** |

* "Complex" includes eye-bead, faceted biconical, triangular-sectioned prism, triangular pendant, irregular pendants and beads, sphere section, coil, and natural shells.

The range of forms and materials among the first-millennium beads is greater than among the third-millennium material (table 76; see plates 169, 171–72, and 179 for a detailed description of the contents of individual strings). Carnelian is the most common medium (18 N 7, 18 N 30, 18 N 36, 18 N 39), followed closely by glass (but all these derive from a single necklace in Burial 2: 18 N 10) and faience (18 N 7, 18 N 30, 18 N 36, 18 N 40). Agate was also very popular (18 N 7, 18 N 30, 18 N 36), as was an agate-related mottled stone (18 N 7). Shells, mostly left in their natural state but pierced for stringing, also often appear (18 N 7, 18 N 30). Lapis lazuli had decreased in availability or popularity since the third millennium B.C. but did still appear with some frequency (18 N 7, 18 N 30, 18 N 36). Quartz and a variety of quartz-related stones of varied colors make up the bulk of the rest of the beads, with equal numbers of amethyst and turquoise,[153] and slightly fewer hematite and marble. Only a few metal beads are represented, comprising nine iron examples (18 N 7), four in bronze (18 N 7, 18 N 30), and three in silver (18 N 127b–d).

---

153. The rarity of turquoise as a medium for cylinder seals has been noted by Collon (1987: 102), and its more general rarity for any objects in Mesopotamia, after relative popularity during the Neolithic and Chalcolithic, has been noted by Potts (1994: 194, 281) and Tosi (1974: 159). This rarity occurs despite sources of turquoise being in the same general area as those of lapis lazuli and no more difficult to exploit. Collon proposes that its scarcity has to do with difficulty

Ring-shaped beads remain the most popular form by a great majority, appearing in all the strings. Double conoid (18 N 7) and cylindrical (18 N 7, 18 N 30, 18 N 37) are the next most common shapes, with slightly smaller numbers of date-shaped, ball-shaped, and elliptical beads (in all strings). The remaining forms are only sparsely represented: lentoid, truncated biconical, biconvex, hub-shaped, plano-convex, rectangular, rhomboid, ovoid, squared elliptical, and hemispherical. There is a single spacer bead (18 N 36) and a fairly large number of unique complex shapes, including irregular pendants and natural shells.

## Baked-clay Objects

### Third Millennium B.C.

A cluster of baked-clay objects came from the southeast room (Locus 40) in Level XIVA: three model chariots (18 N 165, 18 N 162, 18 N 133; pl. 163:1–3) and two sheep figurines (18 N 130, 18 N 166; pl. 163:8, 10). A model boat was found in the same area in Level XIIIC (18 N 128; pl. 163:6), and near it a fragment of a model chair or bed (18 N 167; pl. 163:7). Additional animal figurines were found in the courtyard: the head of a dog figurine (18 N 169; pl. 163:9) from Level XIIIC, and a bird (18 N 168; pl. 163:11) from Level XIB. An animal-shaped rattle (18 N 129; pl. 163:12) came from the narrow space between the two buildings in Level XIA.

The chariots are similar to examples from Kish, Nippur Areas TA and TB, and from farther north at Tepe Gawra and Nuzi. The dates to which these model chariots have been assigned elsewhere vary from the Akkadian through the Old Babylonian periods. Isin-Larsa and Old Babylonian chariots are more likely to bear molded decoration on the front, which is lacking in our examples. Simple model wheels (18 N 163, 18 N 161; pl. 163:4–5) came from the southeast room in Level XIIA and from the courtyard in Level X. These wheels are not date-specific, but had presumably been attached to models of chariots or carts. Model boats can date anywhere between the Akkadian and Isin-Larsa periods, with examples coming from Kish and Nippur Areas TA and TB. The model chair/bed has molded decoration on its upper surface, representing woven support material and the frame from which it was strung. Not enough of the piece is preserved to determine whether there were any human figures in relief on the bed, as is attested elsewhere. Comparanda date from the Akkadian through the Ur III periods, from Nippur Area TB, Kish, and Nuzi.

Animal figurines are usually too schematic to provide precise dating, but versions similar to the sheep from inside the room (18 N 130, 166; pl. 163:8, 10) have been excavated at Kish. The dog figurine (18 N 169; pl. 163:9), with its flat body and head turned to the front, is more distinctive; more complete examples have been found at Nippur in Area TB, in Akkadian through Ur III contexts. The bird figurine (18 N 168; pl. 163:11) is similar to versions from Nippur Areas TB and TA, as well as Kish. The rattle (18 N 129; pl. 163:12) is very close in shape to the sheep figures, with clay pellets contained within its hollow body. This seems to have been a common form in the Akkadian through Ur III periods; examples come from Nippur Areas TB and WA 50c, as well as from Abu Salabikh, Kish, Mari, and Ur.

The single example of a human figurine from the third-millennium levels (18 N 81; pl. 163:13) came from within the mudbrick platform, Wall W, in Level IX. It is a well-known type of the Ur III period: a male figure with a cylindrical lower body and applied and incised features, beard, and necklaces. The possibility exists that this is a foundation deposit, although there is not much evidence for baked-clay figurines being used in this way in the Ur III period. The emphasized sexual attributes of the contemporary, stylistically similar female figures surely indicates that these human figurines are not simply toys but have a religious or symbolic function and meaning. Such clay figures are very frequently found in the houses of Area TB at Nippur and at other sites with levels of Ur III date.

The more enigmatic clay items include a pair of conical, lightly baked "game pieces" (18 N 116, 18 N 115; pl. 163:14–15) from Levels XIIIC and XIIA, respectively. These could have been tokens or counters in a simple system of accounting or even randomly formed, meaningless objects.

---

in carving and with postdepositional degeneration, while Potts argues for a shift from land-based to sea-based trade within the third millennium B.C., which cut off easy access to the sources that had been worked through the fourth millennium. Tosi attributes the scarcity to a change in market demands. There could indeed be a possibility that this stone was consciously avoided. Literary texts indicate that semiprecious stones were frequently used as metaphors for favorable aspects of humans, deities, and buildings; and the way that cylinder seals were worn indicates that they were intended to be seen as well as used. Given the use of amethyst, agate, lapis lazuli, and other brightly colored stones, the long-range visibility and unusual color of turquoise should have been irresistible, unless there was a strong social or symbolic rejection or aversion.

## First Millennium B.C.

The baked-clay figurines of the first-millennium B.C. levels are all mold made, in contrast to the handmade figurines of the third millennium B.C. Two human figurines, both female, belong to distinct and widely represented types. From Level IV, 18 N 26 (pl. 180:1) is a version of the popular motif of the nude female wearing a necklace and holding a flower or some other object in front of her with both hands. The details of the object are worn and unclear, making its identification uncertain. From Level II, 18 N 11 (pl. 180:4) is a more simply formed piece, a female wearing a belt, in this case holding a tambourine at her left shoulder. This pose is less frequently represented than that in which the figure holds an object in front of the body but is widespread in southern Mesopotamia.

There are two plaques with single animals in low relief. The more important of the two, 18 N 51 (pl. 180:3; *Appendix 3*), from Level IIIB, is rectangular, with a depiction of a lion walking to the left, its tail curved up and over its back. The lion stands on a horizontal groundline and above the lion is a line of cuneiform inscription identifying the plaque as the property of Iddina-ahu, son of Ninurta-balat-X. The second plaque, 18 N 15 (pl. 180:5), from Level II, is in an unusual round shape and has a figure in low relief, a schematic, winged scorpion-man walking to the left on a horizontal groundline. The type of figures represented point to an apotropaic function for both these items.

A handmade rattle from Level IIIB (18 N 59; pl. 180:2) is startlingly modern in form, with a rounded hollow head containing clay pellets or small stones and a short cylindrical handle. The rattle has a few circular impressions and pierced holes in the head, to which patches of bitumen also adhere.

## Miniature Vessels

Both whole miniature vessels and a few sherds from miniature vessels were recovered from Area WF. Most had been fired to the same degree as "normal" pottery, but there are a few that appear to have been only lightly fired. The contexts are varied, from a child's burial, through a specialized storage installation, to ordinary occupational material. Some are simply smaller versions of known types that could still have been functional, while others seem to be deliberate imitations of normal-sized vessels, but of such a small size that they could not actually have been used.[154] Some relatively large sherds are included here when they belong to a defined pottery type but are either more delicate in manufacture or substantially smaller than the majority of examples of the type.

The two vessels from a child's burial (Burial 21, Skeleton 1, Level XVIIB) are simply smaller versions of well-known types, rather than nonworking models of such vessels. The small scale of the conical bowl (I686, Type O-1; pl. 132:1) and simple jar (I687, Type C-4; pl. 132:2) are suitable for a child and do seem to have been used (presumably by the child in life), to judge by their worn rims and occasional chipping. There are a number of sherds from occupational material that may have been manufactured specifically for use by children (H877:6, H129:2, H752:2; pl. 164:12–13, 15). These sherds are all from jars with rounded sides that are very much like Type C-21, but with smaller rim diameters, thinner walls, and finer overall morphology; the form suggests they might have been drinking vessels.

The small jars (I113, I354, H1057:12, H1021:16; pls. 127:4, 164:2, 4, 7), conical lid (18 N 164; pl. 164:3), and especially the small incised cups (18 N 137, H1010:7; pls. 127:2, 164:5) also seem to have been functional, although of specialized use. Vessels such as these have been found in other excavations mostly in domestic contexts, although the arrangement of 18 N 137 (pl. 127:2) and I113 (pl. 127:4), both covered by conical bowls (respectively, 18 N 136; pl. 127:3, and I115; pl. 127:5) is assumed to denote a foundation deposit or apotropaic ritual. The two four-footed base fragments (H1021:6, H757:10; pl. 164:8, 14) probably come from cups with incised sides, to judge from the base of 18 N 137.

The piriform hole-mouthed jar (19 N 62; pl. 164:1) does not match any known type among the normal-sized pottery, but this form is known (also in miniature) from other sites. The contexts in which such vessels have been found elsewhere include grave fill and the "Ash-Tip" at Abu Salabikh, Mound A at Kish (where they might or might not have originally derived from a grave), and the architectural model found in a street near to the Ninni-zaza Temple at Mari. These jars are usually just barely large enough to have been actually functional, rather than purely symbolic, though the limited contexts and extremely small size point to a very specialized use.

---

154. The difficulty in making a distinction between very small, usable vessels and miniature models of larger forms is discussed in Green 1993, with regard to examples from Abu Salabikh.

Two of the remaining three vessels could be models of larger vessels. There is a replica of the Akkadian Type C-18, the wide-mouth vessel with large spout at the side (18 N 85; pl. 164:10), comparable to a vessel in the Mari architectural model (Parrot 1967b: 3204). The sherd H126:2 (pl. 164:9) does not match any of the pottery types, but its sharp angles and narrow neck suggest that it could be a much smaller copy of a metal vessel. Both these vessels were made with notable care that is out of all proportion to their size. A votive function for these two vessels and for the piriform jar 19 N 62 is possible, such as has been suggested for the collection of miniature vessels from the Ash-Tip at Abu Salabikh (Green 1993: 114–15). In contrast, the final miniature vessel (18 N 83; pl. 164:11) is a very simple handmade object with a minimal, pinched pouring spout, which could have been a child's toy.

Most of the miniature vessels came from Level XII, Phases B and A, from floors in the courtyard (18 N 85, 18 N 164, H1010:7, H1021:5–6 and 16); a single example was found in the southeast room (H126:2). In the next level, XIB, two more miniatures were represented: one from the courtyard (18 N 83) and a second from the southeast room (H877:6). While the number of miniatures from Area WF is not large, this still represents a distinct clustering in time, and sketches a possible pattern of use (in the southeast room) and disposal (in the courtyard). Interpretation of the function of miniature vessels in third-millennium B.C. Mesopotamia ranges from toys through votive offerings (see Green 1993 for full discussion). The domestic nature of the Area WF context seems to favor the hypothesis that they were for use by children, but the care with which some were made, and the association with other objects found in the southeast room, perhaps bring the vessels into the adult world and give them a symbolic significance.

## Miscellaneous Objects

### Third Millennium B.C.

*Organic*

Shell pairs (*Levicardium*[155]) with green or black cosmetic paste were found with three skeletons: Burial 19 (19 N 81, 19 N 82; pl. 141:1), Burial 14, Skeleton 7 (19 N 105a–b; pl. 141:2), and Burial 14, Skeleton 3 (19 N 27a–b; pl. 141:3). An unworked conoid (*Strombus*) shell (19 N 33; pl. 166:19) was found in association with the animal skeletons in Burial 14, but it is not clear whether this was a chance inclusion in the burial fill or a deliberate deposit. An enigmatic faceted oval object cut from the body of a spider conch (*Lambis*) shell (19 N 100; pl. 166:5) was found loose in Level XVI; the medium suggests that it may have been a piece of inlay, but the object itself is uninformative.

A bone tool made from one end of an equid tibia had been buried at the side of Skeleton 2 of Burial 21 (19 N 144; pl. 132:6).[156] The end is rounded and highly polished, almost certainly from heavy use, but the function to which this tool had been put is unclear. It seems too large and irregular to have been used as a shuttle, but some other function in the weaving process is a possibility, as is leatherworking. It might have been included in the grave not so that its owner could continue to work in the afterlife, but as a marker of profession and identity.

The wood box with bone inlay, found with Skeleton 2 of Burial 14, was in such poor condition that the shape could not be easily reconstructed (19 N 136; pl. 146:7). Only a few fragments of wood were preserved, but from the arrangement of the remaining inlay pieces when in situ it appears that the box was oval. The lid had a border of thin bone strips within which were two rows of triangular pieces set in alternating directions; a knob handle was at the center. Other inlay elements include rosettes with central copper/bronze pins for attachment, smaller rosettes with plain centers, hemispheres, disks, stepped crosses, "ziggurats," squares, and cylinders. A few pieces, which probably were part of the box's sides rather than the lid, were teardrop- and C-shaped, with grooves in their upper surfaces filled with red or black powdery pigment. There are two flat tab handles, also presumably attached to the box itself, rather than the lid. Similar clumps of badly deteriorated inlay were found in several graves at Ur (i.e., PG/543; Woolley 1934: 152) and it is probable that such objects were far more common than the number recorded indicates, their extreme fragility often completely erasing them from the archaeological record.

---

155. All the shells were identified by David Reese during his time as an Associate of the Field Museum of Natural History, Chicago.

156. Again, identification of species is provided by David Reese.

*Inorganic*

A handful of flint blades and scrapers came from Levels XVI through XI, either in floor material or in graves (where they could be chance inclusions, rather than intentional deposits). Some blades are unretouched or retouched along one edge (19 N 150, 19 N 29, 18 N 157, 18 N 66; pl. 166:6–7, 14–15), while others are denticulated (19 N 78, 18 N 156; pl. 166:8, 11). The scrapers are small, made from cores (19 N 68; pl. 166:10) or flakes (19 N 30, 18 N 160; pl. 166:9, 12). The conversion of a depleted core into a tool and the creation of a scraper (18 N 160) and two blades (18 N 66, 19 N 29) from flakes that had retained some of the exterior cortex indicates that there was a conscious effort not to waste any material. Flint in the southern plains was scarce and was often acquired from some distance. Yet evidence of heat-treating in one instance (19 N 29) implies that there was some degree of familiarity with the medium, despite the probable distance to the source (although it must be admitted that the heat-treating may have been performed elsewhere). All flints show traces of heavy use, being worn or chipped on the cutting edges. The flint ranges in color from buff or tan through brown to gray; there is a single obsidian blade (19 N 61; pl. 166:13), also chipped on both cutting edges from frequent use.[157]

Other stone objects include two granitic stone axheads, one unfinished (18 N 139; pl. 166:17) from Level XIVA and a very battered example (18 N 38; pl. 166:18) from Level IIIB. The latter had been used as an ax, grinding stone, and hammer, to judge from the wear, chips, and other damage. Like the comparable signs on the flints, the multiple uses to which the ax was put are indications that, because of its rarity, stone was used to its fullest potential.

A handful of thirty-three hematite, gray stone, steatite, and shell weights and large beads had been placed as a foundation deposit in a broken jar base below the corner of Walls BB and BC in Level XIIIC (19 N 97, pls. 21, 165). As mentioned in *Chapter 3*, a much smaller cluster of rounded river pebbles came from the fill above Skeleton 2 of Burial 14, which may have had a related symbolic aspect. In the case of the foundation deposit, it is surely significant that most of the stones are dark gray or dark brown but are afforded contrast by the white shells and two calcite stones. The symbolic value of lapis lazuli in Mesopotamia, and its use as a metaphor for things glowing and beautiful, are known from texts. The use of bright and clearly visible stones such as lapis lazuli and amethyst for high quality seals carries with it both symbolic and amuletic aspects. The traditional use of hematite for weights, along with the durability of this stone, must have invested the material with a different kind of symbolic association: specifically of stability, strength, and regularity, which are perhaps more relevant to construction.[158]

Several more utilitarian items were recovered from Area WF: a stone disk that could be a spindle whorl or fishnet weight from Level XIIA (18 N 159; pl. 163:19), two carefully shaped stone slabs, probably weights, from Levels XIIIB and XIIB (18 N 158, 18 N 89; pl. 163:16–17), a more irregular pierced stone that could also be a weight from Level XIIA (18 N 141; pl. 163:18), and a much-used whetstone from Level IX (18 N 69; pl. 166:16). A fragment of an inscribed mace-head in Level X (18 N 78; pl. 166:21) was probably redeposited from an Early Dynastic or Akkadian level. As a probable votive object, this is a strange item to have come from a domestic context; it surely had migrated from a temple.

## First Millennium B.C.

Shells appear in a few first-millennium graves: an unworked conoid in Burial 4 (18 N 34; pl. 172:6) and half a freshwater clam in Burial 7 (18 N 41; pl. 173:2). A final object is a heavily worn Seleucid bronze coin from a debris layer in Level II (18 N 28; pl. 179:3). There is a Greek inscription on the reverse, but it is unintelligible; faint traces of a standing figure are visible on the obverse.

---

157. It was not possible to analyze the obsidian or flints to determine their sources. There is a possible source for the flint to the west of Nippur, near Nejef, where a geologic shelf marks the beginning of the Arabian Desert and where there are gravel deposits at the surface. Sources of limestone and steatite/chlorite have been actively sought by archaeologists, in connection with tracking the origins of materials for stone vessels and cylinder seals (Potts 1994), but flint sources are largely ignored once we move into historical periods, despite indications that flint tools continued to be used.

158. The association of hematite with the sun-god, Shamash, and with the concept of justice, is discussed in Postgate 1997. It may be something of a speculative leap from justice and regularity to actual physical stability, but the concepts are related.

Table 77. Concordance of Objects by Level

| Level | Object Number | Description | Level | Object Number | Description |
|---|---|---|---|---|---|
| XVIII | 19 N 106 | Bowl, pottery | | 18 N 192 | Bowl, pottery |
| | 19 N 108 | Cylinder seal, green stone | | 18 N 193 | Jar, pottery |
| XVIIC | 19 N 62 | Miniature vessel, pottery | XIVA | 19 N 13 | Pin, copper/bronze |
| | 19 N 81 | Shell | | 19 N 23 | Bead, stone |
| | 19 N 82 | Shell | | 19 N 29 | Blade, flint |
| | 19 N 83 | Bowl, stone | | 19 N 52 | Bowl, pottery |
| | 19 N 126 | Bowl, pottery | | 19 N 61 | Blade, flint |
| | 19 N 127 | Bowl, pottery | | 19 N 64 | Pin, copper/bronze |
| | 19 N 128 | Bowl, pottery | | 19 N 65 | Pin, copper/bronze |
| XVIIB | 19 N 80 | "Fara" tablet, clay | | 19 N 84 | Jar, pottery |
| | 19 N 144 | Tool, bone | | 19 N 85 | Fruit stand, pottery |
| | 19 N 155 | Jar, pottery | | 19 N 87 | Jar, pottery |
| XVI | 19 N 56 | Bowl, pottery | | 19 N 88 | Jar, pottery |
| | 19 N 57 | Bowl, pottery | | 19 N 89 | Jar, pottery |
| | 19 N 58 | Bowl, pottery | | 19 N 90 | Jar, pottery |
| | 19 N 59 | Bowl, pottery | | 19 N 91 | Bowl, pottery |
| | 19 N 60 | Bowl, pottery | | 19 N 92 | Bowl, pottery |
| | 19 N 63 | Pin, copper/bronze | | 19 N 93 | Bowl, pottery |
| | 19 N 100 | Object, shell | | 19 N 94 | Bowl, pottery |
| | 19 N 105 | Shell pair | | 19 N 95 | Bowl, pottery |
| | 19 N 145 | Jar, pottery | | 19 N 96 | Bowl, stone |
| | 19 N 150 | Blade, flint | | 18 N 111 | Cylinder seal, shell |
| | 19 N 156 | Bowl, pottery | | 18 N 118 | Bracelets, bronze (2) |
| XV B | 19 N 68 | Scraper, flint | | 18 N 119 | Beads, metal and stone |
| | 19 N 74 | Stamp seal, gray stone | | 18 N 120 | Bracelet, bronze |
| XVA | 19 N 22 | Bead, bone | | 18 N 123 | Bowl, pottery |
| | 19 N 30 | Blade, flint | | 18 N 124 | Bowl, pottery |
| | 19 N 34 | Bowl, pottery | | 18 N 130 | Figurine, baked clay |
| | 19 N 39 | Jar, pottery | | 18 N 133 | Model chariot |
| | 19 N 41 | Jar, pottery | | 18 N 134 | Jar, pottery |
| | 19 N 45 | Jar, pottery | | 18 N 136 | Bowl, pottery |
| | 19 N 46 | Bowl, pottery | | 18 N 137 | Miniature jar, pottery |
| | 19 N 78 | Blade, flint | | 18 N 138 | Cup, pottery |
| XIVB | 19 N 55 | Bowl, pottery | | 18 N 139 | Axhead, stone |
| | 18 N 121 | Spearhead, copper/bronze | | 18 N 150 | Pin, copper/bronze |
| | 18 N 122 | Dagger, copper/bronze | | 18 N 153 | Pin, copper/bronze |
| | 18 N 143 | Pin, copper/bronze | | 18 N 162 | Model chariot, baked clay |
| | 18 N 144 | Pin, copper/bronze | | 18 N 165 | Model chariot, baked clay |
| | 18 N 146 | Pin, copper/bronze | | 18 N 166 | Figurine, baked clay |
| | 18 N 147 | Pin, copper/bronze | | 18 N 170 | Vessel, copper/bronze |
| | 18 N 151 | Pin, copper/bronze | | 18 N 189 | Bowl, pottery |
| | 18 N 152 | Bead, shell | | 18 N 190 | Bowl, pottery |
| | 18 N 156 | Blade, flint | XIIIC | 19 N 97 | Foundation deposit, stone weights, and beads (33) |
| | 18 N 160 | Scraper, flint | | | |
| | 18 N 172 | Chisel, copper/bronze | | 18 N 116 | Game piece, baked clay |
| | 18 N 191 | Fruit stand, pottery | | | |

## Table 77. Concordance of Objects by Level (*cont.*)

| Level | Object Number | Description | Level | Object Number | Description |
|---|---|---|---|---|---|
| | 18 N 128 | Model boat, baked clay | | 18 N 182 | Vessel, copper/bronze |
| | 18 N 167 | Model chair, baked clay | | 18 N 183 | Vessel, copper/bronze |
| | 18 N 169 | Figurine, baked clay | | 18 N 184 | Vessel, copper/bronze |
| XIIIB | 19 N 4 | Bowl, stone | | 18 N 185 | Vessel, copper/bronze |
| | 19 N 5 | Pin, copper/bronze | | 18 N 186 | Sieve for drinking straw, copper/bronze |
| | 19 N 7 | Spearhead, copper/bronze | | | |
| | 19 N 9 | Vessel, copper/bronze | | 18 N 187 | Jar, pottery |
| | 19 N 11 | Bowl, pottery | | 18 N 188 | Pin, copper/bronze |
| | 19 N 16 | Bowl, pottery | | 18 N 194 | Bead, stone |
| | 19 N 17 | Bowl, pottery | XIIA | 18 N 85 | Miniature vessel, pottery |
| | 19 N 18 | Necklace | | 18 N 96 | Bead, glass |
| | 19 N 19 | Vessel, copper/bronze | | 18 N 104 | Tablet, clay |
| | 19 N 20 | Necklace | | 18 N 105 | Tablet, clay |
| | 19 N 21 | Bracelets, silver (2) | | 18 N 107 | Tablet, clay |
| | 19 N 24 | Bead, stone | | 18 N 108 | Tablet, clay |
| | 19 N 25 | Bead, bronze | | 18 N 113 | Cylinder seal blank, shell |
| | 19 N 26 | Cylinder seal, lapis lazuli | | 18 N 115 | Game piece, baked clay |
| | 19 N 27 | Shell pair | | 18 N 141 | Weight, stone |
| | 19 N 28 | Pin, copper/bronze | | 18 N 148 | Pin, copper/bronze |
| | 19 N 31 | Bowl, pottery | | 18 N 159 | Disk, stone |
| | 19 N 32 | Bowl, pottery | | 18 N 163 | Model wheel |
| | 19 N 33 | Shell | XIB | 18 N 66 | Blade, flint |
| | 19 N 35 | Jar, pottery | | 18 N 79 | Sherd, inscribed |
| | 19 N 36 | Vessel, copper/bronze | | 18 N 83 | Miniature vessel |
| | 19 N 37 | Earrings, gold (2) | | 18 N 84 | Pin, copper/bronze |
| | 19 N 38 | Fillet, gold | | 18 N 95 | Bead, glass |
| | 19 N 40 | Jar, pottery | | 18 N 114 | Bowl, pottery |
| | 19 N 42 | Jar, pottery | | 18 N 131 | Jar, pottery |
| | 19 N 43 | Jar, pottery | | 18 N 145 | Pin, copper/bronze |
| | 18 N 106 | Tablet, clay | | 18 N 154 | Bead, stone |
| | 18 N 109 | Sealing, clay | | 18 N 168 | Figurine, baked clay |
| | 18 N 112 | Pin, copper/bronze | XIA | 18 N 129 | Rattle, baked clay |
| | 18 N 142 | Pin, copper/bronze | X | 18 N 78 | Mace-head, inscribed stone |
| | 18 N 155 | Bead, stone | | 18 N 90 | Pin, copper/bronze |
| | 18 N 164 | Miniature vessel lid, pottery | | 18 N 161 | Model wheel, baked clay |
| | 18 N 171 | Axhead, copper/bronze | IX | 18 N 69 | Whetstone |
| | 18 N 173 | Cylinder seal, rock crystal | | 18 N 81 | Figurine, baked clay |
| | 18 N 174 | Cylinder seal, green stone | | 18 N 135 | Jar, pottery |
| | 18 N 175 | Fillet, gold | V | 18 N 55 | Jar, pottery |
| | 18 N 176 | Spearpoint, copper/bronze | | 18 N 56 | Jar, pottery |
| | 18 N 177 | Axhead, copper/bronze | | 18 N 102 | Jar, pottery |
| | 18 N 178 | Pin, copper/bronze | | 18 N 103 | Jar, pottery |
| | 18 N 179 | Pin, copper/bronze | IV | 18 N 16 | Jar, glazed pottery |
| | 18 N 180 | Vessel, copper/bronze | | 18 N 22 | Jar, glazed pottery |
| | 18 N 181 | Vessel, copper/bronze | | 18 N 23 | Jar, glazed pottery |

Table 77. Concordance of Objects by Level (*cont.*)

| Level | Object Number | Description | Level | Object Number | Description |
|---|---|---|---|---|---|
| | 18 N 24 | Jar, pottery | | 18 N 41 | Shell |
| | 18 N 26 | Figurine, baked clay | | 18 N 46 | Jar, glazed pottery |
| | 18 N 36 | Necklace | | 18 N 51 | Plaque, baked clay |
| | 18 N 37 | Pins and chain, bronze | | 18 N 53 | Jar, pottery |
| | 18 N 42 | Jar, glazed pottery | | 18 N 54 | Jar, pottery |
| | 18 N 43 | Jar, glazed pottery | | 18 N 59 | Rattle, baked clay |
| | 18 N 44 | Jar, pottery | | 18 N 62 | Bowl, pottery |
| | 18 N 45 | Bowl, pottery | | 18 N 149 | Pin, bronze |
| IIIB | 18 N 10 | Beads, glass | II | 18 N 7 | Necklace |
| | 18 N 17 | Jar, glazed pottery | | 18 N 8 | Scarab, faience |
| | 18 N 25 | Jar, pottery | | 18 N 9 | Stamp seal, stone |
| | 18 N 30 | Necklace | | 18 N 11 | Figurine, baked clay |
| | 18 N 31 | Coffin, baked clay | | 18 N 15 | Plaque, baked clay |
| | 18 N 32 | Jar, pottery | | 18 N 28 | Coin, bronze |
| | 18 N 33 | Palette, stone; and chain, bronze | | 18 N 60 | Tool handle, bronze |
| | 18 N 34 | Shell | | 18 N 126 | Jar, pottery, with metal hoard |
| | 18 N 35 | Bracelet, bronze | | 18 N 127 | Silver objects (6) from metal hoard in 18 N 126 |
| | 18 N 38 | Axhead, stone | | | |
| | 18 N 39 | Bead, stone | | | |
| | 18 N 40 | Beads, faience and stone | | | |

## CHAPTER 4: OBJECTS FROM AREA WF

Table 78. Catalogue of Objects by Object Number
(numbers are not consecutive because objects from operations other than WF were included in the catalogue)

| Object Number | Description | Findspot | Level | Plate |
|---|---|---|---|---|
| 18 N 7 | Necklace | Pit 2 | II | 179:4 |
| 18 N 8 | Scarab, faience | Pit 2 | II | 160:4 |
| 18 N 9 | Stamp seal, stone | Pit 2 | II | 160:5 |
| 18 N 10 | Necklace | Burial 2 | IIIB | 171:3 |
| 18 N 11 | Figurine, terra-cotta | Locus 2 | II | 180:4 |
| 18 N 15 | Plaque, terra-cotta | Pit 1 | II | 180:5 |
| 18 N 16 | Jar, glazed pottery | Burial 6 | IV | 169:1 |
| 18 N 17 | Jar, glazed pottery | Burial 7 | IIIB | 173:1 |
| 18 N 22 | Jar, glazed pottery | Burial 6 | IV | 169:2 |
| 18 N 23 | Jar, glazed pottery | Burial 6 | IV | 169:3 |
| 18 N 24 | Jar, pottery | Burial 6 | IV | 169:4 |
| 18 N 25 | Jar, pottery | Burial 3 | IIIB | 171:4 |
| 18 N 26 | Figurine, terra-cotta | Locus 10, above Floor 1 | IV | 180:1 |
| 18 N 28 | Coin, bronze | Locus 2 | II | 179:3 |
| 18 N 30 | Necklace | Burial 4 | IIIB | 73b, 172:5 |
| 18 N 31 | Coffin, baked clay | Burial 7 | IIIB | 173:3 |
| 18 N 32 | Jar, pottery | Burial 4 | IIIB | 172:1 |
| 18 N 33 | Palette, stone; and chain, bronze | Burial 4 | IIIB | 73b, 172:7 |
| 18 N 34 | Shell | Burial 4 | IIIB | 172:6 |
| 18 N 35 | Bracelet, bronze | Burial 4 | IIIB | 73b, 172:4 |
| 18 N 36 | Necklace | Burial 6 | IV | 169:6 |
| 18 N 37 | Pins and chain, bronze | Burial 6 | IV | 169:5 |
| 18 N 38 | Axhead, stone | Locus 7, above Floor 1 | IIIB | 166:18 |
| 18 N 39 | Bead, stone | Burial 3 | IIIB | 171:5 |
| 18 N 40 | Beads, faience and stone | Burial 3 | IIIB | 171:6 |
| 18 N 41 | Shell | Burial 7 | IIIB | 173:2 |
| 18 N 42 | Jar, glazed pottery | Burial 8 | IV | 71b, 170:1 |
| 18 N 43 | Jar, glazed pottery | Burial 8 | IV | 71c, 170:2 |
| 18 N 44 | Jar, glazed pottery | Burial 8 | IV | 71d, 170:3 |
| 18 N 45 | Bowl, pottery | Burial 8 | IV | 71e, 170:4 |
| 18 N 46 | Jar, glazed pottery | Burial 5 | IIIB | 171:1 |
| 18 N 51 | Plaque, terra-cotta | Locus 7, above Floor 1 | IIIB | 180:3 |
| 18 N 53 | Jar, pottery | Burial 5 | IIIB | 171:2 |
| 18 N 54 | Jar, pottery | Burial 4 | IIIB | 172:2 |
| 18 N 55 | Goblet, pottery | Burial 9 | VA | 69b, 168:1 |
| 18 N 56 | Goblet, pottery | Burial 9 | VA | 69b, 168:2 |
| 18 N 59 | Rattle, terra-cotta | Sand below Wall D | IIIB | 180:2 |
| 18 N 60 | Handle, bronze | Pit 1 | II | 179:2 |
| 18 N 62 | Bowl, pottery | Locus 7, Floor 1 | IIIB | 178:1 |
| 18 N 66 | Blade, flint | Locus 36, above Floor 0 | XIB | 166:15 |
| 18 N 69 | Whetstone | Locus 25, above Floor 1 | IX | 166:16 |
| 18 N 78 | Inscribed mace-head, stone | Locus 27, above Floor 1 | X | 166:21 |
| 18 N 79 | Inscribed sherd, pottery | Locus 36, above Floor 2 | XIB | 166:20 |

Table 78. Catalogue of Objects by Object Number (*cont.*)
(numbers are not consecutive because objects from operations other than WF were included in the catalogues)

| Object Number | Description | Findspot | Level | Plate |
| --- | --- | --- | --- | --- |
| 18 N 81 | Figurine, terra-cotta | Platform W | IX | 163:13 |
| 18 N 83 | Miniature vessel, pottery | Locus 35, above Floor 3 | XIB | 164:11 |
| 18 N 84 | Pin, copper/bronze | Locus 35, above Floor 3 | XIB | 162:20 |
| 18 N 85 | Miniature vessel, pottery | Locus 35, above Floor 5 | XIIA | 164:10 |
| 18 N 89 | Weight, stone | Locus 38, above Floor 2 | XIIB | 163:17 |
| 18 N 90 | Pin, copper/bronze | Doorway between Locus 27, Floor 1, and Locus 33, Floor 1 | X | 162:21 |
| 18 N 95 | Bead, glass | Locus 35, Floor 3 | XIB | 167:1 |
| 18 N 96 | Bead, glass | Locus 38, Floor 1 | XIIA | 167:2 |
| 18 N 102 | Goblet, pottery | Burial 12 | VA | 70b, 168:3 |
| 18 N 103 | Jar, pottery | Burial 12 | VA | 70b, 168:4 |
| 18 N 104 | Tablet, clay | Locus 38, above Floor 1 | XIIA | 192:2 |
| 18 N 105 | Tablet, clay | Locus 38, Floor 1 | XIIA | 192:3 |
| 18 N 106 | Tablet, clay | Locus 38, above Floor 2 | XIIB | 193:1 |
| 18 N 107 | Tablet, clay | Locus 38, on Floor 1 | XIIA | 193:2 |
| 18 N 108 | Tablet, clay | Locus 38, on Floor 1 | XIIA | 193:3 |
| 18 N 109 | Sealing, unbaked clay | Locus 41, above Floor 2 | XIIB | 159:1 |
| 18 N 110 | Sealing, unbaked clay | Locus 43, above Floor 1 | XIIIB | 159:2 |
| 18 N 111 | Cylinder seal, shell | Locus 40, above Floor 2 | XIVA | 160:1 |
| 18 N 112 | Pin, copper/bronze | Locus 38, above Floor 2 | XIIB | 162:16 |
| 18 N 113 | Cylinder seal blank, shell | Locus 35, above Floor 5 | XIIA | 160:3 |
| 18 N 114 | Bowl, pottery | Burial 11 | XIB | 135:8 |
| 18 N 115 | Game piece, clay | Locus 35, above Floor 5 | XIIA | 163:15 |
| 18 N 116 | Game piece, clay | Locus 43, above Floor 3 | XIIIC | 163:14 |
| 18 N 118 | Bracelets (2), copper/bronze | Burial 13 | XIVA | 134:12 |
| 18 N 119 | Beads, metal and stone | Burial 13 | XIVA | 134:13 |
| 18 N 120 | Bracelet, copper/bronze | Locus 40, above Floor 2 | XIVA | 162:6 |
| 18 N 121 | Spearhead, copper/bronze | Locus 40, above Floor 3 | XIVB | 162:3 |
| 18 N 122 | Dagger, copper/bronze | Locus 40, above Floor 4 | XIVB | 162:2 |
| 18 N 123 | Bowl, pottery | Locus 40, on Floor 1 | XIVA | 125:7 |
| 18 N 124 | Bowl, pottery | Locus 40, on Floor 1 | XIVA | 125:8 |
| 18 N 126 | Jar, pottery; with metal hoard | Pit 1 | II | 178:4, 5 |
| 18 N 127 | Silver objects (6) from hoard in 18 N 126 | Pit 1, inside 18 N 126 | II | 179:1 |
| 18 N 128 | Model boat, terra-cotta | Locus 39, above Floor 1 | XIIIC | 163:6 |
| 18 N 129 | Rattle, terra-cotta | Locus 34, above Floor 1 | XIA | 163:12 |
| 18 N 130 | Figurine, terra-cotta | Locus 40, above Floor 1 | XIVA | 163:8 |
| 18 N 131 | Jar, pottery | Locus 36, in drain from Floor 4 | XIB | 121:1 |
| 18 N 133 | Model chariot, terra-cotta | Locus 40, above Floor 1 | XIVA | 163:3 |
| 18 N 134 | Jar, pottery | Locus 40, on Floor 2 | XIVA | 126:3 |
| 18 N 135 | Jar, pottery | In Platform Z | IX | 127:1 |
| 18 N 136 | Bowl, pottery | Locus 40, feature on Floor 2 | XIVA | 127:3 |
| 18 N 137 | Miniature jar, pottery | Locus 40, feature on Floor 2 | XIVA | 127:2 |
| 18 N 138 | Cup, pottery | Locus 40, on Floor 1 | XIVA | 125:12 |

Table 78. Catalogue of Objects by Object Number (*cont.*)
(numbers are not consecutive because objects from operations other than WF were included in the catalogues)

| Object Number | Description | Findspot | Level | Plate |
|---|---|---|---|---|
| 18 N 139 | Axhead, stone | Locus 40, above Floor 1 | XIVA | 166:17 |
| 18 N 141 | Weight, stone | Locus 38, above Floor 1 | XIIA | 163:18 |
| 18 N 142 | Pin, copper/bronze | Locus 41, above Floor 1 | XIIB | 162:17 |
| 18 N 143 | Pin, copper/bronze | Locus 40, above Floor 3 | XIVB | 162:10 |
| 18 N 144 | Pin, copper/bronze | Locus 40, on Floor 3 | XIVB | 162:9 |
| 18 N 145 | Pin, copper/bronze | Wall U, Y, or X | XIB | 162:19 |
| 18 N 146 | Pin, copper/bronze | Locus 40, above Floor 4 | XIVB | 162:12 |
| 18 N 147 | Pin, copper/bronze | Locus 40, above Floor 4 | XIVB | 162:11 |
| 18 N 148 | Pin, copper/bronze | Locus 35, above Floor 4 | XIIA | 162:18 |
| 18 N 149 | Pin, copper/bronze | Burial 4 | IIIB | 73b, 172:3 |
| 18 N 150 | Pin, copper/bronze | Locus 40, above Floor 1 | XIVA | 162:15 |
| 18 N 151 | Pin, copper/bronze | Locus 40, above Floor 3 | XIVB | 162:8 |
| 18 N 152 | Bead, shell | Locus 40, above Floor 1 | XIVB | 166:2 |
| 18 N 153 | Pin, copper/bronze | Locus 40, above Floor 2 | XIVA | 162:14 |
| 18 N 154 | Bead, stone | Locus 36, in drain from Floor 4 | XIB | 166:4 |
| 18 N 155 | Bead, stone | Locus 41, above Floor 2 | XIIB | 166:3 |
| 18 N 156 | Blade, flint | Locus 40, above Floor 3 | XIVB | 166:11 |
| 18 N 157 | Blade, flint | Locus 43, above Floor 1 | XIIIB | 166:14 |
| 18 N 158 | Weight, stone | Locus 43, above Floor 1 | XIIIB | 163:16 |
| 18 N 159 | Disk, stone | Locus 35, above Floor 5 | XIIA | 163:19 |
| 18 N 160 | Scraper, flint | Locus 40, above Floor 3 | XIVB | 166:12 |
| 18 N 161 | Model wheel, terra-cotta | Locus 27, above Floor 1 | X | 163:5 |
| 18 N 162 | Model chariot, terra-cotta | Locus 40, on Floor 1 | XIVA | 163:2 |
| 18 N 163 | Model wheel, terra-cotta | Locus 38, above Floor 2 | XIIA | 163:4 |
| 18 N 164 | Miniature vessel lid, pottery | Locus 41, above Floor 1 | XIIB | 164:3 |
| 18 N 165 | Model chariot, terra-cotta | Locus 40, on Floor 1 | XIVA | 163:1 |
| 18 N 166 | Figurine, baked clay | Locus 40, on Floor 1 | XIVA | 163:10 |
| 18 N 167 | Model chair, terra-cotta | Locus 43, above Floor 3 | XIIIC | 163:7 |
| 18 N 168 | Figurine, terra-cotta | Locus 35, above Floor 3 | XIB | 163:11 |
| 18 N 169 | Figurine, terra-cotta | Locus 43, above Floor 3 | XIIIC | 163:9 |
| 18 N 170 | Vessel, copper/bronze | Locus 40, above Floor 2 | XIVA | 161:5 |
| 18 N 171 | Axhead, copper/bronze | Locus 41, above Floor 2 | XIIB | 162:5 |
| 18 N 172 | Chisel or adze, copper/bronze | Locus 40, on/above Floor 4 | XIVB | 162:1 |
| 18 N 173 | Cylinder seal, rock crystal | Burial 14, Skeleton 1 | XIIB | 157:1 |
| 18 N 174 | Cylinder seal, green stone | Burial 14, Skeleton 1 | XIIB | 157:2 |
| 18 N 175 | Fillet, gold | Burial 14, Skeleton 1 | XIIB | 66a, 152:10 |
| 18 N 176 | Spearpoint, copper/bronze | Burial 14, Skeleton 1 | XIIB | 66b, 152:1 |
| 18 N 177 | Axhead, copper/bronze | Burial 14, Skeleton 1 | XIIB | 66b, 152:2 |
| 18 N 178 | Pin, copper/bronze | Burial 14, Skeleton 1 | XIIB | 66a, 152:7 |
| 18 N 179 | Pin, copper/bronze | Burial 14, Skeleton 1 | XIIB | 66a, 152:8 |
| 18 N 180 | Bowl, copper/bronze | Burial 14, Skeleton 1 | XIIB | 67b, 155:4 |
| 18 N 181 | Bowl, copper/bronze | Burial 14, Skeleton 1 | XIIB | 67a, 156:3 |
| 18 N 182 | Bowl, copper/bronze | Burial 14, Skeleton 1 | XIIB | 67a, 156:4 |

Table 78. Catalogue of Objects by Object Number (*cont.*)
(numbers are not consecutive because objects from operations other than WF were included in the catalogues)

| Object Number | Description | Findspot | Level | Plate |
|---|---|---|---|---|
| 18 N 183 | Cauldron, copper/bronze | Burial 14, Skeleton 1 | XIIB | 67b, 156:1 |
| 18 N 184 | Bucket, copper/bronze | Burial 14, Skeleton 1 | XIIB | 67b, 156:2 |
| 18 N 185 | Vessel, copper/bronze | Burial 14, Skeleton 1 | XIIB | 67a, 155:5 |
| 18 N 186 | Sieve for drinking straw, copper/bronze | Burial 14, Skeleton 1 | XIIB | 152:9 |
| 18 N 187 | Jar, pottery | Burial 14, Skeleton 1 | XIIB | 68b, 154:2 |
| 18 N 188 | Pin, copper/bronze | Burial 14, Skeleton 1 | XIIB | 66a, 152:3 |
| 18 N 189 | Bowl, pottery | Locus 40, on Floor 1 | XIVA | 125:10 |
| 18 N 190 | Bowl, pottery | Locus 40, on Floor 1 | XIVA | 125:9 |
| 18 N 191 | Fruit stand, pottery | Burial 15 | XIVB | 135:2 |
| 18 N 192 | Bowl, pottery | Burial 15 | XIVB | 135:7 |
| 18 N 193 | Jar, pottery | Burial 15 | XIVB | 135:1 |
| 18 N 194 | Bead, stone | Burial 14, Skeleton 1 | XIIB | 66a, 152:11 |
| 19 N 4 | Bowl, stone | Burial 14, Skeleton 4 | XIIIB | 61b, 145:2 |
| 19 N 5 | Pin, copper/bronze | Burial 14, Skeleton 2 | XIIIB | 63, 151:2 |
| 19 N 6 | Daggers (2) and pin, copper/bronze | Burial 14, Skeleton 1 | XIIB | 66b, 152:4–6 |
| 19 N 7 | Spearhead, copper/bronze | Burial 14, Skeleton 4 | XIIB | 61b, 145:4 |
| 19 N 8 | Setting, gold | Burial 14, Skeleton 1 | XIIB | 66a, 152:12 |
| 19 N 9 | Bowl, copper/bronze | Burial 14, Skeleton 2 | XIIIB | 64a, 148:8 |
| 19 N 10 | Bowl, pottery | Burial 14, Skeleton 1 | XIIB | 68a, 153:2 |
| 19 N 11 | Bowl, pottery | Burial 14, Skeleton 4 | XIIIB | 142:2 |
| 19 N 12 | Bowl, pottery | Feature above Burial 14, Skeleton 1 | XIIB | 125:11 |
| 19 N 13 | Pin, copper/bronze | Below Wall AO | XIVA | 162:13 |
| 19 N 14 | Blade, copper/bronze | Locus 39, above Floor 0 | XIIIB | 162:4 |
| 19 N 16 | Bowl, pottery | Burial 14, Skeleton 4(?) | XIIIB | 142:6 |
| 19 N 17 | Bowl, pottery | Burial 14, Skeleton 2 | XIIIB | 64b, 147:11 |
| 19 N 18 | Necklace | Burial 14, Skeleton 2 | XIIIB | 63, 146:5 |
| 19 N 19 | Box, copper/bronze | Burial 14, Skeleton 2 | XIIIB | 64a, 148:7 |
| 19 N 20 | Necklace | Burial 14, Skeleton 2 | XIIIB | 63, 146:4 |
| 19 N 21 | Bracelets (2), silver | Burial 14, Skeleton 2 | XIIIB | 63, 146:3 |
| 19 N 22 | Bead, bone | Burial 14, Skeleton 5 | XVA | 133:7 |
| 19 N 23 | Bead, stone | Burial 14, Southwest shaft | XIVA | 166:1 |
| 19 N 24 | Bead, stone | Burial 14, Skeleton 4 | XIIIB | 145:5 |
| 19 N 25 | Bead, copper/bronze | Burial 14, Skeleton 2 | XIIIB | 63, 146:6 |
| 19 N 26 | Cylinder seal, lapis lazuli | Burial 14, Skeleton 2 | XIIIB | 63, 158:1 |
| 19 N 27 | Shell pair | Burial 14, Skeleton 3 | XIIIB | 60c, 141:3 |
| 19 N 28 | Pin, copper/bronze | Burial 14, Skeleton 3 | XIIIB | 60c, 145:1 |
| 19 N 29 | Blade, flint | Burial 14, Southwest shaft | XIVA | 166:7 |
| 19 N 30 | Blade, flint | Burial 14, Skeleton 5 | XVA | 166:9 |
| 19 N 31 | Bowl, pottery | Burial 14, Skeleton 2 | XIIIB | 64b, 148:5 |
| 19 N 32 | Bowl, pottery | Burial 14, Skeleton 2 | XIIIB | 64b, 147:5 |
| 19 N 33 | Shell | Burial 14, with animal skeleton | XIIIB | 166:19 |
| 19 N 34 | Bowl, pottery | Burial 14, Skeleton 5 | XVA | 53b, 133:5 |
| 19 N 35 | Jar, pottery | Burial 14, Skeleton 2 | XIIIB | 64b, 149:2 |

Table 78. Catalogue of Objects by Object Number (*cont.*)
(numbers are not consecutive because objects from operations other than WF were included in the catalogues)

| Object Number | Description | Findspot | Level | Plate |
|---|---|---|---|---|
| 19 N 36 | Bucket, copper/bronze | Burial 14, Skeleton 2 | XIIIB | 64a, 150:3 |
| 19 N 37 | Earrings, gold (2) | Burial 14, Skeleton 2 | XIIIB | 63, 146:2 |
| 19 N 38 | Fillet, gold | Burial 14, Skeleton 2 | XIIIB | 63, 146:1 |
| 19 N 39 | Jar, pottery | Burial 14, Skeleton 5 | XVA | 53b, 133:1 |
| 19 N 40 | Jar, pottery | Burial 14, Skeleton 2 | XIIIB | 64b, 149:3 |
| 19 N 41 | Jar, pottery | Burial 14, Skeleton 5 | XVA | 53b, 133:2 |
| 19 N 42 | Jar, pottery | Burial 14, Skeleton 2 | XIIIB | 64b, 150:1 |
| 19 N 43 | Jar, pottery | Burial 14, Skeleton 2 | XIIIB | 64b, 151:1 |
| 19 N 44 | Goddess-handled jar, pottery | Burial 14, Skeleton 3 | XIIIB | 143, 144 |
| 19 N 45 | Jar, pottery | Burial 14, Skeleton 5 | XVA | 53b, 133:3 |
| 19 N 46 | Bowl, pottery | Burial 14, Skeleton 5 | XVA | 53b, 133:6 |
| 19 N 47 | Jar, pottery | Burial 14, Skeleton 2 | XIIIB | 64b, 150:2 |
| 19 N 48 | Bowl, pottery | Burial 14, Skeleton 2 | XIIIB | 64b, 148:1 |
| 19 N 49 | Bowl, pottery | Burial 14, Skeleton 2 | XIIIB | 64b, 147:9 |
| 19 N 50 | Bowl, pottery | Burial 14, Skeleton 2 | XIIIB | 64b, 147:4 |
| 19 N 51 | Jar, pottery | Burial 14, Skeleton 2 | XIIIB | 64a, 149:1 |
| 19 N 52 | Bowl, pottery | Burial 14, Southwest shaft | XIVA | 142:1 |
| 19 N 53 | Jar, pottery | Burial 14, Skeleton 2 | XIIIB | 64b, 149:4 |
| 19 N 55 | Bowl, pottery | Locus 47, on Floor 5 | XIVB | 125:6 |
| 19 N 56 | Bowl, pottery | Locus 59, on Floor 2 | XVI | 125:3 |
| 19 N 57 | Bowl, pottery | Locus 59, on Floor 2 | XVI | 125:5 |
| 19 N 58 | Bowl, pottery | Locus 59, on Floor 3 | XVI | 125:2 |
| 19 N 59 | Bowl, pottery | Locus 59, on Floor 3 | XVI | 125:1 |
| 19 N 60 | Bowl, pottery | Burial 18 | XVI | 132:7 |
| 19 N 61 | Blade, flint | Locus 44, above Floor 1 | XIVA | 166:13 |
| 19 N 62 | Miniature jar, pottery | Locus 64, above Floor 1 | XVIIC | 164:1 |
| 19 N 63 | Pin, copper/bronze | Locus 59, on Floor 3 | XVI | 162:7 |
| 19 N 64 | Pin, copper/bronze | Burial 14, Skeleton 6 | XIVA | 136:1 |
| 19 N 65 | Pin, copper/bronze | Burial 14, Skeleton 6 | XIVA | 136:2 |
| 19 N 68 | Scraper, flint | Locus 60, above Floor 1 | XVB | 166:10 |
| 19 N 71 | Bowl, copper/bronze | Burial 14, Skeleton 2 | XIIIB | 64a, 148:9 |
| 19 N 72 | Bowl, copper/bronze | Burial 14, Skeleton 4 | XIIIB | 61b, 145:3 |
| 19 N 73 | Pan, copper/bronze | Burial 14, Skeleton 2 | XIIIB | 64a, 149:5 |
| 19 N 74 | Stamp seal, stone | Locus 60, above Floor 1 | XVB | 160:2 |
| 19 N 78 | Blade, flint | Burial 14, Skeleton 5 | XVA | 166:8 |
| 19 N 80 | Tablet, clay | Locus 62, above Floor 1 | XVIIB | 192:1 |
| 19 N 81 | Shell | Burial 19 | XVIIC | 141:1 |
| 19 N 82 | Shell | Burial 19 | XVIIC | 141:1 |
| 19 N 83 | Bowl, stone | Burial 19 | XVIIC | 128:5 |
| 19 N 84 | Jar, pottery | Burial 14, Skeleton 6 | XIVA | 136:7 |
| 19 N 85 | Fruit stand, pottery | Burial 14, Skeleton 6 | XIVA | 136:5 |
| 19 N 87 | Jar, pottery | Burial 14, Skeleton 6 | XIVA | 136:6 |
| 19 N 88 | Jar, pottery | Burial 14, Skeleton 6 | XIVA | 138:2 |

Table 78. Catalogue of Objects by Object Number (*cont.*)
(numbers are not consecutive because objects from operations other than WF were included in the catalogues)

| Object Number | Description | Findspot | Level | Plate |
|---|---|---|---|---|
| 19 N 89 | Jar, pottery | Burial 14, Skeleton 6 | XIVA | 136:3 |
| 19 N 90 | Jar, pottery | Burial 14, Skeleton 6 | XIVA | 138:1 |
| 19 N 91 | Bowl, pottery | Burial 14, Skeleton 6 | XIVA | 137:12 |
| 19 N 92 | Bowl, pottery | Burial 14, Skeleton 6 | XIVA | 137:7 |
| 19 N 93 | Bowl, pottery | Burial 14, Skeleton 6 | XIVA | 137:6 |
| 19 N 94 | Bowl, pottery | Burial 14, Skeleton 6 | XIVA | 137:3 |
| 19 N 95 | Bowl, pottery | Burial 14, Skeleton 6 | XIVA | 137:4 |
| 19 N 96 | Bowl, stone | Burial 14, Skeleton 6 | XIVA | 136:4 |
| 19 N 97 | Foundation deposit, stone weights, and beads (33) | Below Walls BB and BC | XIIIC | 165 |
| 19 N 100 | Object, shell | Locus 59, above Floor 3 | XVI | 166:5 |
| 19 N 103 | Pan, copper/bronze | Burial 14, Skeleton 2 | XIIIB | 64a, 151:3 |
| 19 N 105 | Shell pair | Burial 14, Skeleton 7 | XVI | 141:2 |
| 19 N 106 | Bowl, pottery | Burial 20 | XVIII | 128:2 |
| 19 N 108 | Cylinder seal, green stone | Locus 65, above Floor 1 | XVIII | 158:2 |
| 19 N 126 | Bowl, pottery | Burial 19 | XVIIC | 129:7 |
| 19 N 127 | Bowl, pottery | Burial 19 | XVIIC | 129:4 |
| 19 N 128 | Bowl, pottery | Burial 19 | XVIIC | 129:2 |
| 19 N 136 | Inlaid box, wood and bone | Burial 14, Skeleton 2 | XIIIB | 146:7 |
| 19 N 144 | Tool, bone | Burial 21, Skeleton 2 | XVIIB | 132:6 |
| 19 N 145 | Jar, pottery | Burial 14, Skeleton 8 | XVI | 56b, 139:1 |
| 19 N 150 | Blade, flint | Burial 14, Skeleton 8 | XVI | 166:6 |
| 19 N 155 | Jar, pottery | Burial 21, Skeleton 2 | XVIIB | 132:4 |
| 19 N 156 | Cup, pottery | Burial 14, Skeleton 8 | XVI | 56b, 139:2 |

# CHAPTER 5

## CONCLUSION

The sounding in Area WF was intended primarily to investigate the transition between the Early Dynastic and Akkadian periods, and in effect to test the validity of the Diyala sequence at a site more central to southern Mesopotamia. The Diyala pottery and artifactual sequence has been the standard since the 1930s, but more recent excavations have shown that there may be both internal problems with dates originally assigned to parts of the sequence and external difficulties when using the sequence for parallels for sites farther south. The Area WF sounding offers a potential solution to some of these problems. Although a larger sample of all aspects of material culture would have been ideal, the nature of the chronological question being asked and the complexity of Nippur, a massive multi-period site, heavily influenced the kind of sounding that was both planned and possible, and its results.

The excavation of Area WF provides important new information on the late third-millennium B.C. artifactual sequence for the site and region. It also offers useful supporting information for other parts of the southern Mesopotamian sequence, such as the first millennium B.C., which is already well established from excavations at Nippur itself and in the surrounding region. As well as providing a mass of detailed chronological data, the sounding contributes to both our biography of the city and our general picture of Mesopotamian domestic occupation.

The settlement history of Nippur includes two gaps in occupation when the entire site was temporarily abandoned. The first of these occurred during the Old Babylonian period, from the reign of Samsuiluna until perhaps ca. 1400 B.C.; the second occurred after the Kassite period, from the twelfth century until sometime in the early first millennium B.C. These hiatuses are reconstructed from evidence present in other previously excavated areas. The two major breaks in the Area WF sequence (between Level V, Phases B and A, and between Levels VA and IV) correspond in date to those lapses in occupation. The Area WF sounding thus lends additional conviction to those reconstructions and supports the conclusion that the entire site was abandoned.

The artifactual sequence for the third millennium B.C. is the most important result of the Area WF sounding. The extension into the Akkadian period of specific pottery types that have long been associated only with the late Early Dynastic period is significant. This extension is logical but not unproblematic, given the volume of material from southern Mesopotamia that must now be considered for reassessment. The same is true for the extension of previously "Akkadian" types into the Ur III period. We have also identified types that could belong primarily to either the early or to the later Akkadian period.

A particular problem for the later third millennium B.C. is that there is very little that can be used for direct comparison with the Area WF sequence as a whole. Arguments that could be marshaled in response to the changes proposed here rest too exclusively on material excavated some time ago when the Mesopotamian artifactual sequence was still under construction, or on material from contexts that are not appropriate for sequence reconstruction, such as graves. No other complete domestic sequence for the Early Dynastic through the Akkadian period has been excavated in southern Mesopotamia. Until another full sequence is revealed, the Area WF sequence must stand as the best revision of the periods under scrutiny, however much it throws accepted datings into question. It is time to reassess the labeling and categorization of those parts of the sequence that have been excavated at other sites.

I am certain that there is no stratigraphic break present in the Area WF sequence for the crucial late Early Dynastic through Ur III periods, a fact reflected in the level-to-level continuity of sherd assemblages from occupation layers, as well as continuity of specific types. The unbroken stratigraphy is also evidenced in consistent use of space and frequent reuse of walls from level to level. There has already been some resistance to the proposed redating of types and redefinition of assemblages of the Early Dynastic III and Akkadian periods as published in the necessarily abridged preliminary report (see Gibson and McMahon 1995; Matthews 1997; Gibson and McMahon 1997; Roaf 2001). There may be further resistance to the proposed changes to traditional typologies.

Notably, it has been possible to outline a transitional Early Dynastic III–Akkadian assemblage (that from Level XVII). Given the continuities of artifacts and ceramics, such a transitional assemblage and a transitional label must be acknowledged, to be used in the absence of written evidence or objects that allow precise dating to one or the other historic period. Early Dynastic III–early Akkadian material excavated from southern Mesopotamia suffers from misidentification and overly rigid period division to a greater extent than for material of virtually all other periods, with type continuities being denied or discounted. There are problems with the traditional picture of the late Akkadian to Ur III transition as well. Area WF supplies a transitional assemblage for these periods (that of Level XI).

A potentially "transitional" label in "Early Dynastic IIIb" already exists; this label was created for levels at Lagash/al-Hiba that correspond to the last independent kings of that city's dynasty. The Nippur "Early Dynastic–Akkadian" must be construed to cover much the same period, or at least the time period during which rulers such as Urukagina at Lagash, Lugalzagesi at Umma and Uruk, and Sargon at Agade claimed sovereignty, each in his own region.

It is certainly easier to conceptualize historic periods as having clear artifactual markers and far more difficult to accept the continuity of types from one period to the next. The concept of sets of "transitional" types can also be extremely discomforting. The term "transitional" implies that a change is afoot somewhere, and that we expect that change to soon become visible; this has an inevitable effect on our vision of transitional assemblages. While such a set should be viewed as a useful well-defined group with a specific identity, it is too often seen as a collection of things that actually belong primarily elsewhere in time.

The length of transitional periods is a further issue. Might a "transition" at an important urban site such as Nippur be shorter than that at a neighboring village or at an urban site elsewhere in the southern plains? We should be accustomed to the dynamic nature of archaeological material, but for some reason, at historical boundaries we tend to falter and look for "moments of transition," rather than the more realistic "periods of transition." We must be aware of the possibilities of continuity over historical borders in all forms of artifacts, both public and private, and of the variable nature of those continuities, no matter how important and apparently abrupt major social changes seem to have been. These continuities are unfortunately not quantifiable and will not be consistent across the entire range of artifacts and ceramic types. It remains to be seen whether depth of type continuity could vary from site to site as well, necessitating a degree of location specificity many could find frustrating.

The Area WF sequence has shown identifiable changes in the ceramic assemblage approximately contemporary with major political changes in southern Mesopotamia. Changes in the ceramic assemblage are visible around the times of the shifts from late Early Dynastic to early Akkadian, from early to late Akkadian, and from late Akkadian to Ur III. In each case, the key information supplied by the Area WF assemblage is that there is continuity of virtually all types from the earlier period, but that these are supplemented by new types. (Seven new forms appeared in Level XVII, six in Level XIVB, four in Level XIVA, and nine in Level XI. These numbers stand in sharp contrast to the more customary one to three new types per level in the rest of the sequence.) Continuity is expected, but the simultaneous sudden development of sets of new types is not; these are the results of conflicting strategies of conservatism and diversification.

In the first case, around the time of the transition from Early Dynastic city-states to the Akkadian nation-state, Level XVII sees five new jar and two open forms. No notable architectural change or alteration of the nature of the context in Area WF explains the sudden appearance of new types. I argue for a recognition of a political and historical overlap of the Early Dynastic and Akkadian periods (see *Chapter 1*) and argue further that changes implicit in the shift to the Akkadian period, even if experimental and partial in this transitional period, could have had an effect on population movements and densities and on local economies — effects that could have registered in the ceramic record. The ten new forms in Level XIVB and A could reflect further economic and social changes linked to the rule of Naram-Sin, when it seems many Akkadian royal policies were consolidated. It must be acknowledged that a change in plan occurred in Area WF from Level XV to Level XIVB, but the fact that further new types appeared in Level XIVA, which has an identical plan to Level XIVB, seems to indicate that the ceramic assemblage was responding to external aspects, not a localized context change.

The collapse of the Akkadian state, the brief Guti period, and the disruption engendered by the establishment of the Ur III state must surely have occurred approximately across Levels XII through X in Area WF. The ceramic assemblage (and material culture in general) of these levels might be expected to show signs of "collapse," traditionally associated with impoverishment of material culture, both public and, to a lesser extent, private. That it does not is evidence that the political turmoil did not lead to a cultural collapse, even at an urban center such as Nippur, where one might expect to see the greatest impact. Nippur may have escaped, however, because of its religious role, while surely the impact would have been more visible at Agade and Ur. Again, no change in plan or context occurred in Area WF across these levels. The bureaucratic nature of the Ur III state could in part explain the sudden increase in number of types of vessels in Level XI. The standardization of writing, weights, and measures and the uniform model established for efficient manufacture and industry could have affected pottery production on two levels, the ideal and the practical. But this is a veneer overlying an essentially conservative society.

As well as contributing to the archaeological chronology of the late third millennium B.C., Area WF presents potential evidence for social changes during that period. Subtle changes in the nature of occupation are represented in the very limited exposure of Area WF, although extension of these changes to the site as a whole must remain speculative until we are able to confirm them by additional excavation. The observed changes occur during the later third millennium B.C. (across the Akkadian period) and include the intensified use of space and an increased range of artifacts (as well as pottery types) present. These aspects could reflect changes in structure, size, and status of the family inhabiting the immediate area. Reorganization of space and changes in house contents and family structure could all possibly relate to alterations in the occupation of the wider "neighborhood." Any of these may, in turn, reflect changes specific to the site or could depend on trends in the larger region.

While extension of such changes to all of Nippur must remain speculation, some comparability exists between the roughly contemporary levels in Area WF and in Area TB, the other main location on the site where domestic contexts of the Akkadian period have been exposed. Levels XIII–X in Area TB probably date to the late Akkadian period and can be compared to the late Akkadian levels in Area WF (Levels XIV–XI).[159] These late Akkadian levels in Area WF and Area TB are roughly equivalent in terms of architectural construction techniques (including reuse of walls from one level to the next), range of objects found, building plans, and close relationship of neighboring structures to each other (as far as these can be adduced for the exposure in Area WF). Unfortunately, we cannot compare the crucial late Early Dynastic and early Akkadian periods in these two areas since the excavation in Area TB did not reach this depth.

The Area WF sounding exposed approximately two millennia of domestic occupation at a site that is best known for its religious architecture and is most notable for its religious and symbolic importance. The near-constant occupation of this area, with the exception of the two stratigraphic breaks cited above, offers useful corrections to generalizations about urban settlement in southern Mesopotamia. Area WF is located near the center of Nippur, close to the probable temple of the healing goddess Gula (earlier Nin-Isin-na)[160] and near to both the Inanna and Enlil Temples, situated on the other side of the water channel (Shatt an-Nil) that runs through the site. The results from the Area WF sounding provide a picture of both horizontal and vertical density of urban land use in this part of Nippur. While horizontal density may be fairly typical of urban situations, it is not necessarily a consistent aspect of city life in this region. Density could vary across a site, and overall density could be expected to vary during episodes when sites are in the process of being abandoned and reoccupied. Both horizontal tightness of layout and vertical depth of deposit, with rapid rebuilding and superimposition of structures, surely indicate that the Area WF position was a particularly desirable location within the city. It is worth noting, however, that this vertical and horizontal density was not present in Area WF in the Early Dynastic levels and only developed during the Akkadian period, after Nippur had already undergone both primary and secondary urban development and expansion in the Uruk and Early Dynastic periods.

The continuity of traditions in mudbrick construction, house plans and orientations, burial practices, and the nature of features and room deposits across the two millennia of occupation are striking. The central position of Area WF with respect to the site and some of its key structures may help to explain this persistence of occupation and use traditions. Location near the center of an urban environment may mean traditions of construction and deposition are retained to a greater extent than would be seen on the outskirts of a city, where different values and accessibility of land were found, allowing variability in occupation. Ideally, what is now needed is an expansion of the Area WA/WF excavation to expose successive levels in a wider area. This larger scale would add immeasurably not only to our knowledge of ceramic and artifactual sequences, but also to our picture of the relationship of a major temple to its surroundings and the relationship of that area to the watercourse beside it. Until such an expanded excavation program can be realized, the sequence column represented by the Area WF sounding must stand as a sample of what is to come.

---

159. The initial publication of the Area TB excavation tentatively dates Level XIII to the Early Dynastic or Akkadian, as it was reached in only a small sounding (McCown and Haines 1967: pl. 52c). However, there is a late version of the double-ridged-rim Type C-13 jar in Level XII (McCown and Haines 1967: pl. 80:18), which implies that this level belongs in the late Akkadian period. The superimposition of walls in Levels XIII and XII appears to show that little time had passed between construction of those two levels. Level XIII must belong in the Akkadian period rather than the Early Dynastic.

160. The excavation in Area WA, to the west-northwest of Area WF, exposed a series of superimposed religious structures during the eleventh, twelfth, and nineteenth seasons, with inscriptional and artifactual evidence that links at least one level to Gula. The full report on this excavation is in preparation.

# APPENDIX 1. SCIENTIFIC ANALYSIS OF TWO AKKADIAN GLASS BEADS

*Pamela Vandiver* and *K. Aslıhan Yener*

In 1934 Horace Beck (1934: 7) reviewed the finds of glass objects dating prior to 1500 B.C. and was able to identify only seventeen possible objects. Third-millennium B.C. glass finds from Southwest Asia are limited to beads and manufacturing elements from six sites. Vessels have been excavated only in later mid-second-millennium B.C. contexts. Scholars have tended to ignore the evidence of glass bead manufacture and preferred instead to concentrate on vessels as the prime evidence of early glass technology, probably because beads are small and can move during site formation processes from the loci of their original deposition. However, the archaeological and technological evidence of these early glass beads cannot be ignored in reconstructing the early history of glass technology.

The evidence has been reviewed by P. R. S. Moorey (1985: 194–201) and Vandiver, Gibson, and McMahon (1995: 331–41). Included among early glass finds are an oblate-to-spherical yellow green bead from Tell Judeideh, Syria, attributed to the early third millennium B.C.; one unillustrated, now lost, pinhead from Nuzi with Akkadian grave association; two beads from graves at Ur, one late Akkadian and the other Ur III; a lump of glass from Eridu, probably of Ur III date; a glass rod from Tell Asmar of Akkadian date; and some beads from Assur found in a mixed foundation deposit perhaps of a later fourteenth-century B.C. date. In addition, two beads from Nineveh attributed to a firm context (level 4 of the Great Pit MM) have been discounted by Beck (1931: 427) and Moorey (1985: 195) because one of them, a brilliant green hexagonal cylindrical bead, contained lead, based on Beck's measurement of its high specific gravity. The other bead from Nineveh was spherical and pale blue and did not have an unusually high specific gravity.

A long-standing controversy has surrounded the origins of lead glasses and glazing and the development and use of lead-stannate and lead-antimonate pigments (Partington 1935; Turner and Rooksby 1959 and 1963; Sayre 1963; Sayre and Smith 1967, 1974; Brill 1969, 1970; Brill and Cahill 1988; Hedges and Moorey 1975; Hedges 1976; Pollard and Moorey 1982; Matson 1986; Wainwright et al. 1986; Harley 1970: 85–98). A distinction has been made between glasses with a lead-containing colorant present as crystalline phase inclusions which date to the second millennium B.C., and glasses with lead as a glass-forming constituent which are considered a late Roman, Byzantine, or early Islamic invention. Thus, the earliest use of lead-antimonate as a pigment has been dated to the second millennium B.C., and lead-stannate to the first millennium A.D.

Very few analyses of early third-millennium B.C. glasses have been carried out, and the evidence of manufacture has been recorded only sparsely. The yellow green bead (field no. x3449) from Tell Judeideh was described by Frederick Matson (in Braidwood and Braidwood 1960: 341) as probably having been rolled around a rod because of the uniformity of the cylindrical hole. Matson also remarks that the many seed bubbles and cord (striations of slightly different chemical composition which are visible because of differences in index of refraction and which serve as indicators of viscous flow during formation) means that the glass was worked at a low temperature. No chemical analyses have been conducted, and the present location of the bead is unknown (R. Tindel, pers. comm., May 1989). In grave 5A, pit L4, at Nuzi, Richard Starr (1939: 380) found a copper pin (15.0 cm long) with a large well-preserved glass bead about 1.5 cm in diameter at one end. This artifact was dated by an associated Akkadian cylinder seal (Boehmer 1965, no. 1566). This bead was neither illustrated in the Nuzi volumes nor analyzed, and its current disposition is unknown (G. Pratico, pers. comm., May 1989). A pale blue green chipped glass rod or tube was found at Tell Asmar (As.31.671, now in the Iraq Museum) in the fill of room 16 E 16 in the Northern Palace in association with Akkadian artifacts (Delougaz et al. 1967: 189–90; Gibson 1982: 534; Frankfort 1934: 56–57, fig. 51; Beck 1934: no. 7, figs. 2, 3). This object appeared to Beck to have been formed while molten. The object was characterized by Cecil Desch as a soda-lime-silicate glass through microscopic examination and measurement of refractive index, but no chemical analyses were carried out. At Eridu, Hall (1930: 213–14) excavated a small, translucent blue lump (British Museum no. 1919-10-11, 4039) in fill beneath the pavement associated with Amar-Sin (third king of the Third Dynasty of Ur), which Moorey dates to early Ur III, but which perhaps dates from the Akkadian period. Barag (1985: 111) gives it a date of 2100–2000 B.C. Beck (1934: nos. 6–7, 8, figs. 4, 5) describes the lump as being perhaps a piece of manufacturer's material. Barag (1985: 111, pl. A) describes the lump as very bubbly with one side broken from a larger lump and the other sides probably original. In his analysis Garner (1956) concludes that it is a soda-lime-silicate colored ultramarine blue by cobalt and copper oxides (65% weight $SiO_2$, 17% $Na_2O$, 4.5% $K_2O$, 3.5% CaO, 3.4% MgO, 2.5% $Al_2O_3$, 2.4% FeO or $Fe_2O_3$, 0.49% CuO, 0.15% CoO, 0.15% $B_2O_3$, 0.09% $TiO_2$, 0.04% MnO, 0.02% PbO, and 0.01% NiO).

Previous analyses showing the diversity and complexity of mid-second-millennium B.C. glasses and other soda-lime-silicates, such as frits, faience, and glazed clay-based ceramics from Nuzi, have suggested that the beginnings of glass technology are to be found earlier in the second, or perhaps in the third, millennium B.C. (Vandiver 1982, 1983). There are five lines of evidence that suggest that the glass industry was well developed by about 1500 B.C. Beads in the tens of thousands have been found in Egypt and Southwest Asia, in addition to many vessel fragments. The colors are varied, including yellow, orange, red, blue, white, green, brown, and purple; replication of the different colors requires not only different compositions but also different heat treatments in different atmospheres. The frit compositions diverge the most. The forming technology was complex and included molding, rod forming, fusing of bits of glass, fusing cross sections of rods, combing, cold working, and most other traditional techniques with the singular exception of blowing. However, so little glass from the third millennium has been found and, in general, it has been incompletely characterized, so that it is impossible at present to reconstruct the practices of this industry.

A major problem in studying the early history of the technology of glazing and glass manufacture is that so few of the objects have survived without serious weathering. In Egypt, where conditions are driest, preservation is best. However, most scholars concur that the beginnings and development of early glass and glaze technology occurred in Southwest Asia and that this technology was then transferred to Egypt (Beck 1934; Oppenheim 1970; Moorey 1985, 195; Barag 1970: 132).

Unfortunately, glass and glazed artifacts found in the Near East from the first through third millennia B.C. are so heavily weathered that stylistic and manufacturing traces are virtually unrecognizable in most objects. For instance, among 11,000 glass beads found by Starr from the mid-second-millennium B.C. site of Nuzi, only seven were sufficiently unweathered that they were suitable for bulk chemical analysis (Vandiver 1982, 1983). Thus it is surprising that the eighteenth season of excavations at Nippur should be so fortunate to yield two glass beads with a late third-millennium B.C. context.

## Archaeological Context

The first bead to be excavated was a spherical olive green and white bead (18 N 95, pls. 167:1, 186a), discovered in Area WF on Floor 3 of Locus 35, the courtyard of a mudbrick building (pl. 27). This floor could be traced through a doorway into a small room where it had the designation Locus 36, Floor 4. In this room, a few centimeters below this floor, a second bead was found. This second bead, a bluish green and yellow barrel bead (18 N 96, pls. 167:2, 186b), lay near the doorway in Wall AG on Floor 1 of Locus 38 (pl. 26). On the same floor, about a meter away in the eastern corner, were four Old Akkadian cuneiform clay tablets. In all levels of this stratigraphic trench, excavation was done systematically, floor by floor, with each floor being cleaned for photography and mapping. Thus, any disturbances or pits were readily recognized and recorded. Although there had been some intrusive cuts in the upper strata of Area WF, in the Akkadian levels there was nothing that could have accounted for the presence of the glass beads through contamination from a later level. Above the findspots of both beads was a series of tamped earth floors, comprising an accumulated depth of about a meter, datable by the artifacts to the Akkadian period. Below the beads was another meter's depth of Akkadian debris. There were no signs on the floors of previous archaeological work, ancient pits, animal burrows, or other sources of contamination. The circular cut shown in the eastern end of Locus 38 was made from Floor 4 of Locus 36, the Akkadian period locus immediately above Locus 38, in order to install a shallow drain consisting of two small vats placed one upon the other. The cut was well defined and easily visible and did not extend as far as the findspot of the glass bead.

Arguing most strongly against contamination as a source for the two beads in the Akkadian level is the fact that they were found in different loci more than two meters apart and separated by a wall. In summary, the context of the beads is as sure as is possible using modern methods of archaeological excavation and the judgment of years of experience in excavation.

The significance of the finds from Nippur are their excellent, sealed context allowing assignment of date with confidence, their relatively good preservation, and the potential for analysis using modern probes which allow thorough microstructural and chemical characterization but which require very little sample. A few particles loosened or scratched from the surface amounting to as little as 0.2 cubic mm can be recycled from one test method to another, allowing microstructural characterization by scanning and transmission electron microscopy, bulk and phase chemical composition by wavelength dispersive electron beam microprobe analysis, phase identification by x-ray and electron diffraction, and thermal history by high resolution differential thermal analysis. Our aim here is to present a description of the beads and results of analyses using four of these analytical techniques: diffraction, lead isotope analysis, and scanning electron microscopy and microprobe. In addition, we present documentation of the rapid weathering phenomena that were observed in the first hours and days after excavation and interpretation of the glass technology.

## Description and Material Identification

The first glass bead to be found was the spherical one (18 N 95, pls. 167:1, 186a), translucent dark olive green and opaque white, which measures 8 to 9 mm with a symmetrical 2 mm diameter hole in the center. One end is chipped and exhibits many small facets with clearly visible conchoidal fractures, characteristic of unweathered, pristine glass (pl. 187a). Some pitting corrosion is present on the surface. A meniscus, or region of rounded curvature, occurs at each end where the glass once joined the rod or support armature that was used during forming (pl. 186a). A meniscus is evidence of the high surface tension of the glass, the result of forming at a low temperature relative to the working and melting temperature range of the glass. The bead is not glazed; the color and gloss continue into the interior of the bead where it was chipped, and both colors continue into the hole. Taken together, the spherical and elongated pores or bubbles, the presence of cord elongated in the direction of forming, the meniscuses at each end where the bead once joined the forming rod, and the pitting corrosion and details of design are characteristic of glass. In addition, calcium-magnesium-silicate (diopside) crystals in the glass, identified by x-ray diffraction, were elongated parallel to one another, the result of rotational forming of the bead; and some were broken and separated during forming, showing that the crystals could not have grown in situ after forming.

The second bead (18 N 96) is cylindrical with a hexagonal cross section and measures about 10.0 mm in length and 6.0–7.0 mm in diameter, with an oval hole 1.5–2.0 mm in diameter (pls. 167:2, 186b). The bright, translucent light green color had an opaque yellow decoration trailed and rolled in a linear pattern over the green. Under a microscope some of the yellow areas can be seen to have cracked and lifted away from the green glass beneath. Each end of the bead has a meniscus where the glass joined the presumed rod support, and one end has evidence of an incompletely made joint. Some pitting corrosion and loss of surface are common in the green areas. Upon excavation the yellow areas were unweathered and glossy, appearing almost pristine, as if just made. Unlike the green glass, the yellow surface was shiny and gave a strong specular reflection to incident light. However, freshly fractured surfaces in both the yellow and green areas had a rough texture in addition to some conchoidal fractures (pl. 187b), indicating that the glass contained a considerable amount of crystalline material. The opaque white and olive green glasses, on the other hand, were amorphous, containing very little crystalline material (pl. 187a).

## Weathering Phenomena

The glass beads at the time of excavation were stabilized in their damp soil in plastic containers. They were immediately removed from the sunlight to a high relative humidity field laboratory where they were allowed to acclimatize over a period of one week. However, changes in their appearance did occur due to drying, shrinking, and cracking. No significant powdering or flaking occurred, and there was very little loss of color intensity. For glass beads found in future excavations, I advise extending the period of equilibration to two or three weeks.

Initially brightly colored with much of the surface glossy, these glass beads altered rapidly after excavation until the colors were barely visible, the texture was matte, and some powdering of the surface had occurred. Within hours of excavation much of the color was lost, even though the beads were not washed. The dirt was carefully removed with a blunt wooden needle and brush while being observed beneath a microscope. In general, a fine mesh of cracks grew to cover the surface; sometimes a thin white crust formed which in some areas then powdered. The different colors, however, weathered somewhat differently. For instance, the white area of the spherical bead (18 N 95) cracked into 0.2 mm islands, but the surface stayed shiny on the first day; on the second day the surface became dull and matte. The olive green glass, meanwhile, began to dissolve differentially parallel to the cord or striae, the chemical heterogeneities in the glass composition giving a rope-like pattern of raised and lowered areas parallel to the edges of the stripes of green glass. On the second day, the green glass cracked, especially in the lowered areas with predominant cracks parallel to striae; the green color changed to a grayish black. Next, a light-colored film formed on the green surface, yielding a matte surface and a few small cracks.

The translucent yellow color of the cylindrical bead gradually turned matte by the end of the second day, whereas small patches of the green quite actively self-destructed. Rounded chips spalled and popped from the green areas leaving a pitted surface without a pattern of interconnected or parallel cracks, and corresponding bits of powder surrounded the bead.

These observations indicate that a long-term process of degradation had occurred during burial, which was accelerated by the rapid changes caused by excavation. In the ground the glass structure gradually changes such that silica, alkalies, and alkaline earths dissociate and hydrate. The soapy feel of the beads just after excavation probably indicates that a saturated alkali solution was present at the surface of the beads and may signal that degradation processes had slowed and almost ceased or perhaps that the beads were in a stabilized condition in the ground. During and just after excavation, rapid changes in relative humidity, alkalinity, and probably oxidation state occurred, and a loss of water and alkali occurred by handling and evaporation at the surface, followed by precipitation of some products as a surface layer or crust. Local shrinkage of alkali-depleted regions as well as the presence of residual water in cracks helped propagate the cracks through the glass in various patterns depending on the degree of crystallinity, chemical homogeneity, and prior processing of the glasses.

These weathering phenomena can be generalized to other glazes and glasses from later periods excavated at Nippur. The surfaces of these objects were observed to change from perfectly glossy and brightly colored immediately after excavation, through visible deterioration within a few hours or days, and finally to form matte-textured, opaque, and white surfaces which sometimes powdered, often becoming unrecognizable as glass or glazed materials. One example of a well-preserved Parthian turquoise blue glazed jar with a soda-lime-silicate composition (no. H480) showed regions of alkali depletion along cracks as well as associated shrinkage and crack formation at the boundary of the depleted region. Needlelike or acicular crystals appeared in the calcium-magnesium-silicate phase which appears to be related to the corrosion process, as some were etched into the glass surface. They seem to affect the rate of corrosion because the boundary between corroded and uncorroded glass deflects when these crystals are encountered. Rough areas indicate the crustal formation of weathering products. Similar structures are present in the Akkadian glass beads.

These same phenomena of deterioration were recognized and described by Starr (1939: 442) when excavating levels dated to ca. 1450 B.C. at Nuzi. Here, more than 11,000 glass beads, over forty glazed vessels, a pair of glazed lions, and a glazed ram's head plaque were found. Starr reported changes in glaze surface and colors within hours of excavation in which glazes or glasses would turn from glossy turquoise blue, to light green, to white, and then would sometimes form powder or weathering layers. Some became soapy and liquefied, often decomposing within a week. Starr and the Nippur excavation members also saw shiny yellow glasses turn white within hours while retaining their gloss.

## Fabrication Processes

The spherical bead (18 N 95) consists of two threads or bits of glass that wrap about the interior hole in a spiral pattern. Although soil adhered loosely to the bead, no core material was found inside the hole. Core material has been reported in second-millennium B.C. glass beads and vessels as a white friable layer or as a soapy brown residue consisting primarily of quartz and clay or lime (Brimson and Werner 1967; Brill 1969; Vandiver 1982). The joints of individual glass threads can be seen at three indentations in the meniscus. The large radius of curvature of the meniscuses indicates that a relatively low forming temperature was used. There are three places in which fairly large white regions with pointed shapes are found, but without any evidence of combing with a hooked tool or displacement of the glass with a straight edge. In addition, there are no flat facets from paddling or marvering (i.e., rolling on a flat surface). In some areas the white glass has fused over the green glass, and in others the opposite is true, indicating that one color was not simply applied over the other. I suspect that this is evidence of the melting together of bits of glass which would have initially formed an uneven glass surface and which gradually were drawn flat by surface tension during fusion at a relatively low working temperature of about 900°C. Such shapes were made more quickly in later second-millennium B.C. beads by combing or moving the glass with a hooked tool or straight edge to such pointed shapes. The manufacture of this bead gives no evidence of such a sophisticated tool kit or of refined and rapid working methods.

The cylindrical bead (18 N 96) was made with a yellow thread of glass wrapped on a rod with a green lump or thread added in a pattern over the surface of the yellow, and then a small bit or yellow fritted particles over the green.

Where the green forms a very thin layer over the yellow, it looks yellow green, giving the effect of three colors. The bead was pinched three times when semi-molten, perhaps with flat-ended tongs, to give it the somewhat rounded hexagonal cross section (pl. 167:2). The hexagonal cross section is less distinct at the end where the incompletely formed joint can be seen. No evidence of combing or displacement of the threadlike decoration was found, and no evidence of a parting layer to separate the bead from an inner armature was found. Like the spherical bead, there is no evidence of sophisticated methods or tools common to most second- and first-millennium B.C. glass production.

## Compositional Analysis, Color Chemistry, and Microstructure

Bulk compositions for the four colored glasses, given in table A.1, show unexpected variation in composition. The olive green is a high soda, high calcia, and magnesia glass in the soda-lime-silica system, which is colored by about 3 percent iron oxide. The opaque white glass is of similar composition but contains very little iron (about 0.5%) and a small amount of lead oxide (about 1.3%). These glasses contain a very large amount of soda (16–19%) and we suspect their poor durability is related to this high soda concentration. The olive green glass contains large diopside crystals (table A.2), one 30 microns long, elongated parallel to other such crystals and aligned with the flow of the glass during forming (see table A.2 for composition). These crystals would have taken several hours just below the melting temperature to nucleate and grow, thus indicating that a long heat treatment was required to make these glasses. This information fits well with the multiple-step sintering, cooling, and reheating processes described in early first-millennium B.C. glass texts (Oppenheim 1970). The white glass is opacified mainly with rounded quartz crystals, indicating a low temperature for the melting of this glass that did not dissolve the quartz crystals that remain from the original raw materials.

The yellow and green glasses are made of different mixtures of copper ions in solution in the glass with inclusions of a lead-tin oxide or lead-stannate yellow colorant, $PbSnO_3$ (pl. 188a). The green glass contains up to 3 percent copper oxide in solution. The lead-stannate phase predominates in the yellow glass, especially at the surface (pl. 188b), and was identified by x-ray diffraction with d-spacings at 3.085 (100), 2.680 (30), 1.894 (40), and 1.615 (25) Angstroms (relative intensity) (Wainwright et al. 1986: 241). It is embedded in a magnesium-calcium-silicate phase, diopside as identified by x-ray diffraction (pl. 189a and b). The diopside has undergone partial melting and some deformation in the glass matrix that contains both lead and soda as active fluxes (tables A.1 and A.2). A sodium-calcium-silicate phase (perhaps devitrite) and a high lead-silicate phase also are present. In addition, there are fine, submicron precipitates of a lead-rich phase and some compositional zoning in the bulk of the glass that is probably the result of weathering. A calcium-phosphate lead-silicate phase is included as spherical particles or droplets in the yellow and green glasses (pl. 190). Because there are no pores and no structures characteristic of residual bone particles as a potential source of the calcium-phosphate, we cannot state whether this phase is original or intrusive. Ian Freestone, however, suggests that it is probably post-depositional. Calcium was present in the soil; however, no phosphate was present in the soil at a level of 0.5 percent. This is one of the most complex glass microstructures we have ever seen, containing at least five and possibly six distinct phases (table A.2). Further characterization and replication are required to identify fully and explain the complex interaction and thermal history of these phases. The bulk composition of the barrel bead was melted at 800, 900 and 1000°C for twelve hours (pl. 191), yielding, respectively, an incompletely melted and stiff frothing glass, a glass with incompletely melted quartz floating on the surface, and a well-fused, homogeneous blue glass. Thus, the presence of so many phases indicates that at least some of the mixing occurred during forming.

The large amount of crystalline inclusions in the yellow and green barrel bead would have made it difficult glasses to form, very viscous and resistant to flow. Thus, pinching may have been necessary to form the yellow and green bead. In particular, the crystalline volume fraction extends to 50 microns below the surface of the yellow regions and amounts to about 80 percent volume; whereas the volume fraction in the bulk and in the green regions is about 40 percent volume. In the interior there are regions which appeared white under an optical microscope and which are rich in the magnesium-calcium-silicate phase (pl. 190). Such a high viscosity and poor formability may help explain why the meniscus is so large and why the bead was formed by pincering rather than by heat, surface tension, and gravity as were used for the other bead. The amount of crystals in the glasses could have been lowered in order to make them more workable, but was not. The unusually large volume fraction of crystals argues for a glass technology in an experimental stage with multiple steps in melting and forming the bead.

Lead isotope analysis of the barrel bead (National Institute of Standards and Technology MAN 822) yielded the following ratios: Pb207/Pb206, 0.848458; Pb208/Pb206, 2.092506; and Pb204/Pb206, 0.054217. This sample falls within an isotopic group previously defined as the Trabzon group (Sayre et al. 2001: 84). This ore group, located in the central Black Sea Pontic mountains of northern Turkey, has a slight overlap with another Black Sea group, Küre. The assignment of the ore source to Turkey is provisional. Given the overlap in this region, it is entirely possible that the ores of Iran may also be candidates for the source of the lead. Until these extensive ore deposits are analyzed and the ore bodies of Turkey, Greece, and Cyprus have been thoroughly characterized, the conclusions posited here are tentative. However, no lead sources are present in lowland Mesopotamia, therefore the lead-containing barrel bead from Nippur represents an import from the north. The appearance of this bead is jewel-like, and the colors are bright yellow and various shades of bluish green to greenish blue. Presumably during manufacture the yellow stannate incased in diopside was added to the copper-containing greenish turquoise glass. The materials and technology are imports and are unlike the other, spherical bead. This latter bead is made from local lowland Mesopotamian materials: soda, lime, and silica, and the green is colored with iron, yielding a "bottle"-green color. The spherical bead has a comparatively dull appearance, and the white opaque base glass contains unmelted quartz inclusions. The glass of this bead is not as well melted as the base turquoise glass of the barrel bead. The spherical bead is probably a local imitation of the jewel-like barrel bead that was found in an earlier context and was presumably made at a slightly later date.

## Discussion

This study has been criticized for reporting the earliest evidence of lead-stannate pigment, in this case as inclusions in the yellow and turquoise green glass barrel bead. Mavis Bimson has reported the earliest identification by x-ray diffraction of a lead-stannate colorant from a La Tene site that dates to the fourth century B.C. (Bimson 1958). Many authors (Partington 1935; Turner and Rooksby 1959, 1963; Sayre 1963; Sayre and Smith 1967, 1974; Brill 1969, 1970; Brill and Cahill 1988; Hedges and Moorey 1975; Hedges 1976; Pollard and Moorey 1982; Matson 1986; Wainwright et al. 1986; Harley 1970) report that lead-tin yellows and lead-containing glasses are Roman and Islamic, which would mean that these Nippur beads could be thought to be late in date and intrusive in the Akkadian levels. But the microstructure of the beads is unlike any of the later examples, especially lead-stannate yellow glass (Turner and Rooksby 1959). The forming of the beads does not involve marvering or combing, only gradual fusing at low heat. They contain a larger crystalline volume fraction than any other glasses, a sufficient amount to be detrimental to fluid forming. In addition, they have a more complex microstructure, with many phases present, which argues for a complex history of the mixing and fusing of several raw materials. In summary, the forming, compositional complexity, and number of crystalline phases all argue, in addition to the sealed archaeological context in association with cuneiform tablets describing textile transactions, for a third millennium date and technology for these glass beads.

The example of the lead-containing bead from Nippur may not be an isolated instance. The evidence of the two beads from Nineveh should be reexamined. One is probably a blue soda-lime composition, and the other, a brilliant green glass bead with a hexagonal shape, was the one with a sufficiently high specific gravity to indicate lead is present (Beck 1931). These two beads from Nineveh have a reasonable third-millennium B.C. context. Yet Beck and Moorey discount them both because of the probable presence of lead in one, as they believe lead is a characteristic only of Roman and Islamic glasses (Moorey 1985; Beck 1934). The presence in the Nippur glass of lead-stannate in characteristic complex microstructures involving diopside suggests that analysis of the bead from Nineveh might show similar microstructural evidence. Such evidence should be pursued because it would either strengthen the conclusion regarding the nature of early glass technology or it would leave the Nippur glass as an isolated and singular instance of a lead-containing glass of the third millennium B.C.

## Interpretation and Conclusions

The two glass beads from Nippur are significant as very early examples of glass technology. Of the six other finds of glass beads from the third millennium B.C., only one has been chemically analyzed and only two of them can presently be located. The context of the two Akkadian glass beads from Nippur is secure, one being found in a room in association with cuneiform tablets, the other in the courtyard of the same building. Both findspots were sealed below multiple floors of Akkadian date.

The significance of these two beads for the history of pyrotechnology consists of relatively low-temperature forming operations (about 800–1000°C), of viscous or semi-viscous materials. The extent and morphology of crystal growth, breakage, and resorbtion imply a total time of many hours in a molten condition. Forming operations included the use of lumps of glass that were fused around a rod armature. The different compositions — one soda-lime-silicate composition, the other perhaps a lead-tin oxide metallurgical residue that was formed as a viscous, partly crystalline material and treated as a glass — opens the definition of ancient glass-working and glassy materials, and implies the possibility of a direct association of glass with metal-working and pigment and/or frit technologies. The extensive crystal growth that would have made these glasses very difficult to form was quite unexpected. The presence of four different colors — olive green, white, yellow, and green — was also quite unexpected and may indicate that from the beginning glasses were made to imitate the colors and shiny surfaces of semiprecious stones, while being able to control the shape and pattern of the colors. Compositional and isotopic analysis showed that the barrel bead has a northern raw material source, provisionally from north central Turkey, and the spherical one, dated to a slightly later floor, has a more local source of raw materials. Variation in appearance, complexity, and technology points to northern source for the manufacture of the barrel bead and to a local, less refined Mesopotamian workshop for the spherical one.

I hope that this study alerts archaeologists and glass technologists to some of the problems and promise of excavating ancient glass remains and, in particular, reaffirms the potential importance of beads with good context for the reconstruction of pyrotechnology. One additional aim has been to develop an awareness of the rapid corrosion phenomena that occur as glassy objects are unearthed.

## Acknowledgments

For help with this article, written in 1991, we thank Eugene Jarosevich and Joseph Neelon of the Mineral Sciences Department Microprobe Facility, Smithsonian Institution National Museum of Natural History, for help with the microprobe analyses; Peggy Sanders for help with the macro-photography of the beads; Martha Goodway for assistance with the photographs taken by optical microscopy; and Blythe McCarthy for her comments and suggestions. we am grateful to the National Geographic Society and the Research Opportunity Fund of the Smithsonian Institution for the generous funding that made this research possible. The lead isotope analyses were conducted at the National Institute of Standards and Technology, Washington, D.C., and were part of a Smithsonian Institution collaborative grant. Emile Joel and Edward Sayre are thanked for their help. We thank the Smithsonian Center for Materials Research and Education where the first draft of this article was written in 1991.

Table A.1. Chemical Compositions of Glass from Nippur by Wavelength Dispersive Microprobe Analysis
(50 analyses for each bead)

|  | *TRANSLUCENT DARK OLIVE GREEN* |  |  | *OPAQUE WHITE* |  |  |
|---|---|---|---|---|---|---|
|  | % Weight | Range | Std. Dev. | % Weight | Range | Std. Dev. |
| $SiO_2$ | 60.64 | (59.0–62.9) | (0.79) | 60.77 | (58.6–62.1) | (0.88) |
| $Al_2O_3$ | 2.10 | (1.88–2.34) | (0.12) | 1.87 | (1.55–2.13) | (0.10) |
| $Na_2O$ | 18.12 | (17.05–19.30) | (0.43) | 17.87 | (16.02–19.21) | (0.59) |
| $K_2O$ | 2.84 | (2.54–3.20) | (0.13) | 2.71 | (2.54–3.20) | (0.13) |
| CaO | 6.23 | (5.69–7.03) | (0.23) | 6.11 | (5.51–6.94) | (0.29) |
| MgO | 7.24 | (6.78–7.96) | (0.23) | 7.18 | (6.90–8.48) | (0.23) |
| FeO | 2.89 | (2.51–3.27) | (0.18) | 0.50 | (0.44–0.58) | (0.03) |
| CuO | *0.05 | (0.00–0.12) | (0.04) | 0.07 | (0.03–0.12) | (0.04) |
| PbO | *0.02 | (0.00–0.30) | (0.01) | 1.32 | (1.04–4.52) | (0.95) |
| MnO | 0.06 | (0.00–0.08) | (0.04) | *0.05 | (0.00–0.16) | (0.03) |
| $TiO_2$ | 0.07 | (0.00–0.18) | (0.04) | *0.05 | (0.00–0.16) | (0.03) |
| $Sb_2O_3$ | 0.08 | (0.00–0.12) | (0.04) | *0.01 | (0.00–0.08) | (0.02) |
| $P_2O_5$ | 0.25 | (0.17–0.33) | (0.04) | 0.23 | (0.13–0.27) | (0.04) |
| $SnO_2$ | *0.03 | (0.00–0.08) | (0.03) | *0.06 | (0.00–0.33) | (0.10) |
| **Total** | **100.62** |  |  | **98.74** |  |  |

|  | *TRANSLUCENT BLUISH GREEN* |  |  | *OPAQUE YELLOW* |  |  |
|---|---|---|---|---|---|---|
|  | % Weight | Range | Std. Dev. | % Weight | Range | Std. Dev. |
| $SiO_2$ | 61.91 | (51.35–72.23) | (6.67) | 63.99 | (15.20–73.23) | (13.90) |
| $Al_2O_3$ | 2.89 | (1.93–3.74) | (0.64) | 3.28 | (1.47–11.37) | (1.51) |
| $Na_2O$ | 5.89 | (0.38–15.45) | (3.97) | 2.51 | (0.11–7.82) | (1.71) |
| $K_2O$ | 1.66 | (0.59–2.55) | (0.33) | 0.74 | (0.25–1.57) | (0.92) |
| CaO | 5.18 | (2.97–11.15) | (1.83) | 4.94 | (1.29–15.80) | (2.57) |
| MgO | 5.69 | (2.90–8.61) | (1.37) | 4.21 | (1.59–7.79) | (1.60) |
| FeO | 0.82 | (0.52–0.95) | (0.21) | 0.55 | (0.13–1.40) | (0.22) |
| CuO | 0.98 | (0.63–2.21) | (0.16) | 0.82 | (0.04–3.18) | (0.64) |
| PbO | 9.81 | (3.56–17.47) | (4.69) | 15.18 | (1.49–37.77) | (6.14) |
| MnO | 0.12 | (0.05–0.31) | (0.07) | 0.15 | (0.00–0.41) | (0.09) |
| $TiO_2$ | 0.12 | (0.03–0.18) | (0.03) | 0.09 | (0.00–0.25) | (0.07) |
| $Sb_2O_3$ | *0.06 | (0.00–0.12) | (0.05) | 0.07 | (0.00–0.23) | (0.07) |
| $P_2O_5$ | 0.25 | (0.10–0.56) | (0.12) | 1.13 | (0.11–3.94) | (1.10) |
| $SnO_2$ | 0.86 | (0.39–1.18) | (0.23) | 1.96 | (0.28–4.56) | (1.06) |
| **Total** | **96.24** |  |  | **99.62** |  |  |

*At or below detection limit

## Sample and Instrument Parameters for Table A.1

Freshly fractured surfaces were mounted in epoxy resin and polished using 600 mesh silicone carbide and 0.5 and 0.03 micron alumina and cleaned ultrasonically. Following examination with an optical microscope, samples were coated with a 200-micron thin film of carbon and analyzed using the Museum of Natural History, Mineral Sciences Department, ARL wavelength dispersive electron microprobe at 15kV accelerating voltage. Spot size was defocused to 30 microns and counting times were 10 seconds to avoid loss of sodium and potassium oxides. Counting times of 30 seconds reduced the sodium concentration to less than 10% of values counted at 10 seconds. Beam current was continuously monitored with a Faraday cup to avoid instrument drift. Hornblende was used as a working standard and analyzed before and after each session, and an analysis was carried out before and after with the beam blanked to be sure totals were null. A ZAF correction program was used with geological standards and Corning Glass standard B. Error bars increased in value with decreasing concentration and vary from 1% relative value for $SiO_2$%, 5% for $Al_2O_3$, CaO, MgO, $Na_2O$, $K_2O$, and FeO; and 10% for the other constituents.

Table A.2. Analyses of Individual Phases Present; Translucent White Crystals in Olive Green Glass Identified by X-Ray Diffraction as Diopside

|  | Calcium-Magnesium-Silicate | | | Calcium-Magnesium-Sodium-Silicate | | |
| --- | --- | --- | --- | --- | --- | --- |
|  | % Weight | Range | Std. Dev. | % Weight | Range | Std. Dev. |
| $SiO_2$ | 56.06 | (54.28–63.08) | (3.69) | 57.78 | (55.47–58.71) | (1.11) |
| $Al_2O_3$ | 0.43 | (0.00–2.02) | (0.73) | 2.99 | (0.27–1.64) | (0.42) |
| $Na_2O$ | Depleted | about 0–2% | — | 7.28 | (2.19–14.47) | (3.29) |
| $K_2O$ | 0.41 | (0.00–2.19) | (0.66) | 1.39 | (0.27–2.21) | (0.52) |
| CaO | 21.38 | (6.15–24.56) | (5.96) | 15.92 | (10.56–23.91) | (3.59) |
| MgO | 15.42 | (6.98–19.01) | (3.72) | 13.16 | (10.22–19.31) | (2.55) |
| FeO | 2.99 | (2.22–5.64) | (0.94) | 2.98 | (2.73–3.35) | (0.17) |
| CuO | Not Measured | — | — | 0.17 | (0.11–0.25) | (0.03) |
| PbO | 0.95 | (0.41–1.24) | (0.25) | Not Measured | — | — |
| $TiO_2$ | Not Measured | — | — | 0.09 | (0.02–0.16) | (0.04) |
| $P_2O_5$ | 0.26 | (0.17–0.31) | (0.05) | Not Measured | — | — |
| $SnO_2$ | *0.03 | (0.00–0.50) | (0.24) | Not Measured | — | — |
| **Total** | **97.95** | | | **100.18** | | |

* At or below detection limit

## Sample and Instrument Parameters for Table A.2

Because of the large size of these crystals, both a 1 micron and 30 micron spot size of the beam on the sample were used. The $SiO_2$ and FeO values are stable, but the CaO and MgO values increase with decreasing spot size which can be explained by the zoning that occurs along the length of the needlelike crystals. Note that the mean values overlap considerably. The sodium values are believable only with the larger beam size. However, the ranges of values in the small spot size analyses are wider and the lower values are more typical of the glass matrix. Two sources of possible variation affect these values: (1) variation within the phase of the material being analyzed, and (2) variation caused by the 3–5 micron depth, it is probable that another phase, the surrounding glassy matrix being higher in soda and lower in calcia and magnesia, could be included in the large spot size analysis.

More important than the composition of these crystals is what they tell us about the formation of the glass in very viscous conditions after a long period of melting at the lower range of possible melting temperatures. From the morphology of the crystals it is obvious that they crystallized from the melt and were subsequently broken and flowed very little during viscous forming. One must note that the composition is very high in fluxes, especially soda, and alkaline earths compared with most Roman or modern glasses, and is essentially a 63-21-14 glass (glass former : alkali or flux : alkaline earth or stabilizer).

## APPENDIX 2. ANIMAL BONES AND SHELLS

### YELLOW AND BLUISH GREEN HEXAGONAL BEAD (18 N 96)

|  | Lead-Stannate Phase | High-lead Silicate Phase | Calcium-Phosphate-Lead-Silicate |
|---|---|---|---|
| PbO | 48.21 | 27.84 | 8.72–32.06 |
| $SnO_2$ | 30.17 | 6.12 | 1.32 –3.39 |
| $SiO_2$ | 15.16 | 49.22 | 29.33–35.51 |
| $Al_2O_3$ | 0.51 | 1.50 | 2.22 |
| CaO | 2.32 | 2.95 | 6.42 – 8.86–11.15 |
| MgO | 1.35 | 3.77 | 3.82 |
| FeO | 0.83 | 0.73 | 0.82 |
| $K_2O$ | 1.07 | 0.27 | 0.79 |
| $P_2O_5$ | 0.38 | 0.31 | 4.68 –8.16 |
| **Total** | **100.00** | **92.71** | **89.85** |

|  | Diopside or Calcium-Magnesium Silicate Phases | Sodium-Calcium Silicate | Mean Glass Matrix Phase |
|---|---|---|---|
| $SiO_2$ | 53.44 | 58.17 | 51.47 | 61.90 |
| $Al_2O_3$ | 0.73 | 1.93 | 0.57 | 2.06 |
| CaO | 13.69 | 15.69 | 23.44 | 5.36 |
| MgO | 14.38 | 14.33 | 4.83 | 4.11 |
| FeO | 0.98 | 1.14 | 0.55 | 0.63 |
| $K_2O$ | 0.52 | 0.62 | 0.39 | 1.67 |
| PbO | 7.64 | 4.62 | 2.07 | 5.80 |
| $SnO_2$ | 0.77 | 1.56 | 4.23 | 1.51 |
| $P_2O_5$ | 0.36 | 0.29 | 0.74 | 0.25 |
| **Total** | **98.84** | **97.35** | **88.29** | **83.29** |
| $Na_2O$ | Not Analyzed |  | About 10% | About 15% |
|  |  |  | Present by E.D.S.* | Presence confirmed by E.D.S. |
| **Total** |  |  | **98.58** | **98.29** |

\* Energy Dispersive Spectroscopy

The lead-tin-rich and the calcium-magnesium-silicate phases both have particle sizes greater than the 3–5 micron sampling volume. Therefore, edge effects are negligible and the totals are high. In the glass matrix and high-lead glass and precipitate areas, the phases are finely divided on a scale of about 0.1 micron and internal scattering and other edge effects reduce the totals. The mean glass matrix phase, however, is quite similar in the ratios of elements to the overall glass phase taken with a 30 micron spot size (table A.1, lower two analyses of hexagonal barrel bead), with the one expected exception of the lower lead oxide concentration.

# APPENDIX 2. ANIMAL BONES AND SHELLS

*David S. Reese*

### AREA WF

#### SELEUCID (360–150 B.C.)

| Level | Locus | Location | Lot | Specimen | Note |
|---|---|---|---|---|---|
| II | 2 | Pit 1 | H63, H64, H66, H81, H90, H94 | 266 Bones | Includes partial animal skeleton |
| II | 2 | Pit 2 | H87 | 12 Bones | — |

#### EIGHTH–SEVENTH CENTURY B.C.

| Level | Locus | Location | Lot | Specimen | Note |
|---|---|---|---|---|---|
| IV | 10 | Fl. 1 inside Jar H367 | H360 | 15 Bones | — |

#### KASSITE (THIRTEENTH CENTURY B.C.)

| Level | Locus | Location | Lot | Specimen | Note |
|---|---|---|---|---|---|
| V | 21 | Burial 10? | H799 | 1 Cowrie (open body) | — |

#### ISIN-LARSA (2000–1800 B.C.)

| Level | Locus | Location | Lot | Specimen | Note |
|---|---|---|---|---|---|
| VI | 14 | Above Fl. 2 | H688, H691 | 14 Bones | — |
| VI | 16 | Above Fls. 1 & 2 | H752 | 16 Bones | — |

#### UR III (2100–2000 B.C.)

| Level | Locus | Location | Lot | Specimen | Note |
|---|---|---|---|---|---|
| VII | 17 | Above Fl. 1 | H758 | 16 Bones | — |
| VIII | 20 | Above Fl. 1 | H764, H772 | 43 Bones, 1 *Unio* | — |
| VIII | 20 | Above Fl. 2 | H775 | 6 Bones, 2 *Unio* | — |
| VIII | 20 | From Fl. 2 to 5 cm above Fl. 3 | H778 | 7 Bones, 1 *Unio* fragment | — |
| VIII | 29 | Above Fl. 1 | H852 | 3 *Unio* | — |
| IX | 26 | Above Fl. 1 | H785 | 5 Bones | — |
| X | 27 | Above Fl. 1 | H798, H828, H893 | 28 Bones | — |
| X | 27 | Above Fl. 2 | H853, H786 | 40 Bones, 1 *Strombus* | — |
| X | 27 | Above Fl. 3, east test trench | H860, H867 | 7 Bones | — |
| X | 27 | Above Fl. 3 | H800 | 250+ Fish Bones | — |

## Ur III (2100–2000 b.c.)

| Level | Locus | Location | Lot | Specimen | Note |
|---|---|---|---|---|---|
| X | 27 | Above Fl. 4 | H839 | 12 Bones | — |
| X | 30 | Above Fl. 1 | H856 | 5 Bones | — |
| X | 33 | Above Fl. 1 | H897 | 12 Bones | — |

## Late Akkadian (2300–2100 b.c.)

| Level | Locus | Location | Lot | Specimen | Note |
|---|---|---|---|---|---|
| XIA | 34 | Above Fl. 1 | H824, H900, H143 | 22 Bones, 1 *Unio* | — |
| XIA | 34 | On Fl. 1 | H505 | 263 Bones | — |
| XIA | 34 | Above Fl. 2 | H521, H524 | 17 Bones | — |
| XIA | 35 | Above Fl. 1 | H880 | 2 Bones | — |
| XIB | 35 | Above Fl. 2 | H140 | 11 Bones | — |
| XIB | 35 | Above Fl. 2A | H142 | 2 Bones | — |
| XIB | 35 | Above Fl. 3 | H507 | 7 Bones | — |
| XIB | 36 | Above Fl. 0 | H831, H864 | 21 Bones | — |
| XIB | 36 | Above Fl. 1 | H869 | 5 Bones | — |
| XIB | 36 | Above Fl. 2 | H872 | 4 Bones | — |
| XIB | 36 | Above Fl. 3 | H878 | 7 Bones | — |
| XIB | 36 | Above Fl. 4 | H882, H886 | 6 Bones, 1 *Unio* | — |
| XIIA | 35 | Above Fl. 4 | H518 | 3 Bones | — |
| XIIA | 35 | Above Fl. 5 | H122, H538 | 38 Bones, 1 *Unio* fragment (1 deer antler) | — |
| XIIA | 38 | Above Fl. 1 | H504 | 3 Bones | — |
| XIIA | 38 | Above Fl. 2 | H120 | 5 Bones, 1 *Unio* | — |
| XIIB | 41 | Above Fl. 1 | H1011, H1018 | 13 Bones, 1 *Unio* | — |
| XIIB | 41 | Above Fl. 2 | H1030 | 6 Bones | — |

## Akkadian (2350–2300 b.c.)

| Level | Locus | Location | Lot | Specimen | Note |
|---|---|---|---|---|---|
| XIII | 39 | Above Fl. 1 | H530, H513 | 9 Bones | — |
| XIII | 43 | Above Fl. 1 | H1051 | 5 Bones | — |
| XIV | 40 | Above Fl. 1 | H1001 | 11 Bones, 1 *Unio* | — |
| XIV | 40 | Above Fls. 1 and 2 | H1013, H1029 | 11 Bones, 1 shell | — |
| XIV | 43 | Above Fl. 2 | H1069 | 7 Bones | — |
| XIV | 43 | On and above Fl. 3 | H1093 | 6 Bones | — |
| XV | 44 | Above Fl. 1 | H1099 | 3 Bones | — |
| XV | 47 | On and above Fl. 1 | H1073 | 21 Bones | — |
| XV | 47 | Above Fl. 2 | H1083 | 11 Bones (1 human molar), 1 *Laevicardium* | — |

## Unknown Dates and Context

| Level | Locus | Location | Lot | Specimen | Note |
|-------|-------|----------|-----|----------|------|
| ? | 24 | Pit 6 | H780 | 9 Bones | — |
| ? | 24 | Above Fl. 1 and Pit 6 | H794 | 16 Bones | — |
| ? | 24 & 25 | Mixed Pit 6 | H782 | Unknown | — |
| ? | 25 & 27 | Above Fl. 1 | H792 | 34 Bones | — |
| ? | 47 | On and above Fl. 3 | H1091 | 1 Bone | — |
| ? | Square 16 | Fls. 1–2 | H753 | 11 Bones, 2 shell fragments | — |

# APPENDIX 3. THE INSCRIPTIONS*

*Robert D. Biggs*

## Dating the Tablets

All my work on these seven texts is based solely on photographs and casts since I have had no opportunity to see the originals, all of which are in the Iraq Museum. I am very grateful to my friend and colleague Walter Sommerfeld for his reading a draft of this section and providing a number of corrections and references. He is in no way responsible for errors or omissions.

Tablets 18 N 104 through 18 N 108, all administrative documents overwhelmingly concerned with textiles, are clearly Akkadian in date, though none have date formulas that would confirm this. Cuneiform palaeography, especially as applied to texts of the third millennium, is a notoriously uncertain science.[1] The forms of the signs, as preserved in these few tablets, suggest to me that they likely date to the time of Naram-Sin or Šar-kali-šarri.[2] The fact that a fragment of a brick stamp of Naram-Sin was found in this level indicates the level is datable to Naram-Sin or later.[3]

Of the personal names attested in these texts, Enlil-da, Na-ba-LUL, and Ur-Enlil (if correctly restored) are attested in other previously published Nippur texts of the Akkadian period.[4]

The tablet 19 N 80 (pl. 192:1) is obviously earlier (a fact confirmed by stratigraphy), specifically Pre-Sargonic. This small administrative tablet, consisting of only seven lines of text and containing only a very small number of signs, is hardly an adequate sample. The tablet is somewhat unusual in that it is inscribed on the sharply rounded side rather than the flatter side as is the normal practice, but it is not certain that this is a factor with chronological importance. My impression — and it is only that — is that this tablet likely is datable to about the same time as the greater part of the Abu Salabikh tablets, that is, in archaeological terms, Early Dynastic IIIa. I likewise believe that it is somewhat later than the bulk of the Fara tablets.

Another tablet, 19 N 51, is a Neo-Babylonian lion plaque.

---

* The following special abbreviations have been used here:

| | |
|---|---|
| BE | Babylonian Expedition of the University of Pennsylvania, Series A: Cuneiform Texts |
| DP | M. Allotte de la Fuÿe, *Documents présargoniques* (Paris, 1908–20) |
| LAK | Anton Deimel, *Liste der archäischen Keilschriftzeichen*, Die Inschriften von Fara, vol. 1 (Leipzig, 1922) (cited by number) |
| MVN | *Materiali per il vocabolario neosumerico* (Rome, 1971–) |
| OAIC | Ignace J. Gelb, *Old Akkadian Inscriptions in Chicago Natural History Museum: Texts of Legal and Business Interest*, Fieldiana Anthropology, vol. 44, no. 2 (Chicago, 1955) |
| OSP 1 | Aage Westenholz, *Literary and Lexical Texts and the Earliest Administrative Documents from Nippur*, Bibliotheca Mesopotamica, vol. 1 (Malibu, 1975) |
| OSP 2 | Aage Westenholz, *Old Sumerian and Old Akkadian Texts in Philadelphia*, Part 2, *The "Akkadian" Texts, the Enlilemaba Texts, and the Onion Archive*, Carsten Niebuhr Institute Publications, vol. 3 (Copenhagen, 1987) |
| PSD | The Sumerian Dictionary of the University Museum of the University of Pennsylvania |
| RTC | F. Thureau-Dangin, *Recueil de tablettes chaldéennes* (Paris, 1903) |
| TMH | Texte und Materialien der Frau Professor Hilprecht-Sammlung |

[1] See Biggs 1973, pp. 39–46, and Edzard 1980, especially the section "Paläographie," pp. 555–61.

[2] Some of the sign forms (NE, for example) are seen to be very similar to the examples in Nippur tablets bearing year dates of Šar-kali-šarri published in Goetze 1968, specifically texts on pp. 57–58.

[3] See Gibson 1975, p. 136, no. 36, and photo p. 98, fig. 69, no. 3.

[4] See the indexes in OSP 1 and 2.

*Field Number:* 18 N 104
*Museum Number:* IM 114990
*Findspot:* Level XIIA, Locus 38, above Floor 1
*Dimensions:* Ht. 4.5 cm, w. 4.0 cm, th. 1.0 cm

*Illustration:* Plate 192:2

DESCRIPTION

Fragment of one side of a small rounded tablet concerning textiles.

TRANSLITERATION

1'. [1 tú]g(?) sag hi ru rí
2'. [1] túg LAK 647
3'. 1 e nu sag

COMMENTARY

2'. For other examples of LAK 647, see Biggs 1974, p. 35, n. 36. Gelb, Whiting, and Steinkeller (1991, p. 113) propose that LAK 647 is a graphic variant of URI. See also the discussion in Krecher 1987; he suggests that the sign may be an epigraphic predecessor of GIŠ.ÉRIN, though Gelb considers this unlikely. For TÚG.URI, see Gelb 1959, p. 190, citing Hilprecht, BE 1 11:5 with additional references, to which one can add MVN 3 95:8.

3'. OAIC 7:21 has an occurrence of e-*nu*, for which Gelb, OAIC, p. 208, suggests a possible connection with Akkadian *unūtu* "utensil," though I do not see that our passage provides any support for this suggestion.

*Field Number:* 18 N 105
*Museum Number:* IM 114991
*Findspot:* Level XIIA, Locus 38, Floor 1
*Dimensions:* Ht. 4.3 cm, w. 3.5 cm, th. 1.5 cm

*Illustration:* Plate 192:3

DESCRIPTION

Small tablet, both obverse and reverse preserved, listing various items (textiles, an aromatic substance, silver, oil, a *hazinnu*-ax, and one sheep) for an unstated purpose.

TRANSLITERATION

1. 1 túg bar-dul$_5$
2. 1 túg nì-lám
3. 4 ma-na šim-gúg
4. 4 gín kù-babbar
5. 10 túg bar-sig
6. 5 sìla ì
7. 1 ha-zi-núm
8. 1 udu

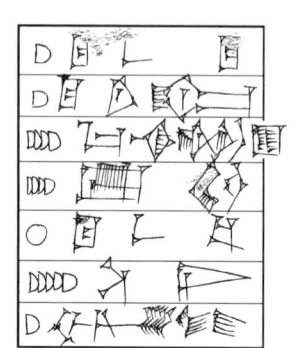

COMMENTARY

5. OAIC 7:8 also lists a túg-bar-sig; Gelb, OAIC, p. 207, cites additional passages. There is also bar-sig-gada in OSP 1 131 v 5.

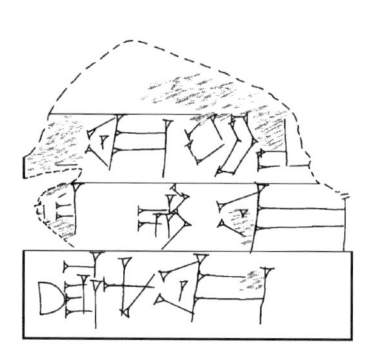

*Field Number:* 18 N 106  *Illustration:* Plate 193:1
*Museum Number:* IM 114992
*Findspot:* Level XIIB, Locus 38, above Floor 2
*Dimensions:* Ht. 4.7 cm, w. 3.9 cm, th. 1.4 cm

DESCRIPTION

Tablet, with obverse relatively well preserved, the reverse destroyed except for x su(?) x at the end of the top line and traces of numerals. List of various commodities, including grain, textiles whose weights are given, and several precious objects, one of gold, one of lapis lazuli, and one of alabaster.

TRANSLITERATION

1. [x +] x še-gu[r]
2. [x] túg aktum(A-SU)
3. ki-lá-bi 6 ma-n[a]
4. 1 túg bar-[dul$_5$]
5. ki-lá-bi 4 ma-na
6. 1 addir LKA 560
7. 1 a-AGA kù-GI
8. 1 gíd-urudu sag za-gìn
9. 1 kišib nu$_{11}$(ŠIR)-gal

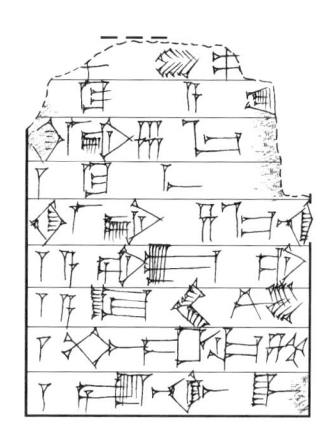

COMMENTARY

4. The restoration [dul$_5$] seems likely since the term is quite common, but there are other possibilities.

6. Walter Sommerfeld points out that this line has one of the many variant writings for addir. See Pomponio 1984, with pages 7–10 devoted to addir; he concludes that the basic meaning is "rent, pay" or "paid hired worker." Selz 1995 proposes that the original meaning was "ferrying, ferry toll, fare." I do not see any passages comparable to ours s.v. addir in the PSD.

   LAK 560, which Green and Nissen 1987, no. 88, connect with the sign DUG "vessel, pot," is probably a variant of SI.PAD, as Walter Sommerfeld points out to me.

7. It is obviously tempting to assume that aga (qualified as golden) denotes a crown or tiara, but the interpretation of a- (unless possibly meant as a reading gloss) is a problem. The PSD has no entry for a-aga and the entry for a-MIR does not appear to be relevant.

8. See OSP 2 49 i 2 and references in Westenholz's discussion on p. 66. It has a "head" made of lapis lazuli.

9. The term nu$_{11}$-gal is surely equivalent to giš-nu$_{11}$-gal "alabaster." The sign DUB is certainly dub in the Akkadian period and is also kišib as is clear in OSP 2 49 i 4 and 6.

*Field Number:* 18 N 107
*Museum Number:* IM 114993
*Findspot:* Level XIIA, Locus 38, on Floor 1
*Dimensions:* Ht. 7.0 cm, w. 4.0 cm, th. 2.9 cm

*Illustration:* Plate 193:2

DESCRIPTION

Tablet, rather badly damaged, listing various commodities, principally textiles, but likely including other items as well. Lines in which only numerals are legible are omitted in the transliteration below. The signs on the edge are virtually illegible on both the cast and photograph.

TRANSLITERATION

Obverse

1–2. traces
3. [x] x kù [x x]
4. [x N]E [x x]
5. ⌜kù⌝ igi-3 [x x]
6. 5 túg x [x x]
7. 1 [+ 4(?)] túg nì-l[ám(?)]
8. 1 [+ x túg í]b-ba-d[ù]
9. 2 + [x] ÙBUR(DAG.KISIM$_5$×IR)
10. 2(?) ⌜túg⌝ SAG×GAG
11. [SA]G-SUG$_5$(?)-gi$_4$
12. [x] túg bar-dul$_5$ gu-la

Reverse

1. 4 túg šu
2. 5 ⌜túg⌝ x si-dul$_5$
3. 5 túg (x) ⌜sag⌝
4. 1 [+ x(?)] túg [x x]
5. 10 + [x] (or 10 lá 1) túg [x x]

   only numerals preserved in remaining lines

Edge

   [x] ⌜ka/sag⌝ [x] hi me ha [x x]

COMMENTARY

9. I owe the identification of the unusual sign here to Walter Sommerfeld. He refers me to the discussion by Selz (1994, p. 224). It is Pre-Sargonic LAK 228.

10. There is a textile túg nì SAG×GAG attested in Ur III texts (see Waetzoldt 1972, p. 119; his reference to TMH NF 1/2 238:5 should instead refer to line 15). It is tempting to suggest that the same term is meant in our text and the Ur III examples. Occurrences of the sign SAG×GAG in personal names (RTC 251:4) and in a descriptive phrase referring to a person (PN SAG×GAG-du$_8$-x in DP 135 iv 17) do not appear to be helpful in determining the reading. Whether the lexical entries mu-uh SAG×GAG = muhhu S$^b$ I 247 and mu-hu-um SAG×[GA]G Proto-Ea 297 are relevant here is uncertain. See also Steinkeller and Postgate 1992, no. 21:10, listing a copper object, possibly a cup; see discussion on ibid., p. 48.

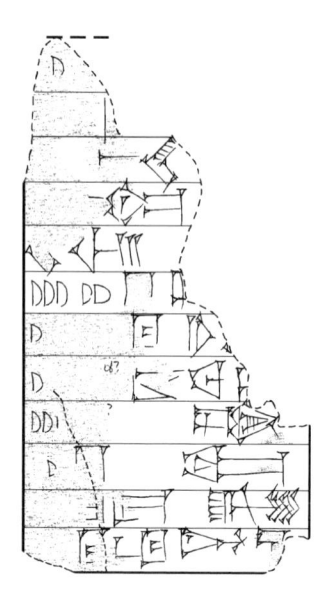

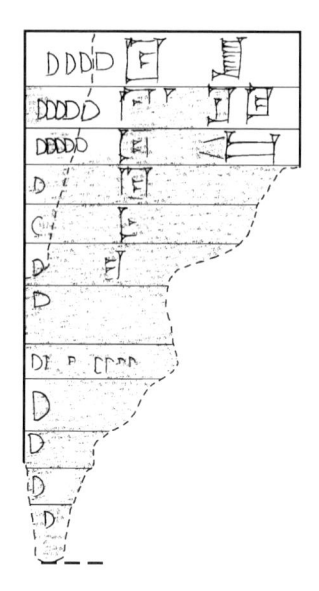

*Field Number:* 18 N 108     *Illustration:* Plate 193:3
*Museum Number:* —
*Findspot:* Level XIIA, Locus 38, on Floor 1
*Dimensions:* Ht. 6.5 cm, w. 4.1 cm, th. 1.9 cm

DESCRIPTION

Small tablet, of which the preserved parts of the obverse consist mostly of the numeral 1 and a personal name. The reverse has two lines, of uncertain interpretation. The areas above and below these two lines are uninscribed.

TRANSLITERATION

Obverse

1. 1 ᵈEn-líl-da
2. 1 x [x x]
3. 1 [x x x]
4. 1 x [x x]
5. 1 ⌈lú⌉ x (possibly [hun-g]á[?])
6. 1 Na-⌈ba⌉-LUL
7. 1 DINGIR.AL-é
8. 1 Ur-še-um-[u]m(?)
9. Lugal-SAR×DIŠ-d[a]
10. x x Ur-ᵈE[n-líl(?)]

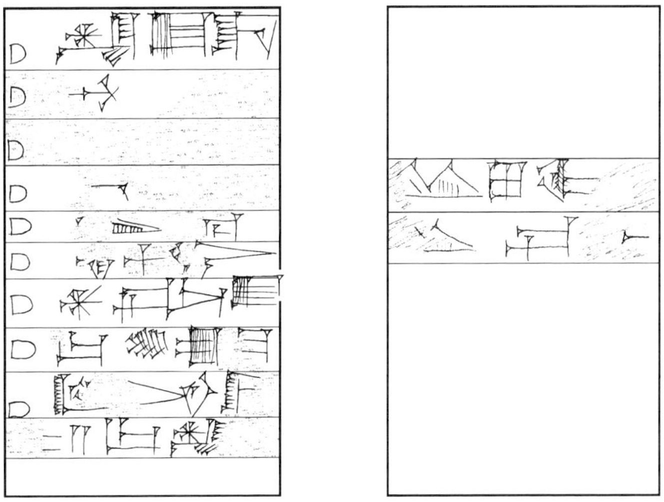

Reverse

1. lú-udu-k[a-x(?)]
2. ⌈lú⌉-aša₃(GÁN)-[gí]d(?)

Rest uninscribed

COMMENTARY

8. Compare the personal name Um-um in, for example, Selz 1993, no. 39 xi 14.


*Field Number:* 18 N 51     *Illustration:* Plate 180:3; not copied
*Museum Number:* —
*Findspot:* Level IIIB, Locus 7, above Floor 1
*Dimensions:* Lgth. 9.4 cm, ht. 6.9 cm, th. 1.9 cm

DESCRIPTION

Neo-Babylonian lion plaque with personal name and patronymic written above the figure: šá ᵐSUM-na-ŠEŠ A šá ᵈMAŠ-DIN-X "belonging to Iddina-aḫu son of Ninurta-balaṭ-X." The last sign in the patronymic is unclear, and hence the Akkadian word corresponding to DIN is likewise uncertain.


*Field Number:* 19 N 80     *Illustration:* Plate 192:1; not copied
*Museum Number:* —
*Findspot:* Level XVIIB, Locus 62, above Floor 1
*Dimensions:* Ht. 5.7 cm, w. 5.6 cm, th. 2.5 cm

DESCRIPTION

See discussion above (p. 165).

# INDEX

Abu Salabikh — 3 nn. 1 and 3, 38, 42 n. 48, 44 n. 53, 48 and n. 59, 50, 51 n. 72, 59, 60 n. 83, 64 and n. 88, 65–71, 72 and n. 100, 73, 74 and nn. 102, 104, and 106; 75 and n. 114, 76, 78–79, 82, 123–27, 132, 133 and n. 154, 134, 163

Agade — 59, 146

Agrab, Tell — 124

Alalakh — 126

Amar-Sin — 26 n. 29, 60, 149

Anatolia — 126

Asmar, Tell — xvii, 1, 3 n. 3, 9, 59–60, 64, 66, 68, 72 n. 100, 73–76, 78–80, 83, 120, 129, 149

Assur — 60 n. 83, 73, 79, 84 n. 123, 149

Assyria — xx, 56

Atiqeh, Tepe al- — xix, 3 nn. 1 and 3, 15, 72–73, 78

Babylon — 56 n. 80, 85

Babylonia — 56, 59 n. 82, 126

Boğazköy — 126

Brak, Tell — 3 n. 3, 60 n. 83, 73, 76, 81, 83, 84 n. 123, 126, 129

British Museum — 149

Chagar Bazar — 74, 81, 83, 84 n. 123, 126

Chuera, Tell — 3 n. 3, 67, 69

D.O.G. — 78

Der, Tell ed- — 85, 126

Deylam, Tell — 3 n. 1, 64 n. 88, 65 and n. 92, 75 n. 114, 125

Deylam, Tell ed-

Deylam, Tell ad-

Diyala — xvii–xix, 1, 4, 9, 47, 59 and n. 82, 60 n. 83, 64 and n. 89, 65–67, 69, 71, 72 n. 100, 73, 75 and n. 107, 78–79, 83, 145

Egypt — 150

Enanatum II — 4

Enentarzi — 4

Enlil — 123 and nn. 145 and 149, 147

Enlil-da — 163

Enmenanna, priestess of the moon-god — 121 n. 137, 122

Eridu — 129, 149

Fara — 3 nn. 1 and 3, 4, 14, 60 n. 83, 64–65, 67–69, 72, 78, 136, 163

Gawra, Tepe — 73, 125, 127, 132

Gula — xviii, 147 and n. 160

Hammam et-Turkman — 126

Hamrin — xviii–xx, 1, 59 n. 82, 65, 72 and n. 100, 77–78

171

Hiba, Tell al- — 3 n. 1, 9, 59, 67–68, 70–71, 73, 77–78, 81, 146

Ibbi-Sin — 60

Iddina-ahu — 133, 167

Inanna Temple — xvii–xviii, 3 n. 3, 5, 59, 64 and n. 90, 66–69, 147

Indus Valley — 128

Iraq Museum — 149, 163

Isin — 3 n. 3, 60, 70 n. 97, 79–80, 82

Judeideh, Tell — 129, 149

Khafajah — 1, 49 n. 64, 59 and n. 81, 64, 68–70, 72–73, 75 and nn. 107–109, 76, 78, 81, 124–25, 127

Kish — xvii, xix, 3 nn. 1 and 3, 4 and n. 4, 47, 48 and n. 62, 49, 59, 64 and n. 88, 65–68, 72–74 and nn. 103 and 105–06, 75 and n. 114, 76, 78–79, 124–27, 132–33

Lagash (modern al-Hiba) — 4 and n. 4, 146

Levant — 126

Lugalanda — 4

Lugal-DÚR — 51, 52 and n. 77, 121

Lugalzagesi — 4 and n. 4, 146

Madhhur, Tell — 3 n. 1, 48 n. 62, 49, 59, 64 n. 88, 74, 79

Manishtushu — 4 and n. 4, 17

Mari — 65, 67, 69, 72 n. 100, 126, 132–34

Megiddo — 126

Mesopotamia — xvii, 1, 3 and n. 3, 4–5, 7, 28 n. 32, 38 and n. 43, 39, 42, 48, 51 and n. 72, 52–53, 59, 60 n. 83, 61, 63–65, 69, 71, 73–74, 76, 78–81, 83, 84 n. 123, 123, 126–27, 129, 131 n. 153, 133–35, 145–47; fig. 1

Na-ba-LUL — 163

Naram-Sin — 4, 19, 59, 71, 74, 75 n. 109, 76, 78 n. 120, 79, 120, 121 nn. 129 and 137–38, 146, 163

Near East — 150

Nimrud — 49 n. 66, 129

Nineveh — 3 n. 3, 73, 81, 83, 84 n. 123, 149, 153–54

Nin-Isin-na — *see* Gula

Nippur — passim

Nuzi — 73, 81, 129, 132, 149–50, 152

Oriental Institute — xvii, 64 n. 89, 67 n. 94, 78

Pazuzu — 129

Puzurum, scribe — 120

Razuk, Tell — xix, 3 n. 1, 47 n. 55, 48–49, 64 and n. 88, 65–67, 69, 72 n. 99, 74, 75 n. 114, 79, 125

Rimush — 4 n. 4, 17

Sabra, Tell — 65, 69, 72 n. 100, 77–78

Samsuiluna — 28 n. 32, 145

Sargon — 4 and n. 4, 20 n. 21, 52 n. 77, 121 n. 138, 146

Shamash — 17, 119, 121 n. 136, 122–23, 135 n. 158

Sharkalisharri — 21 n. 24, 52 n. 77, 78 n. 120, 79, 80, 121 n. 129

Shatt an-Nil — 147

Sin — 51, 121 and nn. 136 and 138, 122–23

Sippar — 85

Southwest Asia — 149–50

Susa — 3 n. 3, 69, 72 n. 100, 73, 76, 79–84, 123, 126–27

Syria — 42, 69, 149

Tello — 72 n. 100, 76, 79, 83, 121 n. 137

Tigris — 59

Ubaid, Tell al- — 64

Umm al-Hafriyat — xviii–xx, 1, 3 and n. 3, 5, 15 n. 14, 60 and n. 83, 63, 69–70, 72–73, 76, 78–80 and n. 121, 82–84

Umm el-Jīr — xvii, 3 nn. 1 and 3, 23 n. 26, 43, 60 n. 83, 67, 69–71, 74, 79–81, 83

Umma — 4 n. 4, 50 n. 70, 146

University of Chicago — 1, 5

University of Pennsylvania — xvii, 78, 163

Pennsylvania Expedition — xvii

Uqair, Tell — 3 n. 1, 64, 123, 125

Ur — xvii, 3 nn. 1 and 3, 44, 47 and n. 56, 48 and n. 62, 49 and n. 66, 50 n. 69, 52 and n. 78, 59, 60 and n. 83, 64–65, 67, 69–73, 75 n. 114, 76, 78–81, 83, 85, 120 and n. 128, 121 nn. 136 and 138, 122, 124–25, 126 and n. 152, 127–29, 132, 134, 146, 149

Ur-Enlil — 163

Ur-Namma — 60

Uruk — 3 nn. 1 and 3, 4 and n. 4, 60, 73, 76, 79–80, 82–83, 85, 124, 146

# PLATES

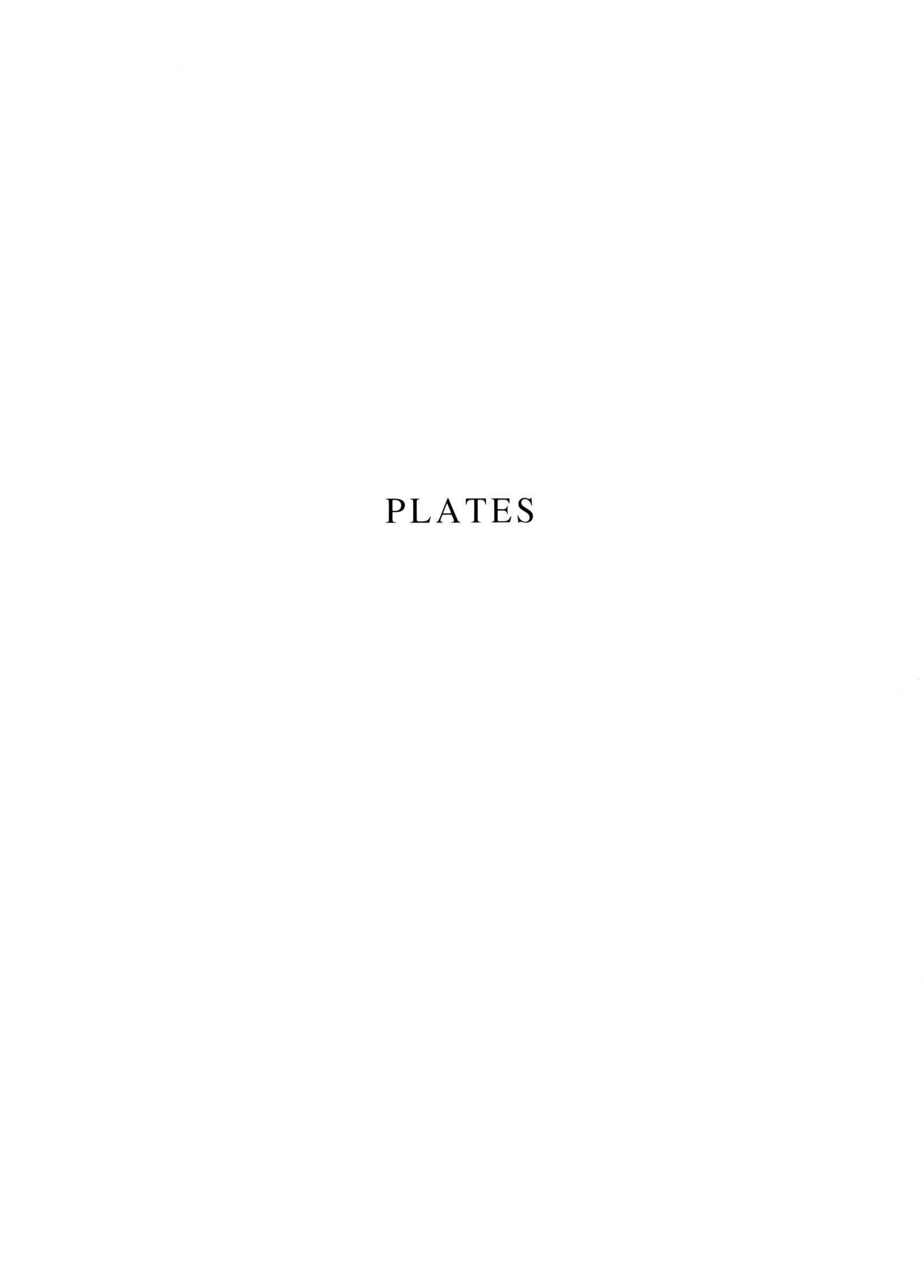

Plate 1

a

b

(*a*) General View of Area WF, from Northeast, Showing Dune on Left, Pennsylvania Dump on Right, Area WA in Center Background, and (*b*) General View of Area WF, from Southwest, Showing Pennsylvania Dump to Left, Ziggurat in Upper Left Background, Shatt an-Nil in Center Background, Parthian and Seleucid Remains on Right

Plate 2

(*a*) Area WF, Looking Down into Trench, from Southeast, and (*b*) Area WF, Looking Up from Base of Trench, Northeast Corner

Plan of Level XIXB, Loci 68–70 and 72

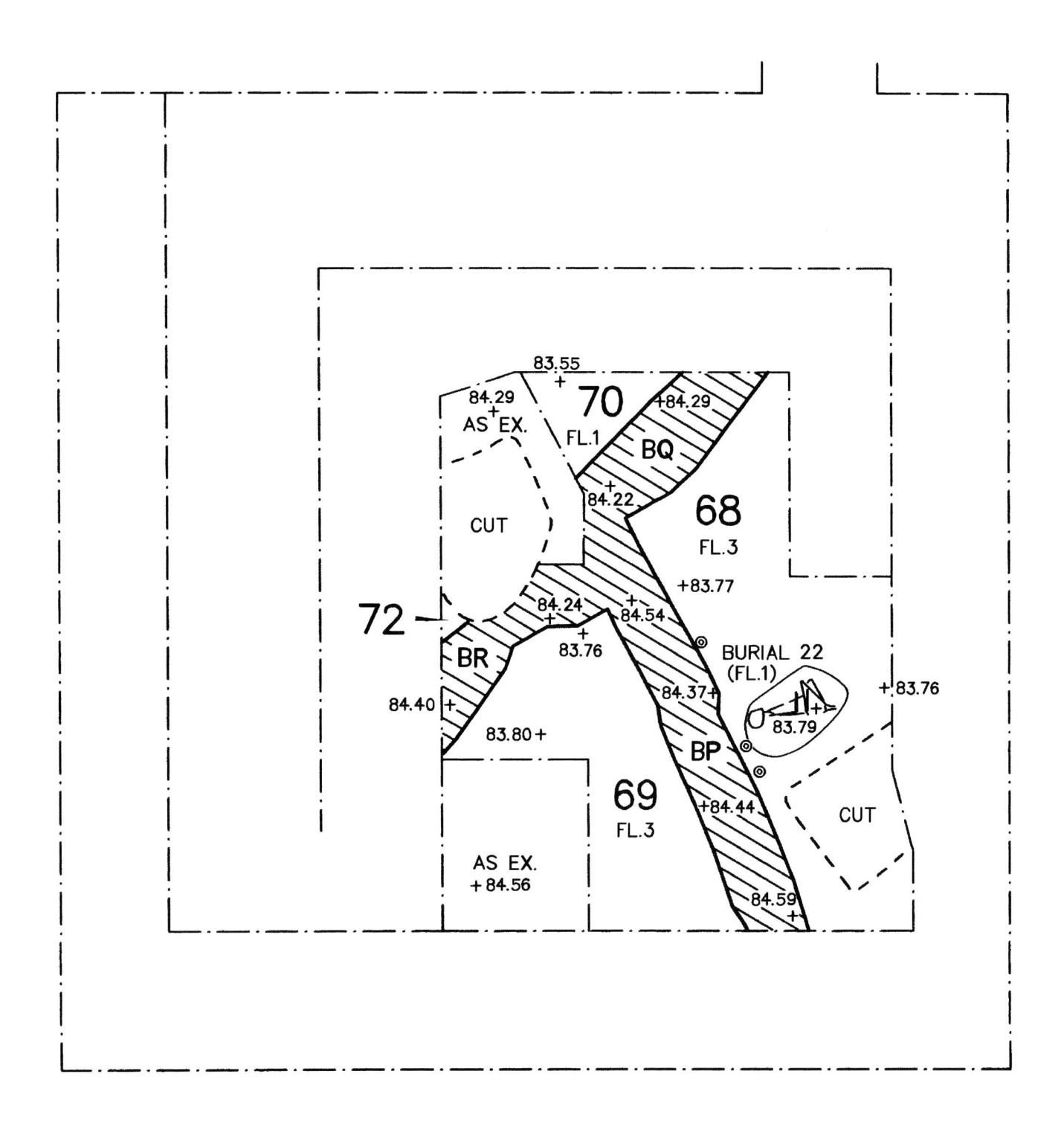

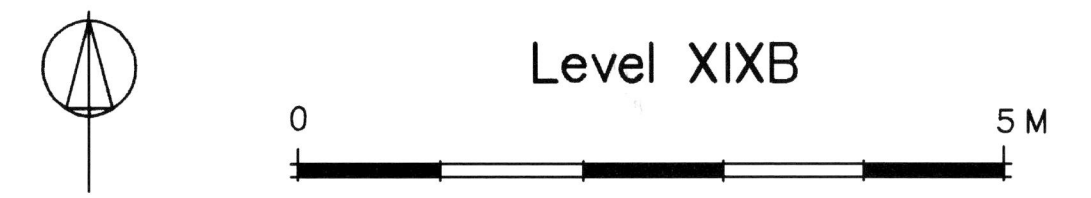

Plate 4

(*a*) Level XIXB, from Above and West (modern stairs at rear, for access), and (*b*) South End of Level XIXB and South Section, from North

Plate 5

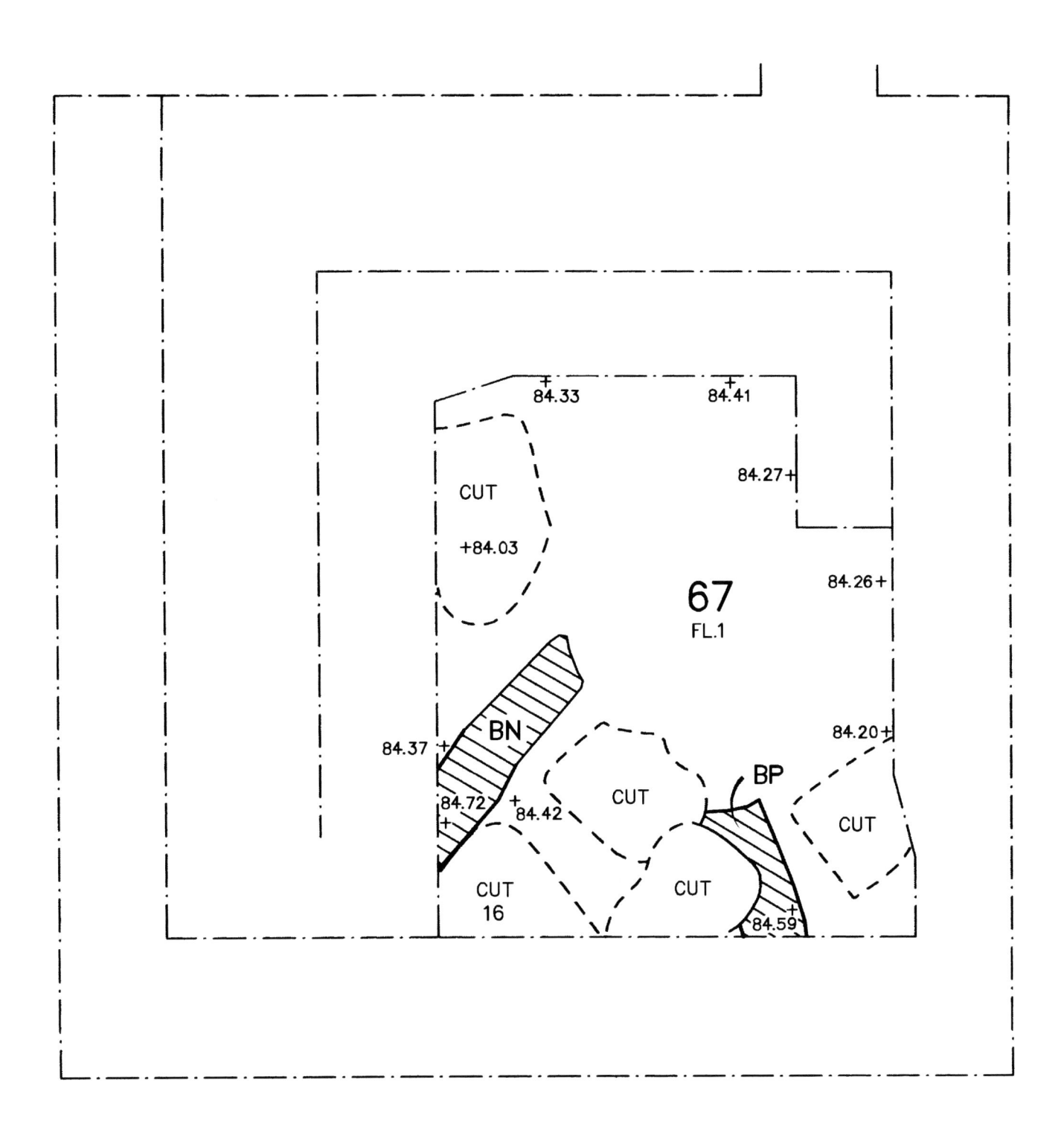

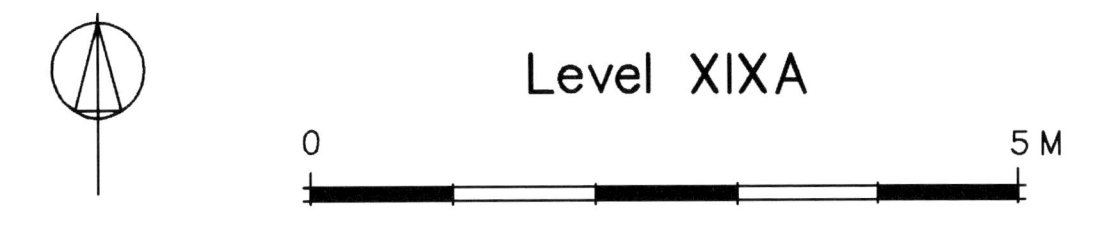

Level XIXA

Plan of Level XIXA, Locus 67

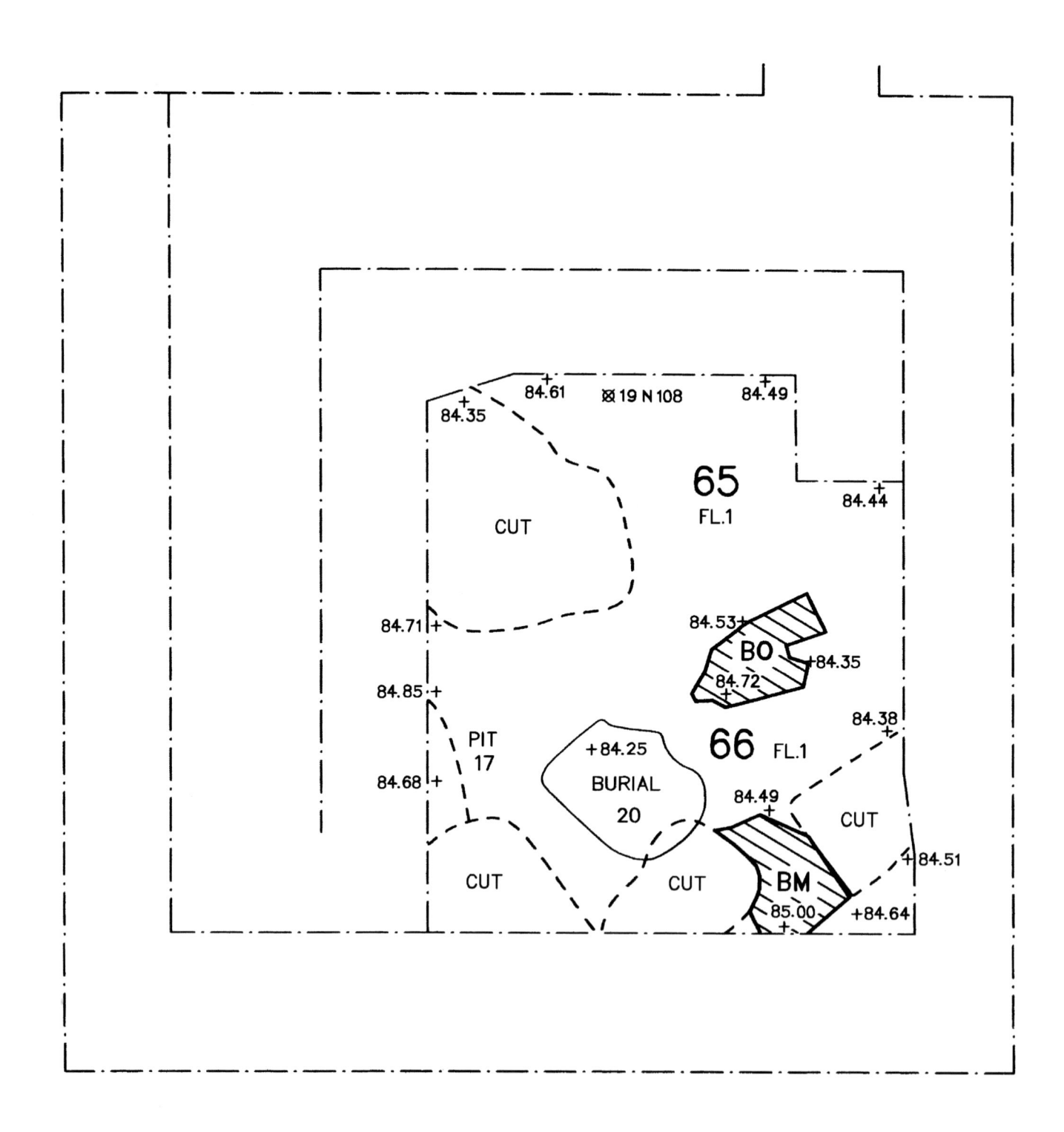

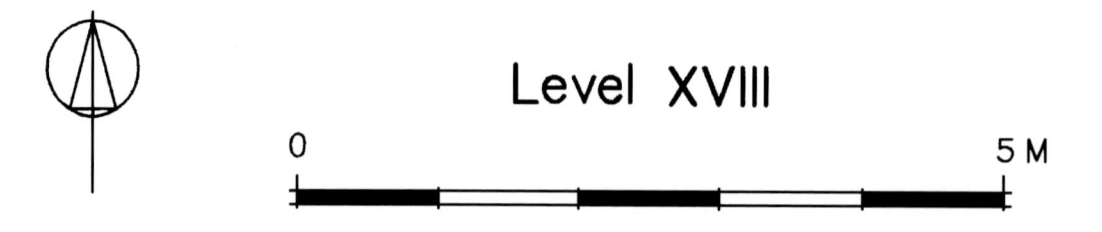

Plate 6

Level XVIII

0 5 M

Plan of Level XVIII, Loci 65–66

Plate 7

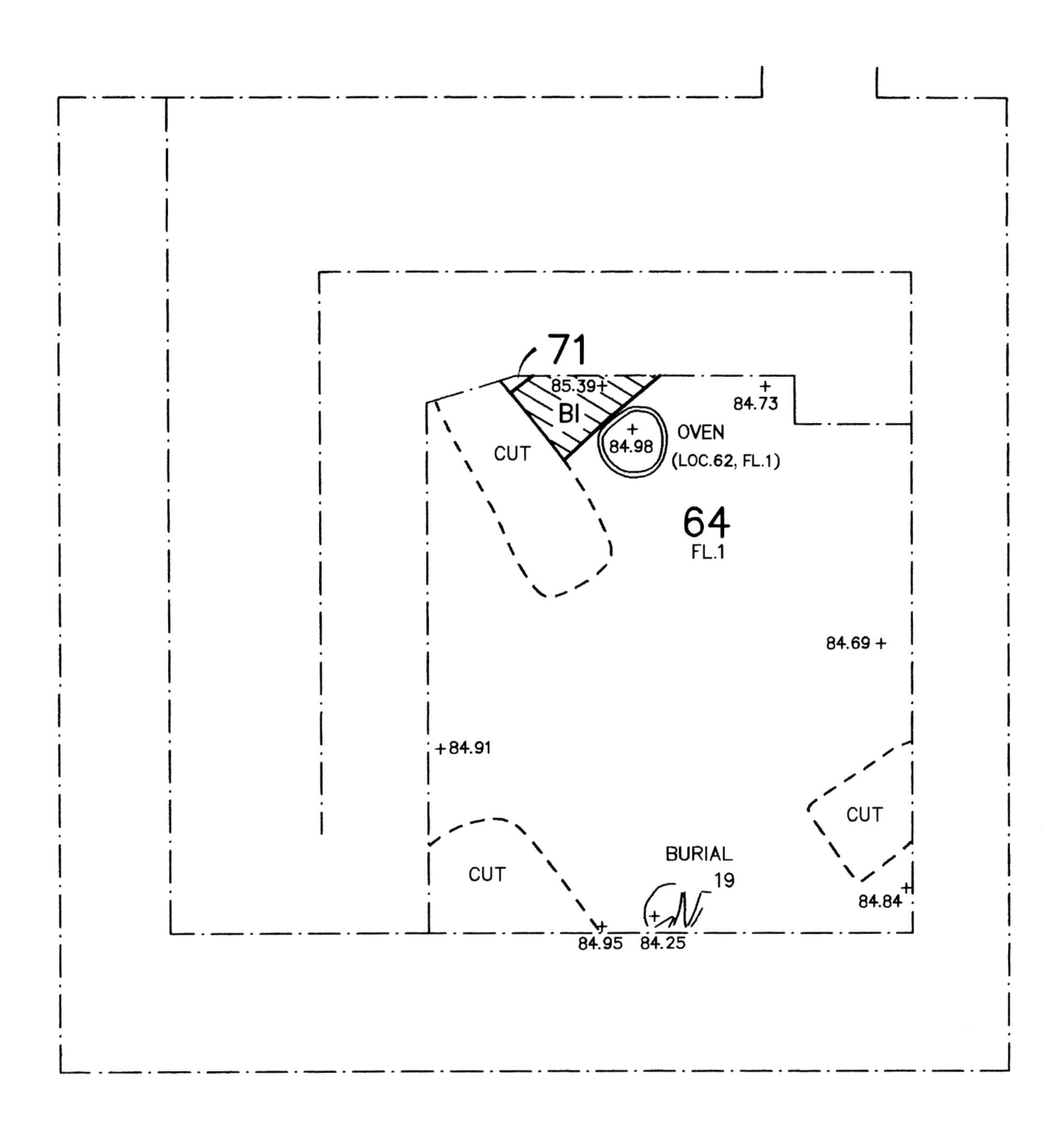

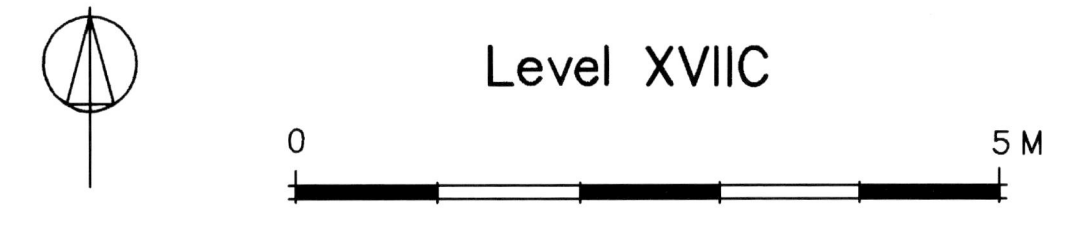

Level XVIIC

Plan of Level XVIIC, Loci 64 and 71

Plate 8

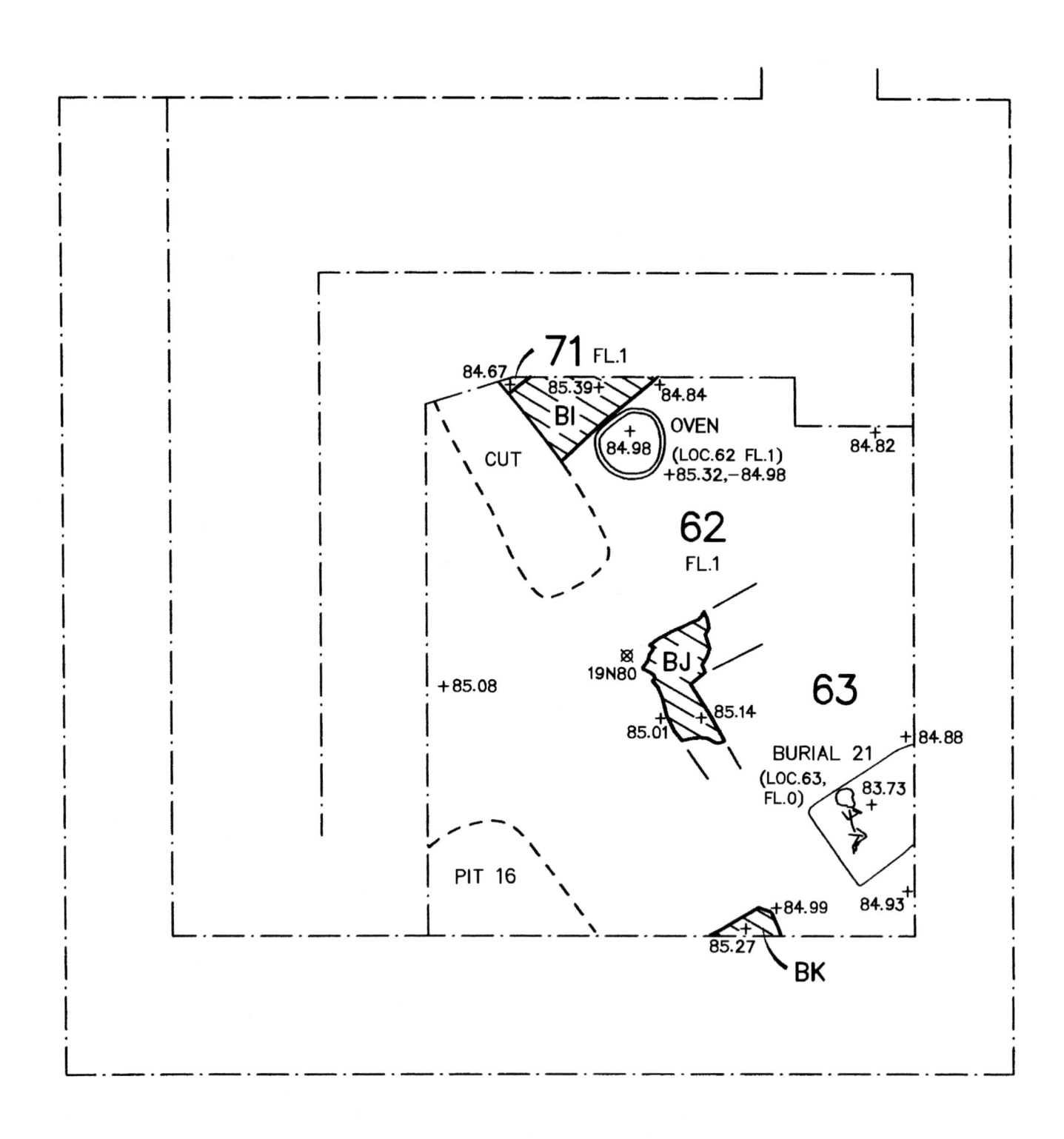

Level XVIIB

Plan of Level XVIIB, Loci 62–63 and 71

Plan of Level XVIIA, Loci 61 and 71

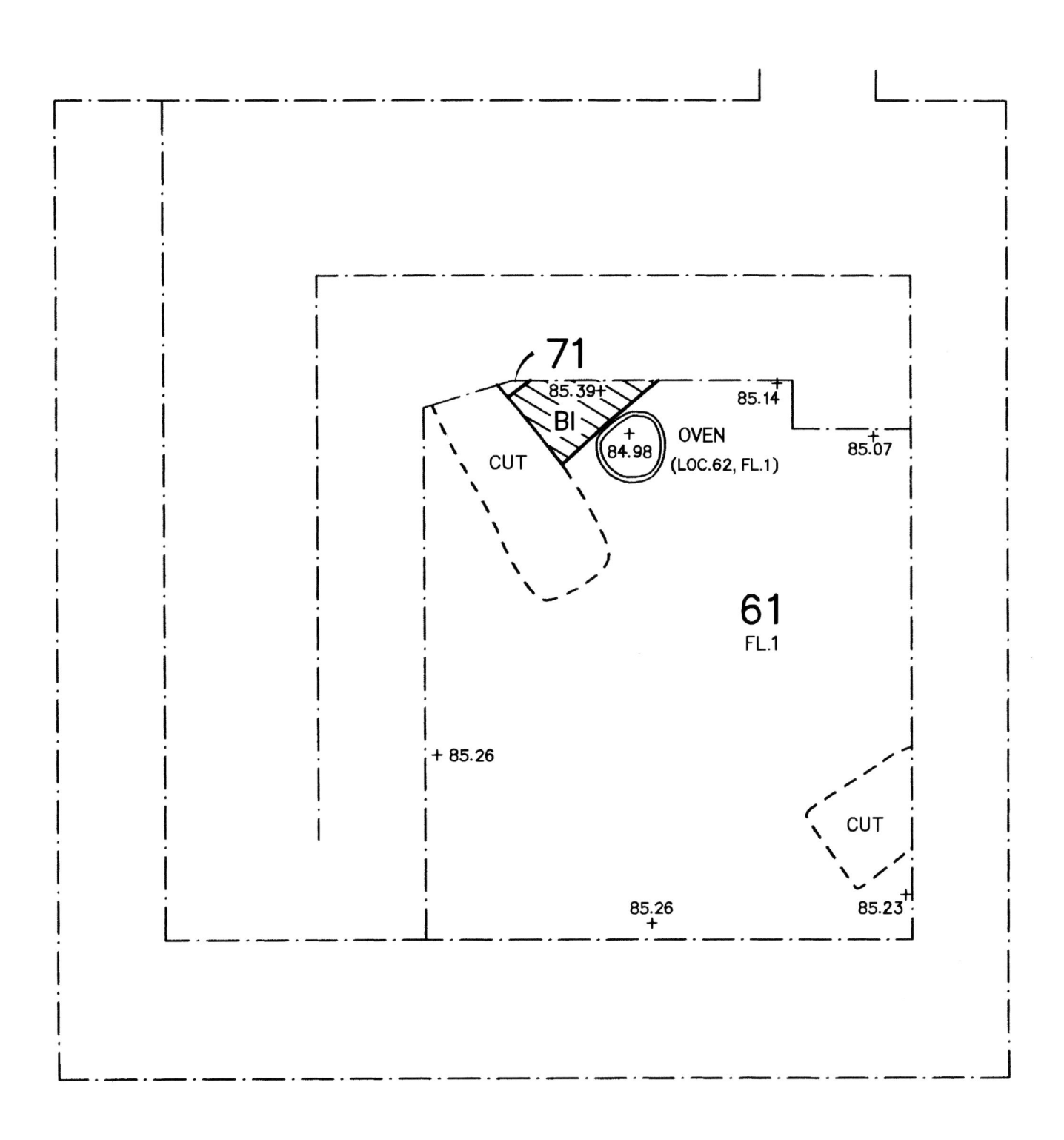

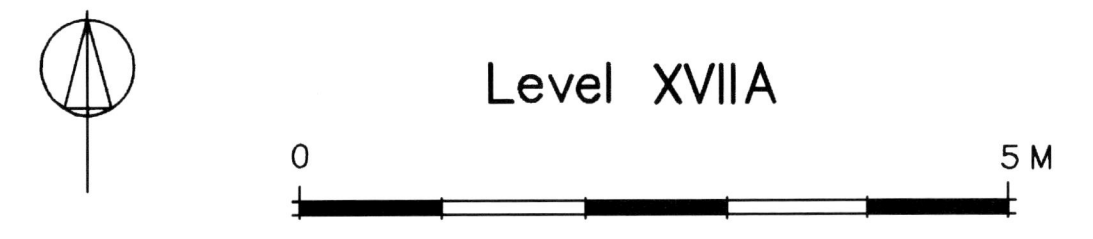

Plate 10

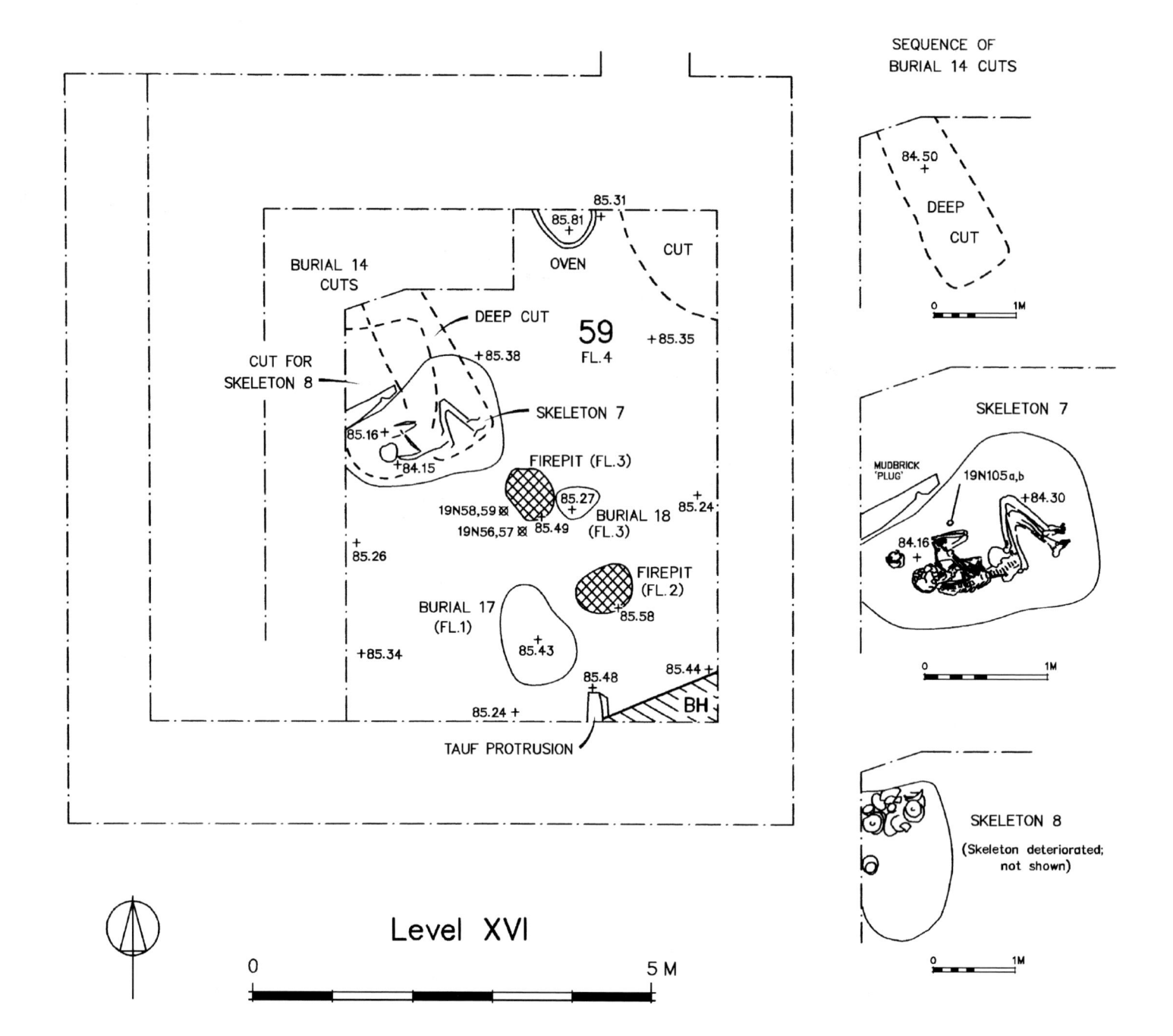

Plan of Level XVI, Locus 59

Plate 11

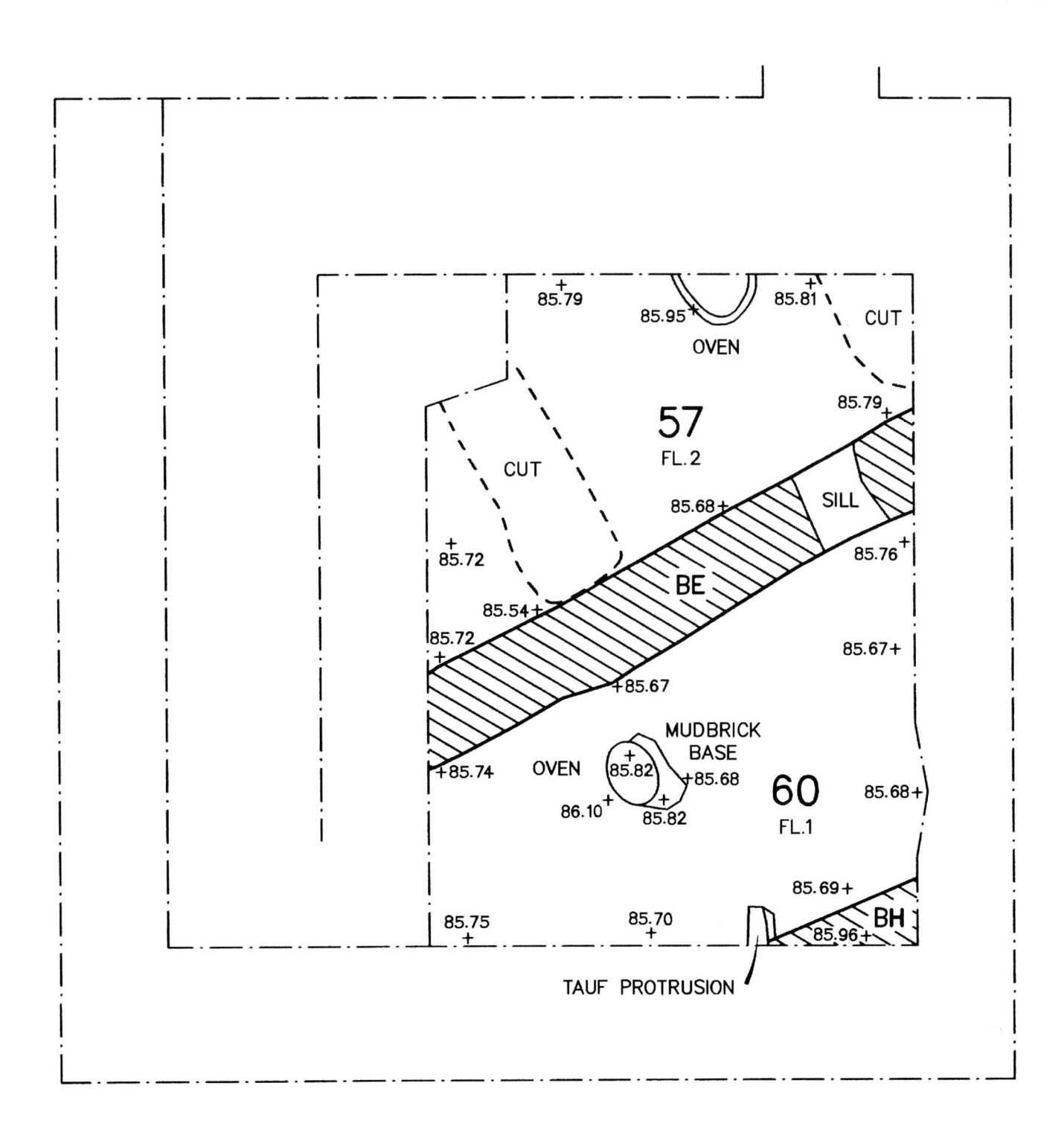

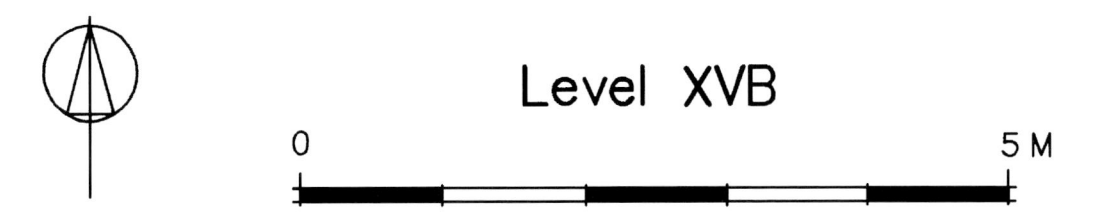

Level XVB

Plan of Level XVB, Loci 57 and 60

Plate 12

a

b

(*a*) Level XV, from Southwest, Bisected by Wall BE, Deep Shaft of Burial 14 Visible on Left, Ovens in Loci 57 (left) and 60 (right), and (*b*) Level XV and South and East Sections, from Northwest

Plate 13

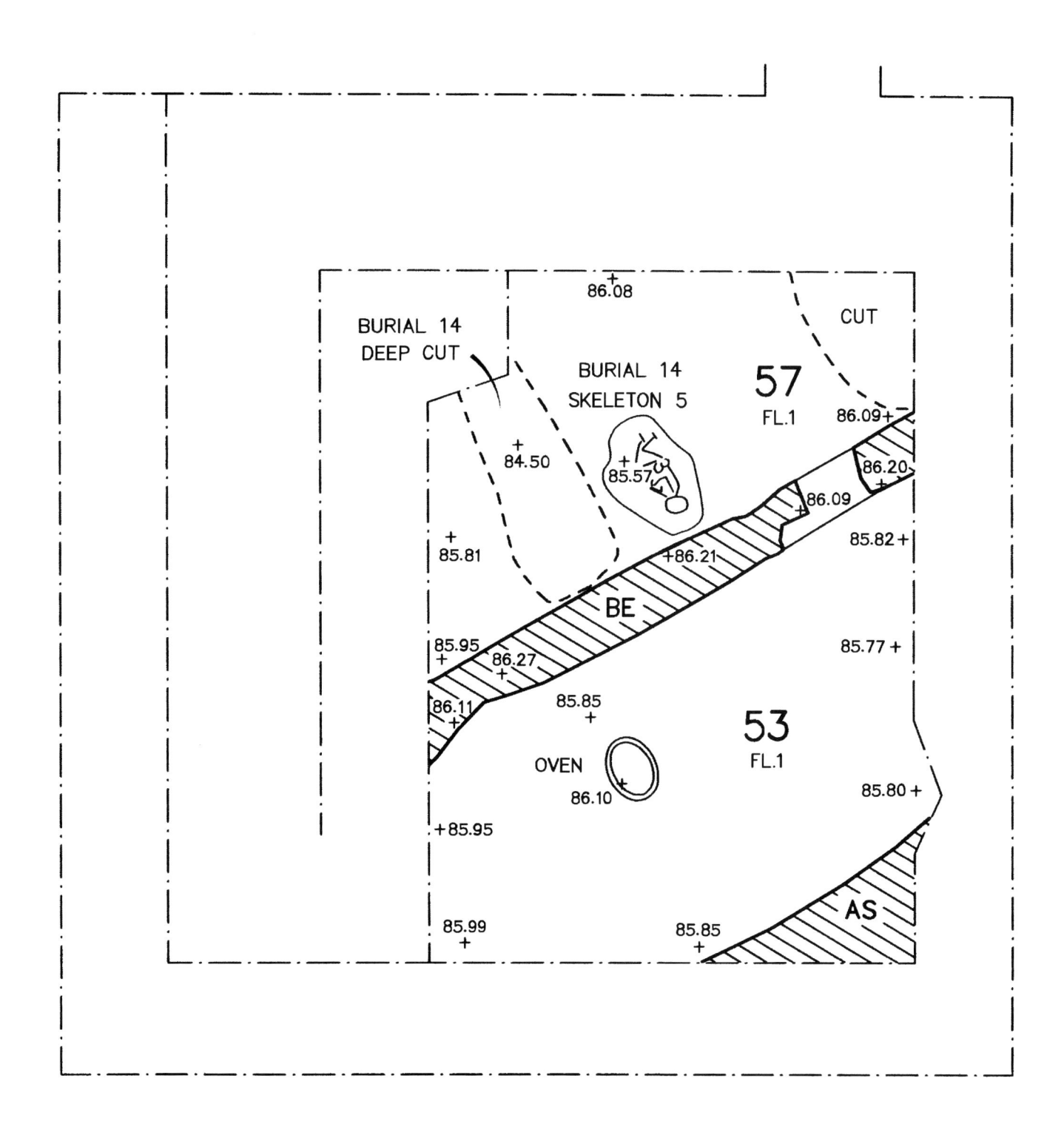

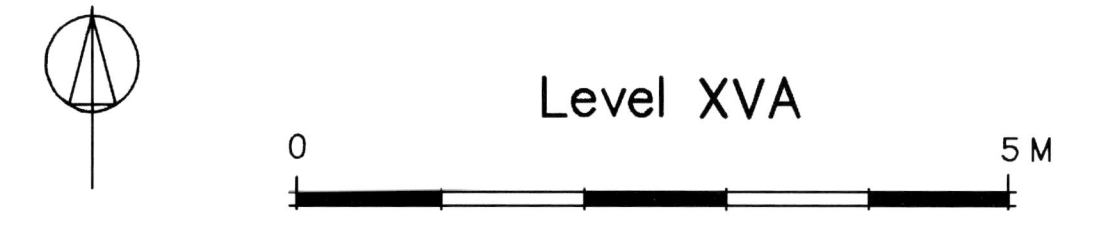

Level XVA

Plan of Level XVA, Loci 53 and 57

Plate 14

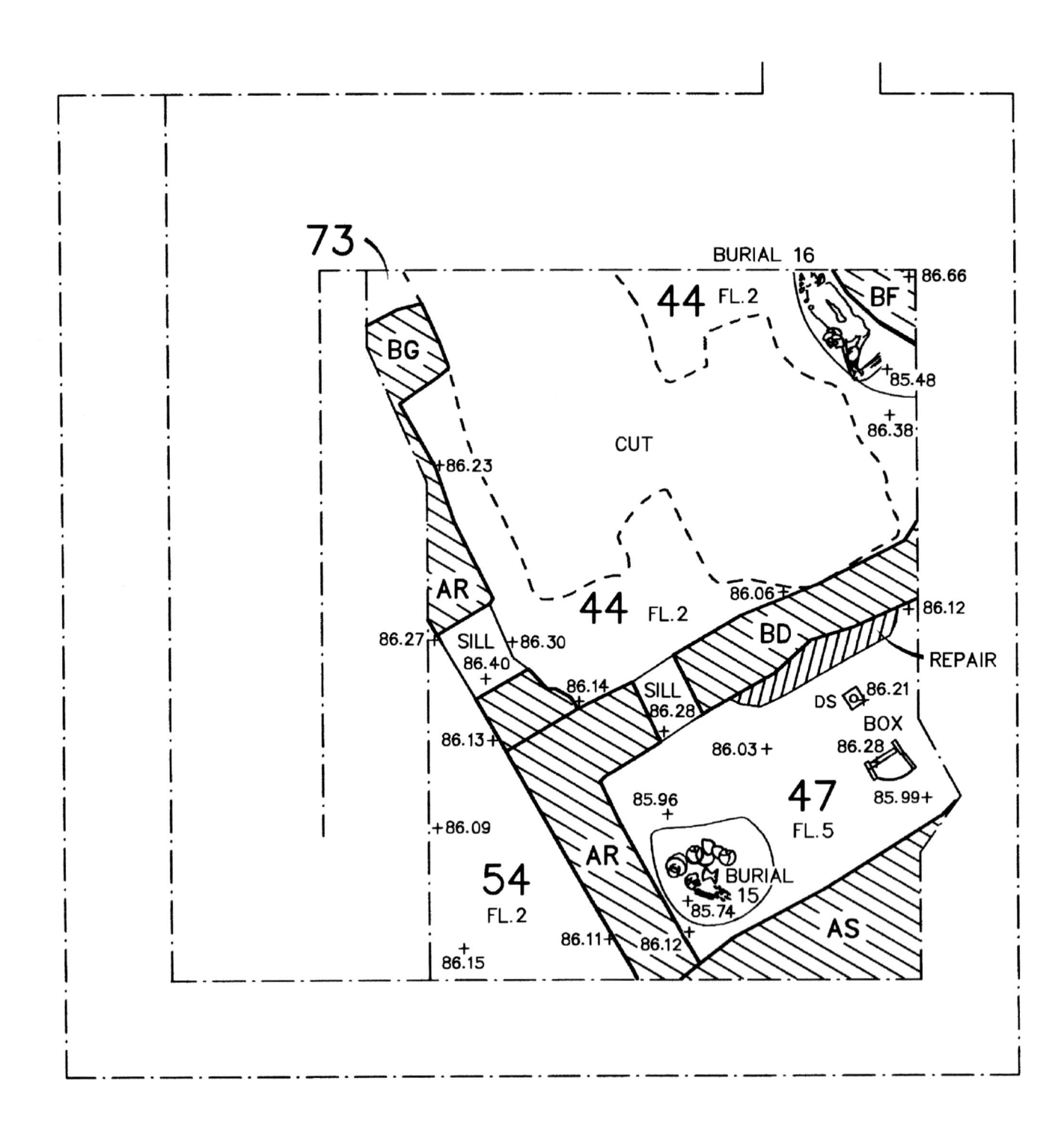

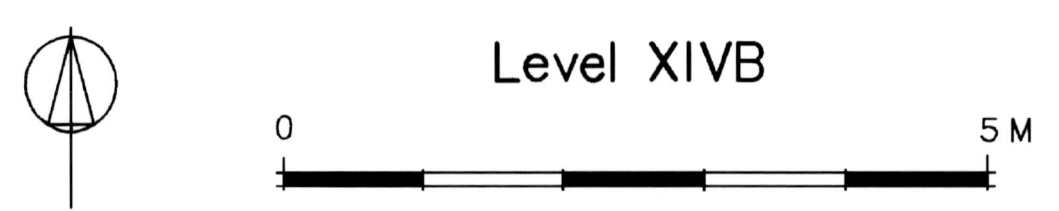

Level XIVB

Plan of Level XIVB, Loci 44, 47, 54, and 73

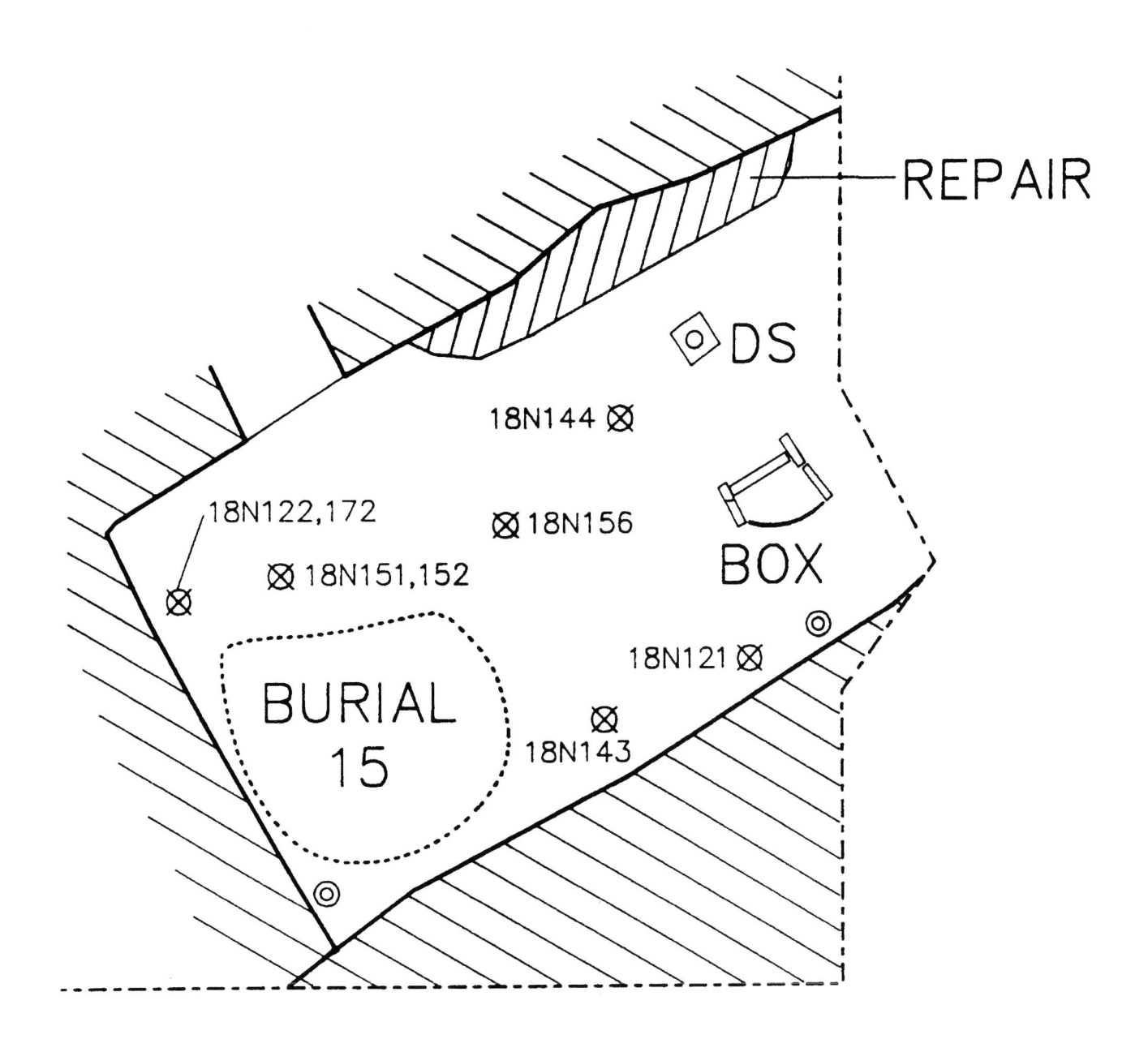

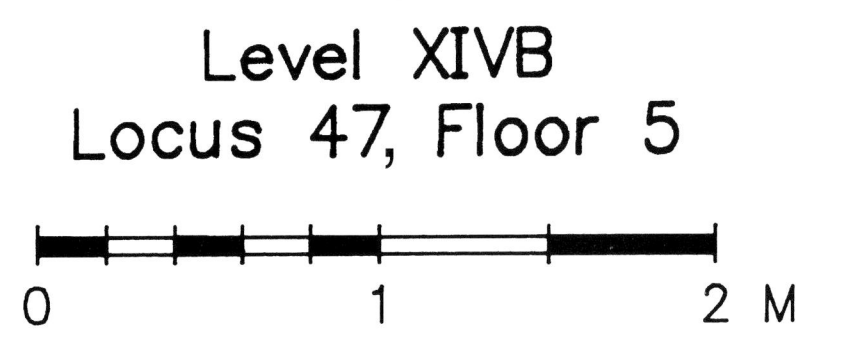

Plate 15

Level XIVB
Locus 47, Floor 5

Detailed Plan of Level XIVB, Locus 47, Objects and Features at Floor 5

Plate 16

Level XIVA

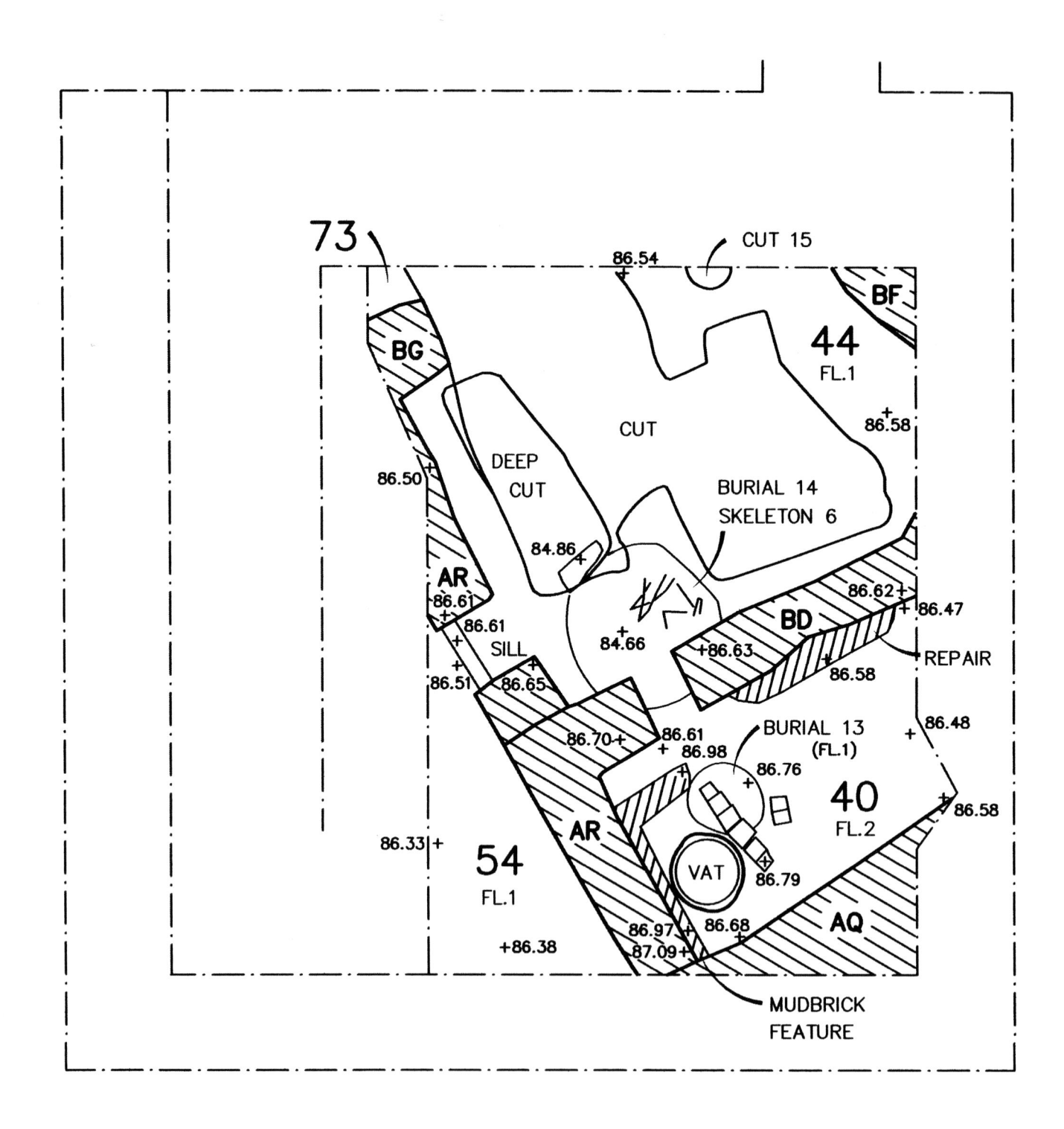

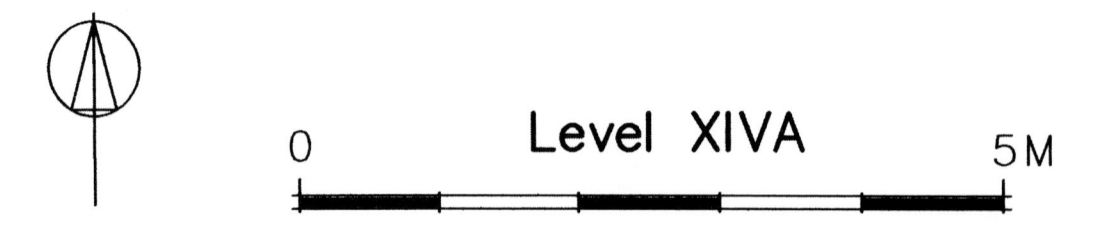

Plan of Level XIVA, Loci 40, 44, 54, and 73

Plate 17

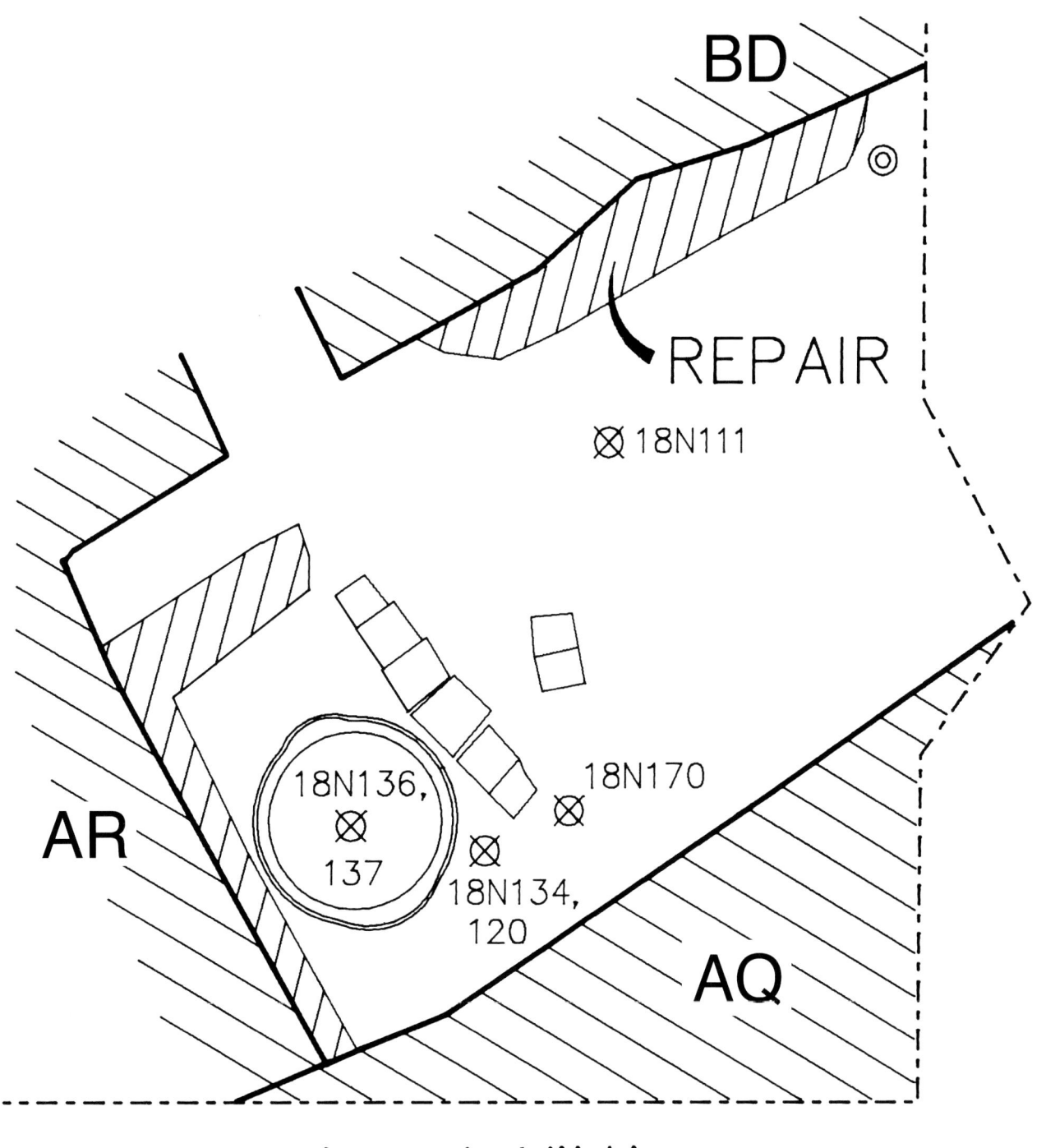

BD

REPAIR

⊗ 18N111

18N170
⊗

AR

18N136,
⊗
137

⊗
18N134,
120

AQ

Level XIVA
Locus 40, Floor 2

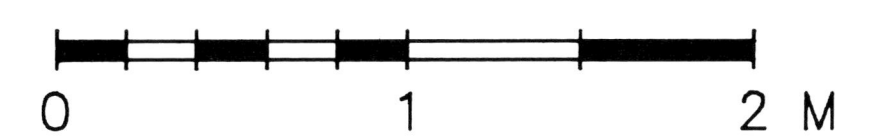

0    1    2 M

Detailed Plan of Level XIVA, Locus 40, Objects and Features at Floor 2

Plate 18

(*a*) Level XIVA, Locus 40, Detail of Western End of Room with Vat and Mudbrick Feature, Bowl Inverted over Cup at Center of Vat, and (*b*) Level XIVA, Locus 40, Northwest Corner of Room with Foundation Deposit Bowls at Floor 1

Plate 19

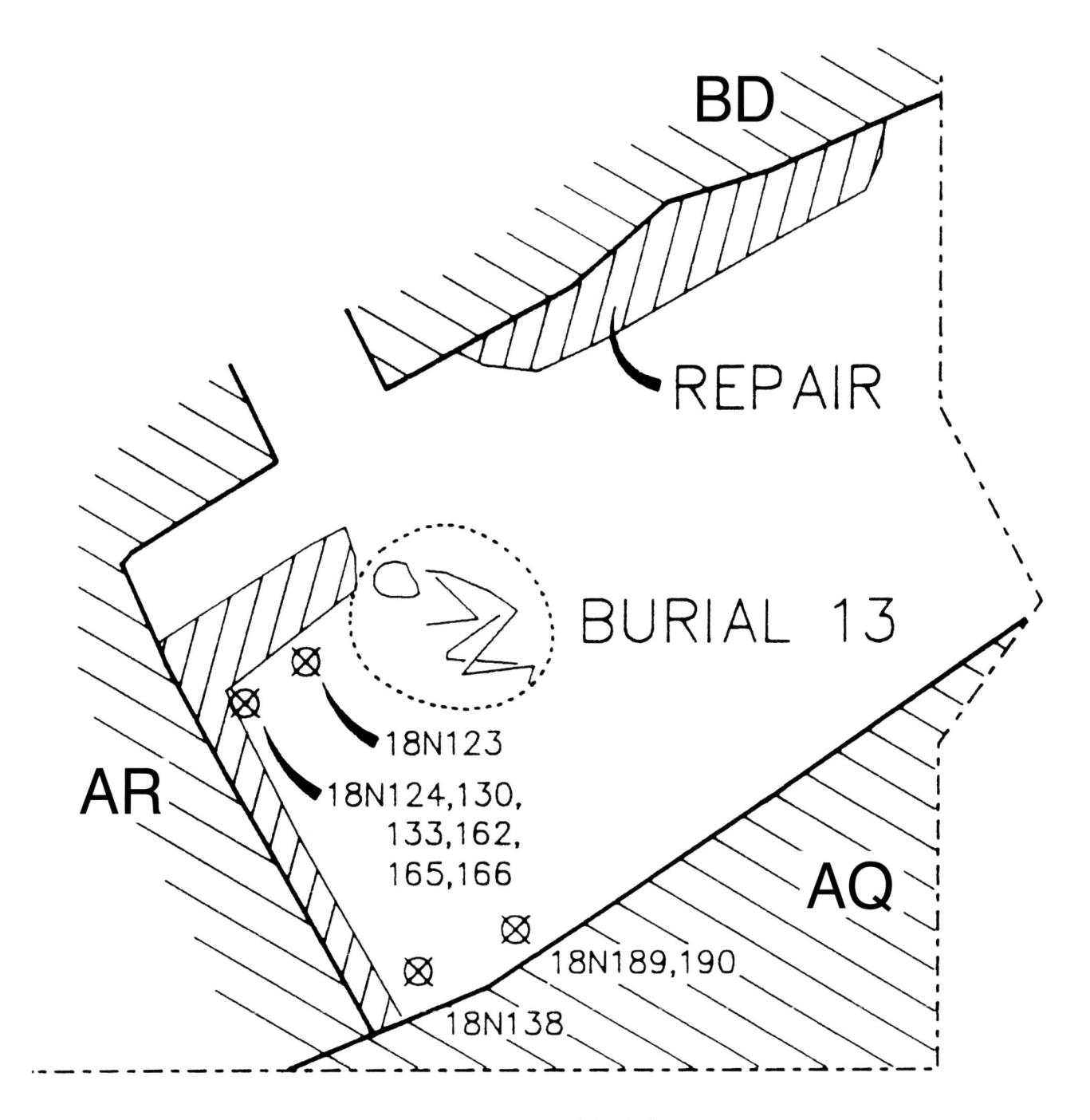

Level XIVA
Locus 40, Floor 1

Detailed Plan of Level XIVA, Locus 40, Objects and Features at Floor 1

Plate 20

*a*

*b*

(*a*) Detail of Superimposed Walls AS, AQ, and AM in Southeast Corner, and (*b*) Detail of East End of Locus 40, Superimposed Floors and Baked-brick Box Below Floor 4 of Level XIV

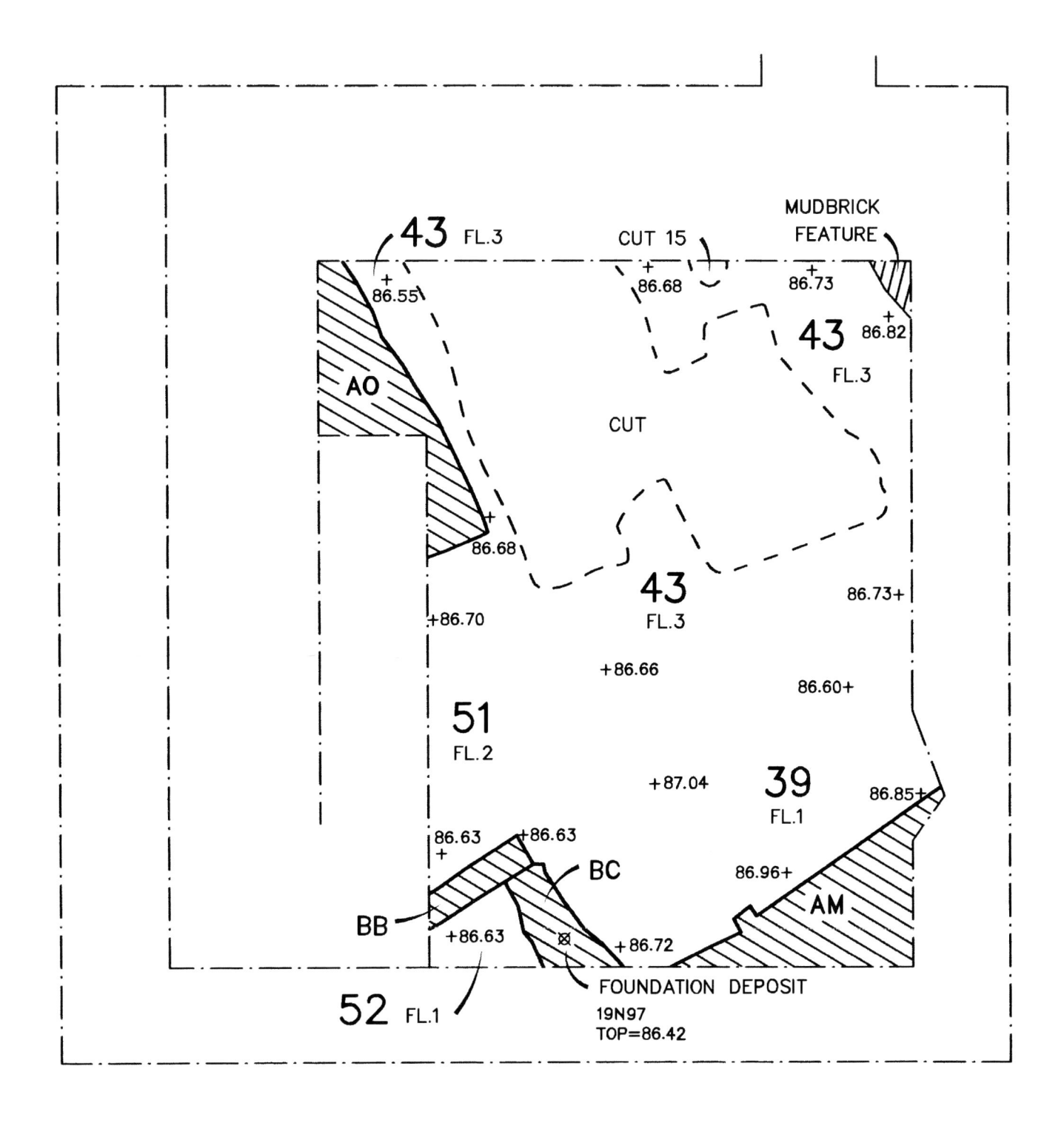

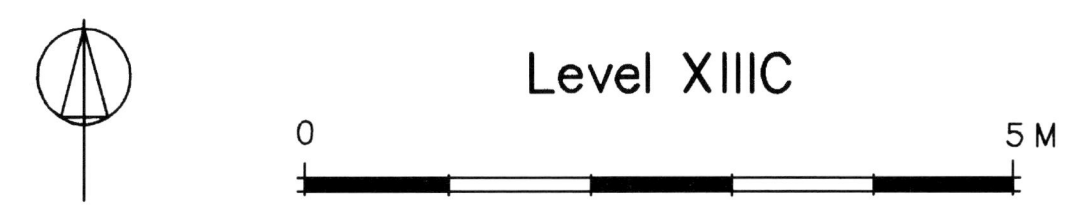

Plate 21

Level XIIIC

0    5 M

Plan of Level XIIIC, Loci 39, 43, and 51–52

Plate 22

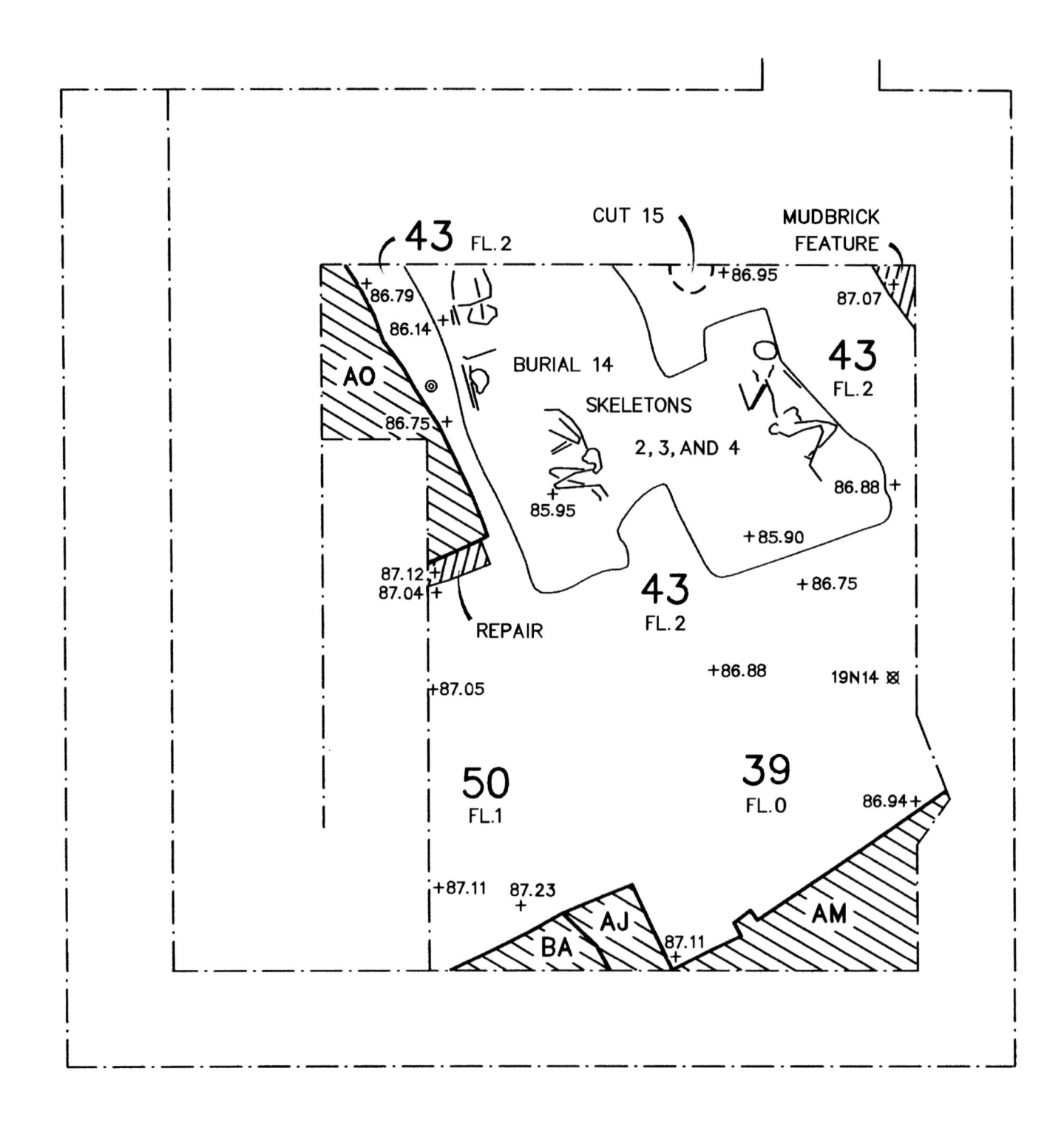

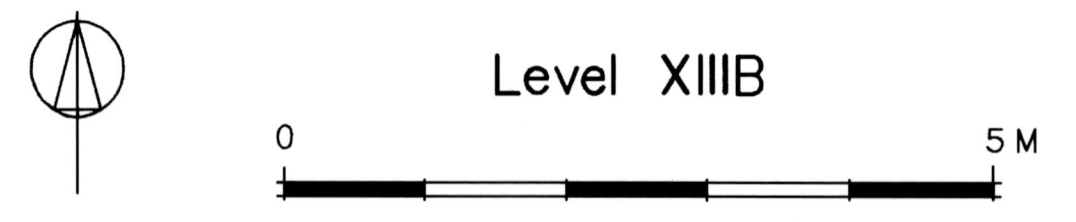

Level XIIIB

Plan of Level XIIIB, Loci 39, 43, and 50

Plate 23

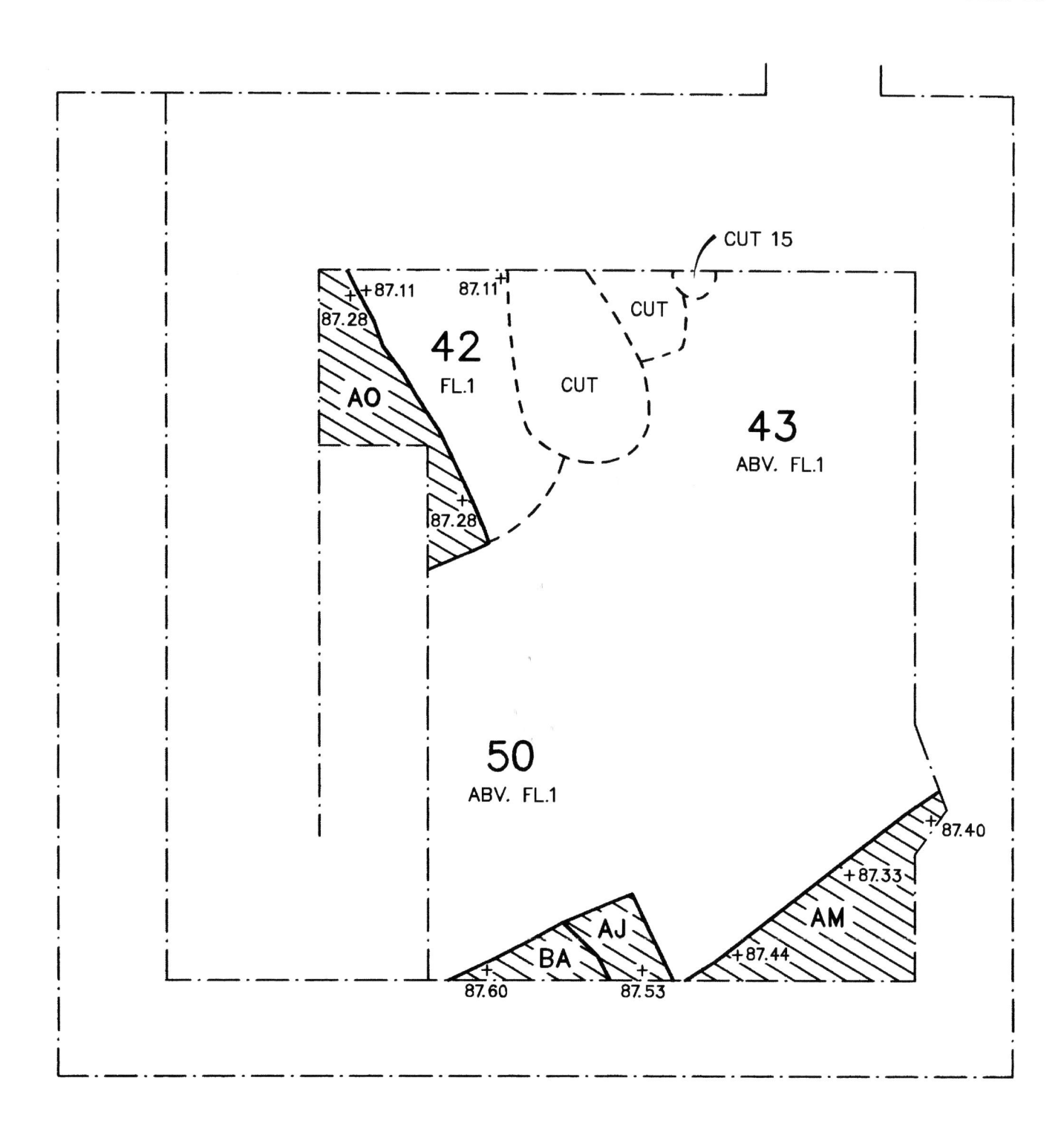

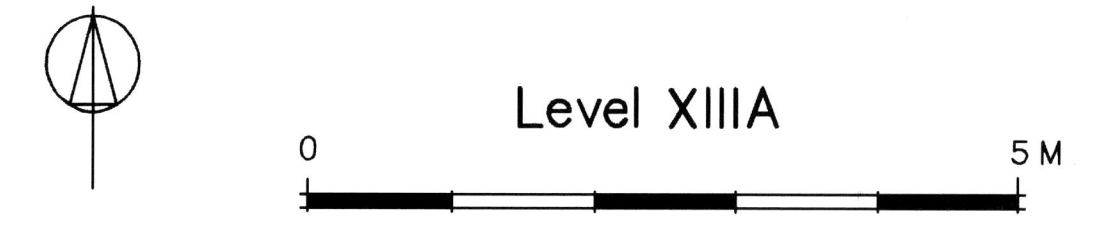

Level XIIIA

Plan of Level XIIIA, Loci 42–43 and 50

Plate 24

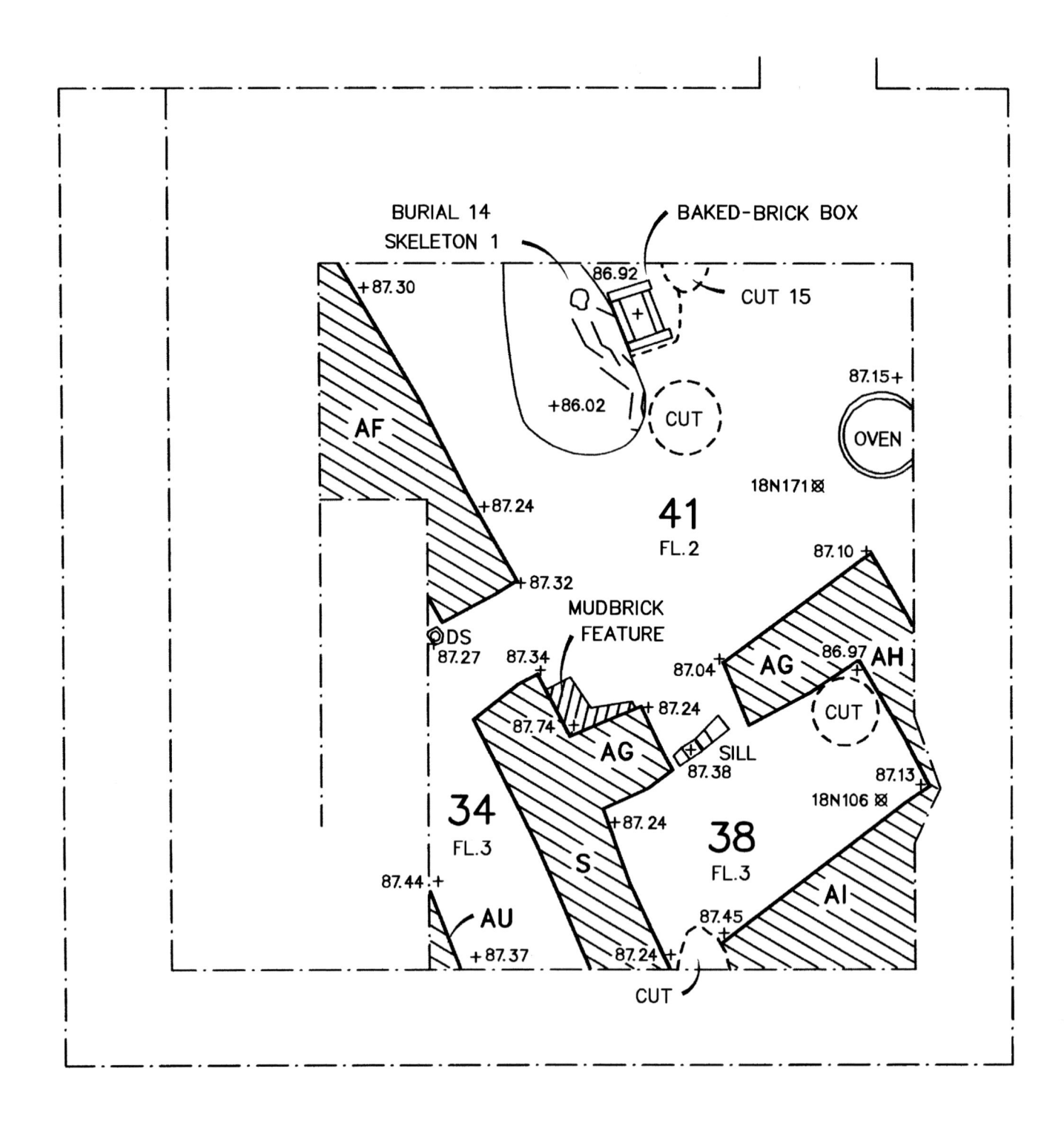

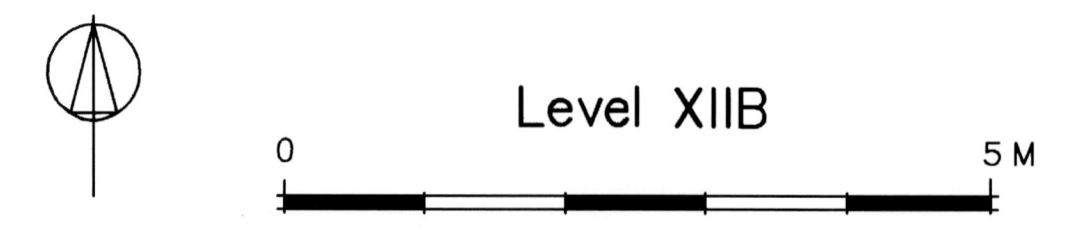

Level XIIB

Plan of Level XIIB, Loci 34, 38, and 41

Plate 25

(*a*) Level XIIB, Wall AG Leaning Outward into Courtyard Locus 41, Buttress at Corner of Walls AG and S, from East-Northeast (modern stairs at right); and (*b*) Level XIIB, from Above and Northwest

Plate 26

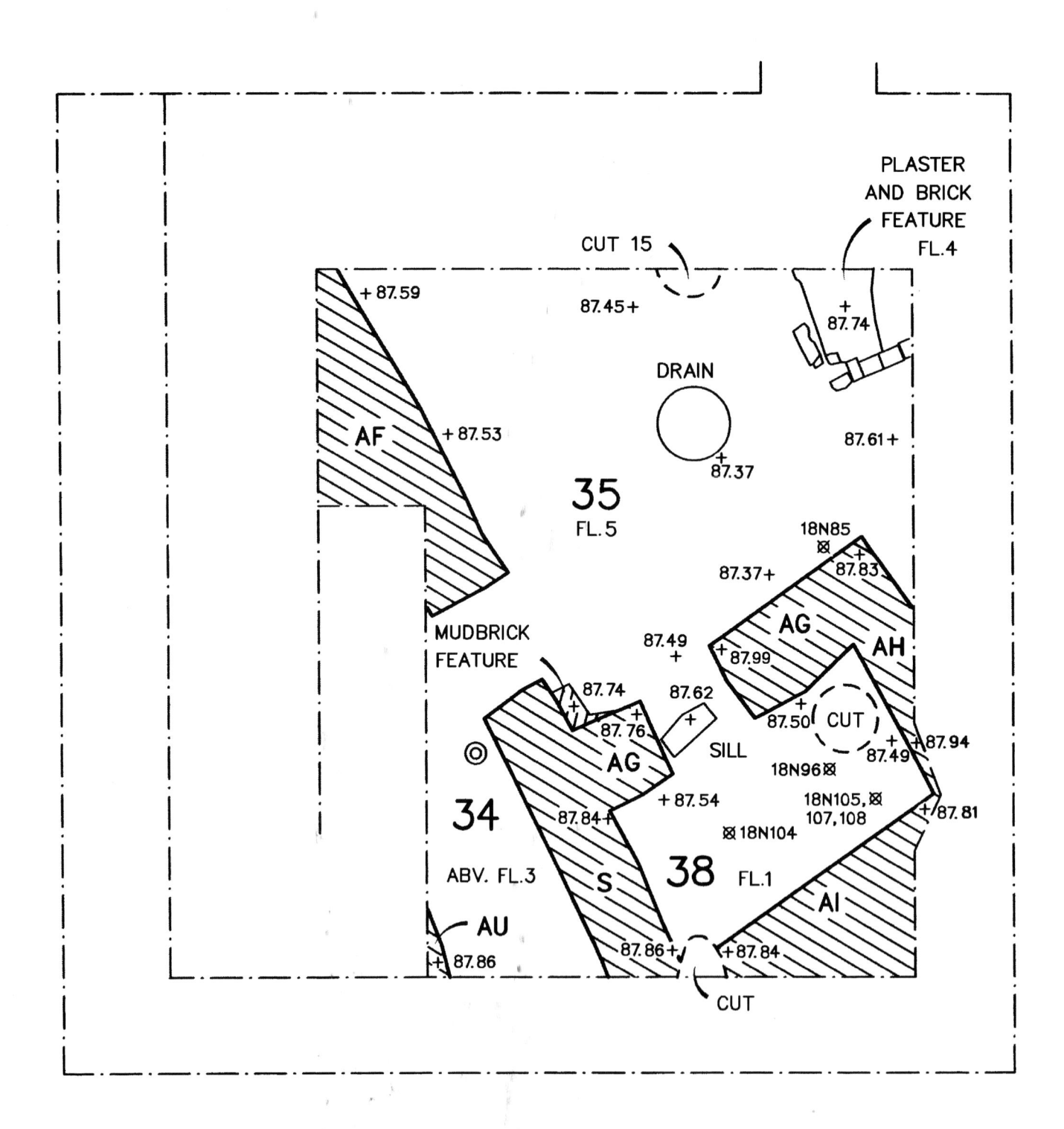

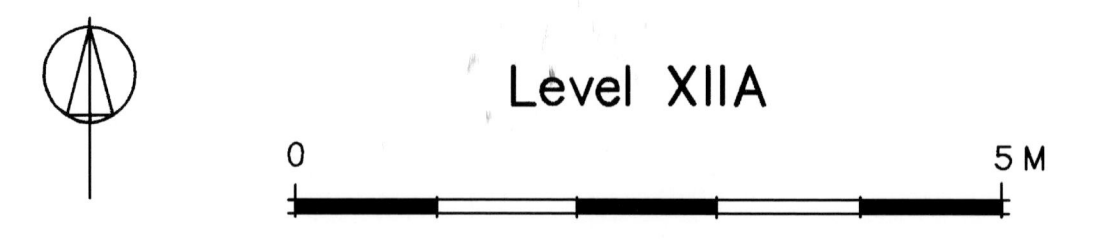

Plan of Level XIIA, Loci 34–35 and 38

Plate 27

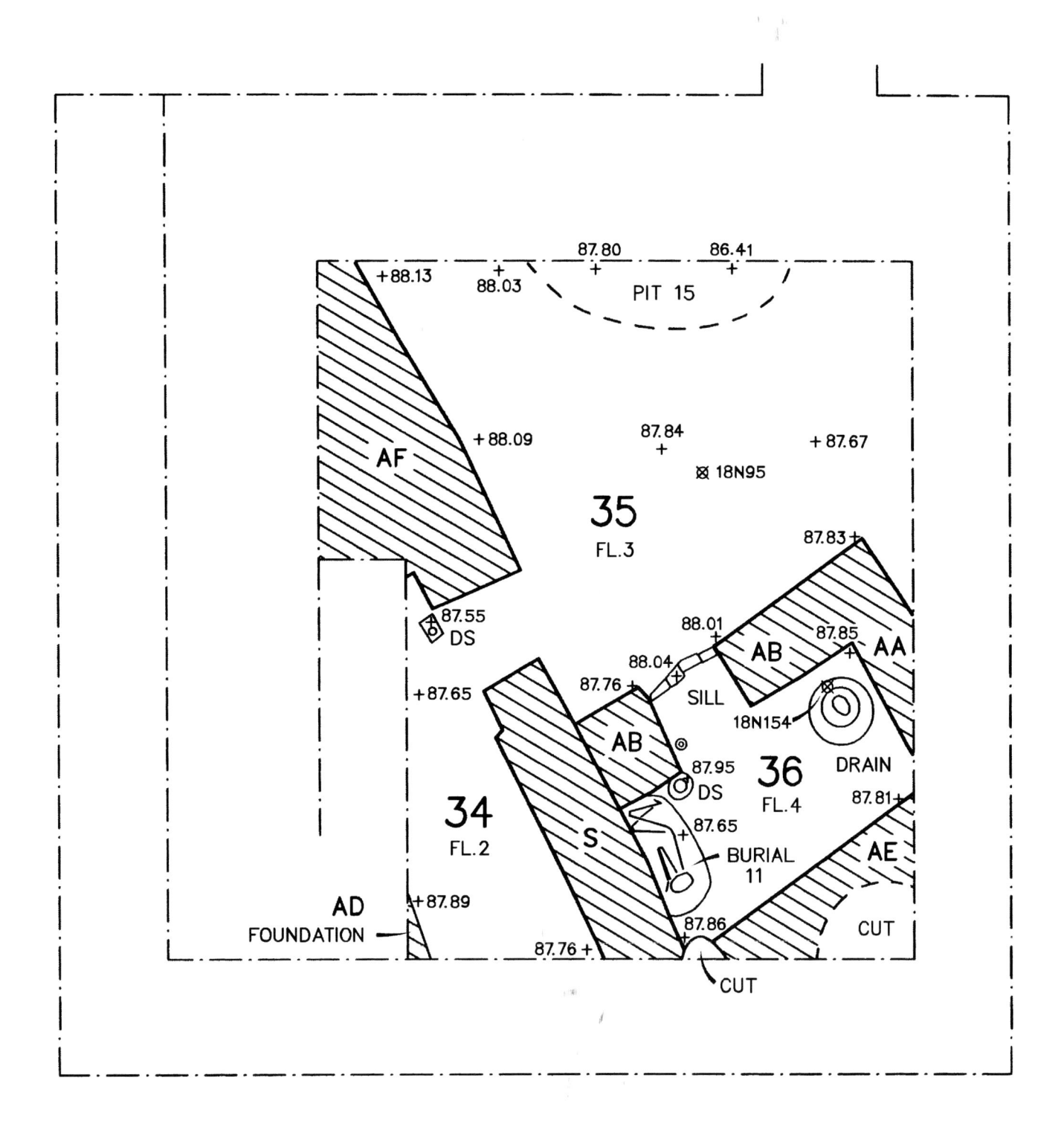

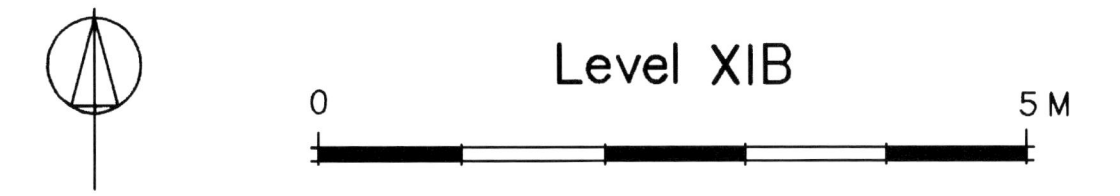

Level XIB

Plan of Level XIB, Loci 34–36

Plate 28

(*a*) Level XIB, Toilet in Locus 36, Upper Vat Partly Removed to Show Details of Construction, and (*b*) Level XIA, Upper Part of Equid Skeleton in Locus 34

Plate 29

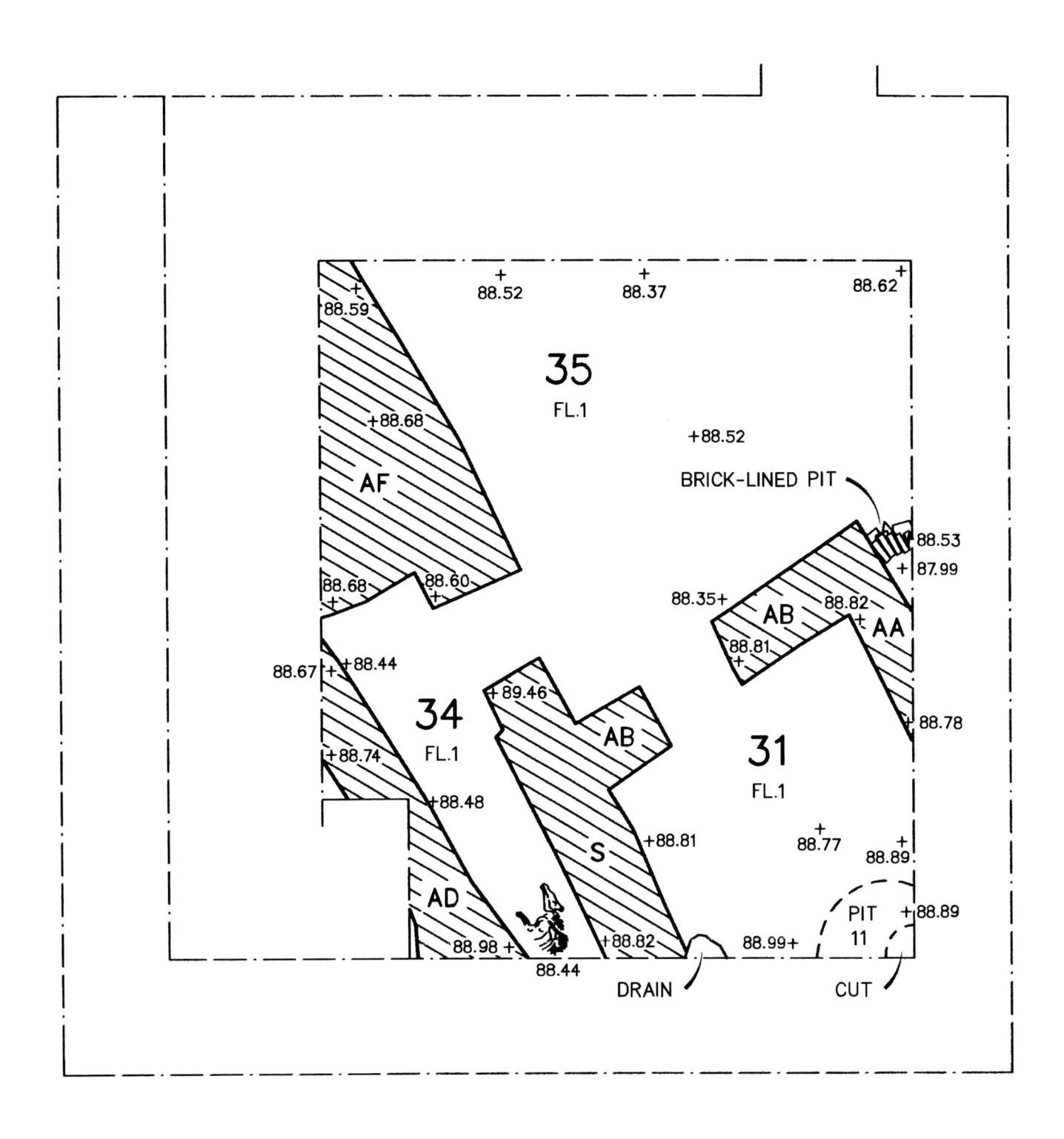

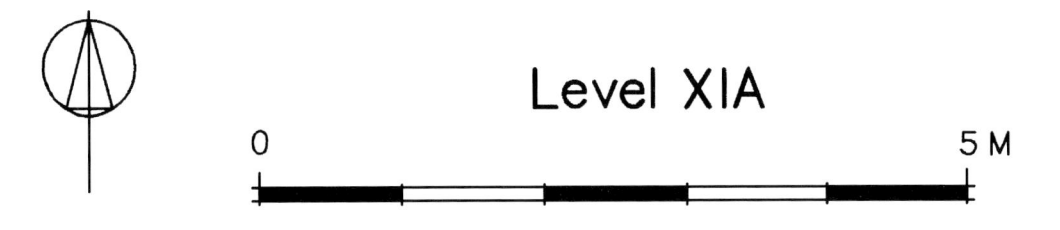

Level XIA

Plan of Level XIA, Loci 31 and 34–35

Plate 30

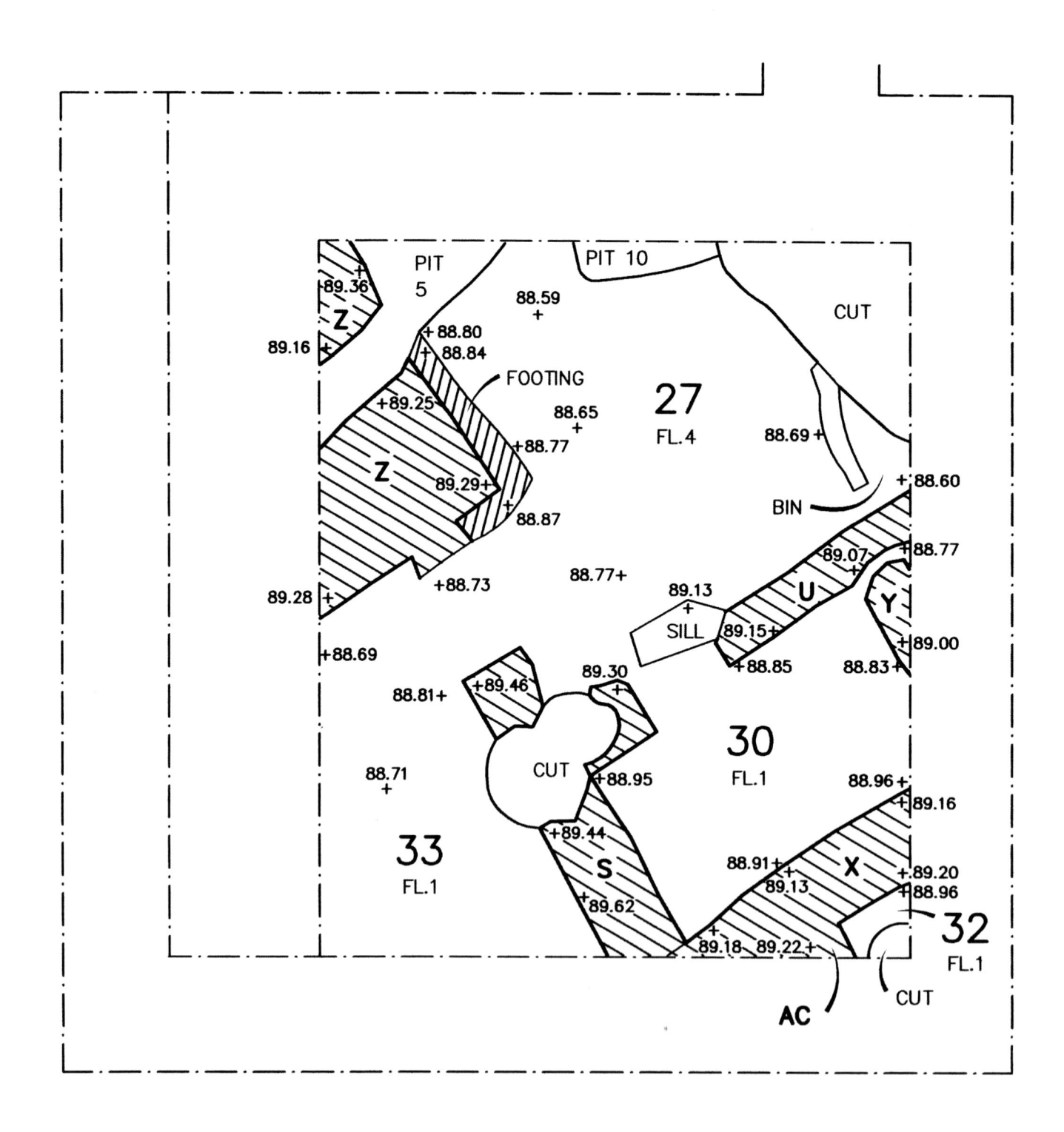

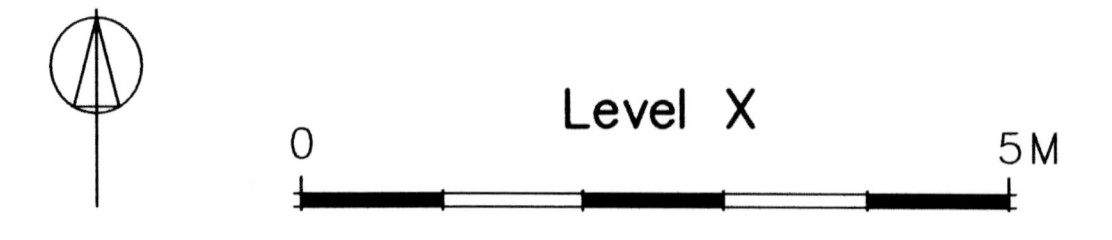

Plan of Level X, Loci 27, 30, and 32–33

Plate 31

(*a*) Level X, from Above and South, with Deeper Excavation into Earlier Levels in Lower Right and Pedestal of Unexcavated Material at Upper Right (later removed), and (*b*) Level X, from Northeast, Showing Detail of Footing at Base of Wall Z on Right and Damage Done to Junction of Walls S and U by Later Burial on Left

Plate 32

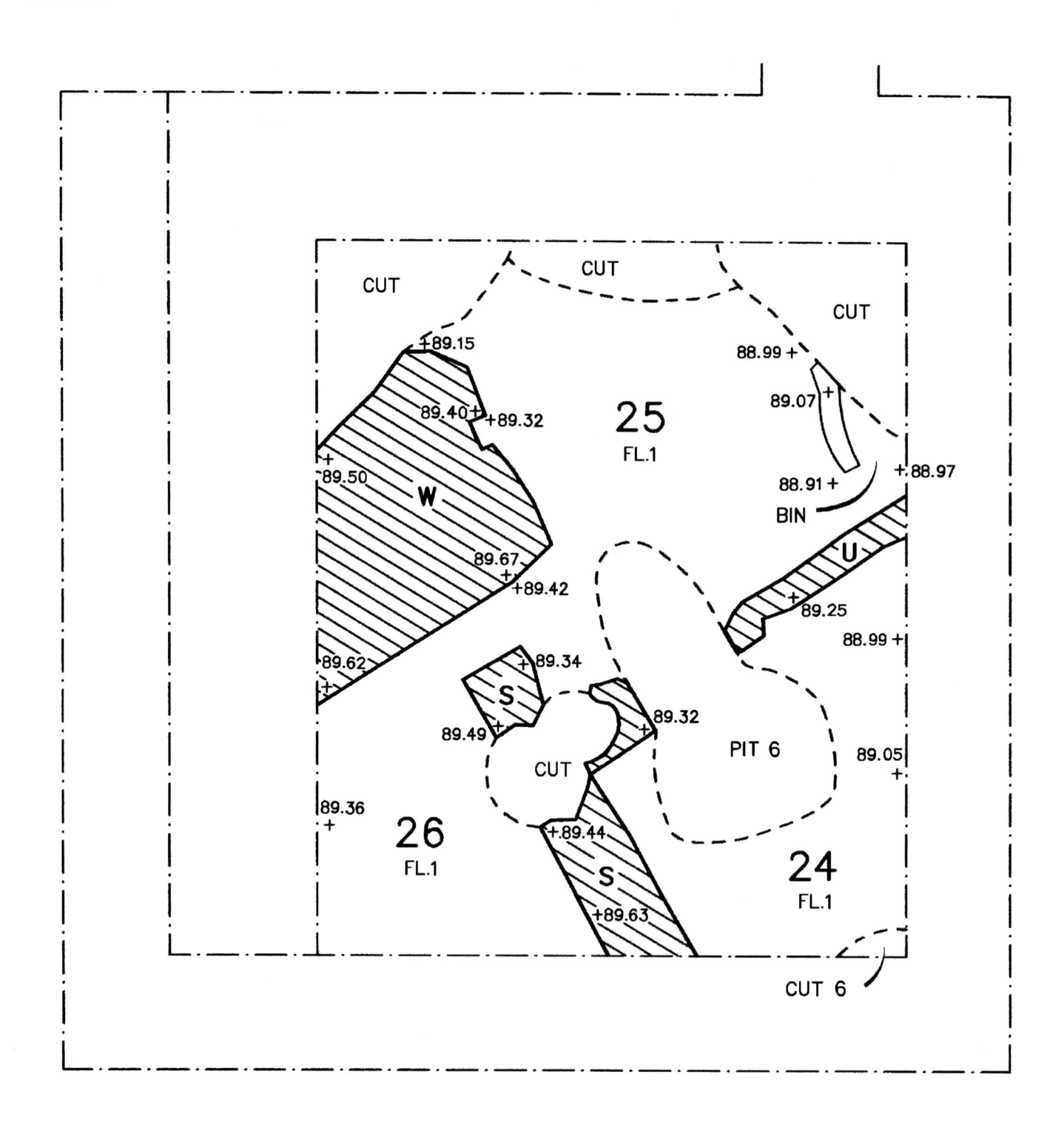

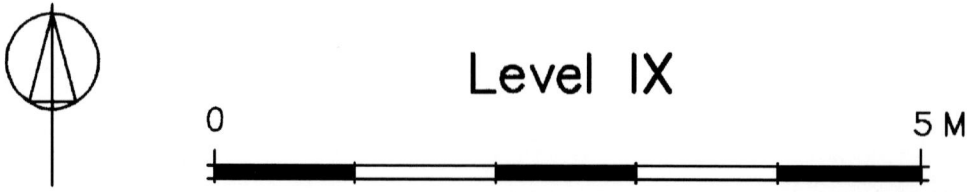

Plan of Level IX, Loci 24–26

Plate 33

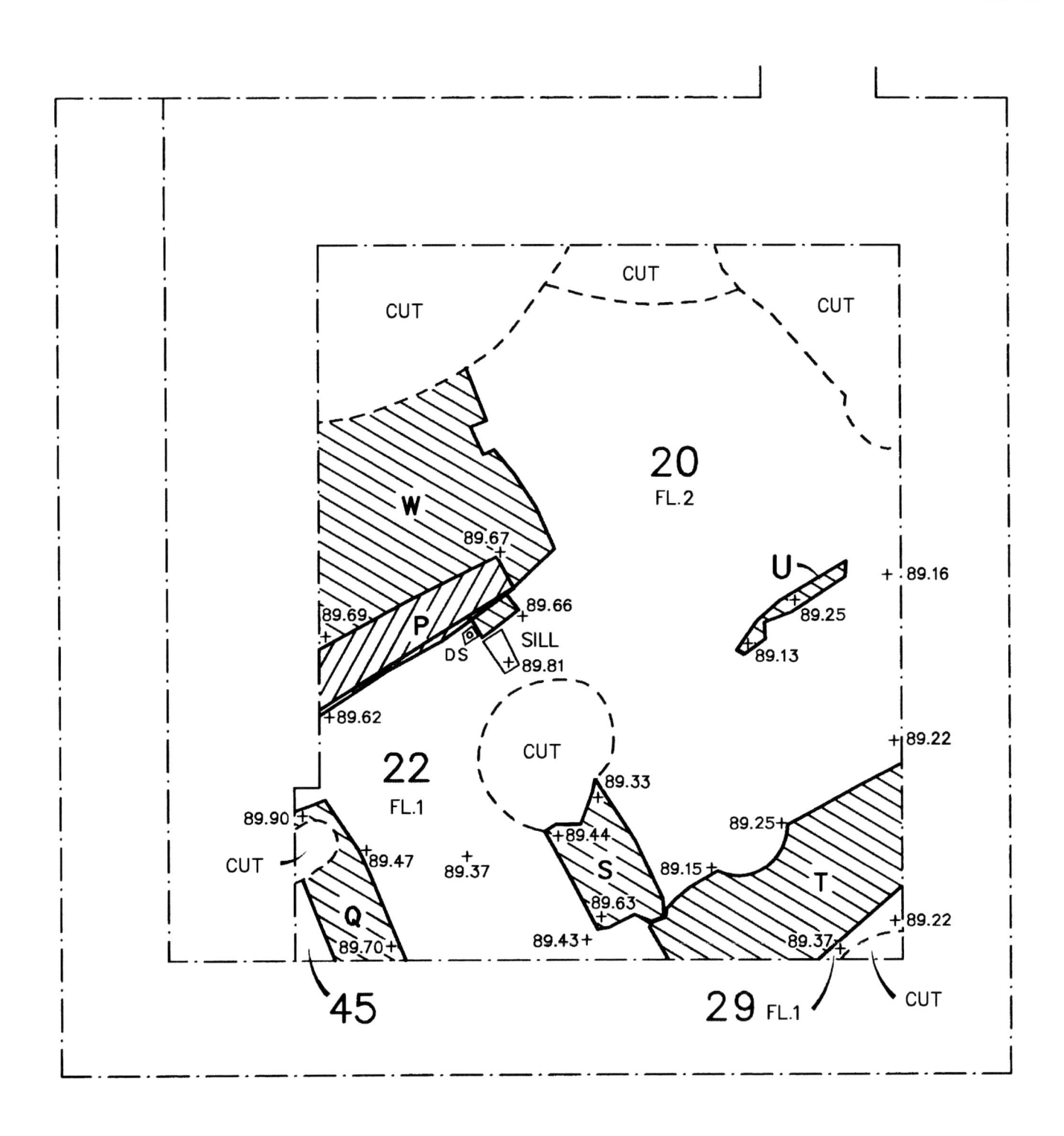

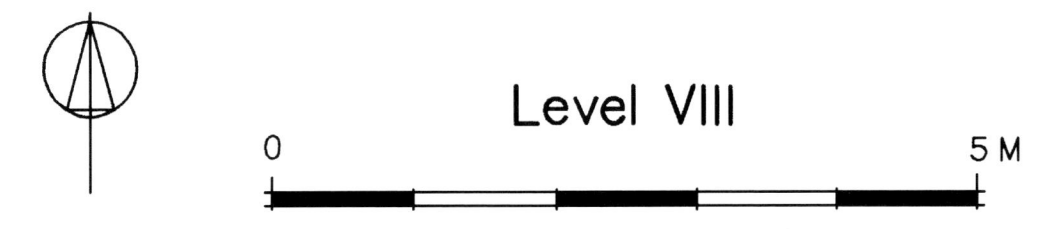

Level VIII

Plan of Level VIII, 20, 22, 29, and 45

Plate 34

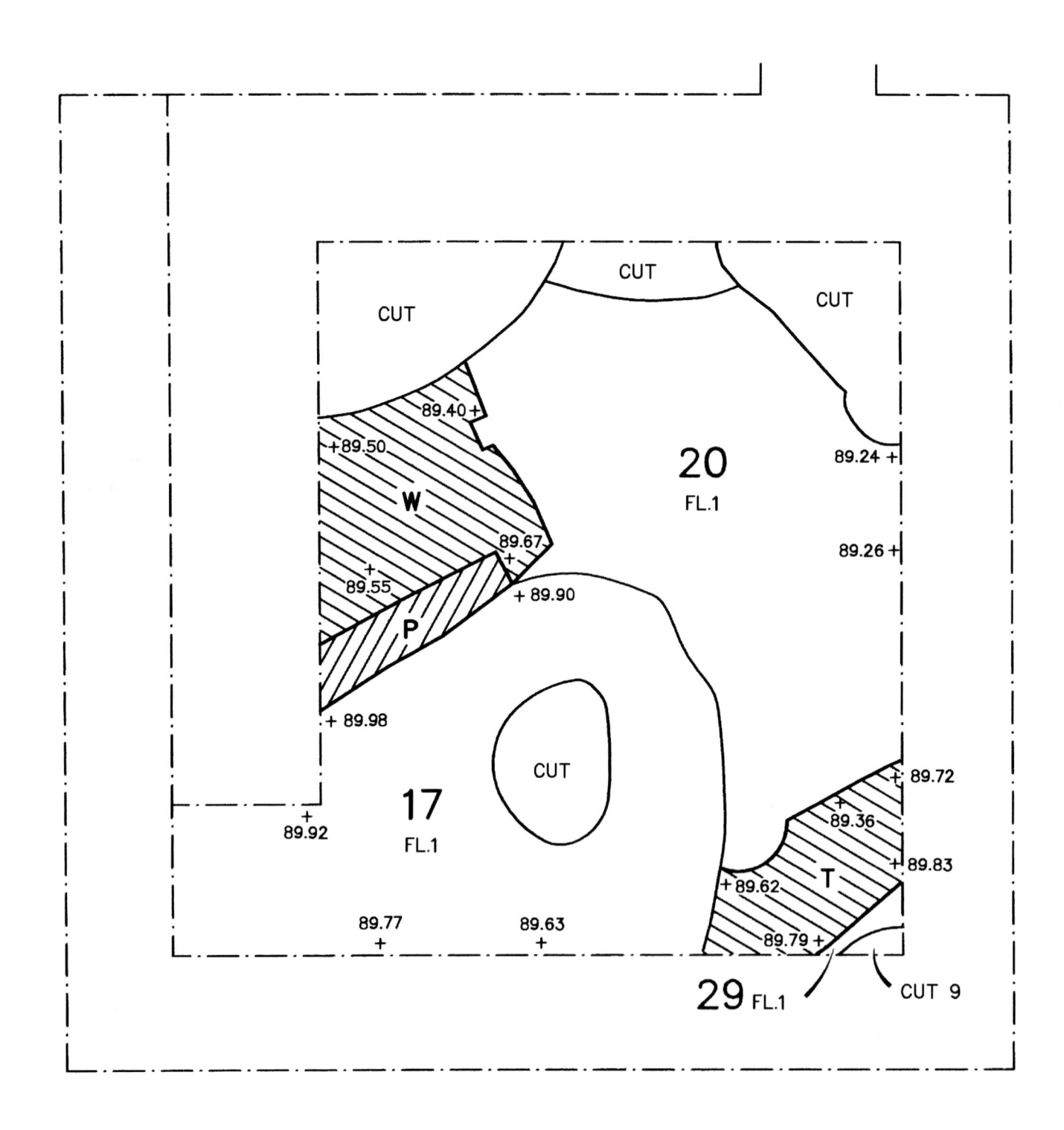

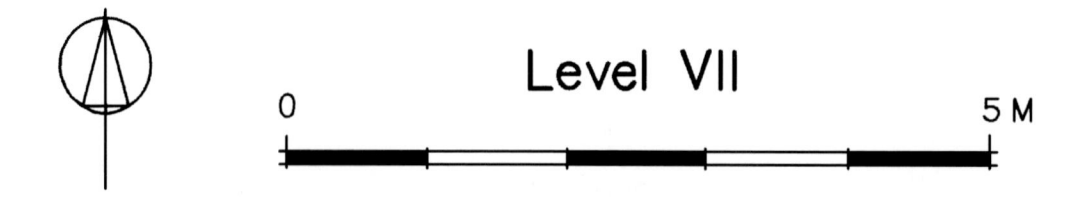

Plan of Level VII, Loci 17, 20, and 29

Plate 35

a

b

(*a*) East Section at Level VI Showing Superimposition of Wall M (square bricks) on Wall T (plano-convex bricks) in Background, and the Slope Down toward North on Which the Walls were Constructed, Visible in Section on Left, and (*b*) South Section Showing Walls of Levels VII and VI, Pit Cutting Locus 19

Plate 36

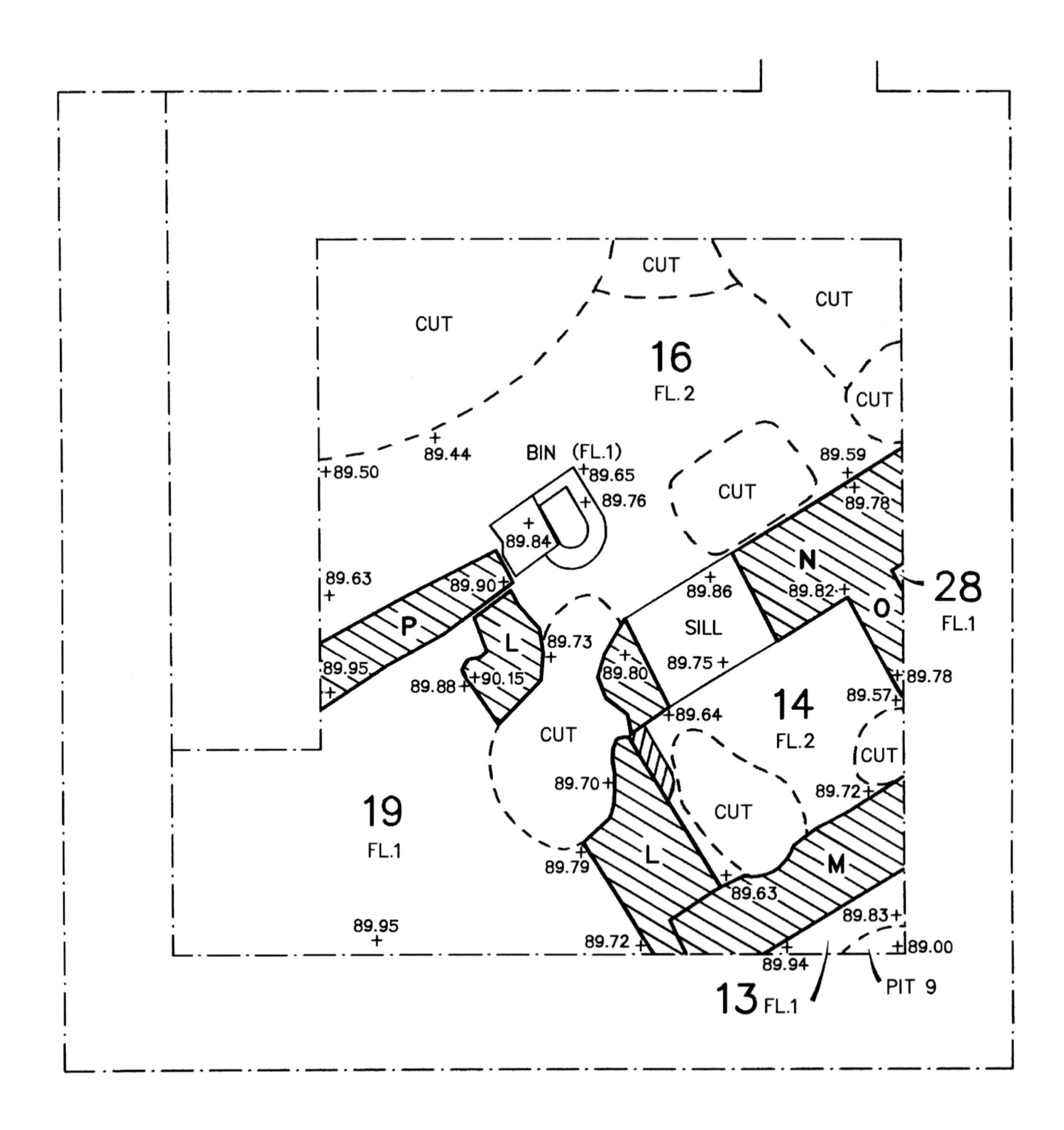

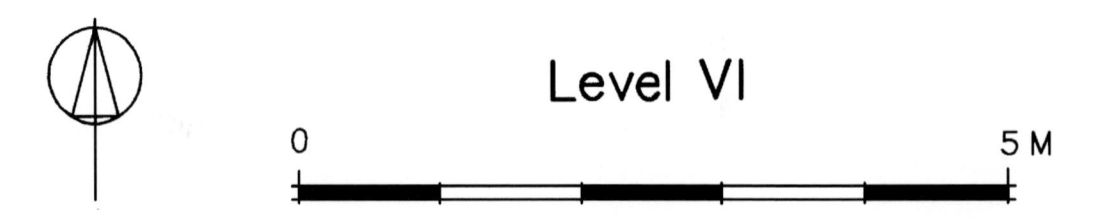

Plan of Level VI, Loci 13–14, 16, 19, and 28

Plate 37

(*a*) Level VI from Above and North and (*b*) Level VI, Detail of Mudbrick Bin and Walls P and L, Damage to Wall L by Later Burial on Left

Plate 38

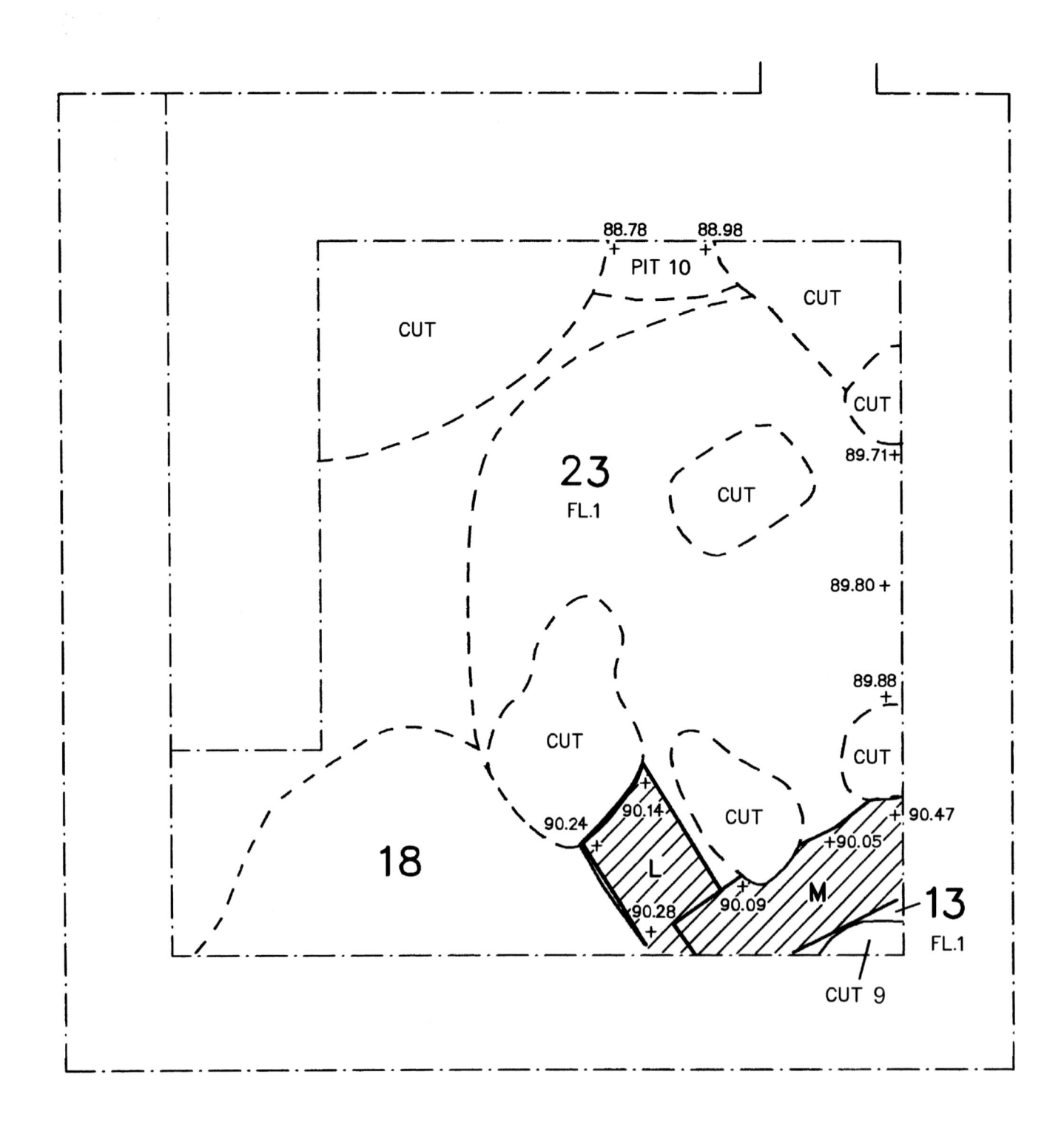

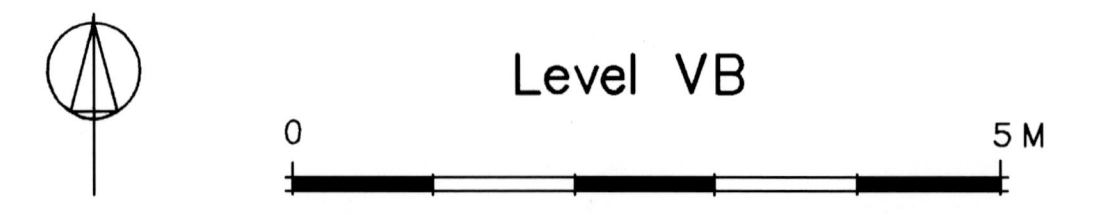

Plan of Level VB, Loci 13, 18, and 23

Plate 39

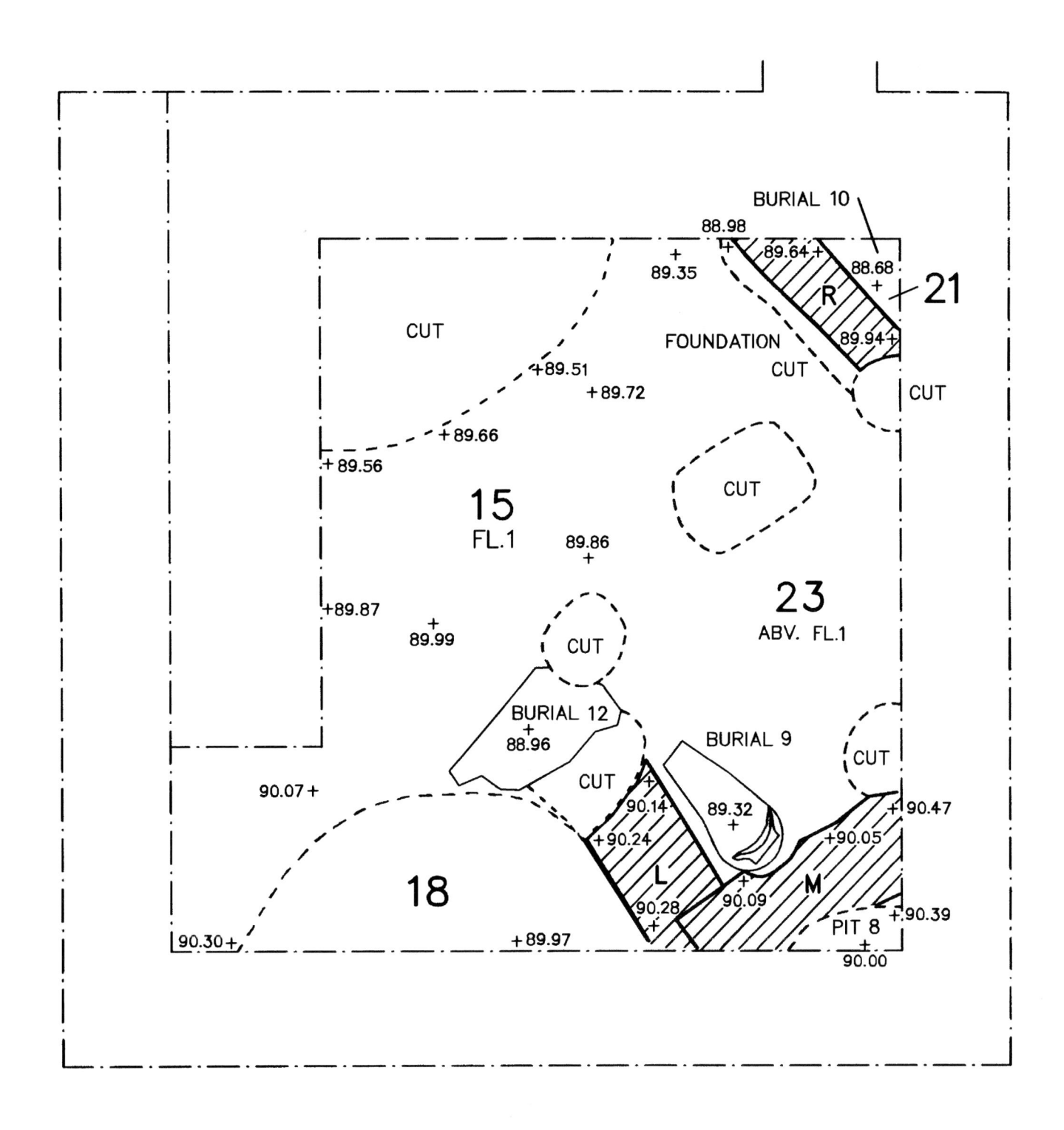

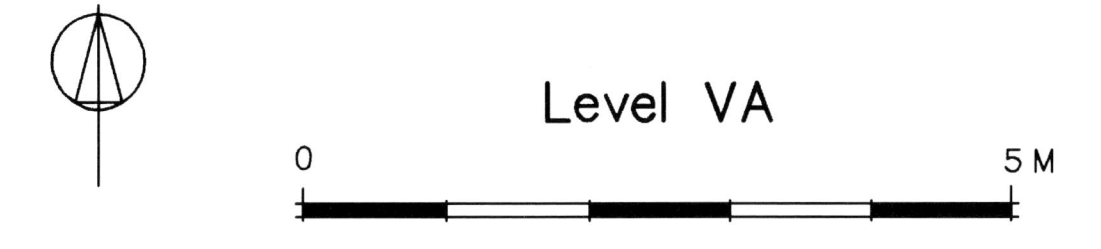

Level VA

Plan of Level VA, Loci 15, 18, 21, and 23

Plate 40

North Section Showing Multiple Pits, Wall R, and Its Foundation Cut and Erosion Layer, Locus 15

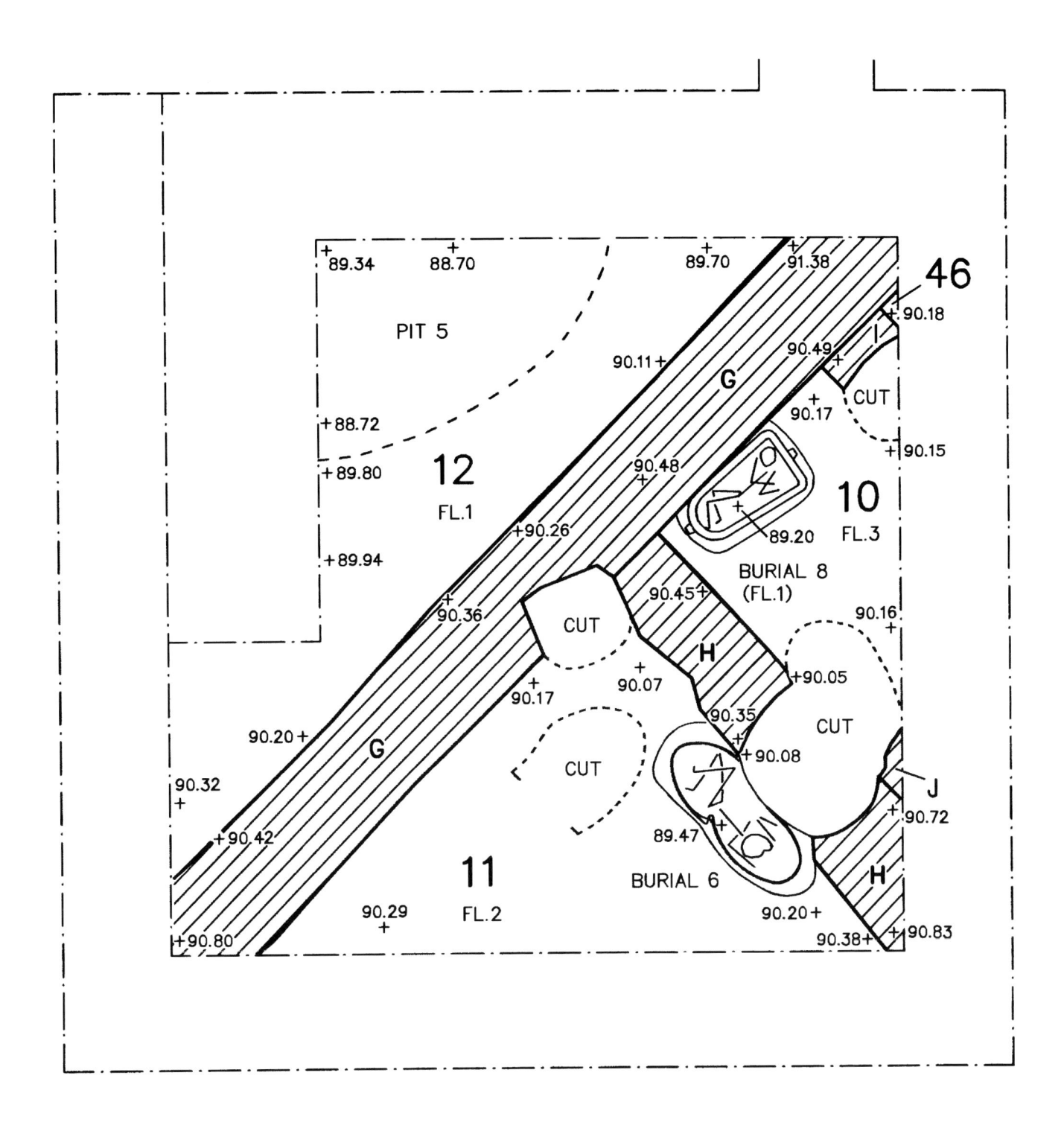

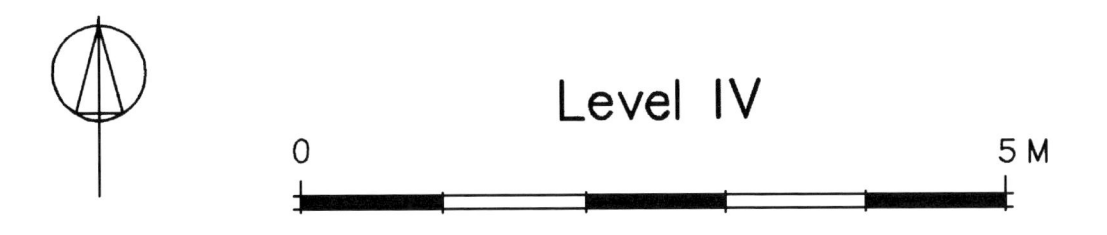

Plate 41

Level IV

0                    5 M

Plan of Level IV, Loci 10–12 and 46

Plate 42

Level IV from Above and South

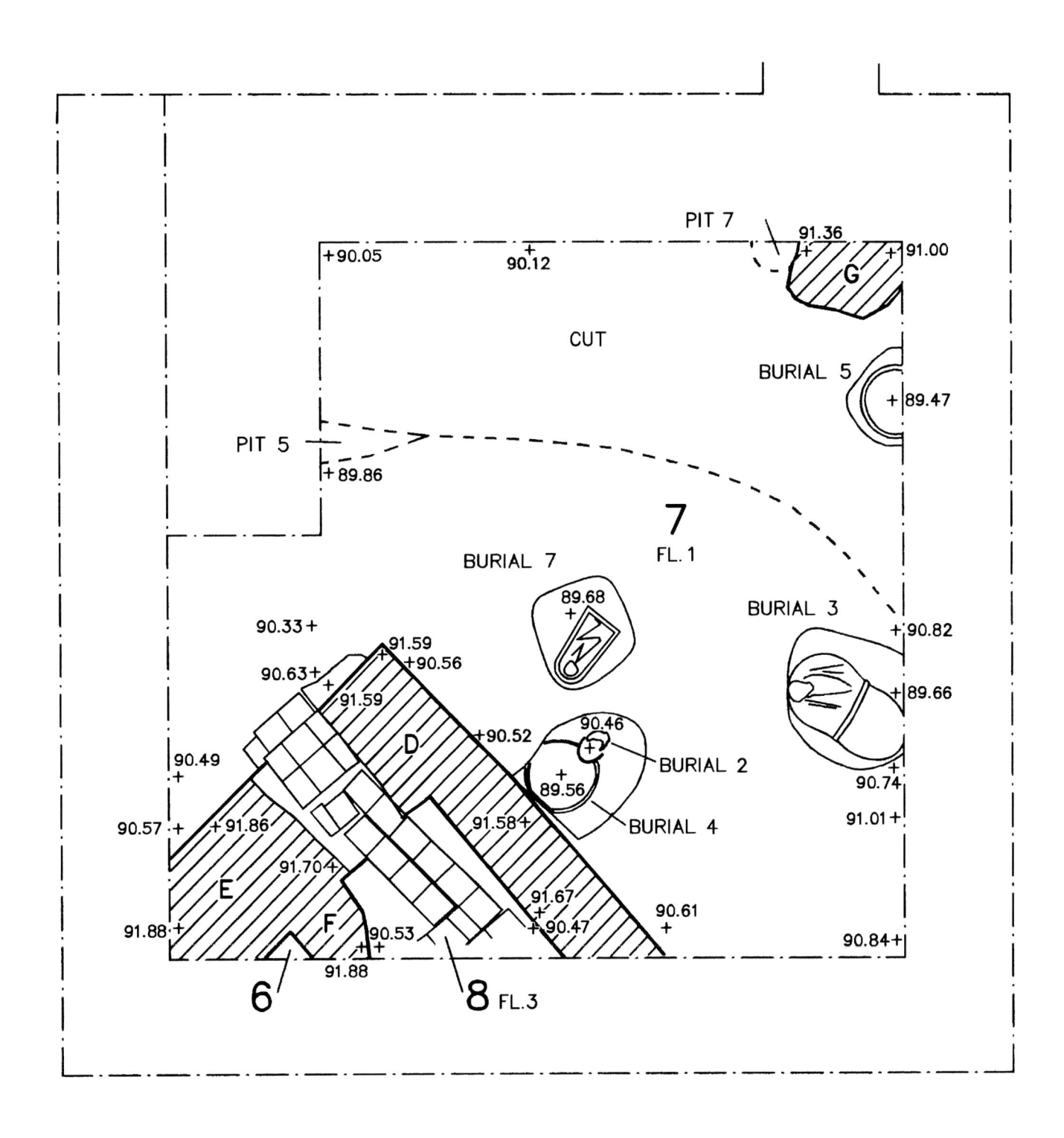

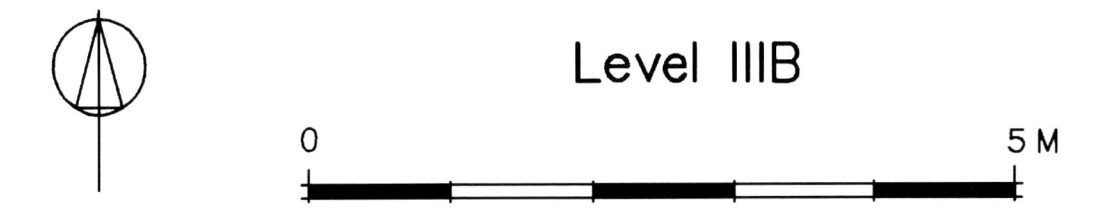

Plate 43

Level IIIB

0    5 M

Plan of Level IIIB, Loci 6–8

Plate 44

*(a)* Level IIIB, Drain at Locus 8, Floor 4, with Baked-brick Cover, and *(b)* Level IIIB, Drain at Locus 8, Floor 4, with Cover Removed and Bitumen-lined Channel Exposed

Plate 45

a

b

(*a*) Level IIIB, Exterior of Building, Detail of Drain Extending Beyond Building and Mudbricks Placed to Protect Base of Wall, and (*b*) Level IIIB, Outlet of Drain at Locus 8, Floor 3

Plate 46

a

b

(*a*) Level IIIB, Corner of Building from Above and East, with Drain at Locus 8, Floor 3, and (*b*) Level IIIB, Drain at Locus 8, Floor 3, Close-up from North

Plate 47

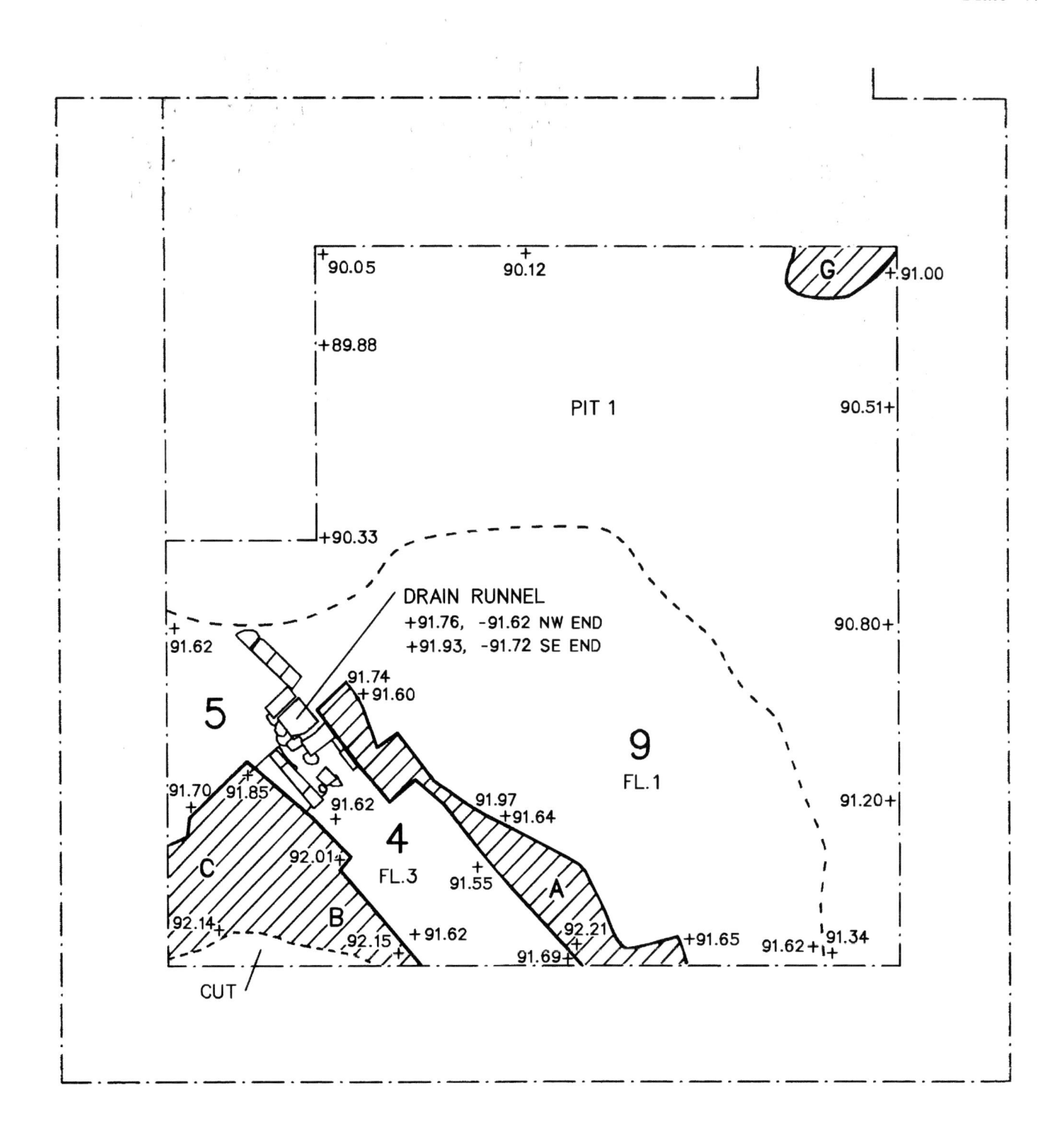

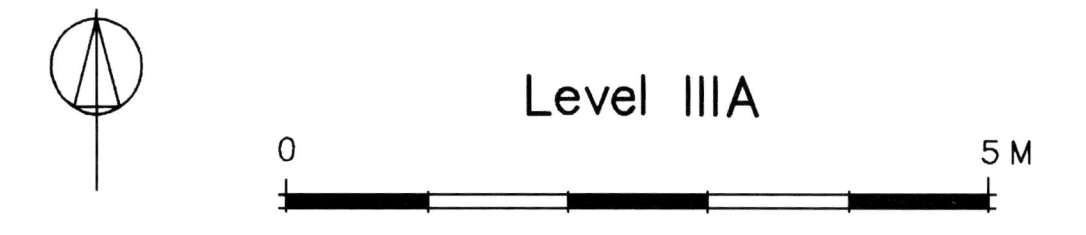

Level IIIA

Plan of Level IIIA, Loci 4–5 and 9

Plate 48

a

b

(*a*) Level IIIA, Building from Above and Northeast, with Drain in Locus 4, and (*b*) Level IIIA, Close-up of Drain in Locus 4, from Northwest

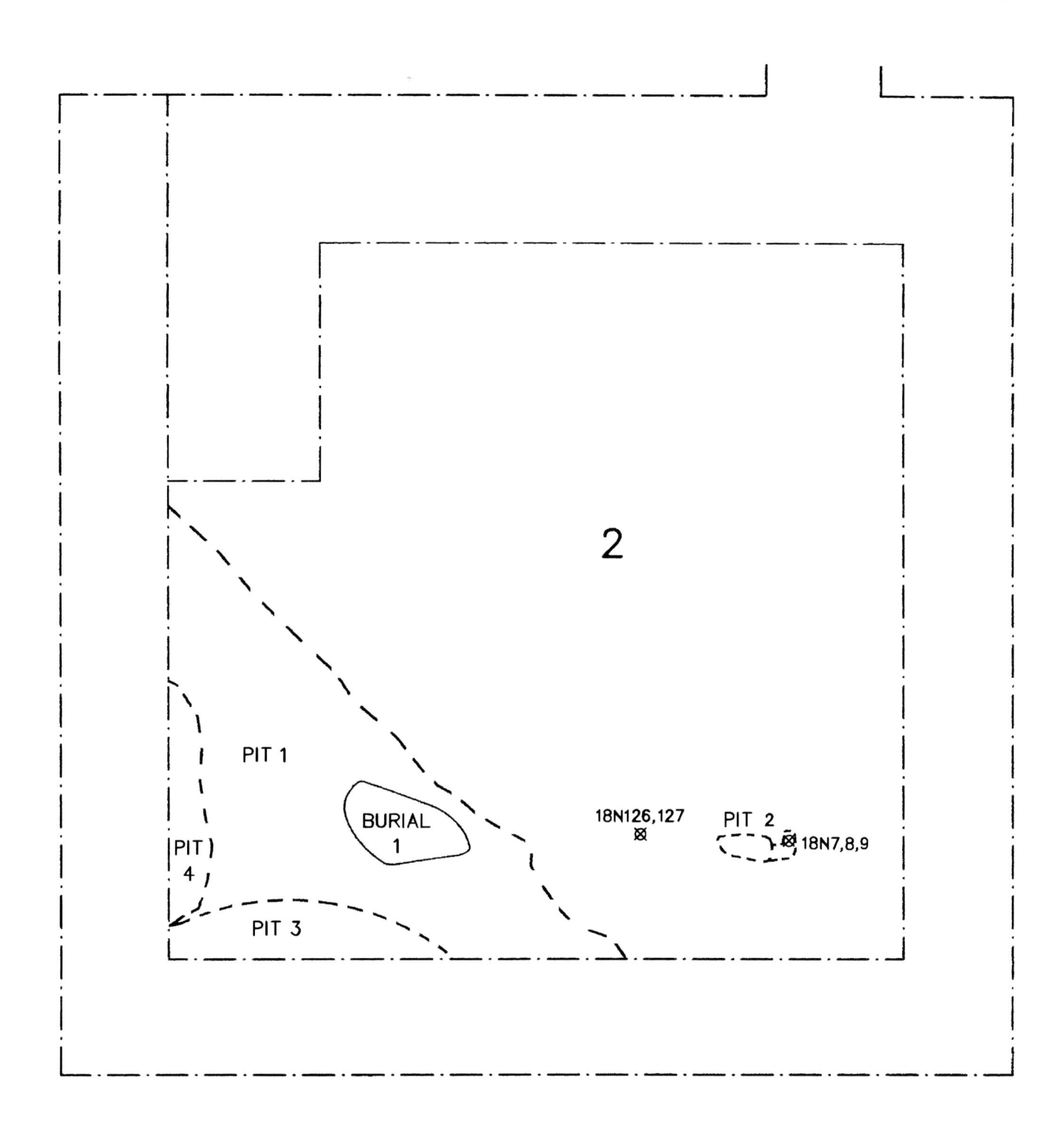

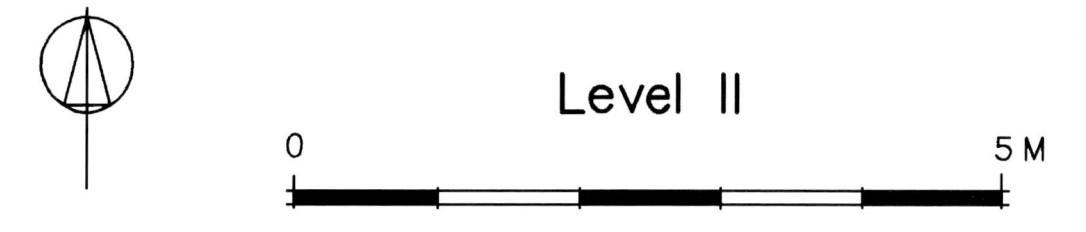

Plate 49

Level II

0                                    5 M

Plan of Level II, Locus 2

Plate 50

(*a*) Burial 22 and (*b*) Burial 19

Plate 51

(*a*) Burial 21, Skeleton 2, and (*b*) Burial 21, Skeleton 1

Plate 52

(*a*) Burial 18 and (*b*) Burial 17

Plate 53

(*a*) Burial 14, Skeleton 5, and (*b*) Burial 14, Skeleton 5 Grave Goods

Plate 54

(*a*) Burial 16 and (*b*) Burial 11

Plate 55

(*a*) Burial 15 and (*b*) Burial 15, Registered Grave Goods

Plate 56

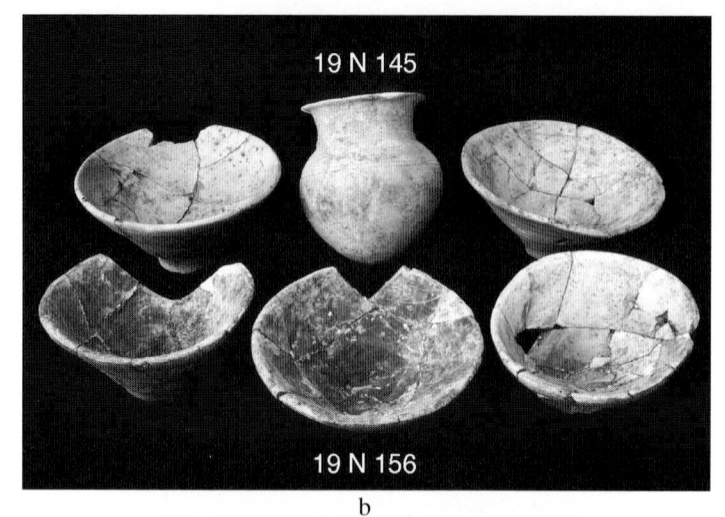

(*a*) Burial 14, Skeleton 8, (*b*) Burial 14, Skeleton 8, Registered Grave Goods, and (*c*) Burial 14, Skeleton 7

Plate 57

(*a*) Deep Shaft of Burial 14 in Foreground with Mudbrick Blocking of Entrance to Chamber for Burial 14, Skeleton 6, and (*b*) Burial 14, Skeleton 6

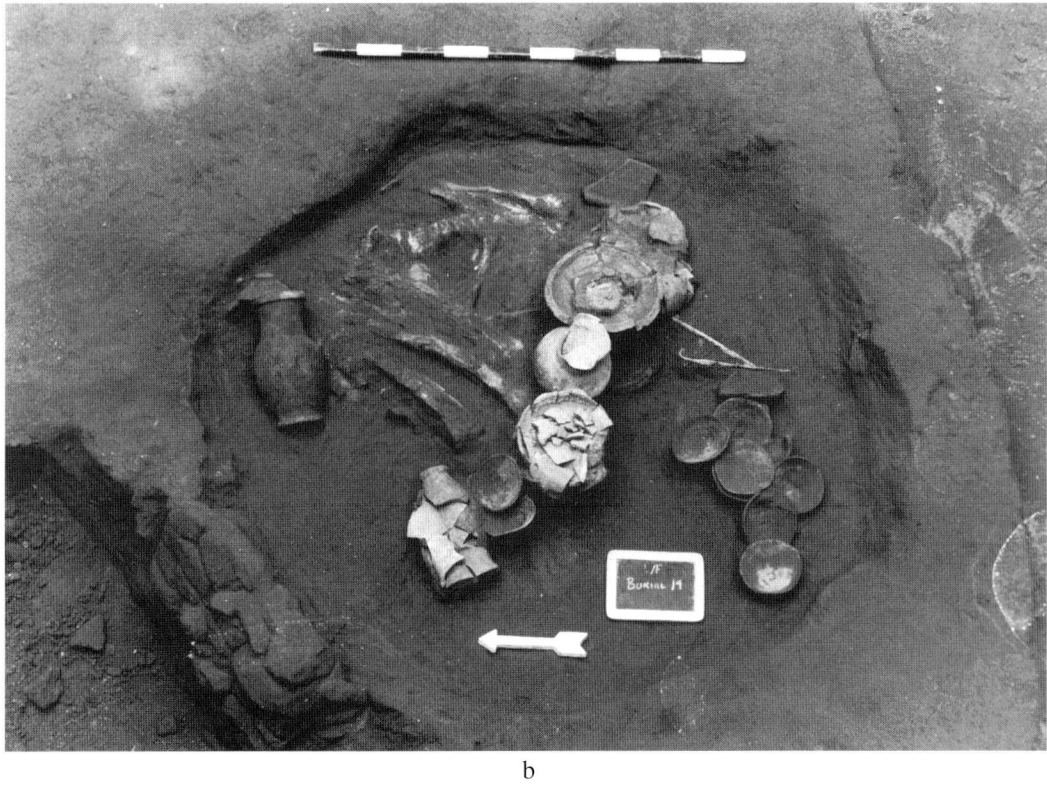

Plate 58

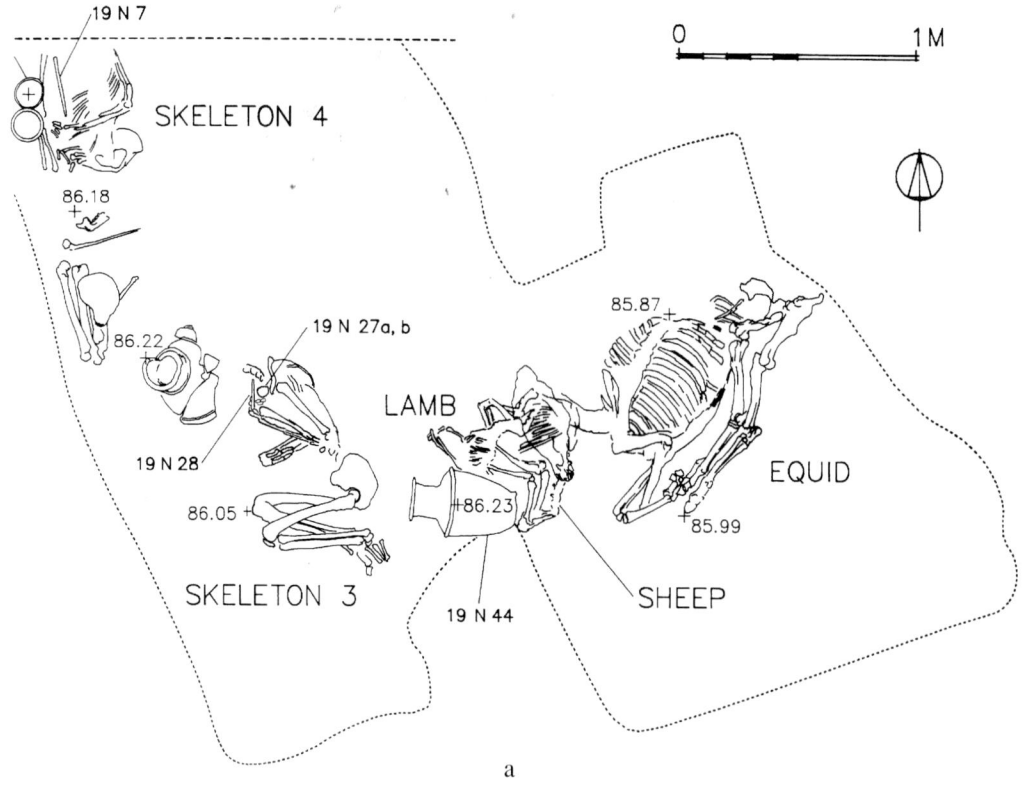

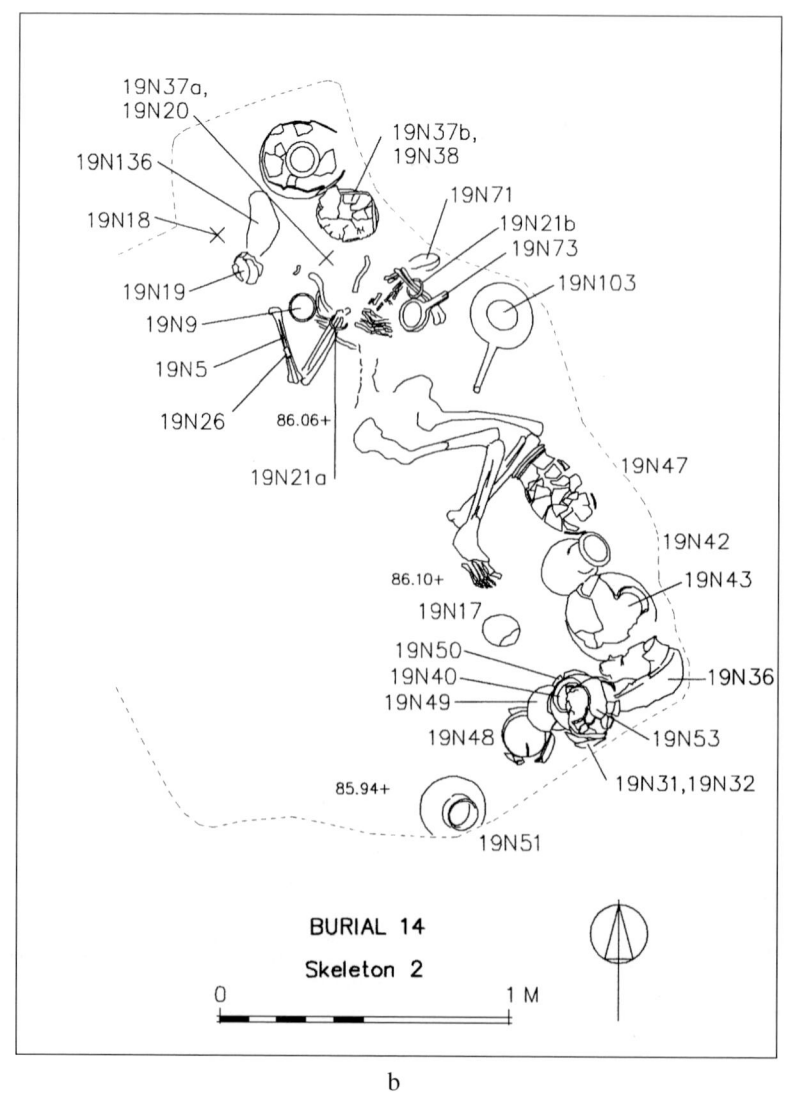

(a) Plan of Burial 14, Level XIIIB Chamber, and (b) Detailed Plan of Burial 14, Skeleton 2

Plate 59

Burial 14, Level XIIIB Chamber

Plate 60

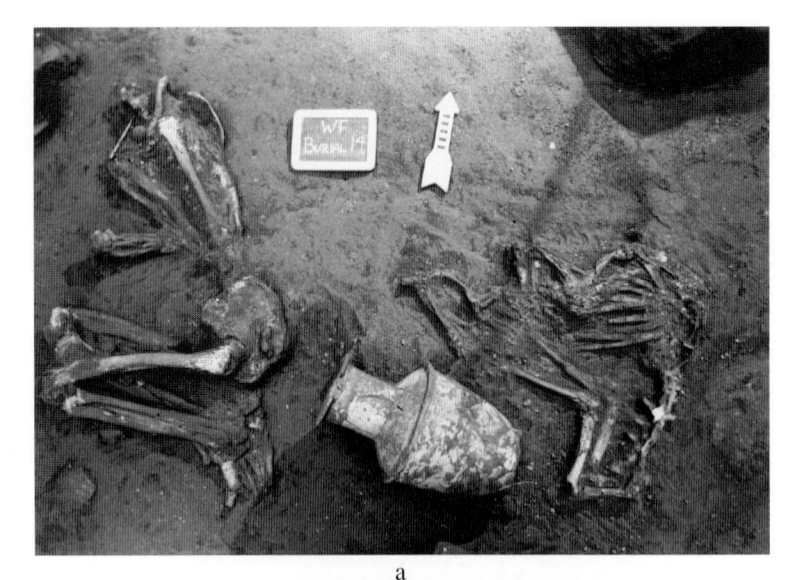

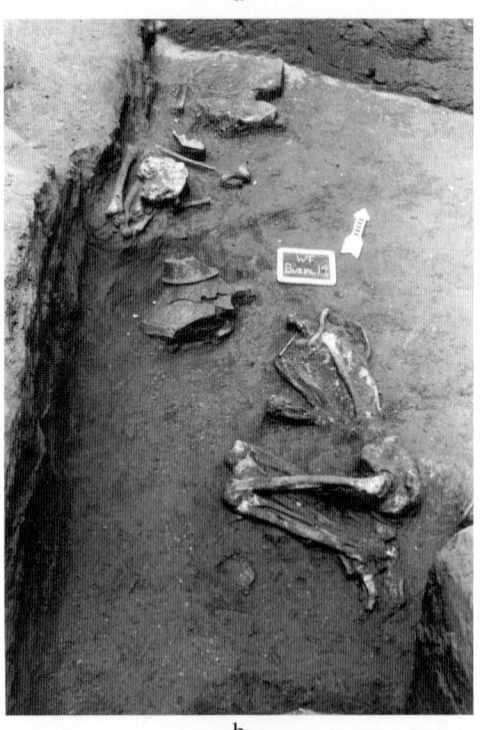

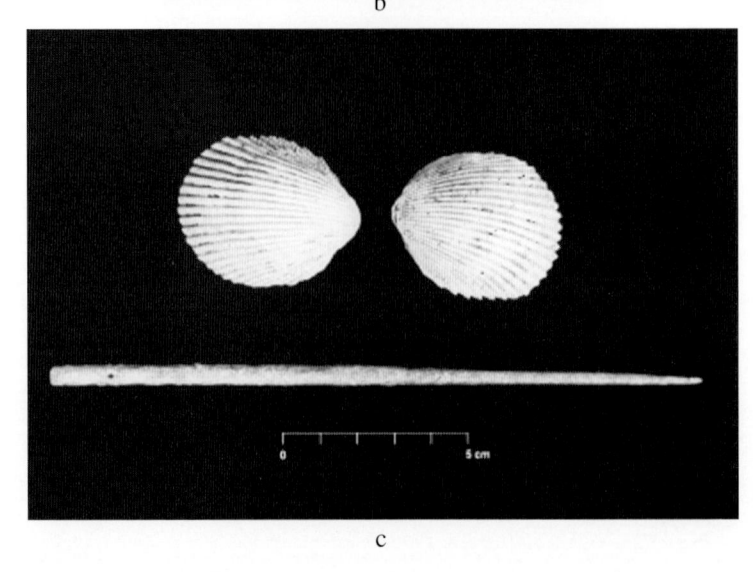

(*a*) Burial 14, Skeleton 3, Goddess-handled Jar 19 N 44 and Sheep Skeletons, (*b*) Burial 14, Skeleton 3, with Base of Fruit-Stand H1097, Head of Skeleton 3, Legs of Skeleton 4 to Left, Torso of Skeleton 4 in Background, and (*c*) Burial 14, Skeleton 3, Grave Goods, 19 N 27 and 19 N 28

Plate 61

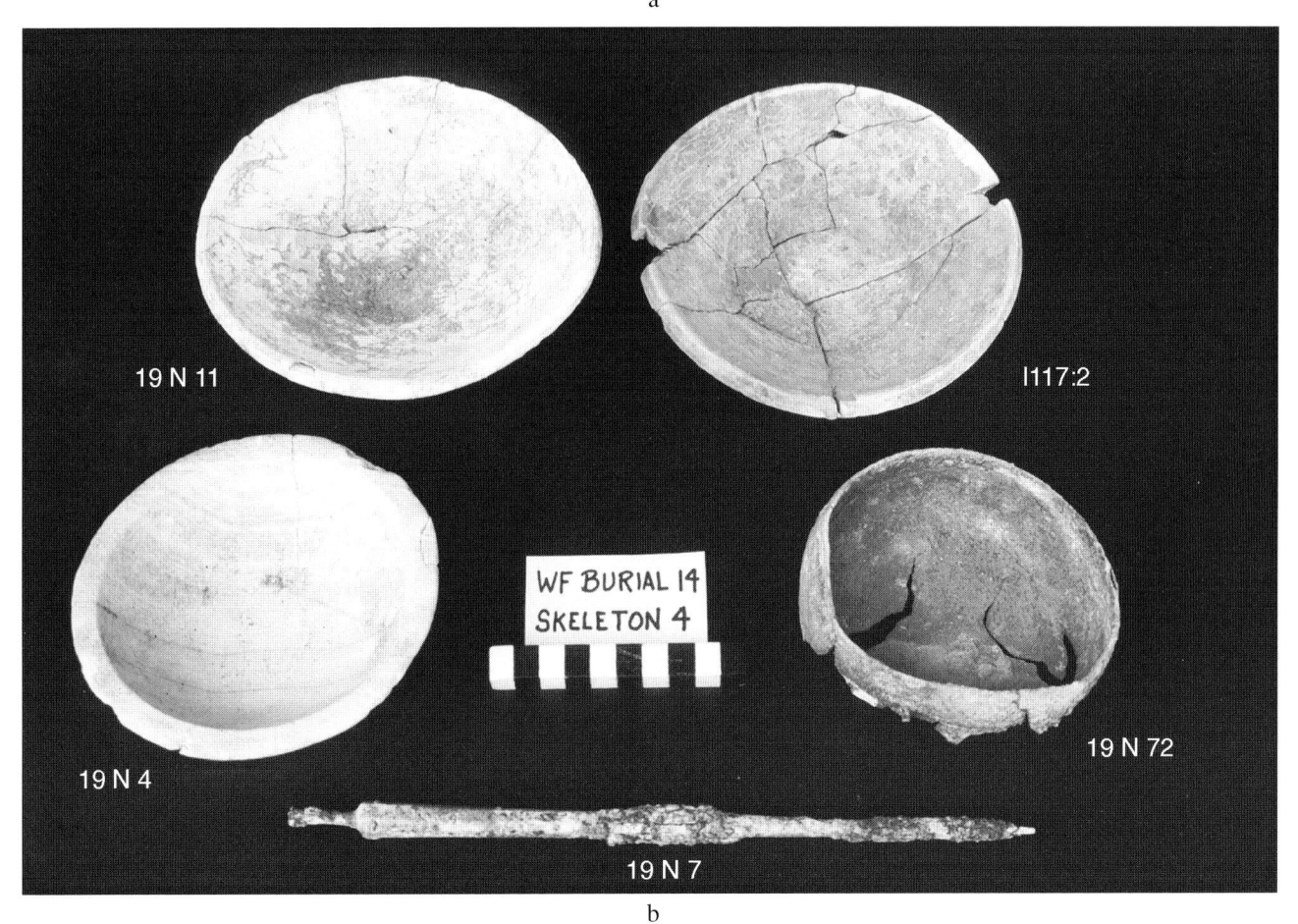

(*a*) Burial 14, Skeleton 4, and (*b*) Burial 14, Skeleton 4, Grave Goods

Plate 62

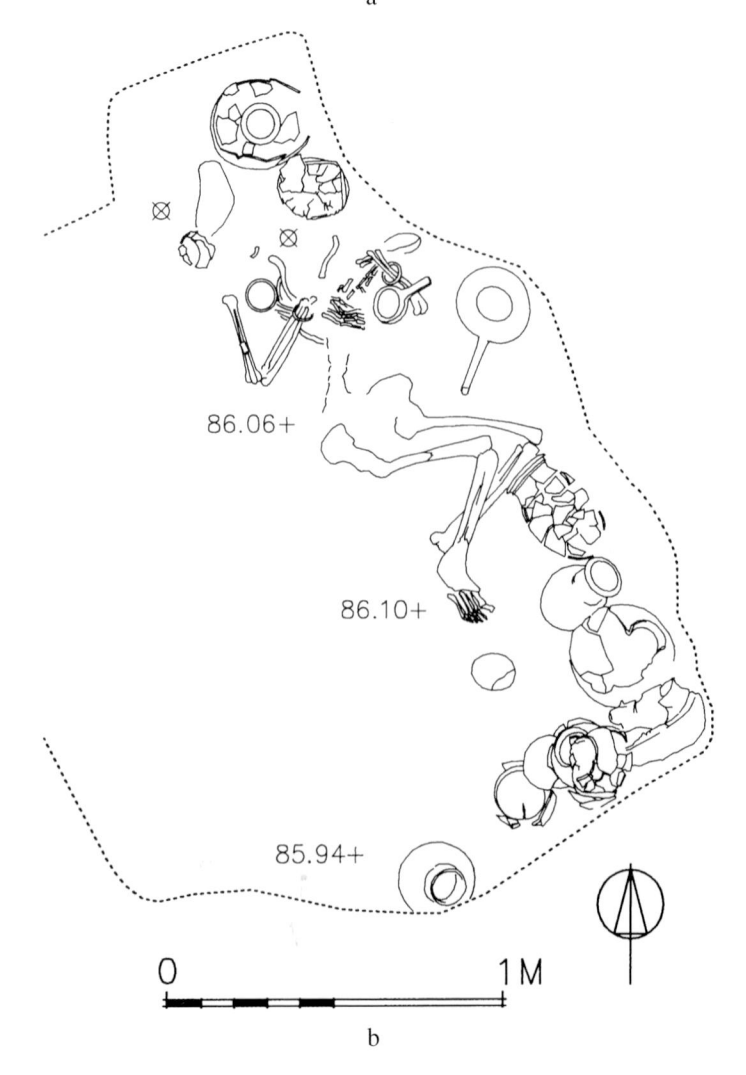

(*a*) Burial 14, Skeleton 2, and (*b*) Plan of Burial 14

Plate 63

(*a*) Burial 14, Equid Skeleton, and (*b*) Burial 14, Skeleton 2 Jewelry and Cylinder Seal

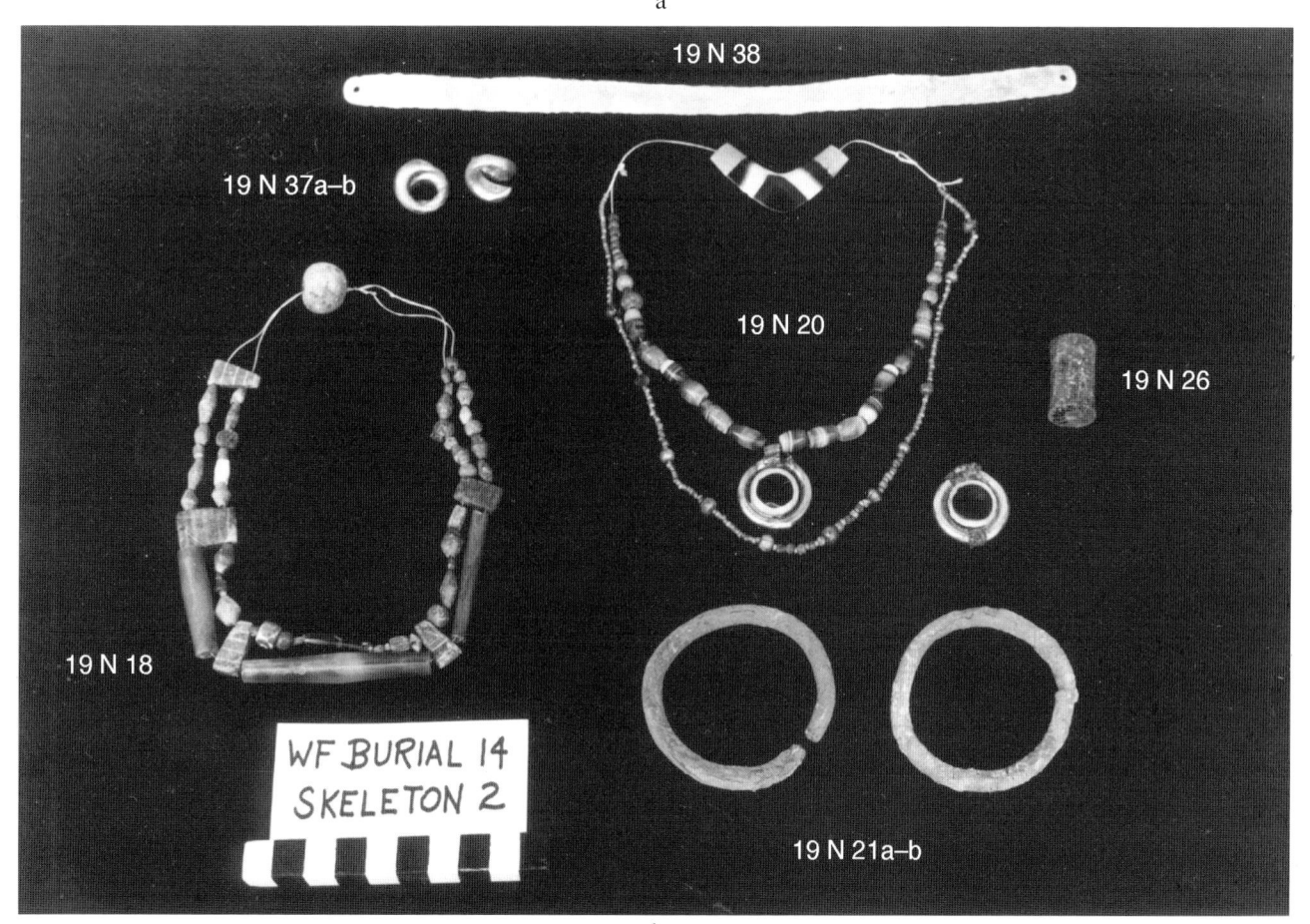

Plate 64

(*a*) Burial 14, Skeleton 2, Copper/Bronze Vessels, and (*b*) Burial 14, Skeleton 2, Pottery

Plate 65

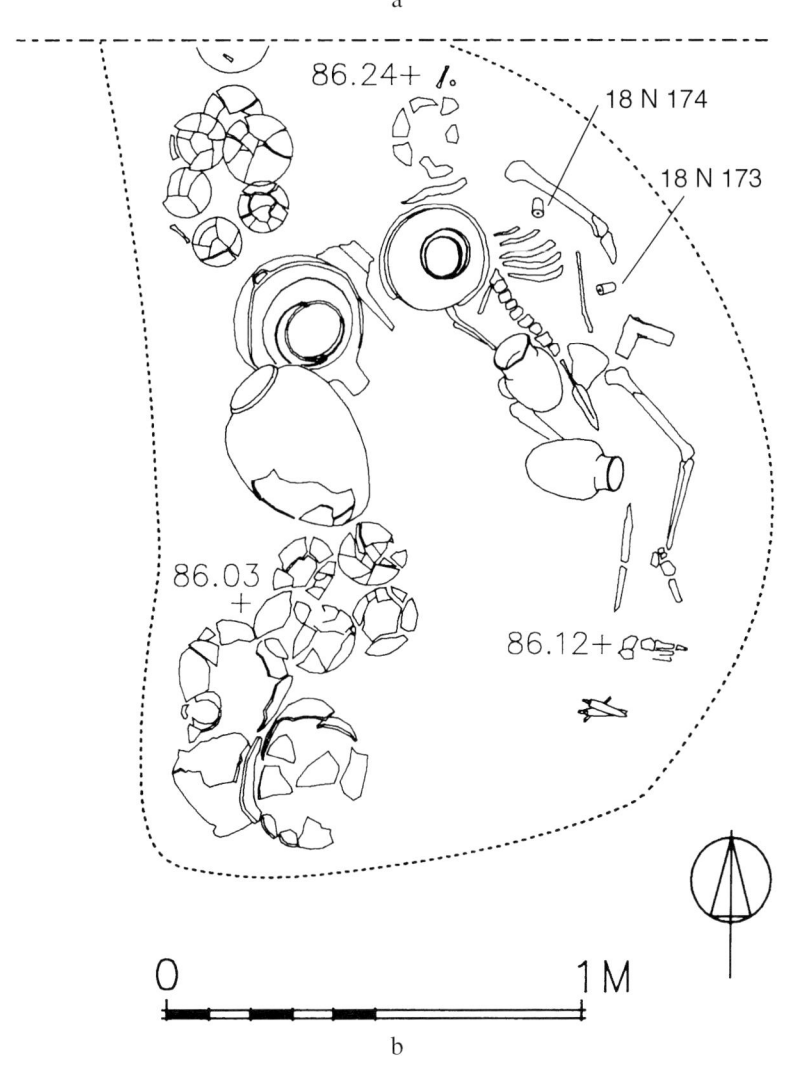

(*a*) Ash-filled Baked-brick Box above Burial 14, with Bowl 19 N 12, and (*b*) Plan of Burial 14, Skeleton 1

Plate 66

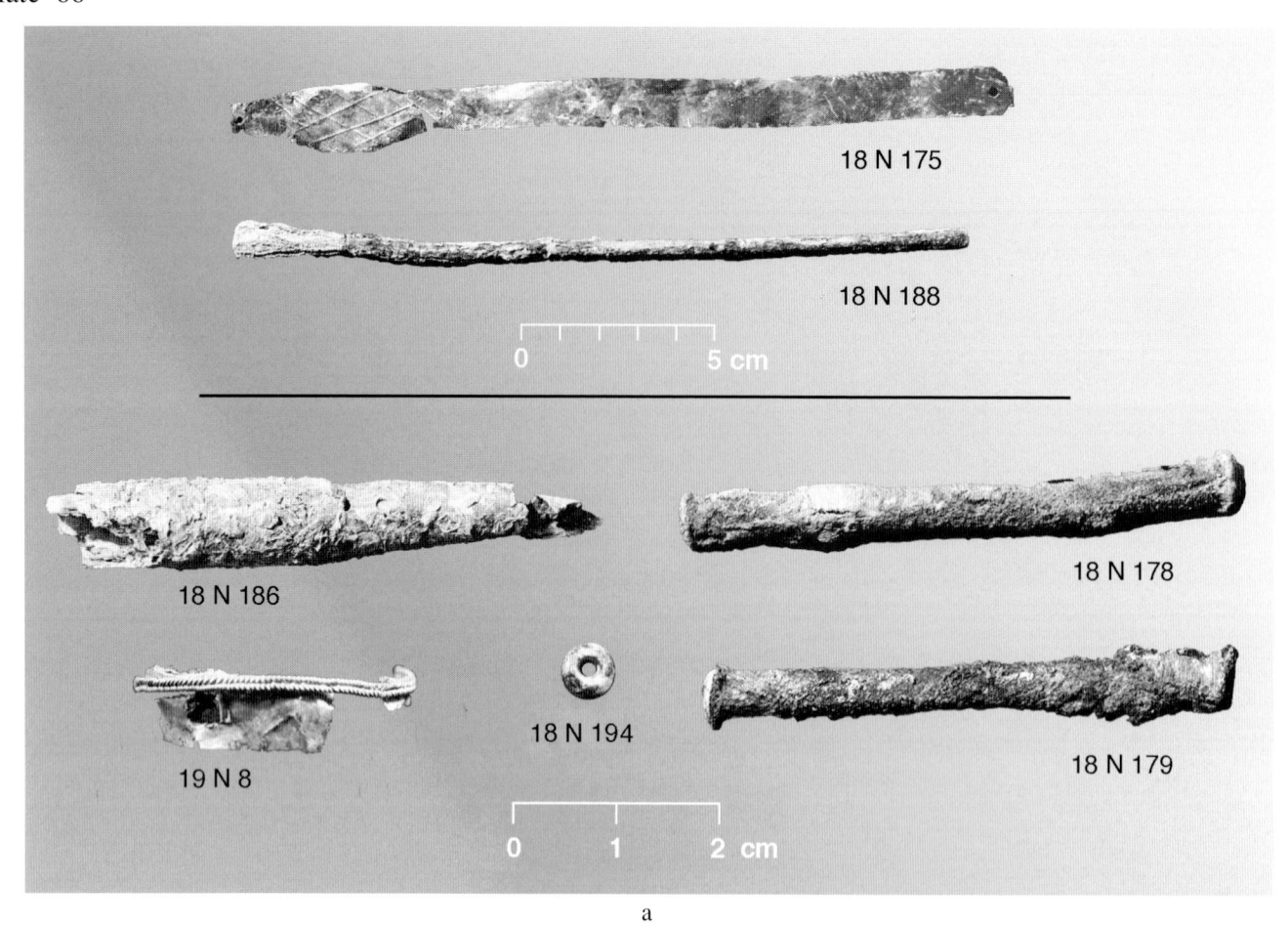

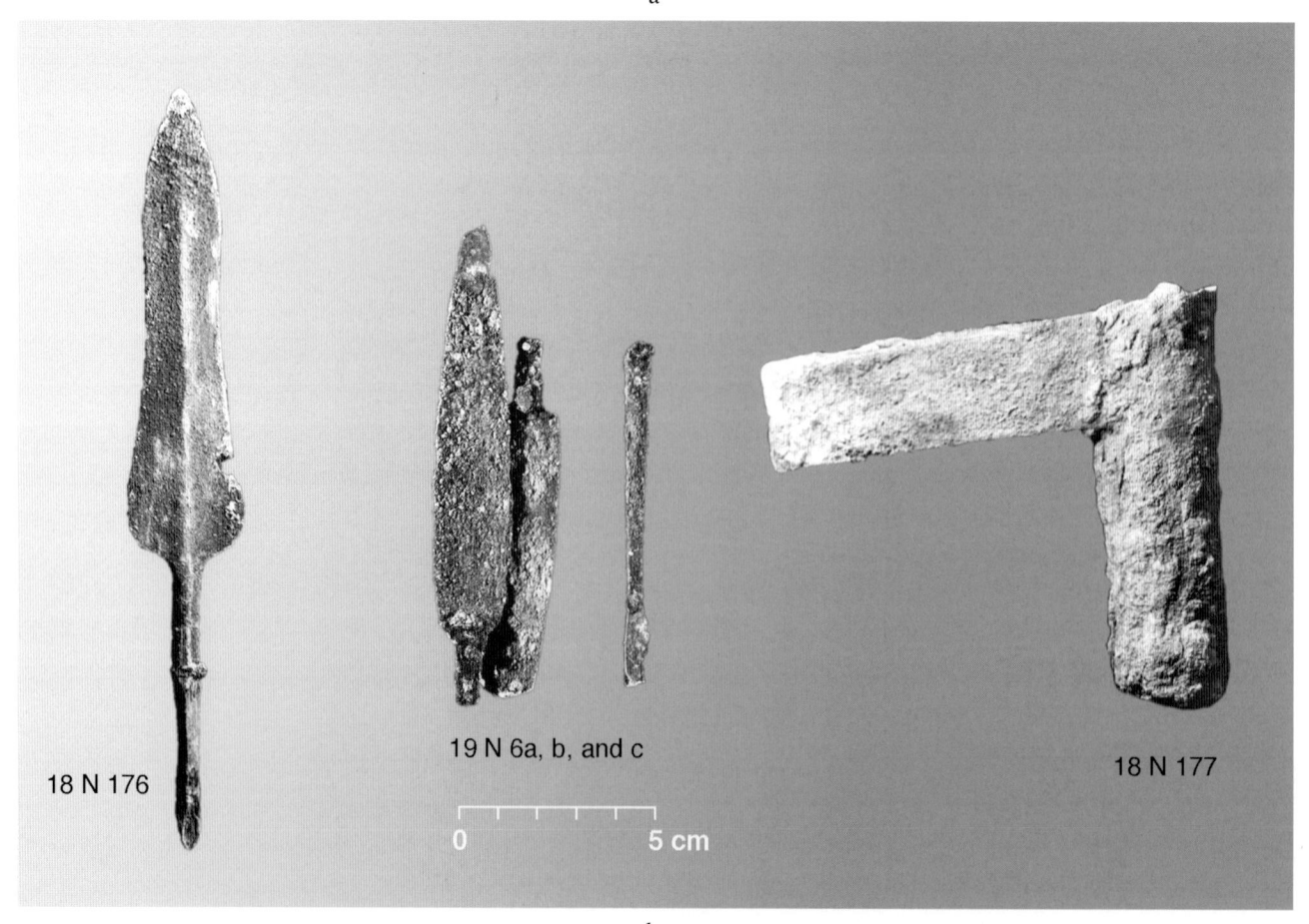

(*a*) Burial 14, Skeleton 1, Jewelry and Bronze Filter, and (*b*) Burial 14, Skeleton 1, Weapons

Plate 67

18 N 185

18 N 181          18 N 182

18 N 180

18 N 183          18 N 184

Burial 14, Skeleton 1, Copper/Bronze Vessels

Plate 68

(*a*) Burial 14, Skeleton 1, Registered Pottery, 19 N 10, and (*b*) Burial 14, Skeleton 1, Registered Pottery, 18 N 187

Plate 69

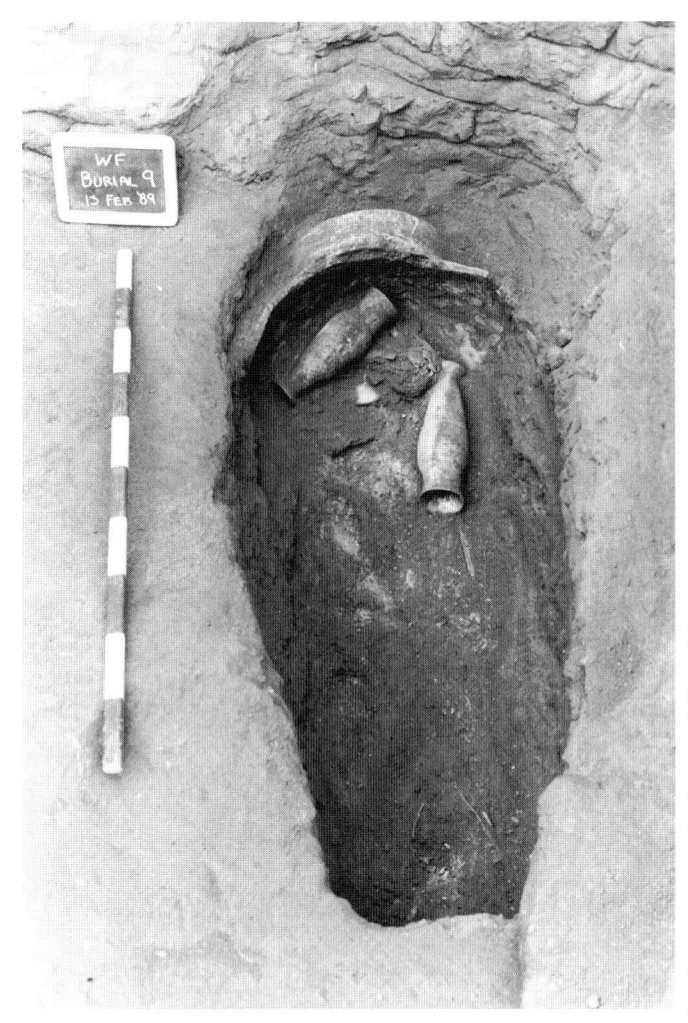

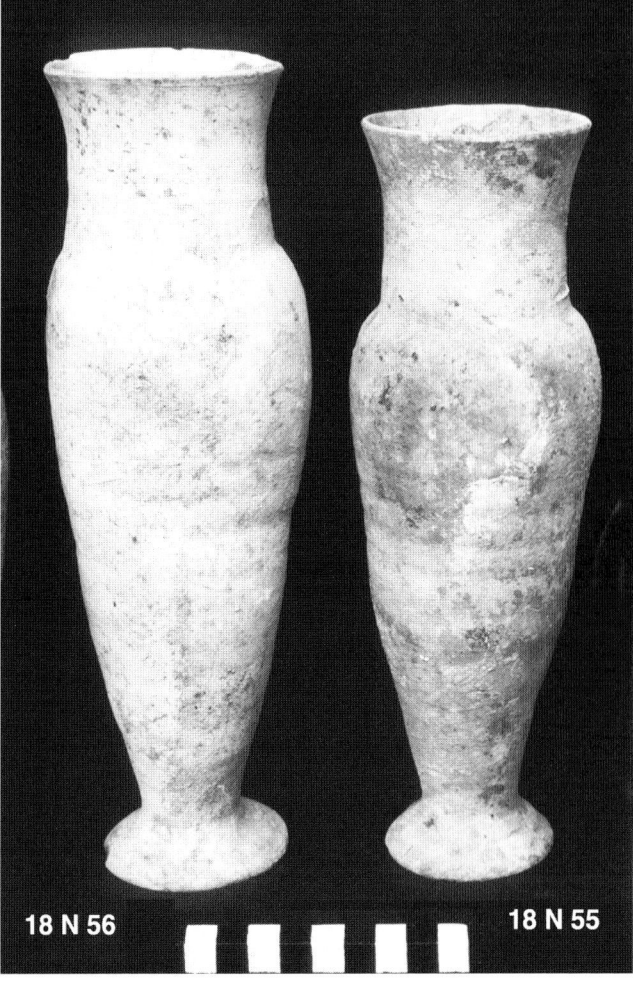

(*a*) Burial 9 and (*b*) Burial 9 Pottery

Plate 70

(*a*) Burial 12 and (*b*) Burial 12 Pottery

Plate 71

(*a*) Burial 8 and Associated Grave Goods: (*b*) 18 N 42, (*c*) 18 N 43, (*d*) 18 N 44, and (*e*) 18 N 45

Plate 72

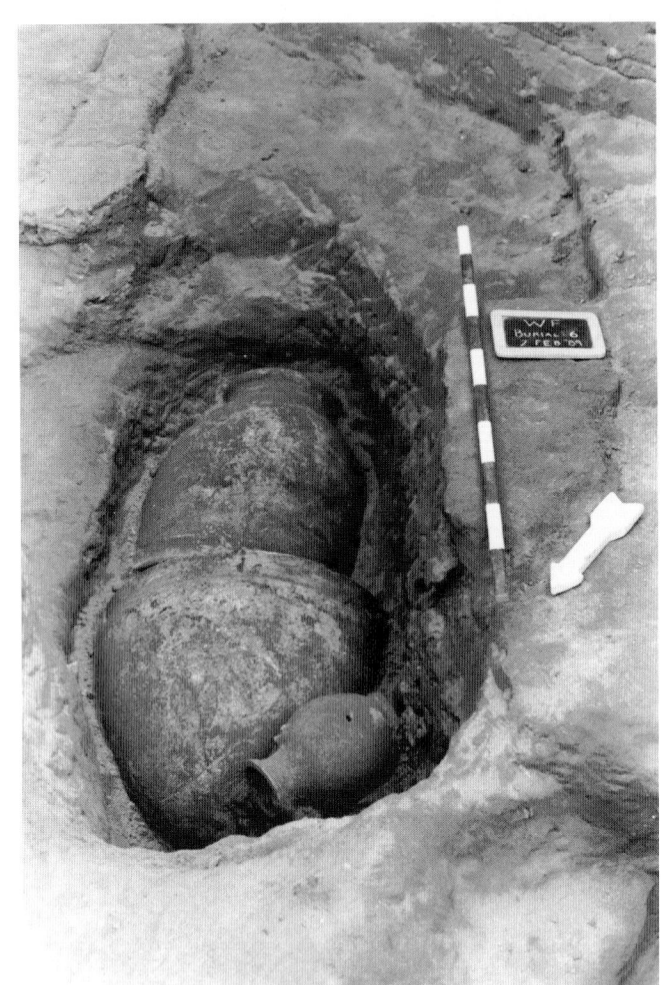

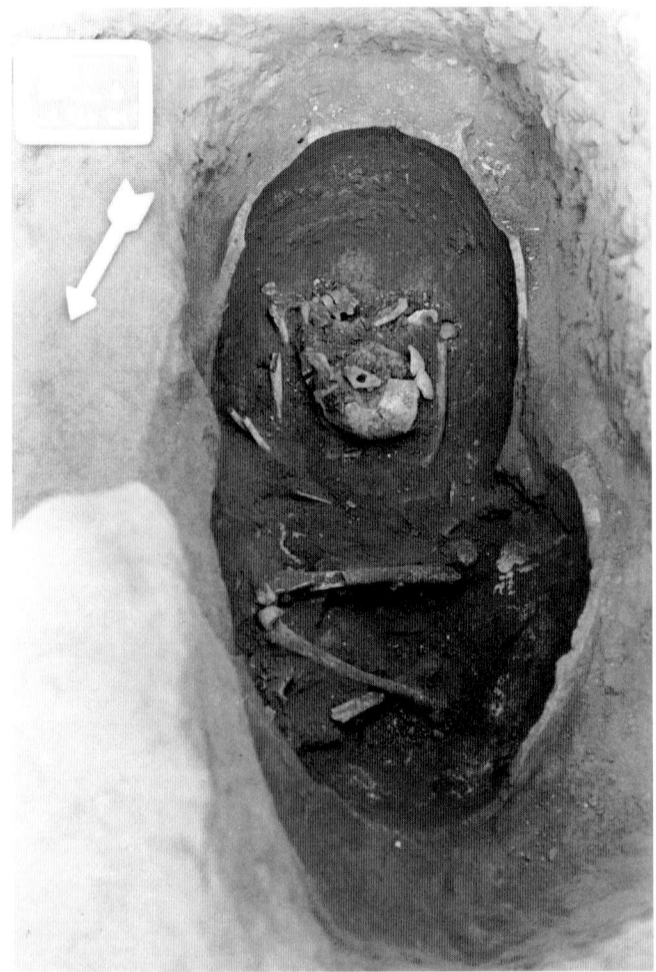

(*a*) Burial 6, Unopened, and (*b*) Burial 6, Opened

Plate 73

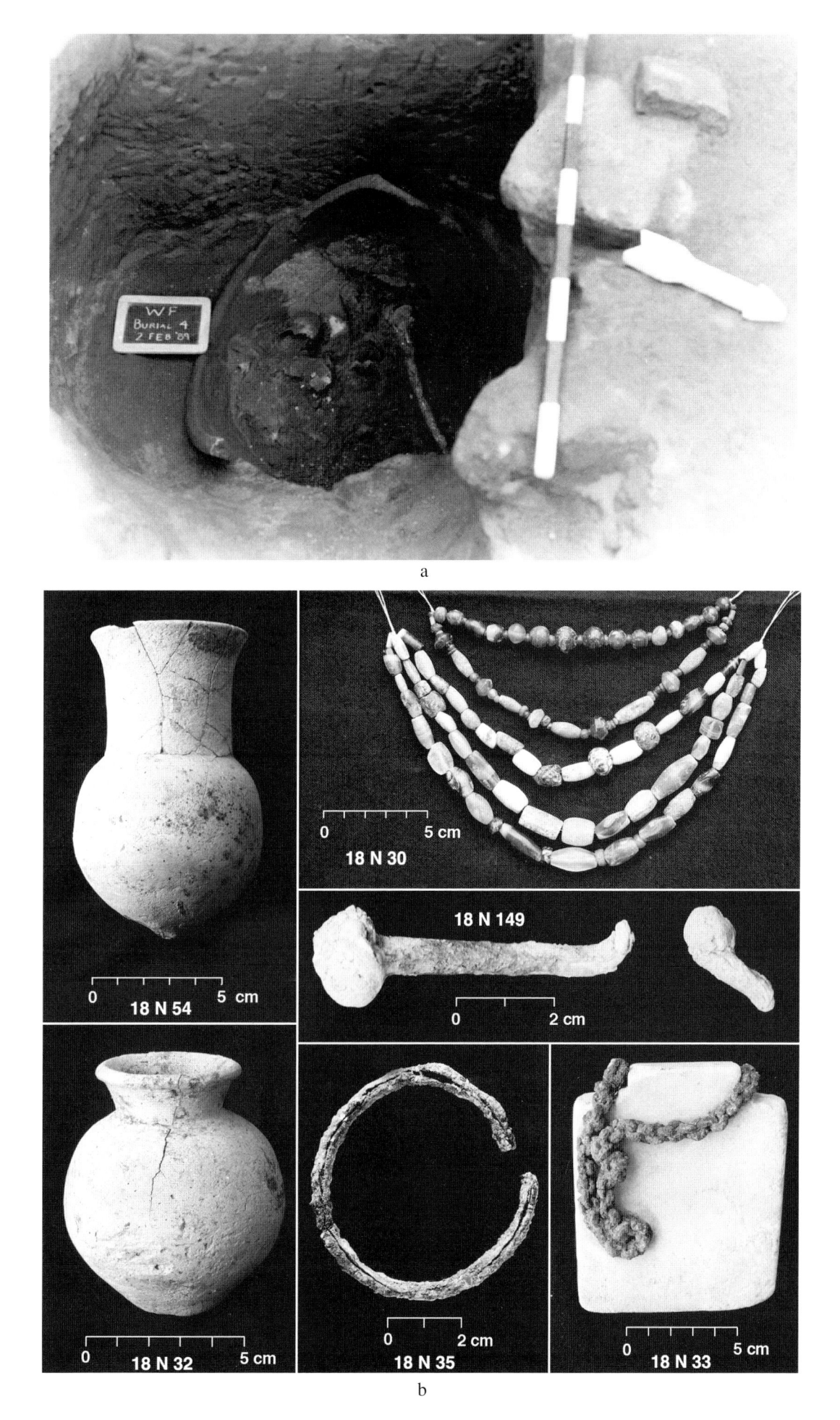

(*a*) Burial 4 and (*b*) Burial 4 Grave Goods

Plate 74

*(a)* Burial 3, Unopened, and *(b)* Burial 3, Opened

Plate 75

(*a*) Burial 5, (*b*) Burial 7, and (*c*) Burial 1

Plate 76. Type O-1: Conical Bowl

|   | Lot Number | Level | Dimension | Description |
|---|---|---|---|---|
| 1 | I329:1 | XVA | Rim diam. 13.0 cm, base diam. 4.5 cm, ht. 6.0 cm | Pale red, cream surface, sand temper |
| 2 | I378:2 | XVA | Rim diam. 15.0 cm, base diam. 4.5 cm, ht. 6.4 cm | Dark buff, cream surface, sand temper, mica inclusions |
| 3 | I326:3 | XIVB | Rim diam. 12.0 cm, base diam. 4.5 cm, ht. 5.7 cm | Buff, cream surface, sand temper |
| 4 | H1028:1 | XIVA | Rim diam. 14.0 cm, base diam. 4.0 cm, ht. 4.0 cm | Buff, sand and light organic temper |
| 5 | I34:1 | XIIIC | Rim diam. 14.0 cm, base diam. 6.0 cm, ht. 5.1 cm | Red, pink surface, sand temper |
| 6 | I34:3 | XIIIC | Rim diam. 12.0 cm, base diam. 4.5 cm, ht. 4.6 cm | Dark red, pink to cream surface, sand temper |
| 7 | H1057:2 | XIIIB | Rim diam. 13.0 cm, base diam. 3.5 cm, ht. 4.2 cm | Buff, sand and light organic temper |
| 8 | I156:2 | XIIIB | Rim diam. 14.0 cm, base diam. 7.0 cm, ht. 5.0 cm | Pink, pink to buff surface, sand temper |
| 9 | H1021:2 | XIIB | Rim diam. 15.0 cm, base diam. 5.0 cm, ht. 5.2 cm | Pink buff, sand and light organic temper |
| 10 | H119:2 | XIIB | Rim diam. 12.0 cm, base diam. 5.0 cm, ht. 4.5 cm | Pink, sand and light organic temper |
| 11 | H539:2 | XIIA | Rim diam. 14.0 cm, base diam. 5.0 cm, ht. 3.2 cm | Red, sand and light organic temper |
| 12 | H539:1 | XIIA | Rim diam. 14.0 cm, base diam. 5.0 cm, ht. 4.4 cm | Red brown, sand temper |
| 13 | H509:1 | XIB | Rim diam. 12.0 cm, base diam. 3.5 cm, ht. 4.2 cm | Buff, sand and light organic temper |
| 14 | H887:2 | XIB | Rim diam. 14.0 cm, base diam. 4.0 cm, ht. 3.7 cm | Red, sand and light organic temper |
| 15 | H857:1 | XIA | Rim diam. 14.0 cm, base diam. 5.0 cm, ht. 2.9 cm | Pink, sand and light organic temper |
| 16 | H129:1 | X | Rim diam. 14.0 cm, base diam. 4.5 cm, ht. 3.4 cm | Red, sand and light organic temper |
| 17 | H777:6 | IX | Rim diam. 13.0 cm, base diam. 4.0 cm, ht. 3.7 cm | Red, sand temper |
| 18 | H781:1 | IX | Rim diam. 14.0 cm, base diam. 5.0 cm, ht. 4.4 cm | Buff, sand temper |
| 19 | H771:1 | VIII | Rim diam. 12.0 cm, base diam. 4.5 cm, ht. 3.5 cm | Buff, sand temper |
| 20 | H754:11 | VIII | Rim diam. 16.0 cm, base diam. 7.0 cm, ht. 4.8 cm | Dark buff, sand temper |
| 21 | I326:1 | XIVB | Rim diam. 8.0 cm, base diam. 3.8 cm, ht. 6.5 cm | Pale red, buff surface, sand temper |

Plate 76

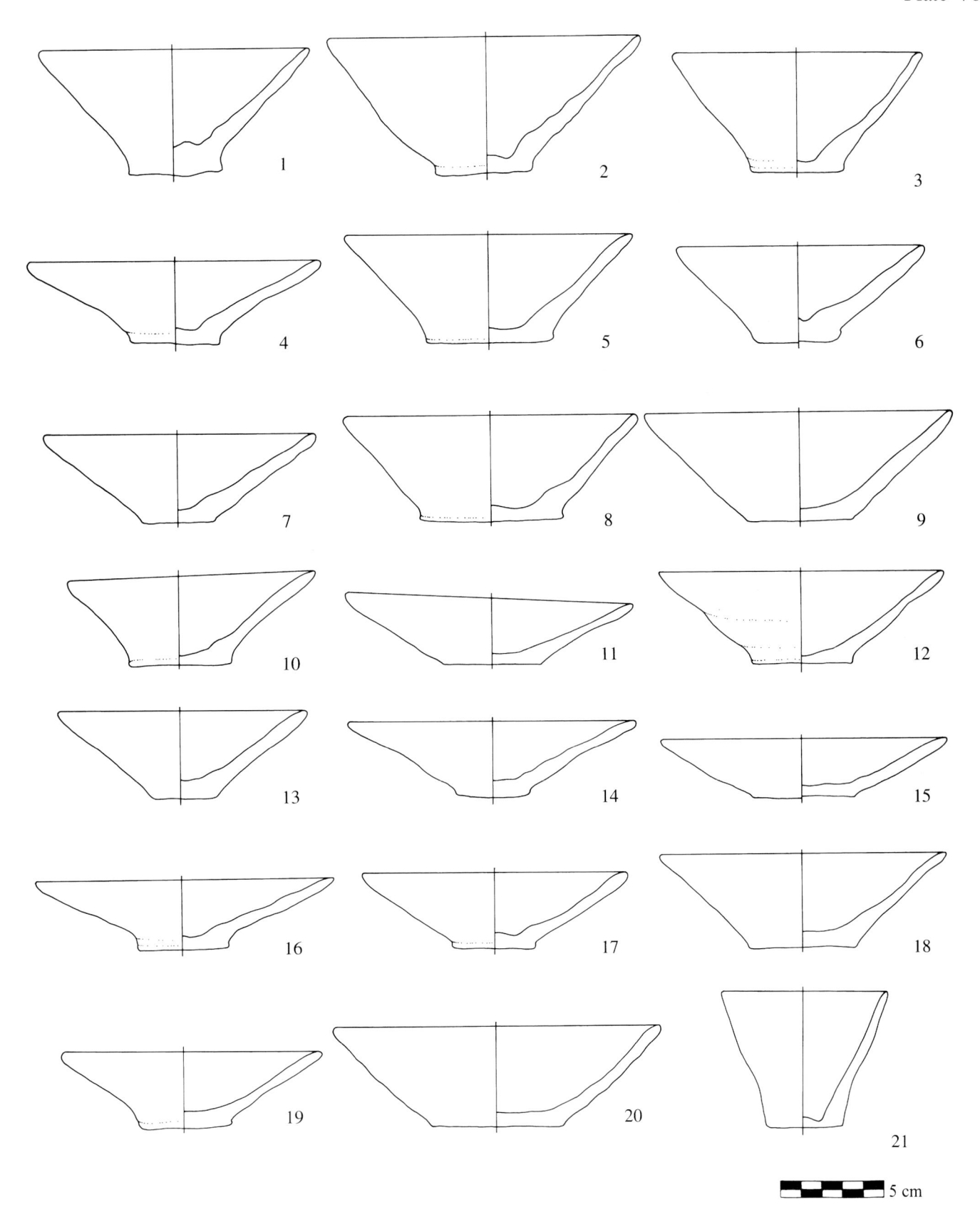

Type O-1: Conical Bowl. Scale 2:5

Plate 77. Type O-2: Fruit Stand or Stemmed Dish

|   | Lot Number | Level | Dimension | Description |
|---|---|---|---|---|
| 1 | I765:4 | XIXB | Rim diam. 28.0 cm | Buff green, sand temper |
| 2 | I776:6 | XIXB | Rim diam. 29.0 cm | Red, cream surface, sand and light organic temper, finger-impressed ridge |
| 3 | I676:1 | XVIII | Rim diam. 30.0 cm | Red, cream surface, sand temper, finger-impressed ridge |
| 4 | I475:3 | XVIIC | Rim diam. 36.0 cm | Buff, cream surface, sand temper, finger-impressed ridge |
| 5 | H540:6 | XIV | Rim diam. 26.0 cm | Pink, sand and light organic temper |
| 6 | H110:6 | XIIA | Rim diam. 26.0 cm | Pink, sand and light organic temper, finger-impressed ridge |
| 7 | H1038:2 | XIIIB | Rim diam. 26.0 cm | Pink, sand and light organic temper |
| 8 | H145:2 | XIB | Rim diam. 36.0 cm | Red, pink surface, sand and light organic temper |
| 9 | H523:3 | XIB | Rim diam. 30.0 cm | Buff, pink surface, sand and light organic temper |

COMPARANDA FOR TYPE O-2

Nippur: McCown, Haines, and Biggs 1978: pl. 48:6 (ED I); Gibson, Armstrong, and McMahon 1998: fig. 25:10, fig. 27:3–5 (ED); Uch Tepe: Gibson 1981: pl. 76:10–16 (ED I–II); Uruk: Pongratz-Leisten 1988: 63–64, 69, 118, 148 (ED); nos. 1, 5, 7 are similar to large bowls from Abu Salabikh: Moon 1987: 162–63

Plate 77

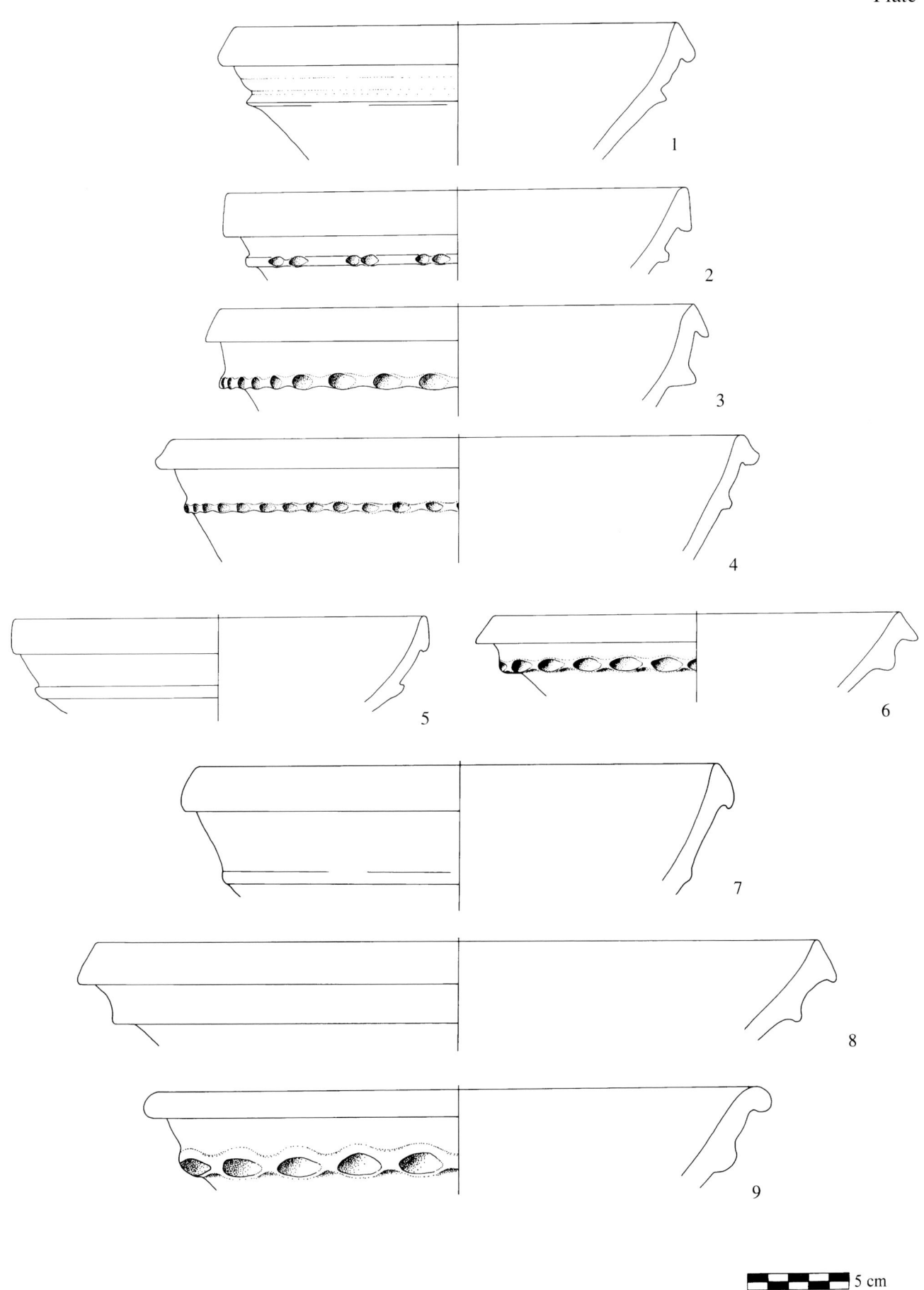

Type O-2: Fruit Stand or Stemmed Dish. Scale 2:5

Plate 78. Type O-3: Large Bowl

|    | Lot Number | Level | Dimension | Description |
|----|------------|-------|-----------|-------------|
| 1  | I677:1     | XIXB  | Rim diam. 36.0 cm | Pink, sand temper |
| 2  | I668:1     | XIXA  | Rim diam. 34.0 cm | Pale red, buff surface, sand temper |
| 3  | I454:4     | XVIIB | Rim diam. 28.0 cm | Red, organic temper |
| 4  | I420:1     | XVI   | Rim diam. 24.0 cm | Cream greenish, sand temper |
| 5  | H1012:5    | XIVA  | Rim diam. 22.0 cm | Pale red, pink surface, sand and light organic temper |
| 6  | H526:3     | XIIIC | Rim diam. 30.0 cm | Cream buff, sand and light organic temper |
| 7  | H1038:5    | XIIIB | Rim diam. 26.0 cm | Red, cream surface, sand and light organic temper |
| 8  | H1021:4    | XIIB  | Rim diam. 24.0 cm | Red, buff surface, organic temper |
| 9  | I9:1       | XIIB  | Rim diam. 24.0 cm | Pink, sand and light organic temper |
| 10 | H502:5     | XIB   | Rim diam. 24.0 cm | Pink, sand and light organic temper |
| 11 | I6:3       | XIB   | Rim diam. 22.0 cm | Red, cream surface, sand temper |
| 12 | H777:3     | IX    | Rim diam. 28.0 cm | Buff pink, sand temper |

COMPARANDA FOR TYPE O-3

Sherds of this type may also derive from bases of fruit stands. Nippur: Gibson, Armstrong, and McMahon 1998: fig. 25:8–9 (ED); Diyala: Delougaz 1952: C.084.310 (ED III), but this example is deeper than most; Uch Tepe: Gibson 1981: pl. 99:1 (early Akk.); Umm el-Jīr: Gibson 1972b: fig. 43:B-3a:4–5, B-4:5, B-5:3, B-6:9, fig. 44:B-8:4–6, fig. 45:B-22:1, B-24:2, fig. 46:D IV:5, D I:3, fig. 47:E-2:3 (ED III–Ur III); Abu Salabikh: Martin, Moon, and Postgate 1985: grave 14:2, grave 22:2, grave 26:35, grave 42:7, grave 48:5, grave 73:29, grave 96:3, grave 97:5 (ED III); Moon 1987: nos. 152–63 (ED III); Uruk: Pongratz-Leisten 1988: 254 (ED)

Plate 78

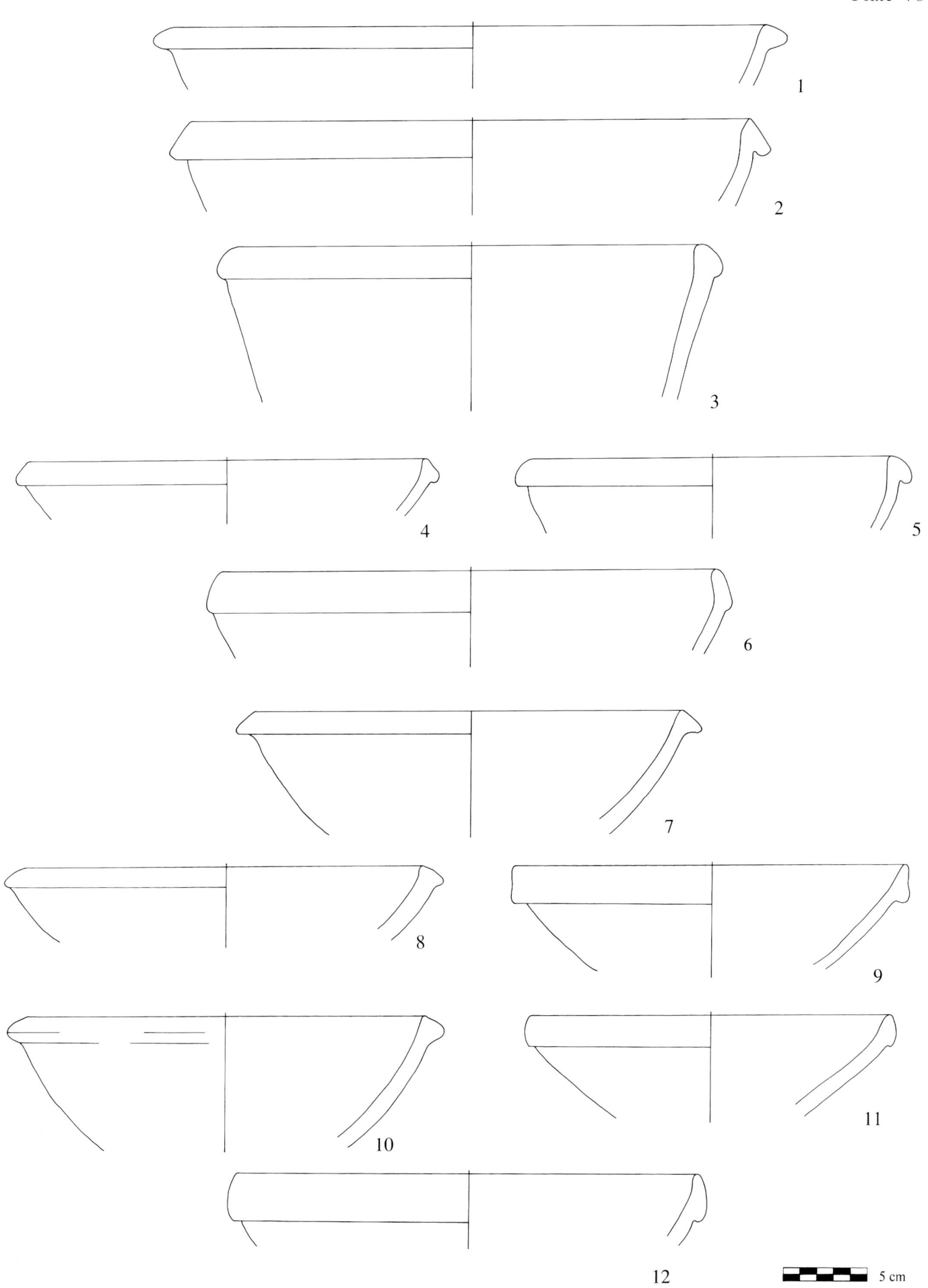

Type O-3: Large Bowl. Scale 1:3

Plate 79. Type O-4: Fruit Stand or Stemmed Dish, Shallow with Band Rim

|   | Lot Number | Level | Dimension | Description |
|---|---|---|---|---|
| 1 | I763:2 | XIXB | Rim diam. 24.0 cm | Buff, cream surface, sand temper |
| 2 | I669:5 | XIXB | Rim diam. 30.0 cm | Buff, cream surface, sand temper |
| 3 | I470:2 | XVIIC | Rim diam. 28.0 cm | Pale red, pink surface, sand and light organic temper |
| 4 | I436:6 | XVIIB | Rim diam. 22.0 cm | Buff, cream surface, sand and light organic temper |

<u>Comparanda for Type O-4</u>

Nippur: McCown, Haines, and Biggs 1978: 44:11 (ED III–early Akk.); unpublished examples from Area EA (ED IIIa); Diyala: Delougaz 1952: C.366.810, C.367.810 (ED II); Kish: Mackay 1929: pl. 49:20 (B. 51, ED III); Ur: Moon 1982: nos. 49, 52, 55, 57 (Ur graves, ED III–early Akk.)

Plate 79

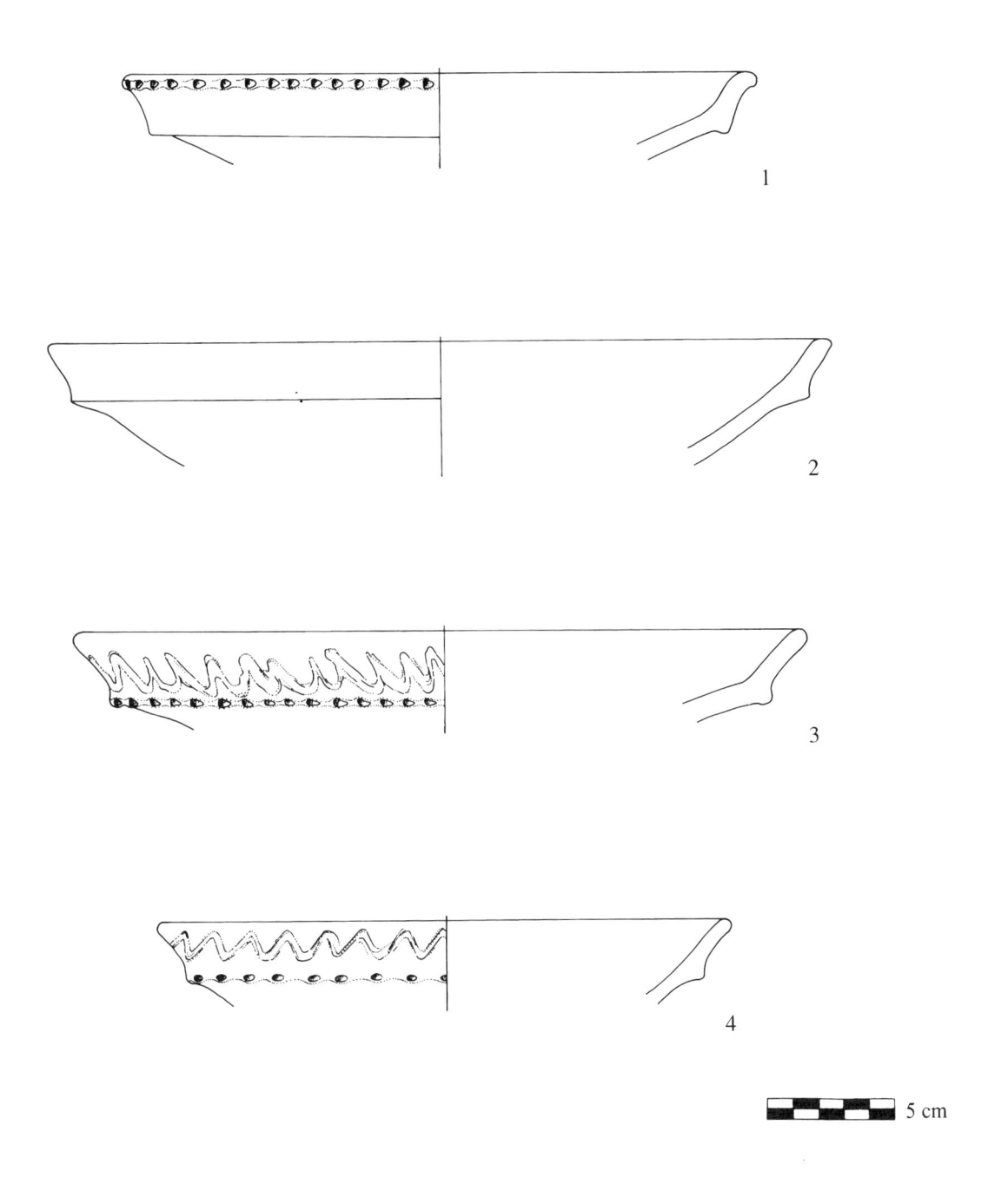

Type O-4: Fruit Stand or Stemmed Dish, Shallow with Band Rim. Scale 2:5

Plate 80. Type O-5: Fruit Stand Stem or Base

|   | Lot Number | Level | Dimension | Description |
|---|---|---|---|---|
| 1 | I772:1 | XIXB | Minimum diam. 7.8 cm | Red, pink surface, sand temper |
| 2 | I439:3 | XVIIB | Base diam. 26.0 cm | Red, pink surface, sand and light organic temper, single-point incision |
| 3 | I370:3 | XVI | Base diam. 26.0 cm | Pale red, buff surface, sand and light organic temper, single-point incision |
| 4 | I406:5 | XVI | Base diam. 22.0 cm | Buff, cream pink surface, sand temper, single-point incision |
| 5 | H1084:1 | XIIIC | Minimum diam. 11.0 cm | Pink, cream surface, sand and light organic temper, single-point incision, palm tree motif |
| 6 | H1098:4 | XIIIB | Base diam. 30.0 cm | Pale red, pink surface, sand and light organic temper, comb incision |
| 7 | H1057:5 | XIIIB | Base diam. 24.0 cm | Pink, buff surface, sand and light organic temper, single-point incision |

Plate 80

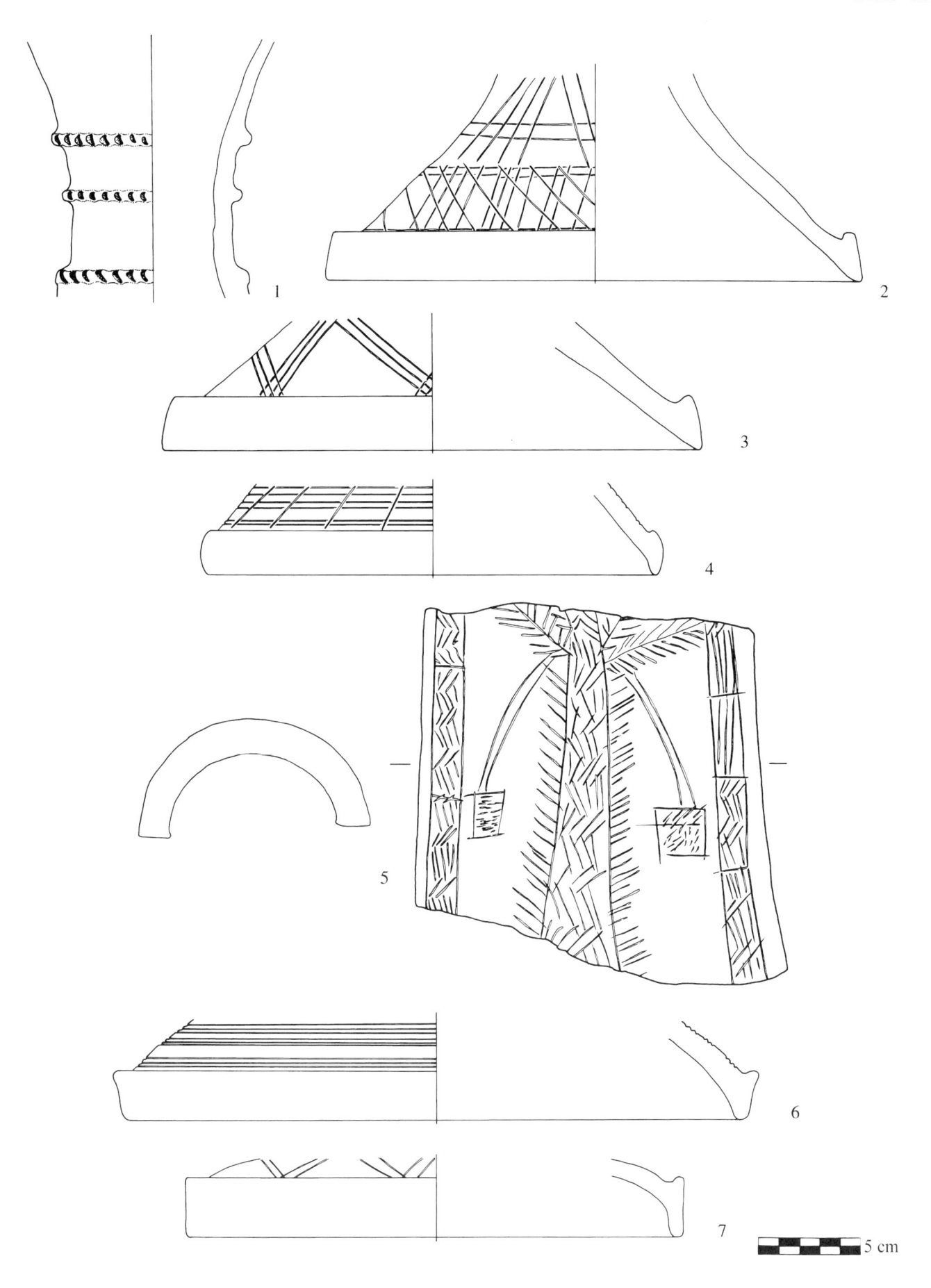

Type O-5: Fruit Stand Stem or Base. Scale 2:5

Plate 81. Type O-6: Feeder Tray

|   | Lot Number | Level | Dimension | Description |
|---|---|---|---|---|
| 1 | I656:2 | XVIII | Rim diam. 32.0 cm, base diam. 33.0 cm, ht. 9.0 cm | Greenish, overfired, heavy organic temper |
| 2 | I388 | XIV | Rim diam. 30.0 cm, base diam. 26.0 cm, ht. 9.5 cm | Dark brown, heavy organic temper |
| 3 | H514:1 | XIIIC | Rim diam. 34.0 cm, base diam. 31.0 cm, ht. 14.0 cm | Green buff, heavy organic temper |
| 4 | H793:8 | IX | Rim diam. 34.0 cm, base diam. 34.0 cm, ht. 10.0 cm | Buff, red core, heavy organic temper |
| 5 | H690:1 | VI | Rim diam. 37.0 cm, base diam. 37.0 cm, ht. 11.5 cm | Buff, pink core, heavy organic temper |

Plate 81

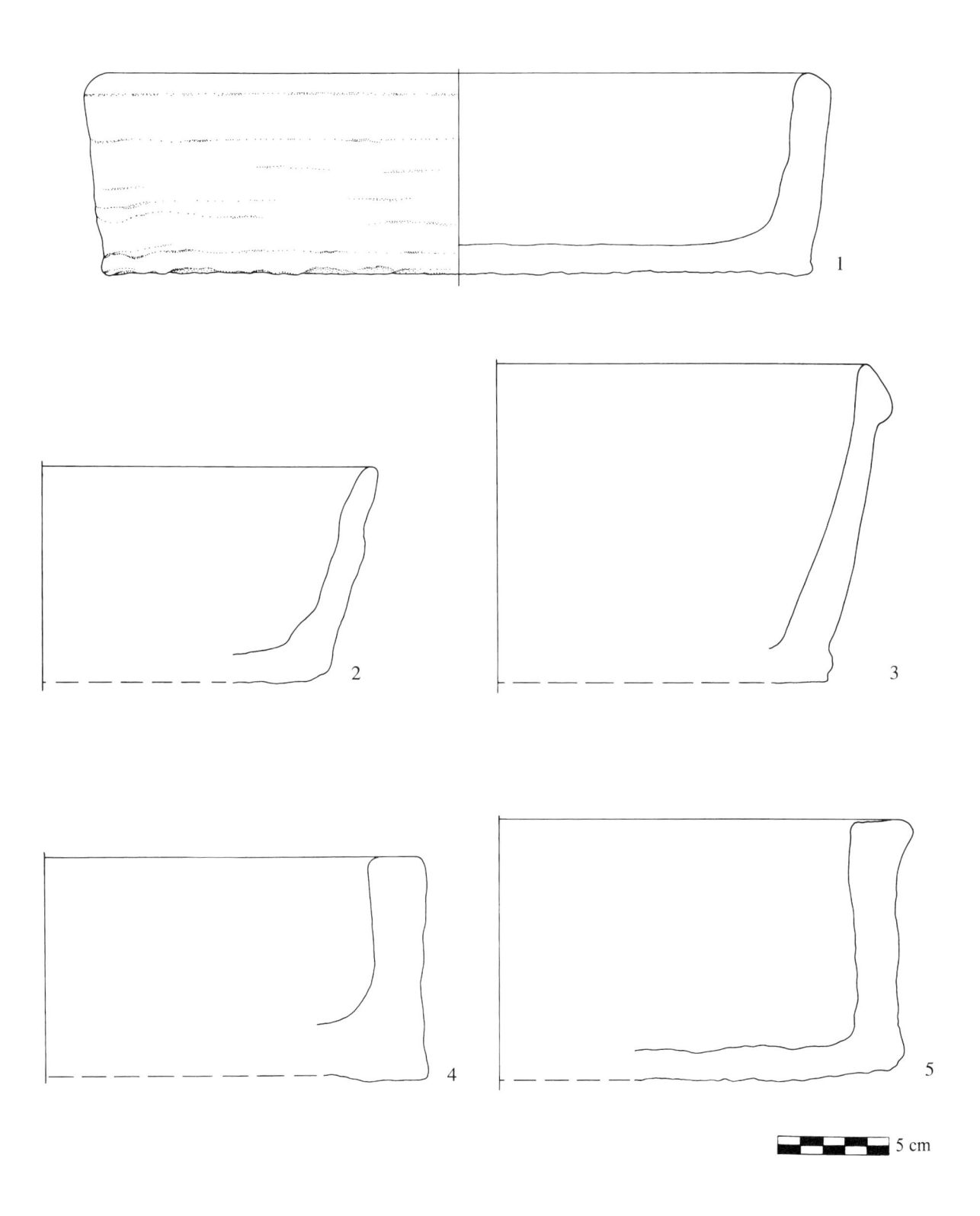

Type O-6: Feeder Tray. Scale 2:5

Plate 82. Type O-7: Large Cylindrical Strainer and Type O-8: Cylindrical Stand

| | Lot Number | Level | Dimension | Description |
|---|---|---|---|---|
| TYPE O-7: LARGE CYLINDRICAL STRAINER | | | | |
| 1 | I681:1 | XVIII | Rim diam. 32.0 cm | Buff green, sand and light organic temper |
| 2 | I436:3 | XVIIB | Rim diam. 26.0 cm | Buff green, sand and light organic temper |
| 3 | H857:3 | XIA | Rim diam. 14.0 cm | Greenish, overfired, organic temper |
| TYPE O-8: CYLINDRICAL STAND | | | | |
| 4 | I433:8 | XVIIA | Rim diam. 9.5 cm, stem diam. 7.0 cm | Pink, cream surface, sand temper |
| 5 | I458:9 | XVIIB | Rim diam. 10.0 cm, stem diam. 7.5 cm | Buff, cream surface, sand and light organic temper |
| 6 | I420:9 | XVI | Rim diam. 10.0 cm, stem diam. 9.0 cm | Buff, sand and light organic temper |
| 7 | I21:1 | XIIIC | Base diam. 8.0 cm, stem diam. 7.0 cm | Pale red, pink surface, sand temper |

COMPARANDA FOR TYPE O-7

Nippur: McCown, Haines, and Biggs 1978: pl. 46:1 (ED III–early Akk.); Gibson, Armstrong, and McMahon 1998: fig. 27:8–9 (ED); Uch Tepe: Gibson 1981: pl. 77:8–9 (ED II), pl. 97:4 (early Akk.); Tell Sabra: Tunca 1987: pl. 89:2–3 (ED III); Abu Salabikh: Moon 1987: nos. 302–05 (ED III)

COMPARANDA FOR TYPE O-8

Possibly should be inverted so that the bowl is at the base and the top is open. Tell al-Hiba: Bahrani 1989: pl. 9:3, possibly 5 (ED IIIB); Fara: Martin 1988: type 99 (ED IIIA); Abu Salabikh: Moon 1987: no. 293 (ED IIIA)

Plate 82

Type O-7: Large Cylindrical Strainer and Type O-8: Cylindrical Stand. Scale 2:5

Plate 83. Type O-9: Fruit Stand or Stemmed Dish

|   | Lot Number | Level | Dimension | Description |
|---|---|---|---|---|
| 1 | I433:3 | XVIIA | Rim diam. 30.0 cm | Buff, cream surface, sand and light organic temper |
| 2 | I406:4 | XVI | Rim diam. 28.0 cm | Red, pink surface, sand temper |
| 3 | I322:1 | XIVB | Rim diam. 28.0 cm | Buff greenish, sand and light organic temper |
| 4 | H514:5 | XIII | Rim diam. 40.0 cm | Red, sand and light organic temper |
| 5 | I5:3 | XIIB | Rim diam. 36.0 cm | Red, cream surface, sand temper |
| 6 | H1010:6 | XIIB | Rim diam. 20.0 cm | Buff, sand and light organic temper |
| 7 | H862:6 | XIA | Rim diam. 20.0 cm | Buff, cream surface, sand and light organic temper |

COMPARANDA FOR TYPE O-9

Diyala: Delougaz 1952: C.365.810b–d (ED III–early Akk.); Tell Sabra: Tunca 1987: pl. 20:12 (= pl. 41:5, ED III–early Akk.?); Umm el-Jīr: Gibson 1972b: fig 34: ED H; Kish: Mackay 1925: pl. 11:2–4, 6–12, pl. 12:13–15, 17; Mackay 1929: pl. 49: especially 16–19, pl. L:1–5 (ED–Akk.); Abu Salabikh: Martin, Moon, and Postgate 1985: grave 1:6, 52, grave 2:4, grave 26:34, grave 28:20, grave 32:8, grave 35:2, grave 73:9, 41, grave 75:6, grave 84:1 (ED IIIa and b); Moon 1981: nos. 51, 54, 62–64, 66, 68–70, 75, 77, 79 (ED III); Moon 1987: nos. 232–40, 244–54 (ED III); Moon 1982: 17–18, 30–31, 46–48, 53, 58 (Kish B.2, 140; Uqair grave 12 and 33: Susa, Ur); Tell al-Hiba: Bahrani 1989: pl. 8:1–4 (ED IIIb)

Plate 83

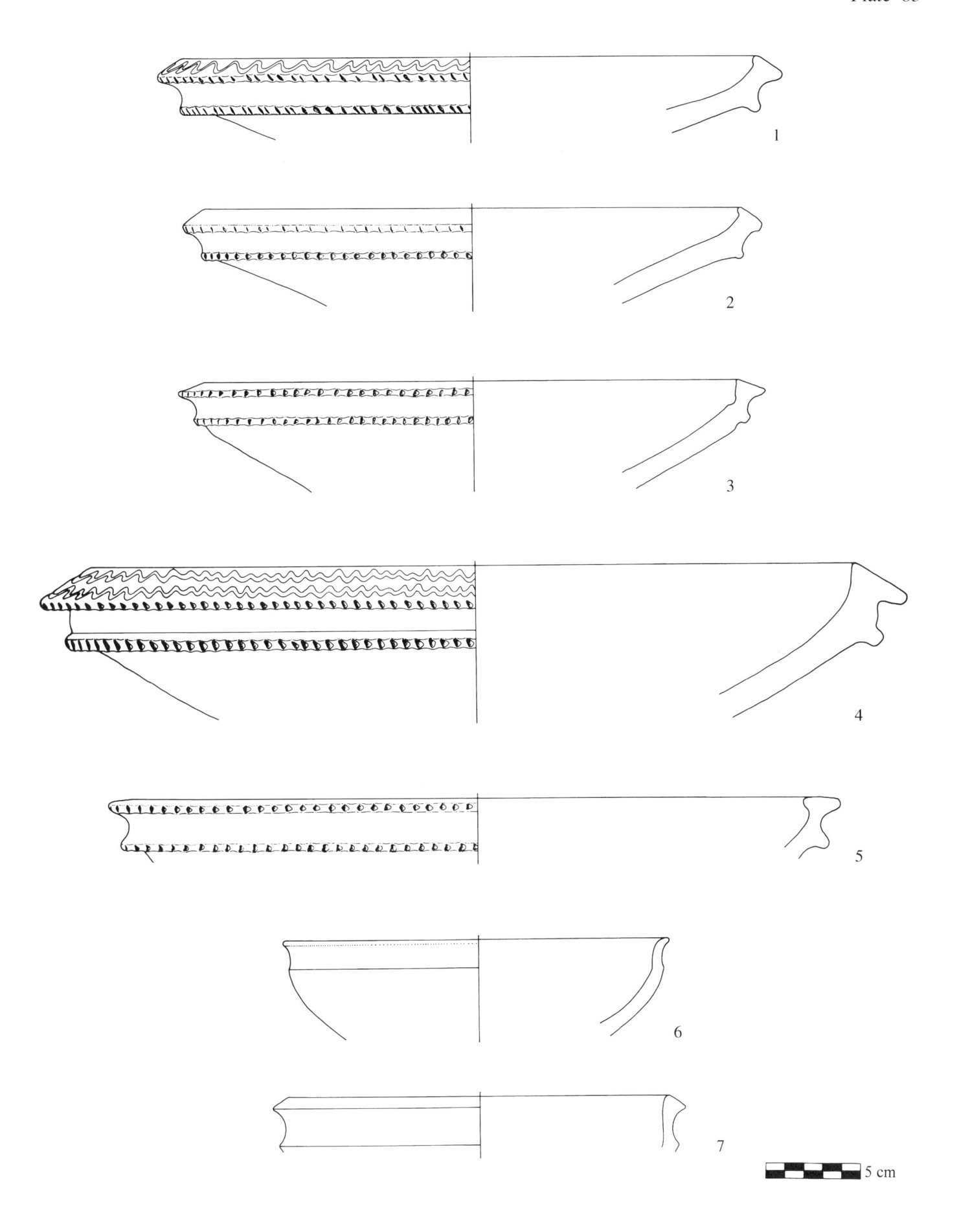

Type O-9: Fruit Stand or Stemmed Dish. Scale 2:5

Plate 84. Type O-10: Conical Bowl with Overhanging Rim

|    | Lot Number | Level | Dimension | Description |
|----|------------|-------|-----------|-------------|
| 1  | I424:1     | XVI   | Rim diam. 17.0 cm | Buff, cream surface, sand and light organic temper |
| 2  | H1082:4    | XIVB  | Rim diam. 18.0 cm, base diam. 5.0 cm, ht. 6.0 cm | Pale red, buff surface, sand and light. organic temper |
| 3  | H540:4     | XIVA  | Rim diam. 18.0 cm | Buff, sand temper |
| 4  | I119:1     | XIVA  | Rim diam. 17.0 cm, base diam. 6.0 cm, ht. 6.0 cm | Pink, cream surface, sand temper |
| 5  | I17:1      | XIIIC | Rim diam. 15.0 cm | Red, cream surface, sand temper |
| 6  | H1078      | XIIIB | Rim diam. 17.0 cm, base diam. 5.0 cm, ht. 5.0 cm | Buff, cream surface, sand and light organic temper. Paired with H1077 as a foundation deposit, Locus 43 below Floor 2, near Wall AO |
| 7  | H1077      | XIIIB | Rim diam. 18.0 cm, base diam. 6.0 cm, ht. 5.5 cm | Buff pale red, sand and light organic temper. Paired with H1078 as a foundation deposit, Locus 43 below Floor 2, near Wall AO |
| 8  | I162:2     | XIIIB | Rim diam. 15.0 cm, base diam. 4.0 cm, ht. 4.5 cm | Buff, sand temper |
| 9  | H1017:1    | XIIB  | Rim diam. 14.0 cm, base diam. 4.5 cm, ht. 5.0 cm | Pale red, sand and light organic temper |
| 10 | H1010:5    | XIIB  | Rim diam. 16.0 cm | Red, sand and light organic temper |
| 11 | H529:2     | XIIA  | Rim diam. 14.0 cm, base diam. 5.5 cm, ht. 5.0 cm | Red, sand and light organic temper |
| 12 | H110:4     | XIIA  | Rim diam. 16.0 cm | Pink, cream surface, sand temper |

COMPARANDA FOR TYPE O-10

Nippur: McCown and Haines 1967: pl. 80:1 (Akk.); Umm el-Jīr: Gibson 1972b: fig. 44:B-7:6, fig. 46:D 4:3, fig. 47:C-2:4, C-5:1, E-2:2, E-3:2, E-5:2 (Akk.); Tell al-Hiba: Bahrani 1989: pl. 1:3 (ED IIIb); unpublished examples from Nippur WC-3 (Ur III), Umm al-Hafriyat (Akk.–Ur III)

Plate 84

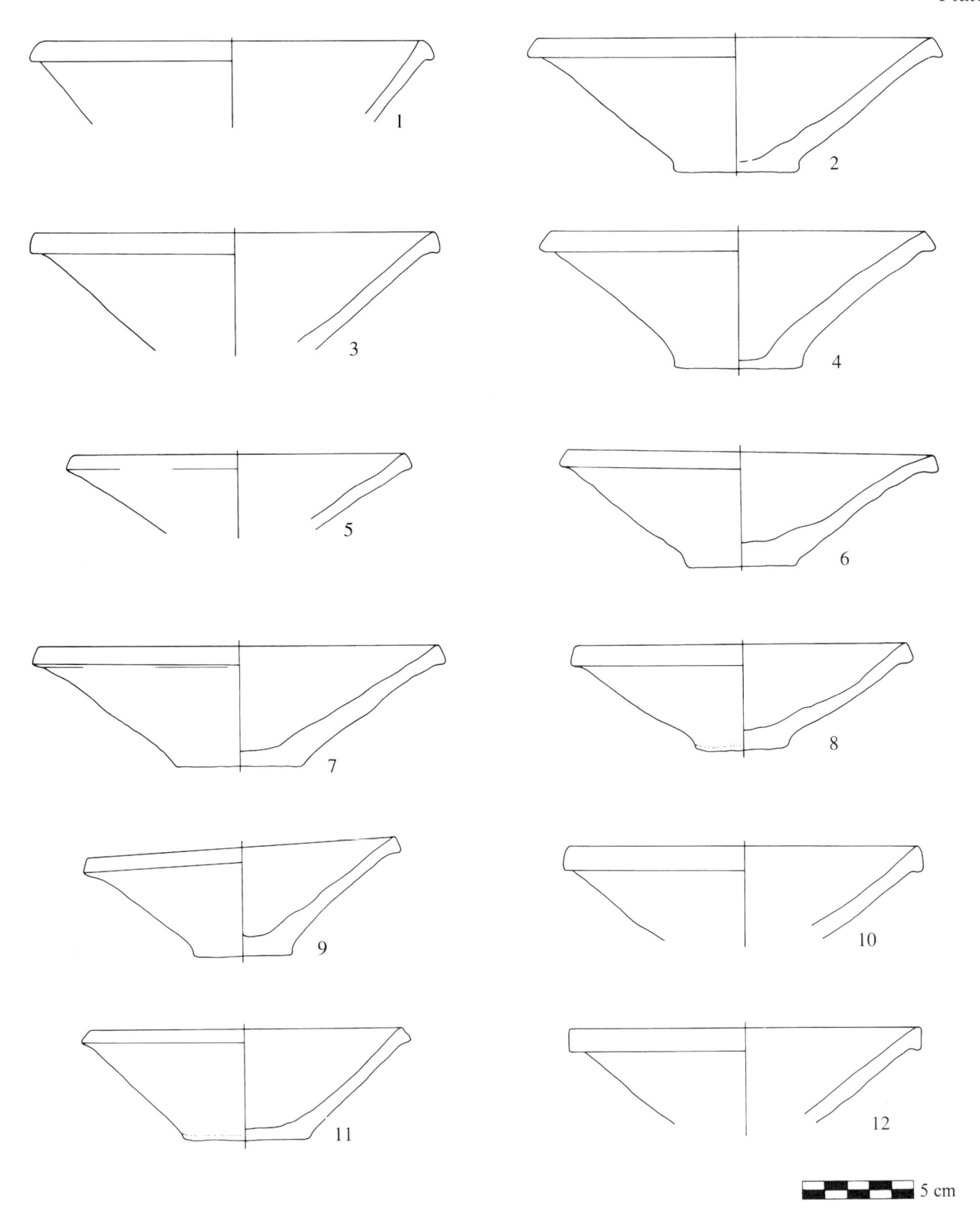

Type O-10: Conical Bowl with Overhanging Rim. Scale 2:5

Plate 85. Type O-10: Conical Bowl with Overhanging Rim (*cont.*)

|   | *Lot Number* | *Level* | *Dimension* | *Description* |
|---|---|---|---|---|
| 1 | H523:1 | XIB | Rim diam. 16.0 cm | Red, sand and light organic temper |
| 2 | H887:3 | XIB | Rim diam. 14.0 cm | Pink, sand temper |
| 3 | H898:1 | XIA | Rim diam. 16.0 cm | Pink, buff surface, sand and light organic temper |
| 4 | I2:1 | X | Rim diam. 14.0 cm, base diam. 5.0 cm, ht. 5.0 cm | Buff, sand temper |
| 5 | H857:1 | X | Rim diam. 16.0 cm | Red, pink surface, sand and light organic temper |
| 6 | H793:3 | IX | Rim diam. 14.0 cm | Buff, cream surface, sand temper |
| 7 | H771:3 | VIII | Rim diam. 14.0 cm | Buff, sand temper |
| 8 | H757:2 | VII | Rim diam. 18.0 cm | Buff, sand temper |

Plate 85

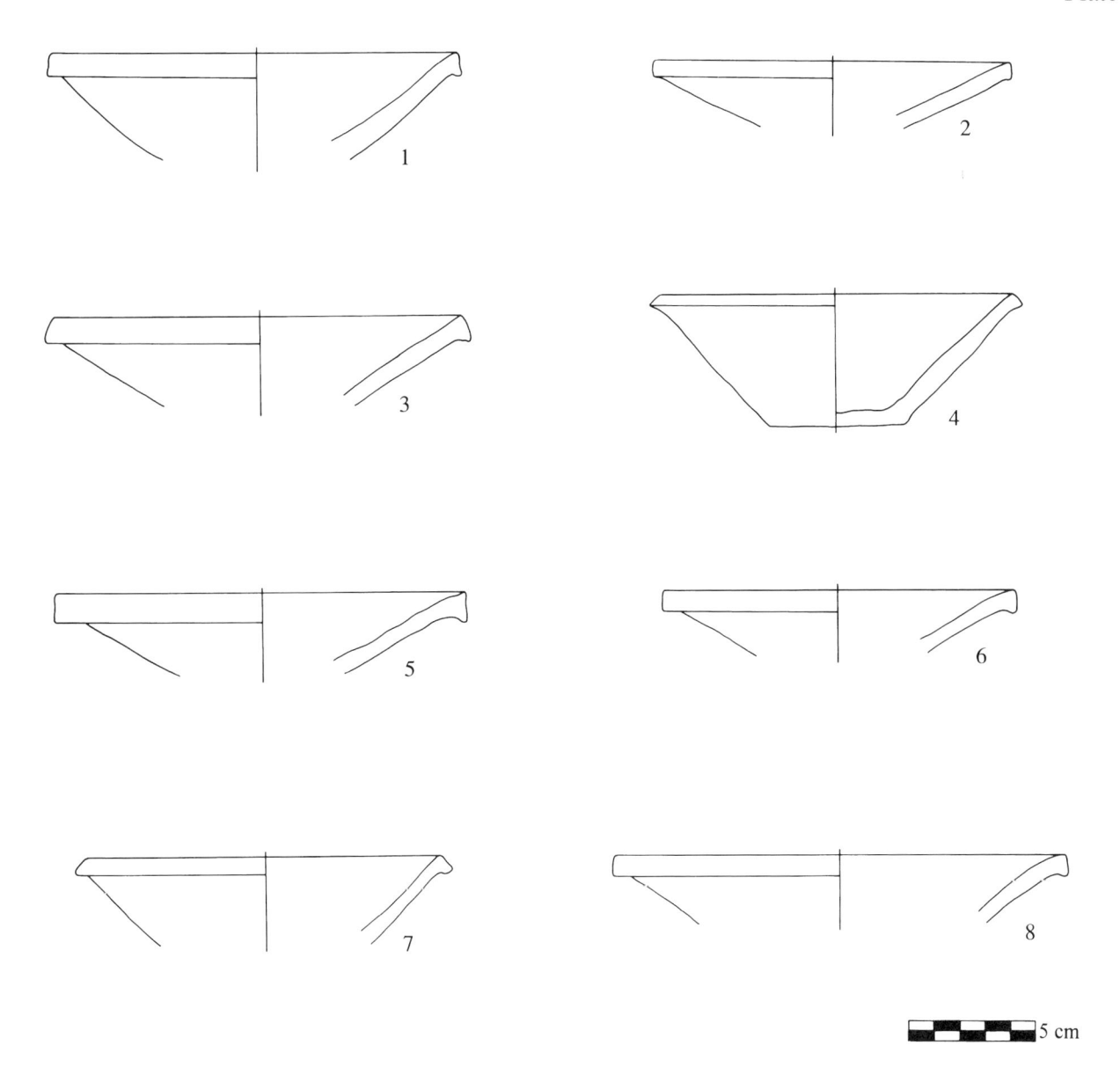

Type O-10: Conical Bowl with Overhanging Rim (*cont.*). Scale 2:5

Plate 86. Type O-11: Conical Bowl with Upturned Rim

|   | Lot Number | Level | Dimension | Description |
|---|---|---|---|---|
| 1 | I20:5 | XIIA | Rim diam. 16.0 cm | Buff, sand temper |
| 2 | H525:3 | XIIA | Rim diam. 14.0 cm | Buff, sand and light organic temper |
| 3 | H539:3 | XIIA | Rim diam. 14.0 cm | Red, sand temper |
| 4 | H502:3 | XIB | Rim diam. 16.0 cm | Pink, sand and light organic temper |
| 5 | H137:5 | XIA | Rim diam. 15.0 cm | Buff, cream surface, sand and light organic temper |
| 6 | H874:1 | X | Rim diam. 12.0 cm | Red, sand and light organic temper |
| 7 | H793:4 | IX | Rim diam. 12.0 cm | Red, sand temper |
| 8 | H771:5 | VIII | Rim diam. 16.0 cm | Buff, sand temper |

COMPARANDA FOR TYPE O-11

Susa: Carter 1980: fig. 49:8 (Ur III); unpublished examples from Nippur WC-3 (Ur III) and Umm al-Hafriyat (Akk.–Ur III)

Plate 86

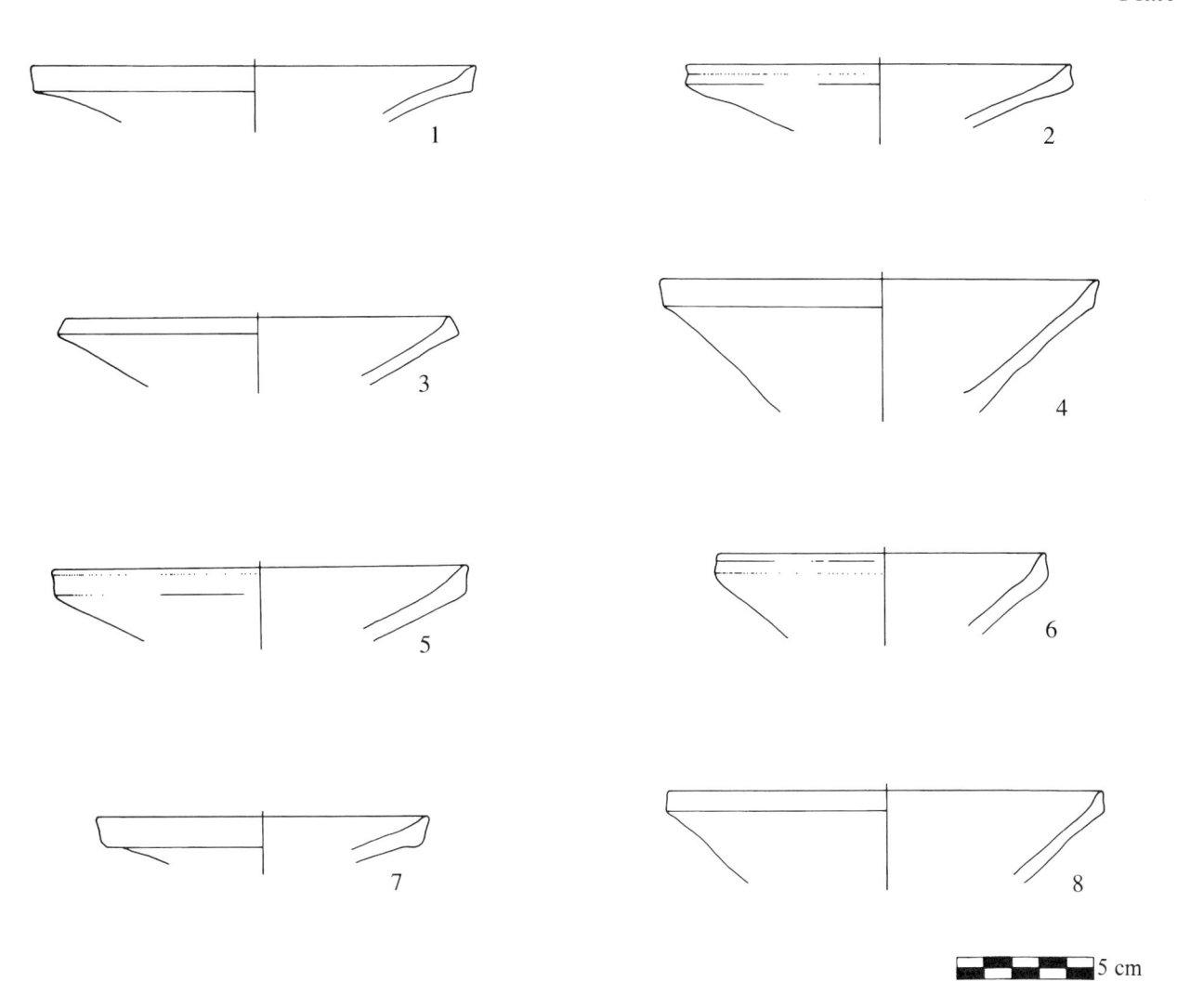

Type O-11: Conical Bowl with Upturned Rim. Scale 2:5

Plate 87. Type O-12: Conical Bowl with Thickened Rim

|    | *Lot Number* | *Level* | *Dimension* | *Description* |
|----|----------|-------|-----------------------------------------------|--------------------------------------------------------|
| 1  | H1028:2  | XIVA  | Rim diam. 18.0 cm                             | Dark red, sand temper                                  |
| 2  | H1012:2  | XIVA  | Rim diam. 16.0 cm                             | Pink, sand and light organic temper                    |
| 3  | I13:1    | XIIIB | Rim diam. 14.0 cm, base diam. 6.0 cm, ht. 4.5 cm | Buff, sand temper                                  |
| 4  | H539:4   | XIIA  | Rim diam. 13.0 cm, base diam. 4.5 cm, ht. 5.0 cm | Red, sand and light organic temper                |
| 5  | H511:2   | XIIA  | Rim diam. 10.0 cm                             | Pink, sand temper                                      |
| 6  | H887:4   | XIB   | Rim diam. 18.0 cm                             | Red, sand temper                                       |
| 7  | H881:3   | XIB   | Rim diam. 14.0 cm                             | Buff, sand temper                                      |
| 8  | H847:3   | XIB   | Rim diam. 16.0 cm                             | Dark buff, sand temper                                 |
| 9  | H859:2   | X     | Rim diam. 18.0 cm                             | Pink, pale buff surface, sand and light organic temper |
| 10 | H874:2   | X     | Rim diam. 14.0 cm                             | Buff, cream surface, sand and light organic temper     |
| 11 | H789:4   | IX    | Rim diam. 18.0 cm                             | Red, sand temper                                       |
| 12 | H773:1   | VIII  | Rim diam. 14.0 cm                             | Buff yellow, sand temper                               |

Comparanda for Type O-12

Nippur: Hansen 1965: fig. 40 (Akk.); Abu Salabikh: Postgate and Moon 1984: no. 2 (post-ED); unpublished examples from Nippur WC-3 (Ur III) and Umm al-Hafriyat (Akk.–Ur III)

Plate 87

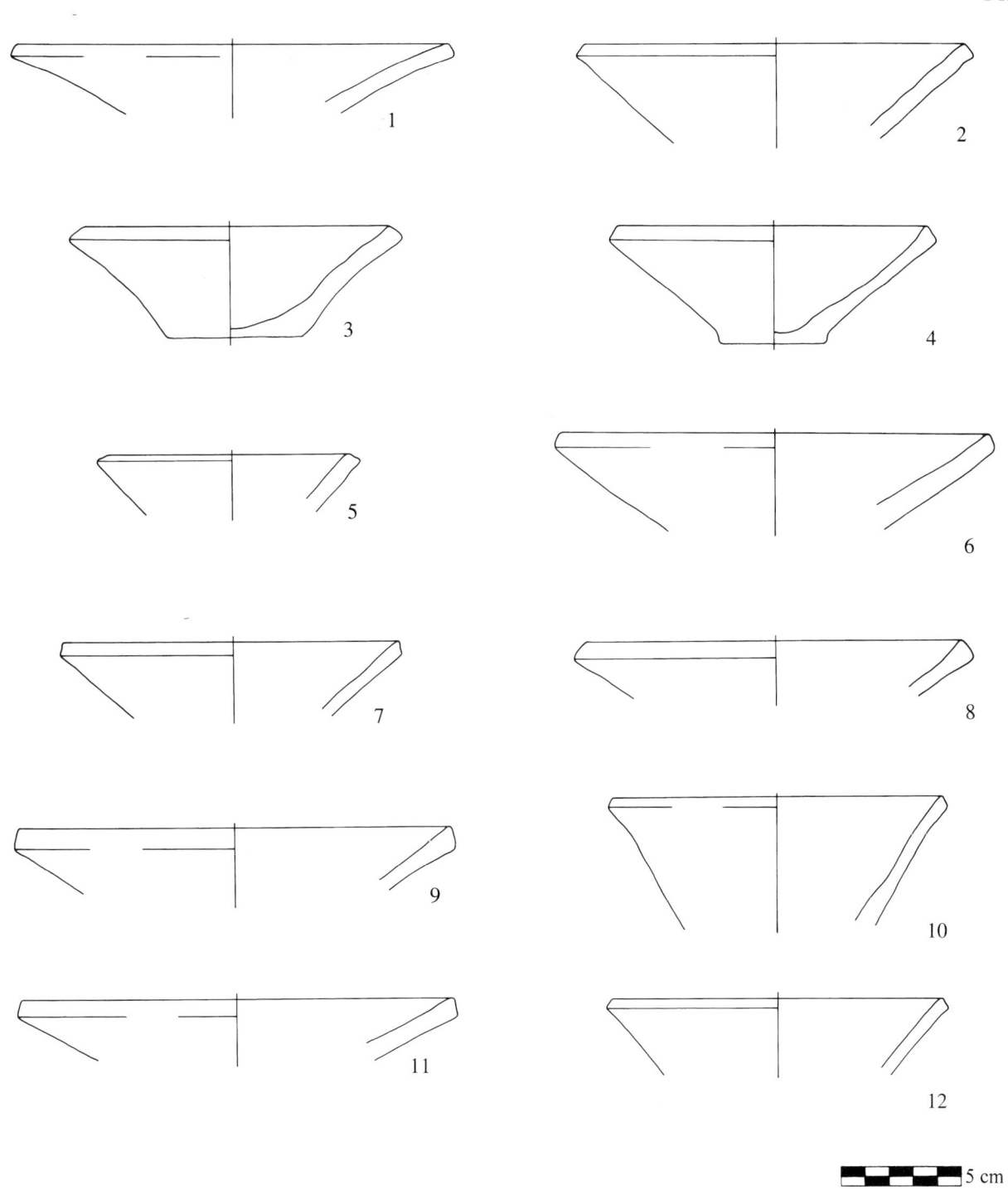

Type O-12: Conical Bowl with Thickened Rim. Scale 2:5

Plate 88. Type O-13: Bowl with Inturned Rim

|   | Lot Number | Level | Dimension | Description |
|---|---|---|---|---|
| 1 | H1012:1 | XIV | Rim diam. 16 cm | Buff pink, sand and light organic temper |
| 2 | H110:2 | XIIA | Rim diam. 14 cm | Cream pink, sand and light organic temper |
| 3 | H881:2 | XIB | Rim diam. 20 cm | Cream buff, sand temper |
| 4 | I6:2 | XIB | Rim diam. 18 cm | Buff, cream surface, sand temper |
| 5 | H838:1 | X | Rim diam. 12 cm | Buff, cream surface, sand temper |
| 6 | H771:2 | VIII | Rim diam. 14 cm | Pale buff, sand temper |

COMPARANDA FOR TYPE O-13

Diyala: Delougaz 1952: B.043.200a, B.052.200a–c (Ur III and later); Umm el-Jīr: Gibson 1972b: fig. 46:D 3:1, fig. 47:C-2:3 (Akk.); Uruk: van Ess 1988: form 8a (Ur III–Isin-Larsa); Ur: Woolley 1934: type 21 (late Akk.–Ur III); Susa: Carter 1980: fig. 45:1–3, (Ur III); Tell Brak: Oates, Oates, and McDonald 2001: nos. 219, 538–39, 570 ff. (Akk.–post-Akk.); unpublished examples from Umm al-Hafriyat (Akk.–Ur III) and Chagar Bazar (post-Akk). In the absence of bases, these inturning rims could come from hemispherical sieves such as those found at Abu Salabikh: Moon 1987: 118–27 (ED III)

Plate 88

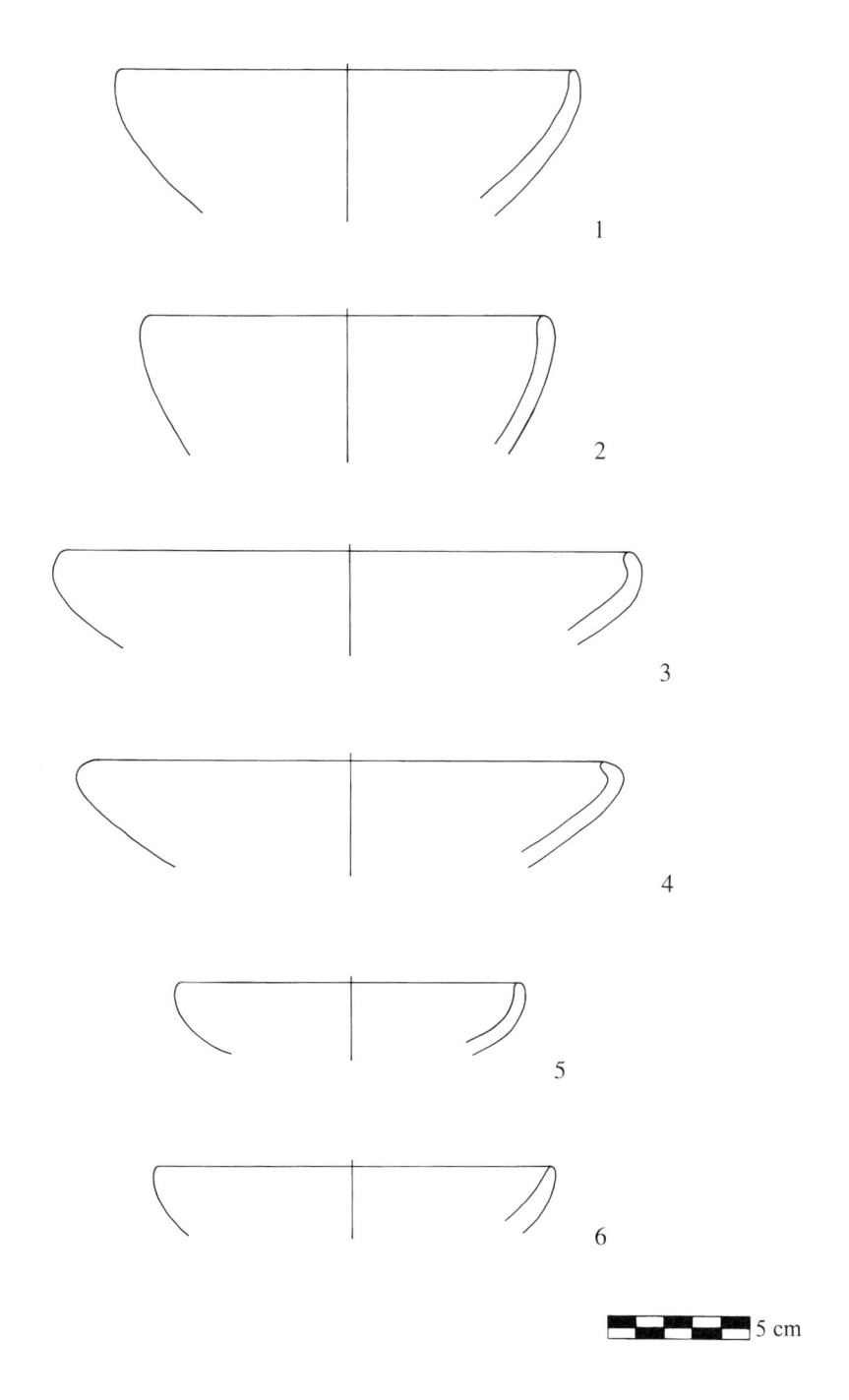

Type O-13: Bowl with Inturned Rim. Scale 2:5

Plate 89. Type O-14: Beveled-rim Cup, Type O-15: Large Carinated Bowl, and Type O-16: Flared-rim Lid

|   | Lot Number | Level | Dimension | Description |
|---|---|---|---|---|
| **Type O-14: Beveled-rim Cup** | | | | |
| 1 | H112:5 | XIIA | Rim diam. 9.5 cm | Red, sand temper |
| 2 | H1021:8 | XIIB | Rim diam. 10.0 cm | Greenish, overfired, sand and light organic temper |
| 3 | H119:5 | XIIB | Rim diam. 10.0 cm | Pink, sand temper |
| **Type O-15: Large Carinated Bowl** | | | | |
| 4 | H1057:6 | XIIIB | Rim diam. 24.0 cm | Red, buff surface, organic temper |
| 5 | H1079:3 | XIIIB | Rim diam. 34.0 cm | Red, cream surface, organic temper |
| 6 | H1021:9 | XIIB | Rim diam. 30.0 cm | Red, buff surface, organic temper |
| **Type O-16: Flared-rim Lid** | | | | |
| 7 | H1021:15 | XIIB | Max. diam. 5.0 cm | Buff, sand and light organic temper |
| 8 | H883:2 | XIB | Rim diam. 9.0 cm | Red, sand and light organic temper |

COMPARANDA FOR TYPE O-14

Nippur: McCown and Haines 1967: pl. 80:5, 7 (Akk.–Ur III); Diyala: Delougaz 1952: B.024.210, B.084.210a–b, B.086.210 (late ED III–Akk.); Tell Sabra: Tunca 1987: pl. 39, group 3, variant b (ED–Akk.); Kish: Gibson 1972a: fig. 34:Akk. E; Umm el-Jīr: Gibson 1972b: fig. 42:e (late Akk.), fig. 48: fl. 1:2 (Akk.); Abu Salabikh: Martin, Moon, and Postgate 1985: grave 79:18–19 (ED III); Uruk: van Ess 1993: fig. 14:173; unpublished examples from Umm al-Hafriyat (Akk.–Ur III). Nos. 1 and 3, inverted, may actually be trumpet bases from small globular jars

COMPARANDA FOR TYPE O-15

Tell Sabra: Tunca 1987: pl. 47:2 (Akk.); Tell al-Hiba: Bahrani 1989: pl. 13:6 (ED IIIb)

COMPARANDA FOR TYPE O-16

Nippur: McCown and Haines 1967: pl. 83:2–3 (Ur III); unpublished examples from Area WC-3 (Ur III); Diyala: Delougaz 1952: B.032.210 (Larsa–OB), B.061.210, B.062.210a (late Akk.–Larsa); Isin: Hrouda 1981: pl. 32:43 (Ur III); Uruk: van Ess 1988: form 19a (Akk.–OB); van Ess 1993: fig. 8:128; Boehmer, Pedde, and Salje 1995: pl. 11:c (Ur III); Ur: Woolley 1934: type 249; Susa: Carter 1980: fig. 49:5 (Ur III)

Plate 89

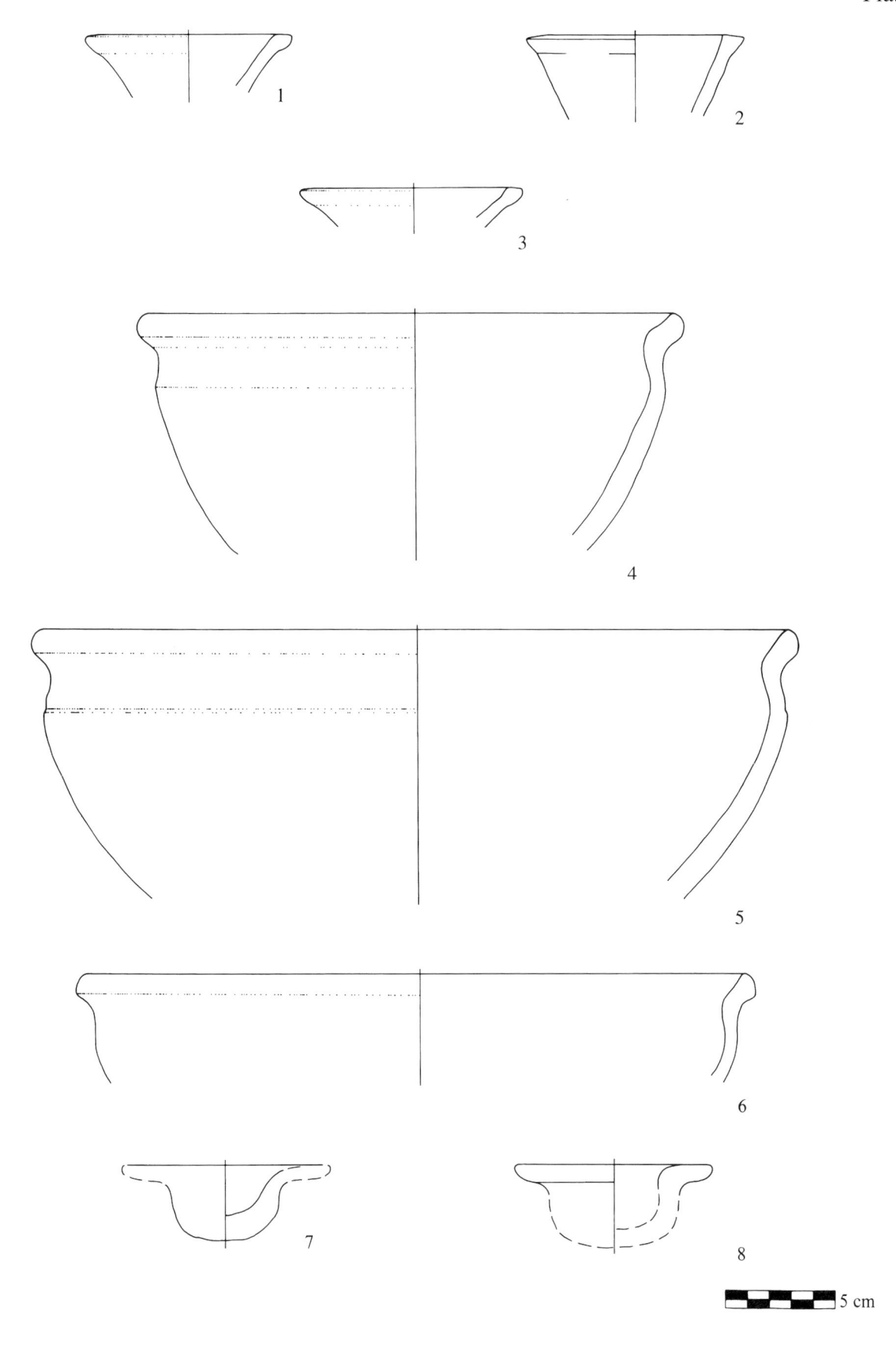

Type O-14: Beveled-rim Cup, Type O-15: Large Carinated Bowl, and Type O-16: Flared-rim Lid. Scale 2:5

Plate 90. Type O-17: Carinated Bowl

|   | Lot Number | Level | Dimension | Description |
|---|---|---|---|---|
| 1 | H899:2 | X | Rim diam. 14.0 cm | Red, sand and light organic temper |
| 2 | H892:1 | X | Rim diam. 13.0 cm | Buff, cream surface, sand and light organic temper |
| 3 | H854:2 | X | Rim diam. 12.0 cm | Red, sand temper |
| 4 | H838:2 | X | Rim diam. 14.0 cm | Buff, sand temper |
| 5 | H763:2 | VIII | Rim diam. 16.0 cm | Pink, sand and light organic temper |
| 6 | H754:2 | VIII | Rim diam. 16.0 cm | Pale buff, sand temper |
| 7 | H754:1 | VIII | Rim diam. 14.0 cm | Buff, sand temper |
| 8 | H754:12 | VIII | Rim diam. 12.0 cm, base diam. 4.5 cm, ht. 3.0 cm | Buff, sand temper |
| 9 | H763:1 | VIII | Rim diam. 16.0 cm | Red, sand temper |
| 10 | H692:1 | VI | Rim diam. 12.0 cm | Buff, sand temper |
| 11 | H689:2 | VI | Rim diam. 12.0 cm | Buff, sand temper |
| 12 | H679:3 | VI | Rim diam. 14.0 cm | Buff, sand temper |

COMPARANDA FOR TYPE O-17

Nippur: Gibson et al. 1978: fig. 8:1, 3–5 (Isin-Larsa); McCown and Haines 1967: pl. 82:19–20 (Ur III); unpublished examples from Area WC-3 (Ur III); Diyala: Delougaz 1952: B.151.210 (late Akk. and later); Survey: Gibson 1972a: fig. 34: Ur III A; Umm el-Jīr: Gibson 1972b: fig. 42c, fig. 43:B-3 a:3, B-3b:3, B-4:3, B-5:2, fig. 44:B-7:4, fig. 46:D 5:1(Akk.–Ur III); Isin: Hrouda 1977: pl. 27:IB 386, 298 (Ur III); Hrouda 1981: pl. 32:44, 47–48 (Ur III); Tell al-Wilayah: Madhlum 1960: fig. 3:19; Fara: Martin 1988: fig. 41:13 (Akk.–Ur III); Tello: Parrot 1948: fig. 56:1110 (Ur III); Abu Salabikh: Postgate and Moon 1984: nos. 6–7 (post-ED); Uruk: van Ess 1988: form 6a (Akk.–Isin-Larsa); van Ess 1993: fig. 8:129 et passim; Boehmer, Pedde, and Salje 1995: pl. 6:c1–4, pl. 9:a–c, g–i, et passim (Ur III); Ur: Woolley 1934: types 26–27 (late Akk.–Ur III); Susa: Carter 1980: fig. 41:1–4, fig. 45:4–6, fig. 49:9–13 (Ur III); Steve and Gasche 1971: pl. 2:2–8, 28–35, pl. 3:10, pl. 4:2–4 (Ur III), pl. 5:14 (Akk.); Nineveh: McMahon 1998: fig. 7:26–28 (post-Akk.); Brak: Oates, Oates, and McDonald 2001: no. 610 (post-Akk.)

Plate 90

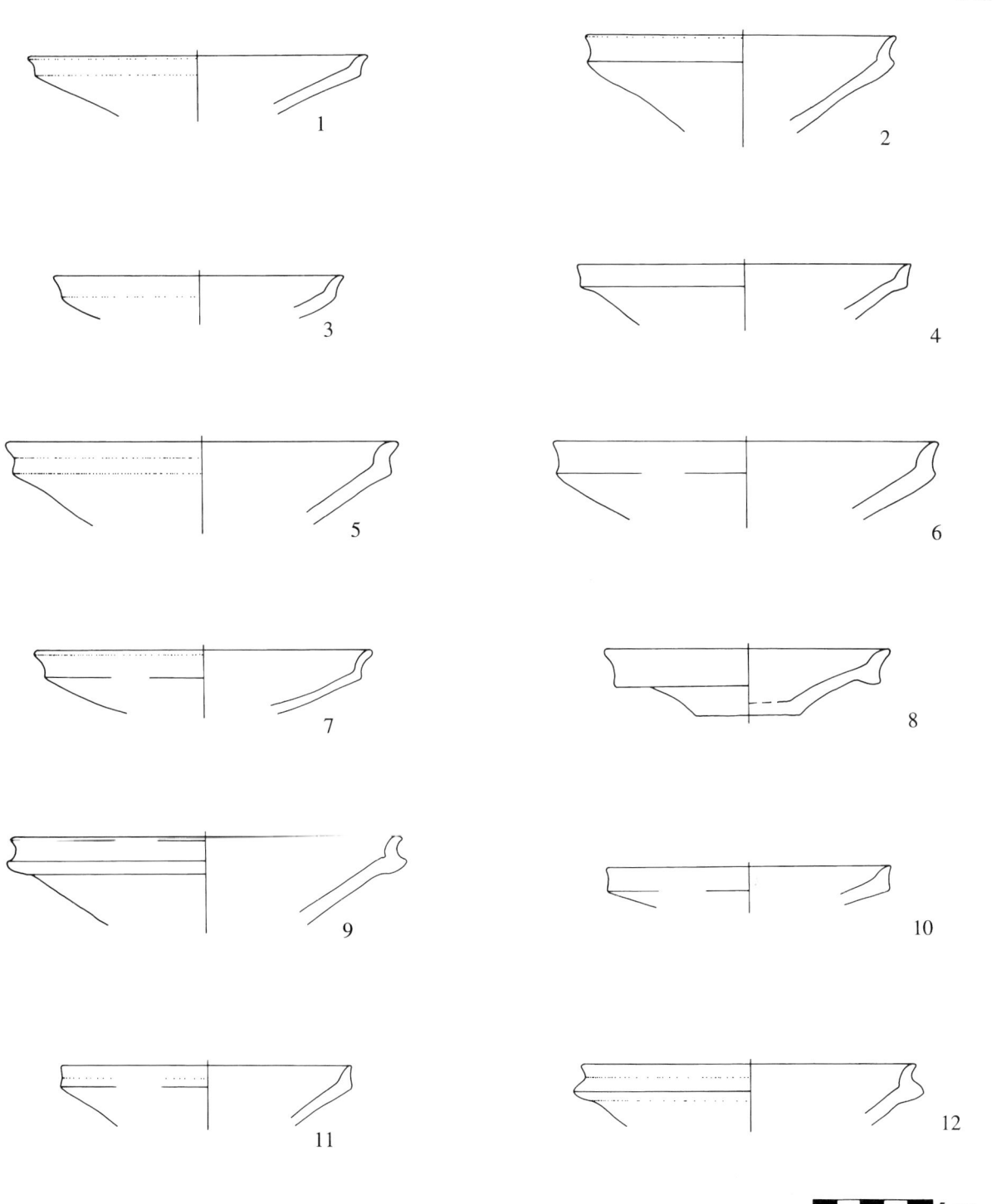

Type O-17: Carinated Bowl. Scale 2:5

Plate 91. Type O-18: Large Ledge-rim Bowl and Type O-20: Large Vessel with Grooved Sides

|   | Lot Number | Level | Dimension | Description |
|---|---|---|---|---|
| TYPE O-18: LARGE LEDGE-RIM BOWL |
| 1 | H887:6 | XIB | Rim diam. 30.0 cm | Red, cream surface, sand and light organic temper |
| 2 | I2:2 | X | Rim diam. 30.0 cm | Pink, buff surface, sand temper |
| TYPE O-20: LARGE VESSEL WITH GROOVED SIDES |
| 3 | H887:9 | XIB | Rim diam. 32.0 cm | Red, cream surface, sand and light organic temper |
| 4 | H879:4 | XIA | Rim diam. 38.0 cm | Buff, cream surface, light organic temper |
| 5 | H783:6 | IX | Rim diam. 36.0 cm | Red, pink surface, sand temper |

COMPARANDA FOR TYPE O-18

Susa: Carter 1980: fig. 49:20 (Ur III)

COMPARANDA FOR TYPE O-20

Nippur: McCown and Haines 1967: pl. 80:9 (Akk.); Abu Salabikh: Postgate and Moon 1984: 49 (post-ED)

Plate 91

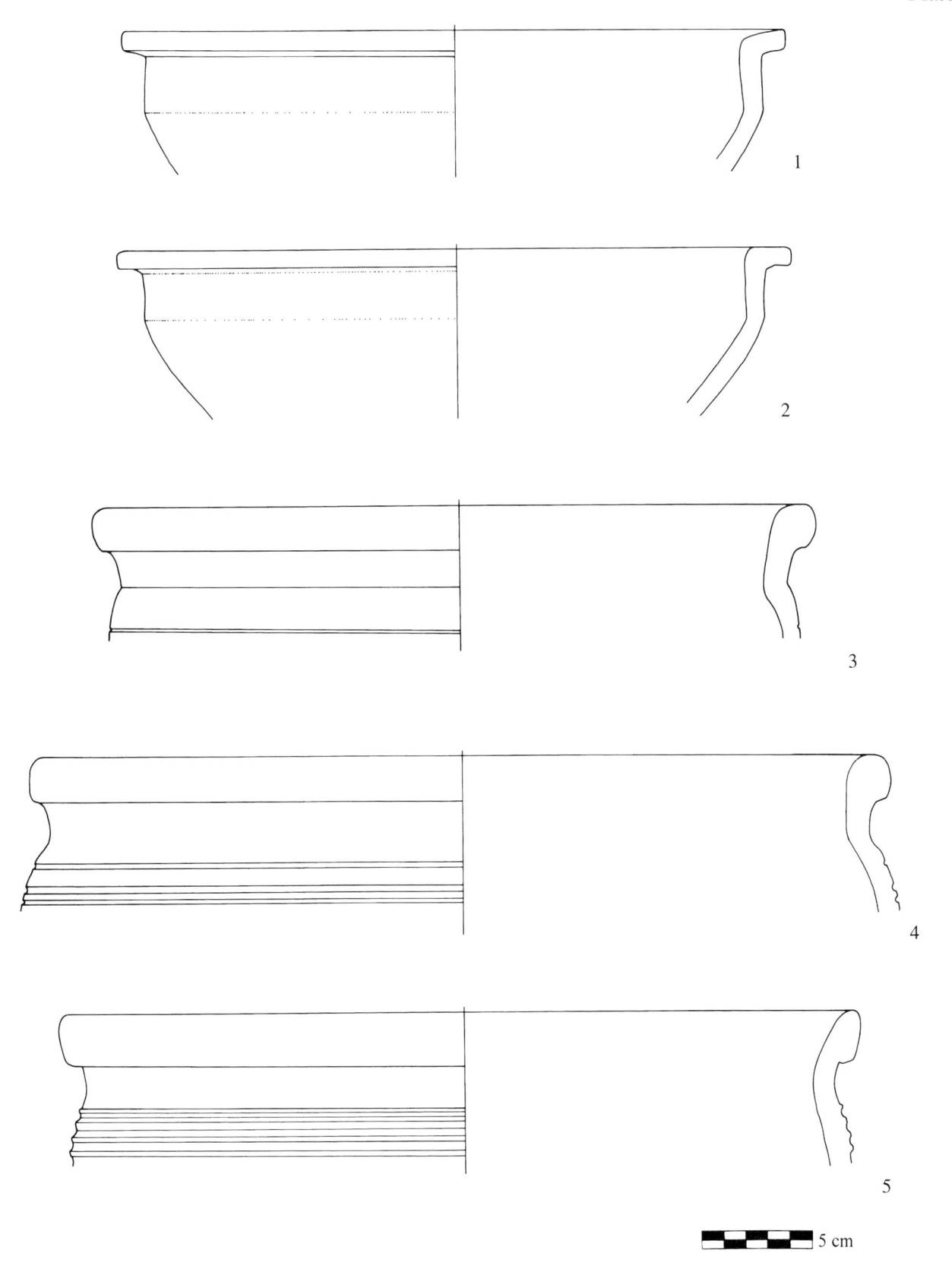

Type O-18: Large Ledge-rim Bowl and Type O-20: Large Vessel with Grooved Sides. Scale 2:5

Plate 92. Type O-19: Large Triangular-rim Bowl

|   | Lot Number | Level | Dimension | Description |
|---|---|---|---|---|
| 1 | H877:3 | XIB | Rim diam. 28.0 cm | Red, sand and light organic temper |
| 2 | H509:3 | XIB | Rim diam. 34.0 cm | Red, sand and light organic temper |
| 3 | H862:4 | XIA | Rim diam. 28.0 cm | Red, buff surface, organic temper |
| 4 | H855:4 | X | Rim diam. 28.0 cm | Pink, pale buff surface, organic temper |
| 5 | H793:5 | IX | Rim diam. 34.0 cm | Pink buff, organic temper |
| 6 | H774:4 | VIII | Rim diam. 28.0 cm | Red, buff surface, organic temper |
| 7 | H768:2 | VII | Rim diam. 30.0 cm | Buff, organic temper |

COMPARANDA FOR TYPE O-19

Abu Salabikh: Moon 1987: nos. 158–60 (ED IIIa). These are the closest published examples, but the WF version is usually shallower.

Plate 92

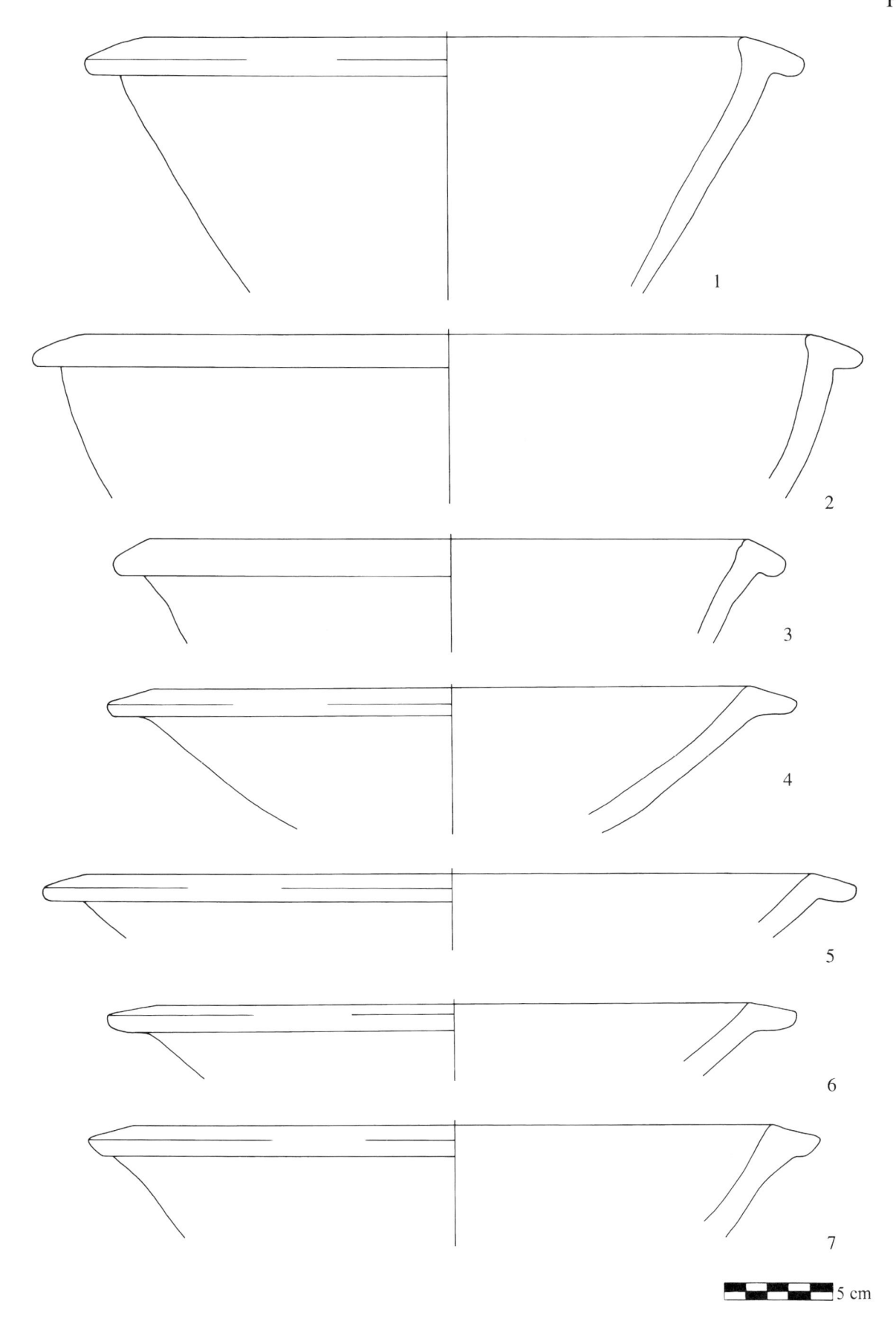

Type O-19: Large Triangular-rim Bowl. Scale 2:5

Plate 93. Type O-21: Large Carinated-sided Bowl

|   | Lot Number | Level | Dimension | Description |
|---|---|---|---|---|
| 1 | H835:1 | XIB | Rim diam. 24.0 cm | Cream, sand and light organic temper |
| 2 | H857:4 | XIA | Rim diam. 24.0 cm | Greenish buff, sand and light organic temper |
| 3 | H862:3 | XIA | Rim diam. 24.0 cm | Buff greenish, sand and light organic temper |
| 4 | H779:2 | IX | Rim diam. 22.0 cm | Yellow buff, sand temper |
| 5 | H789:5 | IX | Rim diam. 24.0 cm | Red, cream surface, sand temper |
| 6 | H763:6 | VIII | Rim diam. 20.0 cm | Red, buff surface, sand and light organic temper |

COMPARANDA FOR TYPE O-21

Umm el-Jīr: Gibson 1972b: fig. 47:C-1:2 (Akk.); Tell al-Hiba: Bahrani 1989: pl. 13:4 (ED IIIb)

Plate 93

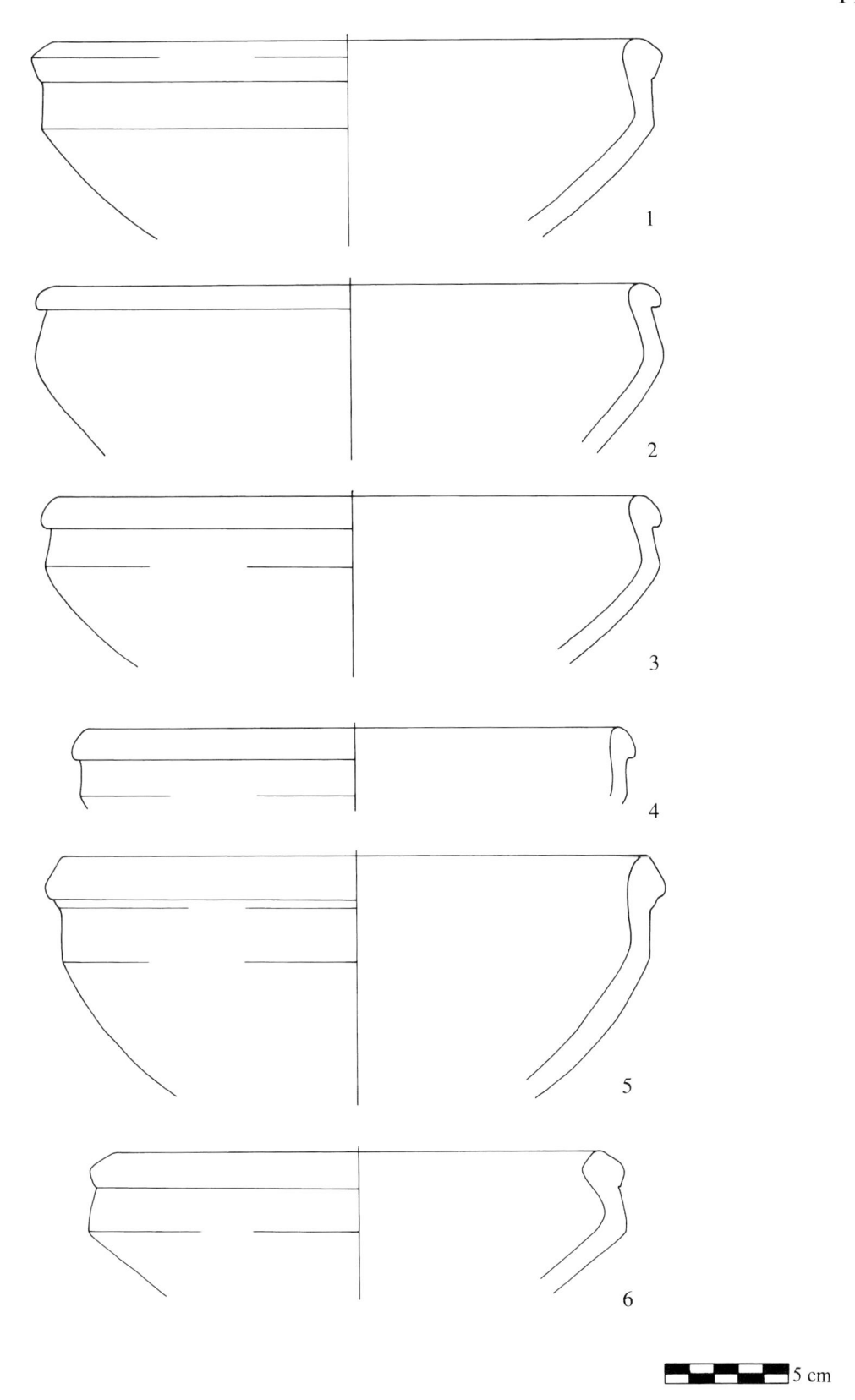

Type O-21: Large Carinated-sided Bowl. Scale 2:5

Plate 94. Type O-22: Band-rim Bowl and Type O-23: Hemispherical Strainer Bowl

|    | Lot Number | Level | Dimension | Description |
|----|------------|-------|-----------|-------------|
| TYPE O-22: BAND-RIM BOWL ||||||
| 1  | H854:1  | X    | Rim diam. 15.0 cm | Red, sand temper |
| 2  | H789:1  | IX   | Rim diam. 13.0 cm | Buff, sand and light organic temper |
| 3  | H754:3  | VIII | Rim diam. 13.0 cm, base diam. 5.0 cm, ht. 4.0 cm | Buff, sand temper |
| 4  | H795:1  | VIII | Rim diam. 16.0 cm | Pink, buff surface, sand temper |
| 5  | H754:13 | VIII | Rim diam. 12.0 cm | Red, sand and light organic temper |
| 6  | H763:8  | VIII | Rim diam. 15.0 cm | Yellow buff, sand temper |
| 7  | H763:7  | VIII | Rim diam. 12.0 cm | Pale buff, sand and light organic temper |
| 8  | H679:2  | VII  | Rim diam. 11.0 cm, base diam. 3.5 cm, ht. 4.0 cm | Yellow buff, sand temper |
| 9  | H696:1  | VII  | Rim diam. 13.5 cm, base diam. 6.0 cm, ht. 4.0 cm | Pink, sand temper |
| 10 | H700:1  | VI   | Rim diam. 12.0 cm, base diam. 4.0 cm, ht. 4.0 cm | Red, sand and light organic temper |
| 11 | H752:1  | VI   | Rim diam. 16.0 cm | Red, cream surface, sand temper |
| TYPE O-23: HEMISPHERICAL STRAINER BOWL ||||||
| 12 | H771:7  | VIII | Rim diam. 8.0 cm | Buff green, sand temper |
| 13 | H388:3  | IV   | Rim diam. 12.0 cm | Buff, sand temper |

COMPARANDA FOR TYPE O-22

Nippur: Gibson et al. 1978: fig. 8:7–8 (Isin-Larsa); McCown and Haines 1967: pl. 82:18, 21–22 (Ur III); Fara: Martin 1988: type 134 (Ur III); unpublished examples from Nippur WC-3 (Ur III) and Umm al-Hafriyat (late Akk.–Ur III)

COMPARANDA FOR TYPE O-23

Nippur: McCown and Haines 1967: pl. 82:10–11 (Akk.–Isin-Larsa); unpublished examples from WC-3 (Ur III); Diyala: Delougaz 1952: B.032.500 (late Larsa), B.041.200, B.042.500a (late Akk.); Survey: Gibson 1972a: fig. 34 (Ur III/Isin-Larsa I); Umm el-Jīr: Gibson 1972b: fig. 46:D I:10 (Akk.); Tell Chuera: Kühne 1976: figs. 327–28 (ED III); Chagar Bazar: unpublished examples (post-Akk.); Brak: Oates, Oates, and McDonald 2001: nos. 1627–45 (mostly Akk.–post-Akk.); Tell Taya: Reade 1968: pl. 85:16 (Akk.); Tepe Gawra: Speiser 1935: pl. 67:97, 100 (ED–early Akk.); Uruk: van Ess 1988: form 18 (Isin-Larsa); Ur: Woolley 1934: type 248 (Ur III)

Plate 94

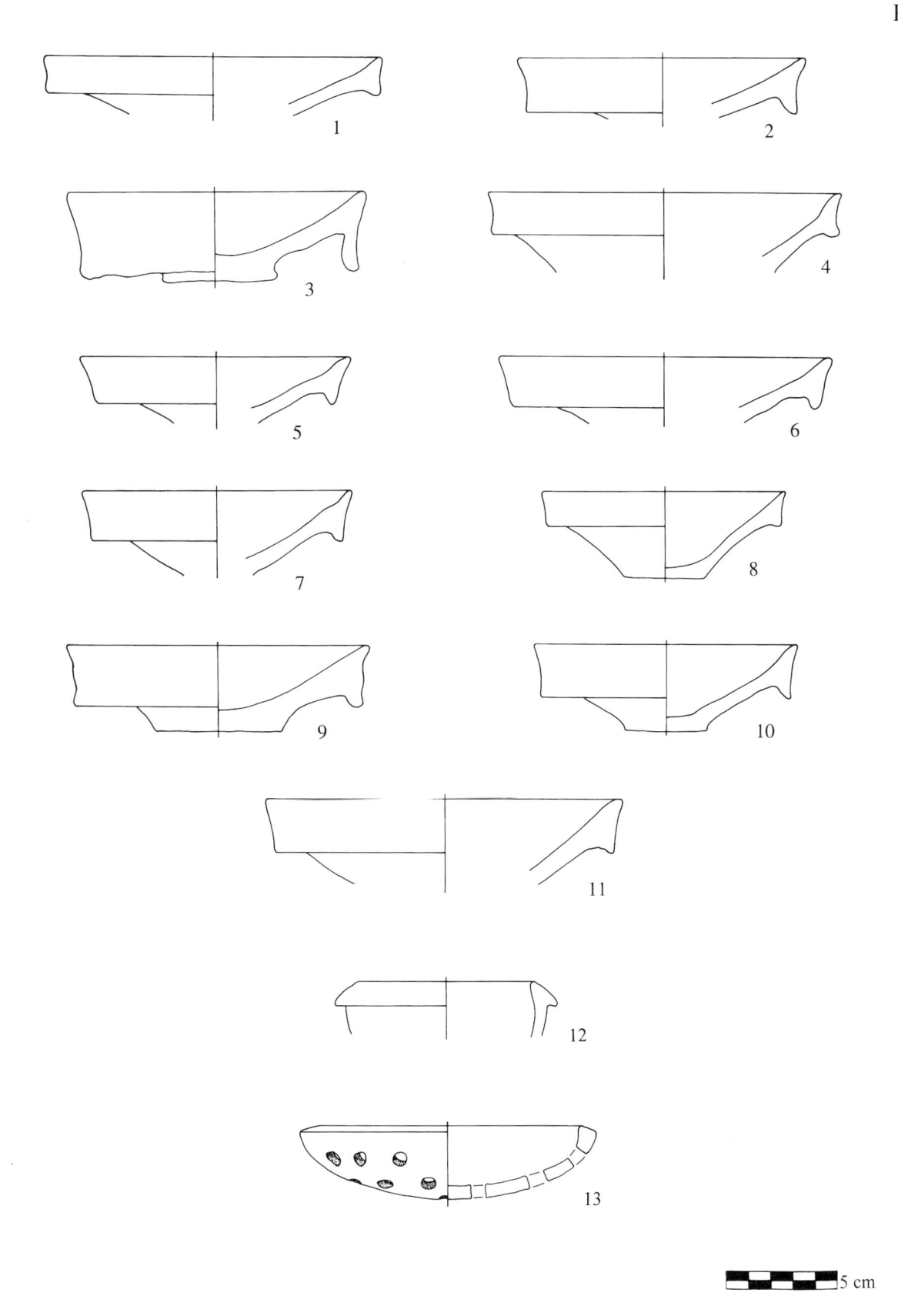

Type O-22: Band-rim Bowl and Type O-23: Hemispherical Strainer Bowl. Scale 2:5

Plate 95. Types O-24 and O-25: Large Vessels with Comb-incised Sides

|   | Lot Number | Level | Dimension | Description |
|---|---|---|---|---|
| TYPE O-24: LARGE VESSEL WITH COMB-INCISED SIDES ||||||
| 1 | H754:8 | VIII | Rim diam. 56.0 cm | Buff, sand and organic temper, bitumen on exterior, comb incision |
| TYPE O-25: LARGE VESSEL WITH COMB-INCISED SIDES ||||||
| 2 | H700:3 | VI | Rim diam. 36.0 cm | Buff, sand temper, bitumen on exterior, comb incision |
| 3 | H365:10 | IV | Rim diam. 30.0 cm | Green, sand temper, comb incision |

COMPARANDA FOR TYPE O-24

Brak: Oates, Oates, and McDonald 2001: no. 336 (post-Akk.)

COMPARANDA FOR TYPE O-25

Nippur: McCown and Haines 1967: pl. 84:21 (Ur III); unpublished examples from Nippur WC-3 and Umm al-Hafriyat (Ur III); Survey: Adams 1981: fig. 7c (Akk.); Fara: Martin 1988: fig. 43:2 (Akk.–Ur III); Abu Salabikh: Postgate and Moon 1984: nos. 21–22, 24 (post-ED); Brak: Oates, Oates, and McDonald 2001: nos. 326, 329–33 (Akk.–post-Akk.); Susa: Steve and Gasche 1971: pl. 2:40, pl. 3:1–2, 6

Plate 95

1

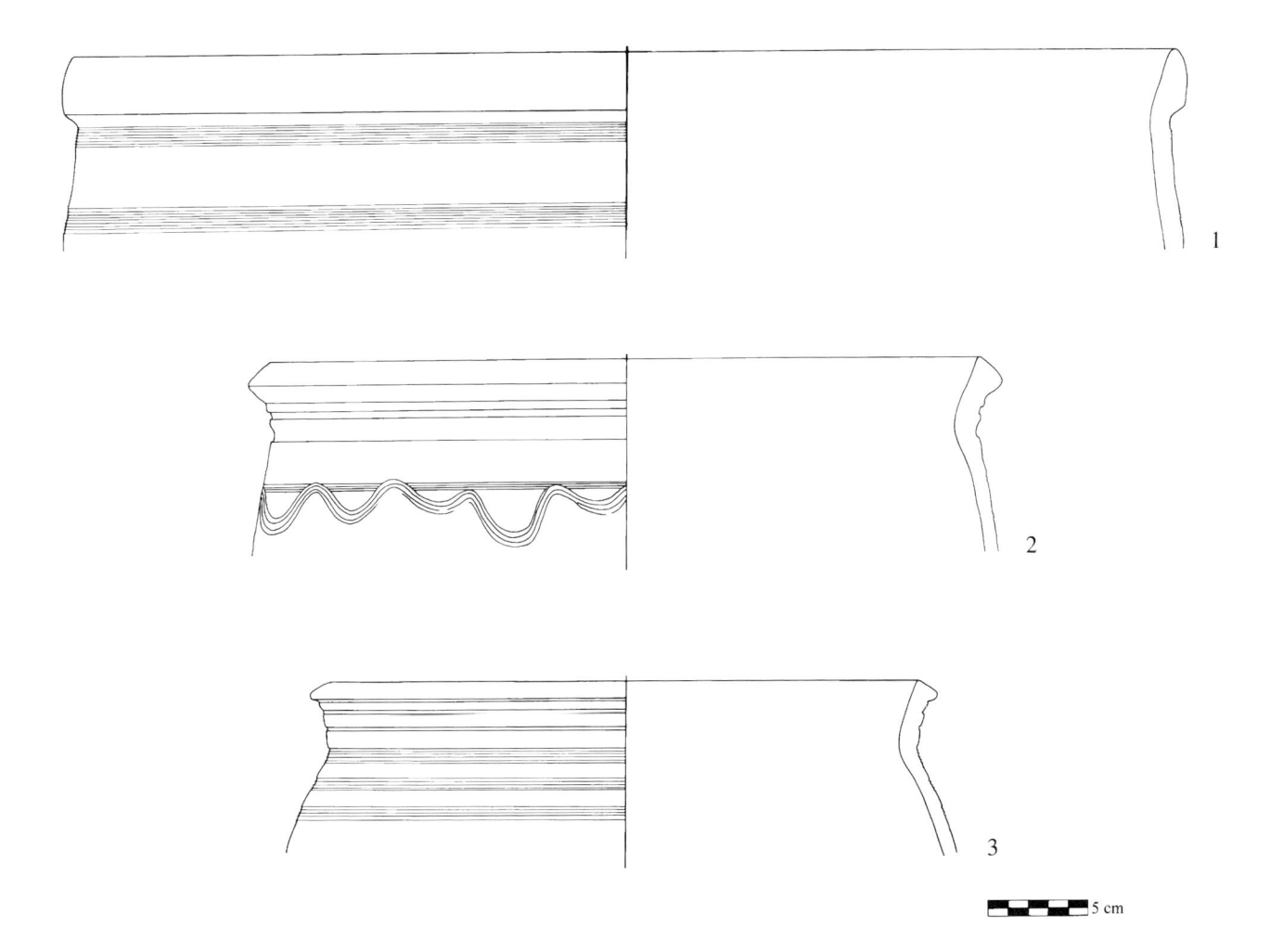

2

3

5 cm

Types O-24 and O-25: Large Vessels with Comb-incised Sides. Scale 1.5:5

Plate 96. Type C-1: Plain-rim Jar

|   | Lot Number | Level | Dimension | Description |
|---|---|---|---|---|
| TYPE C-1: PLAIN-RIM JAR (WIDE) |
| 1 | I669:1 | XIXB | Rim diam. 12.0 cm | Pink, buff surface, sand temper |
| 2 | I656:3 | XVIII | Rim diam. 12.0 cm | Buff, sand temper |
| 3 | I470:5 | XVIIC | Rim diam. 12.0 cm | Buff, sand and light organic temper |
| 4 | I454:5 | XVIIB | Rim diam. 12.0 cm | Buff, cream surface, sand temper |
| 5 | I361:3 | XVB | Rim diam. 12.0 cm | Pale red, cream surface, sand temper |
| 6 | I341:1 | XVA | Rim diam. 10.0 cm | Pale red, buff surface, sand temper |
| 7 | H1098:2 | XIVA | Rim diam. 12.0 cm | Pink, cream surface, sand and light organic temper |
| 8 | H1057:7 | XIIIB | Rim diam. 12.0 cm | Overfired green buff, sand temper |
| 9 | H516:8 | XIIIC | Rim diam. 12.0 cm | Buff, green buff slip, sand and light organic temper |
| 10 | H502:7 | XIB | Rim diam. 11.0 cm | Buff, sand and light organic temper |
| 11 | H895:2 | X | Rim diam. 12.0 cm | Buff, sand and light organic temper |
| TYPE C-1: PLAIN-RIM JAR (NARROW) |
| 12 | I776:2 | XIXB | Rim diam. 10.0 cm | Red, pink surface, sand temper |
| 13 | I417:2 | XVI | Rim diam. 11.0 cm | Buff, pink surface, sand and light organic temper |
| 14 | I406:6 | XVI | Rim diam. 10.0 cm | Buff, sand temper |
| 15 | H540:9 | XIVA | Rim diam. 12.0 cm | Cream, sand and light organic temper |
| 16 | H514:2 | XIIIC | Rim diam. 12.0 cm | Buff, sand and light organic temper |

COMPARANDA FOR TYPE C-1

Nippur: McCown, Haines, and Biggs 1978: pl. 46:2 (early Akk.); Gibson, Armstrong, and McMahon 1998: fig. 26:1, 3 (ED); Diyala: Delougaz 1952: C.526.362b (ED I–III), C.556.322 (early Akk.), C.596.440b (early Akk.); Uch Tepe: Gibson 1981: pl. 64 all, pl. 65:1, 6, 10–11, 13–14, pl. 66:1–10, pl. 67:1–8, 10–13 (ED I–II); Tell Sabra: Tunca 1987: pl. 22:3, pl. 51:1–3, pl. 52:1–5, pl. 70:20, 23–24, 26–27, pl. 71:1, 3–9, 12, 18–19 (ED III–Akk.); Umm el-Jīr: Gibson 1972b: fig. 44:B-15:6–8 (Akk.), fig. 45:B-27:2 (ED I–II), fig. 47:C-1:5 (Akk.); Kish: Mackay 1929: pl. 51:D; Tell el-Wilayah: Madhlum 1960: fig. 3:2; Fara: Martin 1988: types 50–52 (ED II), 86 (ED II), 97 (ED IIIa); Abu Salabikh: Martin, Moon, and Postgate 1985: grave 1:62–90, grave 17:2, grave 26:18–26, grave 28:22, grave 35:6–7, grave 38:24, grave 48:14–15, grave 52:3, grave 61:11–12, grave 81:8, 15, grave 88:10–13, grave 89:14 (ED II–IIIb); Moon 1987: nos. 407–24, 585–87, 618–39, 644–93 (ED II–IIIa); Ur: Woolley 1934: types 65, 67, 110a, 145, 204, 208, 209b, 211–12 (ED–Akk.)

COMPARANDA FOR TYPE C-1

Nippur: Gibson, Armstrong, and McMahon 1998: fig. 26:6 (ED III); Diyala: Delougaz 1952: C.527.362 (ED III)

Plate 96

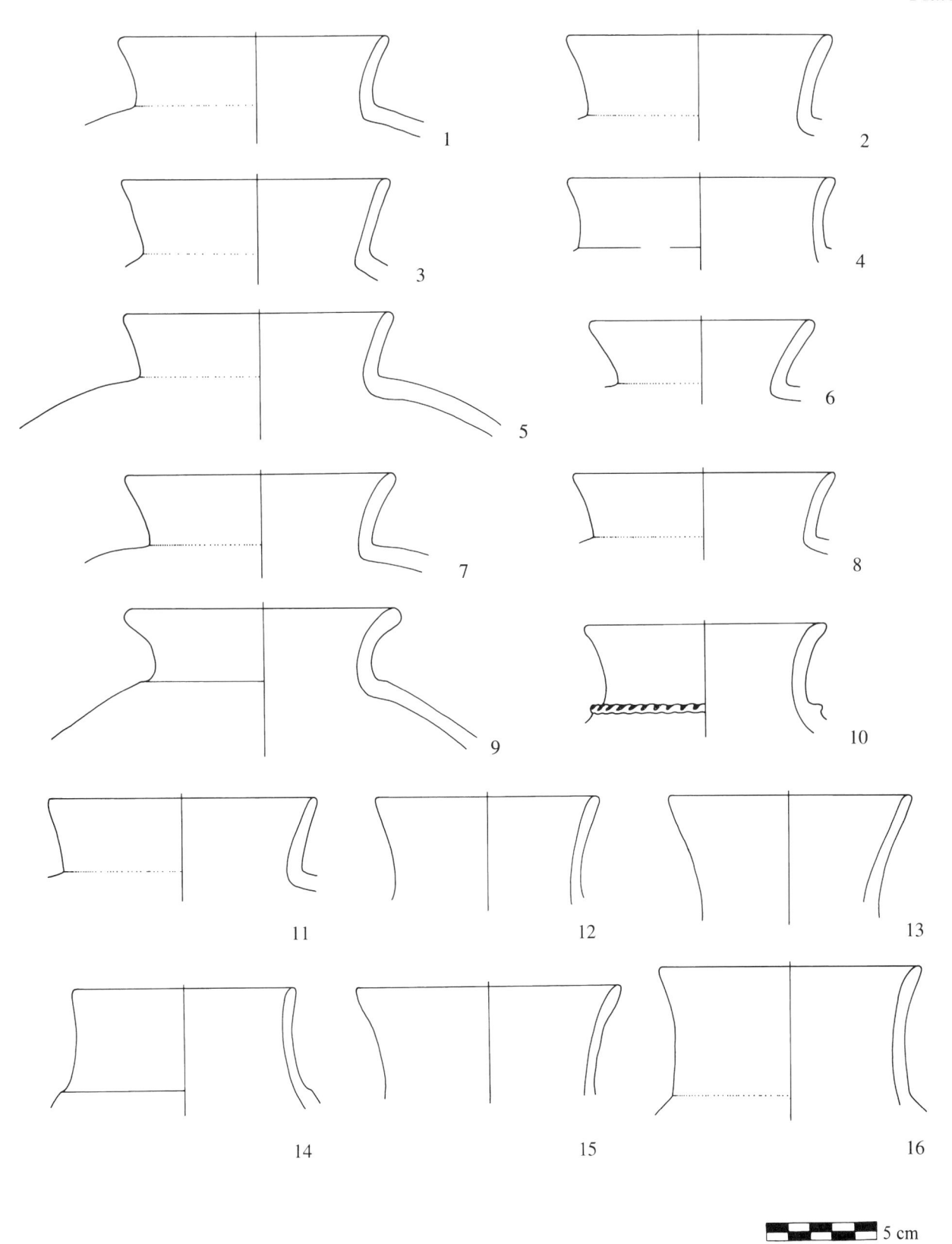

Type C-1: Plain-rim Jar. Scale 2:5

Plate 97. Type C-2: Band-rim Jar

|   | Lot Number | Level | Dimension | Description |
|---|---|---|---|---|
| 1 | I776:3 | XIXB | Rim diam. 12.0 cm | Pink, cream surface, sand temper |
| 2 | I669:2 | XIXB | Rim diam. 12.0 cm | Buff, cream surface, sand temper |
| 3 | I677:2 | XIXB | Rim diam. 15.0 cm | Buff, cream surface, sand temper |
| 4 | I670:1 | XVIII | Rim diam. 12.0 cm | Buff, sand temper |
| 5 | I656:4 | XVIII | Rim diam. 14.0 cm | Buff, cream slip, sand temper |
| 6 | I470:4 | XVIIC | Rim diam. 12.0 cm | Pale red, cream surface, sand temper |
| 7 | I439:1 | XVIIB | Rim diam. 14.0 cm | Dark buff, sand temper |
| 8 | I458:1 | XVIIB | Rim diam. 16.0 cm | Pale red, buff surface, sand temper |
| 9 | I430:1 | XVI | Rim diam. 14.0 cm | Buff greenish, sand temper |
| 10 | I380:2 | XVB | Rim diam. 12.0 cm | Pale red, pink surface, sand temper |
| 11 | I138:1 | XIVA | Rim diam. 15.0 cm | Red, pink surface, sand temper |
| 12 | H516:4 | XIIIC | Rim diam. 14.0 cm | Red, pink surface, sand temper |
| 13 | H1021:7 | XIIB | Rim diam. 10.0 cm | Buff, sand temper |
| 14 | H126:1 | XIIA | Rim diam. 12.0 cm | Buff, sand temper |
| 15 | H865:3 | X | Rim diam. 15.0 cm | Buff greenish, sand temper |
| 16 | H779:4 | IX | Rim diam. 14.0 cm | Pale buff, sand temper |
| 17 | H751:2 | VII | Rim diam. 14.0 cm | Buff, sand temper |

COMPARANDA FOR TYPE C-2

Nippur: Gibson, Armstrong, and McMahon 1998: fig. 26:7–9 (ED); Diyala: Delougaz 1952: C.515.370b (ED I–III), C.526.371b (ED III), D.526.371 (ED III), C.526.471e (ED III); Uch Tepe: Gibson 1981: pl. 68:16–17, pl. 69:8, 15 (ED I–II); Umm el-Jīr: Gibson 1972b: fig. 44:B-15:3 (Akk.), fig. 47:E-3:4 (Akk.); Kish: Mackay 1925: pl. 13:15–17; Mackay 1929: pl. 51:12–17; Abu Salabikh: Martin, Moon, and Postgate 1985: grave 26:29–31, grave 28:10, grave 31:14, grave 32:6, grave 42:10, grave 73:36, 40, grave 80:18–25 (ED IIIa–b); Moon 1981: nos. 9, 31, 36, 39–40; Moon 1987: nos. 446, 519–24, 527–29, 536–37, 541, 564, 567–70, 574, 577–78, 617, 699, 703, 724, 729, 731–32, 799 (ED IIIa–b); Uruk: Pongratz-Leisten 1988: 202 (ED)

Plate 97

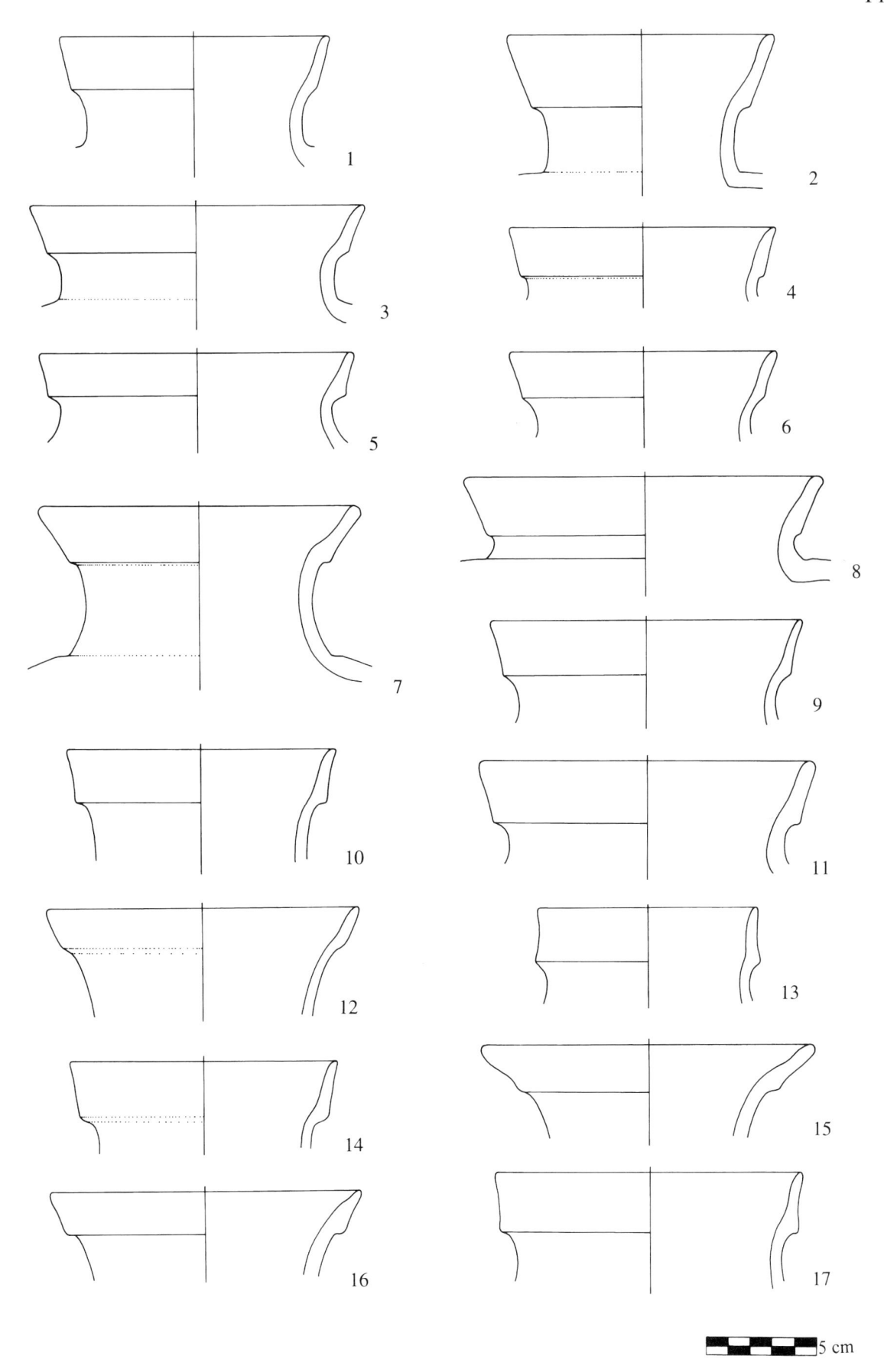

Type C-2: Band-rim Jar. Scale 2:5

Plate 98. Type C-3: Short Plain-rim Jar

|    | Lot Number | Level | Dimension | Description |
| --- | --- | --- | --- | --- |
| 1 | I677:3 | XIXB | Rim diam. 17.0 cm | Pink, cream surface, sand temper |
| 2 | I764:2 | XIXB | Rim diam. 16.0 cm | Buff, cream surface, sand temper |
| 3 | I668:2 | XIXA | Rim diam. 16.0 cm | Buff, sand temper |
| 4 | I662:5 | XIXA | Rim diam. 14.0 cm | Red, buff surface, sand and light organic temper |
| 5 | I486:1 | XVIII | Rim diam. 18.0 cm | Buff, sand and light organic temper |
| 6 | I475:4 | XVIIC | Rim diam. 16.0 cm | Pink, cream surface, sand temper |
| 7 | I439:2 | XVIIB | Rim diam. 14.0 cm | Red, pink surface, sand temper |
| 8 | I453:1 | XVIIB | Rim diam. 14.0 cm | Buff, sand temper |
| 9 | I406:7 | XVI | Rim diam. 14.0 cm | Buff, cream surface, sand temper |
| 10 | I417:3 | XVI | Rim diam. 15.0 cm | Buff, sand temper |
| 11 | I380:4 | XVB | Rim diam. 16.0 cm | Buff, sand temper |
| 12 | H526:11 | XIIIC | Rim diam. 20.0 cm | Buff, sand and light organic temper |
| 13 | H1079:9 | XIIIB | Rim diam. 16.0 cm | Buff, sand and light organic temper |
| 14 | I4:2 | XIA | Rim diam. 18.0 cm | Pink, buff surface, sand temper |

COMPARANDA FOR TYPE C-3

Nippur: Gibson, Armstrong, and McMahon 1998: fig. 24:11–12, fig. 26:2 (ED); Uch Tepe: Gibson 1981: pl. 65:2–5, 7–9, pl. 67:14, pl. 68:1–5, 9–10, pl. 71:11–22, pl. 72:1–10 (ED I–II); Tell Sabra: Tunca 1987: pl. 70:11–16, 18 (ED–Akk.); Tell al-Hiba: Bahrani 1989: pl. 4:1–2, pl. 17:1, 3, pl. 18:1, 7 (ED IIIb); Umm el-Jīr: Gibson 1972b: fig. 44:B-7:23 (Akk.); Uruk: Pongratz-Leisten 1988: 194, 246 (ED)

Plate 98

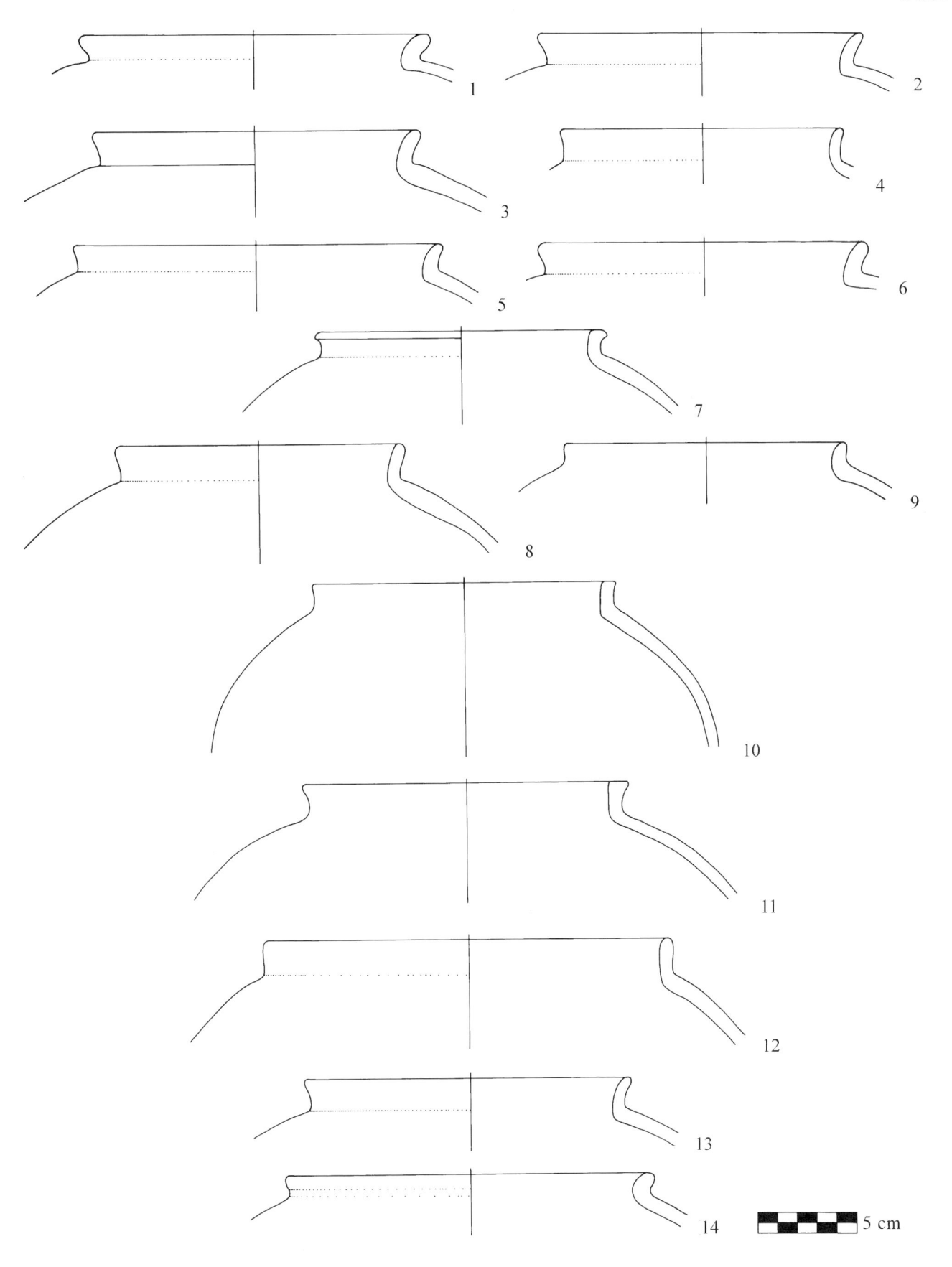

Type C-3: Short Plain-rim Jar. Scale 2:5

Plate 99. Type C-4: Small Plain-rim Jar and Type C-5: Redware Hole-mouth Jar

| | Lot Number | Level | Dimension | Description |
|---|---|---|---|---|
| **Type C-4: Small Plain-rim Jar** | | | | |
| 1 | I764:3 | XIXB | Rim diam. 10.0 cm, max. diam. 13.0 cm | Buff pink, pink surface, sand temper |
| 2 | I458:6 | XVIIB | Rim diam. 8.0 cm, max. diam. 9.5 cm | Pale red, cream surface, sand temper |
| 3 | H112:9 | XIIA | Rim diam. 10.0 cm | Cream, sand and light organic temper |
| 4 | H877:5 | XIB | Rim diam. 6.0 cm, max. diam. 7.5 cm | Buff, sand temper |
| 5 | H137:1 | XIA | Rim diam. 6.0 cm, max. diam. 8.5 cm | Buff, sand temper |
| **Type C-5: Redware Hole-mouth Jar** | | | | |
| 6 | I776:5 | XIXB | Rim diam. 16.0 cm | Scarlet red, dense sand temper |
| 7 | I458:8 | XVIIB | — | Dark red, dense sand temper, horizontal grooves |
| 8 | I765:3 | XIXB | Rim diam. 18.0 cm | Red, sand temper |
| 9 | I656:6 | XVIII | Rim diam. 14.0 cm | Plum red, dense sand temper |
| 10 | I670:2 | XVIII | Rim diam. 16.0 cm | Plum red, dense sand temper |
| 11 | I657:1 | XVIII | Rim diam. 16.0 cm | Scarlet red, dense sand temper |
| 12 | I430:4 | XVI | Rim diam. 18.0 cm | Buff, sand temper |

Comparanda for Type C-4

Diyala: Delougaz 1952: B.184.220c, B.574.220, B.675.220 (ED III–Akk.); Kish: Mackay 1929: pl. 53:1–2; Mackay 1925: pl. 15:19–31; Fara: Martin 1988: types 48–49 (ED II–Akk.); Abu Salabikh: Martin, Moon, and Postgate 1985: grave 1:53–54, grave 3:4, grave 12:7, grave 26:32–33, grave 28:9, grave 31:4, grave 35:5, grave 38:31, grave 42:3, grave 54:4, grave 61:9, 14, grave 75:7, grave 87:2 (ED IIIa–b); Moon 1987: nos. 449, 453, 456–62, 485–92, 496, 508–11 (ED IIIa–b); Ur: Woolley 1934: types 43, 109a, 110c (late ED–Ur III)

Comparanda for Type C-5

Nippur: Gibson, Armstrong, and McMahon 1998: fig. 26:4 (ED); unpublished examples from North Temple IV (ED III–early Akk.); Kish: Y Trench Level 12 (unpublished, M. Gibson, pers. comm.)

Plate 99

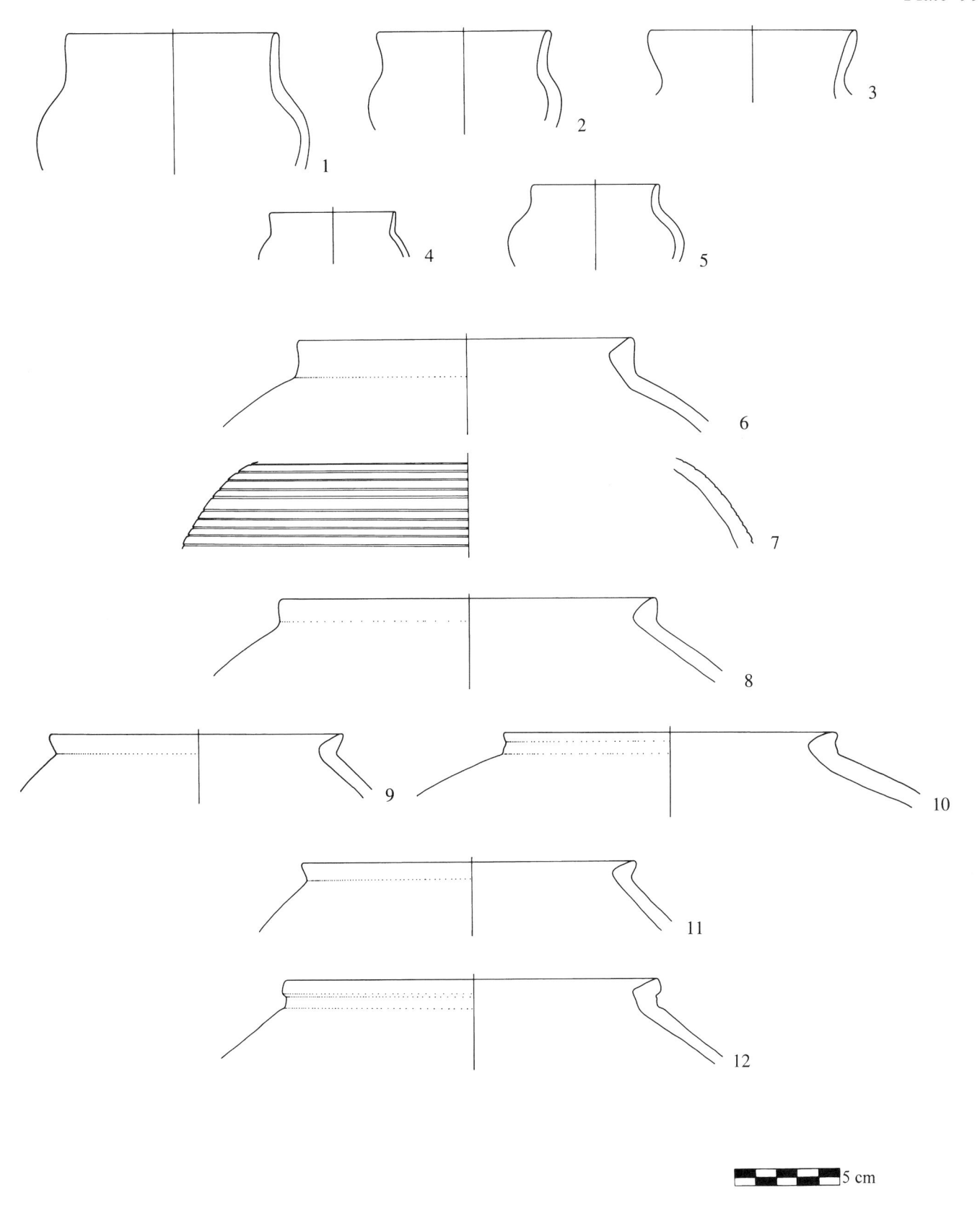

Type C-4: Small Plain-rim Jar and Type C-5: Redware Hole-mouth Jar. Scale 2:5

Plate 100. Type C-6: Elongated Triangular-rim Jar and Type C-7: Small Band-rim Jar

|   | Lot Number | Level | Dimension | Description |
|---|---|---|---|---|
| \multicolumn{5}{l}{TYPE C-6: ELONGATED TRIANGULAR-RIM JAR} |
| 1 | I763:1 | XIXB | Rim diam. 8.0 cm | Buff, sand temper |
| 2 | I662:7 | XIXA | Rim diam. 18.0 cm | Buff, sand and light organic temper |
| 3 | I456:1 | XVIIB | Rim diam. 18.0 cm | Buff, sand temper |
| 4 | I392:3 | XVI | Rim diam. 10.0 cm | Buff, cream surface, sand temper |
| 5 | I361:2 | XVB | Rim diam. 14.0 cm | Buff, sand temper |
| 6 | I22:7 | XIIA | Rim diam. 15.0 cm | Reddish buff, buff surface, sand temper |
| \multicolumn{5}{l}{TYPE C-7: SMALL BAND-RIM JAR} |
| 7 | I662:4 | XIXA | Rim diam. 16.0 cm | Buff green, sand temper |
| 8 | I656:5 | XVIII | Rim diam. 16.0 cm | Buff, sand temper |
| 9 | I454:6 | XVIIB | Rim diam. 14.0 cm | Red, buff surface, sand temper |
| 10 | I122:3 | XIIIB | Rim diam. 14.0 cm | Buff, sand temper |
| 11 | H1034:5 | XIB | Rim diam. 9.0 cm | Pink, sand and light organic temper |
| 12 | H139:2 | XIB | Rim diam. 12.0 cm | Buff green, sand temper |

COMPARANDA FOR TYPE C-6

Nippur: McCown, Haines, and Biggs 1978: pl. 45:2, 4 (ED III–early Akk.); Diyala: Delougaz 1952: C.516.371a, C.516.471, C.526.471 (ED III–early Akk.); Uch Tepe: Gibson 1981: pl. 70:13–14, 18–19, pl. 71:1–2, 4–5 (ED I–II); Kish: Mackay 1925: pl. I:5, 9:1, 6–8, 11–14, 10:16, 18–21; Mackay 1929: pl. 48: especially 1–3, 22–23; Fara: Martin 1988: fig. 41:9(?) (ED II–III), type 68 (ED I–II); Abu Salabikh: Martin, Moon, and Postgate 1985: grave 5:6 (ED III); Moon 1981: nos. 1, 7–8, 37; Moon 1982: nos. 6, 8–9; Moon 1987: nos. 573, 593, 738–43 (ED III); Uruk: Pongratz-Leisten 1988: 23, 107–08, 129, 133, 196–98, 231 (ED)

COMPARANDA FOR TYPE C-7

Diyala: Delougaz 1952: D.526.370a (early Akk.), D.535.542, D.545.542 (ED I–III); Tell Sabra: Tunca 1987: pl. 19:7, pl. 72:19, 22–23, pl. 83:19–20 (ED–Akk.); Uch Tepe: Gibson 1981: pl. 69:1–7, 19–20, pl. 70:1–11 (ED I–II); Isin: Hrouda 1981: pl. 31:7 (ED); Abu Salabikh: Martin, Moon, and Postgate 1985: grave 1:55, grave 94:6 (ED III); Moon 1987: nos. 702, 705, 720, 730 (ED III); Moon 1981: nos. 3–4, 33–34; Uruk: Pongratz-Leisten 1988: 160, 201 (ED)

Plate 100

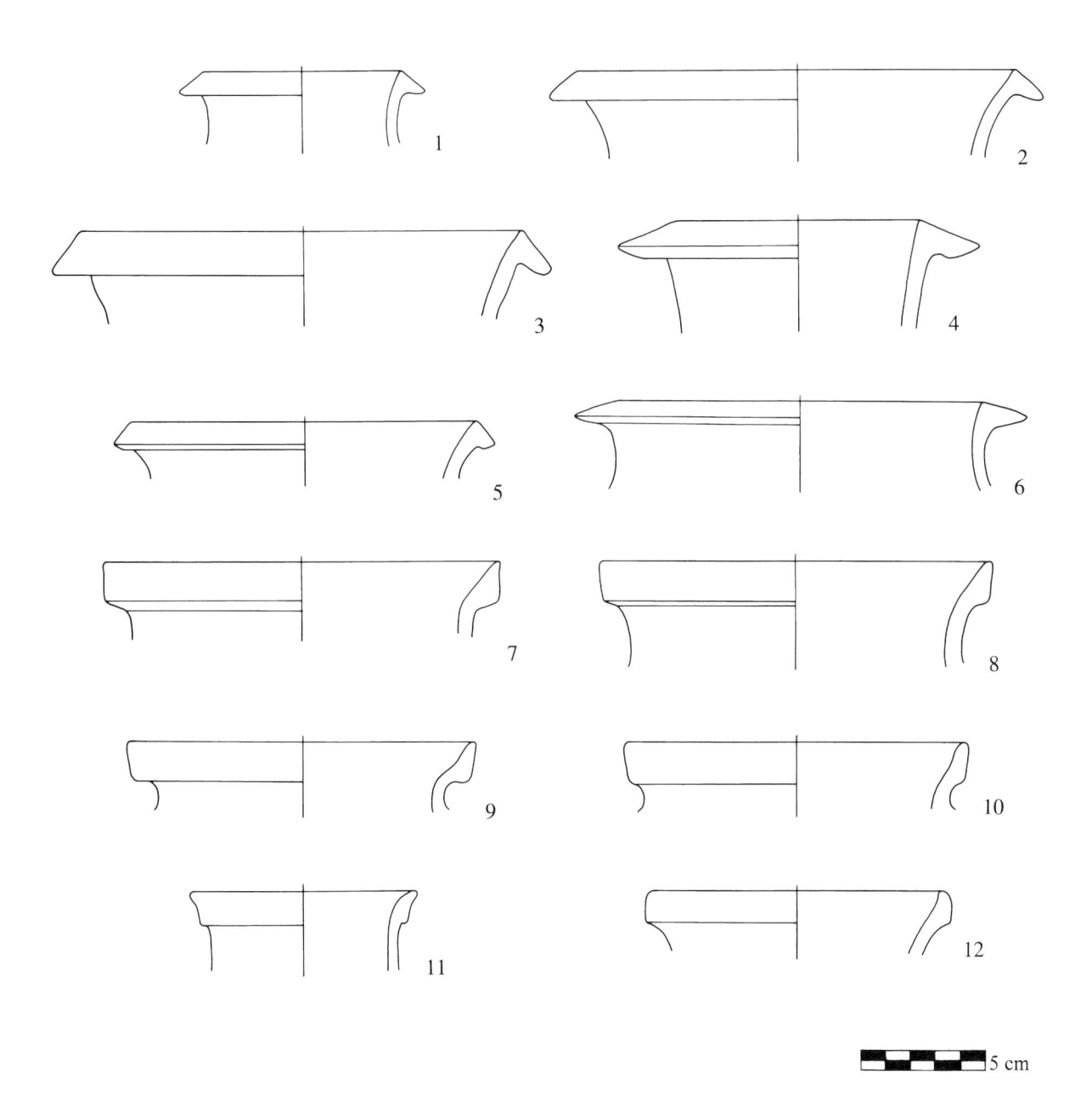

Type C-6: Elongated Triangular-rim Jar and Type C-7: Small Band-rim Jar. Scale 2:5

Plate 101. Type C-8: Tab-handled Jar and Type C-11: Fine Ware Jar

| | Lot Number | Level | Dimension | Description |
|---|---|---|---|---|
| TYPE C-8: TAB-HANDLED JAR | | | | |
| 1 | I657:2 | XVIII | Rim diam. 10.0 cm | Buff, sand temper |
| 2 | I469 | XVIIB | Rim diam. 12.0 cm | Pink, sand temper |
| 3 | I453:4 | XVIIB | Rim diam. 12.0 cm | Pale red, sand temper |
| TYPE C-11: FINE WARE JAR | | | | |
| 4 | I453:3 | XVIIB | Rim diam. 10.0 cm | Buff, sand temper |
| 5 | I436:5 | XVIIB | Rim diam. 10.0 cm | Buff, cream slip, sand temper, shallow horizontal grooves and scarlet paint stripe |
| 6 | I458:7 | XVIIB | Rim diam. 12.0 cm | Pink cream, sand temper |
| 7 | I401:2 | XVI | Max. diam. 14.0 cm | Pale red, cream slip, sand temper, horizontal comb incision and pale scarlet paint stripes |

COMPARANDA FOR TYPE C-8

Nippur: Gibson, Armstrong, and McMahon 1998: fig. 24:10 (ED); Abu Salabikh: Moon 1987: nos. 331–37 (ED I); Uruk: Pongratz-Leisten 1988: 44, 100, 106, 126–27, 131, 136–37, 155–56, 168, 245 (ED)

COMPARANDA FOR TYPE C-11

Diyala: Delougaz 1952: C.545.340a–b, with small ring bases (ED III–early Akk.); Abu Salabikh: Martin, Moon, and Postgate 1985: grave 48:11, grave 73:7 (ED IIIa); Moon 1987: nos. 361–85, 387–99 (ED IIIa–b); Postgate 1977: pl. 33b, grave 100 (ED IIIa); Postgate and Moon 1982: 131, grave 183 (ED IIIa); Fara: Martin 1988: type 85 (ED II); Ur: Woolley 1934: PG/1068, pl. 58 top left, PG/1273, PG/1248 (ED III–early Akk.); Mari: Parrot 1956: fig. 107:1548–49; Lebeau 1985: pl. 16:1, 3, pl. 27:29; Tell Chuera: Kühne 1976: 67–70, fig. 89, pl. 4:6, pl. 5:5; Moortgat-Correns 1988: fig. 4 (ED III)

Plate 101

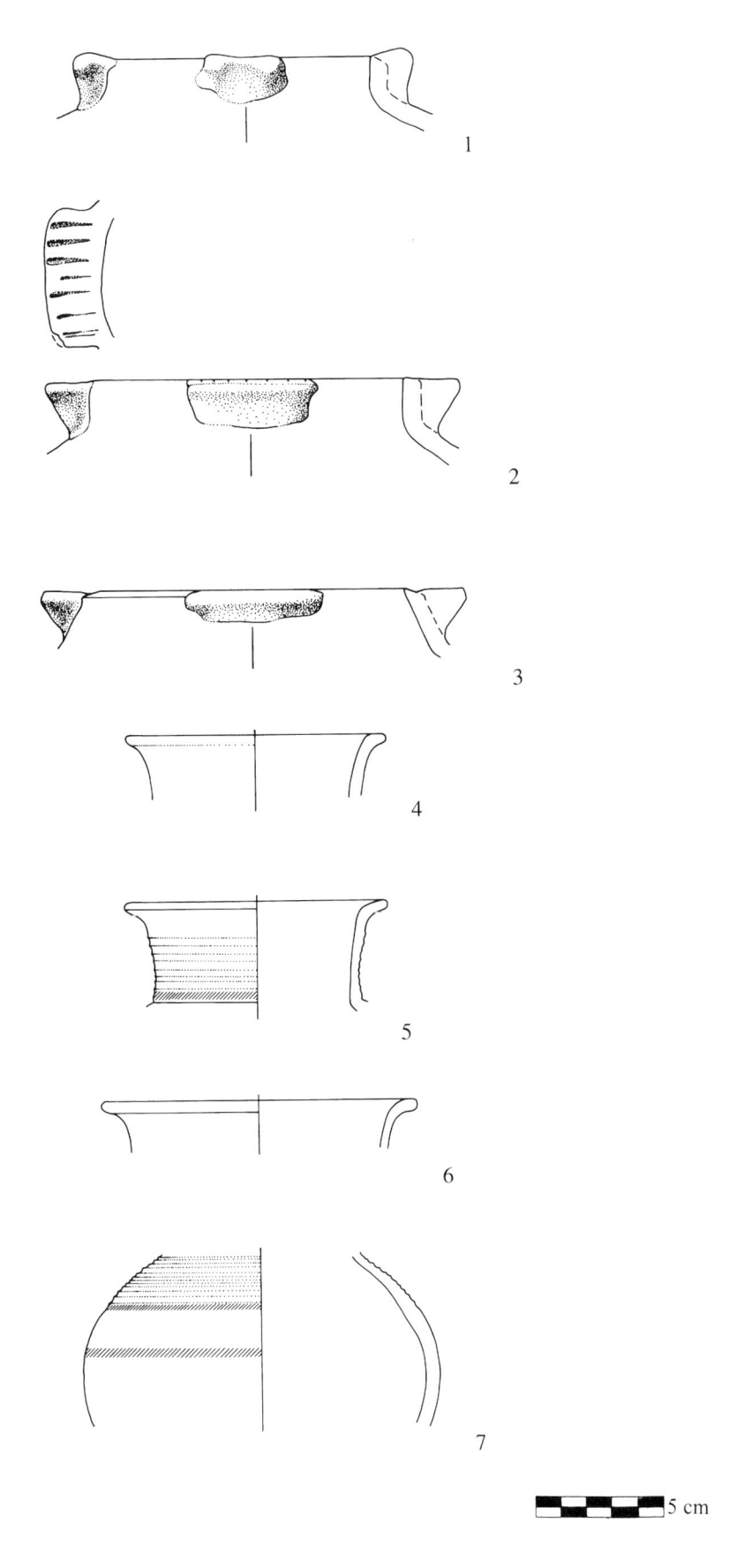

Type C-8: Tab-handled Jar and Type C-11: Fine Ware Jar. Scale 2:5

Plate 102. Type C-9: Rounded-rim Jar

|    | Lot Number | Level | Dimension | Description |
|----|-----------|-------|-----------|-------------|
| 1  | I436:2    | XVIIB | Rim diam. 10.0 cm | Buff, sand temper |
| 2  | I386:2    | XVI   | Rim diam. 10.0 cm | Buff, cream surface, sand temper |
| 3  | I417:4    | XVI   | Rim diam. 12.0 cm | Buff, cream surface, sand temper |
| 4  | I384      | XVB   | Rim diam. 14.0 cm | Buff, sand temper |
| 5  | I380:3    | XVB   | Rim diam. 12.0 cm | Buff, sand temper |
| 6  | H1082:6   | XIVB  | Rim diam. 11.0 cm | Red, sand and light organic temper |
| 7  | H1126:3   | XIIIB | Rim diam. 12.0 cm | Greenish buff, sand temper |
| 8  | I9:2      | XIIB  | Rim diam. 12.0 cm | Red, cream surface, sand temper |
| 9  | H112:8    | XIIA  | Rim diam. 16.0 cm | Overfired green, sand temper |
| 10 | H523:4    | XIB   | Rim diam. 12.0 cm | Pink, buff surface, sand and light organic temper |
| 12 | H868:5    | XIB   | Rim diam. 12.0 cm | Overfired gray green, sand temper |
| 11 | H841:4    | XIA   | Rim diam. 12.0 cm | Pale pink, sand and light organic temper |
| 13 | H862:8    | XIA   | Rim diam. 12.0 cm | Pink buff, sand temper |
| 14 | H895:3    | X     | Rim diam. 10.0 cm | Cream, sand and light organic temper |
| 15 | H855:2    | X     | Rim diam. 12.0 cm | Overfired green, sand temper |
| 16 | H779:9    | IX    | Rim diam. 13.0 cm | Red, pink surface, sand temper |
| 17 | H789:8    | IX    | Rim diam. 12.0 cm | Buff, sand temper |
| 18 | H763:19   | VIII  | Rim diam. 12.0 cm | Pale buff, sand temper |
| 19 | H754:18   | VIII  | Rim diam. 12.0 cm | Red, buff surface, sand temper |
| 20 | H689:6    | VI    | Rim diam. 12.0 cm | Pink, buff surface, sand temper |

COMPARANDA FOR TYPE C-9

Tell al-Hiba: Bahrani 1989: pl. 16:7 (ED IIIb); Uruk: Boehmer, Pedde, and Salje 1995: pl. 9:d–e (Ur III); Tell Sabra: Tunca 1987: pl. 84:9 (Akk.?); unpublished examples from Nippur WC-3 (Ur III) and Umm al-Hafriyat (Akk.–Ur III)

Plate 102

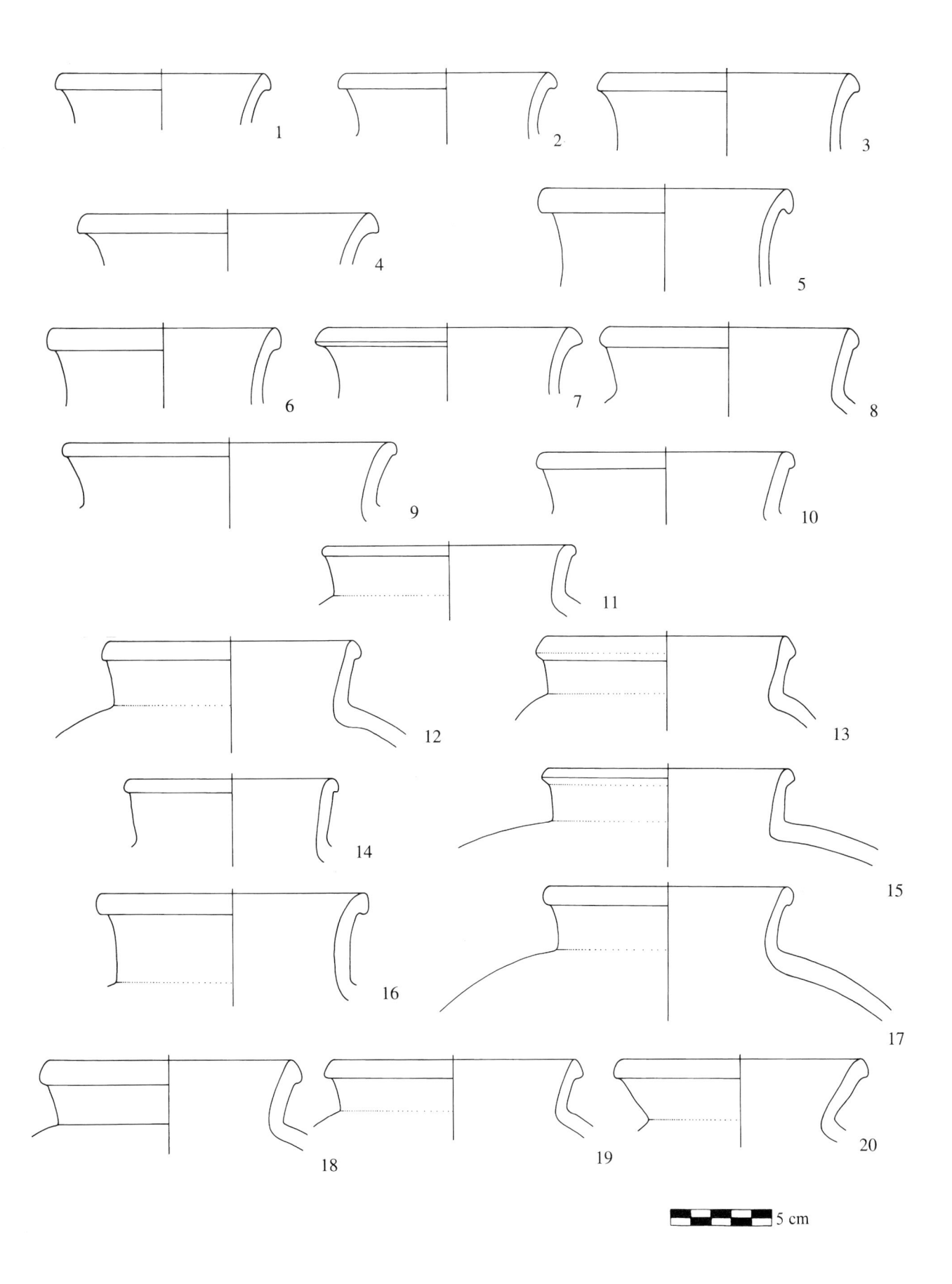

Type C-9: Rounded-rim Jar. Scale 2:5

Plate 103. Type C-10: Large Triangular-rim Jar

|    | Lot Number | Level | Dimension | Description |
|----|------------|-------|-----------|-------------|
| 1  | I436:4     | XVIIB | Rim diam. 16.0 cm | Buff, cream surface, sand temper |
| 2  | I386:3     | XVI   | Rim diam. 14.0 cm | Red, cream surface, sand temper |
| 3  | I417:5     | XVI   | Rim diam. 16.0 cm | Buff, cream surface, sand temper |
| 4  | I110       | XVA   | Rim diam. 14.0 cm | Buff yellow, sand and light organic temper |
| 5  | I373:1     | XVA   | Rim diam. ca. 17.0 cm (warped) | Overfired green, sand temper |
| 6  | H1092:7    | XIIIC | Rim diam. 14.0 cm | Gray green, sand temper |
| 7  | H1017:4    | XIIB  | Rim diam. 14.0 cm | Buff, sand and light organic temper |
| 8  | H1010:10   | XIIB  | Rim diam. 16.0 cm | Overfired green, sand and light organic temper |
| 9  | H539:9     | XIIA  | Rim diam. 18.0 cm | Buff, sand and light organic temper |
| 10 | H525:8     | XIIA  | Rim diam. 18.0 cm | Pale buff, sand and light organic temper |
| 11 | I12:1      | XIB   | Rim diam. 16.0 cm | Buff, sand temper |
| 12 | H779:6     | IX    | Rim diam. 18.0 cm | Buff pink, sand temper |

COMPARANDA FOR TYPE C-10

Diyala: Delougaz 1952: C.515.370a (ED I–III), C.526.471f (ED III); Uch Tepe: Gibson 1981: pl. 69:18, pl. 71:3, 6, 10 (ED I–II); Tell Sabra: Tunca 1987: pl. 72:9, pl. 73:25, pl. 84:2 (ED–Akk.); Umm el-Jīr: Gibson 1972b: fig. 44:B-7:11, 14–15, fig. 46:D III:12 (Akk.); Abu Salabikh: Moon 1987: no. 573, 723, 730 (ED II–III); Tell al-Hiba: Bahrani 1989: pl. 16:8, 10 (ED IIIb); Susa: Steve and Gasche 1971: pl. 12:4, 19 (Akk.)

Plate 103

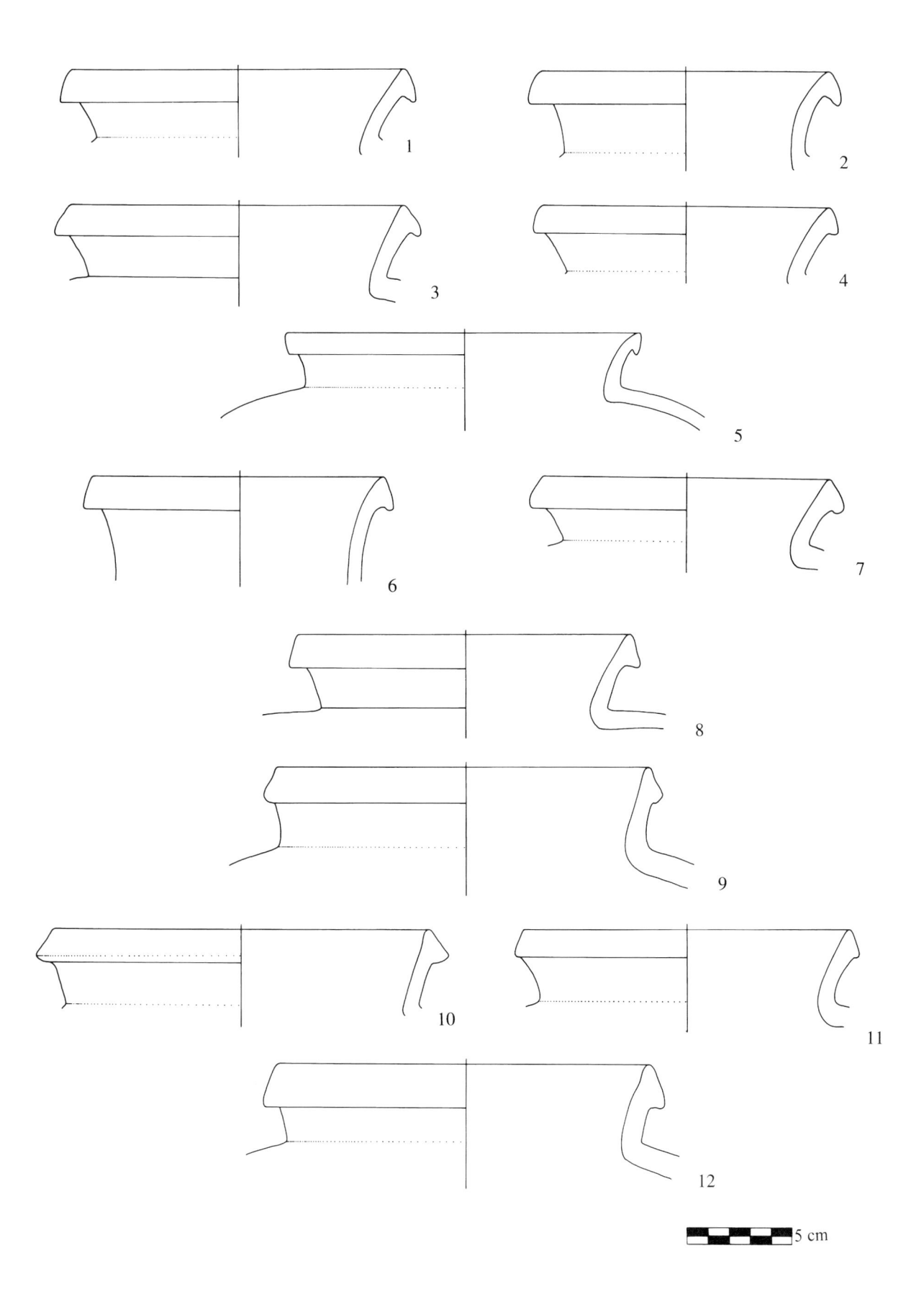

Type C-10: Large Triangular-rim Jar. Scale 2:5

Plate 104. Type C-12: Rolled-rim Storage Jar

|   | Lot Number | Level | Dimension | Description |
|---|---|---|---|---|
| 1 | I458:2 | XVIIB | Rim diam. 16.0 cm | Buff, green surface, sand and light organic temper |
| 2 | H514:4 | XIIIC | Rim diam. 14.0 cm | Pink, cream surface, sand and light organic temper |
| 3 | H526:13 | XIIIC | Rim diam. 14.0 cm | Buff, sand temper |
| 4 | H1021:18 | XIIB | Rim diam. 15.0 cm | Buff, sand and light organic temper |
| 5 | H511:7 | XIIA | Rim diam. 20.0 cm | Red orange, black and white grit temper |
| 6 | H847:5 | XIB | Rim diam. 18.0 cm | Red, black core, sand temper |
| 7 | H509:7 | XIB | Rim diam. 20.0 cm | Buff, sand and light organic temper, incised potter's mark inside rim |
| 8 | H873:1 | XIB | Rim diam. 16.0 cm | Red, cream surface, sand and light organic temper |

COMPARANDA FOR TYPE C-12

Diyala: Delougaz 1952: D.555.510a (late Akk.); Abu Salabikh: Postgate and Moon 1984: 12, 46–47 (post-ED)

Plate 104

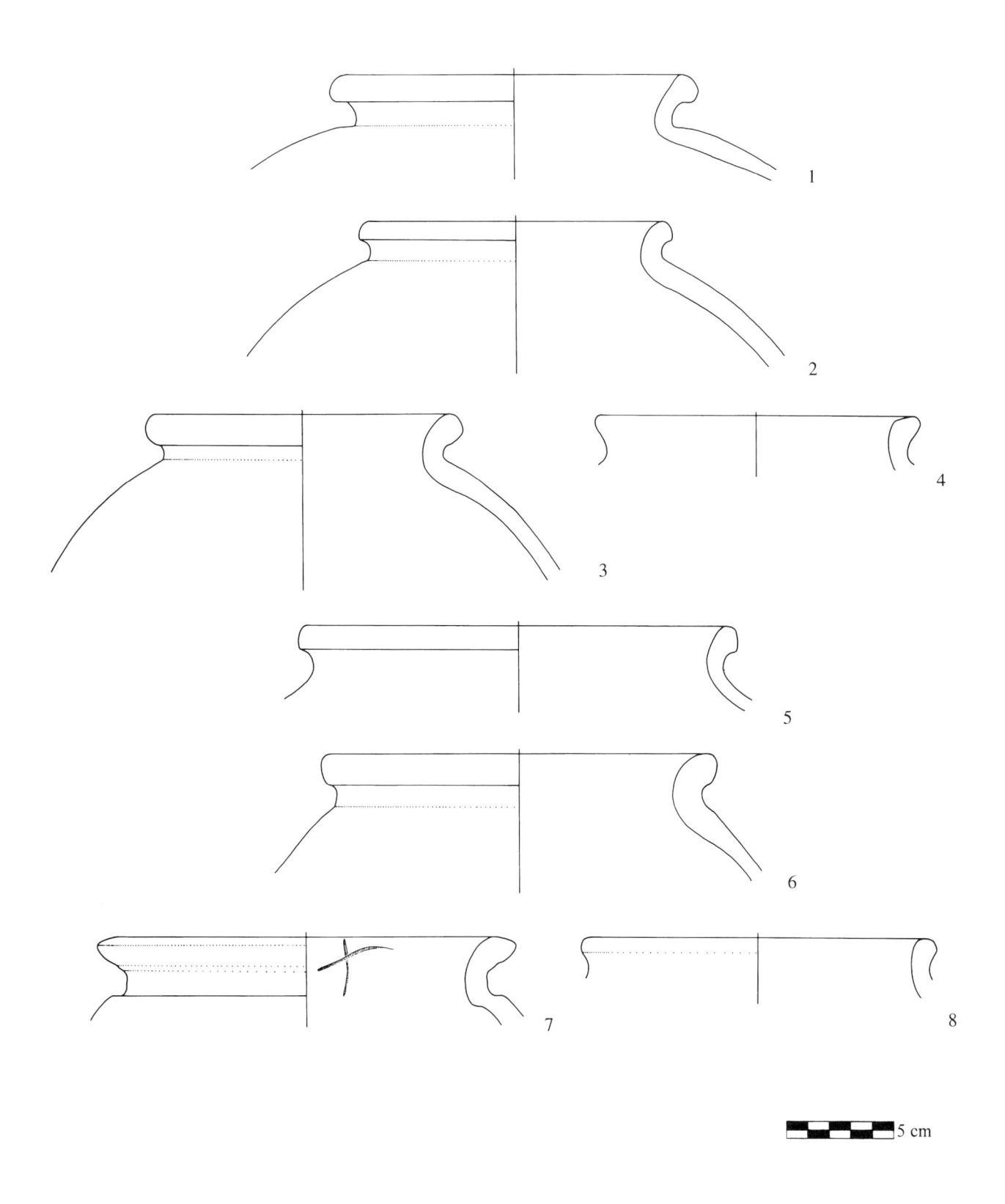

Type C-12: Rolled-rim Storage Jar. Scale 2:5

Plate 105. Type C-13a: Double-ridged-rim Jar with Wide Neck

|   | Lot Number | Level | Dimension | Description |
|---|---|---|---|---|
| 1 | I433:6 | XVIIA | Rim diam. 16.0 cm | Buff, cream surface, sand temper |
| 2 | I433:4 | XVIIA | Rim diam. 16.0 cm | Pink, buff surface, sand temper |
| 3 | I433:5 | XVIIA | Rim diam. 20.0 cm | Pink, sand temper |
| 4 | I361:1 | XVB | Rim diam. 20.0 cm | Buff, sand and light organic temper |
| 5 | I329:2 | XVA | Rim diam. 18.0 cm | Buff, cream surface, sand temper |
| 6 | I43 | XIIB | Rim diam. 18.0 cm | Buff, sand temper |

COMPARANDA FOR TYPE C-13A

Diyala: Delougaz 1952: D.565.310 (ED III–early Akk.); Umm el-Jīr: Gibson 1972b: fig. 44:B-13:8 (Akk.); Fara: Martin 1988: fig. 42:7 (Akk.–Ur III); Abu Salabikh: Moon 1987: nos. 579, 581, 584 (ED IIIa–b); Postgate and Moon 1984: no. 17; Tell al-Hiba: Bahrani 1989: pl. 16:2, pl. 40:1 (ED IIIb); Ur: Woolley 1934: types 44a–c

Plate 105

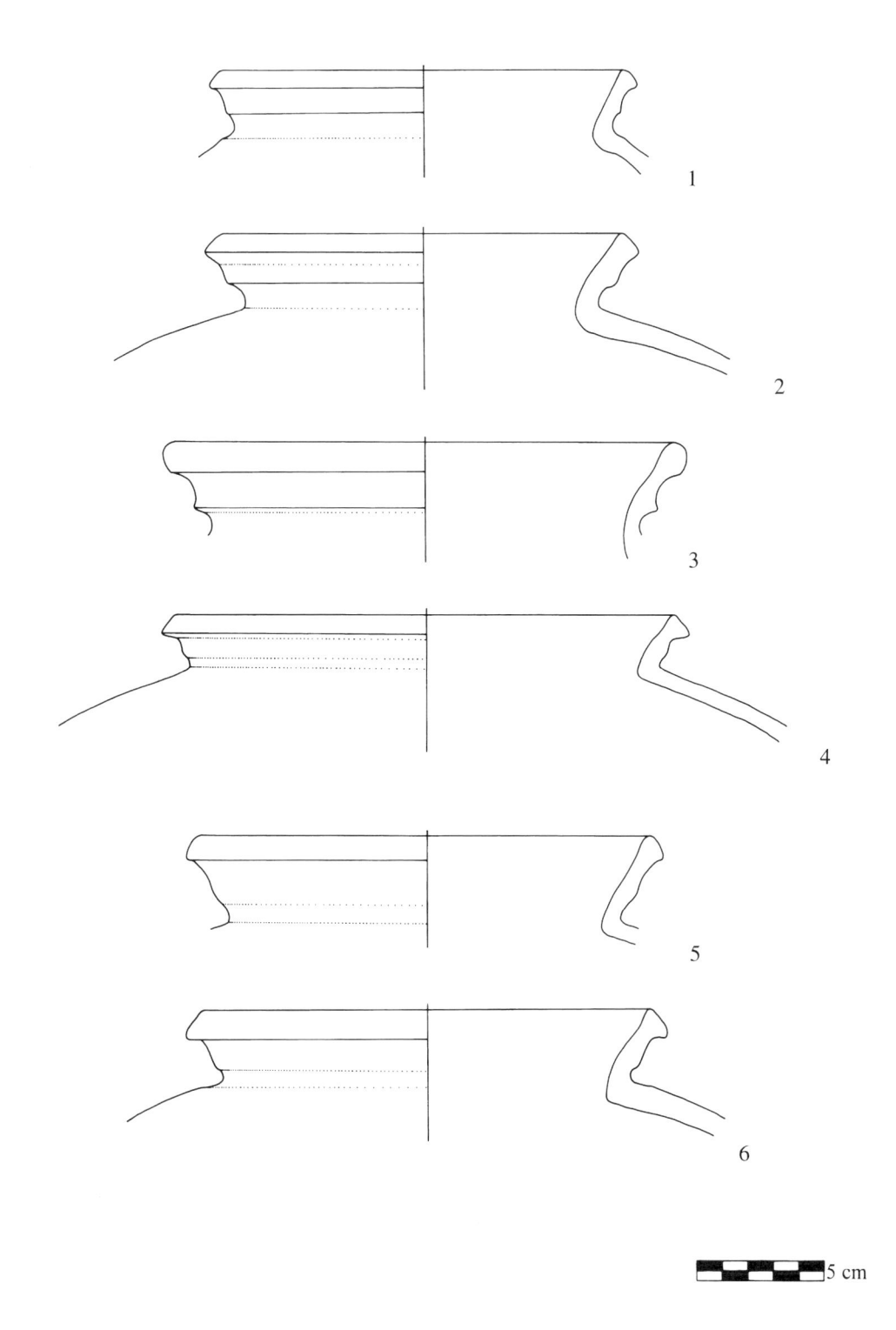

Type C-13a: Double Ridged-rim Jar with Wide Neck. Scale 2:5

Plate 106. Type C-13b: Double-ridged-rim Jar with Narrow Neck

|   | Lot Number | Level | Dimension | Description |
|---|---|---|---|---|
| 1 | I162:3 | XIIIB | Rim diam. 14.0 cm | Pink, cream surface, sand temper |
| 2 | H529:4 | XIIA | Rim diam. 8.0 cm | Overfired green, sand and light organic temper |
| 3 | H539:6 | XIIA | Rim diam. 10.0 cm | Buff red, cream surface, sand temper |
| 4 | H787:1 | X | Rim diam. 11.0 cm | Buff, sand temper |
| 5 | H793:16 | IX | Rim diam. 10.0 cm | Buff, cream surface, sand and light organic temper |
| 6 | H783:5 | IX | Rim diam. 13.0 cm | Pale buff, sand temper |
| 7 | H793:15 | IX | Rim diam. 12.0 cm | Red, buff, surface, sand and light organic temper |
| 8 | H777:8 | IX | Rim diam. 12.0 cm | Buff, sand temper |
| 9 | H763:24 | VIII | Rim diam. 11.0 cm | Red, sand and light organic temper |

COMPARANDA FOR TYPE C-13B

Nippur: McCown and Haines 1967: pl. 80:18 (Akk.); Umm el-Jīr: Gibson 1972b: fig. 42:j–l; fig. 43:B-4:9 (Akk.–Ur III); fig. 47:C-3:16 (Akk.), E-6:2 (ED–Akk.); Isin: Hrouda 1977: pl. 27, IB 685, IB 276a (Ur III); Ur: Woolley 1934: type 162 (Akk.); Brak: Oates, Oates, and McDonald 2001: no. 302 (Ur III)

Plate 106

Type C-13b: Double Ridged-rim Jar with Narrow Neck. Scale 2:5

Plate 107. Type C-14: Oval-rim Jar

|   | Lot Number | Level | Dimension | Description |
|---|---|---|---|---|
| 1 | I380:1 | XVB | Rim diam. 16.0 cm | Buff green, sand temper |
| 2 | H1028:5 | XIVA | Rim diam. 10.0 cm | Yellow buff, sand and light organic temper |
| 3 | I138:2 | XIVA | Rim diam. 10.0 cm | Red, pink surface, sand temper |
| 4 | H526:14 | XIIIC | Rim diam. 14.0 cm | Cream, sand temper |
| 5 | H1079:11 | XIIIB | Rim diam. 12.0 cm | Pale red, buff surface, sand and light organic temper |
| 6 | H1057:13 | XIIIB | Rim diam. 11.0 cm | Buff red, sand and light organic temper |
| 7 | H110:9 | XIIA | Rim diam. 12.0 cm | Overfired green, sand temper |
| 8 | I16:2 | XIIA | Rim diam. 14.0 cm | Buff, sand temper |
| 9 | H847:4 | XIB | Rim diam. 16.0 cm | Red, buff surface, sand and light organic temper |
| 10 | H841:3 | XIA | Rim diam. 12.0 cm | Pale buff, sand temper |
| 11 | H857:9 | XIA | Rim diam. 16.0 cm | Pink, pale buff surface, sand and light organic temper |
| 12 | H763:23 | VIII | Rim diam. 18.0 cm | Dark buff, sand and light organic temper |
| 13 | H899:4 | X | Rim diam. 10.0 cm | Buff gray, sand temper |

COMPARANDA FOR TYPE C-14

Nippur: McCown and Haines 1967: pl. 81:4 (Akk.); Umm el-Jīr: Gibson 1972b: fig. 43:B-5:8, 12, fig. 44:B-9:2, B-15:4, fig. 47:C-3:7, fig. 48:fl.2:4 (Akk.–Ur III); Kish: Mackay 1925: pl. 13:5–6; Mackay 1929: pl. 51:1; Abu Salabikh: Martin, Moon, and Postgate 1985: grave 1:51, grave 38:29 (ED IIIa and b); Moon 1987: nos. 549, 552, 555 (ED III); Postgate and Moon 1984: no. 14; Susa: Steve and Gasche 1971: pl. 6:4, pl. 12:1 (Akk.); Ur: Woolley 1934: type 187 (Akk.–Ur III)

Plate 107

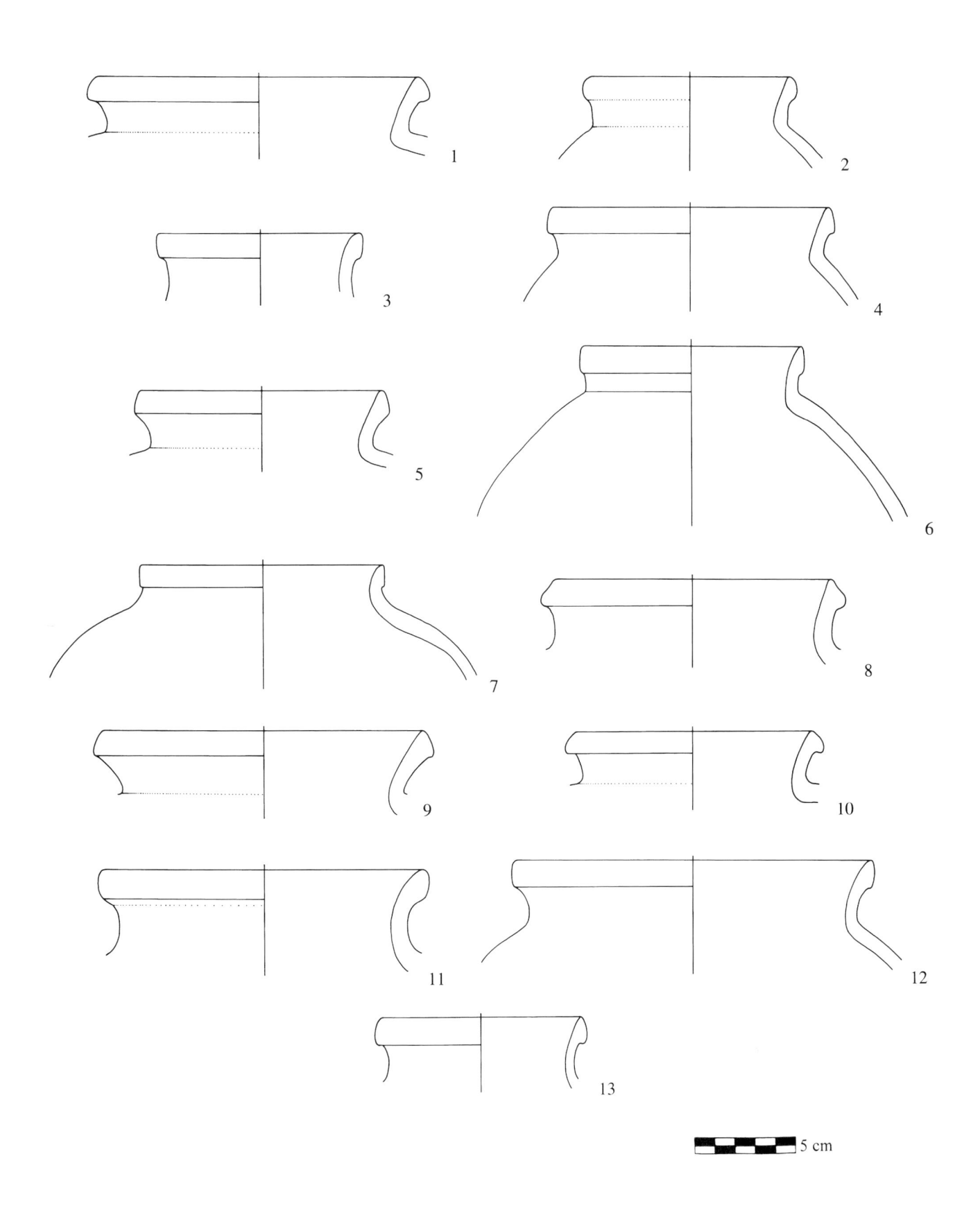

Type C-14: Oval-rim Jar. Scale 2:5

Plate 108. Type C-15: Rounded and Overhanging Band Rim

|   | Lot Number | Level | Dimension | Description |
|---|---|---|---|---|
| 1 | I158:1 | XIVB | Rim diam. 14.0 cm | Buff, cream surface, sand temper |
| 2 | H1084:3 | XIIIC | Rim diam. 12.0 cm | Buff, sand temper |
| 3 | H1079:12 | XIIIB | Rim diam. 14.0 cm | Red, pink surface, sand and light organic temper |
| 4 | H826:2 | XIA | Rim diam. 16.0 cm | Overfired green, sand temper |
| 5 | H854:3 | X | Rim diam. 12.0 cm | Pale buff, sand temper |

COMPARANDA FOR TYPE C-15

Abu Salabikh: Martin, Moon, and Postgate 1985: grave 90:3 (ED III); Moon 1981: no. 2 (ED III)

Plate 108

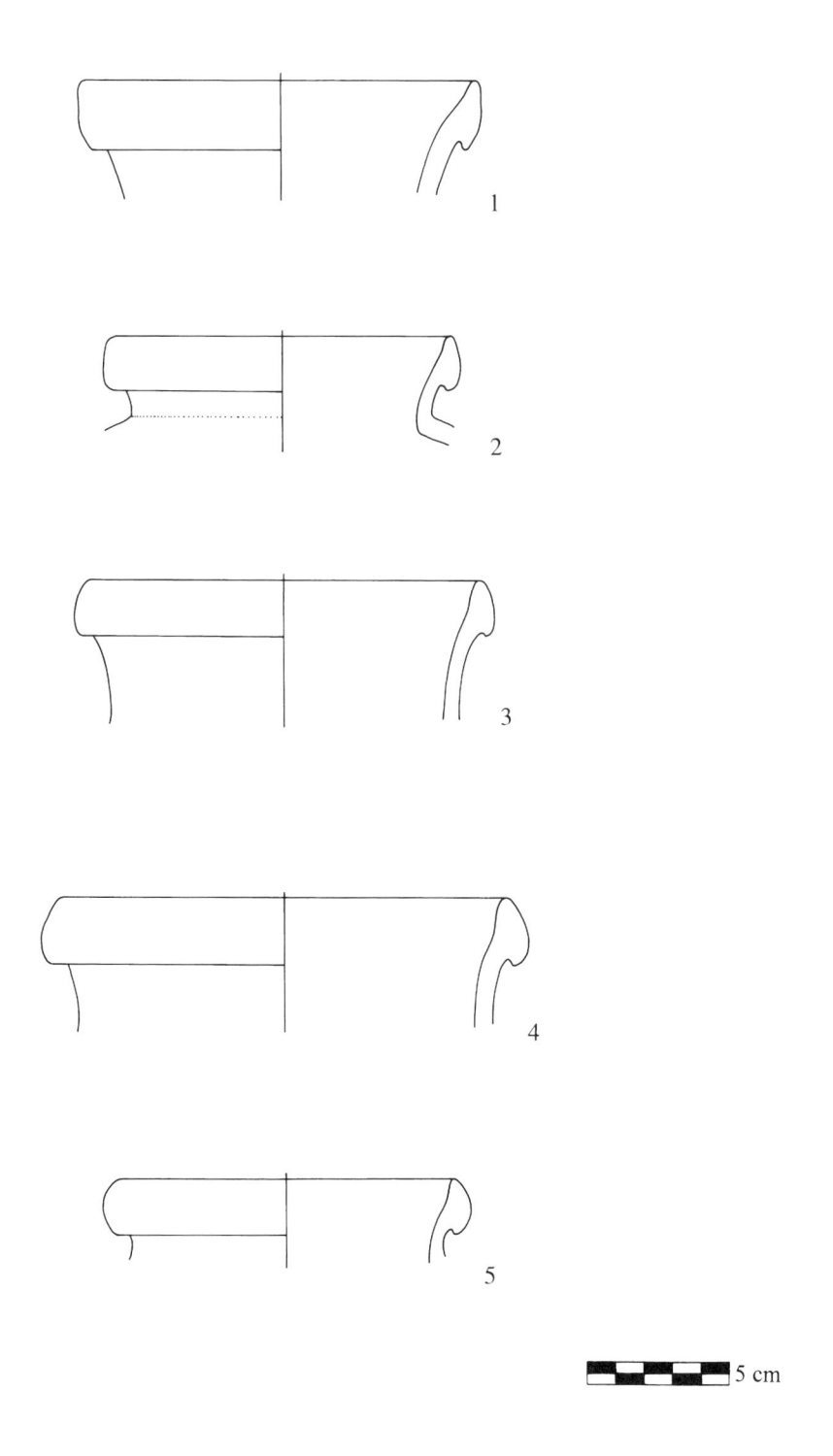

Type C-15: Rounded and Overhanging Band Rim. Scale 2:5

Plate 109. Type C-16a: Triangular-rim Jar with Plain Shoulder

|    | Lot Number | Level | Dimension | Description |
|----|------------|-------|-----------|-------------|
| 1  | H1090:3    | XIVA  | Rim diam. 12.0 cm | Yellow buff, sand and light organic temper |
| 2  | H516:10    | XIIIC | Rim diam. 12.0 cm | Pink, buff surface, sand and light organic temper |
| 3  | H1038:7    | XIIIB | Rim diam. 14.0 cm | Pink, sand and light organic temper |
| 4  | H119:6     | XIIB  | Rim diam. 14.0 cm | Red, greenish buff surface, "textured" slip on shoulder, sand and light organic temper |
| 5  | H1021:11   | XIIB  | Rim diam. 14.0 cm | Buff, sand and light organic temper |
| 6  | I12:5      | XIB   | Rim diam. 13.0 cm | Green, sand temper |
| 7  | H881:7     | XIB   | Rim diam. 14.0 cm | Buff, cream surface, sand and light organic temper |
| 8  | H857:5     | XIA   | Rim diam. 13.0 cm | Buff, sand temper |
| 9  | H859:4     | X     | Rim diam. 14.0 cm | Dark buff gray, sand and light organic temper |
| 10 | H855:1     | X     | Rim diam. 12.0 cm | Pale buff, sand temper |
| 11 | H888:4     | X     | Rim diam. 14.0 cm | Pink, cream surface, sand temper |
| 12 | H789:6     | IX    | Rim diam. 16.0 cm | Buff, sand and light organic temper |
| 13 | H793:12    | IX    | Rim diam. 13.0 cm | Buff gray, sand and light organic temper |
| 14 | H754:14    | VIII  | Rim diam. 12.0 cm | Dark buff, sand temper |
| 15 | H697:2     | VII   | Rim diam. 14.0 cm | Buff, sand and light organic temper |
| 16 | H679:6     | VI    | Rim diam. 14.0 cm | Red, pale buff surface, sand temper |
| 17 | H692:3     | VI    | Rim diam. 14.0 cm | Overfired greenish, sand temper |

COMPARANDA FOR TYPE C-16A

Diyala: Delougaz 1952: C.466.370 (late Akk.), C.466.470 (late Akk.), C.477.350 (early Akk.), C.596.440a (early Akk.); Uch Tepe: Gibson 1981: pl. 96:1–7 (ED–Akk.); Tell Sabra: Tunca 1987: pl. 72:15, pl. 73:10, 14 (ED–Akk.); Umm el-Jīr: Gibson 1972b: fig. 47:C-2:10 (Akk.); Tell al-Hiba: Bahrani 1989: pl. 16:6 (ED IIIb); Assur: Andrae 1970: pl. 60 (Ur III); Haller 1954: pl. 1:b (Ur III); Nineveh: McMahon 1998: fig. 8:22–24; Brak: Oates, Oates, and McDonald 2001: nos. 815, 819 (Akk.–post-Akk.); Nuzi: Starr 1937: pl. 53:C (Akk.); unpublished examples from Nippur WC-3 (Ur III) and Umm al-Hafriyat (Akk.–Ur III)

Plate 109

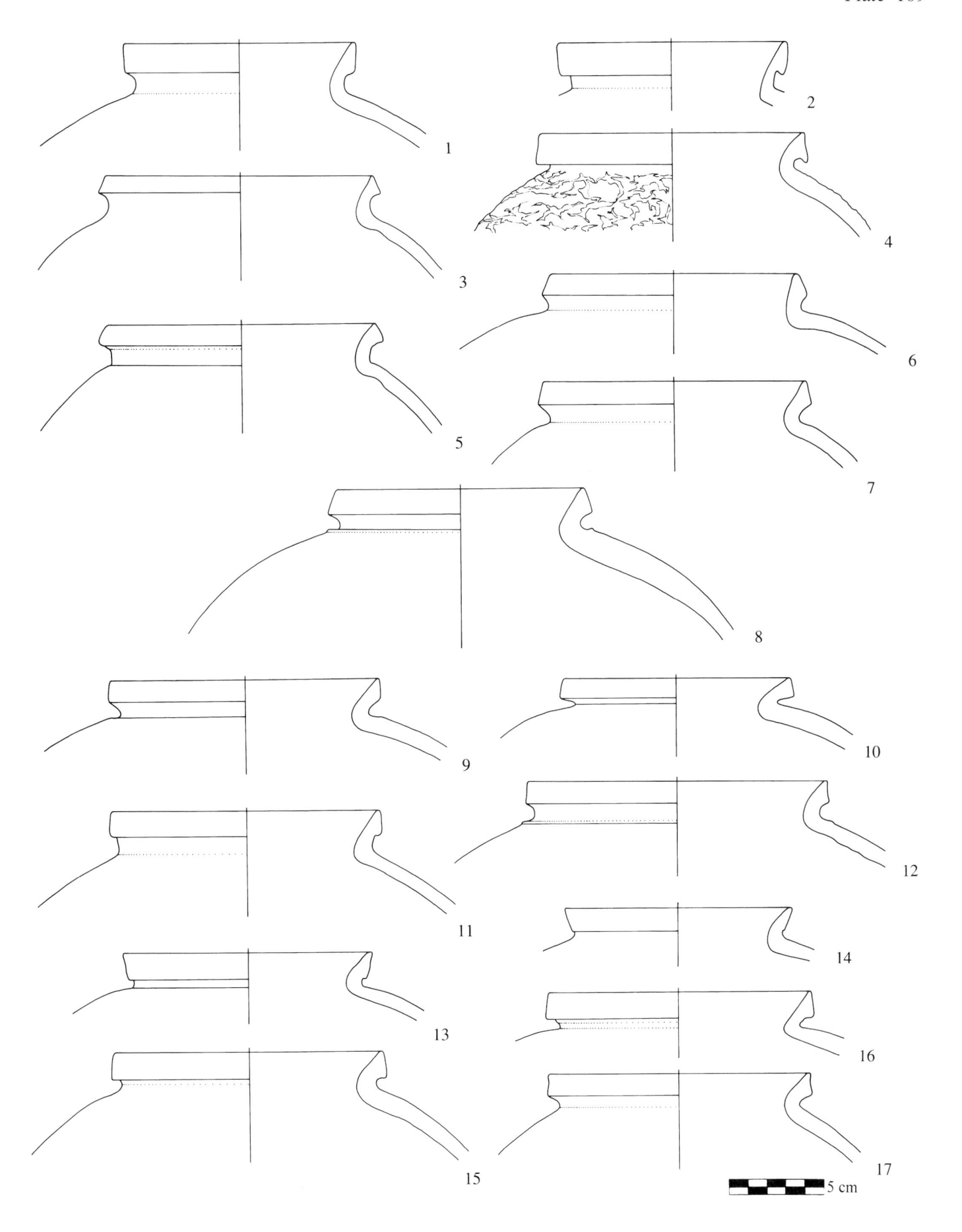

Type C-16a: Triangular-rim Jar with Plain Shoulder. Scale 2:5

Plate 110. Type C-16b: Triangular-rim Jar with Ridged Shoulder

|    | Lot Number | Level | Dimension | Description |
|----|------------|-------|-----------|-------------|
| 1  | H1092:2    | XIIIC | Rim diam. 12.0 cm | Overfired green, sand temper |
| 2  | H1057:8    | XIIIB | Rim diam. 20.0 cm | Buff, sand and light organic temper |
| 3  | H523:2     | XIB   | Rim diam. 14.0 cm | Pink, buff surface, sand and light organic temper, bitumen on exterior |
| 4  | H868:3     | XIB   | Rim diam. 14.0 cm | Buff pink, sand temper |
| 5  | I2:5       | X     | Rim diam. 15.0 cm | Buff pink, sand temper |
| 6  | H874:5     | X     | Rim diam. 14.0 cm | Buff green, sand and light organic temper |
| 7  | H793:13    | IX    | Rim diam. 12.0 cm | Red, pink surface, sand and light organic temper |
| 8  | H779:5     | IX    | Rim diam. 12.0 cm | Pink, buff surface, sand temper |
| 9  | H763:12    | VIII  | Rim diam. 16.0 cm | Dark buff, sand temper, bitumen on exterior |
| 10 | H689:7     | VI    | Rim diam. 10.0 cm | Yellow buff, sand temper |

COMPARANDA FOR TYPE C-16B

Nippur: McCown and Haines 1967: pl. 81:9 (Akk.); Diyala: Delougaz 1952: C.466.450 (late Akk.), C.467.350, C.477.350 (early Akk.), D.465.360 (Akk.), D.465.550 (late Akk.), D.466.360 (Akk.); Tell Sabra: Tunca 1987: pl. 54:2–4 (Akk.); Survey: Gibson 1972a: fig. 34: Akk. A; Umm el-Jīr: Gibson 1972b: fig. 42i, fig. 43:B-2:5, B-3b:12, B-4:11, B-5:13, fig. 44:B-10:12, fig. 46:D IV:23, D I:7, fig. 47:C-1:6 (Akk.–Ur III); Ur: Woolley 1934: type 197–98 (Akk.–Ur III); Uruk: van Ess 1993: fig. 14:174 (Ur III); Tepe Gawra: Speiser 1935: pl. 70:143 (ED–Akk.); Nuzi: Starr 1937: pl. 52:I (Akk.); Susa: Carter 1980: fig. 32:1, fig. 33:1, fig. 35:3, fig. 39:16 (early Akk.–Ur III); Steve and Gasche 1971: pl. 5:33–37, especially 35, pl. 12:6–7, 10, 25 (Akk.); Brak: Oates, Oates, and McDonald 2001: nos. 816–18 (post-Akk.); unpublished examples from Nippur WC-3 (Ur III), Umm al-Hafriyat (Akk.–Ur III) and Nineveh

Plate 110

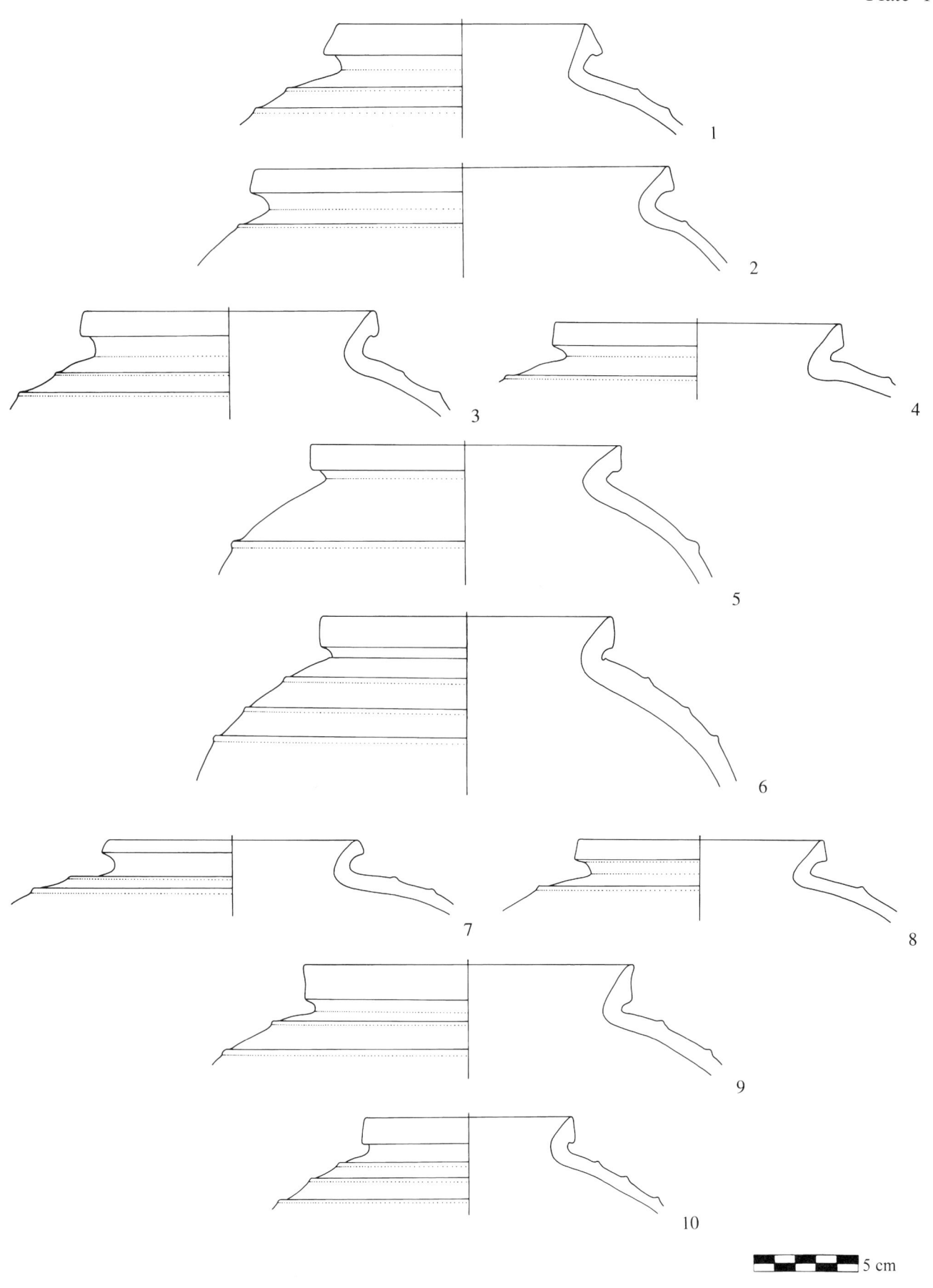

Type C-16b: Triangular-rim Jar with Ridged Shoulder. Scale 2:5

Plate 111. Type C-16c: Large Triangular-rim Jar with Ridged Shoulder

|   | Lot Number | Level | Dimension | Description |
|---|---|---|---|---|
| 1 | I6:5 | XIB | Rim diam. 27.0 cm | Buff yellow, sand temper |
| 2 | H862:5 | XIA | Rim diam. 18.0 cm | Green gray, sand and light organic temper |
| 3 | H870:1 | X | Rim diam. 36.0 cm | Red, sand and light organic temper, bitumen on exterior |
| 4 | H781:3 | IX | Rim diam. 34.0 cm | Red, sand temper |
| 5 | H793:14 | IX | Rim diam. 38.0 cm | Red, cream surface, sand and light organic temper |

COMPARANDA FOR TYPE C-16C

Survey: Adams 1981: 311, fig. 7d (Akk.); Gibson 1972a: fig. 34: Ur III–Isin-Larsa C; Umm el-Jīr: Gibson 1972b: fig. 46: D IV:21, fig. 48: fl. 2:7 (Akk.)

Plate 111

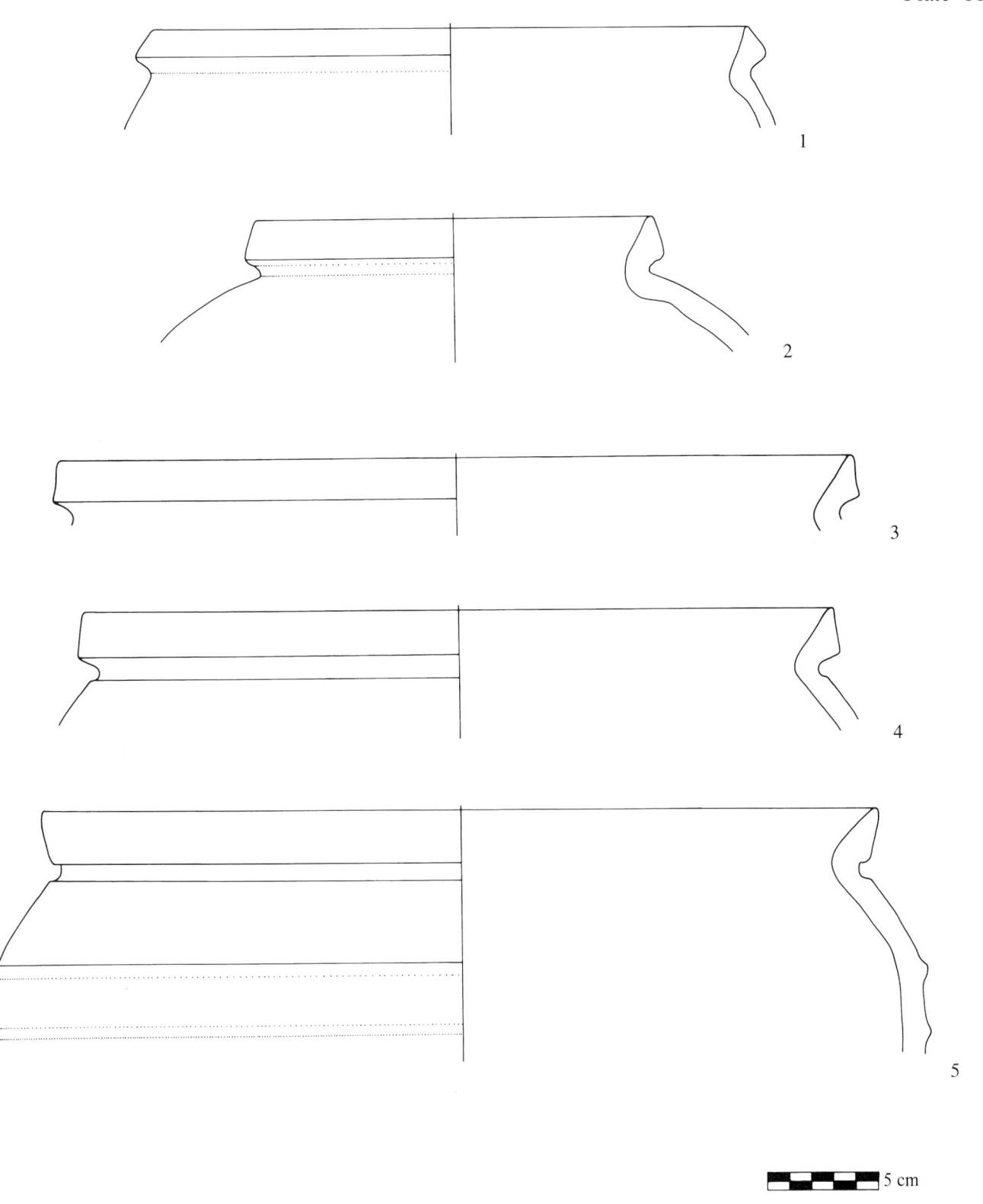

Type C-16c: Large Triangular-rim Jar with Ridged Shoulder. Scale 2:5

Plate 112. Type C-17: Band-rim Jar with Long Neck

|   | Lot Number | Level | Dimension | Description |
|---|---|---|---|---|
| 1 | H1082:8 | XIVA | Rim diam. 14.0 cm | Buff, sand and light organic temper |
| 2 | H540:8 | XIVA | Rim diam. 16.0 cm | Buff green, sand and light organic temper |
| 3 | I37:4 | XIVA | Rim diam. 13.0 cm | Buff, cream surface, sand temper |
| 4 | I119:2 | XIVA | Rim diam. 14.0 cm | Buff, greenish surface, sand temper |
| 5 | H526:5 | XIIIC | Rim diam. 14.0 cm | Greenish, sand temper |
| 6 | H1079:8 | XIIIB | Rim diam. 14.0 cm | Buff, sand and light organic temper |
| 7 | H1071:2 | XIIB | Rim diam. 12.0 cm | Pale buff, sand and light organic temper |
| 8 | H511:5 | XIIA | Rim diam. 16.0 cm | Overfired green, sand and light organic temper |
| 9 | H898:4 | XIA | Rim diam. 16.0 cm | Buff, sand and light organic temper |
| 10 | H865:4 | X | Rim diam. 15.0 cm | Cream buff, sand and light organic temper |

COMPARANDA FOR TYPE C-17

Diyala: Delougaz 1952: C.557.470 (early Akk.); Kish: Mackay 1929: pl. 44:1891B; pl. 54:57; Fara: Martin 1988: type 95 (ED IIIa), fig. 42:2 (Akk.–Ur III); Abu Salabikh: Martin, Moon, and Postgate 1985: grave 1:50, grave 28:8, grave 60:6 (ED III); Moon 1987: nos. 438–40, 442 (ED IIIa–b); Tell al-Hiba: Bahrani 1989: pl. 5:6, pl. 16:4 (ED IIIb); Ur: Woolley 1934: type 61 (late ED III–Akk.); al-Ubaid: Hall and Woolley 1927: pl. 53 center, pl. 57:33; unpublished examples from Tepe al-Atiqeh (Akk.)

Plate 112

Type C-17: Band-rim Jar with Long Neck. Scale 2:5

Plate 113. Type C-18: Wide-mouth, Spouted Vessel

|   | Lot Number | Level | Dimension | Description |
|---|---|---|---|---|
| 1 | I1:5 | XIVA | Rim diam. 26.0 cm | Red, buff surface, sand temper |
| 2 | H884:9 | XIB | Rim diam. 26.0 cm | Pale red, pink surface, sand and light organic temper |
| 3 | H1034:1 | XIB | Rim diam. 26.0 cm | Pink, buff surface, sand and light organic temper |
| 4 | H857:12 | XIA | Rim diam. 24.0 cm | Pink, pale buff surface, sand and light organic temper |
| 5 | H862:7 | XIA | Rim diam. 30.0 cm | Pink, cream surface, sand and light organic temper |
| 6 | H1095:1 | X | Rim diam. 28.0 cm | Red, buff surface, sand and light organic temper |

COMPARANDA FOR TYPE C-18

Nippur: McCown, Haines, and Biggs 1978: pl. 47:7 (Akk.); Diyala: Delougaz 1952: B.173.222 (late Akk.), C.053.312 (Akk.), C.544.312 (late Akk.–Ur III); Tell Brak: Fielden 1977: pl. 12:18 (late Akk.–Ur III); Mallowan 1947: pl. 69:8 (late Akk.); Survey: Gibson 1972a: fig. 34: Akk. B–C; Isin: Hrouda 1977: pl. 27:IB 455 (Ur III); Fara: Martin 1983: fig. 2:3 (Akk.–Ur III); Abu Salabikh: Moon 1987: no. 192 (post-ED); Uruk: van Ess 1988: form 20b (Akk.–Isin-Larsa); Ur: Woolley 1934: types 33, 215 (Akk.–Ur III); unpublished examples from Umm al-Hafriyat (Akk.)

Plate 113

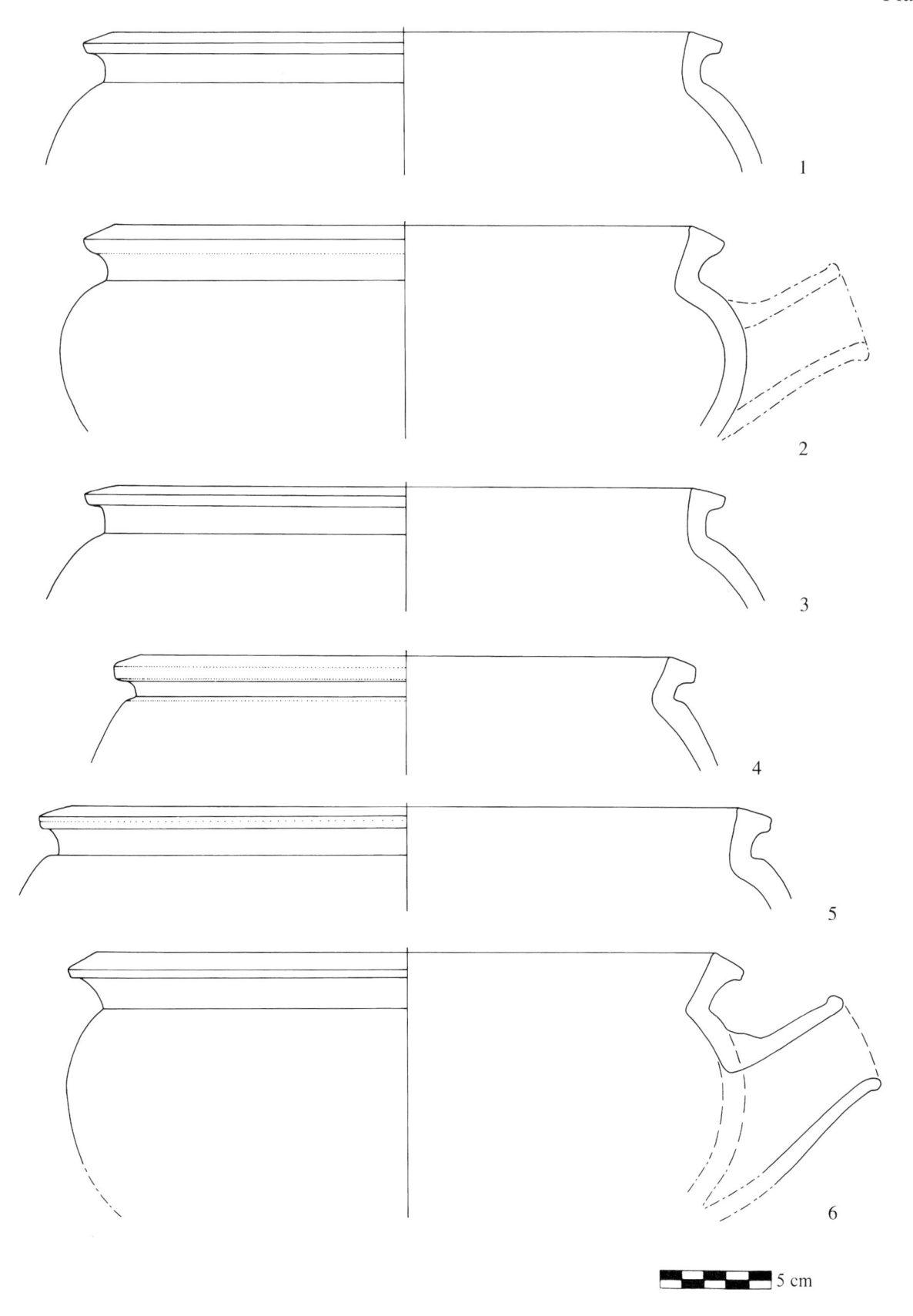

Type C-18: Wide-mouth, Spouted Vessel. Scale 2:5

Plate 114. Type C-18: Wide-mouth, Spouted Vessel (*cont.*) and Type C-19: Bottle

| | *Lot Number* | *Level* | *Dimension* | *Description* |
|---|---|---|---|---|
| TYPE C-18: WIDE-MOUTH, SPOUTED VESSEL (*CONT.*) | | | | |
| 1 | H838:3 | X | Rim diam. 22.0 cm | Buff, sand and light organic temper |
| 2 | H777:10 | IX | Rim diam. 20.0 cm | Pink buff, sand temper |
| 3 | H771:13 | VIII | Rim diam. 28.0 cm | Red, sand and light organic temper |
| TYPE C-19: BOTTLE | | | | |
| 4 | H1082:9 | XIVB | Max. diam. 10.0 cm | Dark red, friable fabric, sand temper |
| 5 | I29 | XIIIC | Max. diam. 11.5 cm | Pale red, sand temper |
| 6 | I17:2 | XIIIC | Max. diam. 10.0 cm | Buff, cream surface, sand temper |
| 7 | H1021:14 | XIIB | Rim diam. 4.0 cm | Buff, sand temper |

COMPARANDA FOR TYPE C-19

Nippur: McCown and Haines 1967: pl. 81:1 (Akk.); Tell al-Hiba: Bahrani 1989: pl. 3:1–2, 6 (ED IIIb); Diyala: Delougaz 1952: pl. 111, B.544.570 (early Akk.), B.633.570 (Akk.–Ur III), B.634.570 (Akk.), B.663.540b (ED II–III), B.703.560 (early Akk.), B.704.570 (Akk.); Kish: Mackay 1925: pl. 16:27–31; Mackay 1929: pl. 54: type N; Tell al-Wilayah: Madhlum 1960: fig. 3:10–12; Fara: Martin 1988: type 84 (ED II); Abu Salabikh: Martin, Moon, and Postgate 1985: grave 41:2, grave 81:7 (ED II–III); Moon 1987: nos. 310, 312, 317–20 (ED II–III); Ur: Woolley 1934: types 51–52 (Akk.–Ur III); al-Ubaid: Hall and Woolley 1927: pl. 57:43–44, pl. 58:45–46; Tepe Gawra: Speiser 1935: pl. 69:126 (ED–Akk.); Nuzi: Starr 1937: pl. 51 D (Akk.); Susa: Steve and Gasche 1971: pl. 12:39; unpublished examples from Umm al-Hafriyat

Plate 114

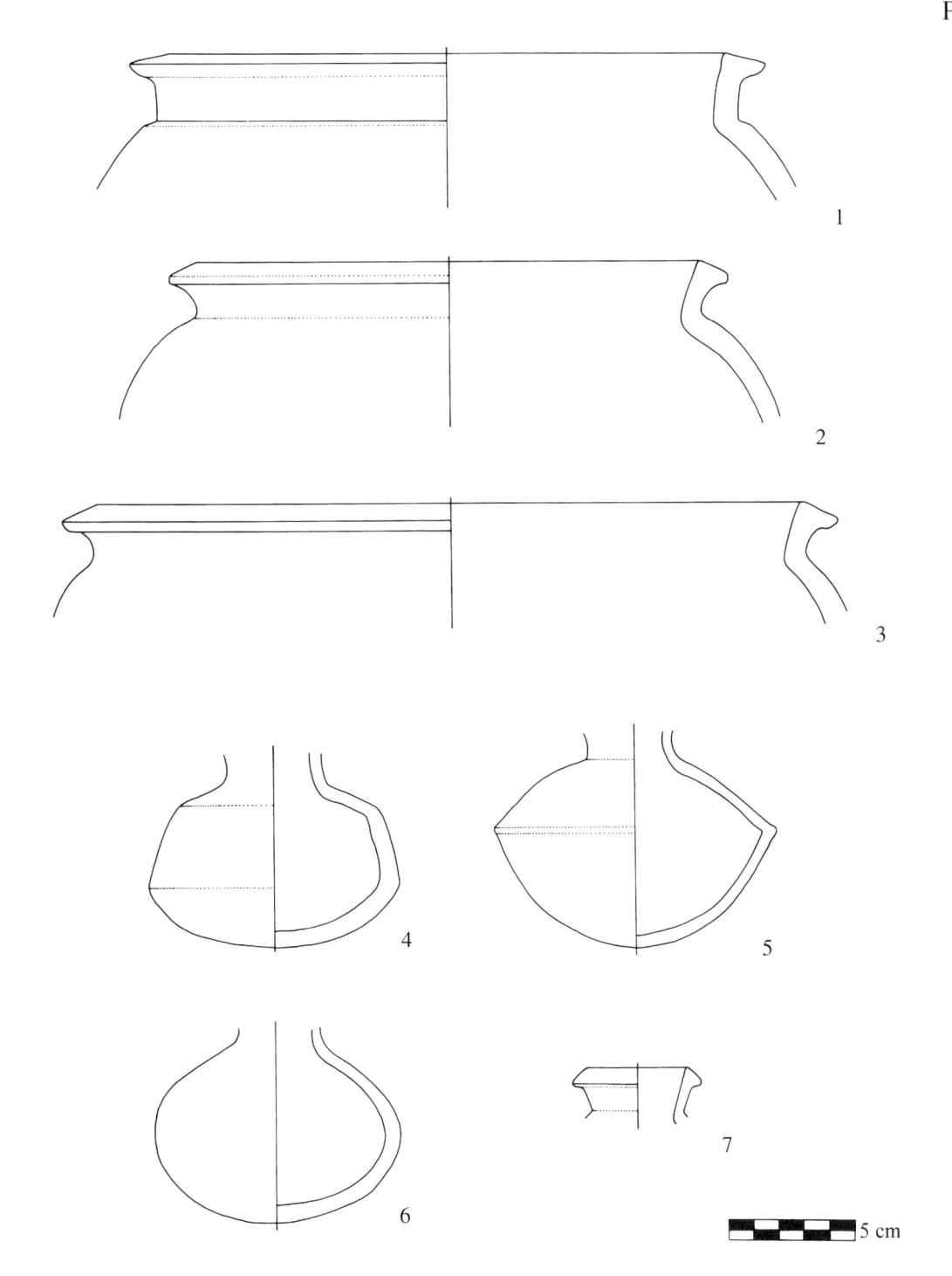

Type C-18: Wide-mouth, Spouted Vessel (*cont.*) and Type C-19: Bottle. Scale 2:5

Plate 115. Type C-20: Carinated-shoulder Jar, Developing to Elongated Jar with Ridge below Rim

|   | Lot Number | Level | Dimension | Description |
|---|---|---|---|---|
| 1 | H1038:10 | XIIIB | Rim diam. 12.0 cm | Red, sand and light organic temper |
| 2 | H511:8 | XIIA | Rim diam. 10.0 cm | Overfired green, sand and light organic temper |
| 3 | H1034:2 | XIB | Rim diam. 10.0 cm | Overfired green, sand and light organic temper |
| 4 | H857:6 | XIA | Rim diam. 11.0 cm | Pink, pale buff surface, sand temper |
| 5 | H779:8 | IX | Rim diam. 11.0 cm | Buff, sand temper |
| 6 | H793:7 | IX | Rim diam. 10.0 cm | Buff, sand temper |
| 7 | H692:7 | VI | Rim diam. 10.0 cm | Greenish buff, sand temper |
| 8 | H697:1 | VII | Rim diam. 12.0 cm | Buff, sand temper |
| 9 | H754:6 | VIII | Rim diam. 12.0 cm | Pale buff, sand temper |

COMPARANDA FOR TYPE C-20

Earlier form: Abu Salabikh: Moon 1987: no. 613 (post-ED); Ur: Woolley 1934: type 160 (late Akk.); Uruk: van Ess 1993: fig. 16:186; Brak: Oates, Oates, and McDonald 2001: nos. 821–22. Later form: Nippur: McCown and Haines 1967: pl. 85:1–6 (Akk.–Isin-Larsa); Survey: Adams 1965: Ur III type F; Gibson 1972a: fig. 34: Ur III–Isin-Larsa F; Diyala: Delougaz 1952: pl. 114 f (Akk.), C.208.440 (Larsa), C.777.340 (late Akk.); Tell al-Wilayah: Madhlum 1960: fig. 3:6; Fara: Martin 1988: fig. 42:1 (Akk.–Ur III); Tello: Parrot 1948: fig. 55:614 (Ur III); Uruk: van Ess 1988: form 51 and nos. 231–32, 234 (Akk.–Isin-Larsa); van Ess 1993: fig. 14:175, fig. 16:186; Boehmer, Pedde, and Salje 1995: pl. 11:a (Ur III); Ur: Woolley 1934: types 75–76 (late Akk.–Ur III); Susa: Steve and Gasche 1971: pl. 2:13, pl. 3:1, 13, pl. 4:11 (Ur III); unpublished examples from Nippur WC-3 (Ur III) and Umm al-Hafriyat (Ur III)

Plate 115

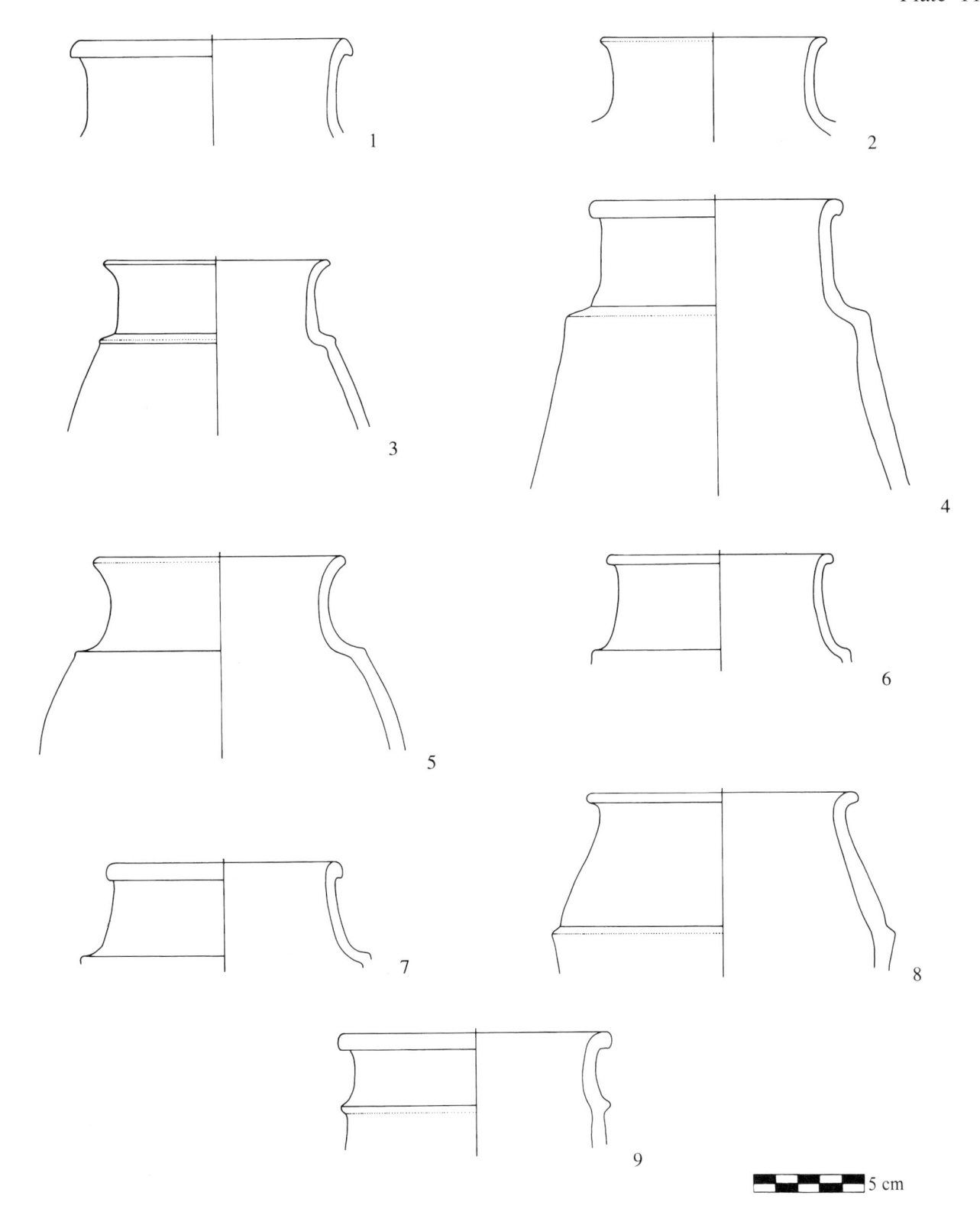

Type C-20: Carinated-shoulder Jar, Developing to Elongated Jar with Ridge below Rim. Scale 2:5

Plate 116. Type C-21: Small Jar with Plain Rim

|   | Lot Number | Level | Dimension | Description |
|---|---|---|---|---|
| 1 | H1052:4 | XIVB | Rim diam. 12.0 cm | Buff, sand and light organic temper |
| 2 | H1012:4 | XIVA | Rim diam. 10.0 cm | Pale buff, sand temper |
| 3 | H540:11 | XIVA | Rim diam. 11.0 cm | Pale red, sand and light organic temper |
| 4 | H516:9 | XIIIC | Rim diam. 12.0 cm | Buff, sand and light organic temper |
| 5 | H526:12 | XIIIC | Rim diam. 10.0 cm | Buff, sand temper |
| 6 | H1038:8 | XIIIB | Rim diam. 10.0 cm | Red, pink surface, sand and light organic temper |
| 7 | H1010:11 | XIIB | Rim diam. 12.0 cm | Buff, sand and light organic temper |
| 8 | H525:9 | XIIA | Rim diam. 10.0 cm | Buff, sand and light organic temper |
| 9 | I20:3 | XIIA | Rim diam. 12.0 cm | Pink, cream surface, sand temper |
| 10 | I12:2 | XIB | Rim diam. 12.0 cm | Green, sand temper |
| 11 | H877:4 | XIB | Rim diam. 12.0 cm | Buff, sand and light organic temper |
| 12 | H144:2 | XIA | Rim diam. 11.0 cm | Buff, sand and light organic temper |
| 13 | H144:4 | XIA | Rim diam. 12.0 cm | Buff, cream surface, sand and light organic temper |
| 14 | I2:6 | X | Rim diam. 12.0 cm | Green cream, sand temper |
| 15 | H774:8 | VIII | Rim diam. 10.0 cm | Buff gray, sand temper |
| 16 | H689:4 | VI | Rim diam. 12.0 cm | Buff yellow, sand temper |

COMPARANDA FOR TYPE C-21

Nippur: McCown and Haines 1967: pl. 80:11, pl. 82:2–3, 5 (Akk.); Diyala: Delougaz 1952: B.174.220b, c (Akk.–Ur III), B.184.220 (ED–Ur III), B.185.220 (Akk.), B.573.240 (Akk.–Ur III), B.574.240 (Akk.–Ur III); Kish: Mackay 1929: pl. 53, type K, especially 1–2, 6, 8; Abu Salabikh: Moon 1987: nos. 463–82 (ED IIIa and b); Tell al-Hiba: Bahrani 1989: pl. 7:10–11 (ED IIIb); Uruk: van Ess 1988: 1 (Akk.); Ur: Woolley 1934: types 32b, 80, 83b–c, 120, 179b, 230 (Akk.–Ur III); unpublished examples from Nippur WC-3 and Umm al-Hafriyat

Plate 116

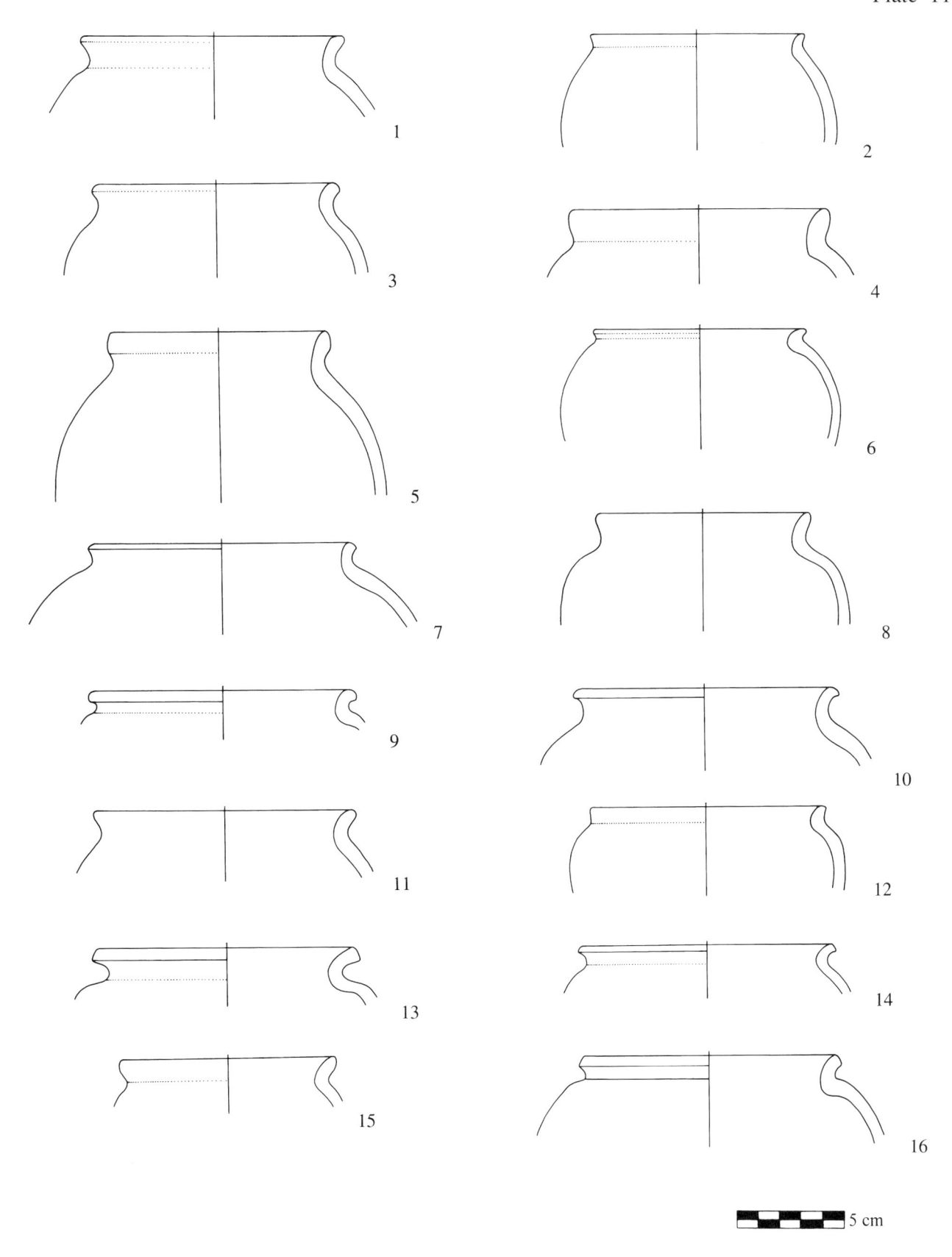

Type C-21: Small Jar with Plain Rim. Scale 2:5

Plate 117. Type C-22: Band-rim Storage Jar

|   | Lot Number | Level | Dimension | Description |
|---|---|---|---|---|
| 1 | I37:7 | XIVA | Rim diam. 13.0 cm | Red, pink surface, sand temper |
| 2 | H516:5 | XIIIC | Rim diam. 12.0 cm | Buff, cream surface, sand and light organic temper |
| 3 | I14:2 | XIIIC | Rim diam. 18.0 cm | Cream, sand temper |
| 4 | I101:11 | XIIIB | Rim diam. 12.0 cm | Buff, cream surface, sand temper |
| 5 | I136:1 | XIIIB | Rim diam. 14.0 cm | Greenish buff, sand and light organic temper |
| 6 | I5:2 | XIIB | Rim diam. 18.0 cm | Red, greenish buff surface, sand temper |
| 7 | H1010:12 | XIIB | Rim diam. 16.0 cm | Buff, cream surface, sand and light organic temper, blackened interior |
| 8 | I16:5 | XIIA | Rim diam. 12.0 cm | Pink, cream surface, sand temper |
| 9 | H511:3 | XIIA | Rim diam. 14.0 cm | Red, pink surface, sand and light organic temper |
| 10 | I11 | XIB | Rim diam. 14.0 cm | Buff, sand temper |
| 11 | H884:7 | XIB | Rim diam. 14.0 cm | Pale buff, sand and light organic temper |
| 12 | H509:6 | XIB | Rim diam. 12.0 cm | Yellow buff, greenish buff surface, sand and light organic temper |
| 13 | H779:3 | IX | Rim diam. 16.0 cm | Buff, sand temper |
| 14 | H771:9 | VIII | Rim diam. 12.0 cm | Overfired greenish, sand temper, bitumen on exterior |

COMPARANDA FOR TYPE C-22

Diyala: Delougaz 1952: D.546.540 (late Akk.), D.555.510b (Akk.), D.556.540b (ED III), D.596.540 (early Akk.); Tell Madhhur: Roaf et al. 1984: fig. 13:3A (grave 5G, early Akk.); Umm el-Jīr: Gibson 1972b: fig. 43:B-3a:7, B-3b:5–6, B-5:9, B-6:2–4, fig. 46:D II:6, fig. 47:C-2:9, C-3:8 (Akk.–Ur III); Kish: Mackay 1929: pl. 54:6; Abu Salabikh: Postgate and Moon 1984:13 (post-ED); Assur: Andrae 1970: pl. 25a (ED–Akk.); unpublished examples from Umm al-Hafriyat (Akk.)

Plate 117

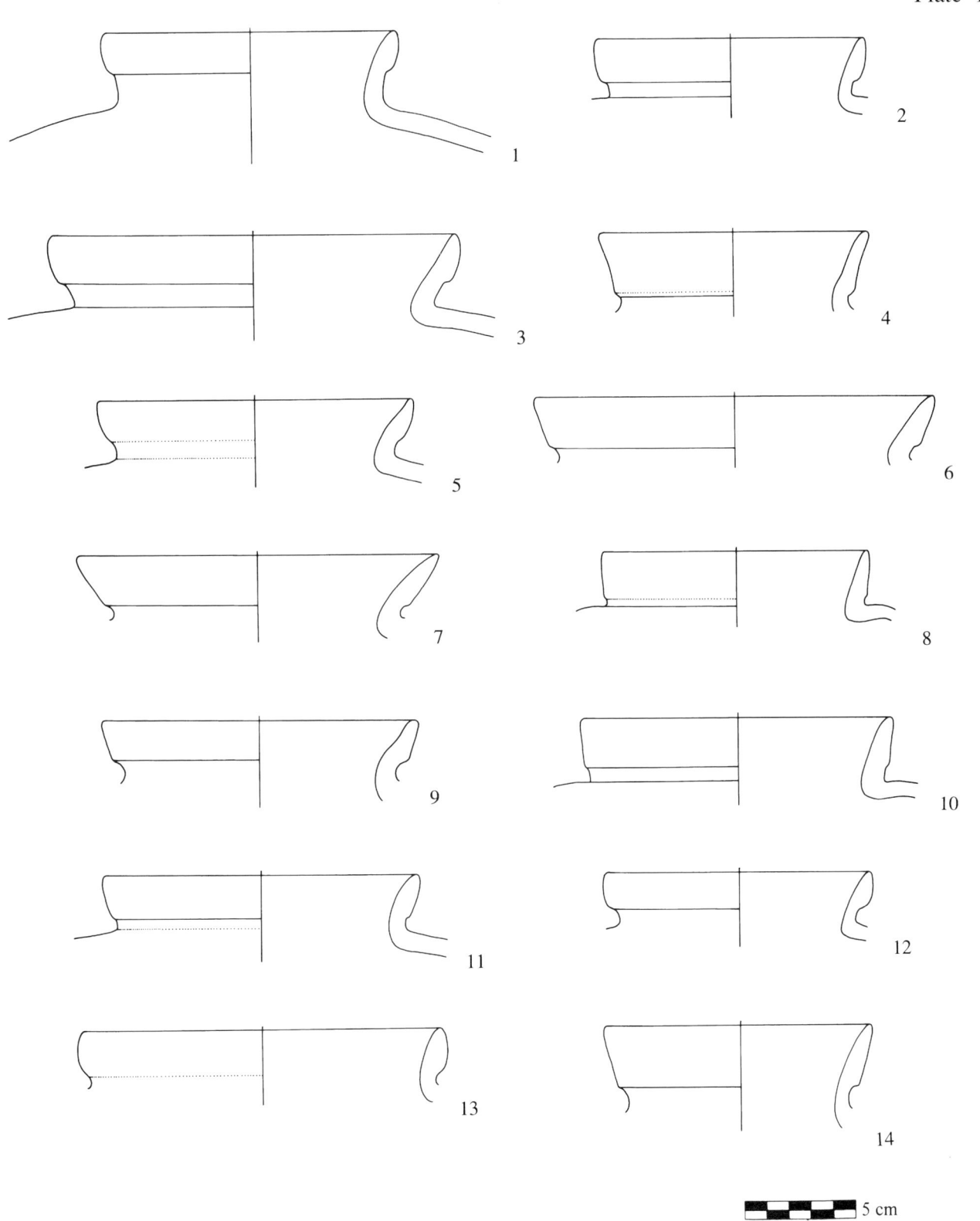

Type C-22: Band-rim Storage Jar. Scale 2:5

Plate 118. Type C-24: Triangular or Rounded Rim on Long Neck

|    | Lot Number | Level | Dimension | Description |
|----|------------|-------|-----------|-------------|
| 1  | I373:2     | XVA   | Rim diam. 12.0 cm | Buff green, sand and light organic temper |
| 2  | I341:3     | XVA   | Rim diam. 9.0 cm  | Pale red, buff surface, sand temper |
| 3  | H1067:3    | XIVB  | Rim diam. 12.0 cm | Red, sand and light organic temper |
| 4  | H1082:7    | XIVB  | Rim diam. 12.0 cm | Pink, sand and light organic temper |
| 5  | I139:1     | XIIIB | Rim diam. 10.0 cm | Overfired green, sand temper |
| 6  | H1052:5    | XIVB  | Rim diam. 12.0 cm | Buff, sand and light organic temper |
| 7  | H540:10    | XIVA  | Rim diam. 12.0 cm | Buff, sand temper |
| 8  | H1057:10   | XIIIB | Rim diam. 13.0 cm | Buff, sand and light organic temper |
| 9  | H1038:9    | XIIIB | Rim diam. 12.0 cm | Yellow buff, sand and light organic temper |
| 10 | H1021:12   | XIIB  | Rim diam. 10.0 cm | Buff, sand and light organic temper |
| 11 | H529:5     | XIIA  | Rim diam. 14.0 cm | Buff, cream surface, sand and light organic temper |
| 12 | H887:10    | XIB   | Rim diam. 12.0 cm | Pale buff, sand and light organic temper |
| 13 | H139:3     | XIB   | Rim diam. 12.0 cm | Cream buff, sand and light organic temper |
| 14 | H877:7     | XIB   | Rim diam. 12.0 cm | Buff green, sand temper |
| 15 | H895:4     | X     | Rim diam. 10.0 cm | Pale buff, sand temper |
| 16 | H771:11    | VIII  | Rim diam. 12.0 cm | Buff pink, sand temper |
| 17 | H757:7     | VII   | Rim diam. 14.0 cm | Buff, sand temper |

COMPARANDA FOR TYPE C-24

Nippur: McCown, Haines, and Biggs 1978: pl. 47:1 (Akk.); Umm el-Jīr: Gibson 1972b: fig. 46:D IV:13 (Akk.); Abu Salabikh: Moon 1987: nos. 434, 436, 603, 609 (ED IIIa and b); Tell al-Hiba: Bahrani 1989: pl. 5:1–5 (ED IIIb); Ur: Woolley 1934: type 63 (ED–Akk.)

Plate 118

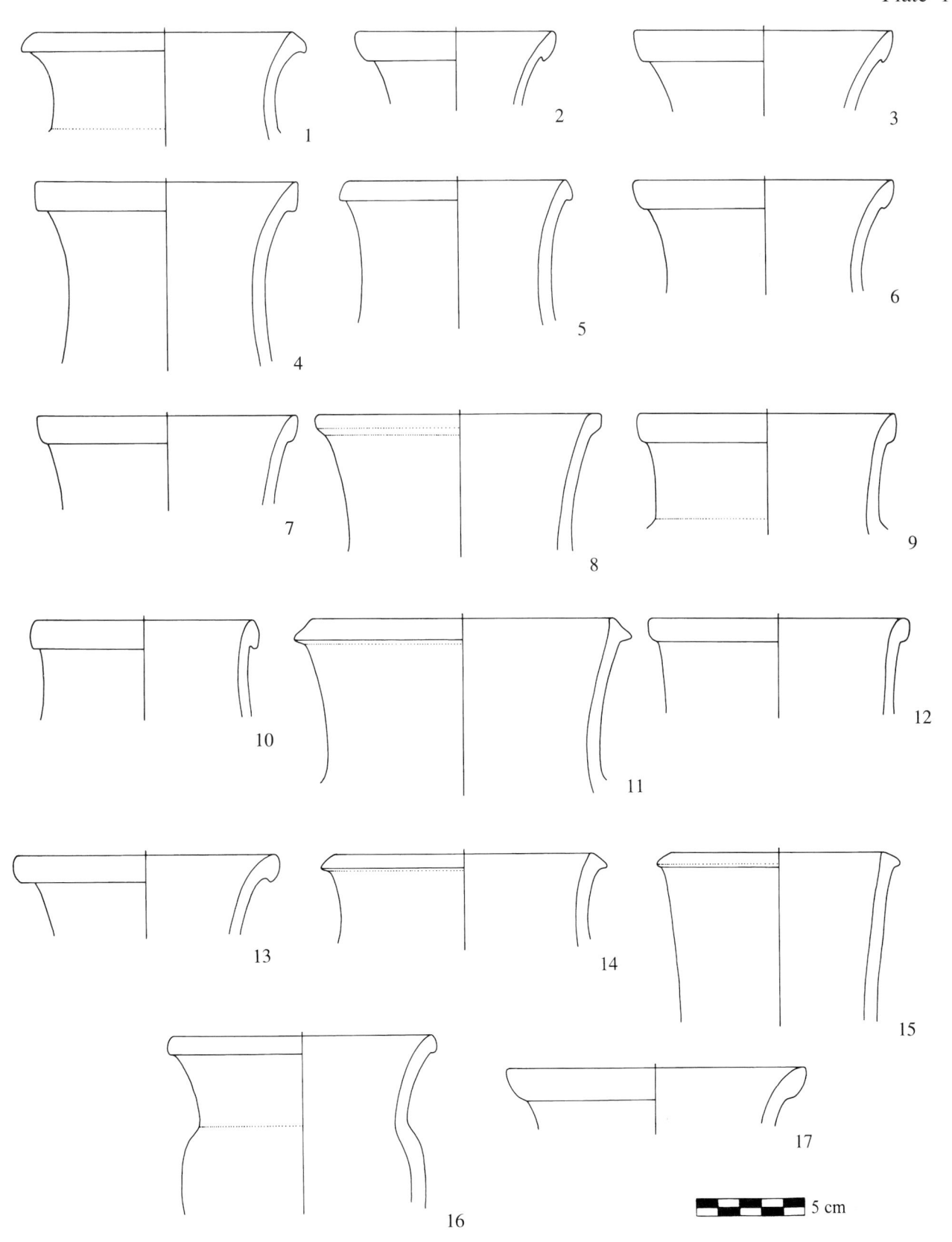

Type C-24: Triangular or Rounded Rim on Long Neck. Scale 2:5

Plate 119. Type C-25a: Squared-rim Vessel

|   | Lot Number | Level | Dimension | Description |
|---|---|---|---|---|
| 1 | H110:5 | XIIA | Rim diam. 12.0 cm | Buff green sand and light organic temper |
| 2 | H868:4 | XIB | Rim diam. 14.0 cm | Greenish gray, sand temper |
| 3 | H884:3 | XIB | Rim diam. 14.0 cm | Buff, sand temper |
| 4 | H833:2 | X | Rim diam. 12.0 cm | Buff, sand temper |
| 5 | H779:7 | IX | Rim diam. 12.0 cm | Buff, sand temper |
| 6 | H793:6 | IX | Rim diam. 14.0 cm | Red, pink buff surface, sand temper |
| 7 | H771:8 | VIII | Rim diam. 12.0 cm | Greenish buff, sand and light organic temper |

COMPARANDA FOR TYPE C-25A

Nippur: McCown and Haines 1967: pl. 84:1–2 (Akk.–Isin-Larsa); Abu Salabikh: Postgate and Moon 1984: no. 19 (post-ED); unpublished examples from Nippur WC-3 and Umm al-Hafriyat

Plate 119

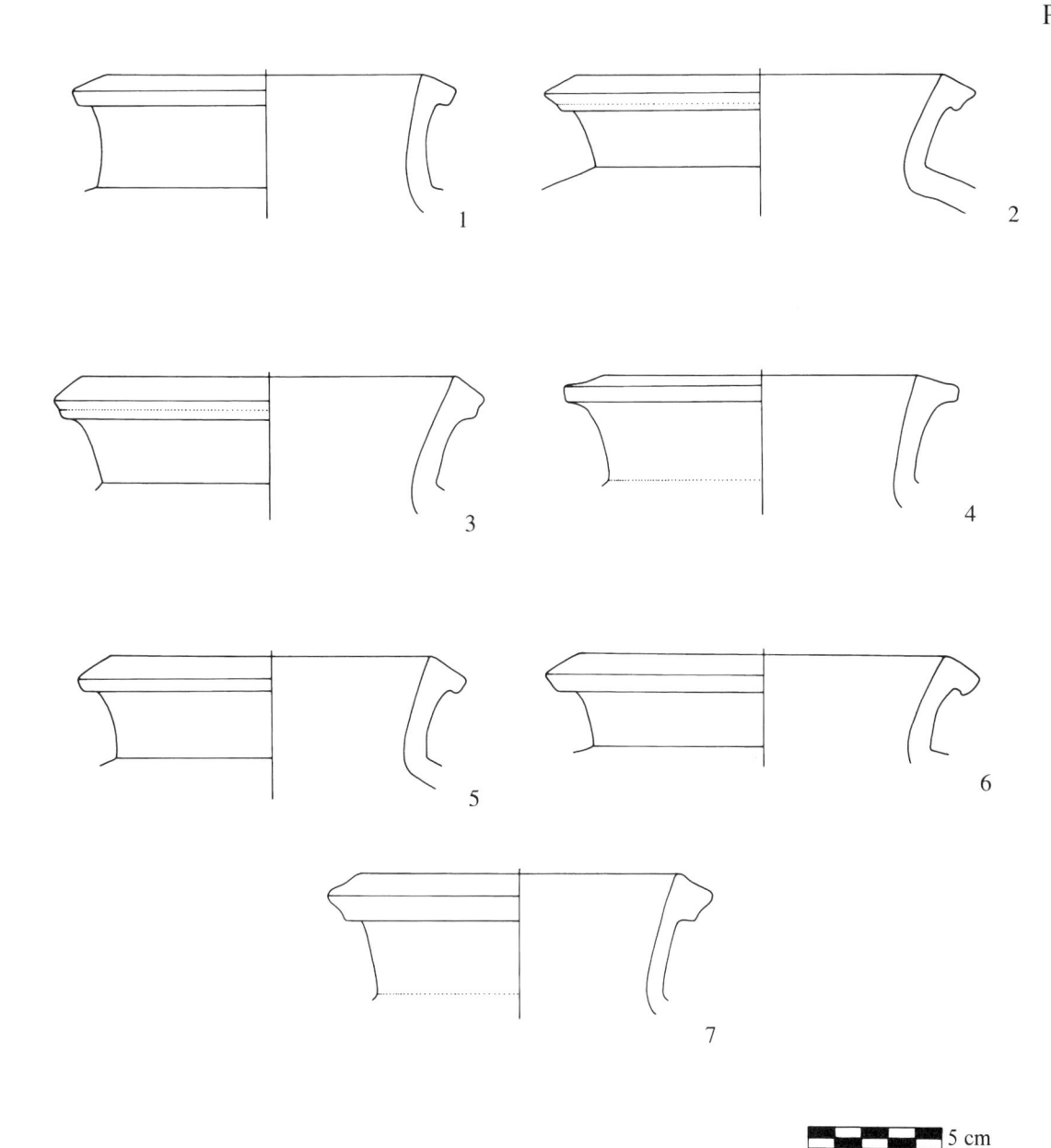

Type C-25a: Squared-rim Vessel. Scale 2:5

Plate 120. Type C-25b: Rectangular-rim Vessel and Type C-28: Triple-ridged-rim Jar

|   | Lot Number | Level | Dimension | Description |
|---|---|---|---|---|
| TYPE C-25B: RECTANGULAR-RIM VESSEL |||||
| 1 | H763:17 | VIII | Rim diam. 16.0 cm | Greenish, sand and light organic temper |
| 2 | H776:1 | VIII | Rim diam. 14.0 cm | Buff, sand temper, bitumen on interior and exterior |
| 3 | H763:16 | VIII | Rim diam. 12.0 cm | Greenish, sand temper |
| 4 | H700:2 | VI | Rim diam. 12.0 cm | Yellow buff, sand temper |
| TYPE C-28: TRIPLE-RIDGED-RIM JAR |||||
| 5 | H898:2 | XIA | Rim diam. 14.0 cm | Red, sand and light organic temper |
| 6 | H757:3 | VII | Rim diam. 12.0 cm | Red, buff surface, sand temper |
| 7 | H680:1 | VB | Rim diam. 16.0 cm | Buff, sand temper |

COMPARANDA FOR TYPE C-25B

Tello: Parrot 1948: fig. 56:1108, 1359 (Ur III); unpublished examples from Nippur WC-3 and Umm al-Hafriyat

COMPARANDA FOR TYPE C-28

Nippur: McCown and Haines 1967: pl. 84:3–4, 7–8 (TB VII–VI, IV, II) (Ur III–Isin-Larsa); Diyala: Delougaz 1952: B.645.540a (Ur III); Survey: Gibson 1972a: fig. 34 (Ur III Ab); Umm el-Jīr: Gibson 1972b: fig. 46:D III:27 (Akk.); Isin: Hrouda 1977: pl. 27:IB 264 (Ur III); Tell al-Wilayah: Madhlum 1960: fig. 3:1; Abu Salabikh: Postgate and Moon 1984: no. 53 (post-ED); Uruk: van Ess 1988: form 32, no. 127 (Ur III–Isin-Larsa); van Ess 1993: fig. 9:143, fig. 15:181; Boehmer, Pedde, and Salje 1995: pl. 6:a1–a2, pl. 9:f (Ur III); Ur: Woolley 1934: types 138, 224–25 (Ur III); Nuzi: Starr 1937: pl. 52:F (Akk.); Susa: Carter 1980: fig. 50:2, 5, 9 (Ur III); Steve and Gasche 1971: pl. 3:8 (Ur III); Assur: Haller 1954: pl. 1:n, r (Ur III); Nineveh: McMahon 1998: fig. 5:25; unpublished examples from Nippur WC-3 (Ur III), Umm al-Hafriyat (Ur III), and Chagar Bazar (late post-Akk.)

Plate 120

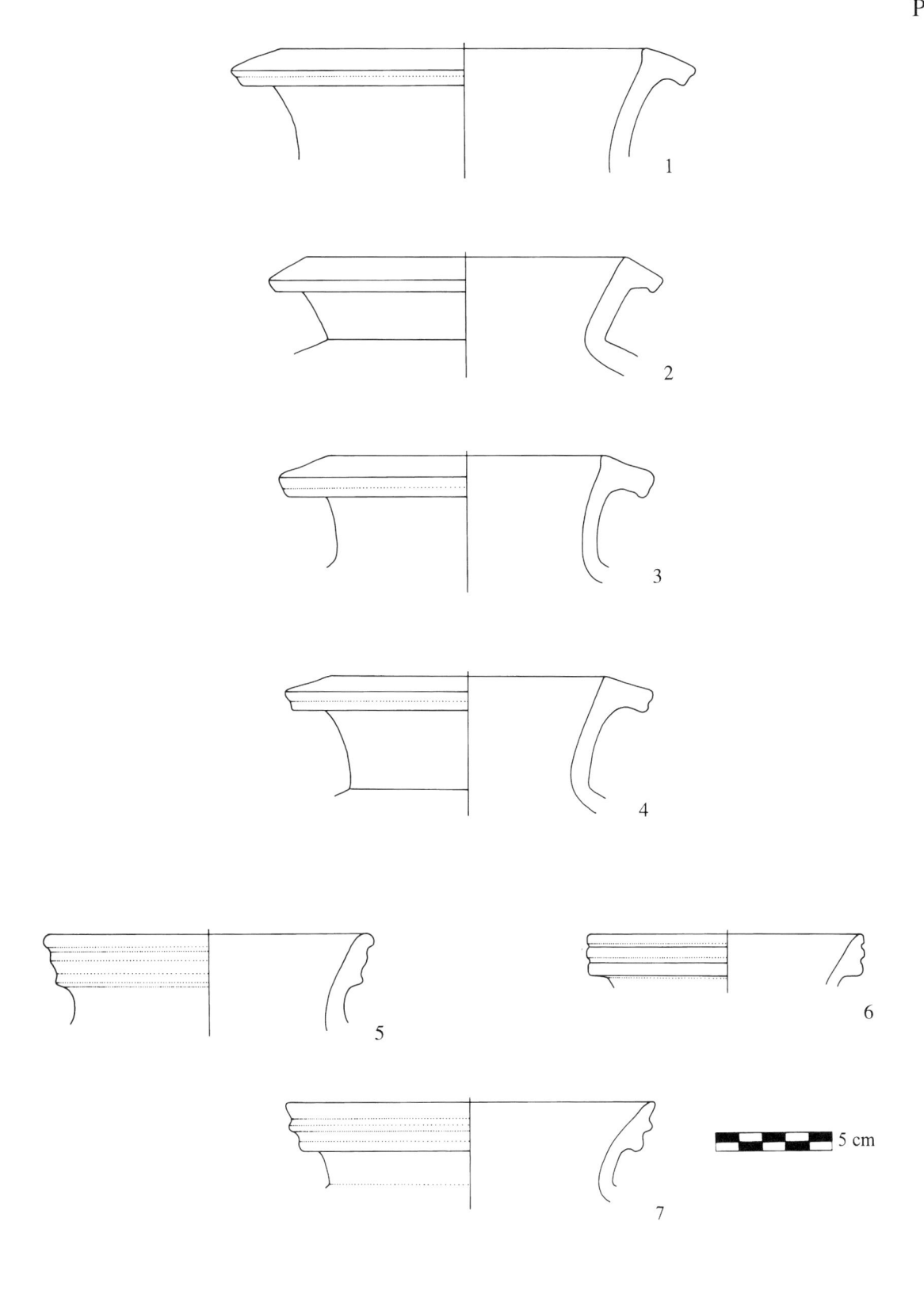

Type C-25b: Rectangular-rim Vessel and Type C-28: Triple-ridged-rim Jar. Scale 2:5

Plate 121. Type C-26: Grooved Rim, Bag-shaped Jar and Type C-27: Oval Rim, Grooved-shoulder Jar

|   | Lot Number | Level | Dimension | Description |
|---|---|---|---|---|
| TYPE C-26: GROOVED RIM, BAG-SHAPED JAR | | | | |
| 1 | 18 N 131 | XIB | Rim diam. 7.6 cm, max. diam. 7.9 cm, ht. 11.0 cm | Pale red, sand temper |
| 2 | H139:6 | XIB | Rim diam. 10.0 cm | Cream green, sand temper |
| TYPE C-27: OVAL RIM, GROOVED-SHOULDER JAR | | | | |
| 3 | H868:6 | XIB | Rim diam. 14.0 cm | Yellow buff, sand and light organic temper |
| 4 | H879:2 | XIA | Rim diam. 20.0 cm | Buff, sand and light organic temper, bitumen on neck |
| 5 | H857:13 | XIA | Rim diam. 16.0 cm | Yellow buff, sand temper |
| 6 | H779:10 | IX | Rim diam. 16.0 cm | Red, buff surface, sand temper |

COMPARANDA FOR TYPE C-26

Nippur: similar vessel form to McCown and Haines 1967: pl. 84:3–4, (Ur III); Diyala: Delougaz 1952: B.555.540a (early Akk.), possibly B.645.540b (ED III–early Akk.); Uruk: similar to van Ess 1993: fig. 9:130 (Ur III); Ur: Woolley 1934: type 222 (Akk.–Ur III)

COMPARANDA FOR TYPE C-27

Diyala: Delougaz 1952: pl. 112 c, B.655.540b (Akk.) is similar but smaller; Tell Brak: Mallowan 1947: pl. 68:17 (Akk.); Nineveh: McMahon 1998: fig. 9:1–3; Abu Salabikh: Moon 1987: nos. 521–22, 529 (ED IIIa)

Plate 121

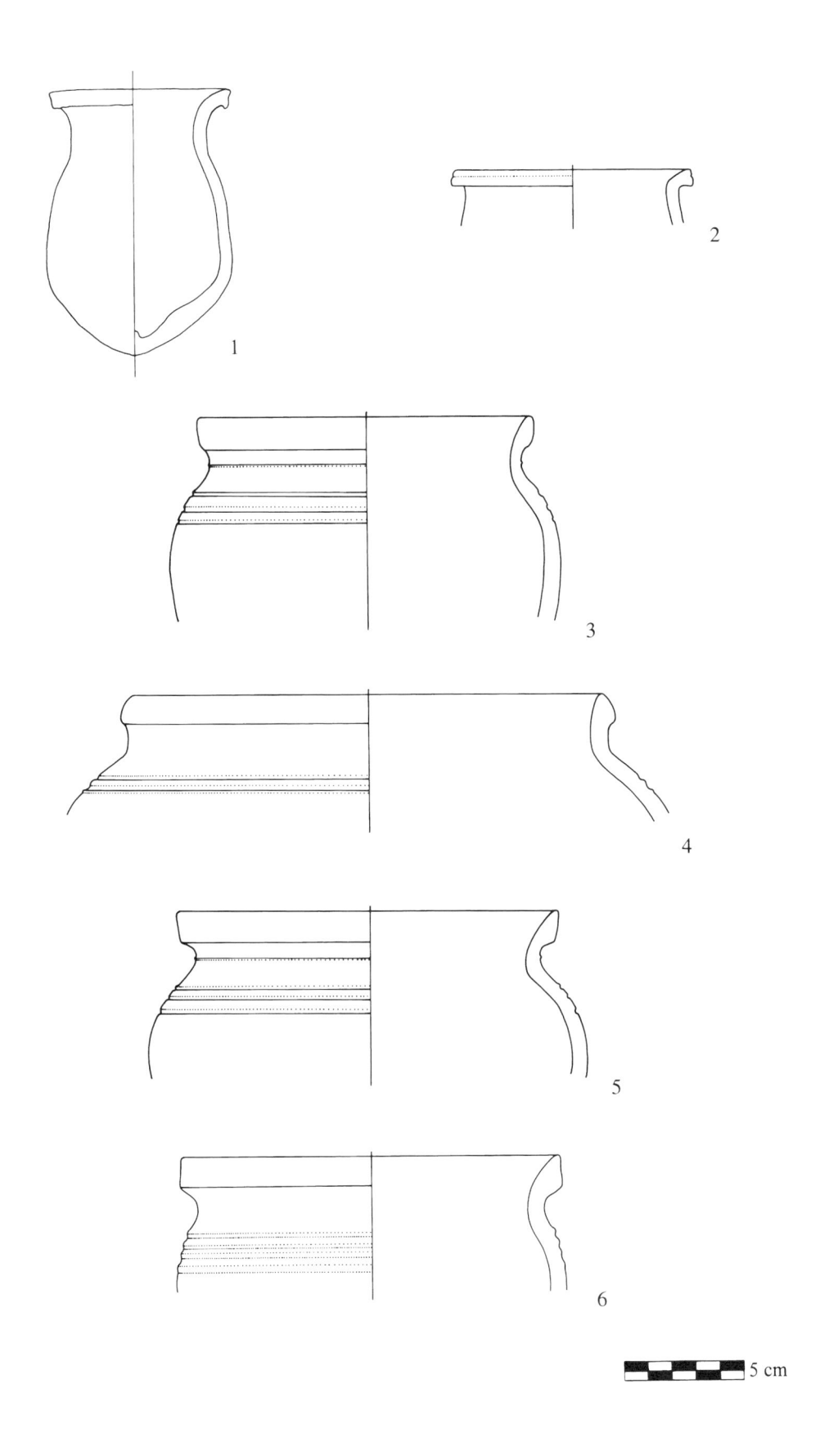

Type C-26: Grooved Rim, Bag-shaped Jar and Type C-27: Oval Rim, Grooved-shoulder Jar. Scale 2:5

Plate 122. Type C-29: Everted Rim with Droop below, Large Jar

|   | Lot Number | Level | Dimension | Description |
|---|---|---|---|---|
| 1 | H797:4 | X | Rim diam. 17.0 cm | Buff, sand and light organic temper |
| 2 | H754:5 | VIII | Rim diam. 19.0 cm | Dark buff, sand temper |
| 3 | H754:4 | VIII | Rim diam. 14.0 cm | Pale buff, sand temper |
| 4 | H754:15 | VIII | Rim diam. 12.0 cm | Pale buff, sand temper |
| 5 | H763:14 | VIII | Rim diam. 15.0 cm | Pale buff, sand temper, comb-incised decoration |
| 6 | H763:13 | VIII | Rim diam. 19.0 cm | Buff, sand and light organic temper, bitumen on rim |
| 7 | H757:5 | VII | Rim diam. 15.0 cm | Red, buff surface, sand temper |
| 8 | H679:4 | VI | Rim diam. 14.0 cm | Red, sand temper |

COMPARANDA FOR TYPE C-29

Fara: Martin 1988: fig. 42:11, 13 (Akk.–Ur III); Martin 1983: fig. 2:5; Abu Salabikh: Postgate and Moon 1984: nos. 15, 20, 35, 38, 51 (post-ED); Uruk: van Ess 1988: form 32 and no. 127 (Ur III–Isin-Larsa); van Ess 1993: fig. 10:146, 148 et passim; Susa: Steve and Gasche 1971: pl. 3:4, 6 (Ur III); unpublished examples from Nippur WC-3 (Ur III) and Umm al-Hafriyat (Ur III)

Plate 122

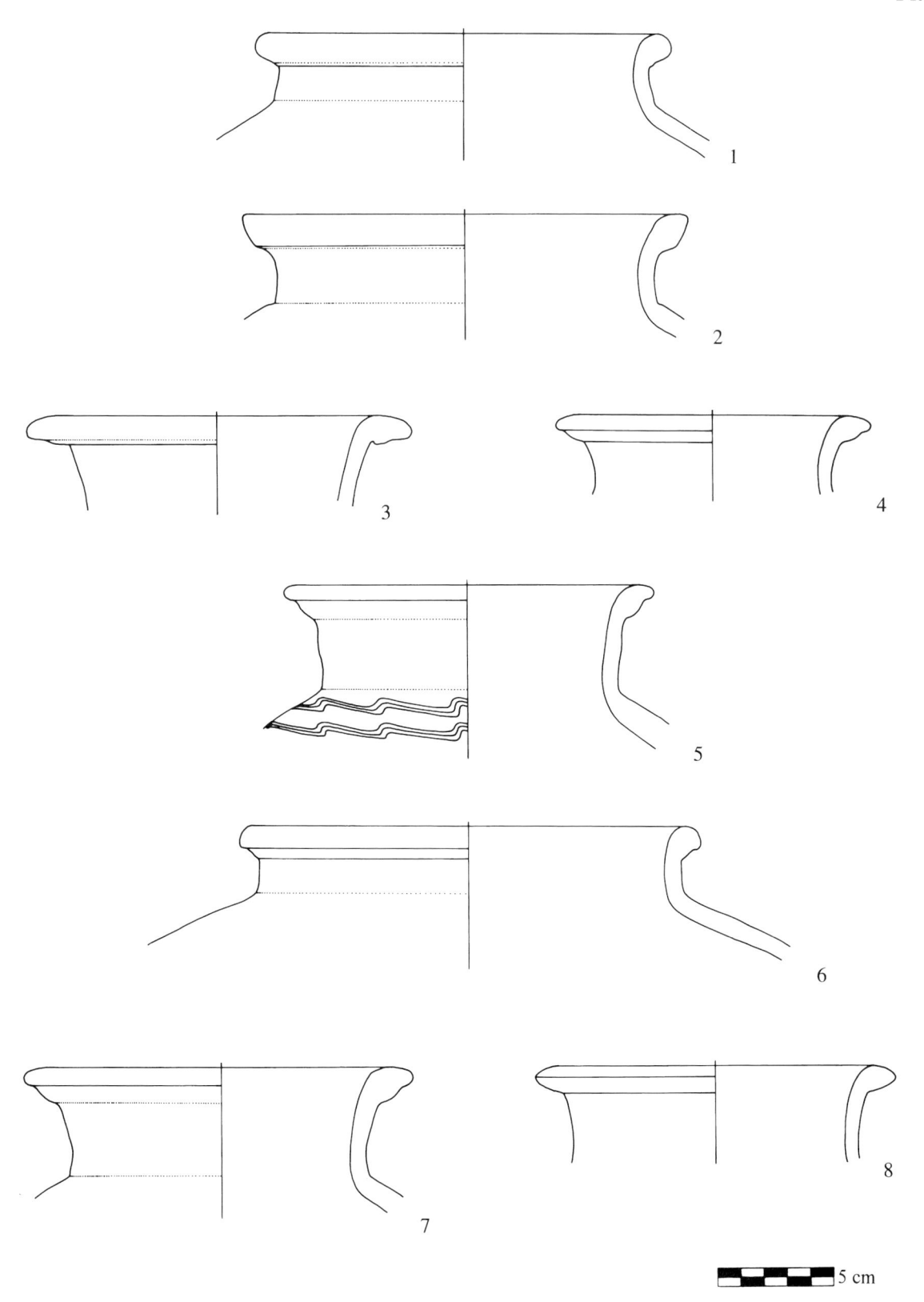

Type C-29: Everted Rim with Droop below, Large Jar. Scale 2:5

Plate 123. Bases and Foundation Deposit Bowls

|    | Lot Number | Level | Form | Location | Dimension | Description |
|----|------------|-------|------|----------|-----------|-------------|
| 1  | I486:4     | XVIII | B-7  | —        | —         | Buff pink, sand temper |
| 2  | I656:7     | XVIII | B-7  | —        | —         | Dark buff, sand temper |
| 3  | I470:10    | XVIIC | B-7  | —        | —         | Buff, sand temper |
| 4  | H1092:1    | XIIIC | B-7  | —        | —         | Buff, sand temper |
| 5  | I759:2     | XIXB  | B-2  | —        | Base diam. 2.6 cm | Buff, sand temper |
| 6  | I669:6     | XIXB  | B-2  | —        | Base diam. 2.6 cm | Pink, cream surface, sand temper |
| 7  | I657:3     | XVIII | B-2  | —        | Base diam. 2.2 cm | Buff, pink surface, sand temper |
| 8  | I774       | XIXB  | O-1  | Locus 68, on Floor 3, near Burial 21 | Rim diam. 16.0 cm, base diam. 5.6 cm, ht. 8.3 cm | Red pink surface, sand temper |
| 9  | I689       | XIXB  | O-1  | Locus 68, on Floor 2, east face of Wall BP | Rim diam. 15.6 cm, base diam. 4.0 cm, ht. 10.0 cm | Red, pink surface, sand temper |
| 10 | I675       | XIXB  | O-1  | Locus 68, above Floor 1, east face of Wall BP | Rim diam. 13.8 cm, base diam. 5.1 cm, ht. 9.1 cm | Pink, sand temper, pronounced interior wheel marks |
| 11 | I385       | XVB   | O-1  | Locus 60, on Floor 1, inside *tannur* | Rim diam. 15.0 cm, base diam. 4.3 cm, ht. 6.0 cm | Buff, sand and light organic temper |
| 12 | I425       | XVI   | O-1  | Locus 59, on Floor 4 | Rim diam. 15.0 cm, base diam. 5.0 cm, ht. 7.5 cm | Buff, cream surface, sand temper |
| 13 | I419:1     | XVI   | O-1  | Locus 59, on Floor 3 | Rim diam. 15.3 cm, base diam. 4.3 cm, ht. 6.8 cm. Paired with I419:2 | Pale red, sand temper |
| 14 | I419:2     | XVI   | O-1  | Locus 59, on Floor 3 | Rim diam. 15.0 cm, base diam. 4.9 cm, ht. 7.3 cm. Paired with I419:1 | Pale red, sand temper |

Plate 123

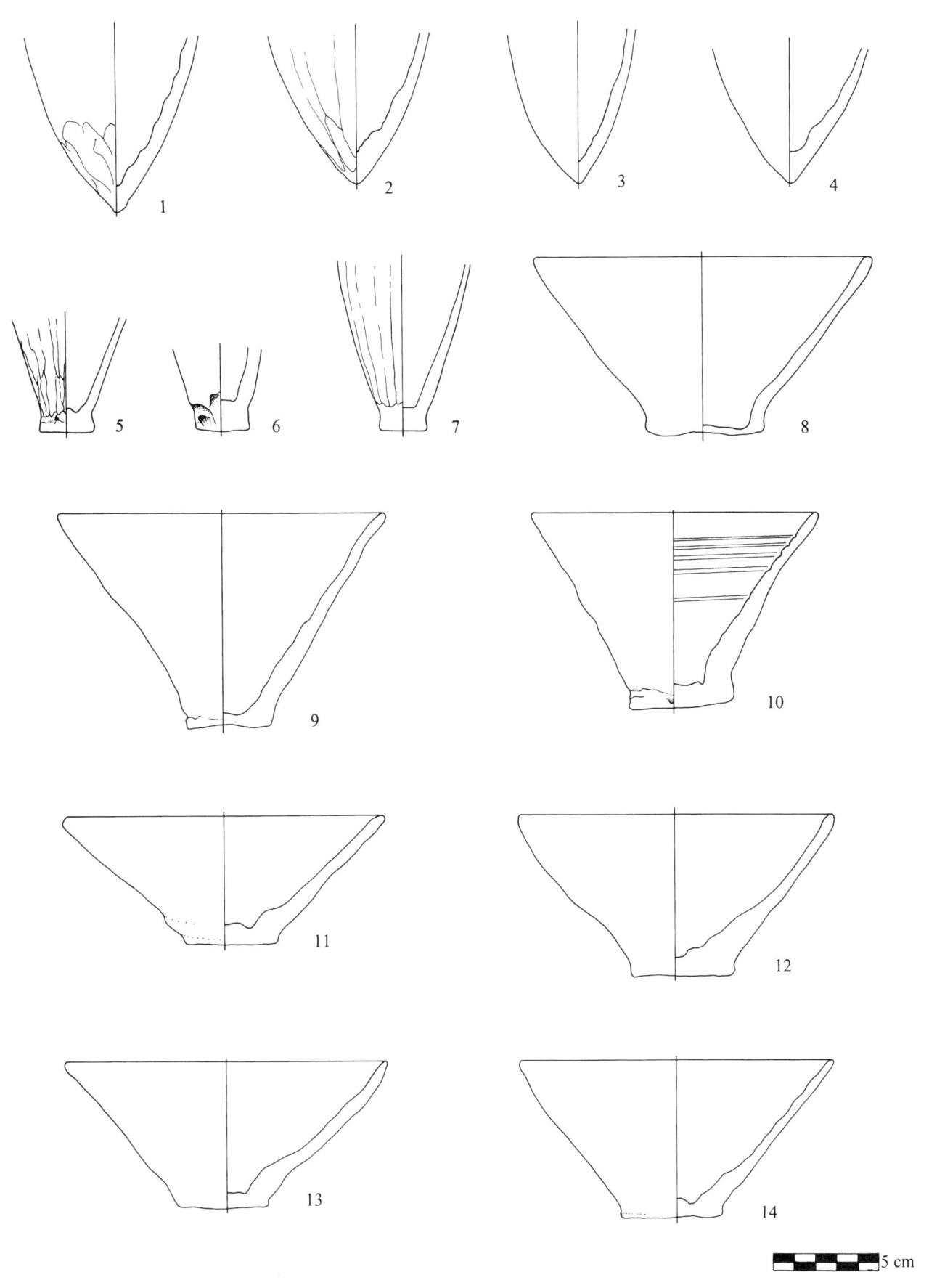

Bases and Foundation Deposit Bowls. Scale 2:5

Plate 124. Foundation Deposit Bowls

| | Lot Number | Level | Form | Location | Dimension | Description |
|---|---|---|---|---|---|---|
| 1 | I410 | XVI | O-1 | Locus 59, on Floor 2 | Rim diam. 15.0 cm, base diam. 4.7 cm, ht. 7.2 cm | Buff, cream surface, sand temper |
| 2 | H1101:1 | XIVB | O-1 | Locus 47, on Floor 2 | Rim diam. 15.5 cm, base diam. 4.2 cm, ht. 6.4 cm. Paired with H1101:2 | Red, light buff surface, sand and light organic temper |
| 3 | H1101:2 | XIVB | O-1 | Locus 47, on Floor 2 | Rim diam. 15.0 cm, base diam. 4.4 cm, ht. 6.7 cm. Paired with H1101:1 | Pale red, cream surface, sand and light organic temper |
| 4 | H536 | XIVA | O-1 | Locus 40, on Floor 1 | Rim diam. 12.0 cm, base diam. 3.7 cm, ht. 4.4 cm | Buff, cream surface, sand and light organic temper |
| 5 | I1:1 | XIVA | O-1 | Locus 44, on Floor 1 east face of Wall AR | Rim diam. 12.0 cm, base diam. 4.2 cm, ht. 4.3 cm | Red, sand temper |
| 6 | I1:2 | XIVA | O-1 | Locus 44, on Floor 1 east face of Wall AR | Rim diam. 13.0 cm, base diam. 4.5 cm, ht. 4.2 cm | Pink, cream surface, sand temper |
| 7 | I1:3 | XIVA | O-1 | Locus 44, on Floor 1 east face of Wall AR | Rim diam. 13.0 cm, base diam. 5.5 cm, ht. 4.3 cm | Pink, sand temper |
| 8 | I1:4 | XIVA | O-1 | Locus 44, on Floor 1 east face of Wall AR | Rim diam. 13.0 cm, base diam. 4.2 cm, ht. 4.3 cm | Pink, sand temper |
| 9 | H138:1 | XIB | O-1 | Locus 36, above Floor 3, in AB doorway | Rim diam. 16.0 cm, base diam. 5.3 cm, ht. 5.2 cm | Pink, sand and light organic temper |
| 10 | I3:1 | XIIA | O-1 | Locus 34, above Floor 3 | Rim diam. 14.0 cm, base diam. 4.3 cm, ht. 5.0 cm. Paired with I3:2 | Pink, sand temper |
| 11 | I3:2 | XIIA | O-1 | Locus 34, above Floor 3 | Rim diam. 16.0 cm, base diam. 4.8 cm, ht. 4.4 cm. Paired with I3:1 | Red, buff surface, sand temper |

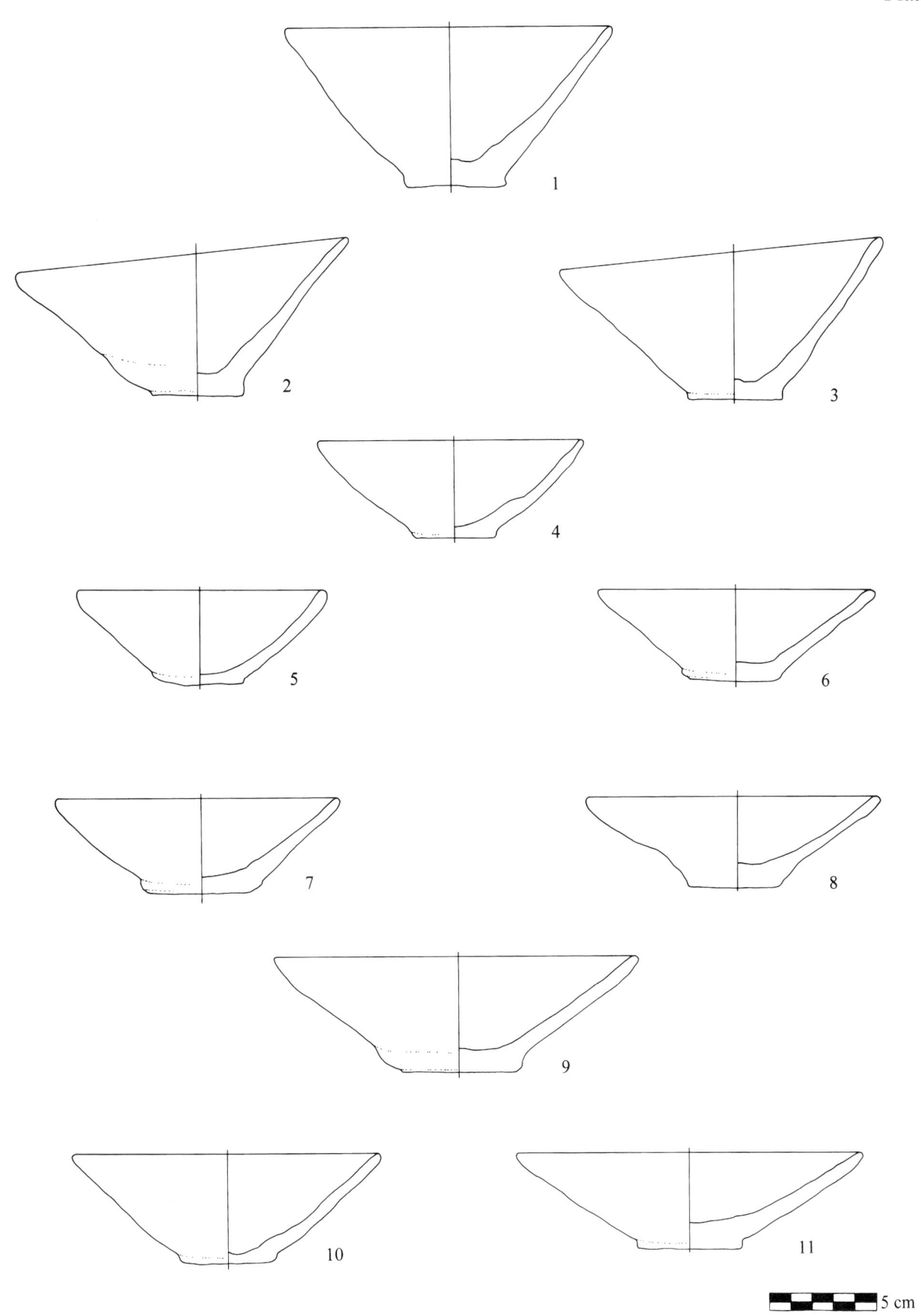

Plate 124

Foundation Deposit Bowls. Scale 2:5

Plate 125. Foundation Deposit Bowls

|   | Lot Number | Level | Form | Location | Dimension | Description |
|---|---|---|---|---|---|---|
| 1 | 19 N 59 | XVI | O-1 | Locus 59, on Floor 3 | Rim diam. 15.8 cm, base diam. 5.0 cm, ht. 6.3 cm. Paired with 19 N 58 | Overfired greenish, sand temper |
| 2 | 19 N 58 | XVI | O-1 | Locus 59, on Floor 3 | Rim diam. 15.3 cm, base diam. 5.0 cm, ht. 5.8 cm. Paired with 19 N 59 | Red, sand temper. String-cut base |
| 3 | 19 N 56 | XVI | O-1 | Locus 59, on Floor 2 | Rim diam. 14.5 cm, base diam. 4.3 cm, ht. 7.9 cm. Paired with I408:1 | Pale red, sand temper. String-cut base |
| 4 | I408:1 | XVI | O-1 | Locus 59, on Floor 2 | Rim diam. 15.0 cm, base diam. 4.6 cm, ht. 7.3 cm. Paired with 19 N 56 | Pale red, pink surface, sand temper |
| 5 | 19 N 57 | XVI | O-1 | Locus 59, on Floor 2 | Rim diam. 10.7 cm, base diam. 4.3 cm, ht. 7.5 cm | Pink, sand temper. String-cut base |
| 6 | 19 N 55 | XIVB | O-1 | In repair on Wall BD | Rim diam. 13.5 cm, base diam. 4.7 cm, ht. 6.3 cm | Pale pink, sand temper. String-cut base |
| 7 | 18 N 123 | XIVA | O-1 | Locus 40, on Floor 1 | Rim diam. 13.5 cm, base diam. 3.8 cm, ht. 5.8 cm. Paired with 18 N 124 | Pink, sand temper. String-cut base |
| 8 | 18 N 124 | XIVA | O-1 | Locus 40, on Floor 1 | Rim diam. 13.0 cm, base diam. 4.4 cm, ht. 5.2 cm. Paired with 18 N 123 | Pink, sand temper. String-cut base |
| 9 | 18 N 190 | XIVA | O-10 | — | Rim diam. 16.0 cm, base diam. 5.5 cm, ht. 6.0 cm. Paired with 18 N 189 | Buff, sand temper. String-cut base |
| 10 | 18 N 189 | XIVA | O-10 | — | Rim diam. 16.0 cm, base diam. 4.0 cm, ht. 6.0 cm. Paired with 18 N 190 | Buff, sand temper. String-cut base |
| 11 | 19 N 12 | XIIB | O-10 | In box above Burial 14 | Rim diam. 15.3 cm, base diam. 5.2 cm, ht. 4.5 cm | Pink, cream surface, sand temper. String-cut base |
| 12 | 18 N 138 | XIVA | O-1 | Locus 40, on Floor 1 | Rim diam. 8.7 cm, base diam. 3.9 cm, ht. 7.5 cm. Paired with H1009:1 | Pink buff, sand temper |
| 13 | H1009:1 | XIVA | O-1 | Locus 40, on Floor 1 | Rim diam. 8.0 cm, base diam. 3.7 cm, ht. 5.6 cm. Paired with 18 N 138 | Pink, sand and light organic temper |

Plate 125

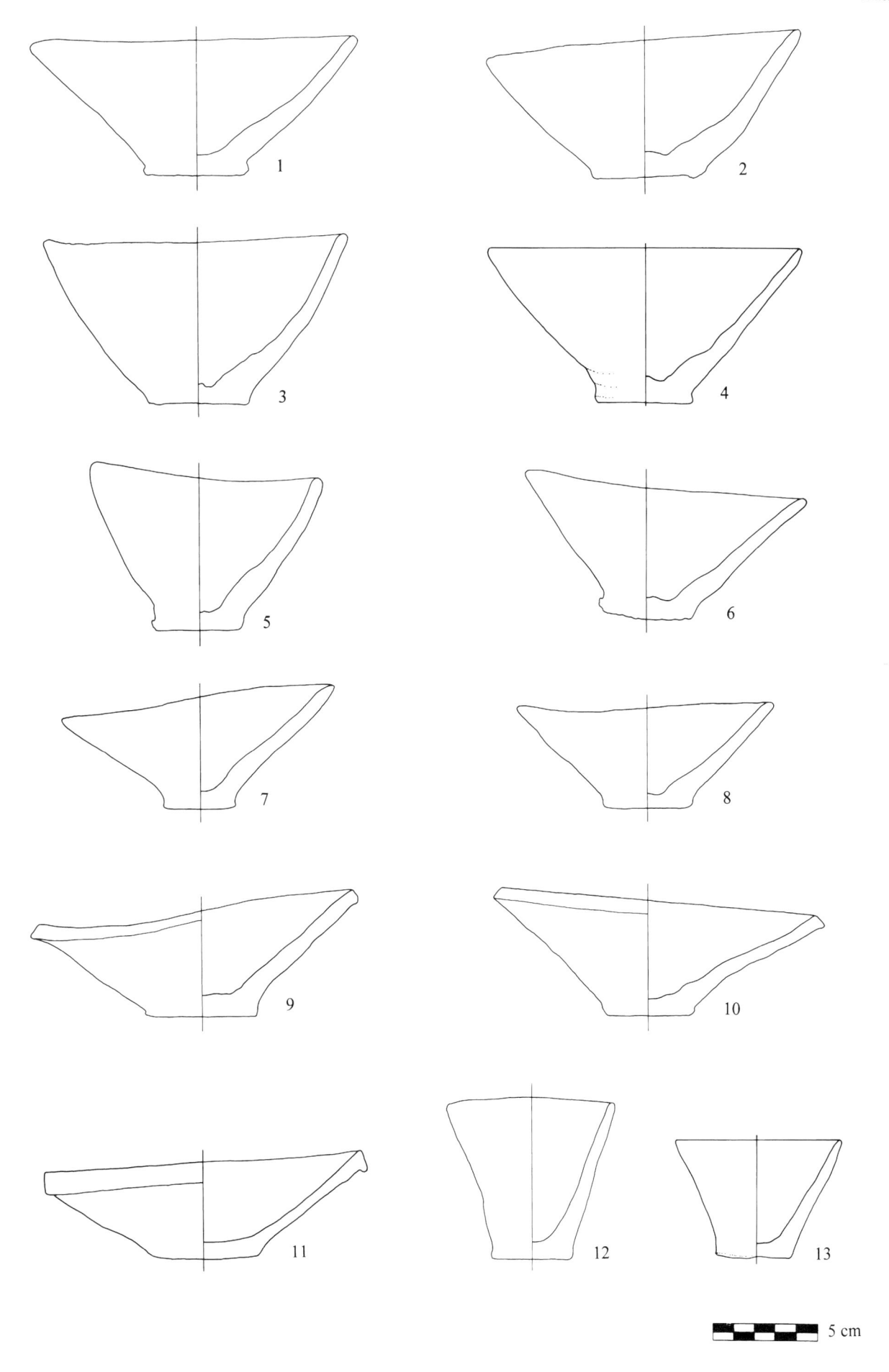

Foundation Deposit Bowls. Scale 2:5

Plate 126. Miscellaneous Third-millennium B.C. Pottery

|   | Lot Number | Level | Form | Dimension | Description |
|---|---|---|---|---|---|
| 1 | I327 | XIVB | C-1 | Rim diam. 8.7 cm, max. diam. 11.4 cm, base diam. 4.9 cm, ht. 20.6 cm | Pale red, pink surface, sand temper. Bismaya: Banks 1912: 175, three examples |
| 2 | I325 | XIVB | C-1 | Rim diam. 6.9 cm, max. diam. 9.8 cm, base diam. 4.8 cm, ht. 17.3 cm | Pale red, pink surface, sand and light organic temper. For comparisons, see I327 |
| 3 | 18 N 134 | XIVA | C-24 | Rim diam. 6.1 cm, max. diam. 14.0 cm, base diam. 9.1 cm, ht. 17.4 cm | Greenish, sand temper. Nippur: McCown and Haines 1967: pl. 81:2 (Akk.) |
| 4 | H537 | XIVA | C-20 early version | Rim diam. 11.5 cm, max. diam. 18.2 cm, base diam. 7.1 cm, ht. 22.5 cm | Greenish buff, sand temper |
| 5 | H515:1 | XIIIC | C-UT | Rim diam. 16.4 cm, max. diam. 19.3 cm, base diam. 10.0 cm, ht. 26.8 cm | Buff green, sand and light organic temper |

Plate 126

Miscellaneous Third-millennium B.C. Pottery. Scale 2:5

Plate 127. Miscellaneous Third-millennium B.C. Pottery

|    | Lot Number | Level | Form | Dimension | Description |
|----|-----------|-------|------|-----------|-------------|
| 1  | 18 N 135 | IX | C-13 | Rim diam. 10.5 cm, max. body diam. 9.8 cm, ht. 11.1 cm | Red, sand temper |
| 2  | 18 N 137 | XIVA | — | Rim diam. 5.4 cm, base w. 5.8 cm, ht. 5.6 cm. Covered with 18 N 136 | Pink, sand temper, handmade. Vertical incised lines on sides, flat base with four pinched feet. Diyala: Delougaz 1952: pl. 141, A.243.900a–b (early Akk.); Nippur: Gibson 1975: fig. 67:3, 7 (Akk.); McCown and Haines 1967: pl. 80:3–4 (Akk.–OB) |
| 3  | 18 N 136 | XIVA | O-1 | Rim diam. 12.7 cm, base diam. 3.6 cm, ht. 5.0 cm. Inverted over 18 N 137 | Red, sand temper. String-cut base |
| 4  | I113 | XIVB | C-4 | Rim diam. 5.0 cm, base diam. 3.5 cm, ht. 6.3 cm. Paired with I115 | Red, pink cream surface, sand temper |
| 5  | I115 | XIVB | O-1 | Rim diam. 13.0 cm, base diam. 4.6 cm, ht. 6.0 cm. Paired with I113 | Pink, sand temper |
| 6  | H1079:6 | XIIIB | O-UT | Rim diam. 14.0 cm | Red, organic temper. See 19 N 52 (Burial 14, southwest shaft) for comparanda |
| 7  | H540:3 | XIVA | — | Rim diam. 10.0 cm | Dark buff, sand temper, burnished exterior, hole below rim. Uch Tepe: Gibson 1981: pl. 72:21 (ED) |
| 8  | I319:3 | XIVA | — | Rim diam. 10.0 cm | Buff, cream surface, sand temper. Double-pierced tab handle |
| 9  | I122:5 | XIIIB | — | Rim diam. 8.0 cm | Dark buff, sand temper, vertical hole through rim. Copy of metal vessel? |
| 10 | H841:5 | XIA | — | — | Gray, very fine, no visible temper. Incised and notched decoration, double-pierced lug handle. Northern Akkadian. Taya: Reade 1968: pl. 84:9, 12 (Akk.); Brak: Oates, Oates, and McDonald 2001: no. 293 (post-Akk.) |
| 11 | H121:3 | XIIA | — | — | Buff, very fine sand temper. Incised lines on shoulder and double-pierced lug handle. Northern Akkadian |
| 12 | H119:4 | XIIB | — | Rim diam. 16.0 cm | Gray, fine sand temper, burnished interior and exterior. Northern Akkadian–post-Akkadian |
| 13 | H1057:4 | XIIIB | — | Rim diam. 22.0 cm. See H119:4 | Gray, burnished interior and exterior |
| 14 | I677:4 | XIXB | D-2 | Max. diam. ca. 10 cm | Red, sand temper. Single-point incision |
| 15 | I486:5 | XVIII | D-5 | — | Pink, cream surface, sand temper. Applied and punctate decoration, possible snake |
| 16 | I31 | XIIIB | D-8 | — | Pale red, buff surface, sand temper. Goddess handle |

Plate 127

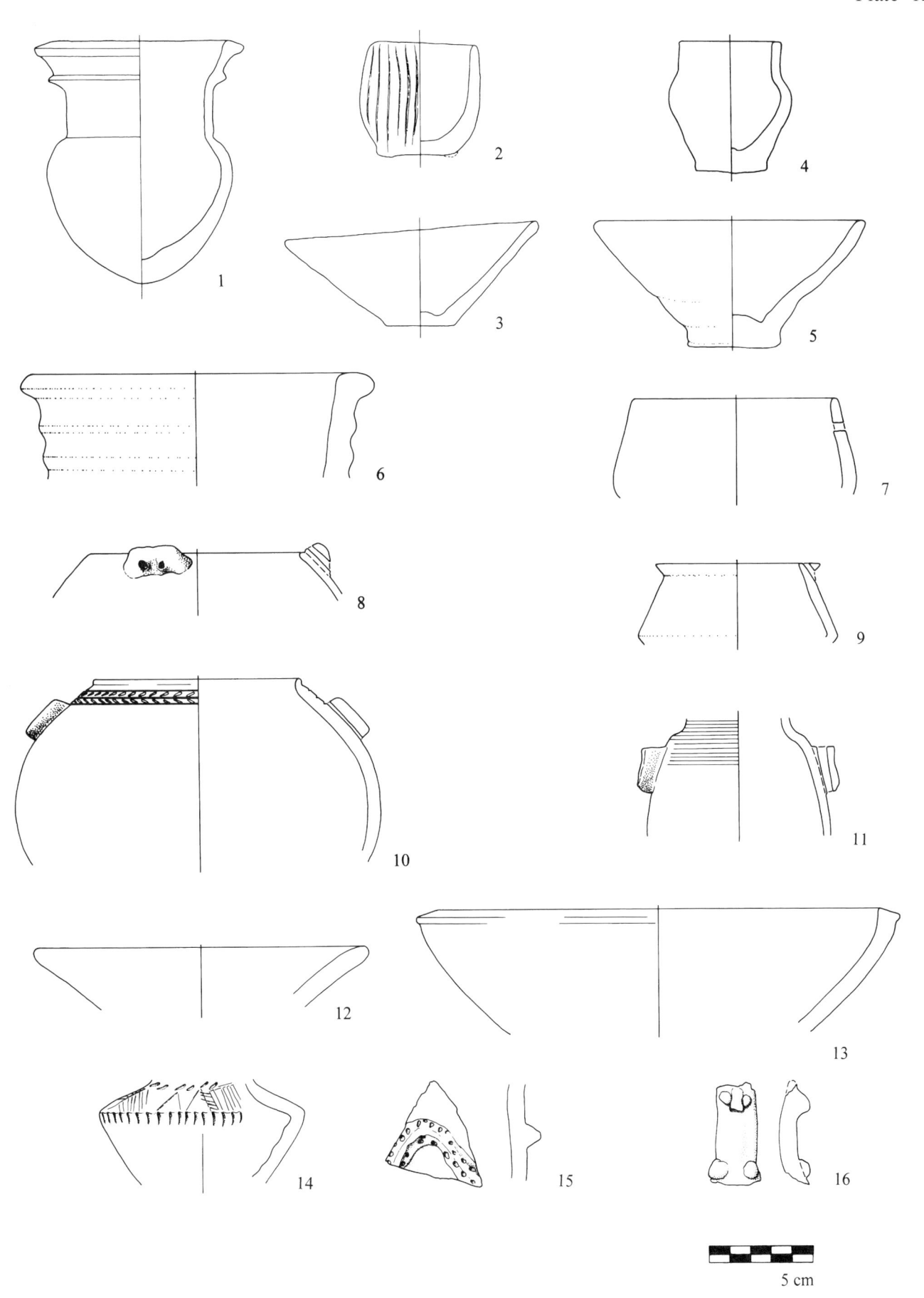

Miscellaneous Third-millennium B.C. Pottery. Scale 2:5

Plate 128. Third-millennium B.C. Grave Groups, Burials 20 and 19

|   | Lot Number | Form | Dimension | Description |
|---|---|---|---|---|
| | BURIAL 20, LEVEL XVIII | | | |
| 1 | I684 | C-1 | Rim diam. 11.0 cm, max. diam. 13.6 cm, base diam. 5.5 cm, ht. 16.3 cm | Pink, buff surface, sand temper |
| 2 | 19 N 106 | O-1 | Rim diam. 13.3 cm, base diam. 4.2 cm, ht. 6.5 cm | Red, red cream surface, sand temper. String-cut base. This bowl has unusual wavy sides; a few examples are known from other sites, so it may be a subtype, rather than a kiln misfire. Abu Salabikh: Martin, Moon, and Postgate 1985: grave 49:7–8 (ED IIIB); Ur: Woolley 1934: pl. 251:8 (Akk.) |
| 3 | I685 | O-1 | Rim diam. 13.6 cm, base diam. 4.0 cm, ht. 6.6 cm | Pink, buff surface, sand temper |
| | BURIAL 19, LEVEL XVIIC | | | |
| 4 | I666 | C-1 | Rim diam. 12.0 cm, max. diam. 15.4 cm, base diam. 6.5 cm, ht. 25.8 cm | Red, sand temper, separately applied ring base with heavy organic temper |
| 5 | 19 N 83 | — | Rim diam. 13.0 cm, base diam. 7.2 cm, ht. 9.6 cm | Banded alabaster bowl. Concave sides, ancient break in rim. Ur: Woolley 1934: pl. 241: type 13 (ED–Akk.) |

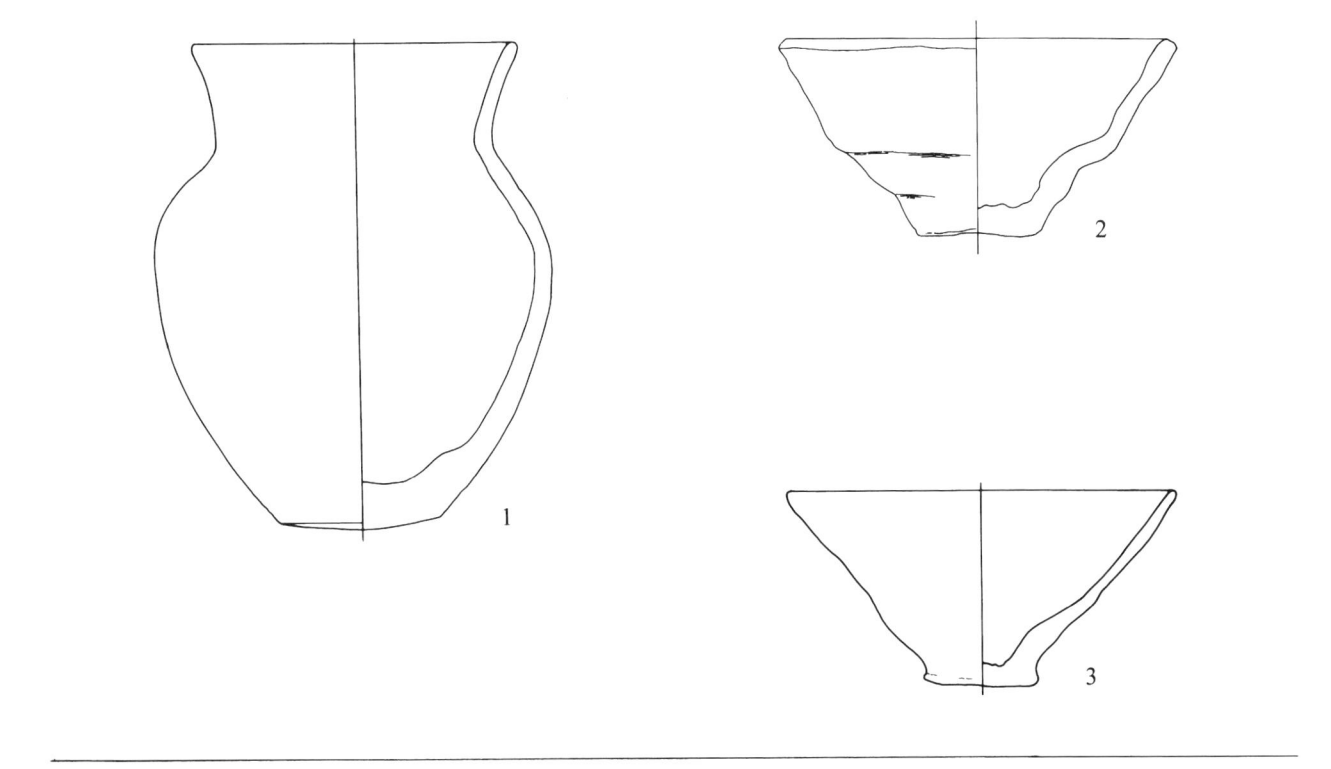

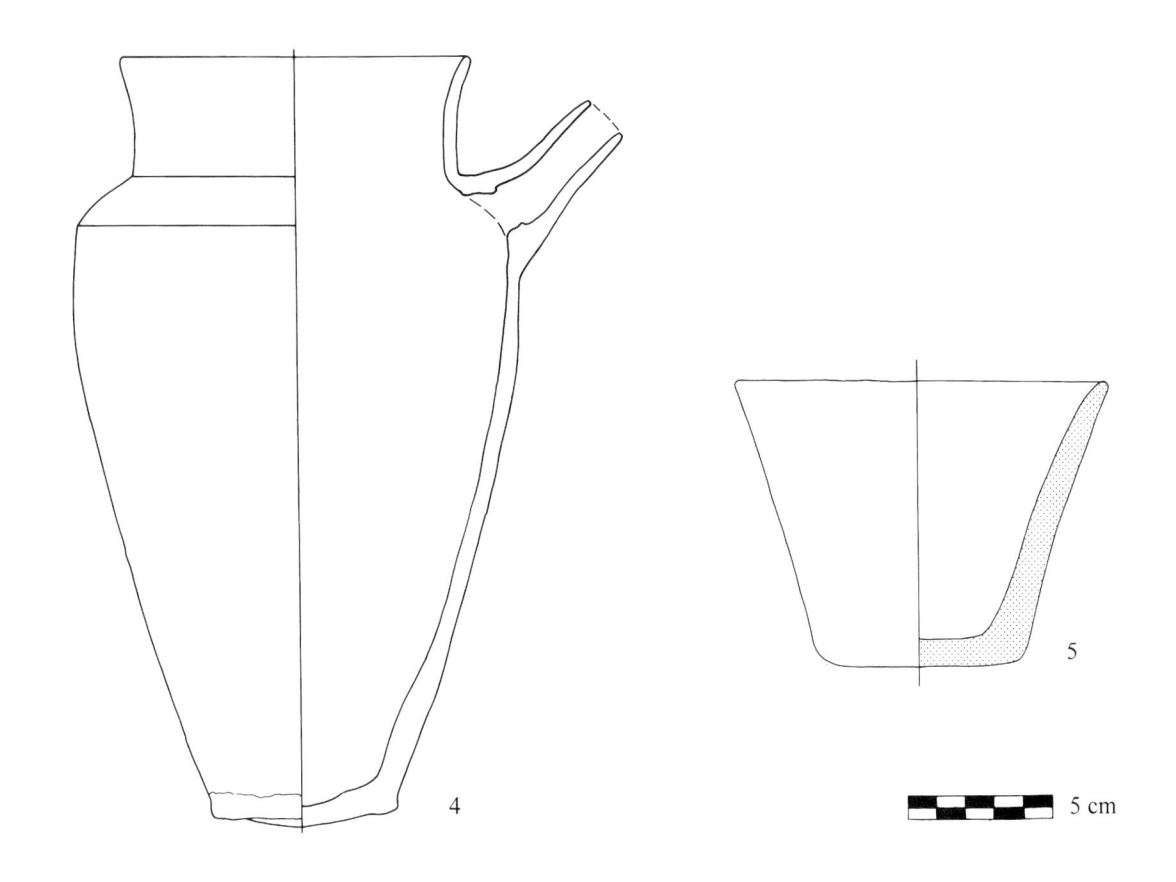

Plate 128

Third-millennium B.C. Grave Groups, Burials 20 and 19. Scale 2:5

Plate 129. Third-millennium B.C. Grave Group, Burial 19 (*cont.*)

|   | Lot Number | Form | Dimension | Description |
|---|---|---|---|---|
| **BURIAL 19, LEVEL XVIIC** | | | | |
| 1 | I664:24 | O-1 | Rim diam. 17.8 cm, base diam. 5.7 cm, ht. 11.9 cm | Buff, cream surface, sand temper |
| 2 | 19 N 128 | O-1 | Rim diam. 16.8 cm, base diam. 5.2 cm, ht. 10.0 cm | Red, pink surface, sand temper. String-cut base |
| 3 | I664:23 | O-1 | Rim diam. 16.3 cm, base diam. 4.7 cm, ht. 10.6 cm | Buff, cream green surface, sand temper |
| 4 | 19 N 127 | O-1 | Rim diam. 15.8 cm, base diam. 5.3 cm, ht. 6.5 cm | Red, sand temper. String-cut base |
| 5 | I664:2 | O-1 | Rim diam. 16.2 cm, base diam. 4.5 cm, ht. 6.8 cm | Pink, sand temper |
| 6 | I664:25 | O-1 | Rim diam. 16.1 cm, base diam. 5.6 cm, ht. 5.3 cm | Buff, pink cream surface, sand temper |
| 7 | 19 N 126 | O-1 | Rim diam. 15.5 cm, base diam. 5.0 cm, ht. 6.2 cm | Red, red cream surface, sand temper. String-cut base |
| 8 | I664:8 | O-1 | Rim diam. 15.4 cm, base diam. 4.0 cm, ht. 7.4 cm | Pink, sand temper |
| 9 | I664:7 | O-1 | Rim diam. 14.5 cm, base diam. 4.5 cm, ht. 8.2 cm | Overfired green ware, sand temper |

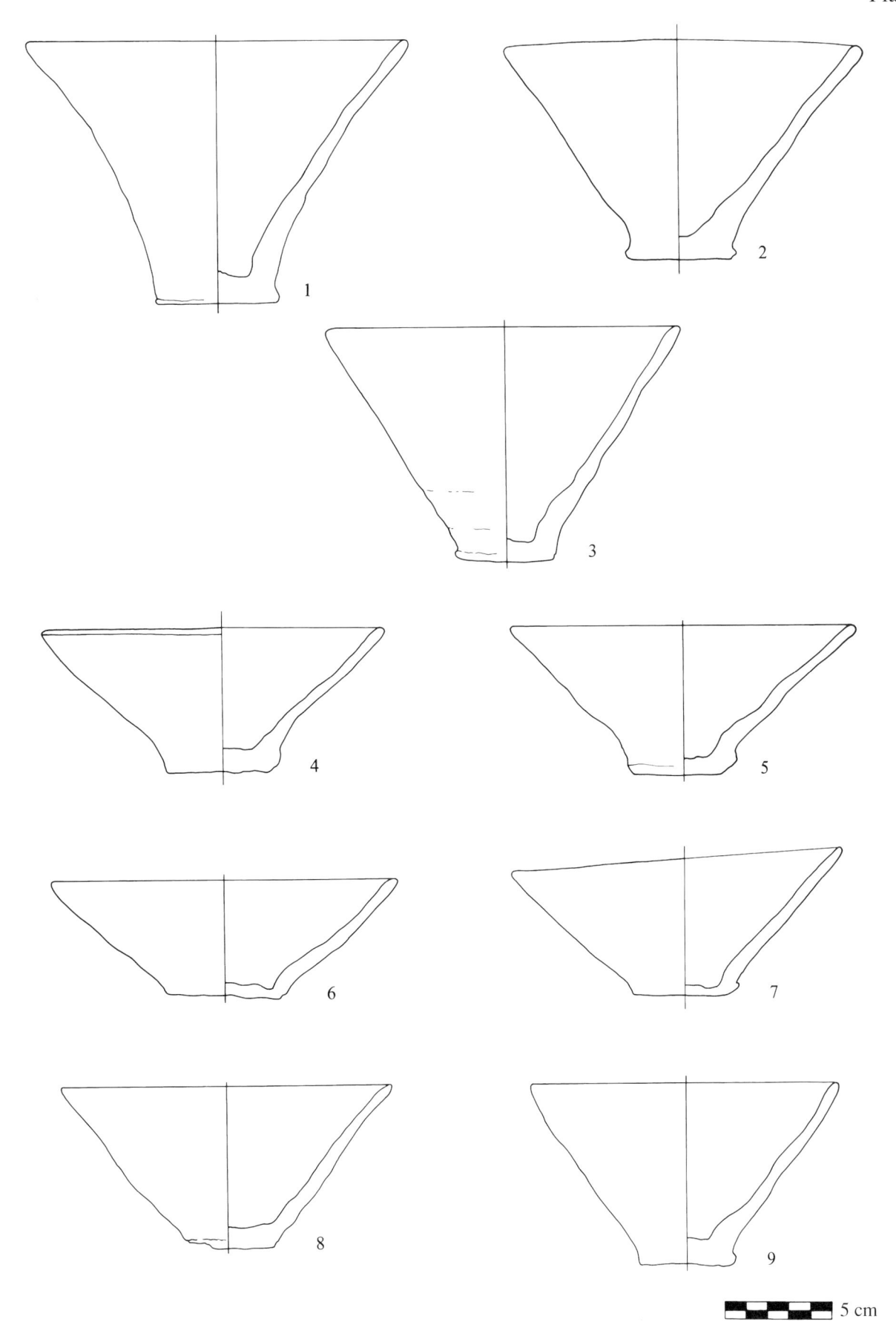

Plate 129

Third-millennium B.C. Grave Group, Burial 19 (*cont.*). Scale 2:5

Plate 130. Third-millennium B.C. Grave Group, Burial 19 (*cont.*)

|    | Lot Number | Form | Dimension | Description |
|----|------------|------|-----------|-------------|
| BURIAL 19, LEVEL XVIIC |||||
| 1  | I664:1  | O-1 | Rim diam. 15.3 cm, base diam. 4.5 cm, ht. 7.0 cm | Pink, sand temper |
| 2  | I664:3  | O-1 | Rim diam. 15.2 cm, base diam. 5.7 cm, ht. 7.4 cm | Pink, sand temper |
| 3  | I664:4  | O-1 | Rim diam. 13.4 cm, base diam. 4.0 cm, ht. 7.9 cm | Pink, sand temper |
| 4  | I664:5  | O-1 | Rim diam. 14.9 cm, base diam. 5.0 cm, ht. 6.4 cm | Pink, sand temper |
| 5  | I664:6  | O-1 | Rim diam. 15.7 cm, base diam. 4.7 cm, ht. 7.2 cm | Pink, sand temper |
| 6  | I664:10 | O-1 | Rim diam. 14.8 cm, base diam. 4.5 cm, ht. 7.0 cm | Pink, cream surface, sand temper |
| 7  | I664:9  | O-1 | Rim diam. 15.0 cm, base diam. 4.5 cm, ht. 7.1 cm | Pink, sand temper |
| 8  | I664:11 | O-1 | Rim diam. 15.0 cm, base diam. 4.7 cm, ht. 7.1 cm | Pink, sand temper |
| 9  | I664:12 | O-1 | Rim diam. 14.8 cm, base diam. 5.0 cm, ht. 6.8 cm | Pink, sand temper |
| 10 | I664:13 | O-1 | Rim diam. 14.6 cm, base diam. 5.0 cm, ht. 7.1 cm | Pink, sand temper |

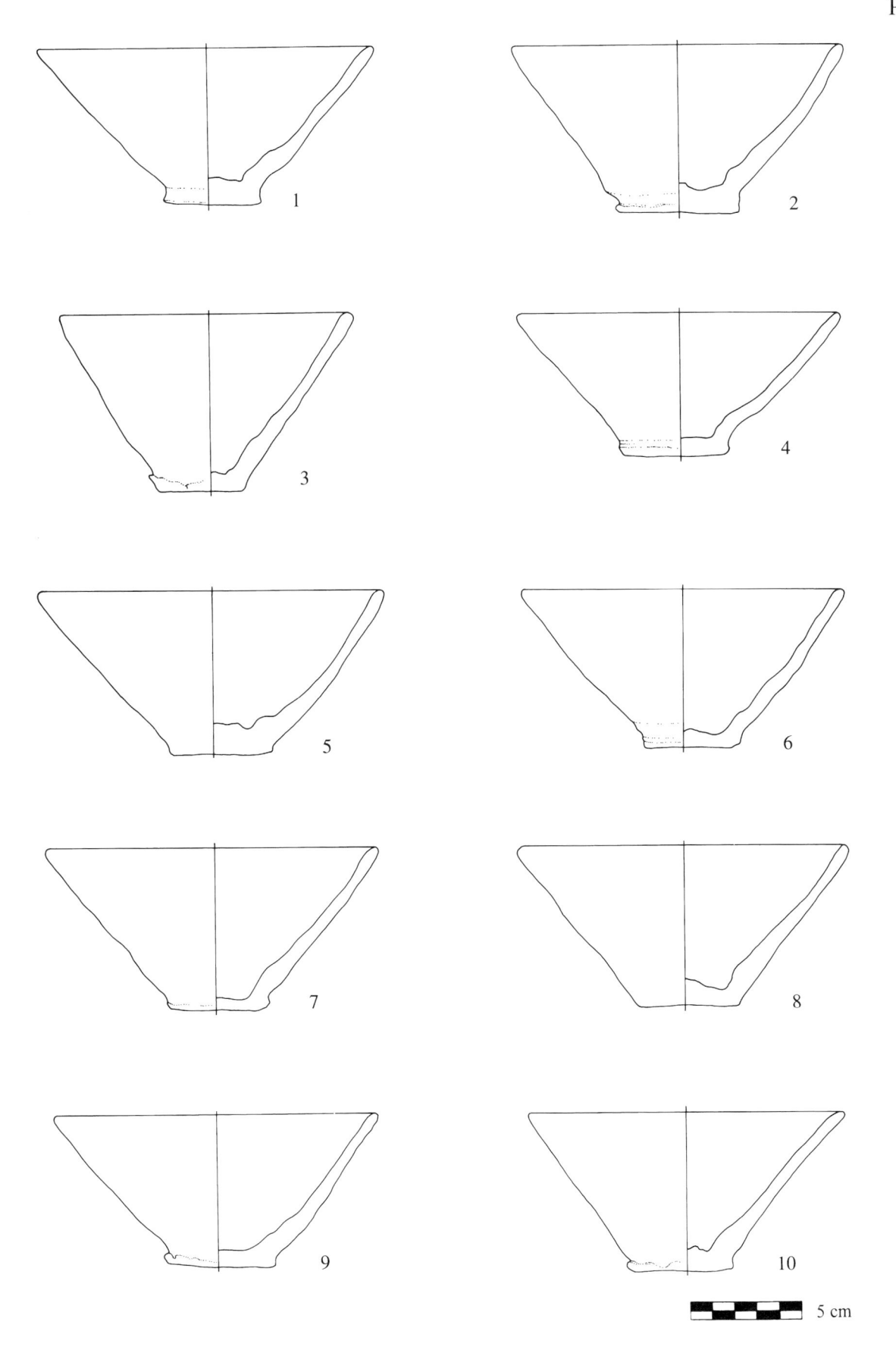

Plate 130

Third-millennium B.C. Grave Group, Burial 19 (*cont.*). Scale 2:5

Plate 131. Third-millennium B.C. Grave Group, Burial 19 (*cont.*)

|   | Lot Number | Form | Dimension | Description |
|---|---|---|---|---|
| | BURIAL 19, LEVEL XVIIC | | | |
| 1 | I664:14 | O-1 | Rim diam. 15.3 cm, base diam. 4.4 cm, ht. 7.0 cm | Pink, cream green surface, sand temper |
| 2 | I664:15 | O-1 | Rim diam. 15.5 cm, base diam. 5.0 cm, ht. 6.9 cm | Pink, sand temper |
| 3 | I664:16 | O-1 | Rim diam. 15.0 cm, base diam. 4.5 cm, ht. 7.1 cm | Pink, sand temper |
| 4 | I664:17 | O-1 | Rim diam. 14.6 cm, base diam. 4.0 cm, ht. 7.2 cm | Pink, buff surface |
| 5 | I664:18 | O-1 | Rim diam. 15.2 cm, base diam. 4.3 cm, ht. 6.5 cm | Buff, sand temper |
| 6 | I664:19 | O-1 | Rim diam. 14.8 cm, base diam. 5.3 cm, ht. 7.9 cm | Pink, buff surface, sand temper |
| 7 | I664:20 | O-1 | Rim diam. 15.4 cm, base diam. 4.3 cm, ht. 6.8 cm | Pink, cream buff surface, sand temper |
| 8 | I664:22 | O-1 | Rim diam. 15.5 cm, base diam. 5.3 cm, ht. 11.2 cm | Buff, cream surface, sand temper |
| 9 | I664:21 | O-1 | Rim diam. 14.9 cm, base diam. 4.9 cm, ht. 7.0 cm | Overfired green, sand temper |

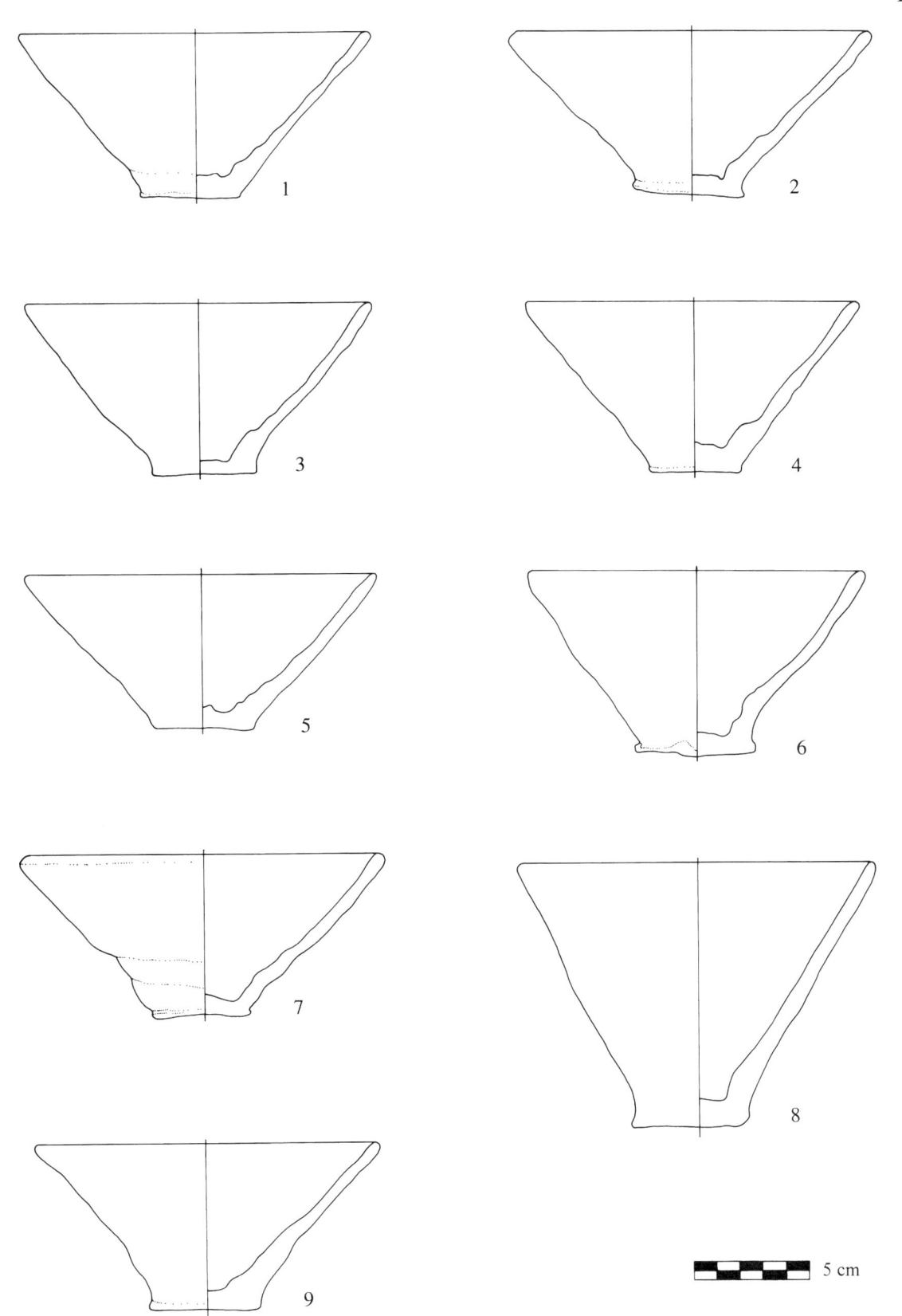

Plate 131

Third-millennium B.C. Grave Group, Burial 19 (*cont.*). Scale 2:5

Plate 132. Third-millennium B.C. Grave Groups, Burial 21, Skeletons 1 and 2, and Burial 18

|   | Lot Number | Form | Dimension | Description |
|---|---|---|---|---|
| **BURIAL 21, SKELETON 1, LEVEL XVIIB** ||||| 
| 1 | I686 | O-1 | Rim diam. 10.6 cm, base diam. 3.0 cm, ht. 3.5 cm | Pink, cream buff surface, sand temper |
| 2 | I687 | C-4 | Rim diam. 7.2 cm, base diam. 6.1 cm, ht. 7.5 cm | Pink, sand temper. Shaved base |
| **BURIAL 21, SKELETON 2, LEVEL XVIIB** |||||
| 3 | I773:2 | C-1 | Rim diam. 11.0 cm, max. diam. 16.0 cm, base diam. 8.1 cm, ht. 28.5 cm | Red, pink surface, sand and light organic temper |
| 4 | 19 N 155 | C-4 | Rim diam. 10.1 cm, max. diam. 12.8 cm, base diam. 7.5 cm, ht. 15.9 cm | Buff, cream surface, sand temper. Slightly taller than the usual form of this type, with a convex, rather than flat, base. Kish: Mackay 1929: pl. 44, B. 117; Abu Salabikh: Moon 1987: nos. 411, 417 (ED IIIb); Ur: Woolley 1934: type 108b (ED–Akk.) |
| 5 | I773:1 | O-1 | Rim diam. 16.4 cm, base diam. 5.1 cm, ht. 7.6 cm | Red, pink surface, sand temper |
| 6 | 19 N 144 | — | Lgth. 17.7 cm, max. w. 5.9 cm, max. th. 4.2 cm | Bone tool made from the distal end of an equid tibia, shaped and polished. Nippur: McCown, Haines, and Biggs 1978: pl. 60:1 (ED III–early Akk.); Tell al-Hiba: Bahrani 1989: pl. 55:1–5 (ED IIIb) |
| **BURIAL 18, LEVEL XVI** |||||
| 7 | 19 N 60 | O-1 | Rim diam. 15.2 cm, base diam. 5.2 cm, ht. 7.0 cm | Red, sand temper. String-cut base |

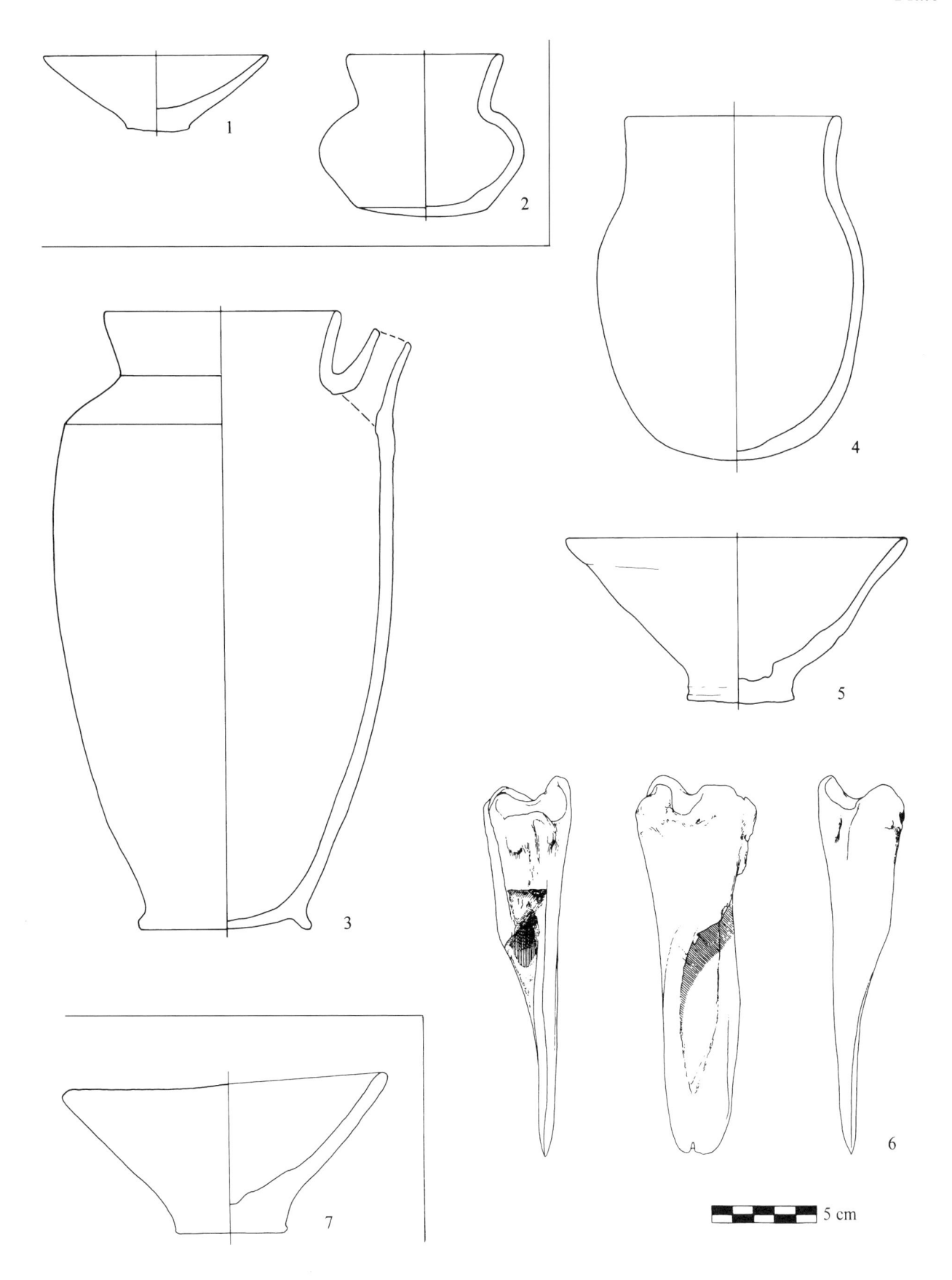

Plate 132

Third-millennium B.C. Grave Groups, Burial 21, Skeletons 1 and 2, and Burial 18. Scale 2:5

Plate 133. Third-millennium B.C. Grave Group, Burial 14, Skeleton 5

|   | Lot Number | Form | Dimension | Description |
|---|---|---|---|---|
| **BURIAL 14, SKELETON 5, LEVEL XVA** ||||||
| 1 | 19 N 39 | C-17 | Rim diam. 12.5 cm, max. diam. 12.5 cm, base diam. 3.5 cm, ht. 24.4 cm | Pale pink, sand temper. Nippur: McCown and Haines 1967: pl. 81:5 (Akk.); McCown, Haines, and Biggs 1978: pl. 46:6 (Akk.); Kish: Mackay 1929: pl. 44:1891B, pl. 54:57; Fara: Martin 1988: type 95 (ED II); Abu Salabikh: Martin, Moon, and Postgate 1985: grave 28:8, grave 60:6 (ED III); Moon 1987: nos. 438–40, 442 (ED III); Ur: Woolley 1934: type 61 (ED–Akk.) |
| 2 | 19 N 41 | C-1 | Rim diam. 9.8 cm, max. diam. 12.8 cm, base diam. 5.5 cm, ht. 17.8 cm | Buff, sand temper. Kish: Mackay 1929: pl. 51:24; Abu Salabikh: Moon 1987: no. 619 (ED IIIa); Ur: Woolley 1934: type 209a (ED) |
| 3 | 19 N 45 | C-4 | Rim diam. 7.6 cm, max. diam. 10.4 cm, ht. 11.2 cm | Pale pink, sand temper. Rim flatter than is usual for this type. Kish: Mackay 1929: pl. 53:35; Abu Salabikh: Moon 1987: nos. 338–39 (ED III); Ur: Woolley 1934: type 43 (Akk.) |
| 4 | I359:1 | O-1 | Rim diam. 14.5 cm, base diam. 5.0 cm, ht. 6.3 cm | Pale red, pink surface, sand temper |
| 5 | 19 N 34 | O-1 | Rim diam. 14.2 cm, base diam. 4.5 cm, ht. 6.5 cm | Red, pink surface, sand temper. String-cut base |
| 6 | 19 N 46 | O-1 | Rim diam. 10.2 cm, base diam. 4.0 cm, ht. 6.9 cm | Pink, cream surface, sand temper. String-cut base |
| 7 | 19 N 22 | — | Diam. 1.0 cm, th. 0.35 cm | Bone bead, ring shaped |

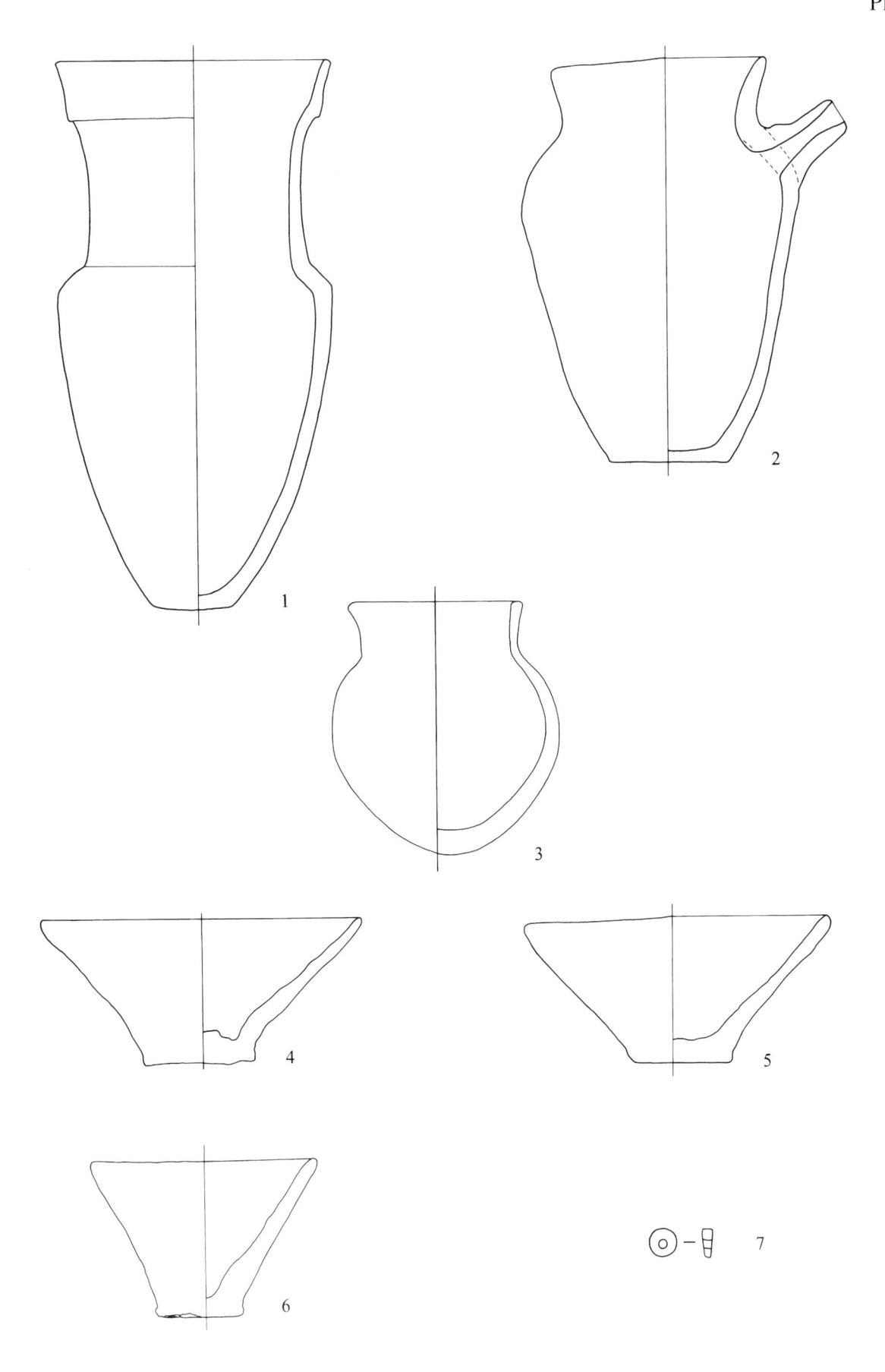

Plate 133

Third-millennium B.C. Grave Group, Burial 14, Skeleton 5. Scales (*1–6*) 2:5 and (*7*) 1:1

Plate 134. Third-millennium B.C. Grave Groups, Burials 16 and 13

|    | Lot Number | Form | Dimension | Description |
|----|------------|------|-----------|-------------|
| **BURIAL 16, LEVEL XIVB** | | | | |
| 1  | I428 | C-24 | Rim diam. 8.0 cm | Buff red, vertically burnished red-slipped surface, sand temper |
| 2  | I403:1 | O-1 | Rim diam. 13.5 cm, base diam. 4.0 cm, ht. 5.7 cm | Buff, cream surface, sand temper |
| 3  | I426:3 | O-1 | Rim diam. 13.6 cm, base diam. 4.8 cm, ht. 5.5 cm | Buff green, sand temper |
| 4  | I422 | O-1 | Rim diam. 13.5 cm, base diam. 4.7 cm, ht. 5.7 cm | Red, pale red to cream surface, sand temper |
| 5  | I426:1 | O-1 | Rim diam. 13.3 cm, base diam. 4.9 cm, ht. 4.0 cm | Buff, sand temper |
| 6  | I426:2 | O-1 | Rim diam. 13.2 cm, base diam. 5.0 cm, ht. 4.6 cm | Buff, sand temper |
| 7  | I403:2 | O-1 | Rim diam. 12.5 cm, base diam. 4.4 cm, ht. 5.6 cm | Buff, cream surface, sand temper |
| **BURIAL 13, LEVEL XIVA** | | | | |
| 8  | H535:2 | O-1 | Rim diam. 14.0 cm, base diam. 4.4 cm, ht. 4.5 cm | Red, sand and light organic temper |
| 9  | H535:3 | O-1 | Rim diam. 13.1 cm, base diam. 4.1 cm, ht. 3.9 cm | Red, cream surface, sand and light organic temper |
| 10 | H535:1 | O-1 | Rim diam. 13.0 cm, base diam. 3.9 cm, ht. 4.5 cm | Buff, sand and light organic temper |
| 11 | H535:4 | O-1 | Rim diam. 12.2 cm, base diam. 3.8 cm, ht. 3.9 cm | Red, sand and light organic temper |
| 12 | 18 N 118a and b | — | (a) diam. 4.7 cm, wire th. 0.5 cm; (b) diam. 4.3 cm, wire th. 0.5 cm | Bracelets, copper/bronze, single loops |
| 13 | 18 N 119 | — | Largest: lgth. 0.8 cm, diam. 0.6 cm; smallest: diam. 0.2 cm, th. 0.1 cm | Necklace, 20 beads: (a) 8 ring-shaped lapis, 1 ring shaped carnelian; (b) 4 ball shaped gold, 1 ball shaped silver; (c) 3 biconvex lapis; (d) 2 date shaped clay, 1 date shaped carnelian |

Plate 134

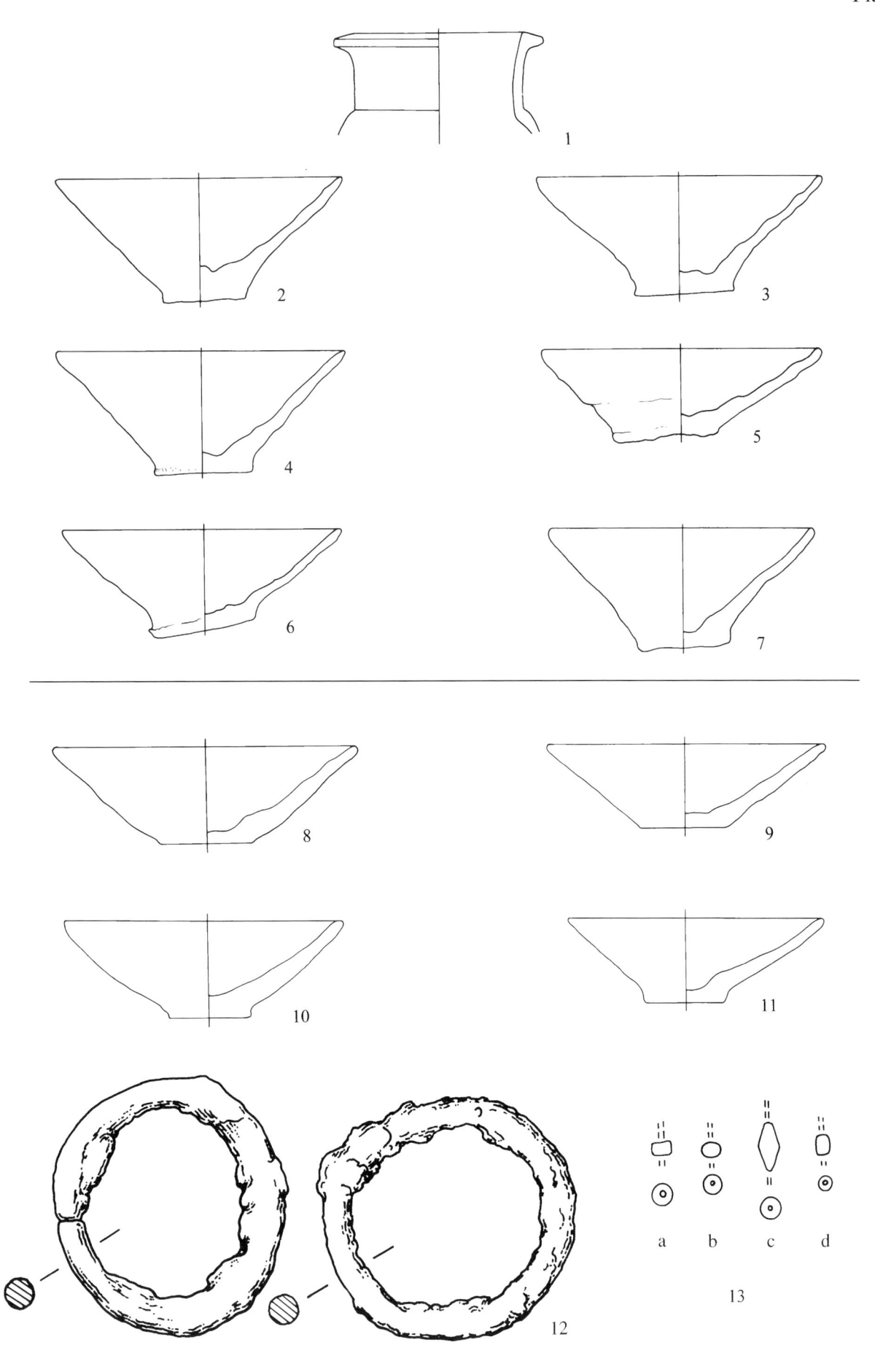

Third-millennium B.C. Grave Groups, Burials 16 and 13. Scales (*1–11*) 2:5 and (*12–13*) 1:1

Plate 135. Third-millennium B.C. Grave Groups, Burials 15 and 11

| | Lot Number | Form | Dimension | Description |
|---|---|---|---|---|
| | BURIAL 15, LEVEL XIVB | | | |
| 1 | 18 N 193 | C-24 | Rim diam. 9.8 cm, max. diam. 19.0 cm, base diam. 12.5 cm, ht. 23.2 cm | Greenish buff, sand temper. For wide body and ring base, see Nippur: McCown and Haines 1967: pl. 82:1 (Akk.); Diyala: Delougaz 1952: pl. 99a, B.515.470 (Akk.); Tell Madhhur: Roaf et al. 1984: fig. 13:2A (early Akk.); Tell Sabra: Tunca 1987: pl. 19:17, pl. 65:6–7 (early Akk.?); Kish: Mackay 1925: pl. 13, nos. 15–19; Mackay 1929: pl. 44, B. 75, 123, pl. 51:12–14, 16–17; Abu Salabikh: Martin, Moon, and Postgate 1985: grave 51:7, 10, grave 73:2, grave 84:3 (ED III); Moon 1987: nos. 563–64, 567–71 (ED III) |
| 2 | 18 N 191 | O-9 variant | Rim diam. 12.5 cm, base diam. 13.0 cm, ht. 11.0 cm | Pink, buff surface, sand temper. Diyala: Delougaz 1952: C.363.810a–b, C.364.810a–b (ED III–early Akk.); Tell Sabra: Tunca 1987: pl. 19:9 (tomb 5310, early Akk.?); Kish: Mackay 1925: pl. 11:1; Mackay 1929: pl. 44:B. 75, 123, pl. 49:8–9, 11, 14; Abu Salabikh: Martin, Moon, and Postgate 1985: grave 4:5, grave 38:22, grave 79:3–4, grave 93:5–6, 9–13 (ED II–III); Moon 1987: nos. 217–31 (ED III); Moon 1982: 14–16 (Kish), 29 (Uqair), 45 (Susa); Ur: Woolley 1934: type 242 |
| 3 | H1103:1 | O-1 | Rim diam. 13.5 cm, base diam. 3.7 cm, ht. 5.9 cm | Buff, sand and light organic temper |
| 4 | H1103:2 | O-1 | Rim diam. 13.0 cm, base diam. 4.7 cm, ht. 6.4 cm | Pale red, sand and light organic temper |
| 5 | H1104 | O-1 | Rim diam. 13.6 cm, base diam. 4.6 cm, ht. 5.6 cm | Cream buff, sand and light organic temper |
| 6 | H1106 | O-1 | Rim diam. 12.6 cm, base diam. 4.3 cm, ht. 6.0 cm | Cream buff, sand and light organic temper |
| 7 | 18 N 192 | O-1 | Rim diam. 13.5 cm, base diam. 4.0 cm, ht. 6.0 cm | Pink buff, sand temper |
| | BURIAL 11, LEVEL XIB | | | |
| 8 | 18 N 114 | O-1 | Rim diam. 14.0 cm, base diam. 5.1 cm, ht. 4.7 cm | Pink, sand temper |
| 9 | H885:1 | O-1 | Rim diam. 12.7 cm, base diam. 4.4 cm, ht. 3.8 cm | Pink, sand and light organic temper |

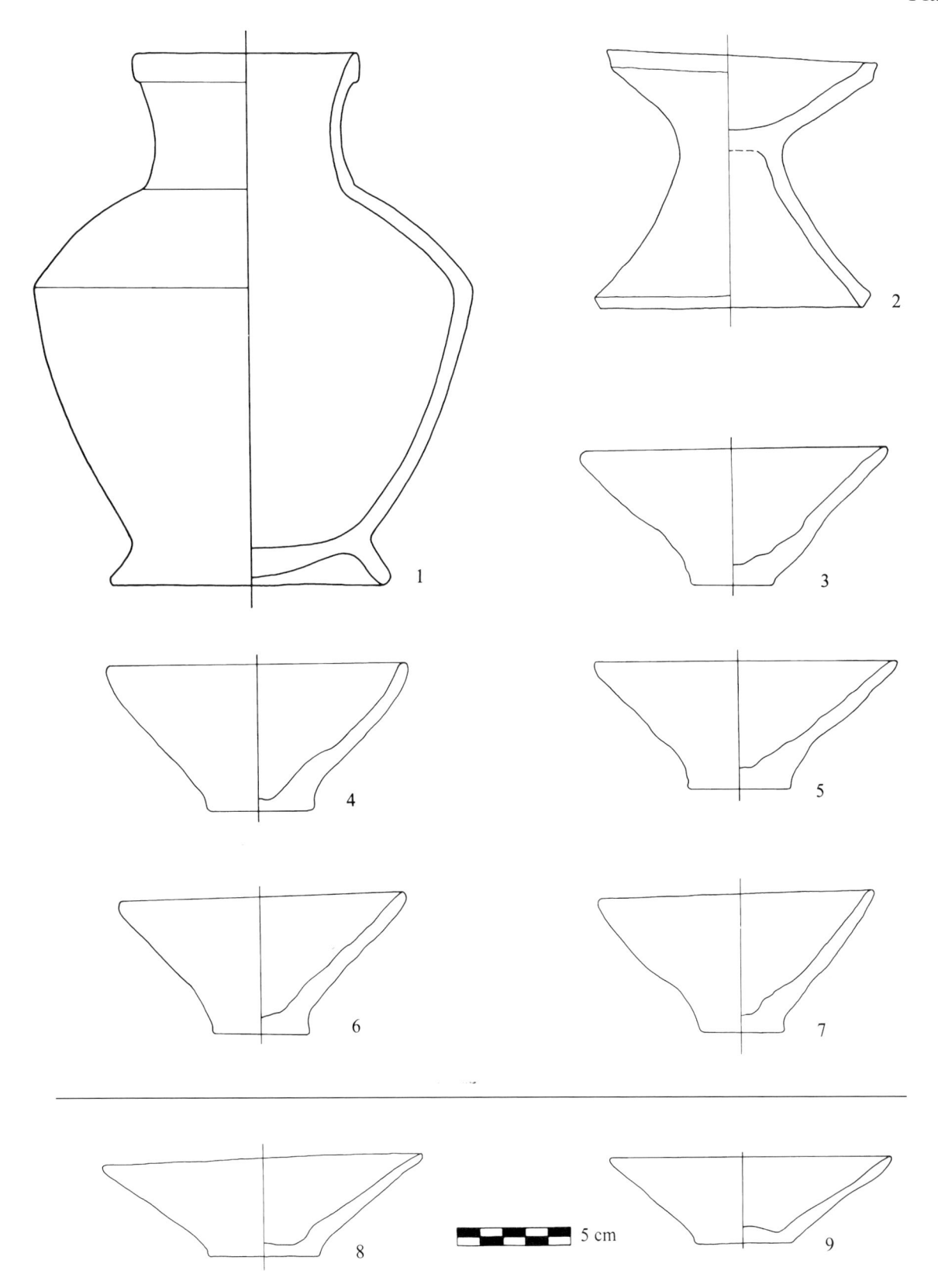

Plate 135

Third-millennium B.C. Grave Groups, Burials 15 and 11. Scale 2:5

Plate 136. Third-millennium B.C. Grave Group, Burial 14, Skeleton 6

| Lot Number | Form | Dimension | Description/Comparison |
|---|---|---|---|
| BURIAL 14, SKELETON 6, LEVEL XIVA–B | | | |
| 1  19 N 64 | — | Lgth. 22.9 cm, max. w. 0.9 cm | Pin, copper/bronze, straight, round cross section, short tang probably originally held a bead. Kish: Mackay 1925: pl. 19:16–18; Mackay 1929: pl. 58:5–10; Mari: Parrot 1956: pl. 44:405; Ur: Woolley 1934: pl. 231, type 1a (ED–Akk.) |
| 2  19 N 65 | — | Lgth. 28.8 cm, max. w. 1.3 cm, average shaft diam. 0.3 cm | Pin, copper/bronze, round cross section, long square-sectioned tang, flattened and pierced central portion. Kish: Mackay 1925: pl. 19:2, 4; Mackay 1929: pl. 58:12–13; Ur: Woolley 1934: pl. 231, type 7 c/d (ED) |
| 3  19 N 89 | C-14 | Rim diam. 9.8 cm, max. diam. 17.7 cm, base diam. 10.0 cm, ht. 23.1 cm | Red, pink surface, sand temper. Kish: Mackay 1925: pl. 53:4–5; Abu Salabikh: Martin, Moon, and Postgate 1985: grave 3:2 (ED IIIb); Ur: Woolley 1934: type 187 (Akk.–Ur III) |
| 4  19 N 96 | — | Rim diam. 10.2 cm, base diam. 3.4 cm, ht. 4.9 cm | Bowl, alabaster, hemispherical, beaded rim. Ur: Woolley 1934: pl. 245, type 49 (ED) |
| 5  19 N 85 | O-9 | Rim diam. 21.4 cm, base diam. 21.6 cm, stem diam. 9.4 cm, ht. 26.0 cm | Pink, cream surface, sand and organic temper. Incised design on base made with four-pointed comb |
| 6  19 N 87 | C-1 | Rim diam. 9.3 cm, max. diam. 12.0 cm, base diam. 5.9 cm, ht. 23.9 cm | Buff, cream surface, sand temper |
| 7  19 N 84 | C-24 | Rim diam. 9.8 cm, max. diam. 12.4 cm, ht. 17.0 cm | Pale pink, sand temper. Kish: Mackay 1929: pl. 53:51; Moon 1987: nos. 376–78, 381, 388 (ED IIIa–b) |

Plate 136

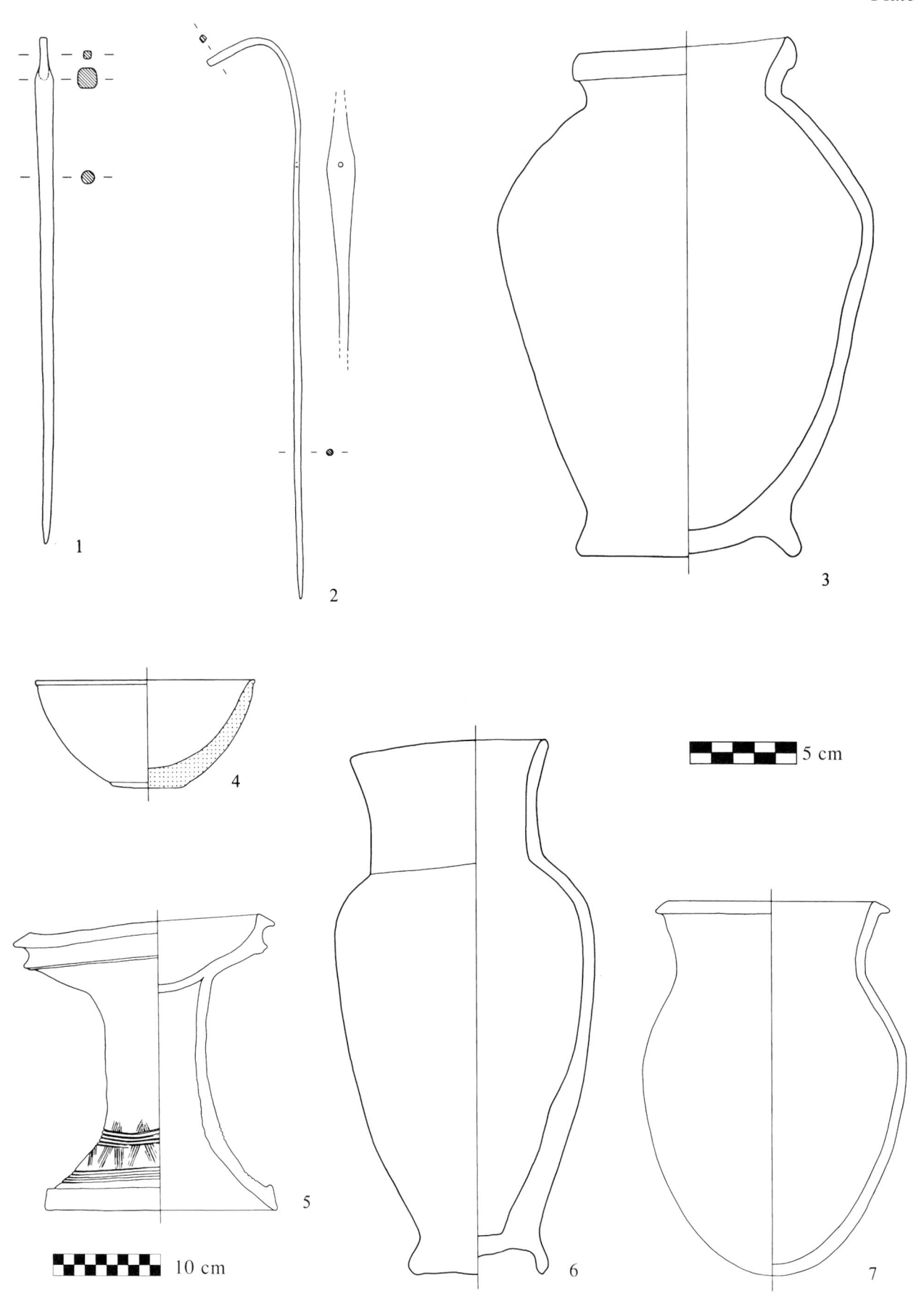

Third-millennium B.C. Grave Group, Burial 14, Skeleton 6. Scales (*1–4, 6–7*) 2:5 and (*5*) 1:5

Plate 137. Third-millennium B.C. Grave Group, Burial 14, Skeleton 6

| | Lot Number | Form | Dimension | Description |
|---|---|---|---|---|
| BURIAL 14, SKELETON 6, LEVEL XIVA–B | | | | |
| 1 | I480 | O-1 | Rim diam. 16.4 cm, base diam. 4.3 cm, ht. 7.7 cm | Buff, sand and light organic temper |
| 2 | I482:2 | O-1 | Rim diam. 13.0 cm, base diam. 4.6 cm, ht. 4.5 cm | Red, cream pink surface, sand temper |
| 3 | 19 N 94 | O-1 | Rim diam. 12.6 cm, base diam. 5.1 cm, ht. 4.1 cm | Buff, cream surface, sand temper |
| 4 | 19 N 95 | O-1 | Rim diam. 12.4 cm, base diam. 4.2 cm, ht. 5.1 cm | Red, cream surface, sand temper |
| 5 | I482:1 | O-1 | Rim diam. 12.3 cm, base diam. 4.1 cm, ht. 5.2 cm | Red, sand temper |
| 6 | 19 N 93 | O-1 | Rim diam. 12.3 cm, base diam. 4.1 cm, ht. 5.0 cm | Buff, red cream surface, sand temper |
| 7 | 19 N 92 | O-1 | Rim diam. 12.1 cm, base diam. 4.5 cm, ht. 4.0 cm | Red, sand temper |
| 8 | I482:5 | O-1 | Rim diam. 13.0 cm, base diam. 4.8 cm, ht. 4.8 cm | Red, sand temper |
| 9 | I482:3 | O-1 | Rim diam. 12.0 cm, base diam. 4.5 cm, ht. 5.6 cm | Buff, cream surface, sand temper |
| 10 | I482:4 | O-1 | Rim diam. 12.0 cm, base diam. 3.5 cm, ht. 4.9 cm | Pale red, cream surface, sand temper |
| 11 | I482:6 | O-1 | Rim diam. 13.0 cm, base diam. 4.5 cm, ht. 4.7 cm | Red, sand temper |
| 12 | 19 N 91 | O-1 | Rim diam. 11.5 cm, base diam. 4.7 cm, ht. 5.2 cm | Buff, pale red surface, sand temper |

Plate 137

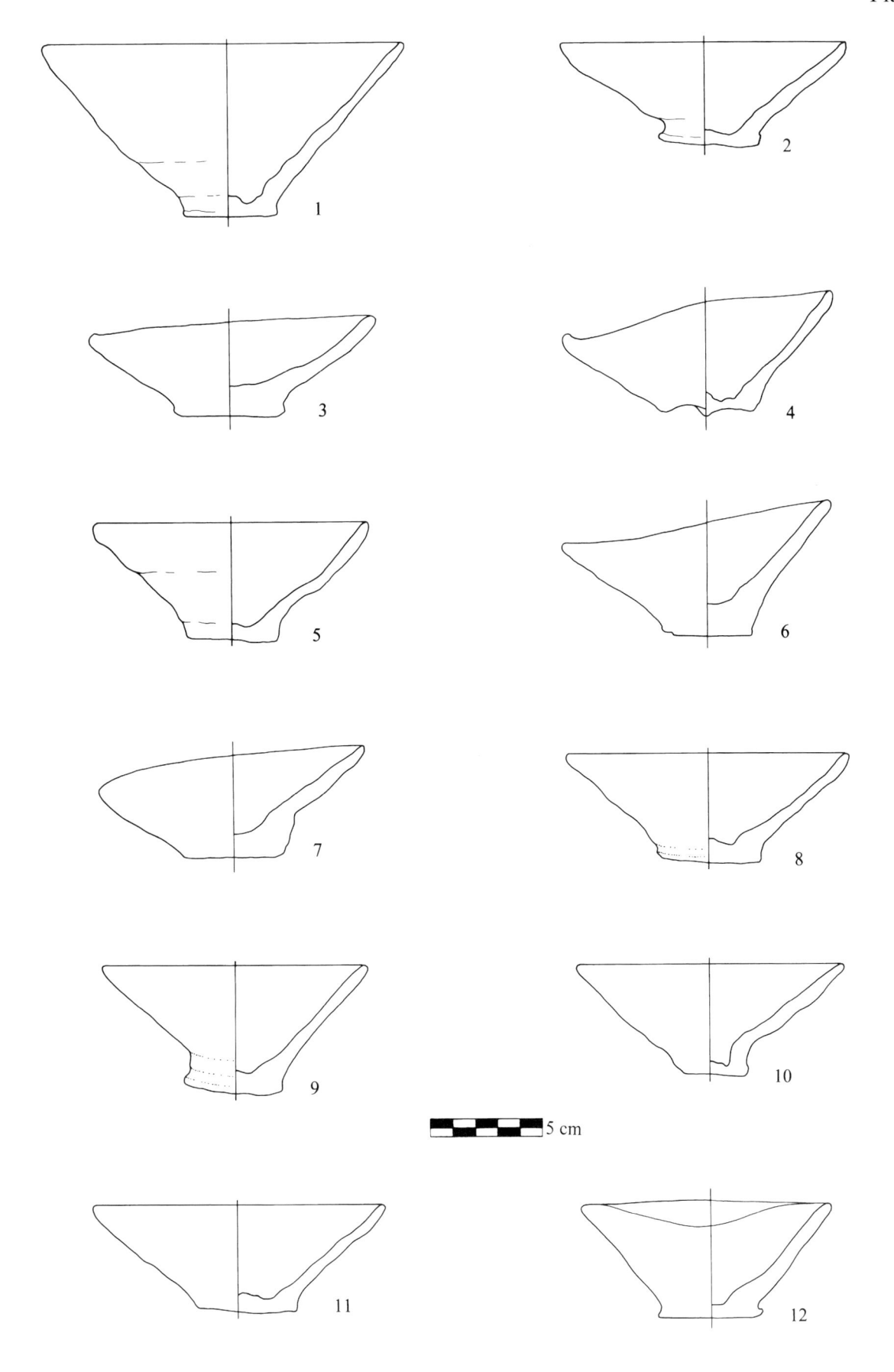

Third-millennium B.C. Grave Group, Burial 14, Skeleton 6. Scale 2:5

Plate 138. Third-millennium B.C. Grave Groups, Burial 14, Skeleton 6, and Burial 14, Skeleton 7

|   | Lot Number | Form | Dimension | Description/Comparison |
|---|---|---|---|---|
| **BURIAL 14, SKELETON 6, LEVEL XIVA–B** ||||||
| 1 | 19 N 90 | C-17 | Rim diam. 11.1 cm, max. diam. 15.5 cm, base diam. 9.2 cm, ht. 28.3 cm | Greenish buff, sand temper, pronounced ridges from wheel-turning on neck and shoulder. Same body shape, different rim: Diyala: Delougaz 1952: C.557.470 (late ED III–early Akk.); same body and rim: Ur: Woolley 1934: type 174 (ED–Akk.) |
| 2 | 19 N 88 | C-17 | Rim diam. 11.2 cm, max. diam. 17.0 cm, base diam. 9.5 cm, ht. 26.5 cm | Buff, cream surface, sand temper, splash of bitumen on shoulder. Ur: Woolley 1934: type 144 (early Akk.) |
| **BURIAL 14, SKELETON 7, LEVEL XVA–B–LEVEL XVI** ||||||
| 3 | I682:2 | C-1 | Rim diam. 11.3 cm, max. diam. 13.2 cm, base diam. 6.7 cm, ht. 17.3 cm | Pink, sand and light organic temper |
| 4 | I682:1 | O-1 | Rim diam. 15.0 cm, base diam. 4.8 cm, ht. 7.3 cm | Pink, sand temper |

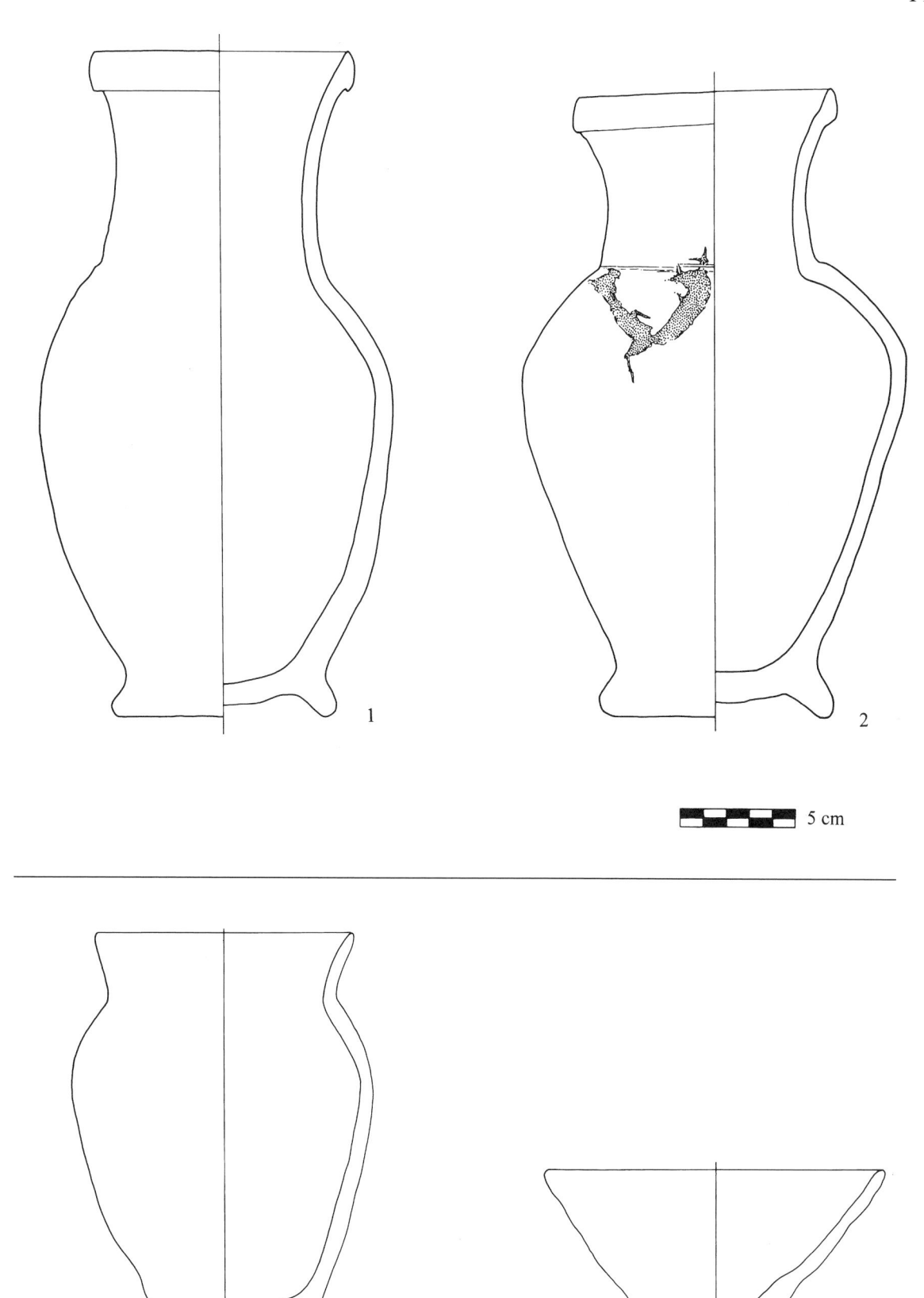

Plate 138

5 cm

Third-millennium B.C. Grave Groups, Burial 14, Skeleton 6, and Burial 14, Skeleton 7. Scale 2:5

Plate 139. Third-millennium B.C. Grave Group, Burial 14, Skeleton 8

|   | Lot Number | Form | Dimension | Description/Comparison |
|---|---|---|---|---|
| **BURIAL 14, SKELETON 8, LEVEL XVI** | | | | |
| 1 | 19 N 145 | C-11 | Rim diam. 10.0 cm, max. diam. 11.4 cm, ht. 12.8 cm | Fine red orange ware, cream slip, sand temper. Horizontal combing on lower neck and shoulder. See Type C-11 for comparanda (pl. 101) |
| 2 | 19 N 156 | O-1 | Rim diam. 10.2 cm, base diam. 4.4 cm, ht. 10.2 cm | Pink, cream red surface, sand temper. String-cut base |
| 3 | I780:10 | O-1 | Rim diam. 10.7 cm, base diam. 3.4 cm, ht. 11.1 cm | Buff, cream pink surface, sand temper |
| 4 | I780:6 | O-1 | Rim diam. 16.4 cm, base diam. 4.8 cm, ht. 7.6 cm | Buff, cream surface, sand temper |
| 5 | I780:11 | O-1 | Rim diam. 16.3 cm, base diam. 3.8 cm, ht. 7.3 cm | Buff, pink cream surface, sand temper |
| 6 | I780:4 | O-1 | Rim diam. 16.3 cm, base diam. 4.8 cm, ht. 6.7 cm | Red, sand temper |
| 7 | I780:3 | O-1 | Rim diam. 16.2 cm, base diam. 4.6 cm, ht. 7.8 cm | Red, pink surface, sand temper |
| 8 | I780:2 | O-1 | Rim diam. 16.0 cm, base diam. 5.1 cm, ht. 7.1 cm | Buff, cream surface, sand temper |
| 9 | I780:16 | O-1 | Rim diam. 16.0 cm, base diam. 4.8 cm, ht. 7.4 cm | Pink, sand temper |
| 10 | I780:17 | O-1 | Rim diam. 16.0 cm, base diam. 4.8 cm, ht. 7.5 cm | Pink, sand temper |
| 11 | I780:9 | O-1 | Rim diam. 15.8 cm, base diam. 4.9 cm, ht. 7.7 cm | Pink, sand temper |

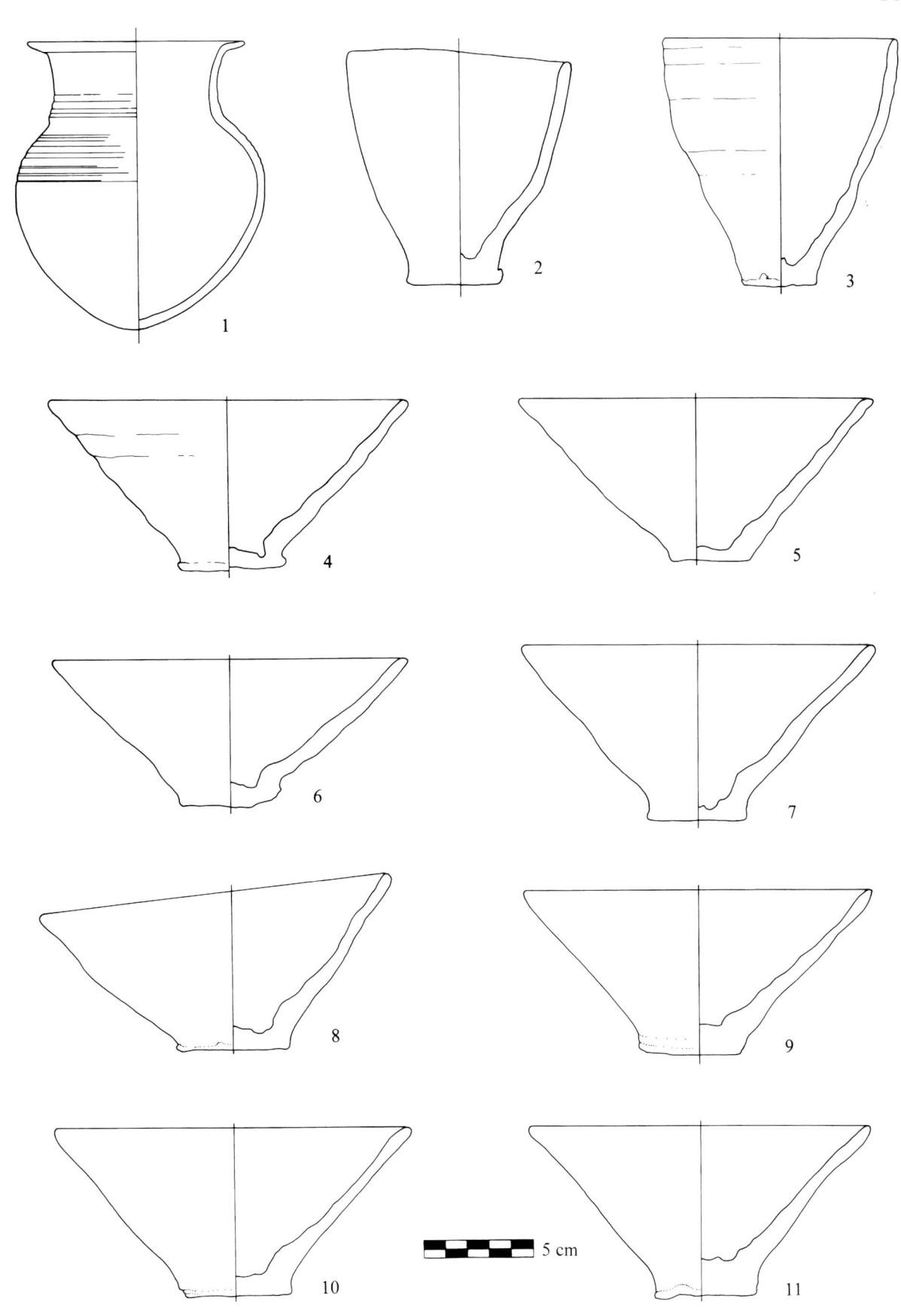

Plate 139

Third-millennium B.C. Grave Group, Burial 14, Skeleton 8. Scale 2:5

Plate 140. Third-millennium B.C. Grave Group, Burial 14, Skeleton 8 (*cont.*)

|   | *Lot Number* | *Form* | *Dimension* | *Description* |
|---|---|---|---|---|
| **BURIAL 14, SKELETON 8, LEVEL XVI** | | | | |
| 1 | I780:14 | O-1 | Rim diam. 15.6 cm, base diam. 5.4 cm, ht. 7.9 cm | Pink, sand temper |
| 2 | I780:15 | O-1 | Rim diam. 15.4 cm, base diam. 4.5 cm, ht. 7.3 cm | Pink, sand temper |
| 3 | I780:8 | O-1 | Rim diam. 15.3 cm, base diam. 3.7 cm, ht. 7.2 cm | Pink, sand temper |
| 4 | I780:7 | O-1 | Rim diam. 15.2 cm, base diam. 5.5 cm, ht. 7.4 cm | Red, pink surface, sand temper |
| 5 | I780:18 | O-1 | Rim diam. 15.2 cm, base diam. 5.0 cm, ht. 7.9 cm | Pink, sand temper |
| 6 | I780:19 | O-1 | Rim diam. 15.0 cm, base diam. 5.0 cm, ht. 7.1 cm | Pink, sand temper |
| 7 | I780:5 | O-1 | Rim diam. 14.9 cm, base diam. 5.0 cm, ht. 7.9 cm | Red, sand temper |
| 8 | I780:1 | O-1 | Rim diam. 14.7 cm, base diam. 5.3 cm, ht. 6.9 cm | Red, pink surface, sand temper |
| 9 | I780:13 | O-1 | Rim diam. 14.5 cm, base diam. 5.3 cm, ht. 6.6 cm | Buff, sand temper |
| 10 | I780:12 | O-1 | Rim diam. 13.5 cm, base diam. 4.2 cm, ht. 6.3 cm | Red, pink surface, sand temper |

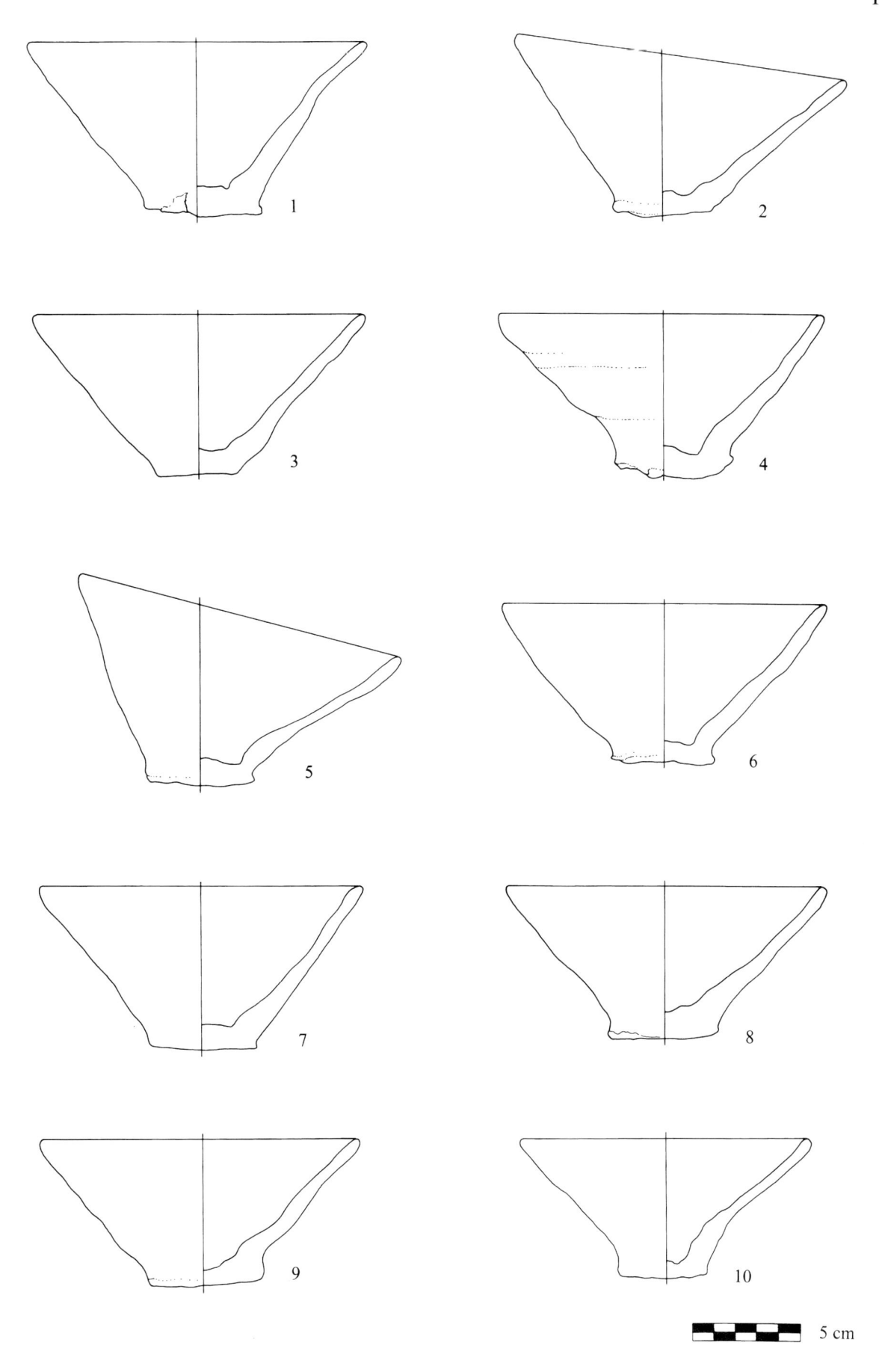

Plate 140

Third-millennium B.C. Grave Group, Burial 14, Skeleton 8 (*cont.*). Scale 2:5

Plate 141. Cosmetic Shells from Burial 19; Burial 14, Skeleton 7; and Burial 14, Skeleton 3

| | Lot Number | Form | Dimension | Description |
|---|---|---|---|---|
| **BURIAL 19, LEVEL XVII** | | | | |
| 1 | 19 N 81 | — | Lgth. 4.6 cm, w. 3.7 cm | Shell, one valve of a *Levicardium* shell, with green cosmetic paste inside |
| | 19 N 82 | — | Lgth. 4.4 cm, w. 3.5 cm | Shell, one valve of a *Levicardium* shell, with green cosmetic paste inside |
| **BURIAL 14, SKELETON 7, LEVEL XVI** | | | | |
| 2 | 19 N 105 | — | (a) Lgth. 4.8 cm, w. 3.9 cm; (b) Lgth. 5.2 cm, w. 4.2 cm | Shell pair, 2 valves of a *Levicardium* shell (not a natural pair), each with traces of green cosmetic paste inside |
| **BURIAL 14, SKELETON 3, LEVEL XIIIA–C** | | | | |
| 3 | 19 N 27 | — | (a) Lgth. 4.5 cm, w. 4.0 cm; (b) Lgth. 5.2 cm, w. 4.1 cm | Shell pair, 2 valves of a *Levicardium* shell (not a natural pair), one with traces of black pigment, the other with white |

Plate 141

19 N 81   19 N 82

1

a   b

2

a   b

3

Cosmetic Shells from Burial 19; Burial 14, Skeleton 7; and Burial 14, Skeleton 3. Scale 1:2

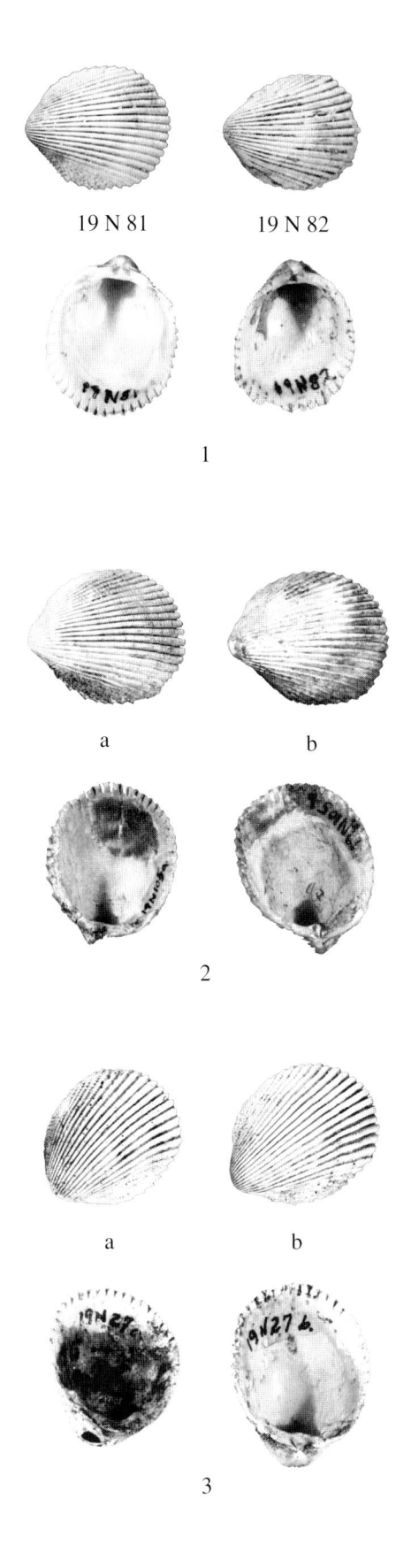

Plate 142. Third-millennium B.C. Grave Groups, Burial 14 Southwest Shaft and Burial 14, Skeleton 3 or 4

| | Lot Number | Form | Dimension | Description/Comparison |
|---|---|---|---|---|
| | | | | |
| BURIAL 14, SOUTHWEST SHAFT, POSSIBLY LEVEL XIV ||||||
| 1 | 19 N 52 | O-UT | Rim diam. 15.0 cm, base diam. 10.0 cm, ht. 8.9 cm | Pale red, sand and light organic temper, horizontally ridged sides. Assur: Andrae 1970: figs. 14–15 (ED–Akk.); Diyala: Delougaz 1952: C.213.200, C.215.210, C.303.200, C.805.210 (late Akk.), C.803.200 (early Akk.); Kish: Mackay 1929: pl. 54:26–27; Tell al-Wilayah: Madhlum 1960: fig. 3:32; Ur: Woolley 1934: type 31 (Akk.) |
| BURIAL 14, SKELETON 3 OR 4, LEVEL XIIIB ||||||
| 2 | 19 N 11 | O-12 | Rim diam. 16.4 cm, base diam. 4.8 cm, ht. 6.0 cm | Buff, sand temper. String-cut base |
| 3 | I117:2 | O-11 | Rim diam. 16.0 cm, base diam. 5.3 cm, ht. 5.0 cm | Pale red, sand temper |
| 4 | I117:1 | O-1 | Rim diam. 13.1 cm, base diam. 5.5 cm, ht. 6.0 cm | Buff green, sand temper |
| 5 | H1097 | O-9 | Rim diam. 43.6 cm, base diam. 38.8 cm, stem diam. 15.0 cm, ht. ca. 64.0 cm | Red, cream surface, organic and sand temper. Two pairs of ventilation holes and comb-incised lines on base, wavy grooved line on rim |
| 6 | 19 N 16 | O-UT | Rim diam. 8.1 cm, base diam. 3.0 cm, ht. 3.5 cm | Olive brown, lightly fired, light sand temper. Single small hole just below rim. Probably a lid |

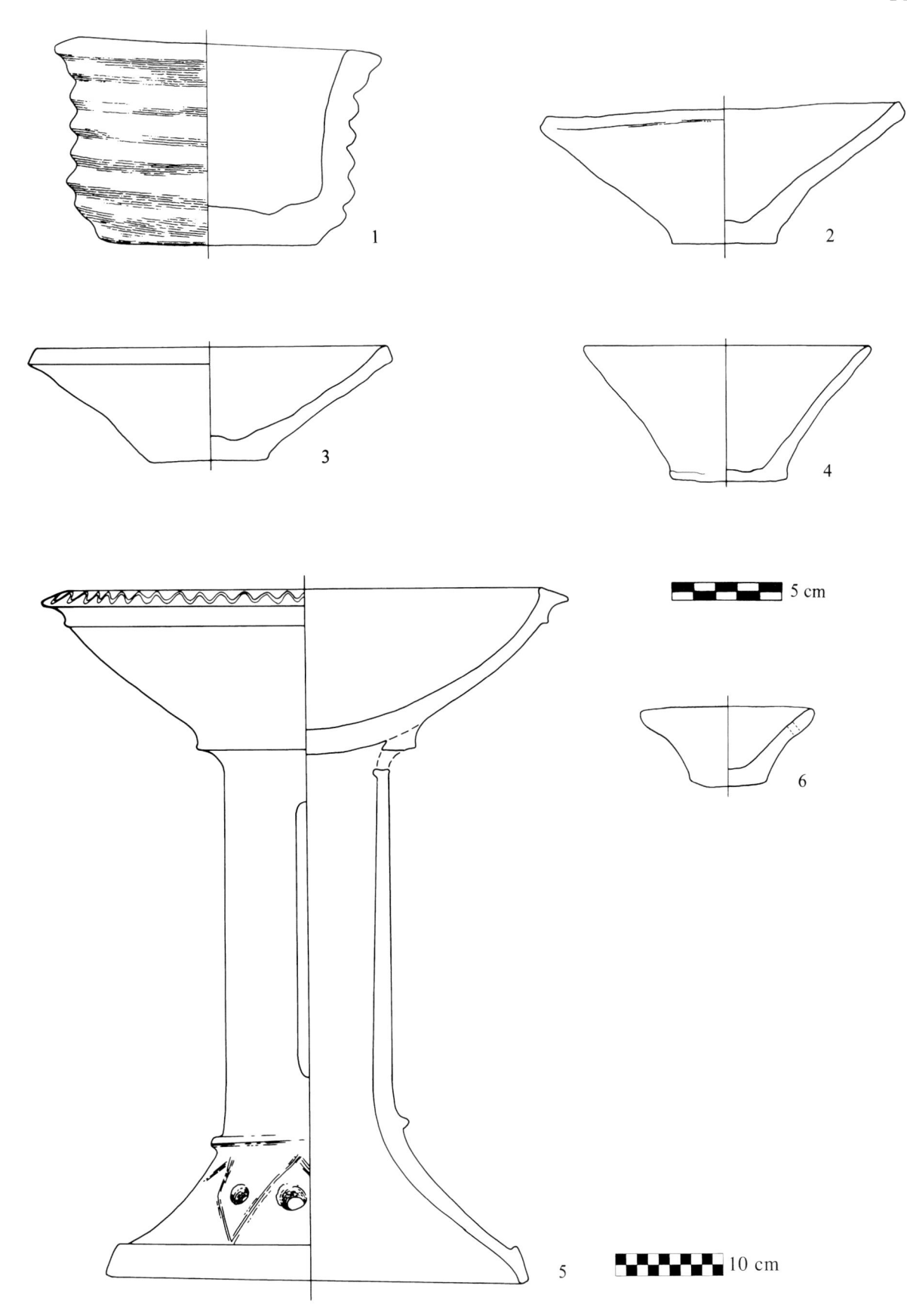

Plate 142

Third-millennium B.C. Grave Groups, Burial 14 Southwest Shaft and Burial 14, Skeleton 3 or 4.
Scales (*1–4, 6*) 2:5 and (*5*) 1:5

Plate 143. Third-millennium B.C. Grave Group, Burial 14, Skeleton 3

| Lot Number | Form | Dimension | Description/Comparison |
|---|---|---|---|
| **BURIAL 14, SKELETON 3, LEVEL XIIIB** | | | |
| 19 N 44 | C-6 | Rim diam. 11.3 cm, max. diam. 24.1 cm, base diam. 14.5 cm, ht. 40.5 cm | "Goddess-handled" jar, wide flat handle, elaborate incised, impressed, and applied features. Shoulder decorated with single-point incision, herringbone pattern within pendant triangles. Base separately applied. For the exaggerated dimensions, especially the tall neck, see Diyala: Delougaz 1952: C.516.471, C.526.471c–d, C.527.471 (early Akk.); Abu Salabikh: Moon 1981: fig. 1; Moon 1987: 742–43 (ED IIIb); Kish: Mackay 1925: pl. 1:5, pl. 2:8; Mackay 1929: pl. 44:7, pl. 45:8, 11, pl. 48:24, pl. 49:3 |

Plate 143

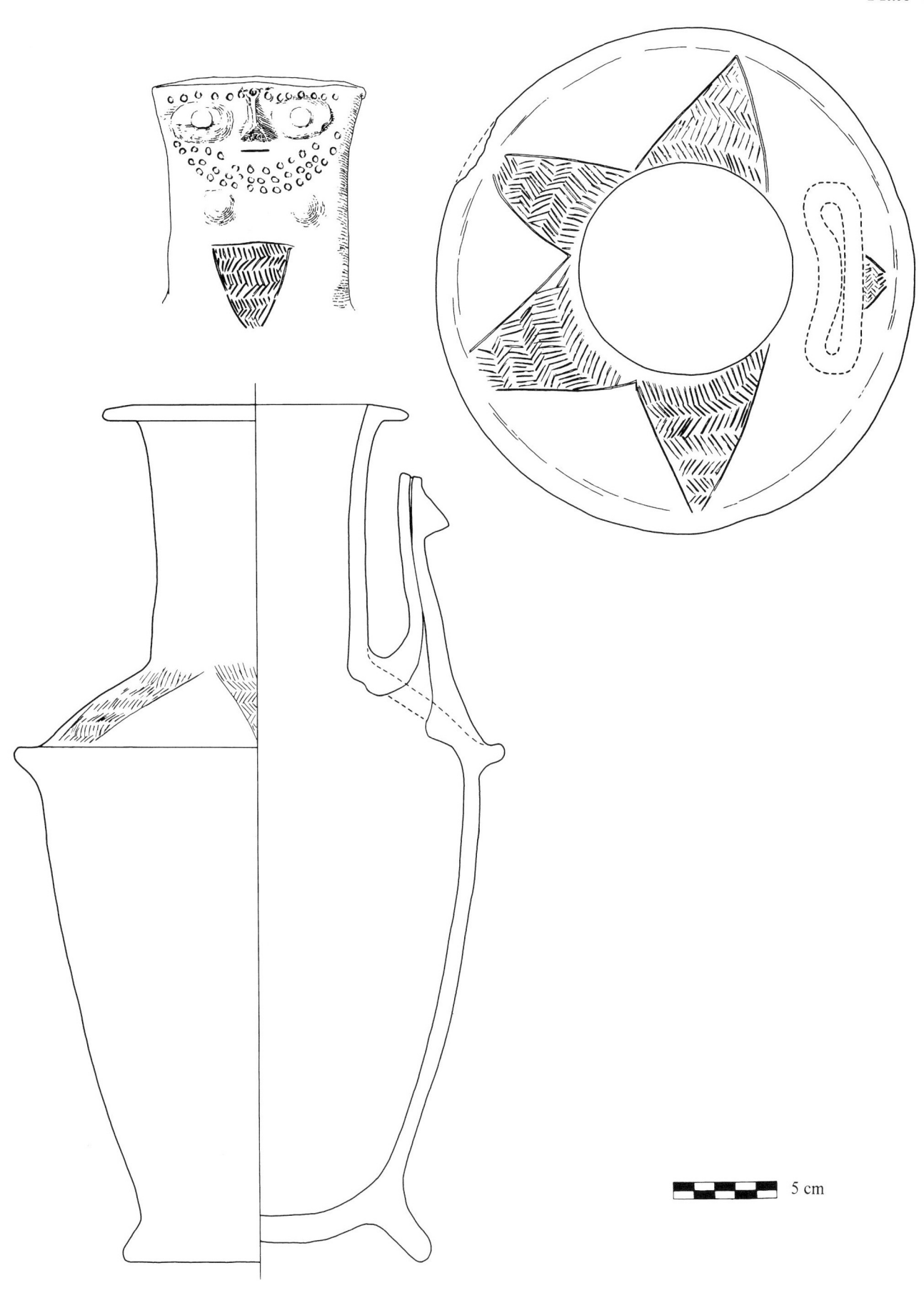

Third-millennium B.C. Grave Group, Burial 14, Skeleton 3. Scale 2:5

Plate 144. Goddess-handled Jar with Burial 14, Skeleton 3

| Lot Number | Form | Dimension | Description |
|---|---|---|---|
| BURIAL 14, SKELETON 3, LEVEL XIIIB | | | |
| 19 N 44 | C-6 | Rim diam. 11.3 cm, max. diam. 24.1 cm, base diam. 14.5 cm, ht. 40.5 cm | "Goddess-handled" jar; see pl. 143 |

Plate 144

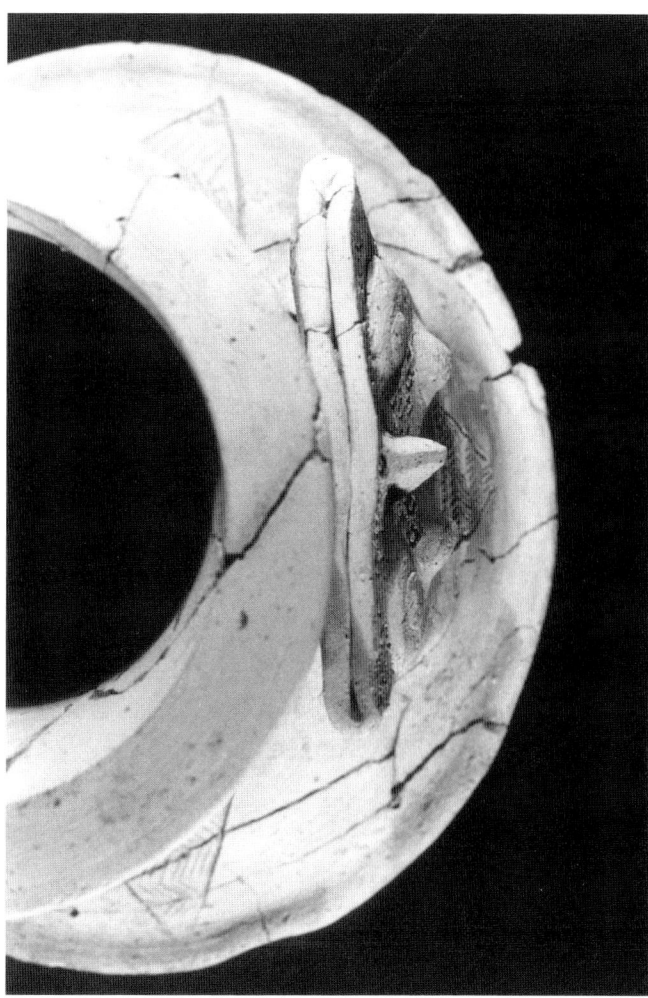

Goddess-handled Jar with Burial 14, Skeleton 3

Plate 145. Third-millennium B.C. Grave Groups, Burial 14, Skeleton 3, and Burial 14, Skeleton 4

|   | Lot Number | Form | Dimension | Description/Comparison |
|---|---|---|---|---|
| BURIAL 14, SKELETON 3, LEVEL XIIIB ||||
| 1 | 19 N 28 | — | Lgth. 18.2 cm, max. diam. 0.5 cm | Pin, copper/bronze, straight, round cross section. For comparisons, see 19 N 5 (pl. 64a) though the example with Skeleton 3 is smaller |
| BURIAL 14, SKELETON 4, LEVEL XIIIB ||||
| 2 | 19 N 4 | — | Rim diam. 14.0 cm, ht. 4.5 cm | Banded alabaster bowl. Carinated sides, everted rim. Abu Salabikh: Martin, Moon, and Postgate 1985: grave 1:48 (ED IIIa early); Ur: Woolley 1934: pl. 178:U.7648, pl. 245: type 54 (late ED–Akk.) |
| 3 | 19 N 72 | — | Rim diam. 12.0 cm, base diam. 10.0 cm, ht. 3.9 cm | Copper/bronze bowl, traces of woven reed on interior and exterior. Müller-Karpe 1993: form 10; Ur: Woolley 1934: pl. 232, type 2 (ED–Akk.) |
| 4 | 19 N 7 | — | Lgth. 28.3 cm, max. w. 1.3 cm | Spearhead, copper/bronze. Ur: Woolley 1934: pl. 227, Type 1a (ED); Susa: Steve and Gasche 1971: pl. 11:32 (Akk.) |
| 5 | 19 N 24 | — | Diam. 1.5 cm, th. 0.6 cm | Bead, carnelian, ring-shaped. Traces of copper corrosion attached to one side |

Plate 145

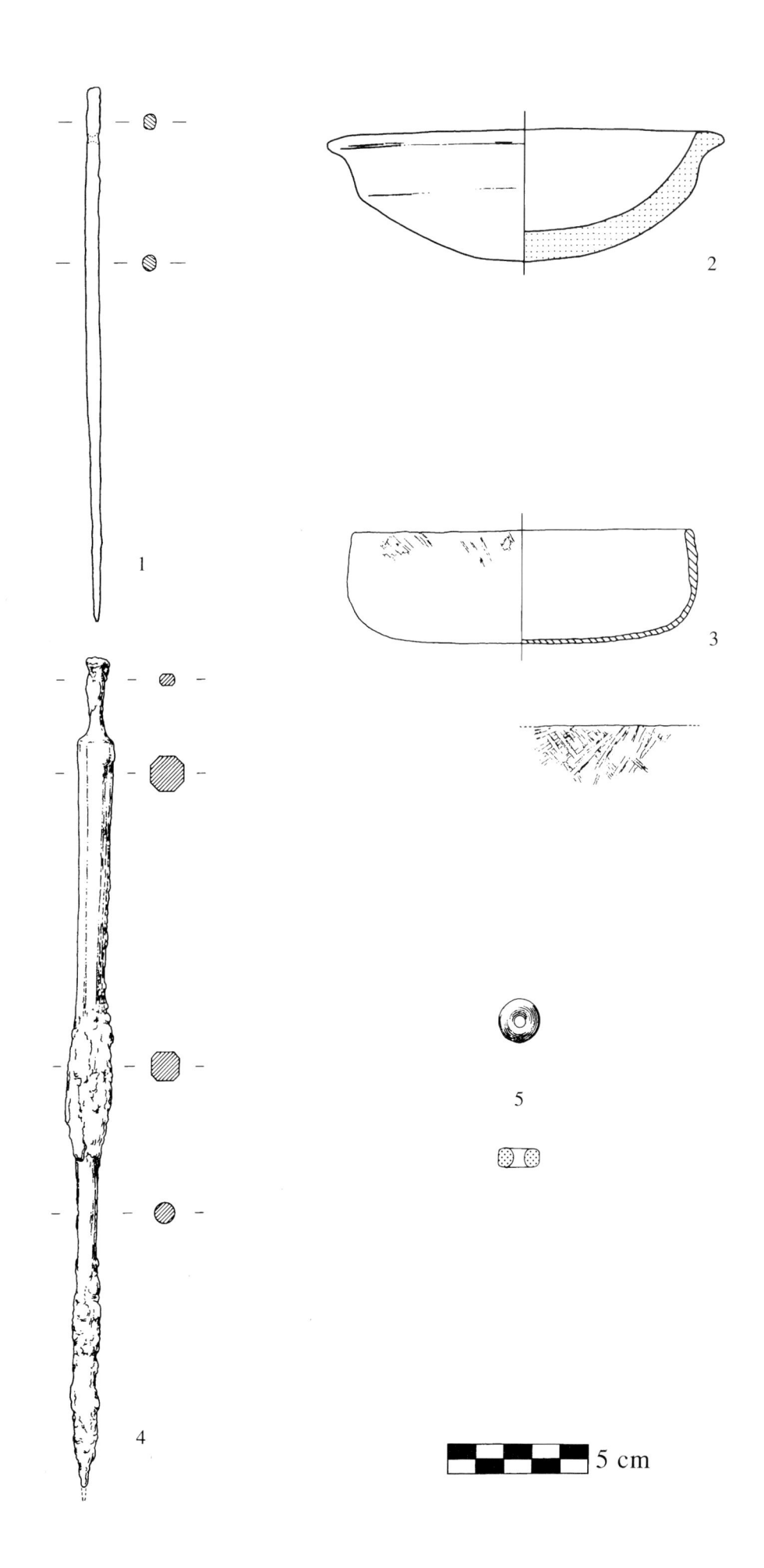

Third-millennium B.C. Grave Groups, Burial 14, Skeleton 3, and Burial 14, Skeleton 4. Scale 1:2

Plate 146. Third-millennium B.C. Grave Group, Burial 14, Skeleton 2

| | Lot Number | Form | Dimension | Description/Comparison |
|---|---|---|---|---|
| | | | | |

BURIAL 14, SKELETON 2, LEVEL XIIIA–C

| | | | | |
|---|---|---|---|---|
| 1 | 19 N 38 | — | Lgth. 29.7 cm, w. 1.3 cm | Gold fillet, thin foil, undecorated surface. Kish: Mackay 1929: pl. 59:8; Ur: Woolley 1934: pl. 146:U.13790 |
| 2 | 19 N 37 | — | (a) diam. 0.9 cm, (b) diam. 0.9 cm | Gold earrings, hollow tubes with tapered ends, formed into loops with overlapping ends. Kish: Mackay 1929: pl. 59:26; Ur: Woolley 1934: pl. 219: type 3 (Akk.) |
| 3 | 19 N 21 | — | (a) diam. 6.9 cm, wire diam. 0.7 cm (b) diam. 6.8 cm, wire diam. 0.7 cm | Bracelets, silver, single wire loops |
| 4 | 19 N 20 | — | (a) diam. 2.8 cm, th. 0.7 cm (b) diam. 2.9 cm, th. 1.2 cm; (c) each arm lgth. ca. 4 cm, max. w. 1.8 cm, th. 0.4 cm | Necklace, pendants, and a selection of beads shown. 317 beads: 13 date-shaped agate, 7 ball-shaped lapis, 15 ball-shaped carnelian, 57 ball-shaped gold foil-covered copper, 3 ribbed ball-shaped gold foil-covered copper, 2 ring-shaped gold foil-covered copper, 23 ring-shaped lapis, 92 ring-shaped carnelian, 101 ring-shaped gold, 1 ring-shaped white stone, 1 ring-shaped brown stone, 1 ring-shaped silver, 1 cylindrical copper-bronze. (a) pendant, brown and white agate center surrounded by gold mount, but those have lapis disks in nearly identical mounts, Woolley 1934: pl. 132: U.12450, PG/1236; agate eye-beads without mounts: Woolley 1934: pl. 132:U.12474, PG/1422; pl. 147, U.17813, PG/1847; (b) pendant, as above but without suspension loop, silver wire wrapped around mount at top and bottom; (c) counterweight, brown and white agate, Woolley 1934: 372, fig. 79; (d) date-shaped bead; (e) ball-shaped bead; (f) ribbed ball-shaped bead; (g) ring-shaped bead (gold) |
| 5 | 19 N 18 | — | (a), (b) trapezoids; (c) lgth. 6.5 cm, diam. 1.1 cm; (d) double conoid; (e), (f), and (g) ball-shaped; (h) large ball-shaped; (i) and (j) cylindrical; (k) etched ring-shaped, (l) ring-shaped; (m) and (n) date-shaped; (o) and (p) diamond-shaped; (q) rectangular; (r) ovoid; (s) hematite ovoid | Necklace, 63 beads: 3 long double-conoid carnelian, 17 double-conoid lapis, 1 date-shaped lapis, 1 date-shaped dark green stone, 4 ring-shaped lapis, 2 ring-shaped carnelian (one etched and filled with white paste), 8 cylindrical lapis, 1 cylindrical shell, 1 incised cylindrical lapis, 1 diamond lapis, one diamond gold foil-covered copper, 1 rectangular lapis, 1 ovoid lapis, 3 ball-shaped lapis, 1 ball-shaped carnelian, 10 ball-shaped copper/bronze, some with gold foil traces, 1 large ball-shaped clay, 1 hematite ovoid, unpierced, and 5 trapezoidal lapis spacers. (a) and (b) trapezoids; Woolley 1934: pl. 145, second from bottom; (c) long double conoid, Woolley 1934: pl. 131; (d) double conoid; (e), (f), and (g) ball-shaped; (h) large ball-shaped; (i) and (j) cylindrical; (k) etched ring-shaped, Kish: Mackay 1929: pl. 43: Group 6:4, Group 9: bottom; Ur: Woolley 1934: pl. 133 center, 134 top; (l) ring-shaped; (m) and (n) date-shaped; (o) and (p) diamond-shaped; (q) rectangular; (r) ovoid; (s) hematite ovoid |
| 6 | 19 N 25 | — | Lgth. 1.6 cm, diam. 0.9 cm | Bead, copper/bronze, cylindrical, traces of organic material inside |
| 7 | 19 N 136 | — | — | Inlaid box fragments. (a) knob handle; (b) B-shaped tab handle; (c) stepped square; (d) ziggurat-shaped; (e) hemisphere; (f) disc; (g) C-shaped; (h) teardrop; (i) rosette with central bronze nail; (j) rosette. Inlaid piece with comparable paste shapes from Nippur: McCown and Haines 1967: pl. 153:26. Individual inlay shapes are paralleled at Mari as parts of larger patches of inlay: Parrot 1956: fig. 93; Parrot 1959: figs. 76–77, pl. 34; Parrot 1967b: fig. 289:2704, 2706, 2711. Single stepped square in shell from Tepe Gawra: Speiser 1935: pl. 53:b, 4. Ur: oval wood box with red paste inlay in PG/730, a patch of inlay in bone and paste with a border of thin strips in PG/556, and other examples in PG/543, 556, 645, and 695 (Woolley 1934: 385–86, pl. 222) |

Plate 146

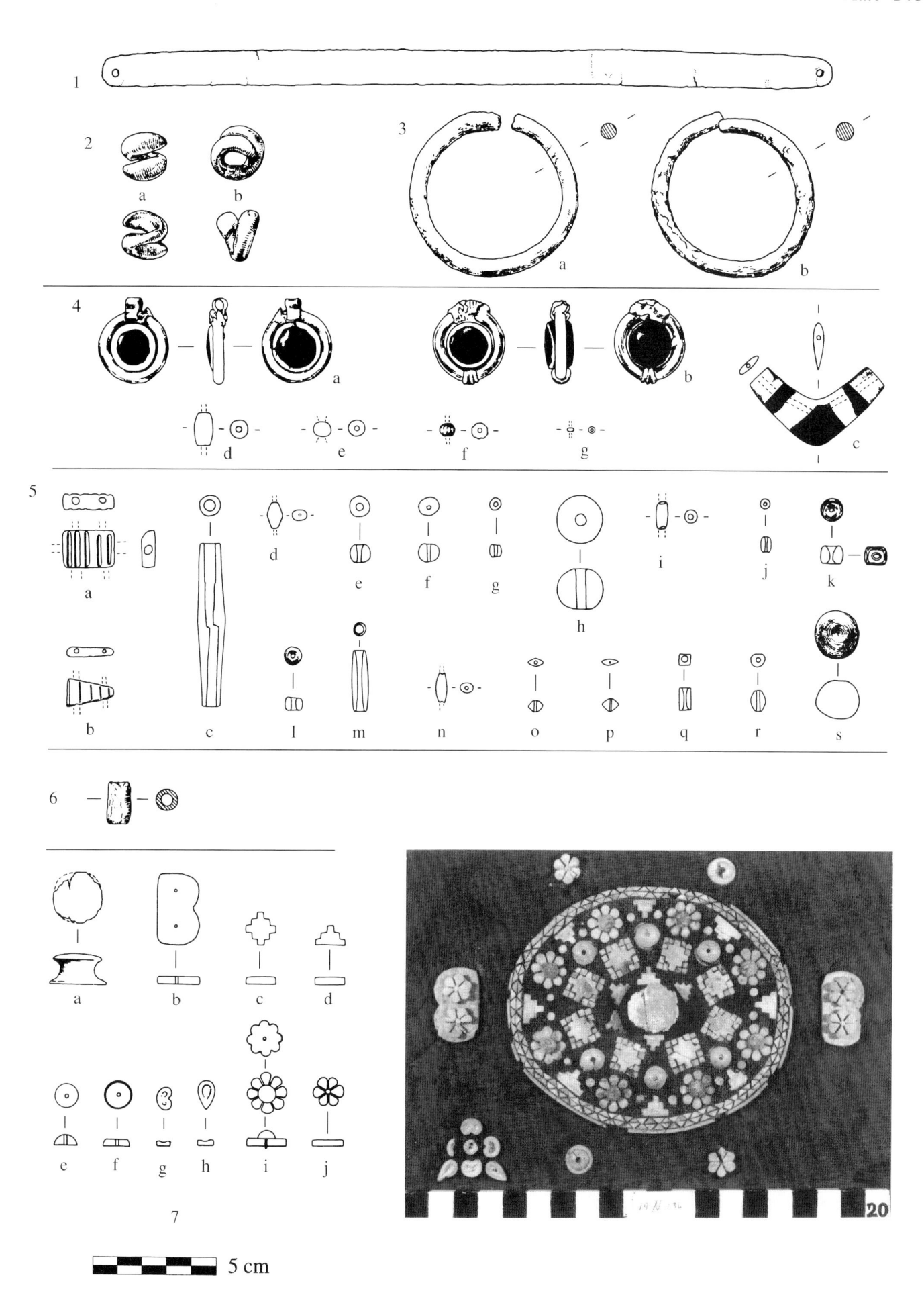

Third-millennium B.C. Grave Group, Burial 14, Skeleton 2. Scale 1:2

Plate 147. Third-millennium B.C. Grave Group, Burial 14, Skeleton 2 (*cont.*)

|    | Lot Number | Form | Dimension | Description |
|----|------------|------|-----------|-------------|
| BURIAL 14, SKELETON 2, LEVEL XIIIA–C ||||
| 1  | I332:2  | O-1 | Rim diam. 16.2 cm, base diam. 5.4 cm, ht. 5.3 cm | Pale red, sand temper |
| 2  | I338:1  | O-1 | Rim diam. 16.0 cm, base diam. 4.4 cm, ht. 4.9 cm | Pink, cream surface, sand temper |
| 3  | I338:3  | O-1 | Rim diam. 16.0 cm, base diam. 6.0 cm, ht. 4.4 cm | Pale red, buff cream surface, sand temper |
| 4  | 19 N 50 | O-1 | Rim diam. 15.8 cm, base diam. 5.2 cm, ht. 5.5 cm | Pale red, pink surface, sand temper. String-cut base |
| 5  | 19 N 32 | O-1 | Rim diam. 15.7 cm, base diam. 4.4 cm, ht. 4.7 cm | Pale pink, sand temper. String-cut base |
| 6  | I338:2  | O-1 | Rim diam. 15.3 cm, base diam. 4.8 cm, ht. 5.5 cm | Pink, sand temper |
| 7  | I184    | O-1 | Rim diam. 15.1 cm, base diam. 4.7 cm, ht. 5.7 cm | Pale red, sand temper |
| 8  | I338:4  | O-1 | Rim diam. 14.5 cm, base diam. 4.4 cm, ht. 4.3 cm | Pink, sand temper |
| 9  | 19 N 49 | O-1 | Rim diam. 14.2 cm, base diam. 4.1 cm, ht. 4.7 cm | Pale red, sand temper. String-cut base |
| 10 | I332:1  | O-1 | Rim diam. 13.4 cm, base diam. 3.9 cm, ht. 4.3 cm | Pale red, cream pink surface, sand temper |

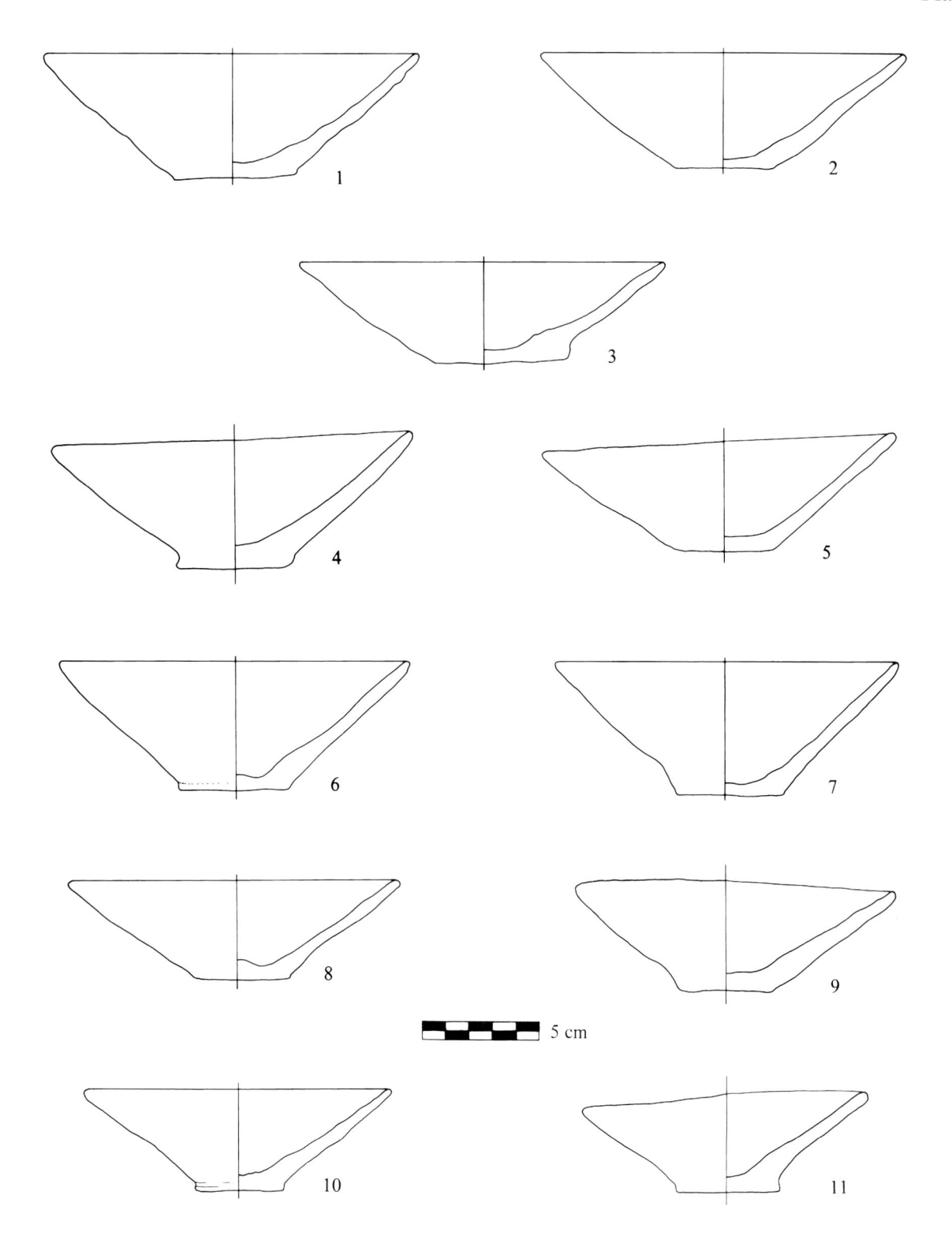

Plate 147

Third-millennium B.C. Grave Group, Burial 14, Skeleton 2 (*cont.*). Scale 2:5

Plate 148. Third-millennium B.C. Grave Group, Burial 14, Skeleton 2 (*cont.*)

|   | Lot Number | Form | Dimension | Description/Comparison |
|---|---|---|---|---|
| **BURIAL 14, SKELETON 2, LEVEL XIIIA–C** | | | | |
| 1 | 19 N 48 | O-10 | Rim diam. 15.2 cm, base diam. 5.0 cm, ht. 4.6 cm | Pink, sand temper. String-cut base |
| 2 | I338:5 | O-10 | Rim diam. 14.3 cm, base diam. 4.3 cm, ht. 4.3 cm | Pale red, pink cream surface, sand temper |
| 3 | I338:6 | O-10 | Rim diam. 13.9 cm, base diam. 4.3 cm, ht. 4.3 cm | Pale red, pink cream surface, sand temper |
| 4 | I338:7 | O-12 | Rim diam. 14.5 cm, base diam. 4.8 cm, ht. 4.0 cm | Pale red, sand temper |
| 5 | 19 N 31 | O-10 | Rim diam. 13.9 cm, base diam. 4.0 cm, ht. 4.5 cm | Red, cream pink surface, sand temper. String-cut base |
| 6 | I159/315 | C-16b | Rim diam. 11.7 cm, max. diam. 25.8 cm, base diam. 11.2 cm, ht. 34.0 cm | Dark red, friable ware, pale red surface, sand temper. Horizontal ridges on shoulder and near base. For the additional set of ridges near the base, see Diyala: Delougaz 1952: D.514.362 (ED III); Abu Salabikh: Moon 1987: 706 (ED IIIa early); Tell Abqa': Trumpelmann 1982: fig. 8 (Akk.) |
| 7 | 19 N 19 | — | Box rim diam. 6.8 cm, box base diam. 7.5 cm, box ht. 4.0 cm, lid diam. 7.2 cm, lid ht. 3.2 cm | Box and lid, copper/bronze. Handle made in one piece with lid. Müller-Karpe 1993: form 46 I; Ur: Woolley 1934: pl. 240: type 110 |
| 8 | 19 N 9 | — | Rim diam. 9.2 cm, ht. 5.3 cm | Bowl, copper/bronze, hemispherical. Müller-Karpe 1993: form 9 I or 9 II; Kish: Mackay 1925: pl. 20:1, 3–4, 6; Susa: Tallon 1987: nos. 700, 702–13 (ED–Akk.); Tell Sabra: Tunca 1987: pl. 32:5 (ED III); Ur: Woolley 1934: pl. 232: type 3 (ED–Akk.) |
| 9 | 19 N 71 | — | Rim diam. 10.0 cm, ht. 6.2 cm | Bowl, copper/bronze, hemispherical. For comparisons, see 19 N 9 |

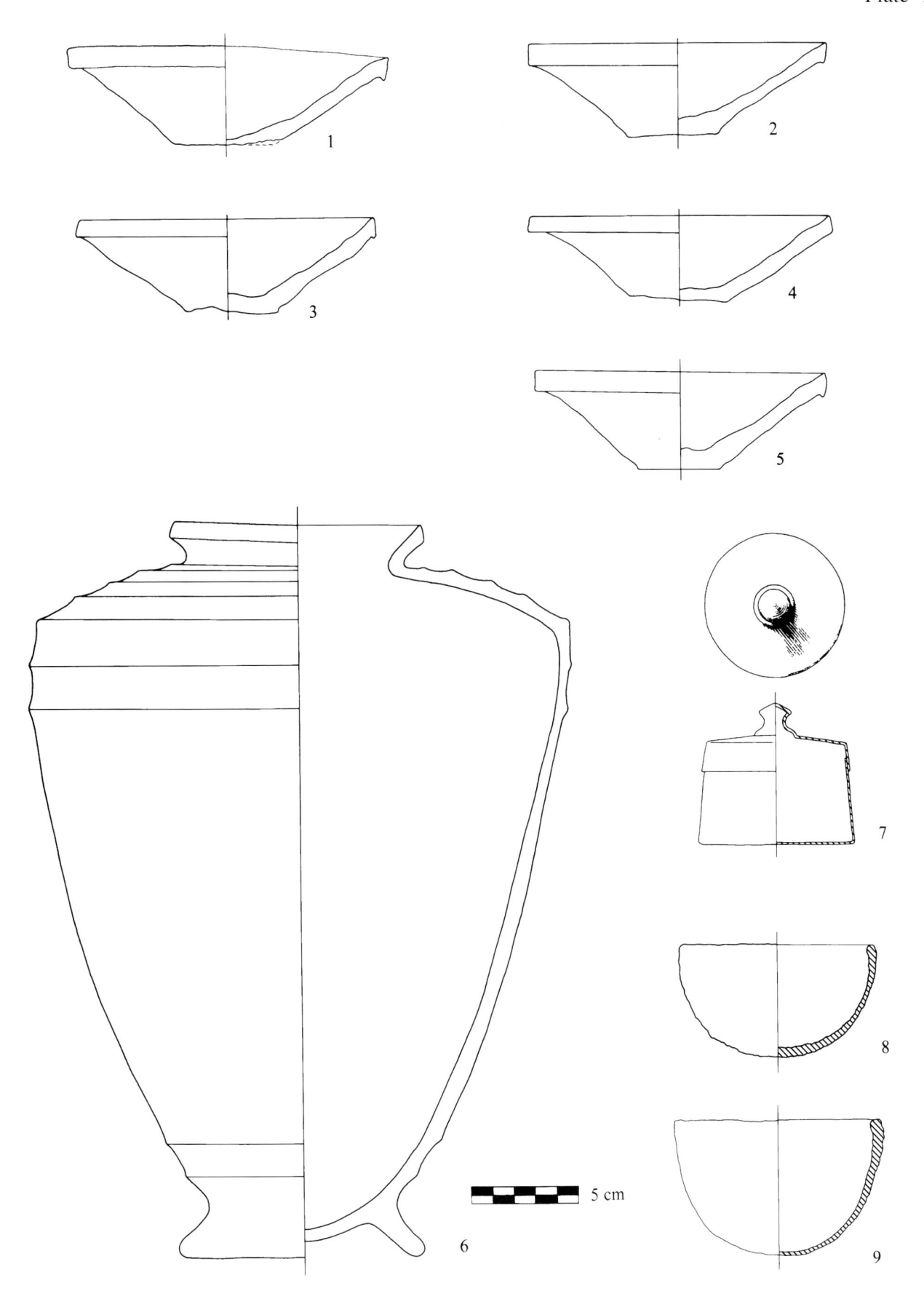

Plate 148

Third-millennium B.C. Grave Group, Burial 14, Skeleton 2 (*cont.*). Scale 2:5

Plate 149. Third-millennium B.C. Grave Group, Burial 14, Skeleton 2 (*cont.*)

| | Lot Number | Form | Dimension | Description |
|---|---|---|---|---|
| \multicolumn{5}{l}{BURIAL 14, SKELETON 2, LEVEL XIIIA–C} |
| 1 | 19 N 51 | C-20 Akkadian variant | Rim diam. 10.6 cm, max. diam. 21.0 cm, base diam. 8.4 cm, ht. 23.7 cm | Cream green, sand and light organic temper. Abu Salabikh: Moon 1987: 613 (post-ED); Ur: Woolley 1934: type 160 (late Akk.) |
| 2 | 19 N 35 | C-21 | Rim diam. 10.8 cm, max. diam. 13.8 cm, ht. 11.6 cm | Pale yellow, sand and light organic temper. Nippur: McCown and Haines 1967: pl. 80: 12 (Akk.); Kish: Mackay 1925: pl. 16:2; Mackay 1929: pl. 53:27, 34; Ur: Woolley 1934: type 83b, late ED through Ur III |
| 3 | 19 N 40 | C-21 | Rim diam. 11.7 cm, max. diam. 20.4 cm, ht. 18.9 cm. Larger version of 19 N 35 | Buff pale yellow, sand and light organic temper. Kish: Mackay 1925: pl. 16:4; Abu Salabikh: Martin, Moon, and Postgate 1985: grave 1:1, grave 61:15, grave 68:6 (ED III); Moon 1987: nos. 341–43 (ED III) |
| 4 | 19 N 53 | C-21 | Rim diam. 12.4 cm, max. diam. 18.5 cm, ht. 16.4 cm | Buff pale yellow, sand and light organic temper. For comparisons, see 19 N 40 |
| 5 | 19 N 73 | — | Rim diam. 10.6 cm, base diam. 8.7 cm, ht. 2.6 cm, handle lgth. 10.7 cm, handle w. 2.3–3.1 cm, handle th. 1.7–2.2 cm | Pan, copper/bronze. Solid handle, plano-convex in section, made in one piece with bowl. No exact parallels, but similar to Ur: Woolley 1934: pl. 240: type 118 (late ED) |

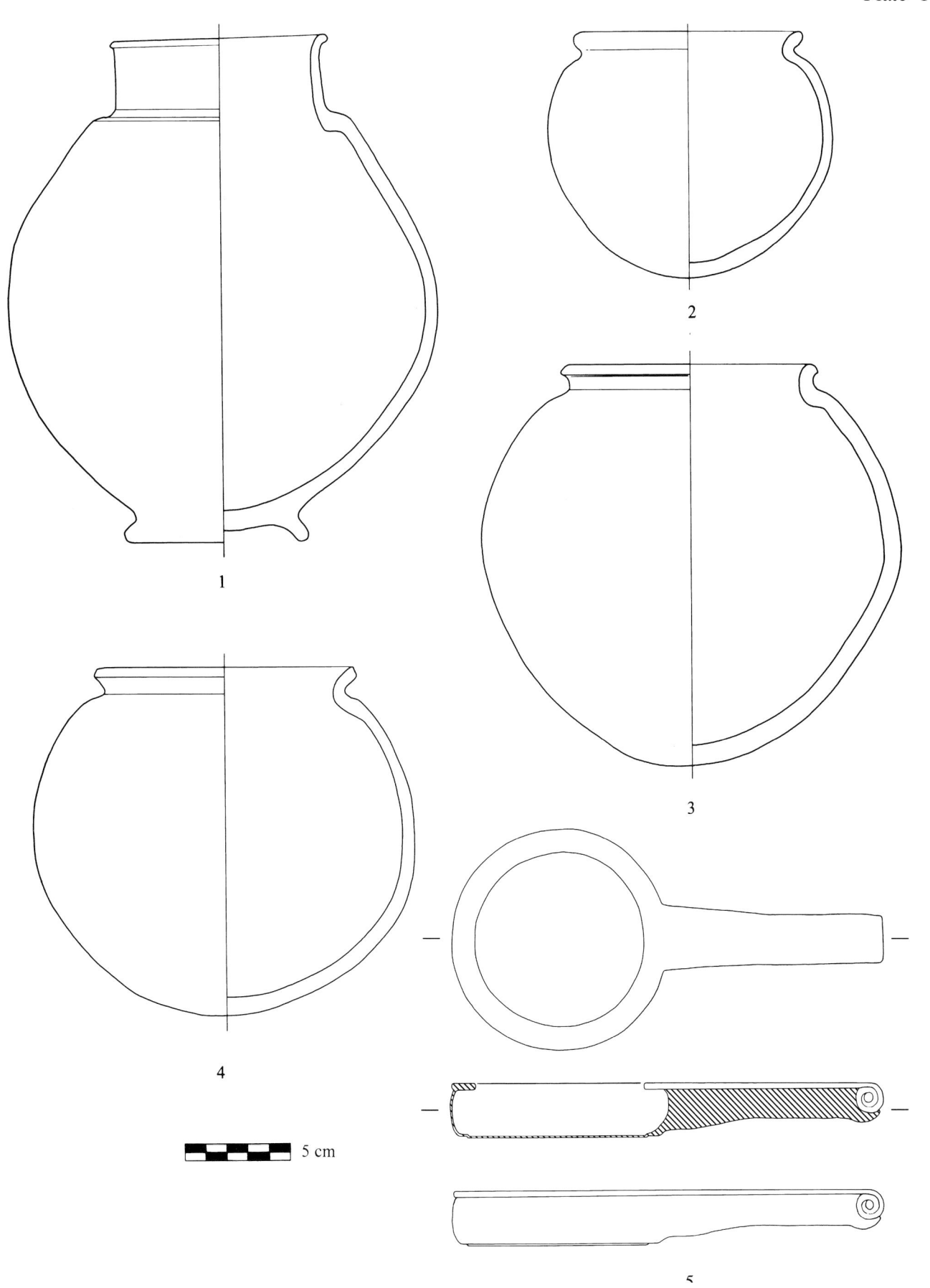

Plate 149

Third-millennium B.C. Grave Group, Burial 14, Skeleton 2 (*cont.*). Scale 2:5

Plate 150. Third-millennium B.C. Grave Group, Burial 14, Skeleton 2 (*cont.*)

| | Lot Number | Form | Dimension | Description |
|---|---|---|---|---|
| BURIAL 14, SKELETON 2, LEVEL XIIIA–C | | | | |
| 1 | 19 N 42 | C-13 | Rim diam. 9.3 cm, max. diam. 17.2 cm, ht. 30.0 cm | Greenish buff, sand and light organic temper |
| 2 | 19 N 47 | C-13 | Rim diam. 9.7 cm, max. diam. 17.0 cm, ht. 26.1 cm | Red, sand temper |
| 3 | 19 N 36 | — | Rim diam. 20.0 cm, max. diam. 29.0 cm, ht. 23.0 cm | Bucket, copper/bronze. Two loops riveted to side for handle attachment; the handle itself is missing. Base covered with ash. Müller-Karpe 1993: form 41 II a; Ur: Woolley 1934: pl. 184 b, right, pl. 235: type 50 (late ED–Akk.) |

Plate 150

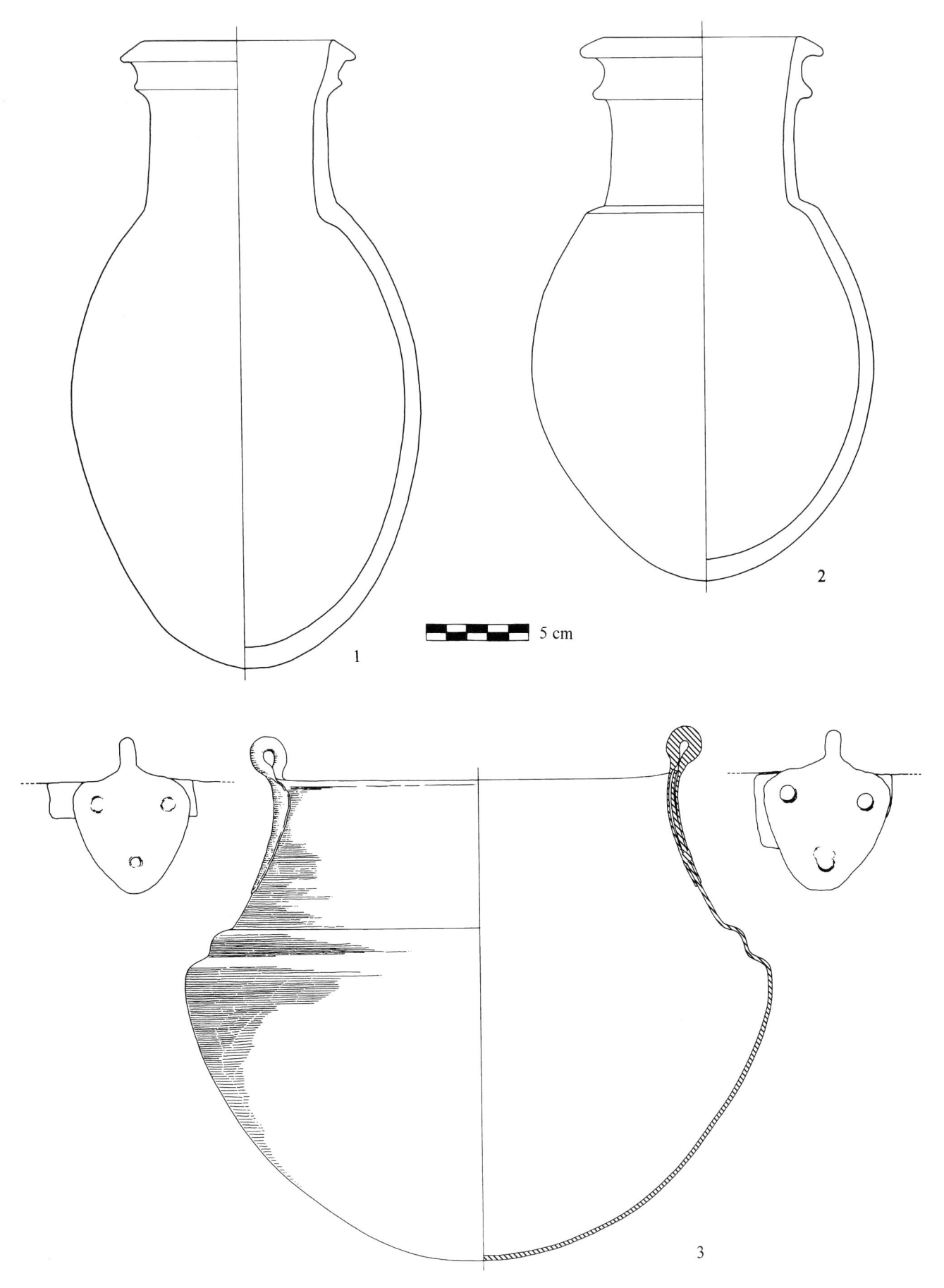

5 cm

Third-millennium B.C. Grave Group, Burial 14, Skeleton 2 (*cont.*). Scale 2:5

Plate 151. Third-millennium B.C. Grave Group, Burial 14, Skeleton 2 (*cont.*)

|   | *Lot Number* | *Form* | *Dimension* | *Description* |
|---|---|---|---|---|
| **BURIAL 14, SKELETON 2, LEVEL XIIIA–C** | | | | |
| 1 | 19 N 43 | C-22 | Rim diam. 12.0 cm, max. diam. 28.8 cm, base diam. 13.0 cm, ht. 31.3 cm. Hole 1.6 cm diam. in one side of base | Buff, sand and organic temper. Kish: Mackay 1929: pl. 54:6; Uch Tepe: Gibson 1981: pl. 96:2, 6 (but with ring bases, rather than convex), pl. 99:3 (also with a ring base) (early Akk.); Tell Madhhur: Roaf et al. 1984: fig. 12:3 (but with ring base and ridge at shoulder); fig. 13:3a (more elongated than 19 N 43) (early Akk.) |
| 2 | 19 N 5 | — | Lgth. 24.5 cm, max. th. 1.3 cm | Pin, copper/bronze, originally straight though now slightly warped, round cross section, laterally pierced. Kish: Mackay 1925: pl. 4:1, 2; Mackay 1929: pl. 58:11; Uruk: van Ess and Pedde 1992: pl. 31:215; Ur: similar to Woolley 1934: pl. 231, type 1 (ED), but without the tang and bead |
| 3 | 19 N 103 | — | Rim diam. 22.5 cm, base diam. 11.1 cm, ht. 6.5 cm, handle lgth. 16.5 cm, handle w. 1.6–2.5 cm, handle th. 2.0–1.1 cm | Pan, copper/bronze. Trough-sectioned handle made in one piece with the bowl. Müller-Karpe 1993: form 42 II; Kish: Mackay 1925: pl. 20:9; Mackay 1929: pl. 43:4, pl. 57:11; Tepe Gawra: Speiser 1935: pl. 51, b (ED–Akk.); Ur: Woolley 1934: pl. 238, type 87 (ED) |

Plate 151

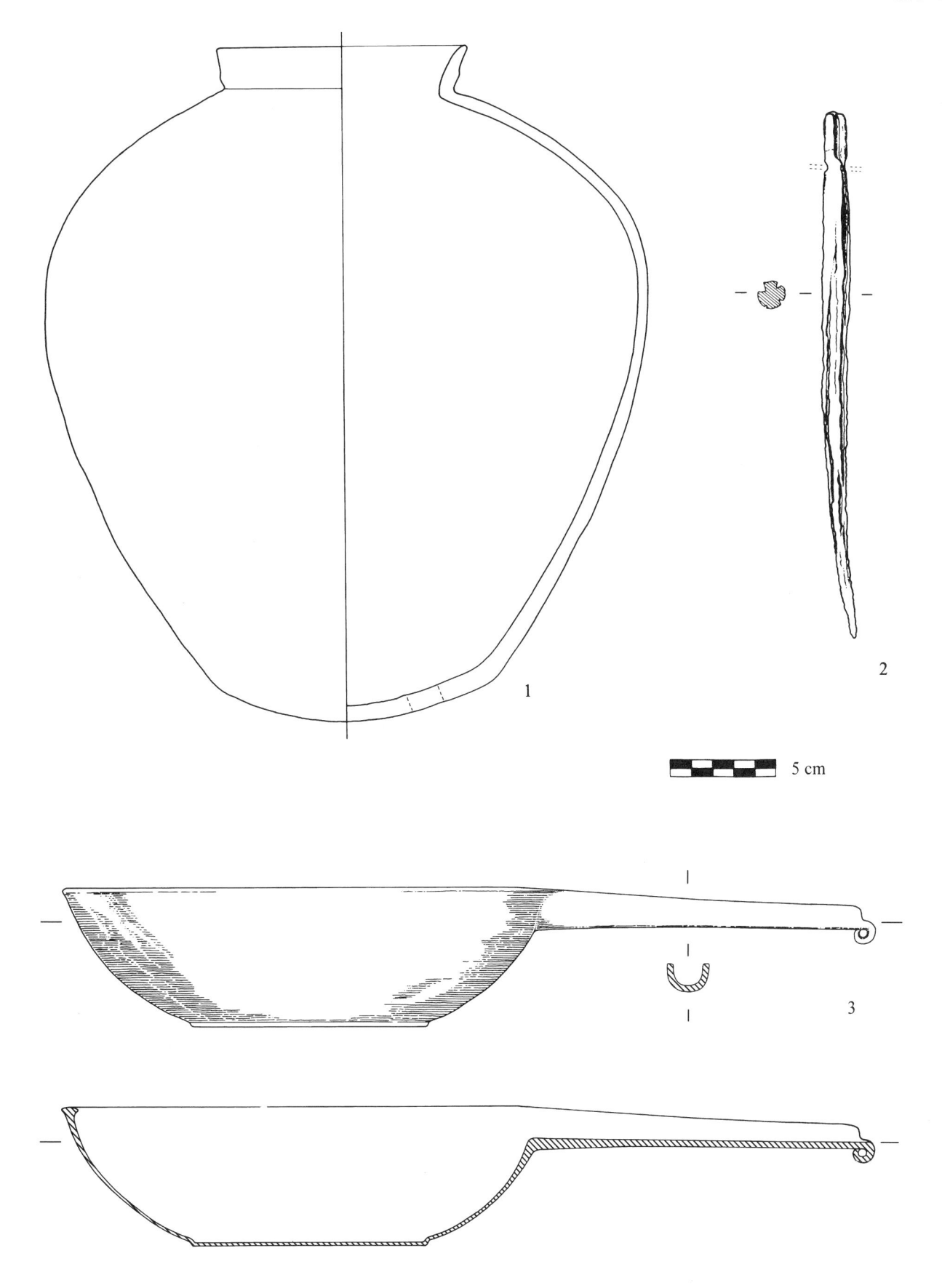

1

2

5 cm

3

Third-millennium B.C. Grave Group, Burial 14, Skeleton 2 (*cont.*). Scale 2:5

Plate 152. Third-millennium B.C. Grave Group, Burial 14, Skeleton 1

|   | Lot Number | Dimension | Description/Comparison |
|---|---|---|---|
| BURIAL 14, SKELETON 1, LEVEL XIIB | | | |
| 1 | 18 N 176 | Lgth. 18.5 cm, max. w. 2.0 cm, max. th. 0.6 cm | Spear point, copper/bronze. Traces of wood handle. Ur: Woolley 1934: pl. 227: type 6 (Akk.) |
| 2 | 18 N 177 | Ht. 10.1 cm, lgth. 12.3 cm, shaft hole diam. 2.8 cm | Ax, copper/bronze. Solid head, traces of wood handle inside shaft hole. Identical to 18 N 171, Level XIIB. Susa: Tallon 1987: nos. 1–18 (late ED–Akk.); Ur: Woolley 1934: pl. 224, U.12484 (Akk.–Ur III) (= Nissen 1966: type A 17, Akk.–Ur III) |
| 3 | 18 N 188 | Lgth. 19.0 cm, diam. 0.4–0.9 cm | Pin, copper/bronze, straight, round cross section |
| 4 | 19 N 6c | Lgth. 8.5 cm, diam. 0.7 cm | Pin, copper/bronze, straight, round cross section, flattened ends |
| 5 | 19 N 6a | Lgth. 11.7 cm, w. 1.9 cm | Dagger, copper/bronze, leaf shaped. Kish: Mackay 1929: pl. 62:20; Abu Salabikh: Martin, Moon, and Postgate 1985: grave 51:13, grave 84:7 (ED IIIb); Ur: Woolley 1934: pl. 228, no. 7a (late ED–Akk.) |
| 6 | 19 N 6b | Lgth. 11.2 cm, w. 2.0 cm | Dagger, copper/bronze, leaf-shaped. For comparisons, see 19 N 6a |
| 7 | 18 N 178 | Lgth. 5.7 cm, diam. 0.5 cm | Pin, copper/bronze, straight, round cross section, flattened ends |
| 8 | 18 N 179 | Lgth. 5.4 cm, diam. 0.5 cm | Pin, copper/bronze, straight, round cross section, flattened ends |
| 9 | 18 N 186 | Lgth. 5.3 cm, max. diam. 0.9 cm | Filter for straw end, copper/bronze. Conical foil tube with vertical rows of perforations, coil of wire around open end for attachment to reed straw, traces of reed inside. Hammam et-Turkman: de Feyter 1988: pl. 190:8–9; Tell Brak: Philip 1997: fig. 144, fig. 235:61, 63; Tell ed-Der: Gasche 1989: pl. 42:2; Chagar Bazar: Mallowan 1937: pl. 14, unpublished examples from 1999–2001 excavations in early second-millennium B.C. levels |
| 10 | 18 N 175 | Lgth. 20.0 cm, band w. 0.8 cm, oval w. 1.8 cm | Fillet, gold. Oval end lightly embossed with cross-hatched lines |
| 11 | 18 N 194 | Diam. 0.4 cm | Bead, lapis lazuli, ball shaped |
| 12 | 19 N 8 | Ht. 0.8 cm, w. ca. 1.8 cm | Fitting, gold. Wire with double herringbone pattern, gold foil strip attached. Part of a ring, a fitting for holding a stone, or a bead; see Ur: Woolley 1934: pl. 138:U.9779, pl. 146:U.9657 |

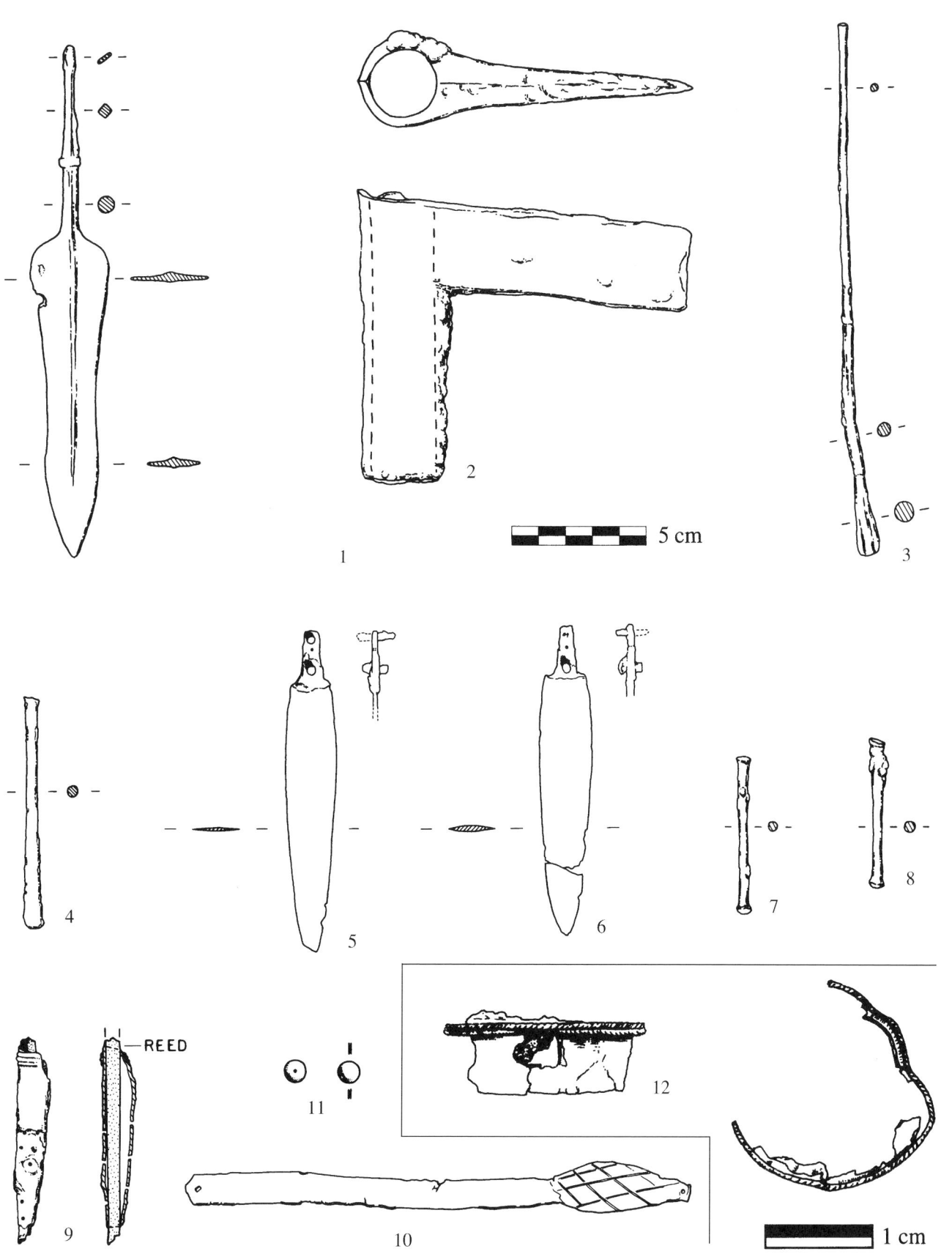

Plate 152

Third-millennium B.C. Grave Group, Burial 14, Skeleton 1. Scales (*1–11*) 1:2 and (*12*) 2:1

Plate 153. Third-millennium B.C. Grave Group, Burial 14, Skeleton 1 (*cont.*)

|   | Lot Number | Form | Dimension | Description |
|---|---|---|---|---|
| **BURIAL 14, SKELETON 1, LEVEL XIIB** | | | | |
| 1 | H1118 | O-1 | Rim diam. 15.0 cm, base diam. 5.5 cm, ht. 5.0 cm | Buff pink, sand and light organic temper |
| 2 | 19 N 10 | O-1 | Rim diam. 13.3 cm, base diam. 4.3 cm, ht. 4.9 cm | Pale pink, sand temper. String-cut base |
| 3 | I36 | O-1 | Rim diam. 13.0 cm, base diam. 5.0 cm, ht. 6.2 cm | Buff, cream surface, sand temper |
| 4 | H1121 | O-1 | Rim diam. 11.9 cm, base diam. 4.0 cm, ht. 4.0 cm | Pink buff, sand and light organic temper |
| 5 | H1120 | O-1 | Rim diam. 11.0 cm, base diam. 4.5 cm, ht. 3.0 cm | Buff pink, sand and light organic temper |
| 6 | H1119 | O-1 | Rim diam. 10.5 cm, base diam. 3.6 cm, ht. 2.7 cm | Buff pink, sand and light organic temper |
| 7 | I107 | O-12 | Rim diam. 16.1 cm, base diam. 5.2 cm, ht. 4.7 cm | Pink, cream surface, sand and light organic temper |
| 8 | H1123 | O-11 | Rim diam. 15.8 cm, base diam. 5.8 cm, ht. 3.7 cm | Dark buff, sand and light organic temper |
| 9 | I102 | O-12 | Rim diam. 14.2 cm, base diam. 4.8 cm, ht. 5.7 cm | Cream pink, sand and light organic temper |
| 10 | I106 | O-10 | Rim diam. 14.5 cm, base diam. 5.6 cm, ht. 5.7 cm | Buff cream, sand temper |
| 11 | I109 | O-10 | Rim diam. 14.3 cm, base diam. 4.3 cm, ht. 5.7 cm | Cream pink, sand temper |
| 12 | H1122 | O-10 | Rim diam. 12.8 cm, base diam. 5.0 cm, ht. 4.2 cm | Buff, sand and light organic temper |

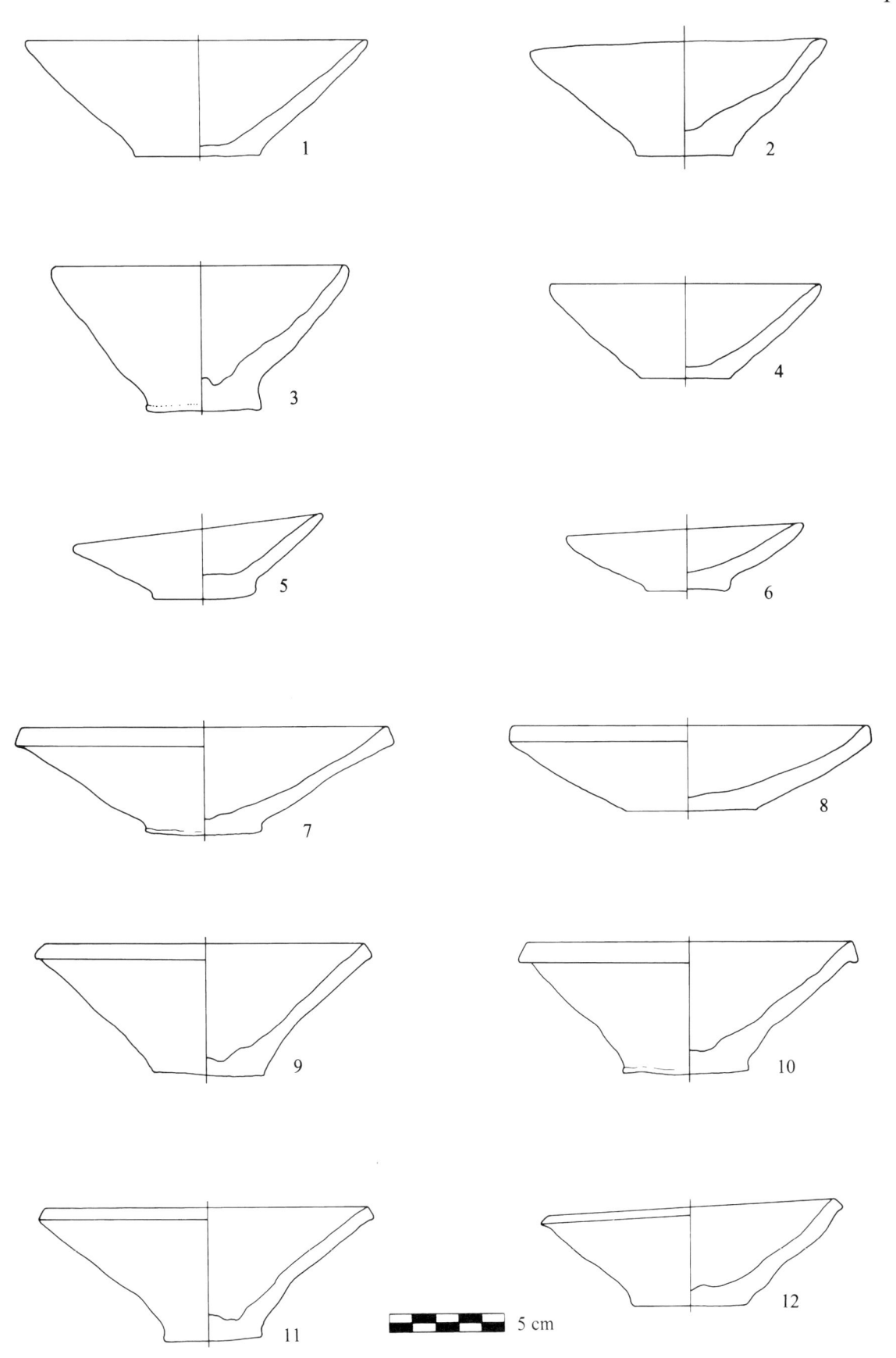

Plate 153

Third-millennium B.C. Grave Group, Burial 14, Skeleton 1 (*cont.*). Scale 2:5

Plate 154. Third-millennium B.C. Grave Group, Burial 14, Skeleton 1 (cont.)

| | Lot Number | Form | Dimension | Description/Comparison |
|---|---|---|---|---|
| BURIAL 14, SKELETON 1, LEVEL XIIB | | | | |
| 1 | I40/103 | C-24 | Rim diam. 10.5 cm, max. diam. 19.4 cm, base diam. 11.4 cm, ht. 33.7 cm | Dark red, pink cream surface, sand temper. Bismaya: Banks 1912: 175 far right |
| 2 | 18 N 187 | C-24 | Rim diam. 10.0 cm, max. diam. 14.4 cm, ht. 25.0 cm | Red pink, sand temper. Separately applied ring base now missing. Nippur: Gibson 1975: fig. 67:2 (Akk.); Kish: Mackay 1929: pl. 53:41; Bismaya: Banks 1912: 175, three examples; Abu Salabikh: Martin, Moon, and Postgate 1985: grave 32:10 (ED IIIb); Moon 1987: nos. 407, 421 (ED III); Ur: Woolley 1934: types 60, 62, and 142 (ED–late Akk.) |
| 3 | H1111 | C-24 | Rim diam. 10.2 cm, max. diam. 12.3 cm, ht. 20.0 cm | Red, vertically burnished exterior, sand temper |
| 4 | H1124 | C-16a | Rim diam. 8.0 cm, max. diam. 17.6 cm, base diam. 11.8 cm, ht. 21.6 cm | Dark red, brittle ware, pink surface, sand and light organic temper |

Plate 154

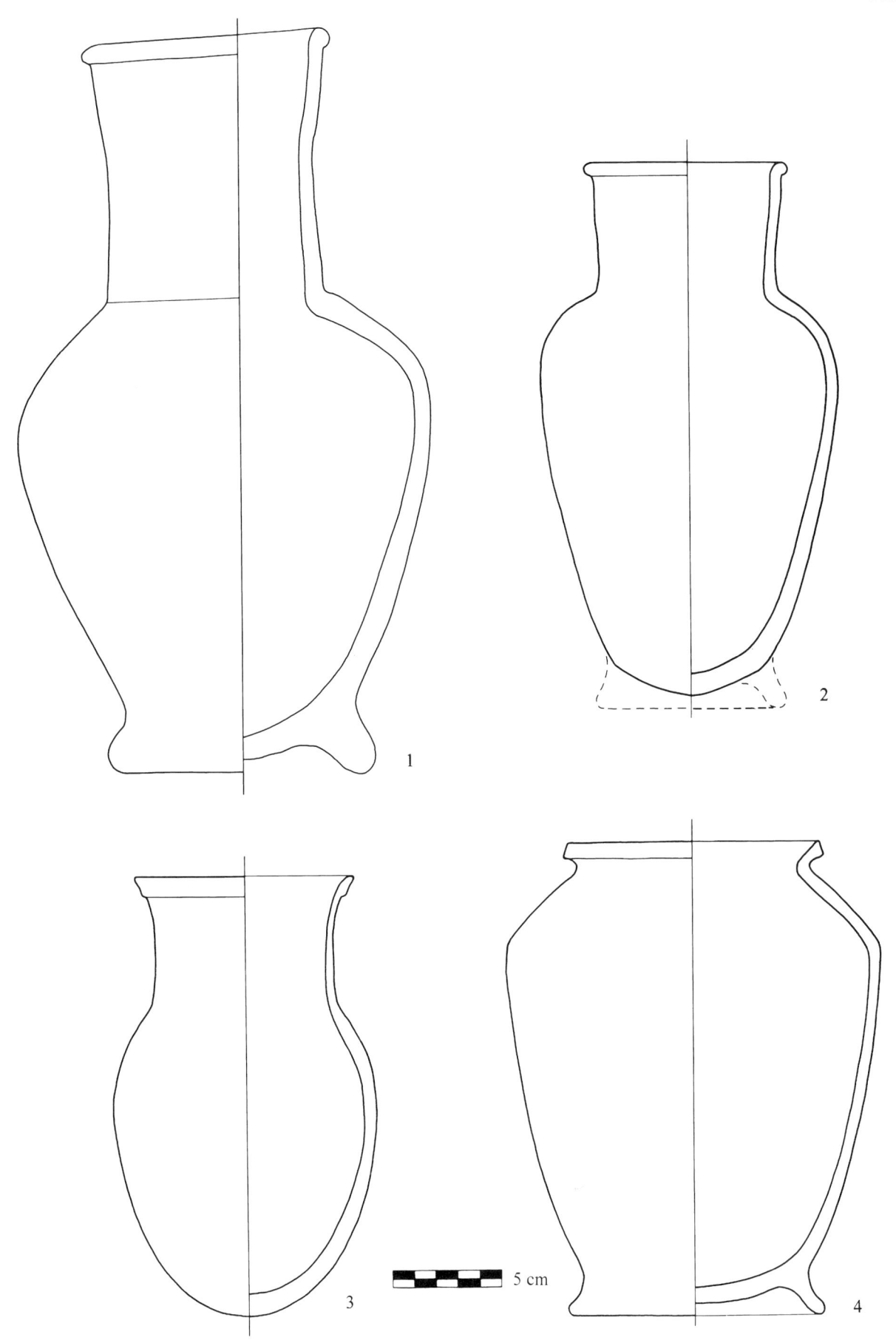

Third-millennium B.C. Grave Group, Burial 14, Skeleton 1. Scale 2:5

Plate 155. Third-millennium B.C. Grave Group, Burial 14, Skeleton 1 (*cont.*)

|   | *Lot Number* | *Form* | *Dimension* | *Description/Comparison* |
|---|---|---|---|---|
| BURIAL 14, SKELETON 1, LEVEL XIIB | | | | |
| 1 | H1109 | C-22 | Rim diam. 13.6 cm, max. diam. 31.0 cm, ht. 39.2 cm. Scale 1:5 | Buff yellowish green, sand and light organic temper |
| 2 | I105 | C-22 | Rim diam. 11.0 cm, max. diam. 28.0 cm, base diam. 13.0 cm, ht. 34.1 cm. Scale 1:5 | Greenish buff, sand and light organic temper |
| 3 | I104 | C-22 | Rim diam. 11.0 cm, max. diam. 30.8 cm, base diam. 13.7 cm, ht. 38.5 cm. Scale 1:5 | Dark red, sand and light organic temper |
| 4 | 18 N 180 | — | Rim diam. 26.5 cm, ht. 7.0 cm, wall th. 0.2 cm | Pan, copper/bronze. Circular, everted rim, raised base made from separate sheet of metal. Müller-Karpe 1993: form 33 II; Ur: Woolley 1934: pl. 233, Type 20, but with a flat base (late ED–Ur III) |
| 5 | 18 N 185 | — | — | Footed bowl with long trough spout/handle, copper/bronze. Lower edge rolled under to form a foot, base made from separate sheet of metal. Müller-Karpe 1993: form 4 VII a–b; Ur: Woolley 1934: pl. 164: U.10451, type 88 (ED), but with different base and more slanted sides; Susa: Carter 1980: fig. 6 (ca. 2600 B.C.); Tallon 1987: 780–83 (twenty-fifth century B.C.) |

Plate 155

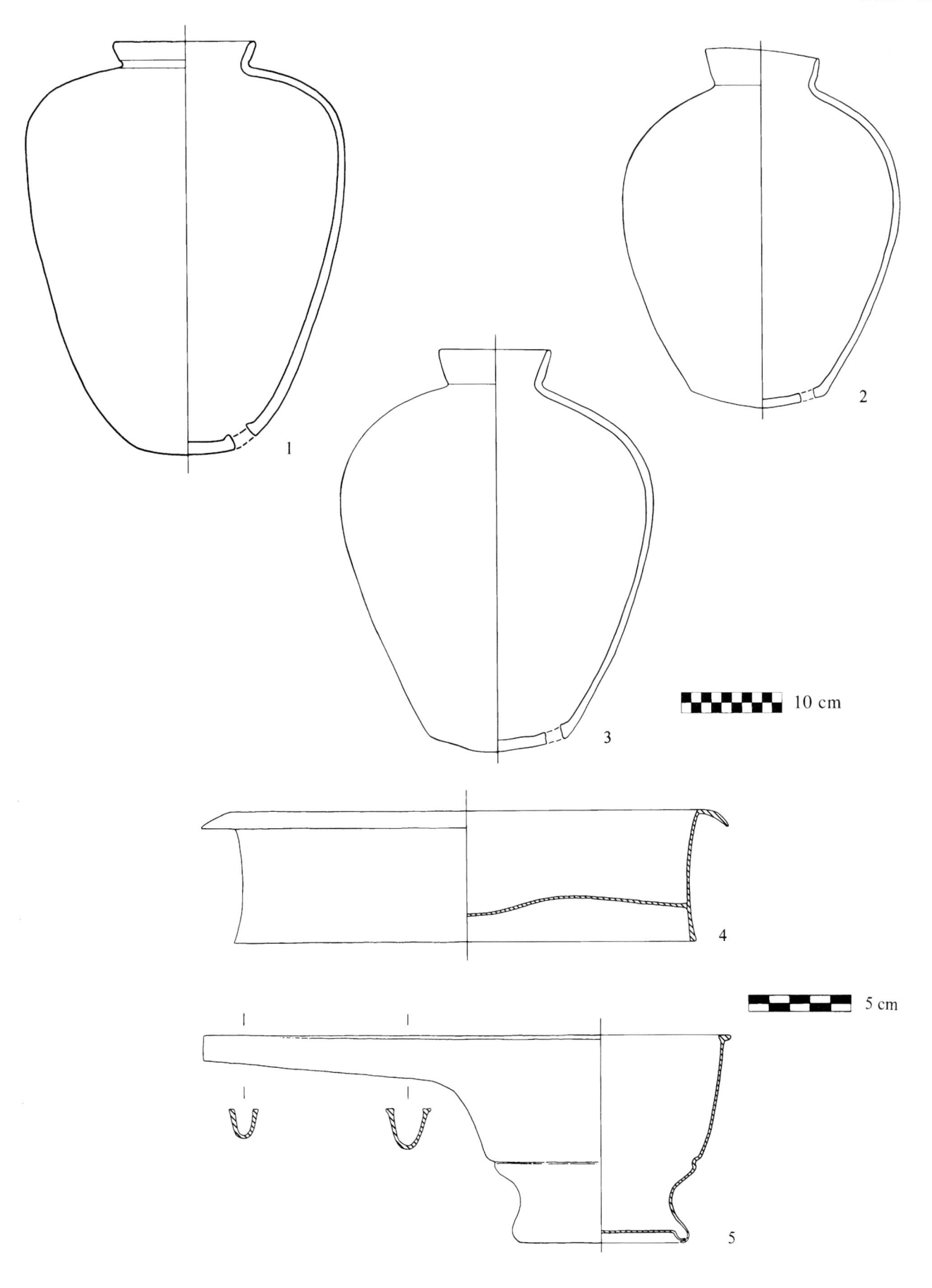

Third-millennium B.C. Grave Group, Burial 14, Skeleton 1 (*cont.*). Scales (*1–3*) 1:5 and (*4–5*) 2:5

Plate 156. Third-millennium B.C. Grave Group, Burial 14, Skeleton 1 (*cont.*)

| | *Lot Number* | *Form* | *Dimension* | *Description/Comparison* |
|---|---|---|---|---|
| BURIAL 14, SKELETON 1, LEVEL XIIB | | | | |
| 1 | 18 N 183 | — | Rim diam. ca. 21.0 cm, ht. ca. 17.0 cm | Pan, copper/bronze. Circular, raised base made from separate sheet of metal. Trough spout and bent loop handle on opposite sides. Similar to Müller-Karpe 1993: forms 33 III and 33 IV and 40; Ur: Woolley 1934: pl. 233, type 19 (Akk.–Ur III) |
| 2 | 18 N 184 | — | Rim diam. 14.5 cm, max. diam. 22.5 cm, ht. 16.5 cm | Bucket, copper/bronze. Müller-Karpe 1993: form 41 II a; Ur: Woolley 1934: pl. 235, type 50 for vessel shape, type 46 for handle attachment; also pl. 184b, right side (ED–Akk.); Susa: Tallon 1987: 779 |
| 3 | 18 N 181 | — | Rim diam. ca. 11.0 cm, ht. ca. 6.0 cm | Bowl, copper/bronze, hemispherical. Kish: Mackay 1925: pl. 20:1, 3–4, 6; Ur: Woolley 1934: pl. 232, type 3 (ED–Akk.); Susa: Tallon 1987: nos. 700, 702–13 (ED–Akk.) |
| 4 | 18 N 182 | — | Rim diam. ca. 9.0 cm, ht. ca. 5.5 cm | Bowl, copper/bronze, hemispherical. For comparisons, see 18 N 181 |

Plate 156

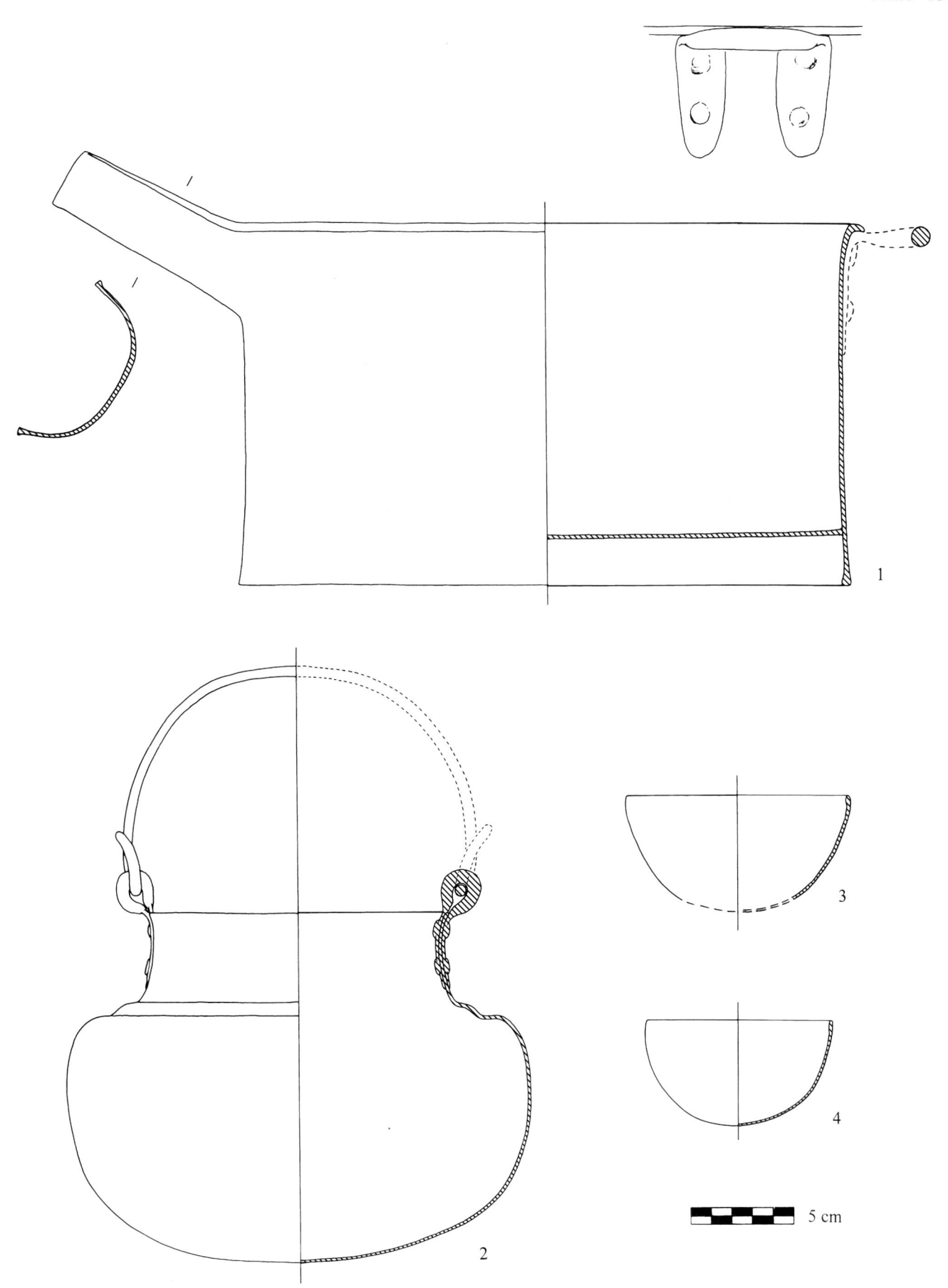

Third-millennium B.C. Grave Group, Burial 14, Skeleton 1 (*cont.*). Scale 2:5

Plate 157. Cylinder Seals, Burial 14, Skeleton 1

| | Lot Number | Dimension | Description/Comparison |
|---|---|---|---|
| | | | |

BURIAL 14, SKELETON 1, LEVEL XIIB

1  18 N 173  Diam. 2.1 cm, ht. 3.4 cm  Translucent white rock crystal with red inclusions. Left to right: two nude six-locked heroes battling addorsed water buffaloes, bull-man thrusting dagger into lion. Inscription same as 18 N 174 (see below). Traces of recutting between legs of bull-man and above tail of lion.

"Akkadisch III" in style; for comparable style and detailing, see Boehmer 1965: especially no. 134, and nos. 152, 163, 165, 175, 178, 191, 202; Buchanan 1981: nos. 417–19, 421, 424; Collon 1982: nos. 10–11, 17–24, 33 et passim, especially 79–80, 83–91, 98, 117; Collon 1987: figs. 98–99; Woolley 1934: pl. 205:168, 181, pl. 209:236–40, pl. 216:372.

2  18 N 174  Diam. 1.9 cm, ht. 3.2 cm  Blue-green marble-like stone with white veins. Left to right: standing human male, facing right, left hand before his face; god with whip and leash standing on lion-griffin that spews fire; god with crescent moon between horns of his crown, ax over right shoulder, standing between mountains, greeting seated god; standard with hoofed feet and staff topped with a mace-head, from which hangs a sandal(?). Double-line inscription: Lugal DÚR, DUB-SAR, "Lugal-Dur, the scribe"; small horned animal in the field below.

The style is Boehmer's Akkadisch III (Naram-Sin or later) and the carving is excellent, comparable to that of royally commissioned "official" seals describing the bearer as "servant" of a king. For the crescent moon above the first standing deity's crown, see Boehmer 1965: pls. 62–63, fig. 275 (Tello), pl. 63, fig. 726 = Legrain 1951: no. 295 (Ur).

For the "sandal" hanging from the standard, see McCown and Haines 1967: pl. 119:11–13 (reconstructed here as pl. 158:1); Woolley 1934: pl. 206:198; (= Boehmer 1965: pl. 46, fig. 548, and Rashid and al-Huri 1982: no. 19), plus Legrain 1951: pl. 17:243; Buchanan 1981: no. 443.

For the deity on the lion-griffin, see Boehmer 1965: nos. 362–74, especially 371; Buchanan 1981: no. 452; Collon 1982: nos. 137, 192, 364–65; Legrain 1951: pl. 7:92.

Plate 157

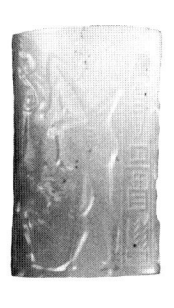

Cylinder Seals, Burial 14, Skeleton 1. Drawings at 2:1, Photographs at 1:1

Plate 158. Cylinder Seals from Burial 14, Skeleton 2, and from Level XVIII

| | Lot Number | Dimension | Description/Comparison |
|---|---|---|---|
| | | | |

BURIAL 14, SKELETON 2, LEVEL XIIIA–C

1    19 N 26    Diam. 1.7 cm, ht. 3.0 cm    Lapis lazuli. Left to right: nude hero battling bull, rampant lion versus bull-man. Blank area between the hero and bull man where inscription was erased; faint unreadable traces of inscription remain. Erasure removed the adjacent ear of the bull-man and curls of the hero.

    Compare Boehmer 1965: pl. 13:137–38, 141, 144 (Akk. II), pl. 15:160–66 (Akk. III), pl. 16:173–80 (Akk. III); Buchanan 1981: nos. 417–21, 424; Gibson et al. 1978: fig. 9:1; Moortgat 1966: pl. 26:179–80, 183–84; Woolley 1934: pl. 205: especially 182, pl. 209:236–38, pl. 212:316, pl. 213:318–19, pl. 216:372–73.

LEVEL XVIII

2    19 N 108    Diam. 2.1 cm, ht. 2.6 cm    Translucent pale green stone. Two horned "masters of animals," each facing right, one holding an inverted goat by the horn with each hand, the other holding a rampant bull by the beard with each hand.

    Early Dynastic II style, Amiet 1961: pl. 65:869, 872, pl. 66:885, pl. 67:892, pl. 72 bis, c; Buchanan 1981: no. 260–61; McCown, Haines, and Biggs 1978: pl. 63:6; Moortgat 1966: pl. 13:79–80, pl. 14:83; Woolley 1934: pl. 195:43, pl. 201:111.

Plate 158

Cylinder Seals with Burial 14, Skeleton 2, and from Level XVIII. Scale: Drawings at 2:1, Photographs at 1:1

Plate 159. Sealings from Levels XIIB and XIIIB

|   | Lot Number | Location | Dimension | Description/Comparison |
|---|---|---|---|---|
| 1 | 18 N 109 | Level XIIB | Lgth. 5.3 cm, w. 4.4 cm, th. 2.0 cm | Sealing, unbaked clay. Obverse: two partial rollings of the same seal. Left to right: lion biting bull held on the opposite side by a hero, head in profile; bull-man versus hero; hero versus bull-man. Lower border of inscription frame, with small scorpion in space below it. Reverse: impression of a cylindrical object and cord.<br><br>Compare Amiet 1961: pl. 85, especially no. 1118, 1120; Boehmer 1965: fig. 2, 6–10; McCown and Haines 1967: pl. 64, especially 5–6; McCown, Haines, and Biggs 1978: pl. 117:3, 9–10; Woolley 1934: pl. 198:73, pl. 207:213, pl. 208:225 |
| 2 | 18 N 110 | Level XIIIB | Lgth. 3.3 cm, w. 3.7 cm, th. 1.4 cm | Sealing, unbaked clay. Obverse: single incomplete rolling of a "Royal Style" seal. Left to right: inverted lion held by the feet by bull-man, nude six-locked hero holding feet of inverted bull. Reverse: impression of cords and possibly some wrinkled material.<br><br>Boehmer's Akkadisch III (Naram-Sin and later); see Boehmer 1965: figs. 153–59, 223–31, 233–35, especially 228, 230; Collon 1982: nos. 105, 121–25; Frankfort 1955: nos. 396, 670; Woolley 1934: pl. 205:180–81, for carving style, also pl. 209:249–50, pl. 213:317, pl. 213:321, 323 |

Plate 159

Sealings from Levels XIIB and XIIIB. Scale 1:1

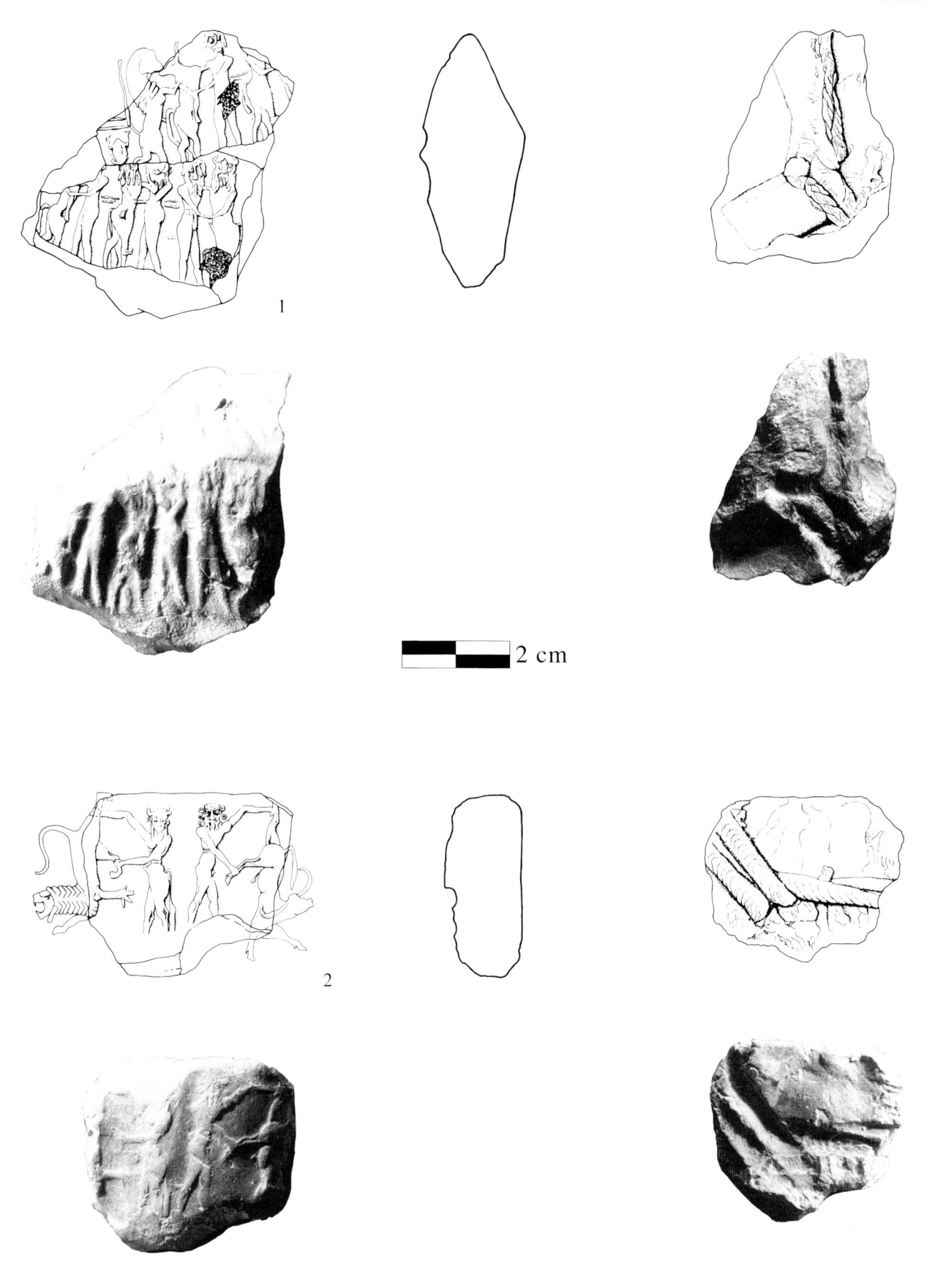

Plate 160. Cylinder Seals, Stamp Seals, and Scarab, Non-burial

|   | Lot Number | Location | Dimension | Description/Comparison |
|---|---|---|---|---|
| 1 | 18 N 111 | Level XIVA | Diam. 1.5 cm, ht. 2.2 cm | Cylinder seal, shell (conch core). Scene, from left to right: Shamash seated in "god-boat" holding steering oar, arms of god-boat hold punting pole; lion in front of boat, with two jars and plow in field above. Amiet 1961: nos. 1411–448, especially 1414, 1417, 1421, 1429; Boehmer 1965: figs. 474–75, (Akk. I b/c–II); Buchanan 1981: no. 346 (ED III); Buchanan 1966: no. 258; Frankfort 1955: especially nos. 331, 339, 516 (early Akk.); Mackay 1925: pl. 6:15; Mackay 1929:198, no. 2555 |
| 2 | 19 N 74 | Level XVB | Orig. diam. 2.0 cm, th. 0.9 cm | Stamp seal, gray stone, hemispherical, pierced lengthwise. Two animals in drilled style, possibly lion and goat, Ubaid period. Amiet 1961: pl. 8:159, 162, 164; Buchanan 1981: fig. 102a; Legrain 1951: pl. 1:12–14, 16 |
| 3 | 18 N 113 | Level XIIA | Lgth. 2.3 cm, diam. 1.6 cm | Cylinder seal blank, shell (conch core) |
| 4 | 18 N 8 | Level II | Lgth. 1.2 cm, w. 0.8 cm, th. 0.6 cm | Scarab, pale green faience, whole. Four Egyptian hieroglyphs on base. Part of 18 N 7 bead hoard |
| 5 | 18 N 9 | Level II | Ht. 1.3 cm, max. base w. 1.3 cm | Stamp seal, olive green stone, loop-end damaged. Conical, oval base with running animal(?); incised branch on side. Part of 18 N 7 bead hoard |

Plate 160

1

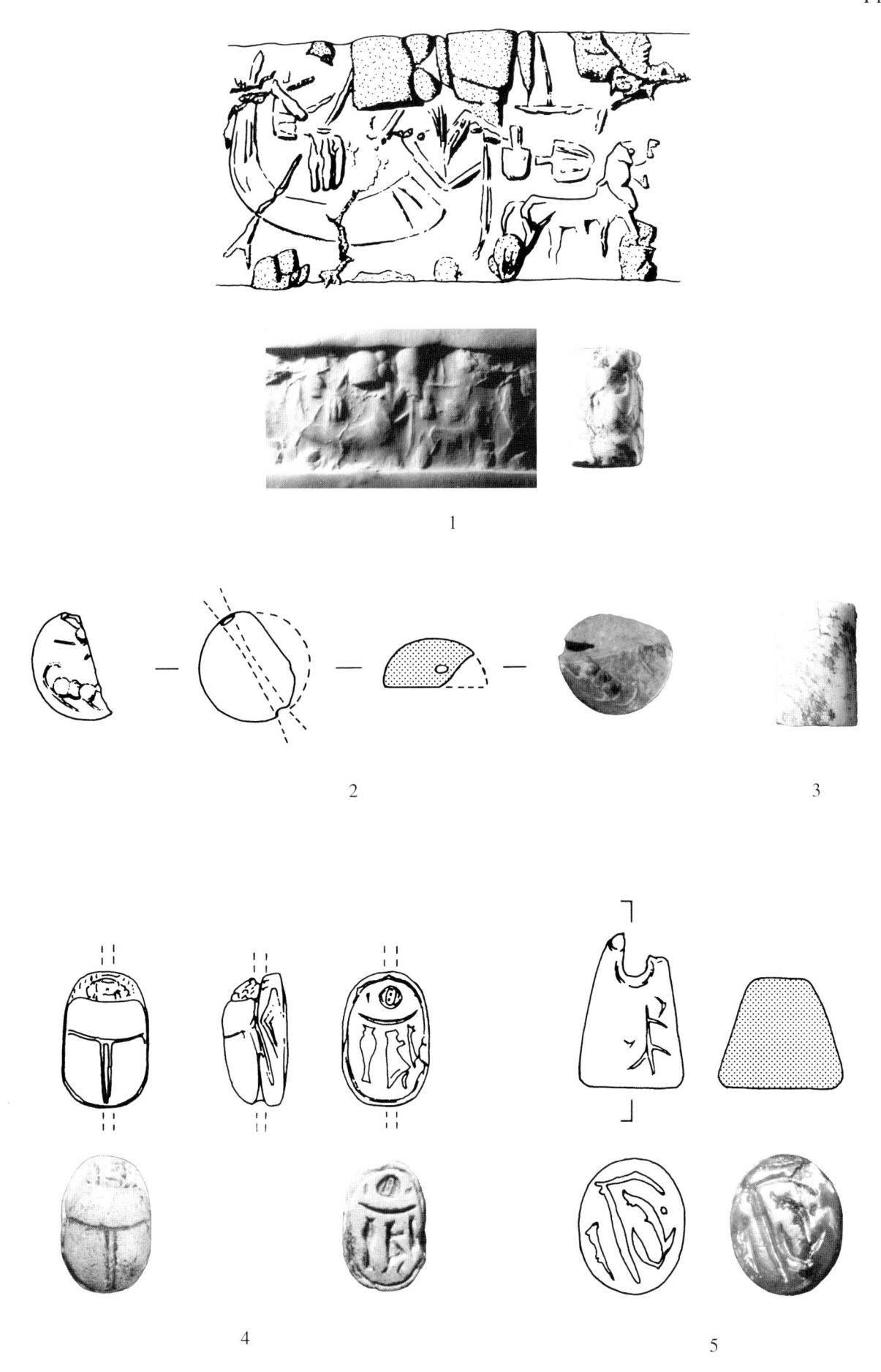

2  3

4  5

Cylinder Seals, Stamp Seals, and Scarab, Non-burial. Scale (*1–3*) 1:1 and (*4–5*) 2:1

Plate 161. Third-millennium B.C. Stone and Copper/Bronze Vessels, Non-burial

|   | Lot Number | Location | Dimension | Description/Comparison |
|---|---|---|---|---|
| 1 | I333 | Level XIVA | Rim diam. 14.0 cm | Bowl rim sherd, white marble-like stone, probably hemispherical, beaded rim. See 19 N 96 |
| 2 | H511:1 | Level XIIA | Rim diam. 18.0 cm | Bowl rim sherd, white translucent marble-like stone with yellow inclusions, plain rim, tapered at end. Abu Salabikh: Potts 1993: 839, 842–43 |
| 3 | H539:5 | Level XIIA | Rim diam. 34.0 cm | Bowl rim sherd, green granitic stone, plain rim. Abu Salabikh: Potts 1993: 841 |
| 4 | H1021:10 | Level XIIB | Base diam. 10.0 cm | Bowl base sherd, white marble, flat base |
| 5 | 18 N 170 | Level XIVA | Rim diam. 11.0 cm, ht. 4.8 cm, handle lgth. 5.0 cm | Ladle, copper/bronze, hemispherical, trough handle. Müller-Karpe 1993: form 4 I, pl. 10:43–44; Kish: Mackay 1925: pl. 20:9–10; Mackay 1929: pl. 57:8, 10–11 (but with flat bases); Ur: Woolley 1934: pl. 238, type 87 (ED III; low ring base); Tello: Parrot 1948: fig. 54c (Ur III) |

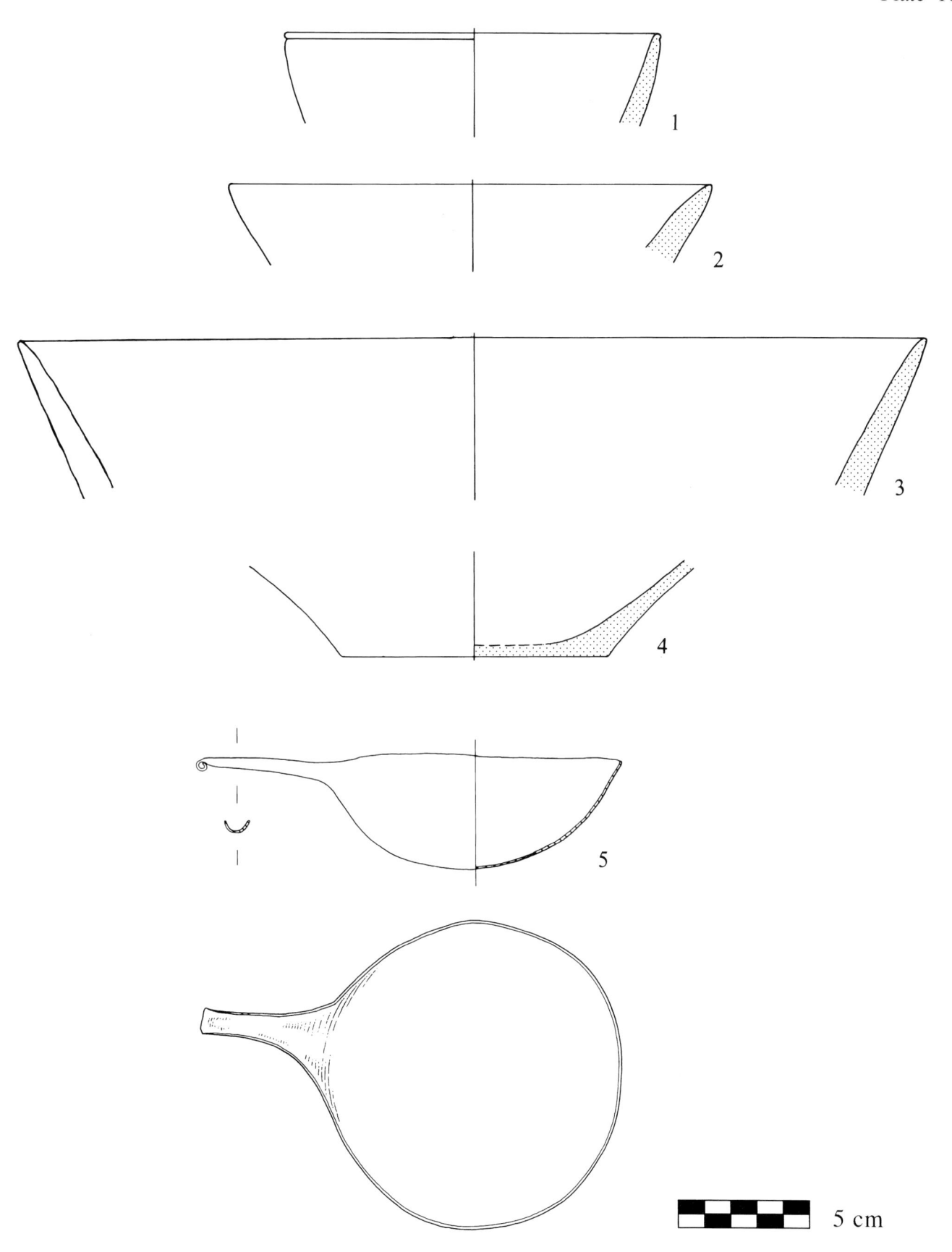

Plate 161

Third-millennium B.C. Stone and Copper/Bronze Vessels, Non-burial. Scale 1:2

Plate 162. Third-millennium B.C. Copper/Bronze Objects, Non-burial

| | Lot Number | Location | Dimension | Description/Comparison |
|---|---|---|---|---|
| 1 | 18 N 172 | Level XIVB | Lgth. 7.0 cm, w. 3.3 cm, th. 0.2–0.5 cm | Chisel or adze, copper/bronze. Traces of wood handle on one side, cords on the other. Susa: Tallon 1987: nos. 472–74 (twenty-eighth century B.C.) |
| 2 | 18 N 122 | Level XIVB | Lgth. 25.7 cm, w. 4.1 cm, th. 0.7 cm | Dagger, copper/bronze. Flat blade with two central grooves, piece of sheath material (leather?) corroded to one side. Nippur: Gibson et al. 1978: fig. 9:3 (I–L); Kish: Langdon 1924: pl. 18:2, bottom; Mackay 1925: pl. 3:5, pl. 17:12–13; Mackay 1929: pl. 39:2396, pl. 42:11, pl. 62:17; Abu Salabikh: Martin, Moon, and Postgate 1985: grave 93:16 (ED IIIb); Ur: Woolley 1934: pl. 228, types 7 c–d (late ED–early Akk.); Mari: Parrot 1956: pl. 64:601 (ED III); Susa: Tallon 1987: nos. 125–27; Tell Sabra: Tunca 1987: pl. 20:7, pl. 33:3–4 (ED III) |
| 3 | 18 N 121 | Level XIVB | Lgth. 36.3 cm, max. th. 1.2 cm | Spearhead, copper/bronze, square cross section. Susa: Tallon 1987: nos. 205–07 (twenty-fifth century B.C.); Ur: Woolley 1934: pl. 154:U.10049, pl. 227, type 1a (ED) |
| 4 | 19 N 14 | Level XIIIB | Lgth. 14.4 cm, w. 3.4 cm, th. 0.3 cm | Blade end, copper/bronze. Ur: Woolley 1934: pl. 225: type S.17, pl. 226: type S.18 (Akk.) |
| 5 | 18 N 171 | Level XIIB | Ht. 9.5 cm, lgth. 11.0 cm, | Ax, copper/bronze. Solid head, traces of wood handle inside hollow shaft. shaft hole diam. 2.5 cm. See 18 N 177 for comparisons |
| 6 | 18 N 120 | Level XIVA | Diam. 4.2 cm, wire th. 0.3 cm | Bracelet, copper/bronze, single loop |
| 7 | 19 N 63 | Level XVI | Lgth. 18.5 cm, max. th. 0.8 cm | Pin, copper/bronze, bent tang, square central section. Abu Salabikh: Martin, Moon, and Postgate 1985: grave 1:33, grave 32:4 (ED IIIa and IIIb); Ur: Woolley 1934: pl. 231: type 7a (late ED–early Akk.) |
| 8 | 18 N 151 | Level XIVB | Lgth. 11.1 cm, w. 0.7 cm | Pin, copper/bronze. The square central section, abruptly tapered to a point at each end, means this may be a broken and reworked longer pin |
| 9 | 18 N 144 | Level XIVB | Lgth. 8.6 cm, diam. 0.2 cm | Pin, copper/bronze, ends broken, straight, round cross section |
| 10 | 18 N 143 | Level XIVB | Lgth. 14.2 cm, diam. 0.3 cm | Pin, copper/bronze, straight, round cross section. Kish: Langdon 1924: pl. 19:2, left; Mackay 1925: pl. 4:1–2; Ur: Woolley 1934: pl. 231, type 8 (ED–Akk.); Uruk: van Ess and Pedde 1992: pl. 31:215 (ED III) |
| 11 | 18 N 147 | Level XIVB | Lgth. 7.3 cm, diam. 0.2 cm | Pin, copper/bronze, both ends broken, straight, round cross section |
| 12 | 18 N 146 | Level XIVB | Lgth. 11.0 cm, max. th. 0.6 cm | Pin, copper/bronze, straight, round cross section, head flattened and rolled. Kish: Mackay 1925: pl. 4:6–8; pl. 19:5–8; Tepe Gawra: Speiser 1935: pl. 82:14, 16 (ED–Akk.); Susa: Tallon 1987: nos. 872–74, 876–77; Ur: Woolley 1934: pl. 231, type 4 (late ED–Akk.) |
| 13 | 19 N 13 | Level XIVA | Lgth. ca. 7 cm, max. th. 0.5 cm | Pin, copper/bronze, head flattened and rolled. For comparisons, see 18 N 146 |
| 14 | 18 N 153 | Level XIVA | Lgth. 16.4 cm, max. diam. 0.8 cm | Pin, copper/bronze, straight, round cross section. Short shaft above hole may have originally held a bead; corrosion bears traces of what might have been a cord wrapped spirally down the length of the pin. Nippur: McCown and Haines 1967: pl. 152:1 (TB XI, Akk.); Kish: Langdon 1924: pl. 19:3, left; Mackay 1925: pl. 4:9–11, pl. 19:16–19, 27–28; Mackay 1929: pl. 40: group 5, pl. 58:4–10, 23, 28–29; Abu Salabikh: Martin, Moon, and Postgate 1985: grave 14:6 (ED III); Mari: Parrot 1956: pl. 64:405 (ED III); Tepe Gawra: Speiser 1935: pl. 82:12; Susa: Steve and Gasche 1971: pl. 10:12, 14 (Akk.); Ur: Woolley 1934: pl. 231, type 1b–d (Akk.) |
| 15 | 18 N 150 | Level XIVA | Lgth. 7.1 cm, diam. 0.7 cm | Pin, copper/bronze, straight, round cross section, tapered end only |
| 16 | 18 N 112 | Level XIIB | Lgth. 8.2 cm, diam. 0.2 cm | Pin, copper/bronze, straight, round cross section, end flattened and rolled. See 18 N 146 for comparisons |
| 17 | 18 N 142 | Level XIIB | Lgth. 5.9 cm, diam. 0.4 cm | Pin, copper/bronze, straight, round cross section, one end broken |
| 18 | 18 N 148 | Level XIIA | Lgth. 9.0 cm, diam. 0.5 cm | Pin, copper/bronze, straight, round cross section, hole and short shaft at larger end. See 18 N 153 for comparisons |
| 19 | 18 N 145 | Level XIB | Lgth. 2.6 cm, max. diam. 1.0 cm, diam. 0.3 cm | Short tack or rivet, copper/bronze. Mari: Parrot 1956: pl. 64:418 |
| 20 | 18 N 84 | Level XIB | Lgth. 12.3 cm, diam. 0.4 cm | Pin, copper/bronze, straight, round cross section, laterally pierced |
| 21 | 18 N 90 | Level X | Lgth. 8.0 cm, diam. 0.4 cm | Pin, copper/bronze, round cross section, end flattened and rolled. See 18 N 146 for comparisons |

Plate 162

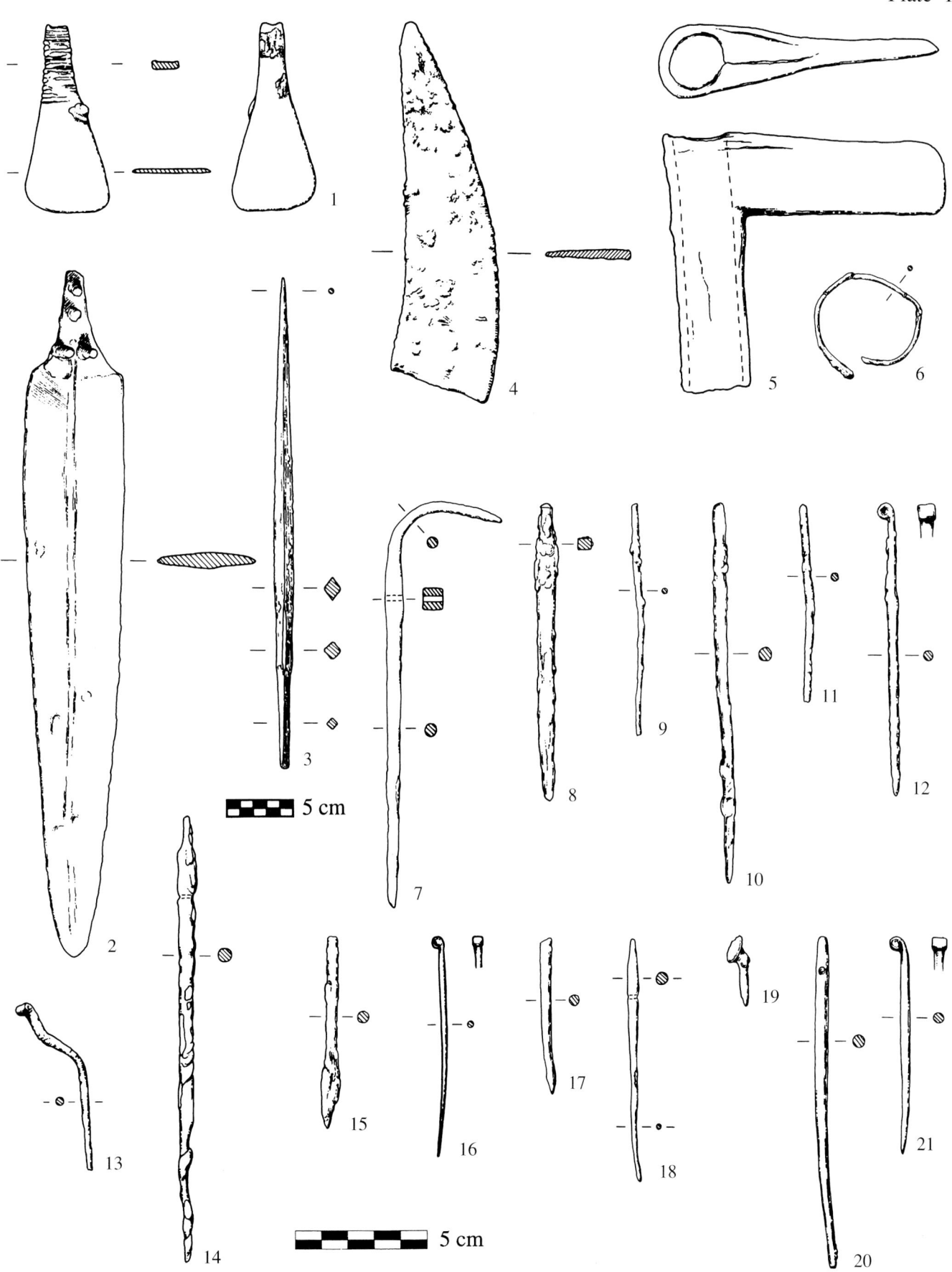

Third-millennium B.C. Copper/Bronze Objects, Non-burial. Scales (*1–2, 4–21*) 1:2 and (*3*) 1:4

Plate 163. Third-millennium B.C. Baked-clay and Stone Objects

|  | Lot Number | Location | Dimension | Description/Comparison |
|---|---|---|---|---|
| 1 | 18 N 165 | Level XIVA | Lgth. 5.7 cm, max. w. 3.4 cm, ht. 6.8 cm | Chariot model, baked clay. Nippur: McCown and Haines 1967: pl. 144:7, pl. 149:8–10 (Akk.–OB); Kish: Mackay 1929: pl. 46:2, 4; Tepe Gawra: Speiser 1935: pl. 34:2, 4; Nuzi: Starr 1937: pl. 54:E–I (Akk.) |
| 2 | 18 N 162 | Level XIVA | Lgth. 4.0 cm, w. 2.5 cm, ht. 4.5 cm | Chariot model, baked clay, handmade |
| 3 | 18 N 133 | Level XIVA | Lgth. 5.6 cm, ht. 6.5 cm, w. 3.8 cm | Chariot model, baked clay, handmade |
| 4 | 18 N 163 | Level XIIA | Diam. 4.5 cm, th. 2.6 cm | Wheel model, baked clay |
| 5 | 18 N 161 | Level X | Diam. 3.8 cm, th. 1.7 cm | Wheel model, baked clay |
| 6 | 18 N 128 | Level XIIIC | Lgth. 8.2. cm, max. w. 3.8 cm, ht. 4.0 cm | Boat model, baked clay. Nippur: Legrain 1930: pl. 70:380; McCown and Haines 1967: pl. 144:9, 11 (Akk.–Isin-Larsa) |
| 7 | 18 N 167 | Level XIIIC | Extant lgth. 3.1 cm, ht. 4.2 cm | Chair model, fragment, baked clay. Handmade with molded upper surface. Cholidis 1992: pl. 8 ff. chairs), pl. 21 ff. (beds) (Ur III and later); Nippur: McCown and Haines 1967: pl. 143:7, pl. 144:3–4 (Ur III); Legrain 1930: pl. 62:346, 348, 350, pl. 64:353; Uruk: Böck et al. 1993: pl. 20:101–02, pl. 21:103–05; Nuzi: Starr 1937: pl. 57u (Akk.) |
| 8 | 18 N 130 | Level XIVA | Lgth. 7.8 cm, ht. 5.0 cm, max. w. 3.2 cm | Figurine, Sheep, baked clay. Kish: Mackay 1929: pls. 47:9, 1114 |
| 9 | 18 N 169 | Level XIIIC | Extant ht. 4.8 cm, w. 2.5 cm | Figurine, dog, baked clay. Flat body with head turned to the front. Nippur: Legrain 1930: pl. 54:288–89; McCown and Haines 1967: pl. 139:5, 14 (Akk.–Ur III) |
| 10 | 18 N 166 | Level XIVA | Lgth. 8.3 cm, ht. 6.3 cm, th. 2.2 cm | Figurine, sheep, baked clay. Flat figure with details incised on one side |
| 11 | 18 N 168 | Level XIB | Lgth. 6.7 cm, w. 5.1 cm, ht. 4.9 cm | Figurine, bird, baked clay. Nippur: Legrain 1930: pl. 62:334–41; McCown and Haines 1967: pl. 142:1–4 (Akk., Ur III, and Kassite); Kish: Mackay 1929: pl. 47:10 |
| 12 | 18 N 129 | Level XIA | Lgth. 6.6 cm, w. 4.1 cm, ht. 4.8 cm | Rattle, baked clay, animal shaped with incised lines on body, hole below tail into hollow center. Nippur: Gibson 1975: fig. 70:2 (Akk.); Legrain 1930: pl. 58:310–11; McCown and Haines 1967: pl. 139:11, pl. 140:10 (Akk.–Ur III); Tello: Parrot 1948: fig. 51d (Ur III); Ur: Woolley 1934: pl. 221:U.17657 (Akk.) |
| 13 | 18 N 81 | Level IX | Ht. 11.1 cm, w. 4.7 cm | Figurine, human male, baked clay, applied and incised details. Nippur: Legrain 1930: pls. 31–35; McCown and Haines 1967: pl. 128:12–15 (Ur III), pl. 129:1–5, 7 (Ur III) |
| 14 | 18 N 116 | Level XIIIC | Diam. 2.0 cm, ht. 1.6 cm | "Game piece," baked clay |
| 15 | 18 N 115 | Level XIIA | Diam. 1.8 cm, ht. 1.7 cm | "Game piece," baked clay |
| 16 | 18 N 158 | Level XIIIB | Ht. 6.6 cm, w. 5.2 cm, th. 1.8 cm, wt. 130 gm | Weight, stone, beveled edges, three incised lines on shoulder, pierced through rounded end. Nippur: McCown and Haines 1967: pl. 156:12 (Isin-Larsa) |
| 17 | 18 N 89 | Level XIIB | Ht. 5.5 cm, w. 3.5 cm, th. 2.7 cm, wt. 88.4 gm | Weight, stone, beveled edges, pierced through rounded end. See 18 N 158 |
| 18 | 18 N 141 | Level XIIA | Ht. 12.9 cm, w. 11.3 cm, th. 7.3 cm, wt. 1,495 gm | Weight, stone, irregular ovoid, pierced through narrower end |
| 19 | 18 N 159 | Level XIIA | Diam. 5.0 cm, th. 1.6 cm | Disk, stone, possible spindle whorl or fishnet weight |

Plate 163

Third-millennium B.C. Baked-clay and Stone Objects. Scale 1:2

Plate 164. Third-millennium B.C. Miniature Pottery Vessels

|   | Lot Number | Location | Dimension | Description/Comparison |
|---|---|---|---|---|
| 1 | 19 N 62 | Level XVIIC | Rim diam. 1.3 cm, max. diam. 4.0 cm, ht. 5.4 cm | Hole mouth, ovoid body, pointed base. Pale pink, sand temper, handmade. Abu Salabikh: Green 1993: 442; Moon 1987: no. 804 (ED IIIa); Kish: Mackay 1929: pl. 54:62; Diyala: Delougaz 1952: A.546.630 (ED III–early Akk.); Mari: Parrot 1967b: fig. 306:2831, figs. 314–15 (ED III) |
| 2 | I354 | Level XVA | Rim diam. 4.5 cm, base diam. 3.0 cm, ht. 5.5 cm | Miniature jar, pale redware, pink surface, sand temper, string-cut base |
| 3 | 18 N 164 | Level XIIB | Diam. 5.7 cm, ht. 2.8 cm | Miniature vessel lid, redware |
| 4 | H1057:12 | Level XIIIB | Rim diam. 4.5 cm | Miniature jar, pale green buff ware, sand and light organic temper |
| 5 | H1010:7 | Level XIIB | Rim diam. 5.0 cm | Miniature cup, buff ware, sand and light organic temper, vertical incisions on sides. See 18 N 137 |
| 6 | H1021:5 | Level XIIB | Rim diam. 6.0 cm | Miniature cup rim, vertical incisions on sides |
| 7 | H1021:16 | Level XIIB | Rim diam. 5.0 cm | Miniature jar, buff ware, sand and light organic temper |
| 8 | H1021:6 | Level XIIB | Base diam. ca. 4.0 cm | Miniature cup base, buff ware, sand and light organic temper. Flat with four pinched feet. See 198 N 137 |
| 9 | H126:2 | Level XIIA | Rim diam. 2.6 cm, max. diam. 4.0 cm | Miniature jar, beaded rim, long neck, base missing, pale redware, pink surface, sand and light organic temper |
| 10 | 18 N 85 | Level XIIA | Rim diam. 1.9 cm, max. diam. 2.9 cm, base diam. 1.2 cm, ht. 1.8 cm | Miniature version of Type C-18. Red, handmade, spout missing. Mari: Parrot 1967b: 3204 (ED III "maquette") |
| 11 | 18 N 83 | Level XIB | Rim diam. 3.8 cm, base diam. 3.8 cm, ht. 2.4 cm | Handmade, pinched spout. Red. Abu Salabikh: Green 1993: 433–35 |
| 12 | H877:6 | Level XIB | Rim diam. 8.0 cm | Miniature jar, buff ware, sand temper |
| 13 | H129:2 | Level X | Rim diam. 8.0 cm | Miniature jar, redware, sand temper |
| 14 | H757:10 | Level VII | Base diam. ca. 3.5 cm | Miniature jar base, buff pink ware, sand temper. Flat base with four pinched feet. Nippur: McCown and Haines 1967: pl. 80:3–4 |
| 15 | H752:2 | Level VI | Rim diam. 10.0 cm | Miniature jar, yellow buff ware, sand temper |

Plate 164

Third-millennium B.C. Miniature Pottery Vessels. Scale 1:2

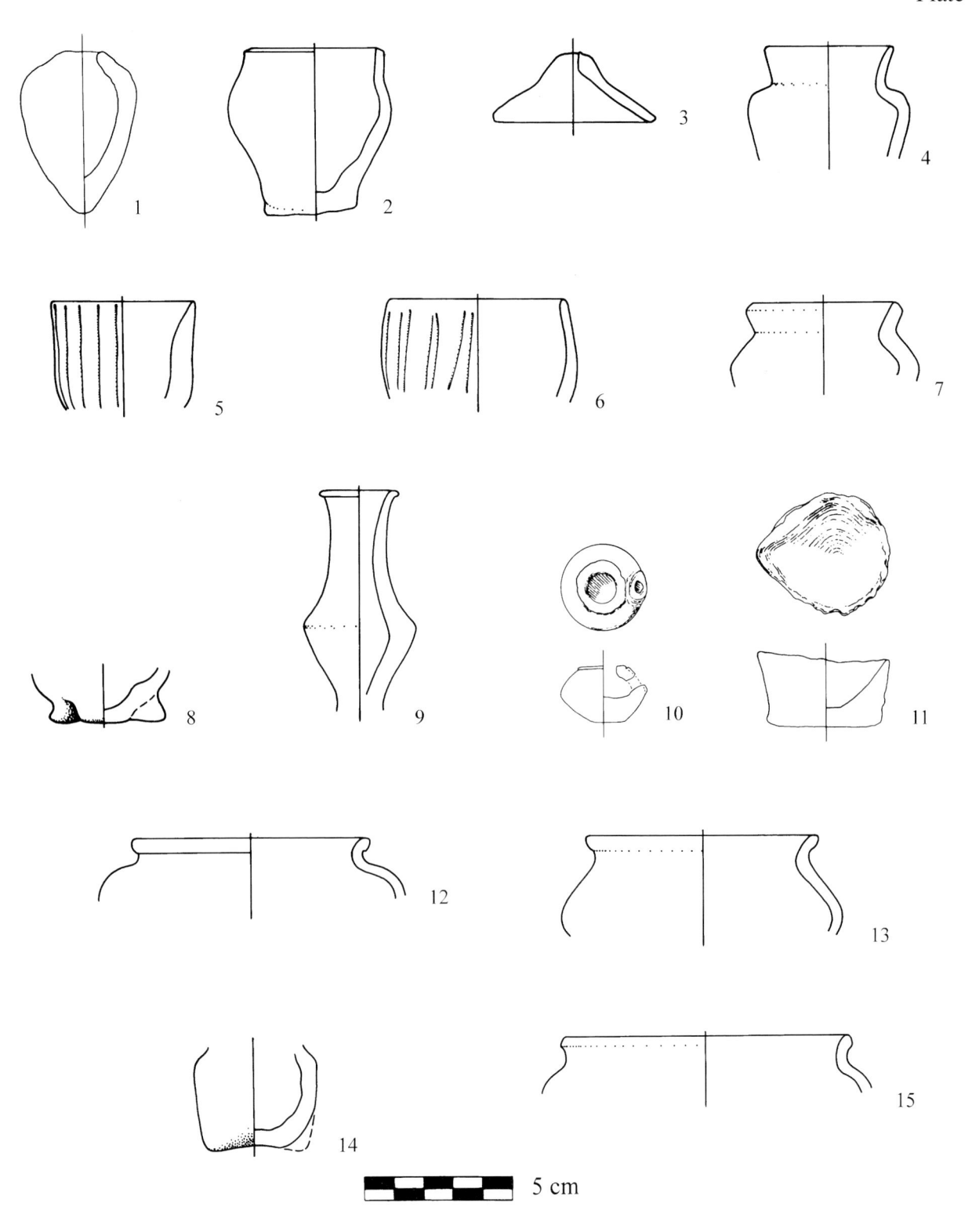

## Plate 165. Foundation Deposit 19 N 97, Level XIIIC

A similar group of hematite weights and pebbles was found in Grave PG 1413 at Ur; a very different context, but possibly with a similar apotropaic purpose (Woolley 1934: 473)

|    | Lot Number | Dimension | Description |
|----|-----------|-----------|-------------|
| 1  | 19 N 97aa | Diam. 0.8 cm, th. 0.45 cm | Ring shaped, *Columella* shell |
| 2  | 19 N 97ag | Diam. 1.0 cm, th. 0.5 cm | Ring shaped, brown stone |
| 3  | 19 N 97ac | Diam. 1.1 cm, th. 1.0 cm | Ball shaped, *Columella* shell |
| 4  | 19 N 97ad | Diam. 1.2 cm, th. 1.1 cm | Ball shaped, *Columella* shell |
| 5  | 19 N 97ab | Diam. 1.3 cm, diam. 0.9 cm | Ball shaped, *Columella* shell |
| 6  | 19 N 97af | Diam. 1.6 cm, lgth. 1.25 cm | Cylindrical, hematite |
| 7  | 19 N 97ae | Diam. 1.75 cm, th. 1.4 cm | Ball shaped, glazed steatite |
| 8  | 19 N 97y  | Lgth. 1.95 cm, max. w. 1.0 cm, max. th. 0.4 cm, wt. 1 gm | Irregular ellipsoid, gray stone |
| 9  | 19 N 97z  | Diam. 1.8 cm, th. 0.3 cm, wt. 2 gm | Disc, gray stone, triangular section missing |
| 10 | 19 N 97p  | Diam. 1.5 cm, ht. 0.9 cm, wt. 3 gm | Hemisphere, black and white stone, patch of copper corroded to one side, slightly chipped |
| 11 | 19 N 97m  | Diam. 1.7 cm, ht. 1.3 cm, wt. 9 gm | Hemisphere, brown hematite, small hole in center of flattened side |
| 12 | 19 N 97k  | Lgth. 1.8 cm, diam. 0.8 cm, wt. 2 gm | Date shaped, black and white stone |
| 13 | 19 N 97j  | Lgth. 2.1 cm, diam. 0.7 cm, wt. 1 gm | Date shaped, gray stone |
| 14 | 19 N 97h  | Lgth. 1.9 cm, diam. 1.0 cm, wt. 4 gm | Date shaped, brown hematite, small chip |
| 15 | 19 N 97g  | Lgth. 2.3 cm, diam. 0.95 cm, wt. 4 gm | Date shaped, brown hematite, chip in one end |
| 16 | 19 N 97i  | Lgth. 1.9 cm, diam. 1.0 cm, wt. 4 gm | Date shaped, calcite |
| 17 | 19 N 97w  | Lgth. 2.8 cm, max. w. 1.2 cm, max. th. 1.2 cm, wt. 4.0 gm | Flattened date-shaped, gray hematite, lightly scratched |
| 18 | 19 N 97e  | Lgth. 3.05 cm, diam. 1.05 cm, wt. 8.90 gm | Date shaped, gray hematite, small chips |
| 19 | 19 N 97f  | Lgth. 2.6 cm, diam. 1.5 cm, wt. 8 gm | Date shaped, gray hematite |
| 20 | 19 N 97o  | Lgth. 2.75 cm, diam. 1.5 cm, wt. 17 gm | Cylindrical, brown hematite, chipped |
| 21 | 19 N 97c  | Lgth. 3.4 cm, diam. 1.3 cm, wt. 9 gm | Date shaped, gray stone, one incised line |
| 22 | 19 N 97d  | Lgth. 4.1 cm, diam. 1.15 cm, wt. 8 gm | Date shaped, gray stone, small chip in one end |
| 23 | 19 N 97q  | Lgth. 2.8 cm, w. 2.7 cm, th. 1.4 cm, wt. 10 gm | Irregular pebble, quartz |
| 24 | 19 N 97u  | Lgth. 2.8 cm, diam. 2.0 cm, wt. 25 gm | Barrel shaped, brown hematite, chipped and scratched |
| 25 | 19 N 97l  | Lgth. 3.0 cm, max. diam. 2.05 cm, wt. 17 gm | Egg shaped, calcite |
| 26 | 19 N 97r  | Lgth. 2.8 cm, max. w. 2.3 cm, max. th. 1.8 cm, wt. 17 gm | Faceted trapezoid, gray stone, chipped |
| 27 | 19 N 97v  | Lgth. 3.8 cm, max. w. 3.0 cm, th. 1.4 cm, wt. 42 gm | Irregular trapezoid, gray stone, chipped, shallow drill hole at wider end |
| 28 | 19 N 97n  | Lgth. 2.2 cm, diam. 2.5 cm, wt. 34 gm | Cylindrical, brown hematite, chipped |
| 29 | 19 N 97t  | Lgth. 3.3 cm, diam. 2.3 cm, wt. 42 g. | Barrel shaped, gray hematite, chipped and scratched |
| 30 | 19 N 97s  | Lgth. 4.1 cm, max. w. 2.7 cm, th. 1.8 cm, wt. 33 gm | Faceted truncated lozenge, gray stone |
| 31 | 19 N 97x  | Lgth. 4.7 cm, diam. 2.5 cm, wt. 83 gm | Date shaped, gray hematite, chipped and scratched |
| 32 | 19 N 97b  | Lgth. 7.35 cm, diam. 1.9 cm, wt. 42 gm | Date shaped, gray stone, traces of copper adhering |
| 33 | 19 N 97a  | Lgth. 7.35 cm, diam. 2.7 cm, wt. 84 gm | Date shaped, gray stone |

Plate 165

Foundation Deposit 19 N 97, Level XIIIC. Scale 1:2

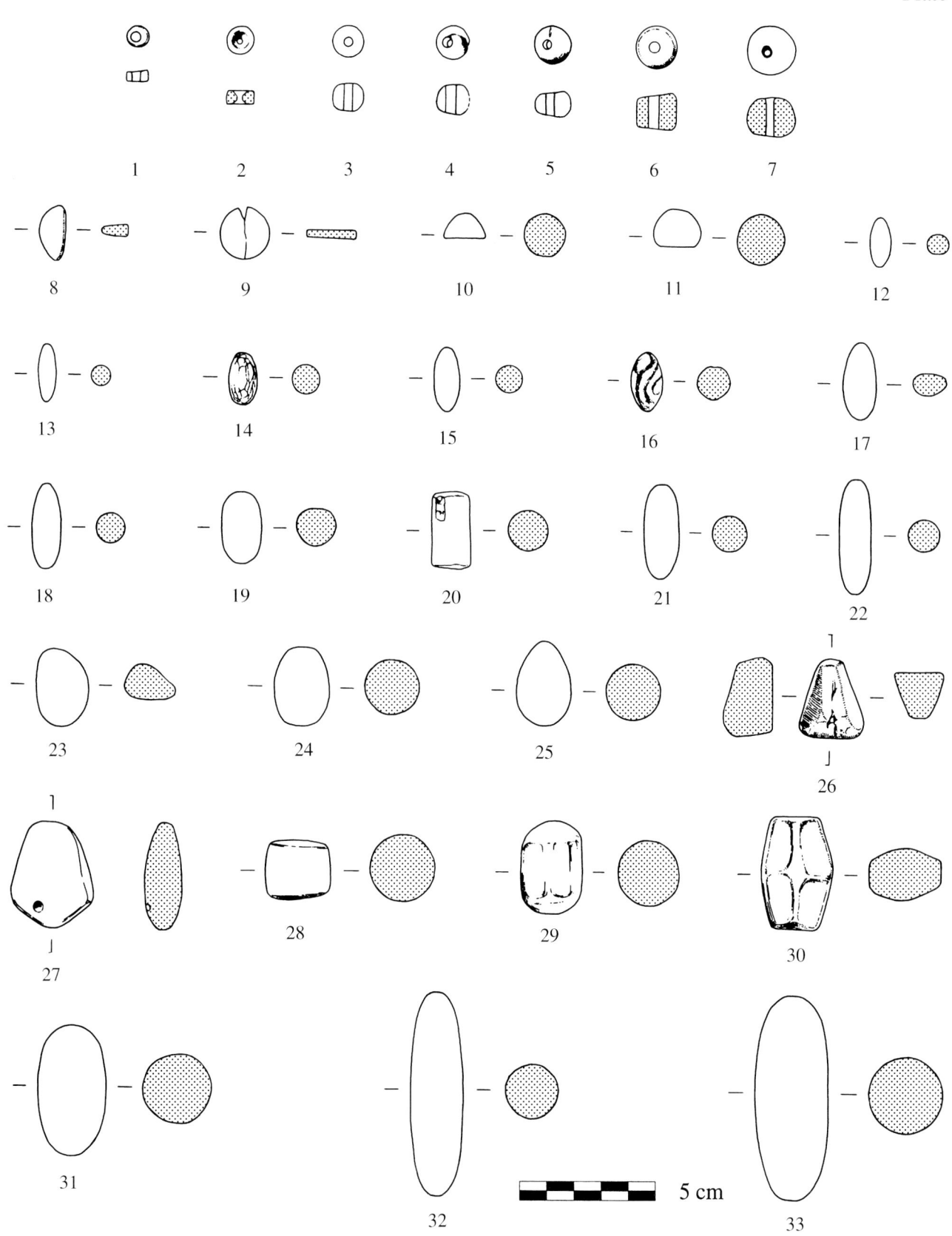

Plate 166. Third-millennium B.C. Miscellaneous Objects

| | Lot Number | Location | Dimension | Description/Comparison |
|---|---|---|---|---|
| 1 | 19 N 23 | Level XIV, Burial 14, Southwest Shaft | Diam. 1.1 cm, th. 0.4 cm | Soft dark gray stone bead, ring shaped |
| 2 | 18 N 152 | Level XIVB | Diam. 2.9 cm | Bead, section through center of conch shell, natural perforation |
| 3 | 18 N 155 | Level XIIB | Lgth. 2.2 cm, w. 0.7 cm, th. 0.5 cm | Spacer bead, gray stone, fragmentary |
| 4 | 18 N 154 | Level XIB | Lgth. 2.3 cm, diam. 0.8 cm | Bead, banded orange red and tan agate, date shaped |
| 5 | 19 N 100 | Level XVI | Diam. 2.0 cm, th. 0.25 cm | Shell object, cut from body of *Lambis* (spider conch), interior natural, convex exterior cut into irregular facets |
| 6 | 19 N 150 | Level XVI, Burial 14, Skeleton 8 | Lgth. 2.1 cm, w. 1.3 cm, th. 0.25 cm | Light buff flint blade, not retouched, both edges lightly chipped from use |
| 7 | 19 N 29 | Level XIV, Burial 14, Southwest Shaft | Lgth. 4.25 cm, w. 2.4 cm, th. 0.6 cm | Heat-treated dark brown flint blade, part of cortex remaining at one end, not retouched, chipped from use |
| 8 | 19 N 78 | Level XVA, Burial 14, Skeleton 5 | Lgth. 4.0 cm, w. 1.8 cm, th. 0.4 cm | Brown gray flint blade, trapezoidal cross section, one long side denticulated. Uch Tepe: Gibson 1981: pl. 51:11 (ED I); Kish: Mackay 1929: pl. 42:17 |
| 9 | 19 N 30 | Level XVA, Burial 14, Skeleton 5 | Lgth. 3.6 cm, w. 2.0 cm, th. 0.8 cm | Tan banded flint, scraper, end with bulb of percussion retouched and chipped from use |
| 10 | 19 N 68 | Level XVB | Lgth. 2.9 cm, w. 1.9 cm | Brown flint, scraper made from a microblade core |
| 11 | 18 N 156 | Level XIVB | Lgth. 1.8 cm, w. 1.3 cm, th. 0.3 cm | Flint blade, one edge unworked, the other denticulated but worn |
| 12 | 18 N 160 | Level XIVB | Lgth. 6.9 cm, w. 3.9 cm, th. 1.2 cm | Flint scraper, large flat flake with some cortex remaining. One end retouched |
| 13 | 19 N 61 | Level XIVA | Lgth. 4.2 cm, w. 1.9 cm, th. 0.3 cm | Obsidian, blade, one long side retouched, both long sides chipped from use |
| 14 | 18 N 157 | Level XIIIB | Lgth. 7.6 cm, w. 0.8 cm, th. 0.3 cm | Flint blade, long narrow blade with unworked edges, chipped from use |
| 15 | 18 N 66 | Level XIB | Lgth. 7.0 cm, w. 2.7 cm, th. 1.2 cm | Gray flint, blade, reddish brown cortex along one edge, retouch and chipping from use on opposite edge |
| 16 | 18 N 69 | Level IX | Lgth. 7.2 cm, w. 1.5 cm, th. 1.5 cm | Whetstone, gray stone, natural pebble flattened on one side, pierced through thinner end |
| 17 | 18 N 139 | Level XIVA | Lgth. 11.5 cm, w. 6.3 cm, th. 4.1 cm | Axhead, gray granitic stone, oblong shape, drill holes begun in top and bottom, but unfinished |
| 18 | 18 N 38 | Level IIIB | Lgth. 12.4 cm, w. 6.4–9.3 cm, th. 2.7–5.0 cm | Axhead, pink granitic stone, whole but badly battered. Vertical bow-drilled shaft hole |
| 19 | 19 N 33 | Level XIIIB | Lgth. 4.8 cm, max. diam. 3.2 cm | Unworked *Strombus* shell found with first sheep skeleton |
| 20 | 18 N 79 | Level XIB | Lgth. 6.1 cm, w. 5.2 cm | Jar shoulder sherd, pale redware. B-shaped potter's mark incised |
| 21 | 18 N 78 | Level X | Diam. 5.2 cm, ht. 2.4 cm | Inscribed mace-head, alabaster, ovoid with collar around pierced end. Only ca. one-quarter of whole remaining. Traces of illegible inscription |

Plate 166

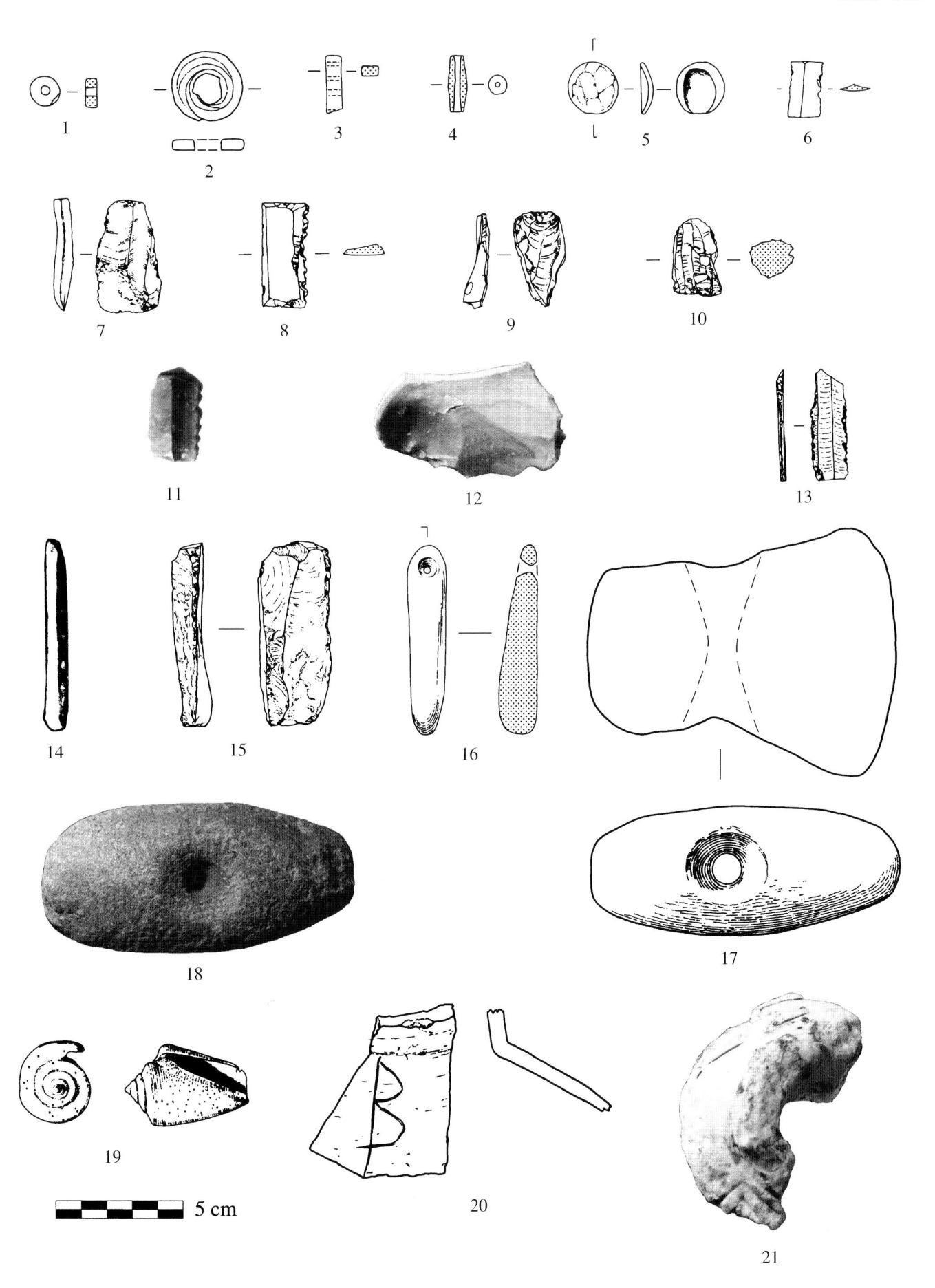

Third-millennium B.C. Miscellaneous Objects. Scales (*1–10, 12–20*) 1:2 and (*11, 21*) 1:1

Plate 167. Third-millennium Glass Beads

|   | *Lot Number* | *Location* | *Dimension* | *Description* |
|---|---|---|---|---|
| 1 | 18 N 95 | XIB | Diam. 0.9 cm | Ball-shaped, spirally wrapped olive green and white glass threads |
| 2 | 18 N 96 | XIIA | Lgth. 1.0 cm, diam. 0.6 cm | Cylindrical, pale green glass with yellow swirls |

Plate 168

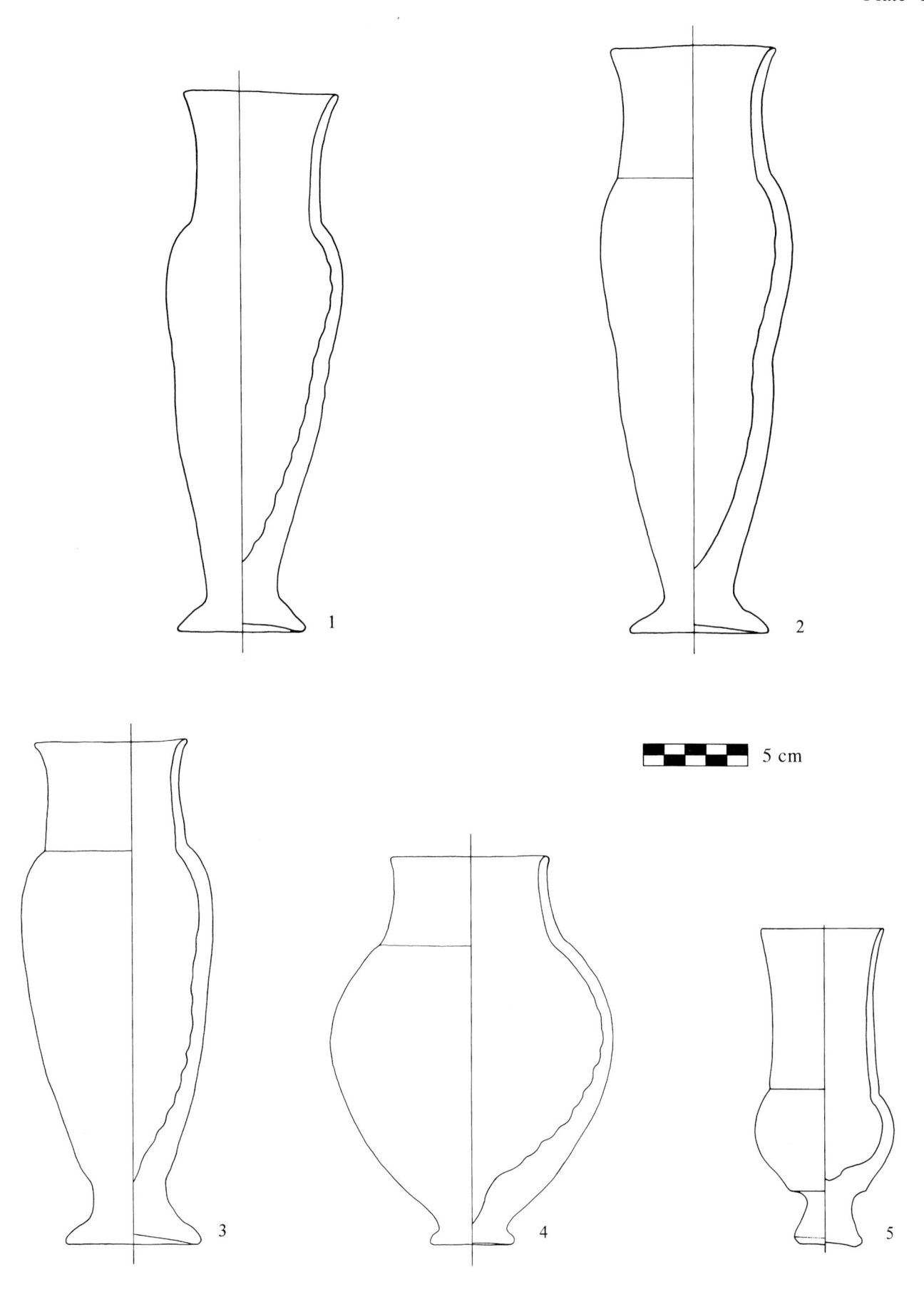

5 cm

Second-millennium B.C. Grave Groups, Burials 9 and 12. Scale 2:5

Plate 169. First-millennium B.C. Grave Group, Burial 6, Level IV

| | Lot Number | Dimension | Description/Comparison |
|---|---|---|---|
| **Burial 6, Level IV** | | | |
| 1 | 18 N 16 | Rim diam. 5.7 cm, max. diam. 8.5 cm, base diam. 3.8 cm, ht. 7.5 cm | Jar, reddish buff ware. Plain rim, ovoid body, small flat base. Fragile glazed zigzag pattern in yellowish green, white, and yellow, radiating design on base. Nippur: McCown and Haines 1967: pl. 101:1–3 (type 57) |
| 2 | 18 N 22 | Rim diam. 4.1 cm, max. diam. 7.4 cm, base diam. 1.4 cm, ht. 7.6 cm | Jar, reddish buff ware. Plain rim, ovoid body, small flat base. Fragile glazed pattern of circles and swags in yellowish green, white, and yellow, vertical lines. See 18 N 16, but with smaller base. Inside 18 N 24 |
| 3 | 18 N 23 | Rim diam. 4.7 cm, max. diam. 7.4 cm, base diam. 0.8 cm, ht. 7.8 cm | Jar, reddish buff ware. Plain rim, ovoid body, nipple base. Fragile glazed pattern of bands of dots and circles in yellowish green, white, and yellow, vertical lines at base. See 18 N 16, but with pointed base. Inside 18 N 24 |
| 4 | 18 N 24 | Rim diam. 9.4 cm, max. diam. 19.2 cm, base diam. 10.7 cm, ht. 27.3 cm | Jar, pottery, buff ware, organic temper. Ridged rim, high neck, ovoid body with sets of horizontal grooves on shoulder, ring base, two lug handles (one broken). Nippur: McCown and Haines 1967: pl. 102:4 (type 60) |
| 5 | 18 N 37 | Chain lgth. ca. 32.0 cm, pin lgth. 6.8 cm, pin diam. 0.6 cm | Pins and chain, bronze, corroded. Two round-sectioned pins connected by a chain of single wire loops |
| 6 | 18 N 36 | (a) lgth. 1.6 cm, w. 0.8 cm; (b) lgth. 0.6–0.7 cm, diam. 0.7–0.8 cm; (c) lgth. 0.9–1.4 cm, diam. 0.5–0.6 cm; (d) lgth. 0.6 cm, w. 0.4 cm; (e) th. 0.1–0.4 cm, diam. 0.2–0.5 cm; (f) lgth. 0.7–1.1 cm, w. 0.4–0.9 cm; (g, l) lgth. 0.9 cm, w. 0.3–0.6 cm; (h) lgth. 0.5–1.3 cm, diam. 0.3–0.5 cm; (i) lgth. 0.6 cm, diam. 0.5 cm; (j) lgth. 0.5 cm, diam. 0.4 cm; (k) lgth. 1.1–1.5 cm, diam. 0.4–0.6 cm; (m) diam. 0.5–0.7 cm; (n) diam. 0.6 cm, th. 0.4 cm | Necklace of 150 stone and faience beads. (a) 1 rectangular spacer (carnelian); (b) 3 ovoid (all carnelian); (c) 3 biconical (2 carnelian, 1 yellow stone); (d) 1 triangular-sectioned prism (lapis); (e) 44 ring-shaped (40 carnelian, 4 faience); (f) 2 biconvex (1 carnelian, 1 banded agate); (g, l) 7 elliptical (3 banded agate, 3 lapis, 1 carnelian); (h) 55 cylindrical (44 carnelian, 9 lapis, 2 banded agate); (i) 1 faceted biconical (carnelian); (j) 1 hub-shaped (carnelian); (k) 5 date-shaped (4 carnelian, 1 banded agate); (m) 24 ball-shaped (all carnelian); (n) 3 lentoid (all carnelian) |

Plate 169

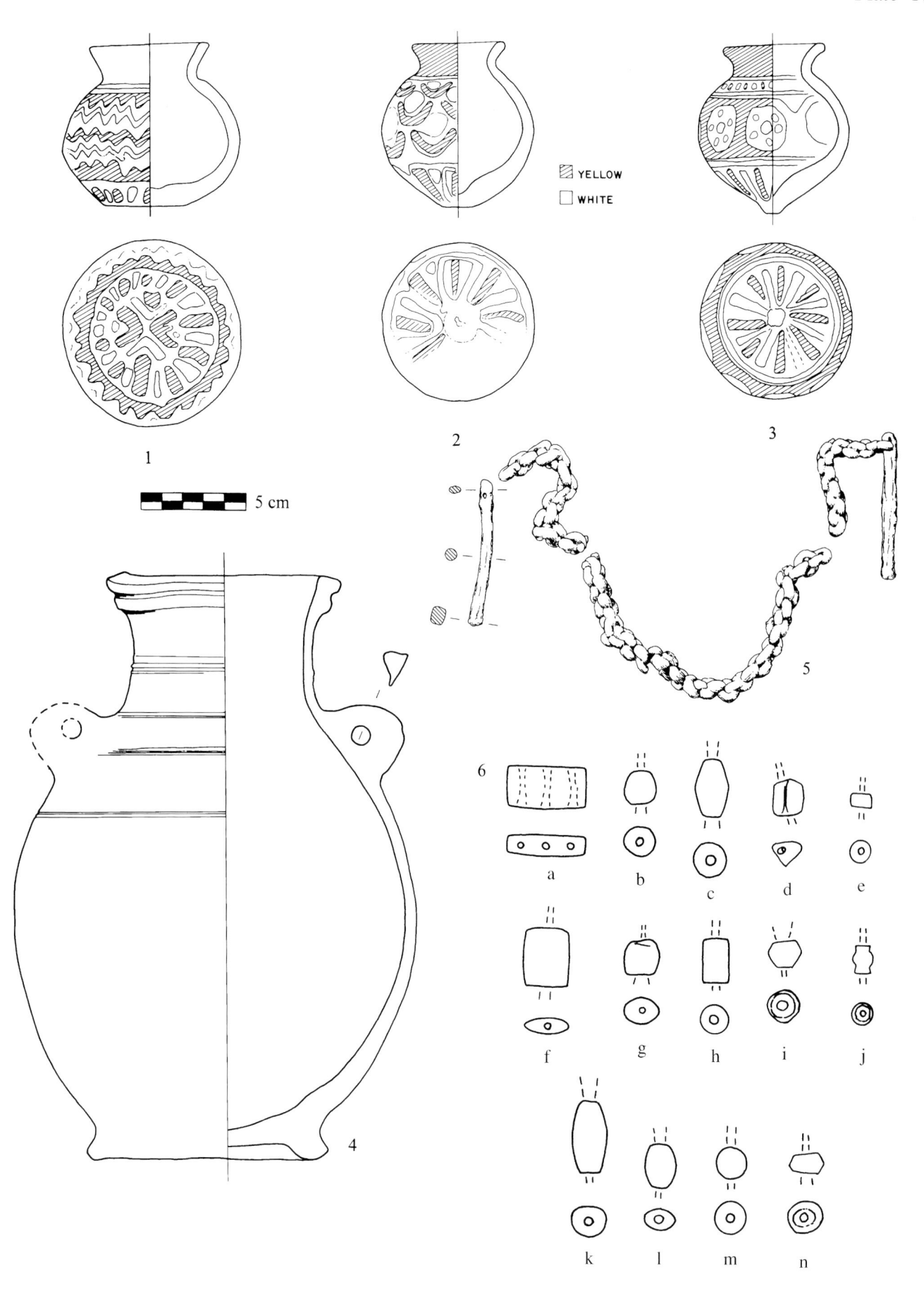

YELLOW
WHITE

First-millennium B.C. Grave Group, Burial 6. Scales (*1–5*) 2:5 and (*6*) 1:1

Plate 170. First-millennium B.C. Grave Group, Burial 8

|   | Lot Number | Dimension | Description/Comparison |
|---|---|---|---|
| **BURIAL 8, LEVEL IV** | | | |
| 1 | 18 N 42 | Rim diam. 2.5 cm, max. diam. 9.2 cm, base diam. 5.0 cm, ht. 10.9 cm | Jar, reddish buff ware. Plain rim, narrow neck, ovoid body, small flat base. Fragile glazed pattern of horizontal bands in light brown and yellow, vertical lines at base. Nippur: McCown and Haines 1967: pl. 101:4–11 (type 58) |
| 2 | 18 N 43 | Rim diam. 6.0 cm, max. diam. 9.7 cm, base diam. 5.0 cm, ht. 10.3 cm | Jar, reddish buff ware. Plain rim, ovoid body, small flat base. Fragile glazed pattern of bands, dots, and concentric circles in yellowish green, pale and dark yellow, concentric circles on base. Nippur: Armstrong 1993: pls. 61c, 87d. See 18 N 16 |
| 3 | 18 N 44 | Rim diam. 10.1 cm, max. diam. 15.7 cm, base diam. 6.5 cm, ht. 22.0 cm | Jar, buff ware, organic temper. Beveled rim, ridged neck, elongated ovoid body with groups of horizontal grooves on shoulder, slightly raised base. Nippur: McCown and Haines 1967: pl. 102:4, 8 (type 60, but without neck ridge) |
| 4 | 18 N 45 | Rim diam. 16.0 cm, base diam. 5.7 cm, ht. 7.0 cm | Bowl, buff ware, organic temper. Club rim, flat base. Nippur: McCown and Haines 1967: pl. 100:11 (type 51); Armstrong 1993: pls. 85b, 87c |
| 5 | H756 | Lgth. 117 cm, w. 67 cm, ht. 55 cm | Coffin, lightly baked heavily straw-tempered clay. "Bathtub" shape, horizontal applied ridge around body, vertical handles at each end. Nippur: McCown and Haines 1967: pl. 157:13 |

Plate 170

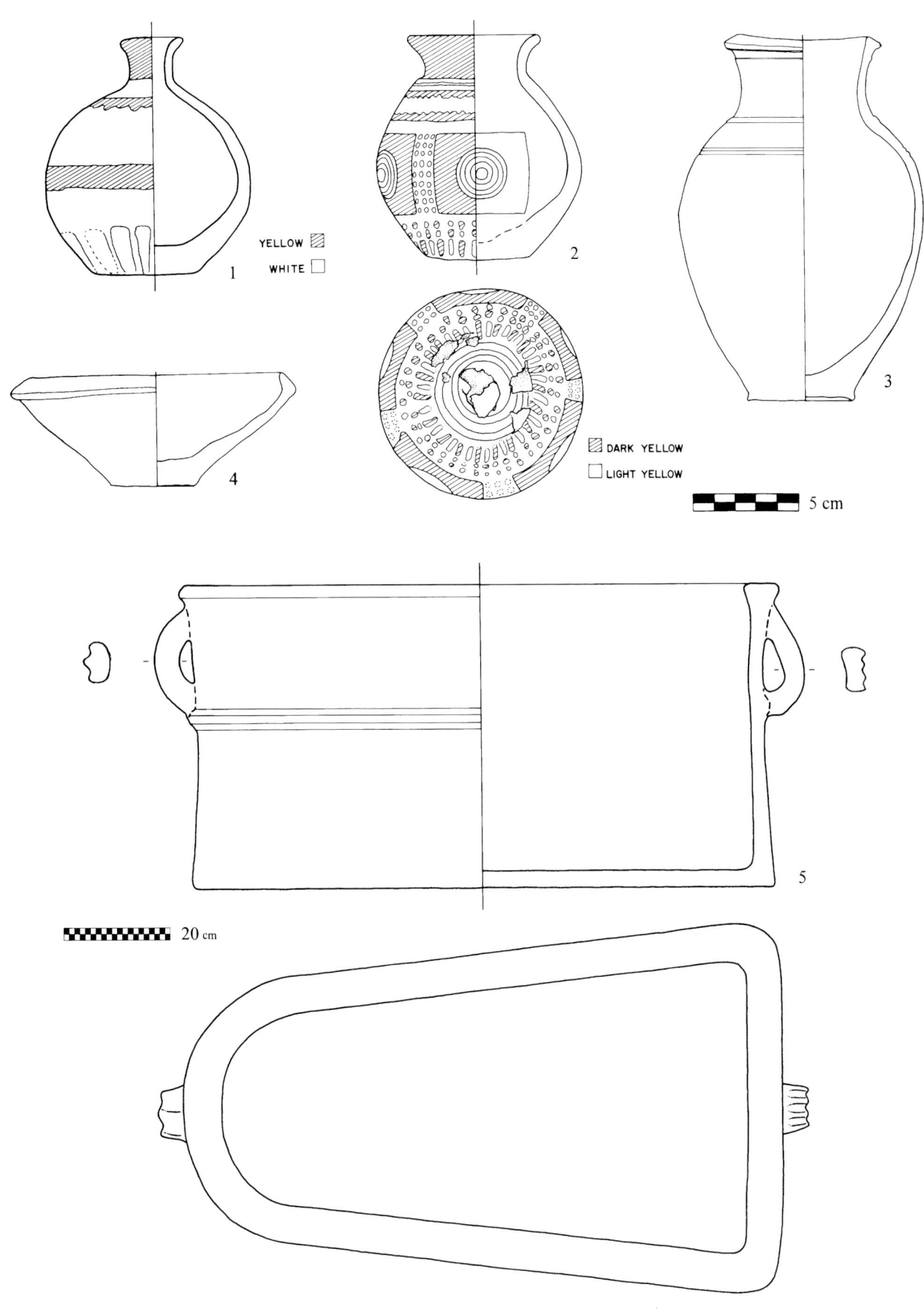

First-millennium B.C. Grave Group, Burial 8. Scales (*1–4*) 2:5 and (*5*) 1:5

Plate 171. First-millennium B.C. Grave Groups, Burials 5, 2, and 3

|  | Lot Number | Dimension | Description/Comparison |
|---|---|---|---|
| **BURIAL 5, LEVEL IIIB** | | | |
| 1 | 18 N 46 | Rim diam. 2.5 cm, max. diam. 8.5 cm, base diam. 3.5 cm, ht. 10.9 cm | Jar, light buff ware. Plain rim, narrow neck, ovoid body, flat base. Fragile glazed pattern of dots, chevrons and bands in brown and black. See 18 N 42 |
| 2 | 18 N 53 | Rim diam. 11.2 cm, max. diam. 20.5 cm, base diam. 17.3 cm, ht. 33.5 cm | Jar, buff ware, light organic temper. Ridged rim, elongated ovoid body with groups of horizontal grooves on shoulder, ring base. See 18 N 24 (but without handles) |
| **BURIAL 2, LEVEL IIIB** | | | |
| 3 | 18 N 10 | (a) Small ring shaped (diam. 0.3 cm, th. 0.1 cm); (b) larger ring shaped (diam. 0.4 cm, th. 0.2 cm); (c) lentoid (diam. 0.7–0.9 cm, th. 0.3 cm) | Necklace, 158 off-white glass beads, very fragile. 112 small ring shaped; 43 larger ring shaped; 3 lentoid |
| **BURIAL 3, LEVEL IIIB** | | | |
| 4 | 18 N 25 | Rim diam. 10.7 cm, max. diam. 16.2 cm, base diam. 5.8 cm, ht. 22 cm | Jar, buff ware, organic temper. Beveled rim, ovoid body, groove at neck to shoulder juncture, flat base. Nippur: Armstrong 1993: pls. 61d, 87f |
| 5 | 18 N 39 | Diam. 0.8 cm, th. 0.6 cm | Bead, carnelian, whole, lentoid |
| 6 | 18 N 40 | (a) diam. 3.6 cm, th. 0.6 cm, (b) diam. 1.2–1.6 cm | Beads (2): (a) disc-shaped faience eye-bead, white with dark blue interior circle, laterally pierced; (b) ball-shaped banded agate bead. Found inside 18 N 25. Uruk: Limper 1988: F. 160 (eye-bead) |

Plate 171

BLACK
REDDISH-BROWN

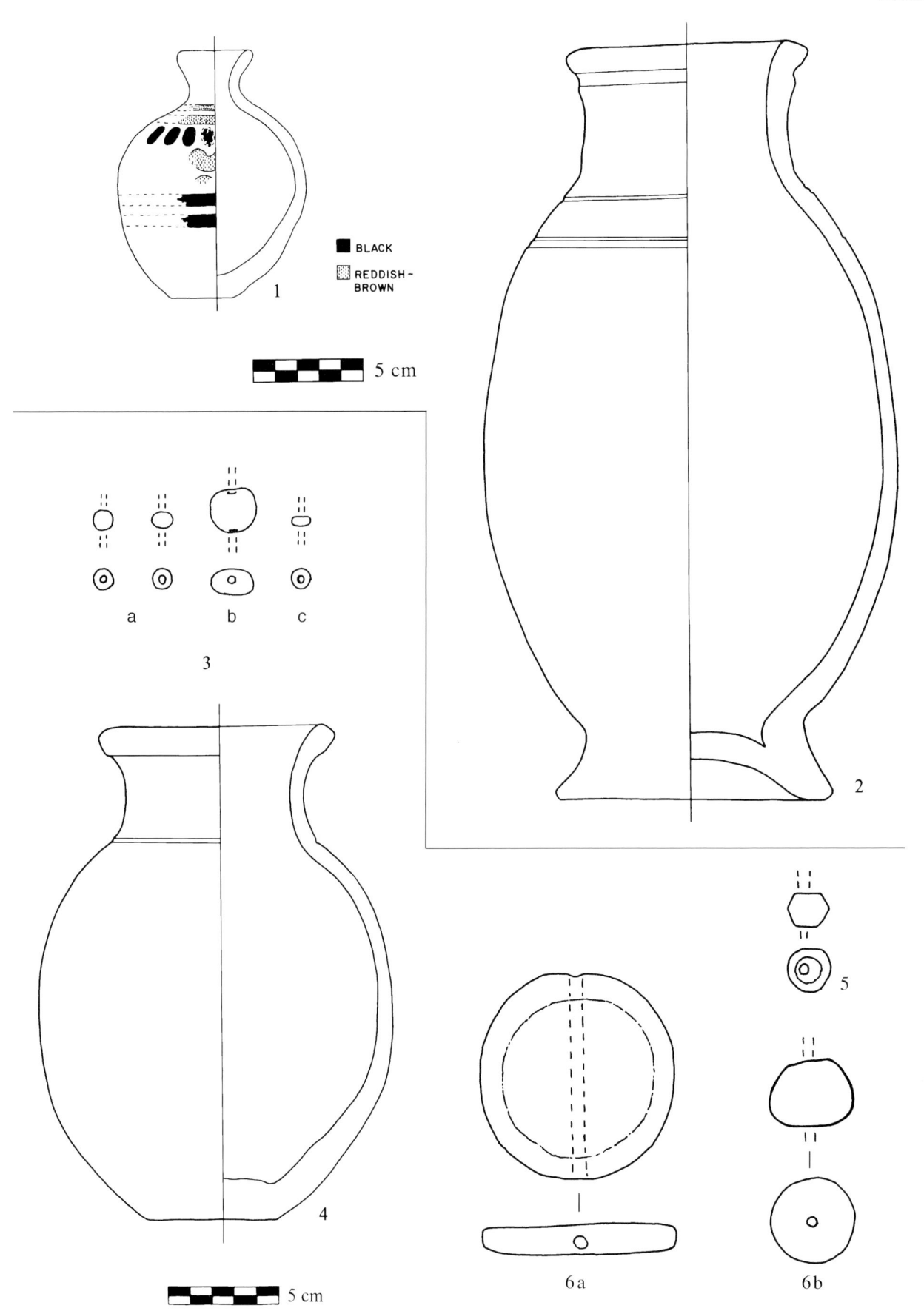

First-millennium B.C. Grave Groups, Burials 5, 2, and 3. Scales (*1, 2, 4*) 2:5 and (*3, 5–6*) 1:1

Plate 172. First-millennium B.C. Grave Group, Burial 4

| | Lot Number | Dimension | Description/Comparison |
|---|---|---|---|
| **BURIAL 4, LEVEL IIIB** | | | |
| 1 | 18 N 32 | Rim diam. 4.8 cm, max. diam. 7.5 cm, base diam. 2.6 cm, ht. 8.3 cm | Jar, buff ware. Rounded rim, ovoid body, small flat base. Shape similar to 18 N 16, but unglazed |
| 2 | 18 N 54 | Rim diam. 6.8 cm, max. diam. 8.0 cm, ht. 13.0 cm. | Jar, buff ware. Plain rim, high neck, ovoid body, nipple base. Nippur: Similar to Armstrong 1993: pl. 86i; McCown and Haines 1967: pl. 102:16 (type 62) |
| 3 | 18 N 149 | Lgth. 6.2 cm, head diam. 1.8 cm, shaft diam. 0.7 cm | Pin, bronze, complete but corroded. Biconical head, round cross-sectioned shaft, tip bent upward. Uruk: van Ess and Pedde 1992: pl. 32:225, pl. 35:330 (NB) |
| 4 | 18 N 35 | Diam. 6.0 cm, wire diam. 0.5 cm | Bracelet, bronze, complete but corroded. Single loop, plano-convex cross section, possible snake-head ends |
| 5 | 18 N 30 | (a) 92 ring shaped (diam. 0.2–0.8 cm, th. 0.1–0.6 cm); (b) 44 date shaped (lgth. 0.6–2.6 cm, diam. 0.4–1.0 cm); (c) 17 elliptical (lgth. 1.0–2.5 cm, diam. 0.3–0.8 cm); (d) 12 ball shaped (diam. 0.7–1.4 cm); (e) 9 truncated biconical (diam. 0.5–1.2 cm, th. 0.7–0.8 cm); (f) 7 cylindrical (lgth. 0.4–1.6 cm, diam. 0.2–0.6 cm); (g) 4 w. 0.3–0.6 cm); (h) 4 plano-convex (lgth. 1.1–1.7 cm, w. 0.5–0.8 cm); (i) rectangular (lgth. 1.0–1.9 cm, w. 0.3–0.7 cm); (j) 4 squat date shaped (lgth. 0.8–1.0 cm, diam. 0.7–0.8 cm); (k) 3 rhomboid (lgth. 1.4–1.6 cm, w. 0.9 cm); (l) 3 square elliptical (lgth. 0.7–1.7 cm, w. 0.5–0.7 cm); (m) 2 irregular pendants (lgth. 0.6–1.1 cm, w. 0.5–0.7 cm); (n) 1 rounded biconvex (lgth. 1.4 cm, w. 0.6 cm); (o) 1 irregular lump (lgth. 1.5 cm, w. 0.7 cm); (p) 1 sphere section (lgth. 1.4 cm, w. 0.8 cm); (q) 1 coil (lgth. 0.7 cm, diam. 0.5 cm); 9 shells: (r) 4 core sections (lgth. 0.6–1.0 cm, diam. 0.3–0.5 cm), (s) 4 other sections (diam. 1.0–1.3 cm, th. 0.3–0.9 cm), (t) 1 cowrie (lgth. 1.9 cm, th. 0.6 cm) | Necklace of 218 stone, faience, metal, and shell beads. 92 ring shaped (44 white faience, 39 carnelian, 5 lapis, 2 hematite, 1 yellow faience, 1 gray stone); 44 date shaped (22 faience, 11 banded agate, 6 marble, 2 lapis, 2 quartz, 1 amethyst); 17 elliptical (4 lapis, 4 banded agate, 2 marble, 2 quartz, 1 brown stone, 1 tan stone, 1 gray stone); 12 ball shaped (7 carnelian, 1 quartz, 1 banded agate, 1 black-and-white stone, 1 orange-and-white stone, 1 faience); 9 truncated biconical (7 carnelian, 1 faience, 1 quartz); 7 cylindrical (2 banded agate, 2 lapis, 2 orange-brown stone, 1 black stone); 4 biconvex (2 orange-black stone, 1 banded agate, 1 carnelian); 4 plano-convex (1 faience, 1 quartz, 1 banded agate, 1 yellow stone); 4 rectangular (2 lapis, 1 faience, 1 banded agate); 4 squat date shaped (3 carnelian, 1 banded agate); 3 rhomboid (1 faience, 1 quartz, 1 banded agate); 3 square elliptical (1 quartz, 1 gray stone, 1 banded agate); 2 irregular pendants (1 pale orange stone, 1 turquoise); 1 rounded biconvex (black-and-white stone); 1 irregular lump (leopard-skin agate); 1 sphere section (banded agate); 1 coil (bronze); 9 shells (4 core sections, 4 other sections, 1 cowrie) |
| 6 | 18 N 34 | Ht. 3.2 cm, w. 2.0 cm | Shell, unworked brown and white conoid shell |
| 7 | 18 N 33 | Ht. 11.5 cm, w. 9.7 cm, th. 3.0 cm, chain lgth. approx. 27 cm, wire diam. 0.8 cm | Marble palette with attached bronze chain |

Plate 172

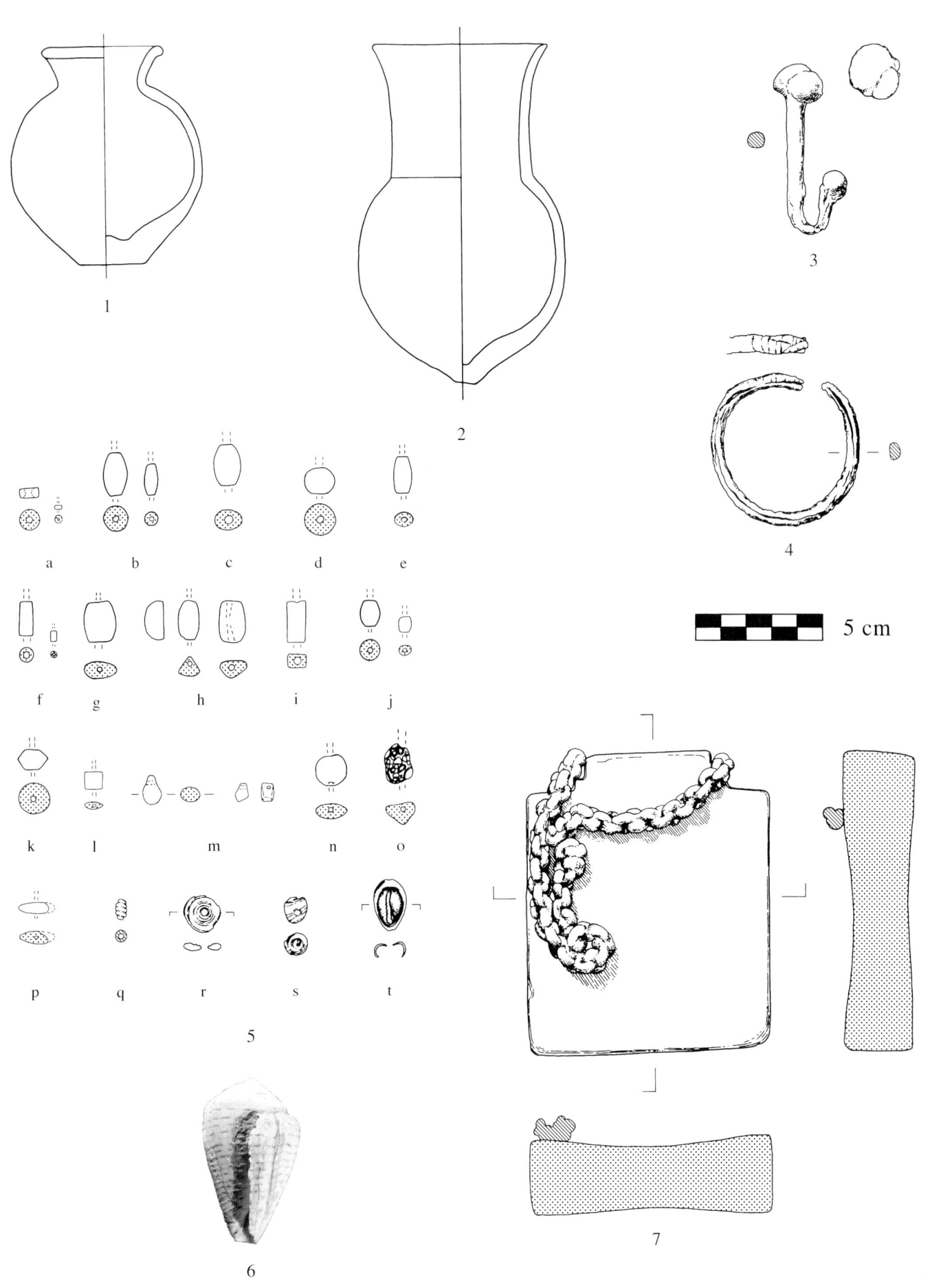

First-millennium B.C. Grave Group, Burial 4. Scales (*1–5, 7*) 1:2 and (*6*) 1:1

Plate 173. First-millennium B.C. Grave Group, Burial 7

|   | Lot Number | Dimension | Description/Comparison |
|---|---|---|---|
| BURIAL 4, LEVEL IIIB | | | |
| 1 | 18 N 17 | Rim diam. 6.2 cm, max. diam. 10.3 cm, base diam. 4.7 cm, ht. 11.5 cm | Jar, buff ware. Plain rim, ovoid body, flat base, pale green glaze on exterior and inside neck. Shape as 18 N 16, but green glaze is post-575 B.C. Nippur: McCown and Haines 1967: pl. 104:19 |
| 2 | 18 N 41 | Lgth. 5.8 cm, w. 3.0 cm | Shell, unworked half of a freshwater clam |
| 3 | 18 N 31 | Lgth. 65.0 cm, w. 39.0 cm, ht. 27.5 cm | Coffin, lightly baked heavily straw-tempered clay. "Bathtub" shape, separately attached rim. Nippur: McCown and Haines 1967: pl. 157: midway between 12 and 13 |

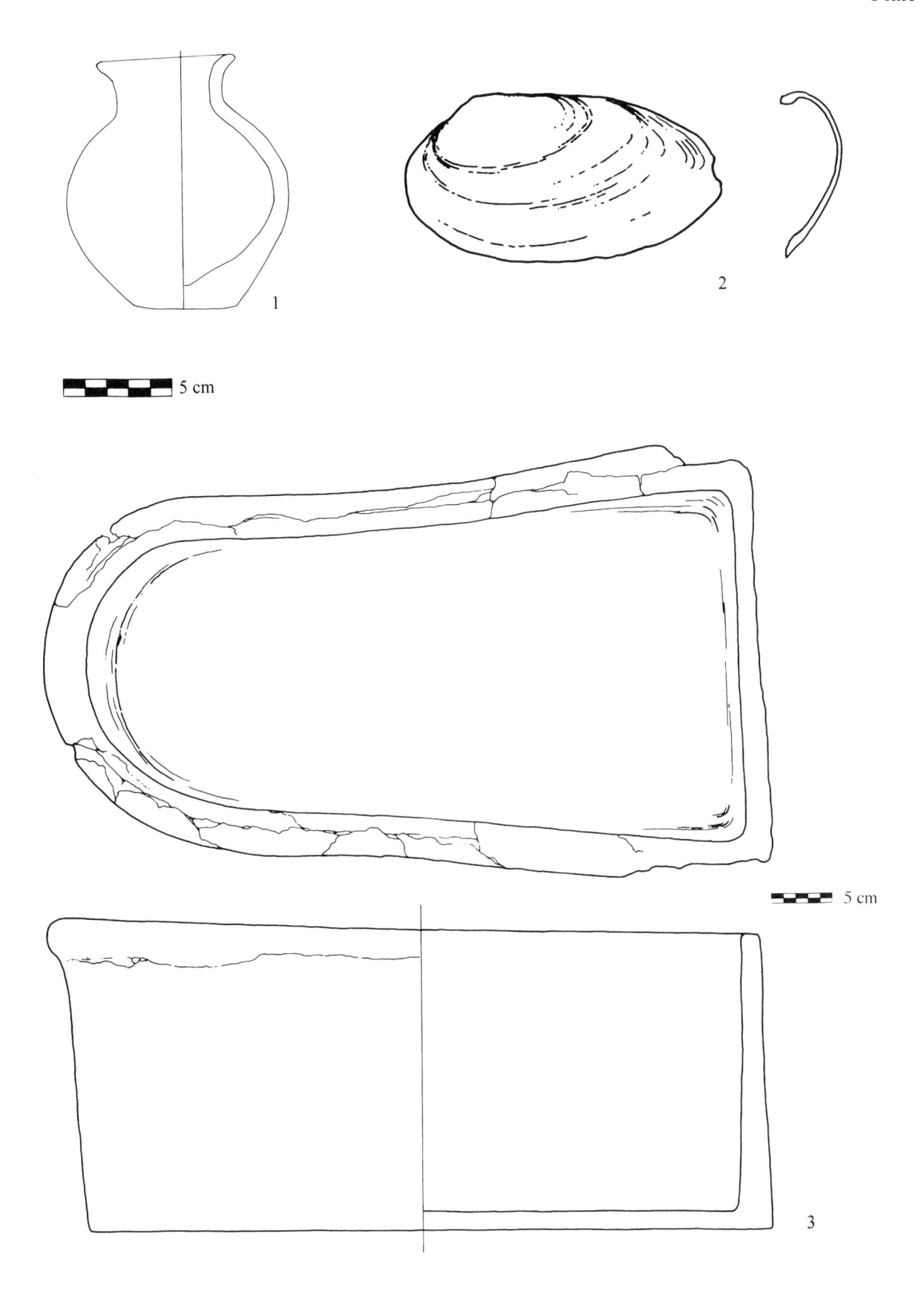

Plate 173

First-millennium B.C. Grave Group, Burial 7. Scales (*1*) 2:5, (*2*) 1:1, and (*3*) 1:5

Plate 174. First-millennium B.C. Pottery Bowls

| | Lot Number | Location | Dimension | Description |
|---|---|---|---|---|
| | INTURNING-RIM BOWL | | | |
| 1 | H365:6 | Level IV | Rim diam. 16.0 cm | Buff, sand and organic temper |
| 2 | H388:4 | Level IV | Rim diam. 16.0 cm | Buff, pale buff surface, organic temper. For distinctive narrowing at rim, see Druc 1989 (Habl as-Sahr): fig. 8:2 |
| 3 | H354:1 | Level IIIB | Rim diam. 14.0 cm | Pink, organic temper |
| | INTURNING BEVELED-RIM BOWL | | | |
| 4 | H365:4 | Level IV | Rim diam. 16.0 cm | Yellow, organic temper |
| 5 | H375:2 | Level IIIB | Rim diam. 14.0 cm | Pink, sand and organic temper |
| 6 | H355:4 | Level IIIB | Rim diam. 22.0 cm | Pale buff, organic temper |
| | CLUB-RIM BOWL | | | |
| 7 | H366:2 | Level IIIB | Rim diam. 14.0 cm | Pink, buff surface, sand temper |
| | INTERNALLY BEVELED RIM BOWL | | | |
| 8 | H91:3 | Level II | Rim diam. 17.0 cm, base diam. 7.5 cm, ht. 5.4 cm | Pink, organic temper |
| | FLAT-RIM BOWL | | | |
| 9 | H354:4 | Level IIIB | Rim diam. 20.0 cm | Pink, buff surface, organic temper |
| | BEVELED-RIM BOWL | | | |
| 10 | H381:7 | Level IIIB | Rim diam. 16.0 cm | Pink, buff surface, organic temper |

COMPARANDA FOR INTURNING-RIM BOWL

Nippur: McCown and Haines 1967: pl. 100:1, 13; Armstrong 1993: pl. 88b (NA–Ach.); Sippar: Haerinck 1980: pl. 10:1 (NB–Ach.); Uruk: Boehmer, Pedde, and Salje 1995: pl. 85h; Salje 1992: no. 47 et passim (NB)

COMPARANDA FOR INTURNING BEVELED-RIM BOWL

Nippur: McCown and Haines 1967: pl. 97:18, pl. 100:11; Armstrong 1993: pl. 86h (NB–Ach.)

COMPARANDA FOR CLUB-RIM BOWL

Sippar: Haerinck 1980: pl. 10:12 (NB–Ach.); Nippur: McCown and Haines 1967: pl. 100:7 (NA)

COMPARANDA FOR INTERNALLY BEVELED-RIM BOWL

Sippar: Haerinck 1980: pl. 10:7 (NB–Ach.); Uruk: Salje 1992: no. 69 (Ach.)

COMPARANDA FOR FLAT-RIM BOWL

Ur: Woolley 1962: pl. 40: type 29 (NB–Ach.)

COMPARANDA FOR BEVELED-RIM BOWL

Nippur NA–NB: McCown and Haines 1967: pl. 100:10; Uruk: Salje 1992: no. 96 (NB)

Plate 174

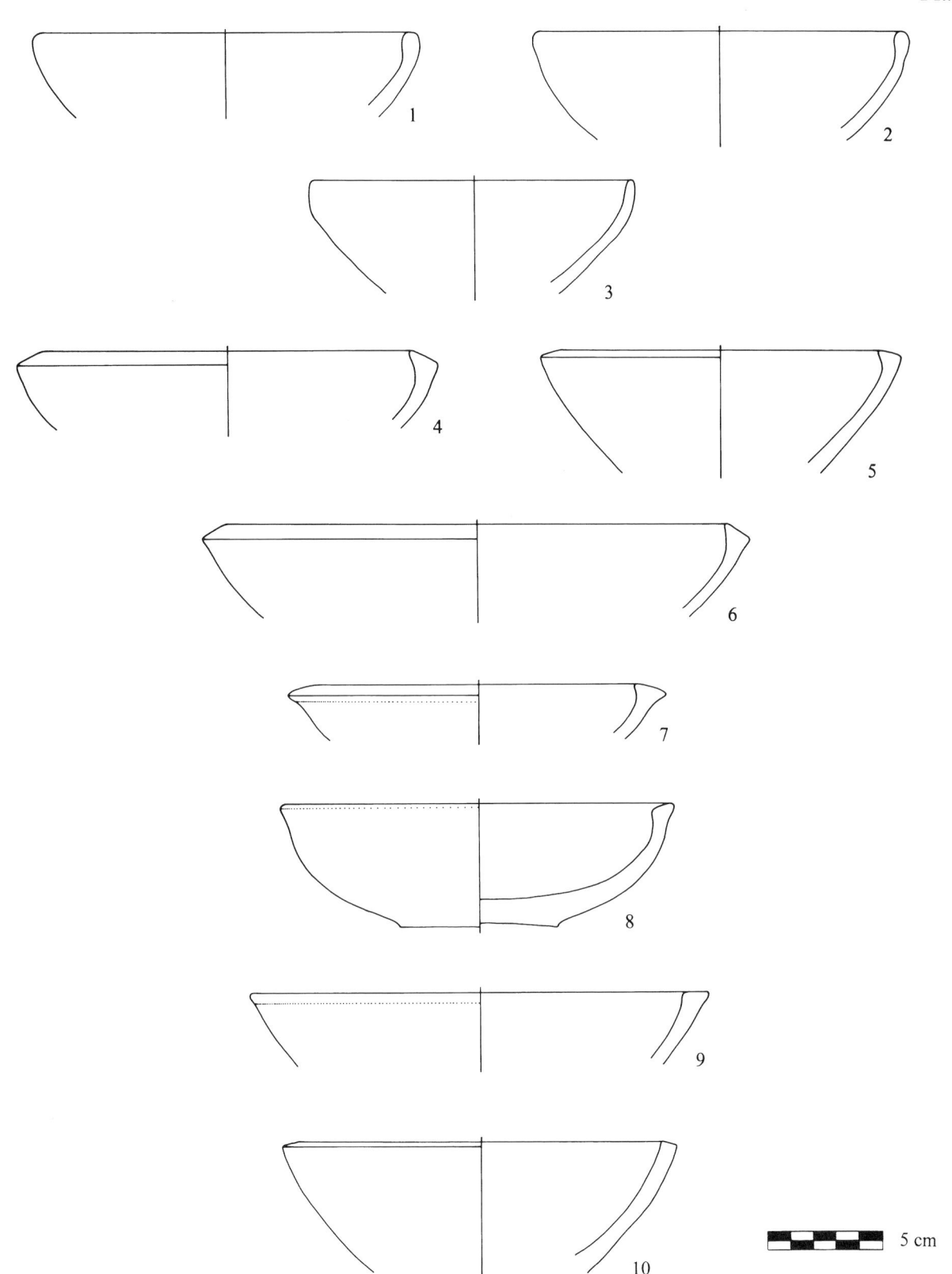

First-millennium B.C. Pottery Bowls. Scale 2:5

Plate 175. First-millennium B.C. Pottery Bowls

| | Lot Number | Location | Dimension | Description |
|---|---|---|---|---|
| \multicolumn{5}{l}{BEVELED-RIM BOWL, EXTERNAL PROJECTION} | | | | |
| 1 | H678:4 | Level IV | Rim diam. 17.0 cm | Yellow, organic temper |
| 2 | H95:1 | Level IIIA | Rim diam. 17.0 cm | Yellow, organic temper, bitumen-coated interior |
| \multicolumn{5}{l}{BOWL WITH PLAIN RIM AND GROOVE BELOW} | | | | |
| 3 | H382:2 | Level IV | Rim diam. 22.0 cm, | Red, sand and organic temper |
| | | | | base diam. 8.0 cm, ht. 8.7 cm |
| 4 | H673:3 | Level IV | Rim diam. 21.0 cm | Pink, buff surface, organic temper |
| 5 | H678:2 | Level IV | Rim diam. 26.0 cm | Red, sand and organic temper |
| \multicolumn{5}{l}{SMALL BEVELED RIM, DEEP BOWL} | | | | |
| 6 | H362:1 | Level IIIB | Rim diam. 13.5 cm, | Pink buff, sand and organic temper |
| | | | | base diam. 6.5 cm, ht. 10.4 cm |
| \multicolumn{5}{l}{CARINATED-SIDE BOWL} | | | | |
| 7 | H354:3 | Level IIIB | Rim diam. 12.0 cm | Pale buff, yellow surface, organic temper |
| 8 | H362:2 | Level IIIB | Rim diam. 13.0 cm, | Pink, cream surface, sand and organic temper |
| | | | | base diam. 4.5 cm, ht. 5.4 cm |
| 9 | H667:3 | Level IV | Rim diam. 9.0 cm | Buff, sand temper |

COMPARANDA FOR BEVELED-RIM BOWL, EXTERNAL PROJECTION

Nippur: McCown and Haines 1967: pl. 100:7 (NA); Habl as-Sahr: Druc 1989: fig. 8:17 (NB); Uruk: Salje 1992: no. 251 (NB)

COMPARANDA FOR BOWL WITH PLAIN RIM AND GROOVE BELOW

Nippur: McCown and Haines 1967: pl. 97:16 (NA); Sippar: Haerinck 1980: pl. 11:1, 3–4 (NB–Ach.); Uruk: Boehmer, Pedde, and Salje 1995: pl. 62a, pl. 111: grave 303a et passim (NB)

COMPARANDA FOR SMALL BEVELED RIM, DEEP BOWL

Similar to Uruk: Salje 1992: no. 97 (NB)

COMPARANDA FOR CARINATED-SIDE BOWL

Very common and widespread form; for geographic and temporal range, see Rutten 1996: figs. 13–14. Nippur: McCown and Haines 1967: pl. 100:14 (NA–Ach.); Sippar: Haerinck 1980: pl. 6:4, pl. 12: 12–14 (Ach.); Pasargadae: Stronach 1978: fig. 106:12–13 (Ach.)

Plate 175

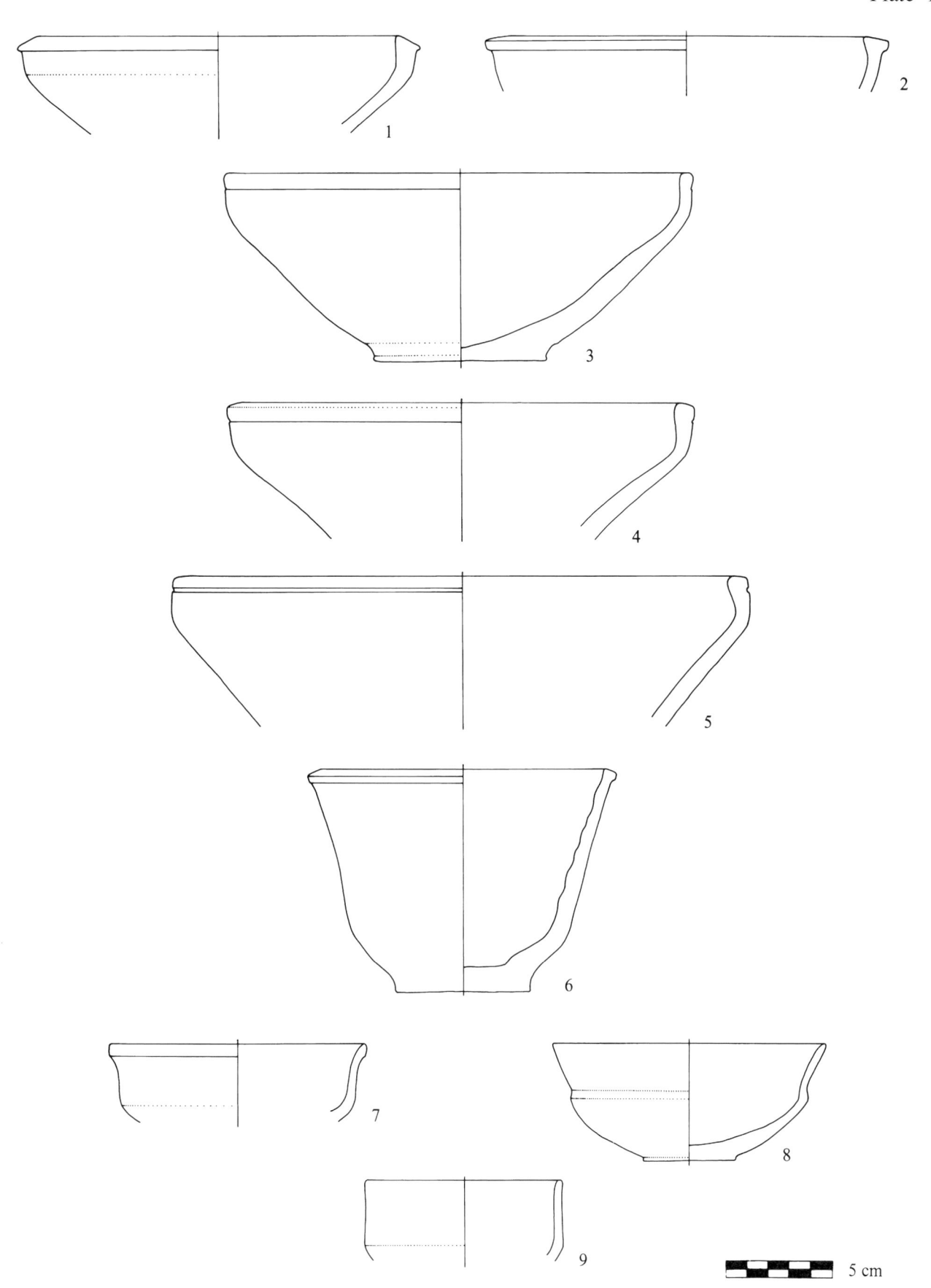

First-millennium B.C. Pottery Bowls. Scale 2:5

Plate 176. First-millennium B.C. Pottery Bowls

| | Lot Number | Location | Dimension | Description |
|---|---|---|---|---|
| | MEDIUM BOWL, BEVELED RIM, RIDGE BELOW | | | |
| 1 | H95:2 | IIIA | Rim diam. 19.0 cm | Yellow, organic temper |
| | MEDIUM BOWL, THICKENED RIM | | | |
| 2 | H98:1 | IIIB | Rim diam. 26.0 cm | Pale buff, organic temper |
| 3 | H371:4 | IV | Rim diam. 24.0 cm | Buff, organic temper |
| | MEDIUM BOWL, BEVELED RIM, GROOVE BELOW | | | |
| 4 | H664:5 | IV | Rim diam. 24.0 cm | Yellow buff, organic temper, bitumen-coated interior and exterior |
| 5 | H371:5 | IV | Rim diam. 24.0 cm | Buff yellow, organic temper |
| | LEDGE RIM, CYLINDRICAL VESSEL | | | |
| 6 | H354:6 | IIIB | Rim diam. 24.0 cm | Buff, yellow surface, organic temper |
| | EGGSHELL-WARE BOWL | | | |
| 7 | H381:10 | IIIB | Rim diam. 16.0 cm | Pale buff, no visible temper |
| 8 | H381:2 | IIIB | Rim diam. 10.0 cm | Gray, no visible temper |
| | GRAY WARE CARINATED BOWL | | | |
| 9 | H354:5 | IIIB | Rim diam. 17.0 cm | Gray, no visible temper |
| | GRAY WARE BEVELED-RIM BOWL | | | |
| 10 | H355:2 | IIIB | Rim diam. 25.0 cm | Gray, no visible temper, burnished interior and exterior |
| | SELEUCID BOWL | | | |
| 11 | H381:4 | IIIB | Rim diam. 23.0 cm | Buff, light sand temper, yellow glaze interior and exterior |
| 12 | H91:1 | II | Rim diam. 21.0 cm | Buff, light sand temper, white glaze interior and exterior |
| 13 | H354:2 | IIIB | Rim diam. 16.0 cm | Yellow, organic temper |

COMPARANDA FOR MEDIUM BOWL, BEVELED RIM, RIDGE BELOW

Uruk: Boehmer, Pedde, and Salje 1995: pl. 103:o, pl. 162:f; Salje 1992: no. 412 (NB)

COMPARANDA FOR MEDIUM BOWL, THICKENED RIM

Nippur: McCown and Haines 1967: pl. 97:17 (NA); Habl as-Sahr: Druc 1989: fig. 8:9 (NB)

COMPARANDA FOR MEDIUM BOWL, BEVELED RIM, GROOVE BELOW

Nippur: McCown and Haines 1967: pl. 97:15 (NA); Habl as-Sahr: Druc 1989: fig. 8:8 (NB); Sippar: Haerinck 1980: pl. 11:9 (NB–Ach.)

COMPARANDA FOR EGGSHELL-WARE BOWL

Very common and widespread form; for geographic and temporal range, see Rutten 1996: fig. 11. Nippur: McCown and Haines 1967: pl. 103:13 (Ach.); Abu Qubur: Warburton 1989: pl. 8:17 (Ach.); Sippar: Haerinck 1980: pl. 6:12 (Ach.); Isin: Hrouda 1987: pl. 31:5 (Ach.)

COMPARANDA FOR GRAY WARE CARINATED BOWL

Nippur: McCown and Haines 1967: pl. 100:3 (Ach.); Sippar: Haerinck 1980: pl. 11:15 (Ach.)

COMPARANDA FOR SELEUCID BOWL

Very common and widespread form; for geographic and temporal range, and form variations, see Rutten 1996: figs. 5–8. Nippur: Gibson et al. 1978: fig. 63:17 (Ach.–Sel.); Abu Qubur: Warburton 1980: pl. 6:13–23 (Ach.); Habl as-Sahr: Druc 1989: fig. 8:13 (NB); Sippar: Haerinck 1980: pl. 11:4, pl. 18:2–4 (Sel.); Ur: Woolley 1962: pl. 41: type 43 (Ach.)

Plate 176

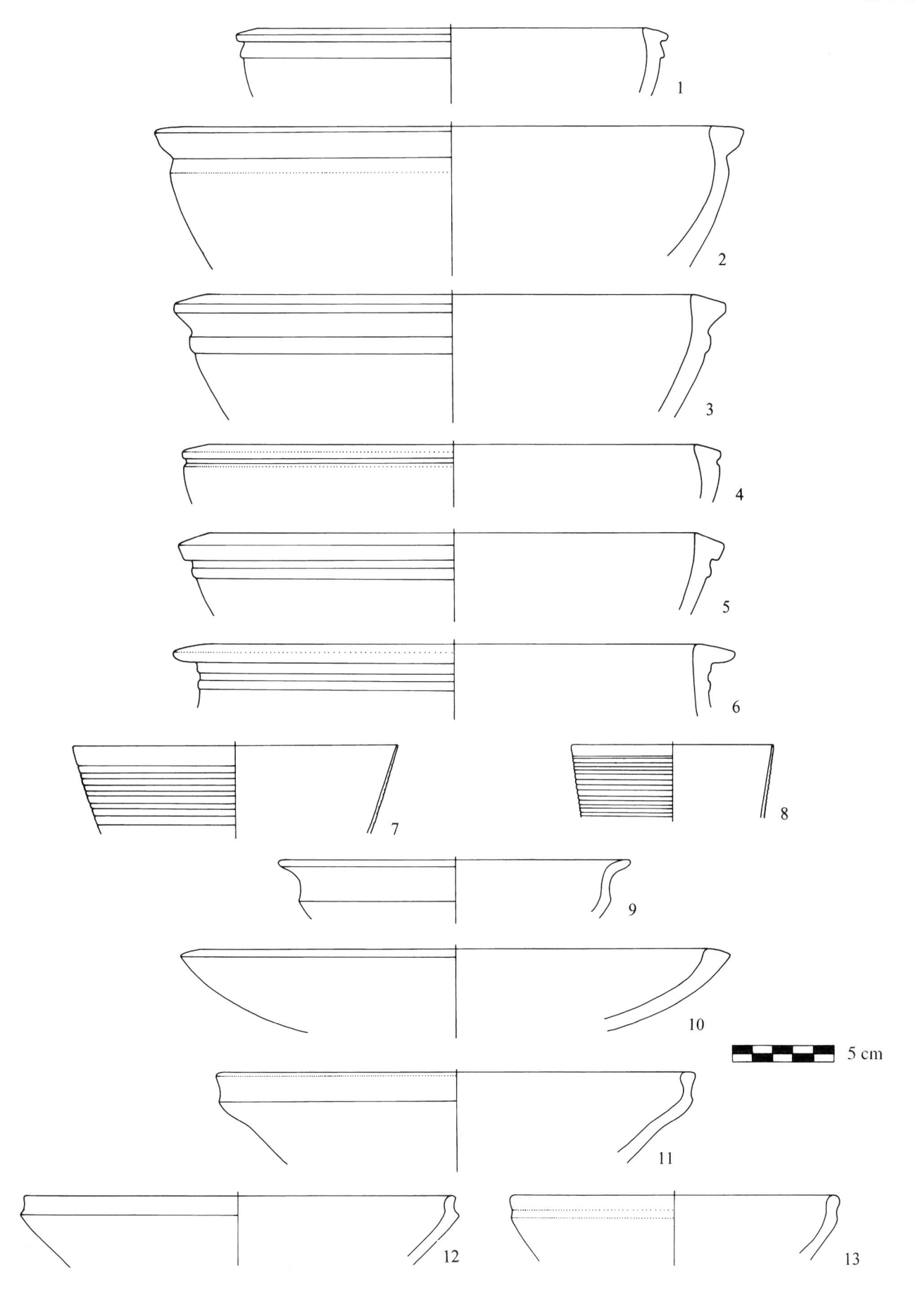

First-millennium B.C. Pottery Bowls. Scale 2:5

Plate 177. First-millennium B.C. Pottery Jars and Other Forms

| | Lot Number | Location | Dimension | Description |
|---|---|---|---|---|
| FLARED-RIM VESSEL | | | | |
| 1 | H388:9 | Level IV | Rim diam. 18.0 cm | Buff yellow, organic temper |
| FLARED PLAIN JAR RIM OR POT STAND | | | | |
| 2 | H381:9 | Level IIIB | Rim diam. 8.0 cm | Gray green, sand and organic temper |
| 3 | H399:5 | Level IV | Rim diam. 6.0 cm | Yellow, sand and organic temper |
| 4 | H399:6 | Level IV | Rim diam. 10.0 cm | Yellow, organic temper |
| CLUB-RIM JAR | | | | |
| 5 | H387:2 | Level IIIB | Rim diam. 8.0 cm | Yellow, organic temper |
| THICKENED JAR RIM, SMALL | | | | |
| 6 | H664:2 | Level IV | Rim diam. 9.0 cm | Pink, sand and organic temper |
| THICKENED JAR RIM, MEDIUM | | | | |
| 7 | H664:1 | Level IV | Rim diam. 9.0 cm | Yellow, organic temper |
| 8 | H375:1 | Level IIIB | Rim diam. 12.0 cm | Pale buff, organic temper |
| THICKENED JAR RIM, RIDGE BELOW | | | | |
| 9 | H91:4 | Level II | Rim diam. 12.0 cm | Buff, organic temper |
| THICKENED JAR RIM, LARGE | | | | |
| 10 | H381:1 | Level IIIB | Rim diam. 12.0 cm | Yellow buff, organic temper |
| DOUBLE-RIDGE RIM | | | | |
| 11 | H664:3 | Level IV | Rim diam. 16.0 cm | Buff yellow, organic temper |
| "HOLE-MOUTH" VESSEL | | | | |
| 12 | H363:6 | Level IIIB | Rim diam. 16.0 cm | Yellow green, sand and organic temper |
| FINE WARE JAR RIMS | | | | |
| 13 | H363:5 | Level IIIB | Rim diam. 16.0 cm | Brown, light sand temper |
| 14 | H95:4 | Level IIIA | Rim diam. 8.0 cm | Greenish buff, light sand temper |
| CYLINDRICAL CUP BASE | | | | |
| 15 | H355:1 | Level IIIB | Base diam. 3.5 cm | Yellow buff, organic temper |

## COMPARANDA

### FLARED-RIM VESSEL
Nippur: McCown and Haines 1967: pl. 100:19 (NA–NB)

### FLARED PLAIN JAR RIM OR POT STAND
For geographic and temporal range, see Rutten 1996: fig. 16. Nippur: Gibson et al. 1978: fig. 33:3, 5, 11, 14, et passim (Ach.–Sel.); Sippar: Haerinck 1980: pl. 13:11, 13 (NB–Ach.); Isin: Hrouda 1987: pl. 31:2 (Ach.); Pasargadae: Stronach 1978: fig. 113:6–7 (Ach.)

### THICKENED JAR RIM, SMALL
Sippar: Haerinck 1980: pl. 13:19 (NB–Ach.); Habl as-Sahr: Druc 1989: fig. 10:11, 15 (NB)

### THICKENED JAR RIM, MEDIUM
Sippar (NB–Ach.): Haerinck 1980: pl. 13:15; Habl as-Sahr (NB): Druc 1989: fig. 10:8

### THICKENED JAR RIM, RIDGE BELOW
Sippar: Haerinck 1980: pl. 15:8 (NB–Ach.); Abu Qubur: Warburton 1989: pl. 10:2 (Ach.)

### THICKENED JAR RIM, LARGE
Sippar: Haerinck 1980: pl. 13:10 (NB–Ach.); Habl as-Sahr: Druc 1989: fig. 11:4–5 (NB)

### "HOLE-MOUTH" VESSEL
Nippur: Gibson et al. 1978: fig. 68:30 (Ach.–Sel.); Sippar: Haerinck 1980: pl. 17:6 (Ach.–Sel.)

### FINE WARE JAR RIMS
Nippur: McCown and Haines 1967: pl. 102:5 (NB–Ach.); Ur: Woolley 1962: pl. 49, type 143 (Ach.); Sippar: Haerinck 1980: pl. 14:2–3 (NB–Ach.)

### CYLINDRICAL CUP BASE
Ur: Woolley 1962: pl. 43: type 74 (NB); Uruk: Boehmer, Pedde, and Salje 1995: pl. 183:c (NB–Ach.)

Plate 177

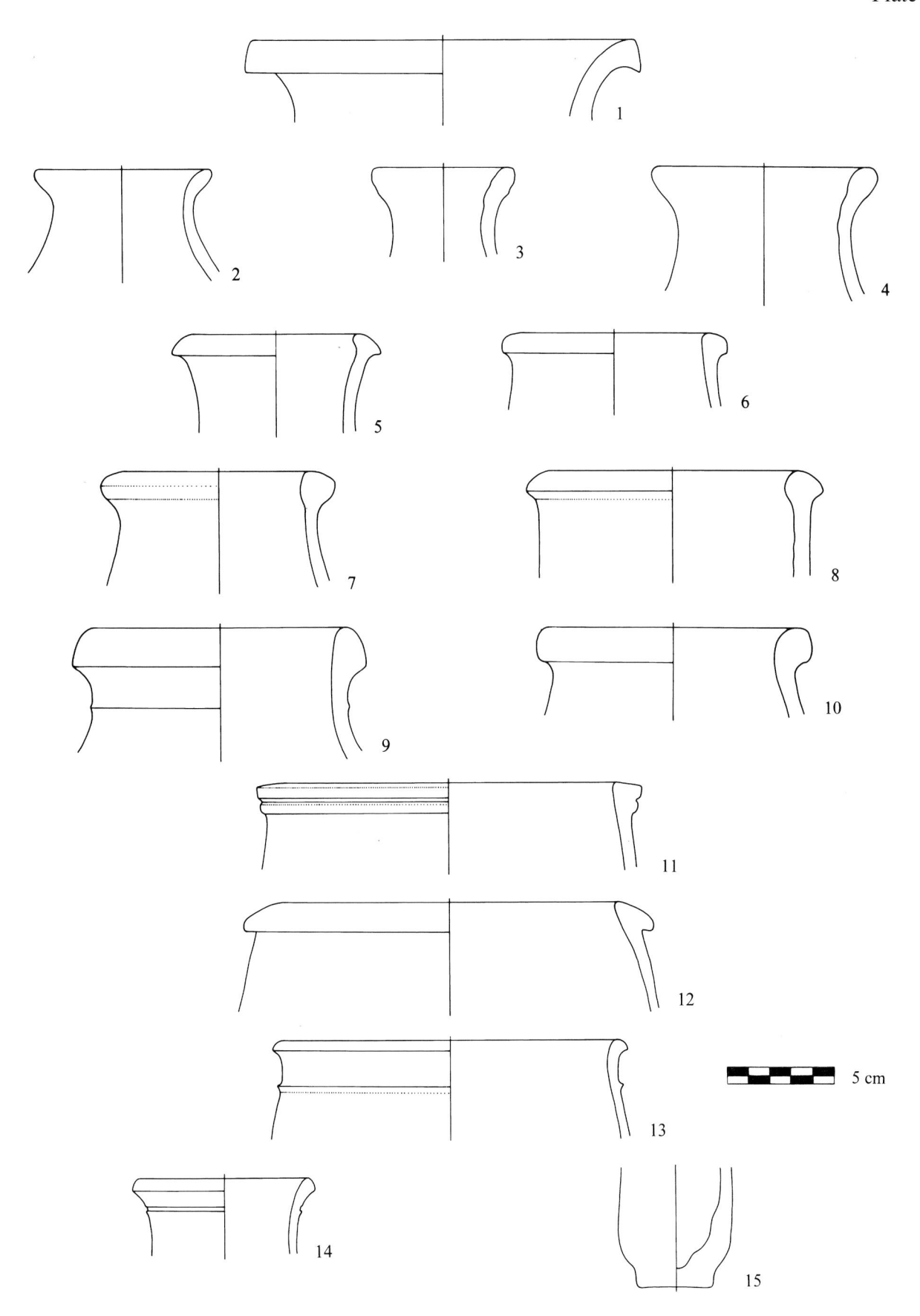

First-millennium B.C. Pottery Jars and Other Forms. Scale 2:5

Plate 178. First-millennium B.C. Pottery and Metal Hoard

|   | Lot Number | Location | Dimension | Description |
|---|---|---|---|---|
| 1 | 18 N 62 | Level IIIB, Locus 7, Floor 1 | Rim diam. 25.2 cm, base diam. 9.4 cm, ht. 9.4 cm | Bowl, buff ware, light organic temper. Rounded, thickened rim, string-cut base. Nippur: Armstrong 1993: pls. 85i, 87c; McCown and Haines 1967: pl. 100:7 (type 50) |
| 2 | H98:4a | Level IIIB | Rim diam. 3.0 cm | Rim sherd of small jar, light buff ware. Plain rim, narrow neck. Fragile glazed pattern of horizontal bands and zigzags in yellow, yellow green, and white. See 18 N 42 |
| 3 | H98:4b | Level IIIB | Base diam. 4.0 cm | Base sherd of small jar, light buff ware. Flat base. Fragile glazed fish-like pattern in yellow, yellow green, and white, vertical lines at base. See 18 N 16 |
| 4 | 18 N 126 | Level II | Rim diam. ca. 5.5 cm, max. diam. 11.0 cm, ht. 18.0 cm | Ovoid jar, rim missing (ancient break), low nipple base, pink buff ware, sand and organic temper. Contained hoard of copper and silver objects. McCown and Haines 1967: pl. 147:1, "Assyrian" hoard of beads and silver chunks in similar jar, TA V |
| 5 | 18 N 126 | Level II | 724 pieces 0.2–2.0 cm long, 106 pieces 2.0–4.0 cm long, 6 pieces 4.0–6.0 cm long, 8 pieces of silver wire, 14 pieces of agglomerated silver and copper. Total wt. 3,262 gm | Hoard of copper and silver objects from inside pottery jar. Mostly corroded together, primarily flat scraps of copper and silver |
| 6 | H352 | Level IIIB | Rim diam. 20.0 cm, max. diam. 22.0 cm, base diam. 14.0 cm, ht. 23.0 cm | Jar containing Burial 2. Ledge rim with ridge below, barrel-shaped body, ring base |

Plate 178

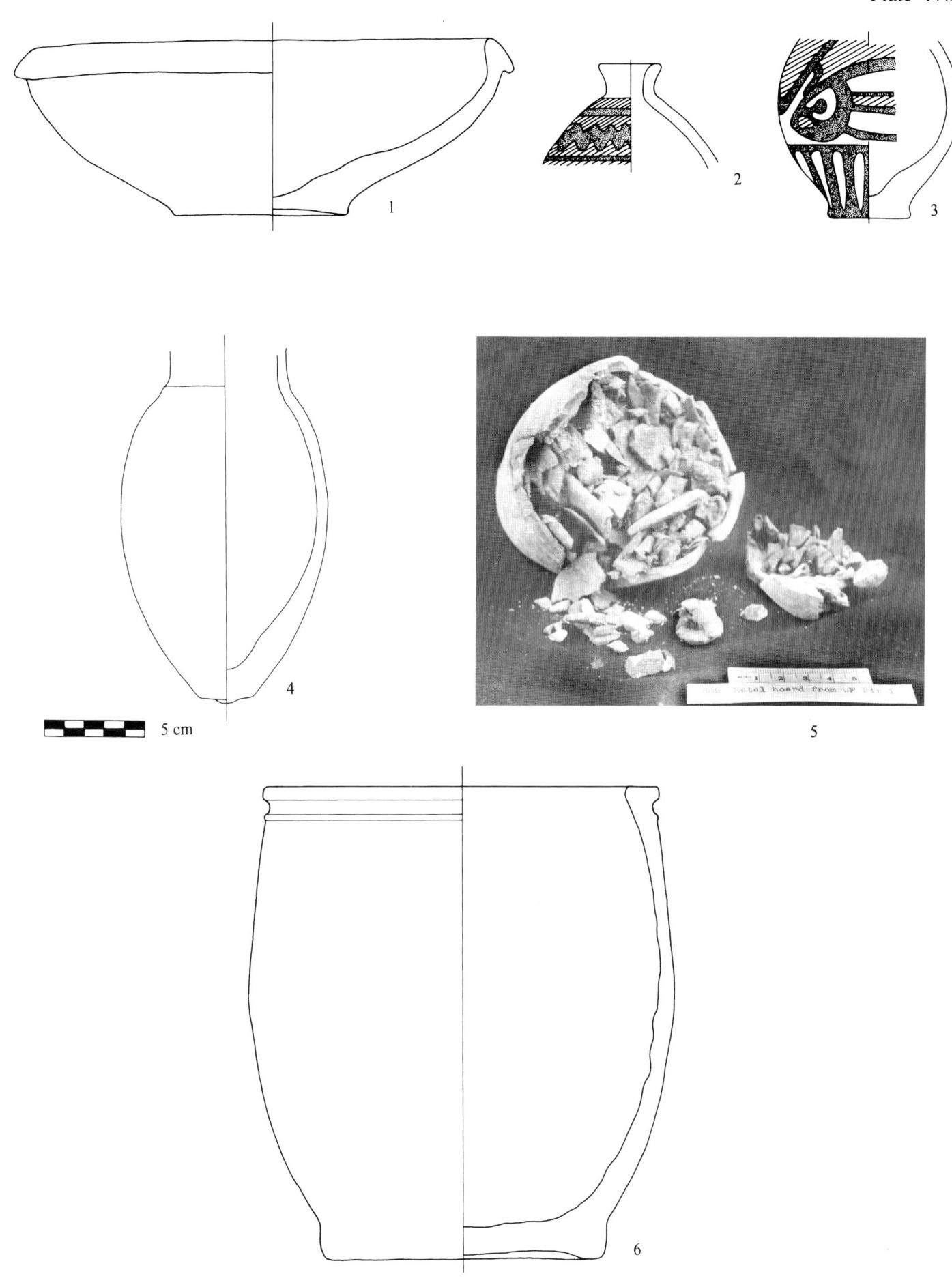

First-millennium B.C. Pottery and Metal Hoard. Scales (*1–4, 6*) 2:5 and (*5*) 1:2

Plate 179. First-millennium B.C. Objects

|   | Lot Number | Location | Dimension | Description |
|---|---|---|---|---|
| 1 | 18 N 127a–f | Level II, inside 18 N 126 | (a) lgth. 3.4 cm, diam. 1.2 cm; (b) max. diam. 1.1 cm; (c) max. diam. 1.1 cm; (e) lgth. 3.0 cm, w. 1.0 cm, th. 0.5 cm; (f) diam. 1.9 cm, th. 0.3 cm | Six silver objects from metal hoard, all slightly corroded. (a) Earring, whole, penannular with spherical pendant, granulated bead, ribbed hub-shaped; (b + c) bead, ribbed hub shaped (c not illustrated); (d) bead, ribbed hub shaped; (e) wire clump; (f) ring fragment, bezel missing, single loop with oval counterweight |
| 2 | 18 N 60 | Level II | Lgth. 9.1 cm, max. diam. 1.6 cm | Tool handle, bronze, broken and corroded. Straight shaft with round cross section tapering to rectangular cross section |
| 3 | 18 N 28 | Level II | Diam. 1.5 cm, th. 0.2 cm, wt. 1.4 g. | Coin, bronze, worn. Obverse: human figure with long skirt and headdress, bending to right, inscription. Reverse: unintelligible |
| 4 | 18 N 7 | Level II | (a) lgth. 0.8 cm, diam. 0.5 cm; (b) lgth. 0.5–1.1 cm, diam. 0.4–0.9 cm; (c) diam. 0.8–1.2 cm, th. 0.4–0.9 cm; (d) lgth. 0.8 cm, w. 0.8 cm; e) l. 0.7–1.4 cm, diam. 0.4–0.5 cm; (f, y, z) lgth. 0.7–1.8 cm, diam. 0.4–0.7 cm; (g) lgth. 1.6 cm, w. 0.9 cm; (h) diam. 1.0 cm, th. 0.5 cm; (i, j) lgth. 0.7–1.8 cm, diam. 0.4–0.8 cm; (k) diam. 0.6–0.9 cm; (l) lgth. 0.9–1.6 cm, w. 0.5–1.0 cm; (m) diam. 0.8–1.0 cm, th. 0.5–0.8 cm; (n) lgth. 0.9–1.3 cm, w. 0.6–0.8 cm; (o) lgth. 1.0 cm, w. 0.8 cm; (p) lgth. 0.6–0.9 cm, diam. 0.3 cm; (q) diam. 0.9 cm, th. 0.2 cm; (r) lgth. 1.6 cm, th. 0.4 cm); (s) diam. 0.6–1.4 cm, th. 0.2–0.8 cm; (t, v, w, x) lgth. 1.0–1.3 cm, diam. 0.5–0.7 cm; (u) lgth. 0.4–1.6 cm, diam. 0.3 cm | Necklace/bead hoard. 285 beads of various stones, metal, faience, and shell: (a) 1 ribbed hub shaped (blue faience); (b) 8 squat date shaped (4 orange brown stone, 2 mottled stone, 1 turquoise, 1 hematite); (c) 12 ring shaped (7 turquoise, 4 carnelian, 1 mottled stone); (d) 1 plano-convex (turquoise); (e) 14 date shaped (4 lapis, 4 turquoise, 3 amethyst, 1 hematite, 1 white quartz, 1 yellow quartz); (f, y, z) 39 cylindrical (19 mottled stone, 9 iron, 3 bronze, 3 banded agate, 2 carnelian, 2 white quartz, 1 turquoise); (g) 1 triangular pendant (amethyst); (h) 1 hemispherical (amethyst); (i, j) 128 double-conoid (34 mottled stone, 32 banded agate, 15 orange brown stone, 12 white quartz, 8 olive yellow stone, 6 carnelian, 6 hematite, 4 amethyst, 4 black stone, 3 marble, 2 lapis, 1 green quartz, 1 orange quartz); (k) 9 ball shaped (5 banded agate, 4 carnelian); (l) 6 elliptical (2 banded agate, 1 turquoise, 1 hematite, 1 olive yellow stone, 1 mottled stone); (m) 6 lentoid (amethyst); (n) 4 faceted double-conoid (orange-brown stone); (o) 1 irregular unshaped (mottled stone); 44 shells: (p) 7 dentalium; (q) 3 ring-shaped core sections; (r) 1 cowrie section; s) 8 conical core sections; (t, v, w, x) 9 unworked shells; (u) 16 cylindrical shell cores |

Plate 179

1

2

3

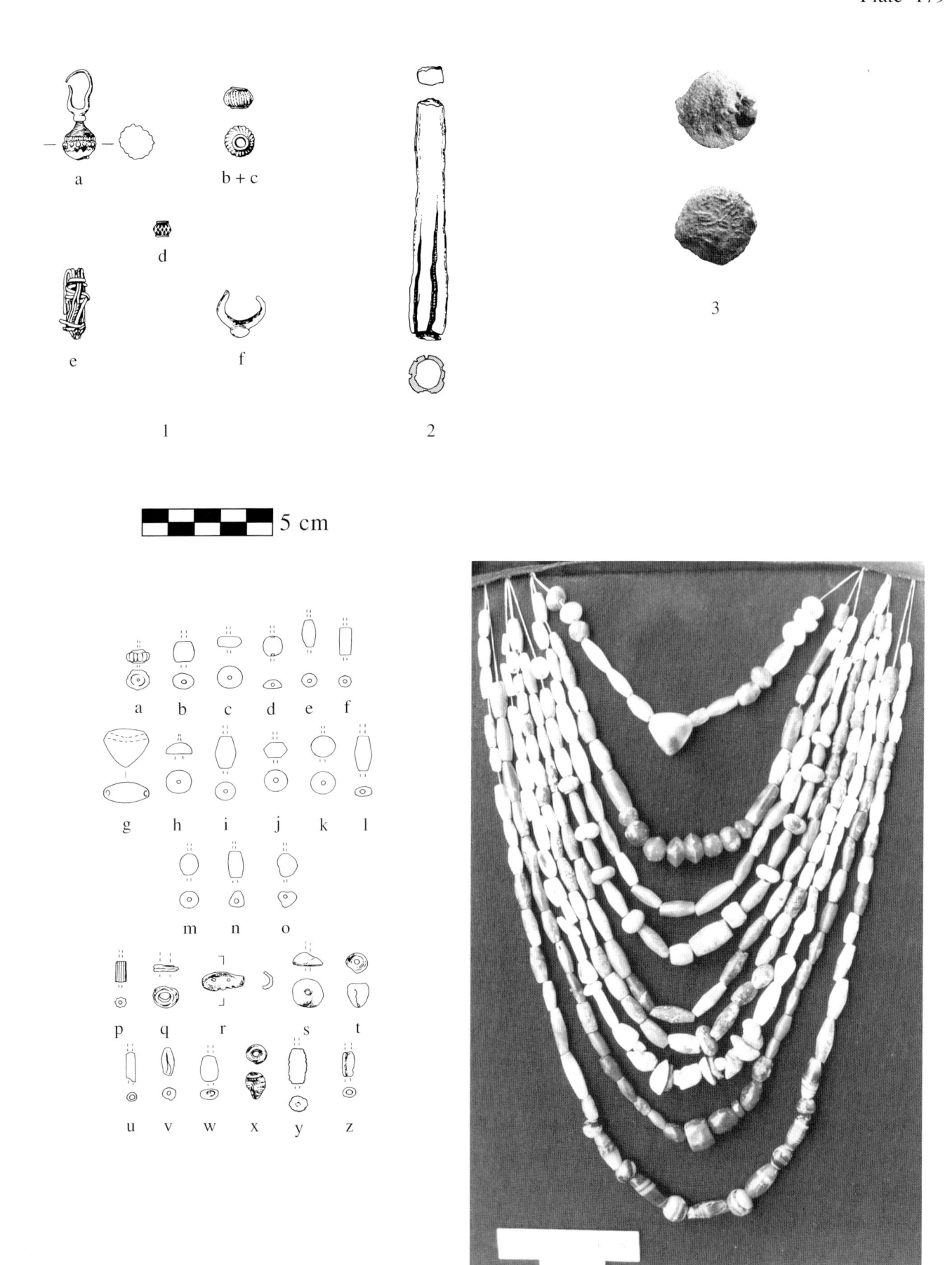

4

First-millennium B.C. Objects. Scales (*1–2, 4*) 1:2 and (*3*) 1:1

Plate 180. First-millennium B.C. Objects

|   | Lot Number | Location | Dimension | Description |
|---|---|---|---|---|
| 1 | 18 N 26 | Level IV | Ht. 7.2 cm, w. 4.3 cm, th. 2.3 cm | Figurine, baked clay, fragment only. Upper body and head of mold-made nude female figure with necklace, holding possible flower, or hands clasped at chest |
| 2 | 18 N 59 | Level IIIB | Lgth. 7.5 cm, max. diam. 4.0 cm, handle diam. 1.5 cm | Rattle, baked clay, whole, handmade. Spherical hollow head with round impressions and holes in surface, clay(?) pellets inside, cylindrical handle. Patches of bitumen on surface |
| 3 | 18 N 51 | Level IIIB | Lgth. 9.4 cm, ht. 6.9 cm, th. 1.9 cm | Plaque, baked clay, corners damaged. Rectangular mold-made plaque with lion in low relief, striding left. Inscription. Nippur: McCown and Haines 1967: pl. 142:9; Gibson 1975: fig. 71:5 |
| 4 | 18 N 11 | Level II | Ht. 9.3 cm, max. w. 5.0 cm, th. 3.0 cm | Figurine, baked clay, head missing. Mold-made female figure, nude, tambourine held at left shoulder. Nippur: Gibson 1975: fig. 74:1, 3 |
| 5 | 18 N 15 | Level II | Diam. 6.6 cm, th. 1.5 cm | Plaque, baked clay, worn. Disc-shaped, mold-made plaque with low relief of scorpion-man, walking left |

Plate 180

1
2
3
4
5

First-millennium B.C. Objects. Scale 1:2

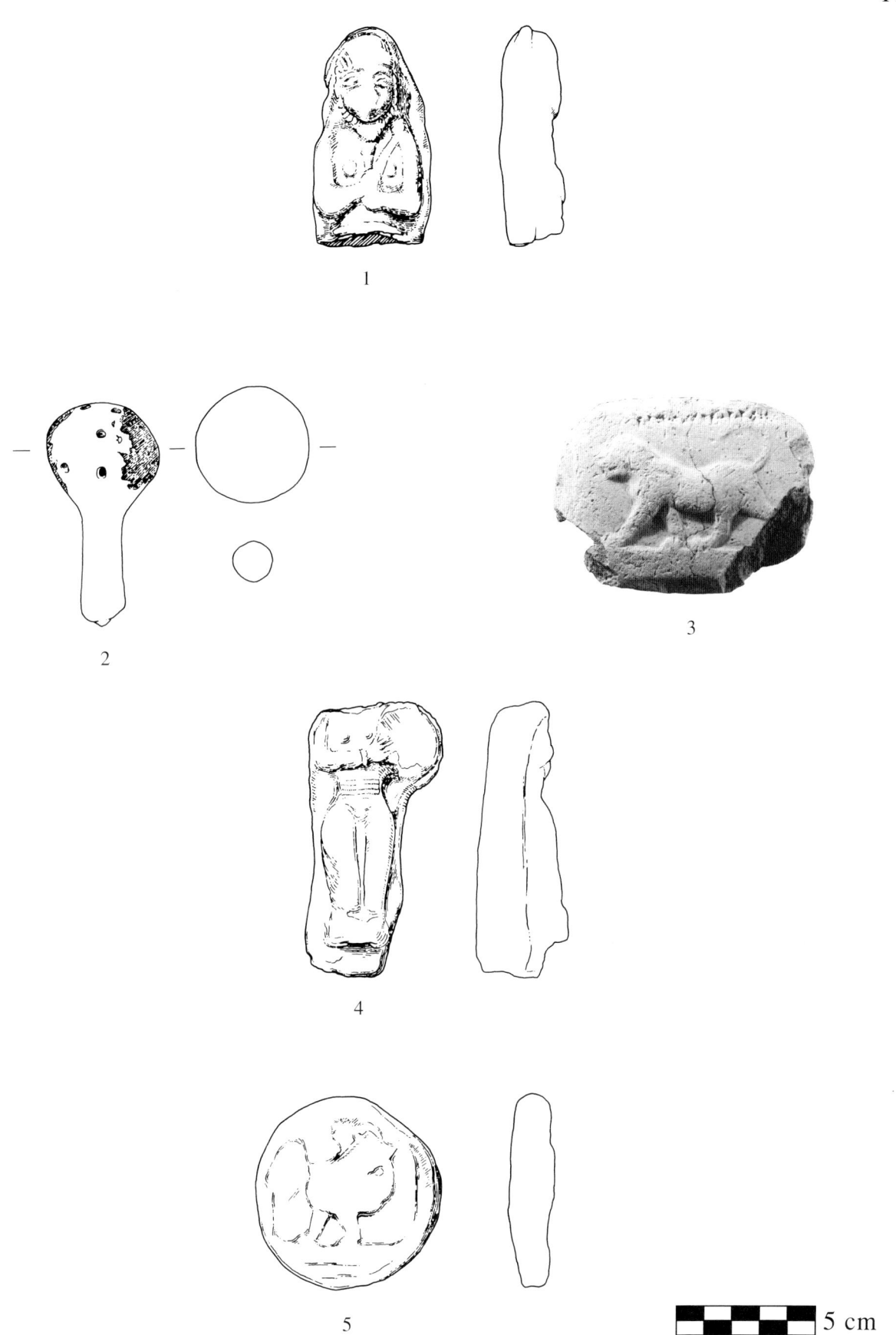

Plate 181

(*a*) West Section, Middle Portion, Levels XI and Above; and (*b*) West Section, Lower Portion, Levels XIII and Below

Plate 182

(*a*) North Section, Lower and Middle Portions, Levels XII and Below; and (*b*) East Section, Lower and Middle Portions, Levels XII and Below

Plate 183

(*a*) South Section, Middle Portion, Levels XI and Above; and (*b*) South Section, Middle Portion, Southeast Corner, Levels V to X

Plate 184

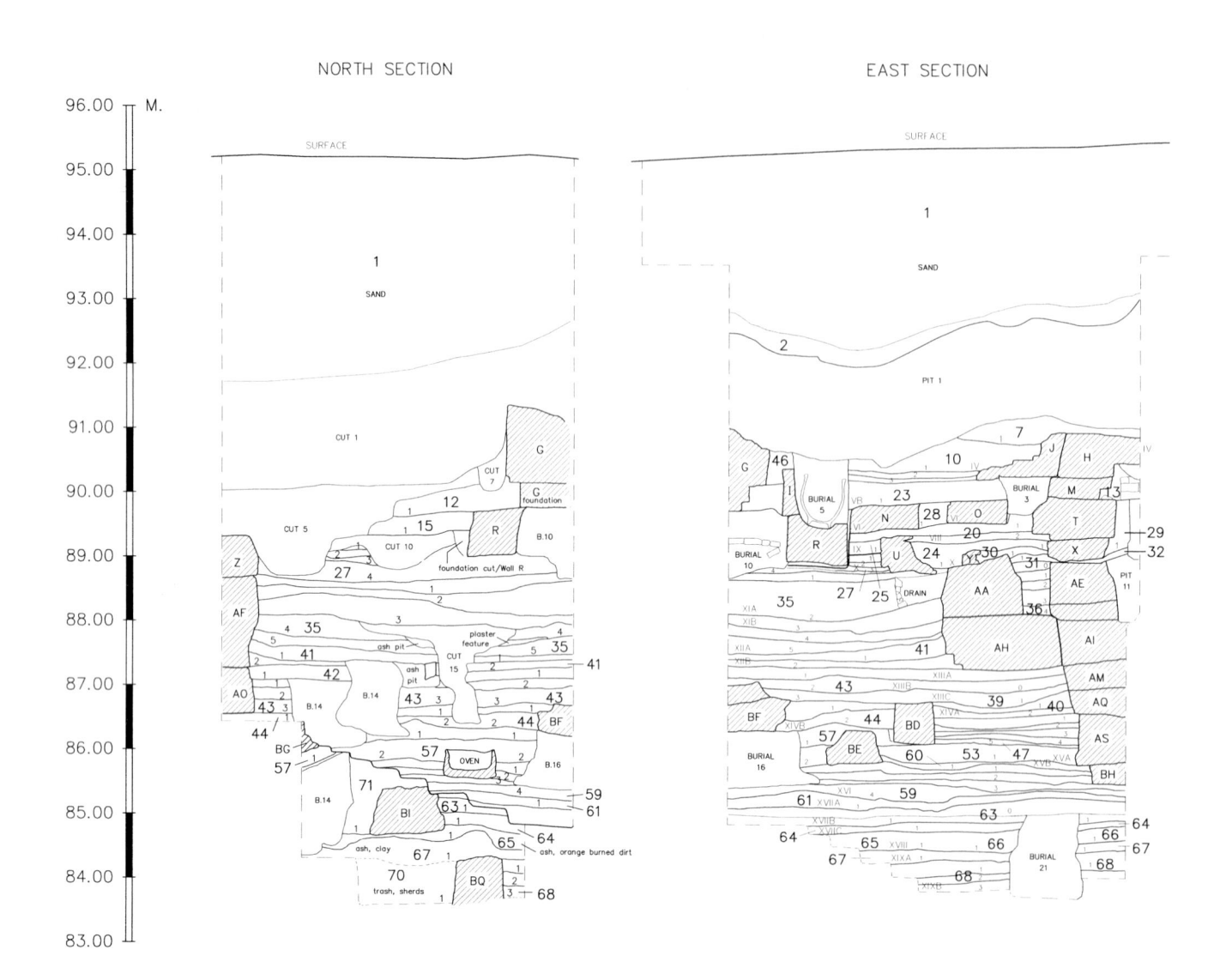

Area WF North and East Sections

Plate 185

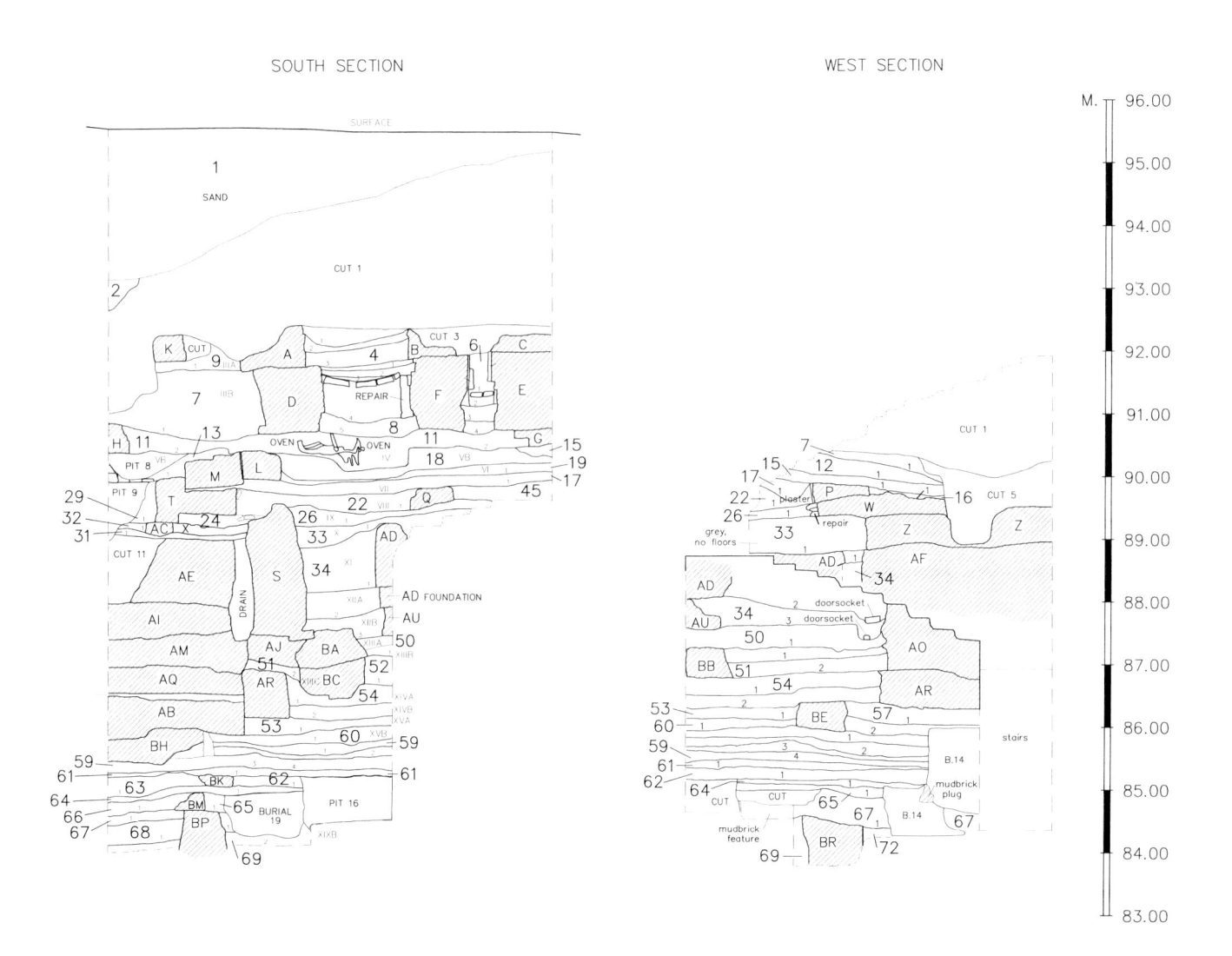

Area WF South and West Sections

Plate 186

(*a*) Spherical Translucent Dark Olive Green and Opaque White Glass Bead (18 N 95, H840, 27.2.89), Side View Showing a Miniscus at Each End, and (*b*) Cylindrical Opaque Yellow and Translucent Bluish Green Bead (18 N 96, H107, 1.3.89), Side View Showing Barrel Shape. Scales in mm

Plate 187

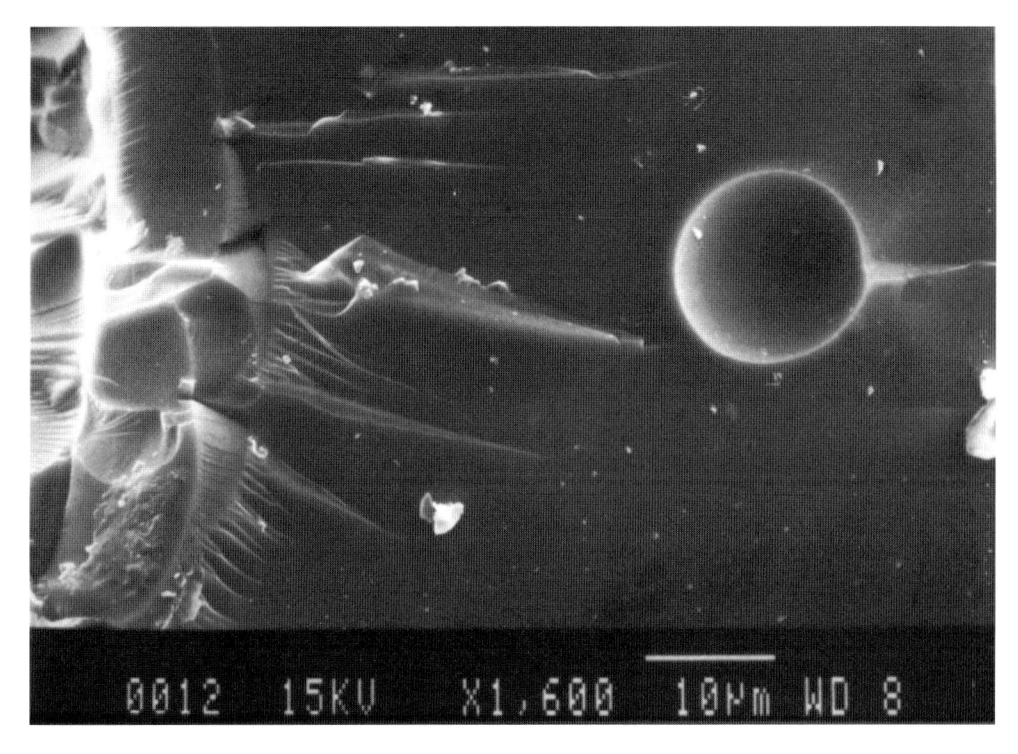

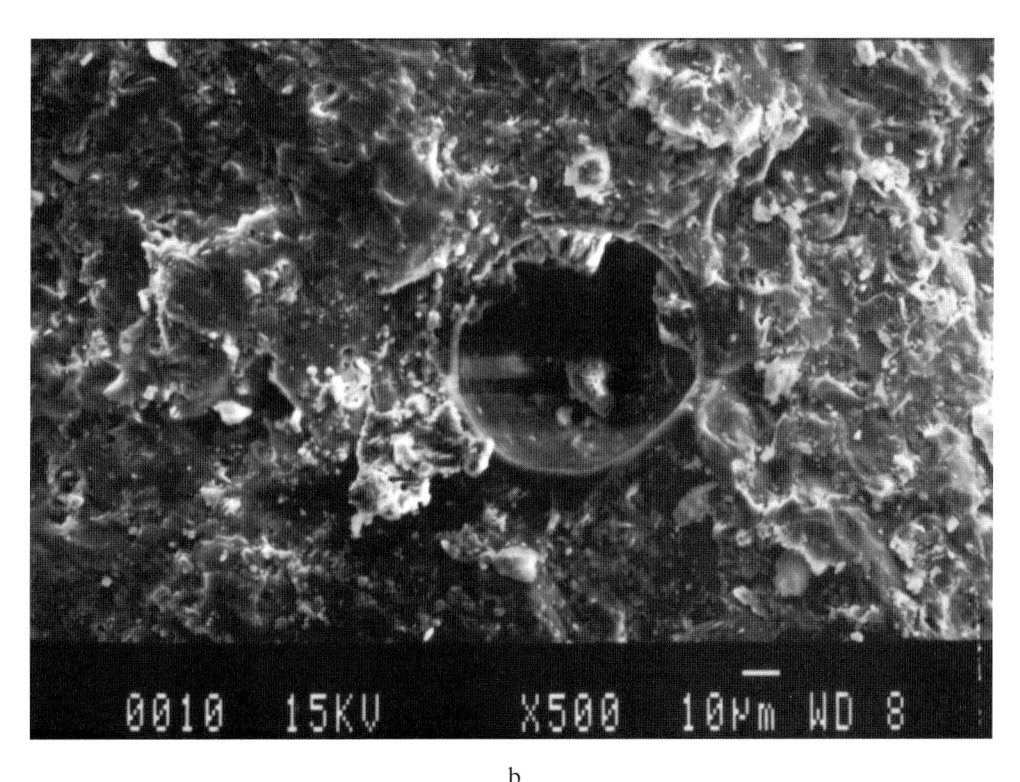

(*a*) Section of Opaque White Glass of 18 N 95 Showing Conchoidal Fracture (left) and Bubble or Pore (right), Taken with Scanning Electron Microscope (S.E.M.) in Secondary Mode at ×1,600, and (*b*) Freshly Fractured Surface of Opaque Yellow Glass of 18 N 96 Showing Rough, Polycrystalline Surface Texture and Round Bubble (right of center). Taken with S.E.M. in Secondary Mode at ×500

Plate 188

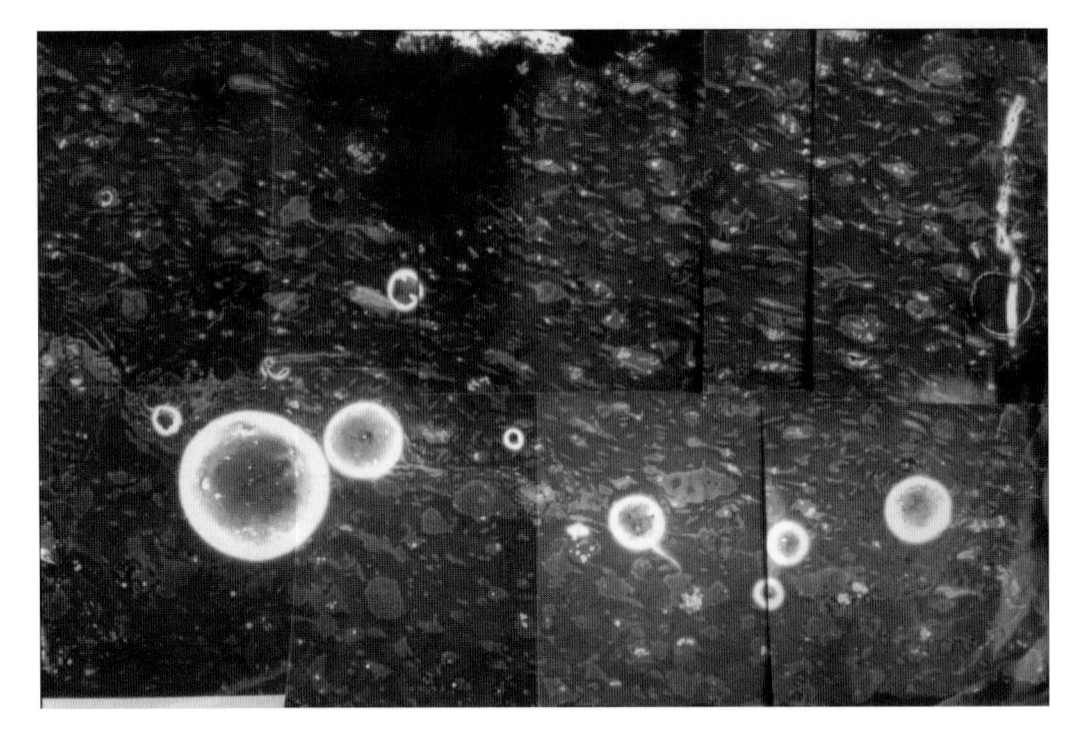

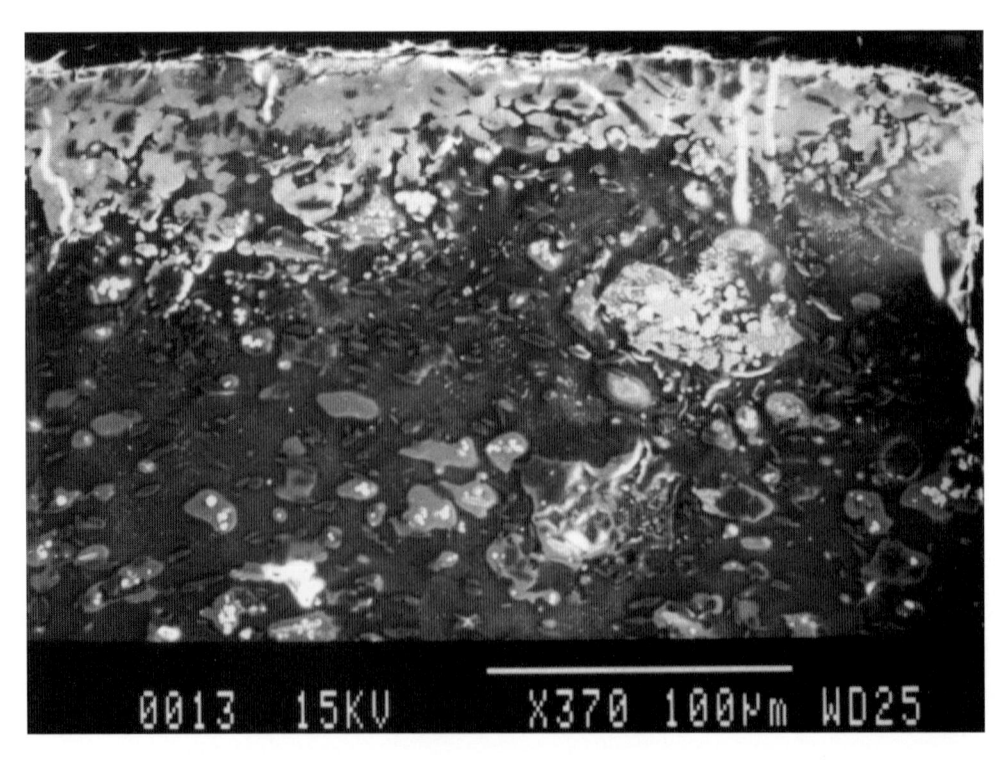

(*a*) Green Glass Showing Lead-tin II or Lead-stannate Phases (small rounded white crystals about 1 to 5 microns in maximum diameter) Surrounded by Calcium-magnesium-silicate Phase Identified by X-ray Diffraction as Diopside (gray). Wispy Edges of Diopside Crystals Show Evidence of Having Been Partially Melted and Having Flowed from Middle Right to Upper Left, Probably During the Viscous Forming of Bead. Surrounding Glass Matrix is High-lime Lead-silicate (see table A.1) Containing Small Crystals (ca. 0.1 micron), which Have Probably Precipitated from the Melt. In Upper Left are a Cluster of Calcium-silicate Crystals and Some Darker Gray Crystals Formed within Diopside Phase (backscattered S.E.M. at ×750). (*b*) Flat Polished Cross Section of Yellow Glass Showing Lead-stannate and Diopside Phases Concentrated at Surface to Give Opaque Yellow Color (backscattered at ×370)

Plate 189

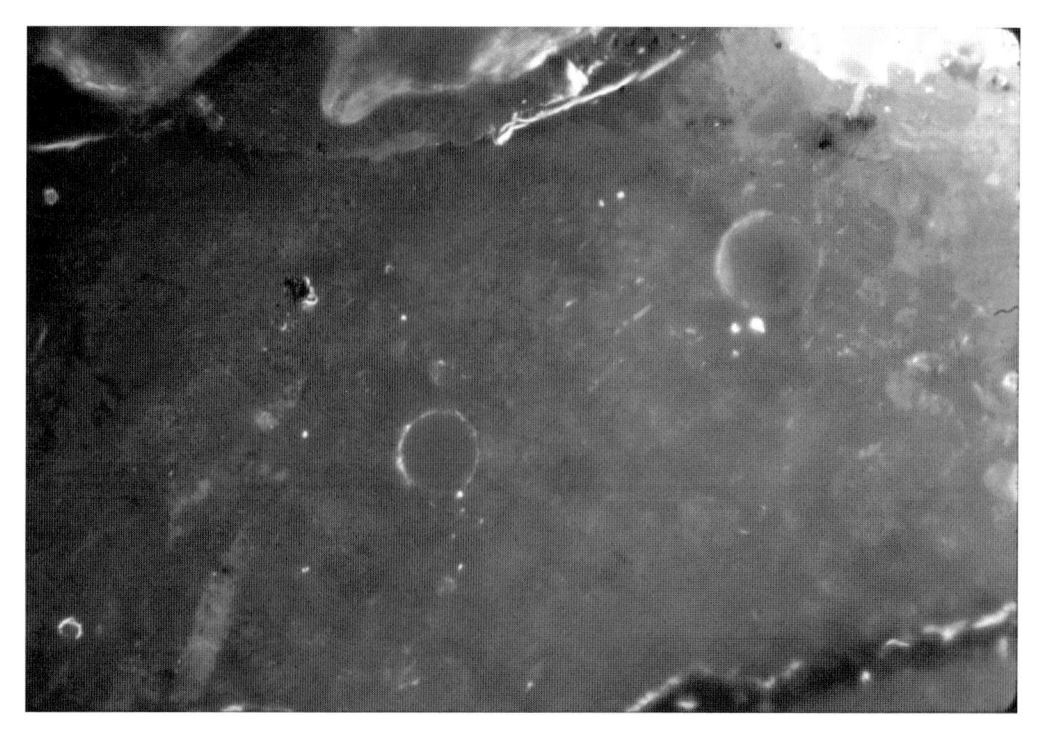

a

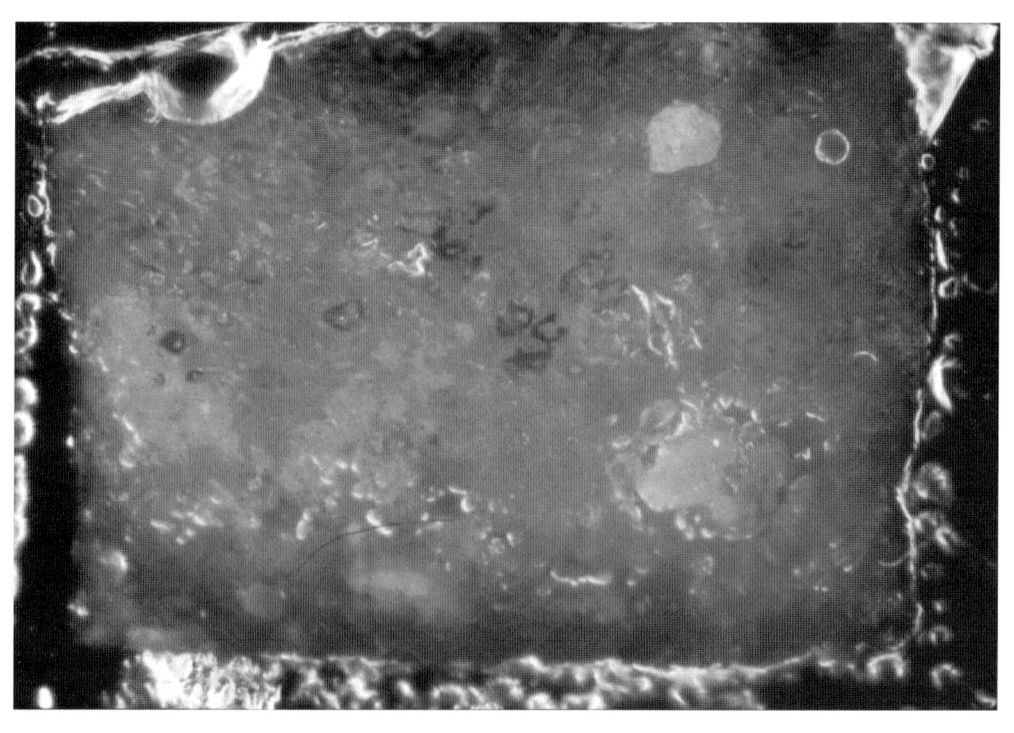

b

The Same 0.3 mm Polished Chip of Yellow Glass Shown Using Optical Microscopy in (*a*) Transmitted and (*b*) Reflected Light at ×400. Yellow Lead-stannate Crystals in Diopside Appear Light Gray and Due to the Limited Depth of Focus They Appear Somewhat Fuzzy. (*b*) In Reflected Light, Glassy Matrix Stands Out with Diopside Appearing with Small Flecks of Lead-stannate and Diopside Appears White, Original Surface at Top

Plate 190

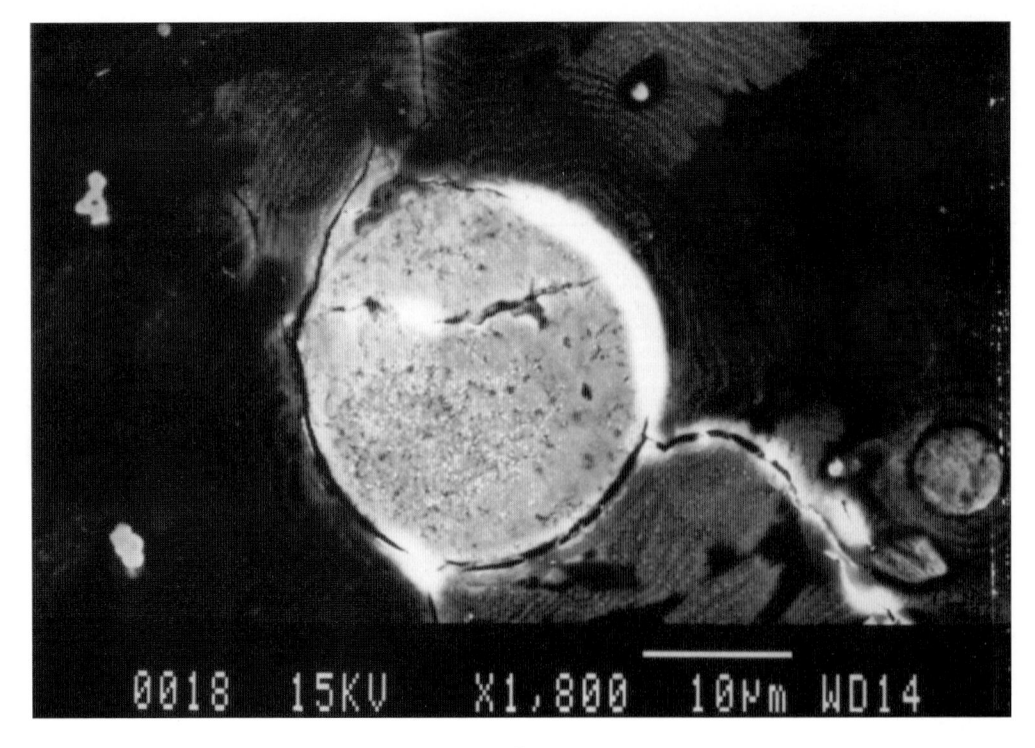

a

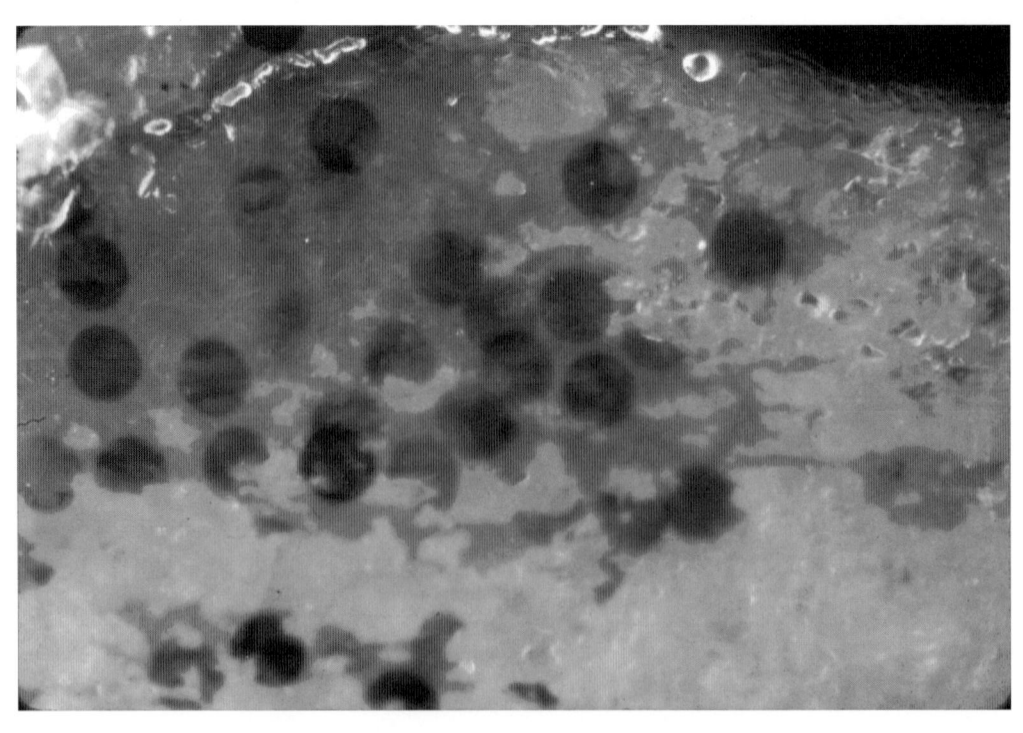

b

(*a*) Two Small Droplets of Lead Phosphate Phase (see table A.2 for composition) Shown in Backscattered S.E.M. at ×1,800 and (*b*) As Concentration of Brown-colored Droplets in Transmitted Light Micrograph at ×400

Plate 191

Replication of the Yellow-green Glass Composition, Melted in a Fireclay Crucible at Three Different Temperatures for Twelve Hours in Oxidation. Left, Glass Heated at 800°C is Poorly Melted. Center, Glass Heated at 900°C is Vitreous but a Silica Scum Floats on the Surface. Right, Glass Heated at 1000°C is Homogeneous and Successfully Melted; Copper Blue Is the Resulting Color. Yellow Lead-stannate Colorant Was Added During Forming

Plate 192. Third-millennium B.C. Tablets

|   | *Lot Number* | *Location* | *Dimension* | *Description* |
|---|---|---|---|---|
| 1 | 19 N 80 | Level XVIIB | Ht. 5.7 cm, w. 5.6 cm, th. 2.5 cm | "Fara" tablet, lightly baked clay, square with rounded corners. Obverse: four columns (last two blank), reverse: blank |
| 2 | 18 N 104 | Level XIIA | Ht. 4.5 cm, w. 4.0 cm, th. 1.0 cm | Old Akkadian tablet, unbaked clay, lower left corner only. Account text. Obverse: 3+ lines, reverse: broken |
| 3 | 18 N 105 | Level XIIA | Ht. 4.3 cm, w. 3.5 cm, th. 1.5 cm | Old Akkadian tablet, unbaked clay, rectangular. Account text. Obverse: 7 lines, reverse: 1 line |

Plate 192

1

2 Obverse 					2 Reverse

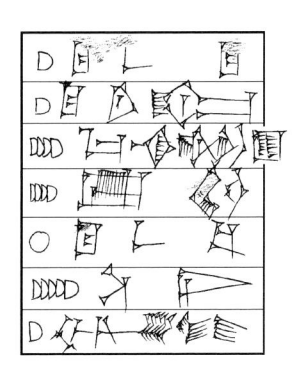

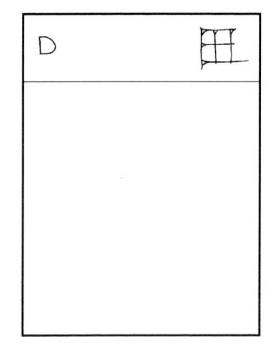

3 Obverse					3 Reverse

Third-millennium B.C. Tablets. Scale 1:1

Plate 193. Third-millennium B.C. Tablets

|   | *Lot Number* | *Location* | *Dimension* | *Description* |
|---|---|---|---|---|
| 1 | 18 N 106 | Level XIIB | Ht. 4.7 cm, w. 3.9 cm, th. 1.4 cm | Old Akkadian tablet, unbaked clay, rectangular. List of cloth weights and personal names. Obverse: 9 lines, reverse: 1 line partially preserved, rest broken |
| 2 | 18 N 107 | Level XIIA | Ht. 7.0 cm, w. 4.0 cm, th. 2.9 cm | Old Akkadian tablet, unbaked clay, rectangular. Account text. Upper right corner missing and left side damaged. Obverse: 12+ lines, reverse: 11+ lines |
| 3 | 18 N 108 | Level XIIA | Ht. 6.5 cm, w. 4.1 cm, th. 1.9 cm | Old Akkadian tablet, unbaked clay, rectangular. List of personal names. Upper edge damaged. Obverse: 10+ lines, reverse: 2 lines |

Plate 193

1

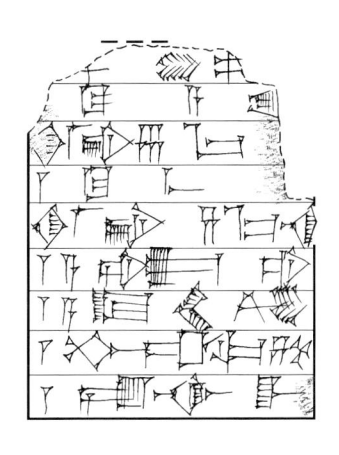

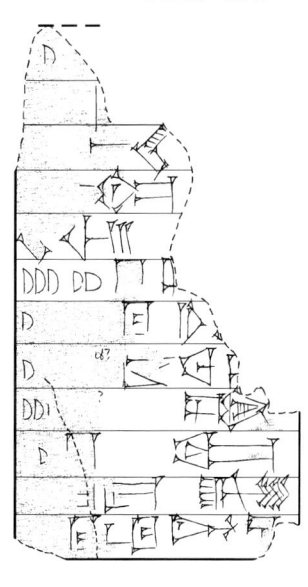

2 Obverse

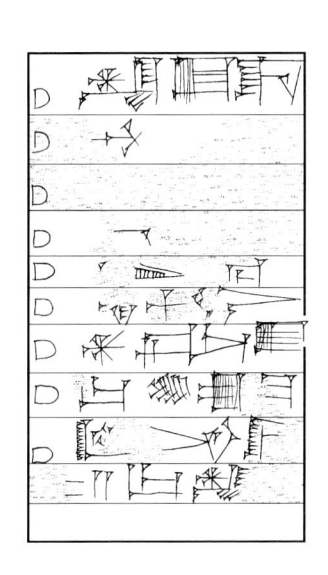

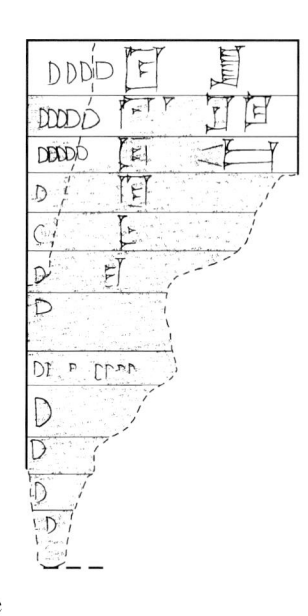

3 Obverse

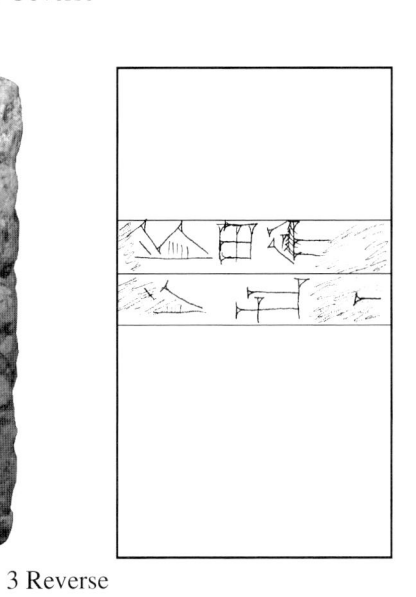

2 Reverse

3 Reverse

2 Edge

Third-millennium B.C. Tablets. Scale 1:1